THE ENGLISH PEOPLE AT WAR
IN THE AGE OF HENRY VIII

Steven Gunn studied at Merton College, Oxford. He has held research fellowships there and at the University of Newcastle, and is now Fellow and Tutor in History at Merton College and Professor of Early Modern History at Oxford. His books include *Charles Brandon, Duke of Suffolk, c.1484–1545* (1988), *Early Tudor Government 1485–1558* (1995), *Henry VII's New Men and the Making of Tudor England* (2016), and, with David Grummitt and Hans Cools, *War, State, and Society in England and the Netherlands, 1477–1559* (2007).

Praise for *The English People at War in the Age of Henry VIII*

'No student of the Tudor world, or of the early modern military, will be unable to find some new, intriguing fact at every turning of the page.'

Eric Klingelhofer, *H-War*

'Readers will find the eight compact chapters filled with fascinating stories and vignettes that reveal the extent to which war touched the lives of men and women from all orders of English society.'

David R. Lawrence, *Renaissance Quarterly*

'...essential reading for anyone hoping to understand not just Tudor warfare, but Tudor society as a whole.'

Jonathan Healey, *Literary Review*

'I can think of no better example of the very best military history.'

Ian F.W. Beckett, *The Society for Army Historical Research Annual Booklist, 2019–2020*

The English People at War in the Age of Henry VIII

STEVEN GUNN

OXFORD
UNIVERSITY PRESS

Great Clarendon Street, Oxford, OX2 6DP,
United Kingdom

Oxford University Press is a department of the University of Oxford.
It furthers the University's objective of excellence in research, scholarship,
and education by publishing worldwide. Oxford is a registered trade mark of
Oxford University Press in the UK and in certain other countries

Published in the United States of America by Oxford University Press
198 Madison Avenue, New York, NY 10016, United States of America

British Library Cataloguing in Publication Data
Data available

Library of Congress Cataloging in Publication Data
Data available

ISBN 978–0–19–880286–0 (Hbk.)
ISBN 978–0–19–886421–9 (Pbk.)

Ad suos Mertonenses: colleagues, students, friends

Preface

This book is based on my Ford lectures, delivered in 2015. The James Ford Lectures in British History, funded by a bequest from the Revd James Ford, were first given in 1896. A glance at the list of those who have delivered them since then should convince anyone that my protestations of unworthiness to follow in their footsteps are not merely a matter of conventional modesty. I thank the electors for asking me to deliver the lectures and the audiences who attended week by week. The lectures are intended both to advance historical understanding and to engage the interest of the general public. I thought it best to take a fairly large subject and one to which people could relate their own experience.

My country has often been to war in my lifetime, yet my personal experience of war is minimal, and I thank God for that. I have never come near to being drafted, I have rarely seen armed soldiers in public, the closest I have come to aerial attack is to watch the Red Arrows, and the most alarming weapon I have ever had at home was a blunted Austrian cavalry sword liberated from a film set by my grandfather. Yet my parents' generation can never forget that they lived through a war of conscription, and rationing, and bombing, and evacuation. What I hoped to explore in the lectures and hope to consider in this book is where the England of Henry VIII stood between these extremes. How regularly, how intensively, how disruptively did the king's wars affect the lives of his subjects?

We shall have to look for evidence of how much Henry's subjects thought about war, heard about war, prepared for war, as well as how much they took part in war or suffered its ill-effects. In the back of our minds will have to stand that perhaps legendary ploughman who had to be asked to move out of the way for the battle of Marston Moor. Hearing, two years into the English Civil War, that the forces of king and parliament were to fight, he asked 'What, has them two fallen out then?'[1] We shall also have to think about the boundaries of war and peace in a society in which the state had only imperfectly achieved its Weberian monopoly on the legitimate use of force. Henry's subjects were habituated to bloodshed across a spectrum of situations from the casual child-beating, wife-beating, and servant-beating of patriarchal domestic discipline, through the bear-baiting and cock-fighting of popular entertainment and the practised slaughter of pigs and chickens in half a million backyards, to feud and duelling, riot and rebellion. They shared the experience summed up by John Keegan, that there was 'considerable congruence between the civil and military facts of medieval life and a minimum—admittedly a very substantial minimum—of divergence between them on the battlefield'.[2] Some would argue that in their world violence against the person was so normal that to be asked to direct it against the king's enemies was more a deployment of transferable skills than the alien butchery for which twentieth-century recruits had to be pumped up by bayonet drill.[3] We shall have to ask how Henry's subjects rehearsed, contemplated, and responded to killing and death in war.

What scope should we cover in asking these questions? The age of Henry VIII is one of those conveniently loose phrases that will, I hope, allow me to include what I want to include and ignore what I want to ignore. As Chapter 1 explains, there are good reasons for stretching it from the 1470s to the 1570s. The English people raise a further problem of definition. Again I hope I shall be excused an imprecise approach. Henry's English subjects, born and bred inside the old Anglo-Saxon kingdom, seem to have thought of the Welsh as English—subjects of the English crown—when it suited them, just as parliament legislated for 'an amicable concorde and unitie' between his English and Welsh subjects, a concord to be furthered by the use of 'the speche or langage of Englisshe', a language many of the Welsh did not understand, in the governance of Wales.[4] In the same way the English of England thought and regularly spoke of the English in Ireland, what would later be thought of as the Old English, as English, at least when they were fighting together against the Gaelic opponents of the English king's rule. We shall have to think in due course about how far the different parts taken by these different peoples in Henry's wars helped to constitute their identities and their attitudes towards one another.

In converting the lectures into a book, I have preserved most of the text of the lectures as delivered in Chapters 2 to 7, while moving parts of the first and last lectures to this preface and to Chapter 1 and Chapter 8. While I have retained original spelling in quotations, I have extended contractions, modernized capitalization, and standardized the use of i, j, u, and v. I have translated other languages into English.

In the thirty or so years I have studied Henry's wars I have benefited from the advice of many colleagues. They include Ian Archer, Ian Arthurson, George Bernard, Jeremy Black, Susan Brigden, Hans Cools, John Currin, Michael Depreter, David Grummitt, Peter Gwyn, Richard Hoyle, Armand Jamme, Neil Murphy, Geoffrey Parker, David Parrott, Simon Payling, Andrew Pettegree, David Potter, David Rundle, Jonathan Thacker, David Trim, Malcom Vale, John Watts, Peter Wilson, and Neil Younger. I am grateful to them for their help, as I am to the three anonymous readers who guided me in turning the lectures into a book, to my editors at Oxford University Press, to the staffs of the libraries and archives in which I have worked, and to the Huntington Library, Merton College, Oxford, and the History Faculty of the University of Oxford for financial support. My graduate students have also been a constant source of inspiration. Those whose research has been particularly relevant to the themes I address here include Tom Boyd, Andy Boyle, Kirsten Claiden-Yardley, Mark Geldof, Yuval Harari, Graham Long, Chris Skidmore, Tracey Sowerby, Monica Stensland, and Annette Walton, but that of David Ashton, Jamie Bartlett, Benjamin Baum, John Baxter, James Berrill, Alice Blackwood, Madeline Briggs, David Burns, Thomas Carter, Paul Cavill, Nick Craft, Lois Day, Edward Geall, Emily Glassford, Tomasz Gromelski, Huw Jones, Allison Kroll, James McComish, and Victoria Smith has also touched on this topic in different ways. I am grateful to Roger Highfield for reading the text of the lectures week by week as I delivered them, and to Steven Ellis for reading the entire revised draft and especially for advice on Ireland. Janet Foot provided invaluable support in finding and reading sources in Welsh and Kirsten Claiden-Yardley searched printed editions of wills. Lastly, and most continually, the loving encouragement of my wife, my daughters, and my mother has sustained me throughout.

Two of the great Tudor historians of the generation that taught mine died in the space between my delivering the lectures and completing the book. Cliff Davies was my doctoral supervisor and a perennial source of encouragement and advice, as well as the scholar whose published work touches most often, most closely, and most inspirationally on the themes I try to address here. David Loades not only published numerous important studies of the political and naval history of the period, but was also constant in his encouragement of younger researchers from the workshops he ran at Bangor in the 1980s to his involvement in Oxford research seminars in his retirement. They will both be sorely missed.

For the dedication of this book I have adopted an expression used by Thomas Bradwardine, fellow of Merton College, Oxford and Archbishop of Canterbury, in his *De causa Dei contra Pelagium* of 1344. It has been and remains a privilege to teach and research in an institution with deep historical roots and a lively commitment to scholarship, and one in which I am grateful for the friendship and encouragement of many academic and non-academic colleagues and many generations of students. The first ever Ford lecturer was a Mertonian, S. R. Gardiner, and he was followed by many more: Arthur Johnson, Maurice Powicke, Michael Wallace-Hadrill, Rodney Hilton, Donald Bullough, Conrad Russell, Paul Slack, James Campbell, and Rees Davies. In my time as a student the Merton history school felt the positive influence of the tutors who had developed it in the previous decades, especially Roger Highfield, John Roberts, and Ralph Davis. Roger Highfield, the anchor of successive teams of history tutors for nearly forty years, died as this book was going to press, warmly remembered by hundreds of Merton historians. As a tutor at Merton it has been a pleasure to work with their successors, Philip Waller, Robert Gildea, Karl Gerth, Matthew Grimley, and Micah Muscolino, and to share in historical debate with them and with a succession of inspirational junior research fellows and other younger colleagues, as well as with our admirable undergraduate and graduate students. I was touched by the numbers of Mertonians of all generations who attended the lectures. Bradwardine's Merton was doubtless a smaller and more closely-focused place than mine, but we have both been blessed in our college.

Contents

List of Figures

List of Abbreviations

ADN	Archives Départementales du Nord, Lille
AO	Archives Office
APC	*Acts of the Privy Council of England*, ed. J. Dasent, 2nd ser., vols i–vii, AD 1542–70 (London, 1890–3)
Bodl.	Bodleian Library
BL	British Library
CA	College of Arms
CCA	Canterbury Cathedral Archives
CEPR*	*Calendar of Entries in the Papal Registers relating to Great Britain and Ireland*, ed. W. H. Bliss et al., 19 vols to date (London and Dublin, 1893–)
CS	Camden Society
CSPDE	*Calendar of State Papers, Domestic Series, of the Reign of Edward VI 1547–1553 preserved in the PRO*, rev. edn, ed. C. S. Knighton (London, 1992)
CSPDM	*Calendar of State Papers, Domestic Series, of the Reign of Mary, 1553–1558*, ed. C. S. Knighton (Chippenham, 1998)
CSPFE	*Calendar of State Papers, Foreign Series, of the Reign of Edward VI, 1547–1553*, ed. W. Turnbull (London, 1861)
CSPFM	*Calendar of State Papers, Foreign Series, of the Reign of Mary, 1553–1558*, ed. W. B. Turnbull (London, 1861)
CUL	Cambridge University Library
EETS	Early English Text Society
ESRO	East Sussex Record Office
EcHR	*Economic History Review*
EHR	*English Historical Review*
HC	History Centre
HJ	*Historical Journal*
HKW	H. M. Colvin (ed.), *The History of the King's Works*, 6 vols (London, 1963–82)
HL	Huntington Library, San Marino, CA
HMC	Historical Manuscripts Commission
HP	*Hamilton Papers*, ed. J. Bain, 2 vols (Edinburgh, 1890–2)
HR	*Historical Research*
HS	Historical Society
KHLC	Kent History and Library Centre, Maidstone
LJ	*Journals of the House of Lords*, 10 vols (London, 1846 edn)
LMA	London Metropolitan Archives
LP*	*Letters and Papers, Foreign and Domestic, of the Reign of Henry VIII*, ed. J. S. Brewer et al., 23 vols in 38 (London, 1862–1932)*

NA	*Norfolk Archaeology*
NRA	National Register of Archives ('NRA report' indicates documents I have not seen in the original)
n.s.	new series
ODNB	*Oxford Dictionary of National Biography*, ed. H. C. G. Matthew and B. Harrison, 60 vols (Oxford, 2004)
PP	*Past and Present*
PRO	The National Archives: Public Record Office
RO	Record Office
RS	Record Society
SHC	Surrey History Centre
SS	Surtees Society
STC	*A Short-Title Catalogue of Books printed in England, Scotland, & Ireland and of English Books Printed Abroad, 1475–1640*, ed. A. W. Pollard, G. R. Redgrave, W. A. Jackson, F. S. Ferguson, and K. F. Pantzer, 2nd edn, 3 vols (London, 1976–91)
StP	*State Papers, King Henry the Eighth*, 5 vols in 11 (London, 1830–52)
TE	*Testamenta Eboracensia*, ed. J Raine and J. W. Clay, 6 vols, SS 4, 30, 45, 53, 79, 106 (London, 1836–1902)
TRHS	*Transactions of the Royal Historical Society*
TRP	*Tudor Royal Proclamations*, ed. P. L. Hughes and J. F. Larkin, 3 vols (New Haven CT and London, 1964)*
UL	University Library
YASRS	Yorkshire Archaeological Society Record Series
YCR	*York Civic Records*, ed. A. Raine, 8 vols, YASRS, 98, 103, 106, 108, 110, 112, 115, 119 (Wakefield, 1939–53)

* references in these sources are usually made to document numbers, rather than to pages.

1

The King's Wars

Henry VIII grew up knowing that great kings won battles and made conquests. Edward I, his great-great-great-great-great-great-grandfather, victor at Evesham and Falkirk, had conquered Wales and almost subdued Scotland. Edward III, his great-great-great-great-grandfather, was victorious at Halidon Hill and Crécy and took Berwick and Calais for England. Henry V, the first husband of his great-grandmother Catherine of Valois, a 'noble predecessour' whose reign he alluded to in a letter with the telling adverb 'lately', won at Agincourt and overran Normandy.[1] His grandfather Edward IV took the throne and kept it at Towton, St Albans, and Tewkesbury, and his father Henry VII did the same at Bosworth, Stoke, and Blackheath.

This was not only true of English kings. Henry's father-in-law Ferdinand of Aragon consolidated his control of Castile after the admittedly inconclusive battle of Toro and conquered Granada, the last outpost of Moorish Spain, in 1492, while his lieutenants beat the French to master Naples. Maximilian of Austria, who accompanied Henry on his own first campaign, saved the Low Countries for the Habsburgs at Guinegatte in 1478. And all the kings of France who reigned in Henry's lifetime mounted campaigns of conquest in Italy, Charles VIII to Naples, Louis XII to Genoa, Francis I to Milan, claiming along the way bloody glory at Marignano over the once invincible Swiss. Conquests placed kings in history. In November 1545, as Henry clung on to his last acquisition in France, Edmund Harvel, English agent at Venice and an accomplished stroker of the royal ego, put it crisply: 'that famous conquest of Bolaigne...shalbe a perpetual monument of the most mightye King Harry the Eight'.[2]

Of course great kings did other things too. They spread justice among their subjects, encouraged learning and godliness, built magnificent palaces, and held great festivals. Henry did, or thought he did, all these. But wherever he turned, war caught his eye. Had not even King David, the Old Testament monarch on whom he increasingly patterned himself as he came to believe in his royal supremacy over the English church and his duty to preside over his subjects' spiritual as well as their temporal welfare, been a great warrior? David, victor over Goliath, was a man of whom the women sang that Saul had slain his thousands, but David his tens of thousands, a king beset by wars on every side until the Lord put his enemies under his feet.[3]

The wars of his English ancestors had shaped the institutions available to Henry should he wish to wage war. Powerful systems of taxation both direct and indirect, able to tap the wealth of the laity, of the clergy, and even of foreign consumers of

English goods, had developed under Edward I and Edward III. So had parliament as a body able to make grants of those taxes to the king with the endorsement of the political nation.[4] The same two kings drew together the hybrid system of military recruitment inherited by Henry. All adult Englishmen had an obligation to serve in the defence of the realm, had to possess arms appropriate to their wealth as defined by Edward I's statute of Winchester of 1285, and could be gathered into armies by commissions of array of the sort Edward pioneered. But effective forces for overseas conquest were better assembled by the issue of contracts to lords, knights, and esquires to raise retinues of cavalry and infantry to fight for generous pay under their command, on the model perfected by Edward III.[5]

Those earlier wars also shaped the strategic context and the ambitions of Henry's wars. Edward I's attempts to subjugate the Scots led to two centuries of conflict punctuated by truces and occasional, fragile peace treaties, like that under which Henry's sister Margaret married James IV in 1503. These struggles left Scottish kings with a grievance over English-held Berwick and a traditional alliance with France. They left English kings with border subjects who complained of Scottish raids and with claims to overlordship that could be dusted off when required. In Wales Edward I had committed all England's resources to complete a conquest begun piecemeal by Anglo-Norman barons, but in Ireland no English king had acted so decisively to build on similar Anglo-Norman expansion and make a reality of the English crown's claim to the lordship of all Ireland. Expeditions were sent from time to time to bolster the English communities of the East and South against the assertive Gaelic lordships of the West and North and to rein in the more independent-minded of the English lords in Ireland, the earls of Ormond, Desmond, or Kildare. Only a king with a high view of royal power like Richard II tried to make much of his sovereignty over Ireland, for campaigns against O'Neills or O'Briens across mountains, forests, and bogs promised neither glamour, profit, nor comfort compared with those elsewhere. But in Ireland as in Scotland, Henry might wish to pursue titles his ancestors had been happy to underplay.

For most of Henry's predecessors and, it seems, for Henry himself, all these struggles were eclipsed by that with France, the strongest monarchy in Europe.[6] Edward I and Edward III inherited from their Angevin forebears a conflict with the French kings over lands in western France, notably Normandy and Gascony. Edward III raised the stakes by claiming that he, rather than Philip of Valois, should have inherited the French crown in 1328. His English successors kept up the claim, and Henry VI was even crowned king of France in Paris, the fruit of his father Henry V's victories, before his feeble kingship, his nobles' rivalries, and his subjects' exhaustion brought disaster and the loss of all England's French territories save Calais in 1450–3. The long war begun by Edward III shaped the imagination of the English elite as they looked back to the heroic deeds of their ancestors and read Froissart's chronicles, a work owned by lawyers and merchants as well as heralds, captains, and kings, and other texts whose contents and very language were shaped by the Anglo-French conflict.[7] The war consolidated English national and political identity, as ordinary men and women were taught to pray for the king's success, honour St George, and pay taxes for the common good, generating a passion that demanded 'justice upon the traitors' when Normandy fell in 1450.[8]

The Anglo-French war also shaped the politics of western Europe for more than a century. Each side sought alliances in Iberia, with Portugal, Castile, or Aragon. Each sought alliances in the Low Countries, with the counts of Flanders, Hainaut, or Holland, or with the great cities that made cloth from English wool. As the various principalities of the Low Countries were drawn together under the Valois dukes of Burgundy and their Habsburg successors, so they became vital partners for any English regime bent on war, or well-defended peace, with France. As Castile and Aragon were united by Ferdinand and Isabella, the same became true of the Trastámara, then Habsburg, monarchy in Spain. Henry's father's shrewdness was never more evident than in the marriages he planned for his son and heir, first Arthur then Henry, to the daughter of Ferdinand and Isabella, and for his younger daughter Mary to Charles of Ghent, heir both to the Habsburg Low Countries and, prospectively, to the Spanish kingdoms.

To understand Henry's wars and his subjects' engagement with them we must set them not just in this general background, but in the context of around a hundred years of change in England's strategic fortunes and military institutions. This has a certain logic in terms of historical analysis. It takes us from 1475, the occasion of the first great English expedition across the Channel after the traumatic collapse of Lancastrian France, to the 1570s and the inauguration of the militia trained bands that would form the basis of English military organization for the following seventy years. It shows us English regimes facing drastic change in international politics, from the consolidation of French royal power and the French invasions of Italy, through the formation and dissolution of the empire of Charles V, the most powerful European ruler since Charlemagne, to the religious civil wars of the 1560s and 1570s in the Low Countries, Scotland, and France. It embraces both English rulers beset by political and religious dissent, from a suspected child-murderer in Richard III to the consort of a foreign king in Mary I and an unmarried and excommunicate queen regnant in Elizabeth I, and those, above all Henry himself, able to draw together the political nation and capitalize on the inherited strengths of English government to pursue ambitious policies at home and abroad. It includes episodes of civil disorder from the last campaigns of the Wars of the Roses to the Northern Rebellion of 1569–70, the occasion of the last great mobilization on English soil for actual combat—as opposed to the preparations to meet successive Spanish armadas—before the civil wars of the late 1630s and 1640s.

To think of this period of a hundred years as the age of Henry VIII also bears some relationship to the experience of Henry's subjects. The men who were wise old warriors when Henry was young had fought in 1475: Thomas Howard, second duke of Norfolk, victor at Flodden, for example, or John Risley, the Yorkist courtier who went on to serve as a loyal councillor to Henry and his father.[9] Some even remembered the switchback campaigns of 1469–71: John de Vere, thirteenth earl of Oxford, who was worsted at Barnet, led the vanguard at Bosworth, and lived on until 1513, or Thomas Butler, seventh earl of Ormond, who may have fought at Towton, was captured at Tewkesbury, and raised troops for naval service in Henry's first French war.[10] In the same way the great commanders of 1569–70 had served their apprenticeships in Henry's last campaigns. Thomas Radcliffe, third earl of Sussex, knighted by Henry at Boulogne in 1544, commanded against the northern rebels. Edward Fiennes, Lord Clinton, knighted at Leith after the burning of Edinburgh that same year, was made earl of Lincoln for his role alongside Sussex.[11] Elizabeth's Irish captains too, Sir Nicholas Arnold, Sir Nicholas Bagenal, Sir James Croft, and Sir William Drury, had all blooded themselves around Boulogne in Henry's closing years.[12] At least one great man, William Paulet, marquess of Winchester, who mustered men for Henry's first wars, gathered supplies for his last campaigns and then struggled to finance Mary's and Elizabeth's wars with France and Scotland, was born around the time Edward IV crossed the Channel and died as the trained bands were nearing birth.[13]

The campaign of 1475 illustrated the complexities of English military enterprise in the wake of the Hundred Years War. Edward sought to use war against France to unite his people after the civil strife that had marked the beginning and middle of his reign, but he had trouble raising money, resorting to extra-parliamentary benevolences as well as parliamentary grants with experimental scales for the assessment of individual wealth, and his army was dominated to an unusual extent by his own close followers at court. He coordinated his invasion carefully with his ally, Charles the Bold, duke of Burgundy, but Charles got bogged down in his siege of Neuss and never came to join Edward. Edward rapidly came to terms with Louis XI, but was this a shameful abandonment of his mission of conquest, as some of his contemporaries seem to have felt, or a clever way to turn a profit—a pension from the French and a great marriage for his daughter—from an otherwise fruitless campaign?[14]

Edward's brother and northern lieutenant, Richard, duke of Gloucester, took more interest than most English kings in Scotland. In the war of 1481–4 he recaptured Berwick, which had been handed back to the Scots by Henry VI, and briefly occupied Edinburgh, but failed to depose James III. Having taken the throne from his nephew Edward V, he defeated one domestic uprising in 1483, but was overthrown by the next, as Henry Tudor returned from exile in France in 1485.[15] Henry VII kept the crown for twenty-four years but never felt entirely secure. Challenges from dynastic rivals, international conflicts, and adverse public reactions to the policies he pursued in the efforts to deal with threats internal and external interacted in frustrating ways.

At the battle of Stoke in 1487 he defeated an invasion by the backers of a boy, Lambert Simnel, whom they had crowned Edward VI at Dublin. Then he sought to neutralize the support of the Habsburgs for such ventures by dispatching small armies in 1489 and 1492 to aid them in their fight against towns and nobles who opposed their rule in the Low Countries. In the same period he sent expeditions to Brittany, trying in vain to bolster the independence of the duchy, often an English ally in the past, against the French monarchy. In 1492 he invaded France himself, but like Edward IV, and similarly let down by his allies in the Low Countries, he cut a financially attractive but inglorious deal and returned home. Meanwhile the heavy taxes he had raised, drawing on, but going beyond Edward's experiments, and amplified by a benevolence, had provoked a large revolt in Yorkshire in 1489 and a smaller one three years later. Against the first he had to mobilize a full-scale army, though the second was dealt with by local forces.[16]

A second wave of troubles followed. Perkin Warbeck, claiming the throne as the supposed younger son of Edward IV, found support in both Ireland and Scotland. Henry sent English troops under one of his leading captains, Sir Edward Poynings, to stabilize the situation in Ireland in 1495–6, and prepared a large campaign by land and sea for 1497 to punish James IV of Scots for his invasions in support of the pretender. Before the blow could fall, the largest tax grants of the fifteenth century, preceded by a forced loan, sparked revolt in the South-West and the rebel army reached Blackheath before it was defeated by the king's forces, recalled from their march towards Scotland. As Warbeck arrived in Cornwall to try to capitalize on the unrest there, Henry headed west and all submitted before him. Those of his captains who remained in the North were left to make token war on the Scots.[17]

Thereafter Henry VII sought peace, but his style of rule would condition his son's strategic options in important ways. He sought military strength for the crown through a navy equipped with large new ships and permanent dockyards and through a scheme to control the recruitment of retinues of military and political followers by noblemen and gentry. He sought financial security by the development of sources of revenue independent of parliamentary grant, above all the crown lands, the feudal dues, and the customs on trade, which, while authorized by parliament, were granted for life rather than one levy at a time. And he sought political control by the manipulation of debts imposed on leading subjects in a way that many found painful and humiliating. This gave Henry VIII at his accession in 1509 both enhanced means to make war and an attraction to the idea that war might unite him and the great men of his realm, consolidating his rule by visibly repudiating his father's ways.[18]

At first Henry, like his father, sent out small forces to aid his friends, to crusade in North Africa with the Spanish, or fight the duke of Guelders with the Dutch. By 1512, however, he was ready for full-scale war with France in alliance with other rulers, led by the pope, who were alarmed at French expansion in Italy. That summer saw an over-optimistic attempt to invade Gascony from Spain and a naval campaign of mixed fortunes in the Channel. French trade was disrupted and Brittany pillaged, but one of Henry's biggest ships, the *Regent*, went up in flames with one of his favourite courtiers, Sir Thomas Knyvet, in command. In 1513 the king, aided by the administrative skill of his rising minister Thomas Wolsey, determined to do better. The spring naval campaign was inauspicious, as Admiral Sir Edward Howard drowned in a quixotic attack in rowing-boats on the becalmed French fleet. But in the summer Henry marched into northern France with a larger English army than any seen since Edward III's siege of Calais, conquered two cities, little Thérouanne and the much larger Tournai, and defeated a French relieving force in what was soon dubbed, mocking the speed of the French flight, as the battle of the Spurs. In Henry's absence James IV invaded Northumberland and was killed together with many of his noblemen in a bloodily decisive encounter on the moors at Flodden.[19]

Henry gave Tournai a large garrison and began to plan its fortification as a new bastion of English power to match Calais, but as his allies wavered he decided to make peace in 1514. By then the enormous cost of even comparatively minor military success was becoming evident. This first war had cost around a million pounds, some ten years' ordinary crown revenue, and grants of taxes had covered only about a third of that. Much may have been financed by reserves accumulated by Henry VII, the scale of which remains shadowy thanks to the old king's habitual concern to keep his cards close to his chest. However large they were, they were now gone, and in the aftermath of war Wolsey had to implement sharp policies to cut royal spending and improve regular income, including in 1518 the return of Tournai to France. This set the tone for the reign: Henry would spend whatever money he could get to register military success, but that money might be hard to find.[20]

Henry's next military venture was in Ireland, with the dispatch in 1520 of a small army under Thomas Howard, earl of Surrey. Instructed, optimistically, to begin with his 500 or so men and limited local contacts a process that might 'reduce this land to obedience and good order', Surrey achieved little.[21] Soon the earl and Henry's other captains were back in the more familiar wars with France and Scotland, as Henry tried to take advantage of the rivalry between Francis I of France and the newly elected Holy Roman Emperor Charles V, while the Scots were drawn in to support the French. The campaigning seasons of 1522 and 1523 saw major raids on the French coast at Morlaix and Tréport and significant forces guarding the North against the Scots. Participation in a failed siege of Hesdin in Artois in 1522 was followed next year by a dramatic thrust across the Somme to threaten Paris, before Charles Brandon, duke of Suffolk, and his colleagues from the Low Countries were forced to retreat amid freezing weather and mutinous men.[22]

These campaigns were funded by new fiscal initiatives. In 1522 a general survey of personal wealth, arms, and military capacity was exploited to levy heavy forced loans, never to be repaid. In 1523 large taxes were raised from the clergy and a more efficiently assessed direct tax on landed income or goods, the lay subsidy, was perfected, though only after considerable parliamentary wrangling.[23] When funds were needed at short notice to renew the war in 1525, however, to take advantage of the capture of Francis I by Charles V's army in Italy, the limits of fiscal expansion were exposed. Henry sent out commissioners to ask his subjects for an 'amicable grant' of a swingeing proportion of their wealth, one-third from the richer clergy, one-quarter from the poorer, and between one-sixth and one-tenth from the laity. The demand was met by widespread refusals and, in some places, popular unrest. Henry backed down, though staging first submission and then pardon for the protesters, and made peace soon afterwards.[24]

From the later 1520s, as Henry concentrated on his divorce campaign and the break with Rome necessary to conclude it, his wars turned to unfamiliar channels and he entangled himself again in the awkward nexus between foreign policy, crown finance, and domestic revolt. In 1527–9 he briefly and unsuccessfully confronted England's traditional allies in the Low Countries in the attempt to press their lord, Charles V, to acquiesce in the divorce, but provoked disorder among cloth-workers unemployed thanks to his efforts at economic warfare.[25] In 1532–4 he fought the Scots in a war for which parliament refused taxes; it was born of border raiding and mutual distrust, uncommonly devoid of major initiatives on either side, and patched up by French mediation.[26] In 1534 he had to send the largest English force seen in Ireland since Richard II's reign to suppress a rebellion by the followers of the earl of Kildare, whom he had planned to remove as governor, as part of a general tightening of central control over outlying parts of his realm as the crisis over the break with Rome deepened.[27]

In 1536 he mobilized the entire South and Midlands against a huge revolt in the North, the Pilgrimage of Grace. The rebels were responding to many and diverse grievances, but prominent among them were the taxation levied to pay for the army in Ireland, the new annual tax of a tenth on clerical incomes, the statute of uses which tried to improve the king's revenue from his feudal rights, and the first phase of the dissolution of the monasteries. The dissolution, though framed in terms of the reform of religious life and the deployment of resources to other pious ends, was a policy Henry justified in his answer to the rebels as compensation for the 'extreme charges' he had to meet for his subjects' 'defence against foreign enemies'.[28] Then in 1538–40, as Francis I and Charles V made peace, he faced the threat of invasion by both major powers at the pope's behest. He responded with a vigorous programme of coastal fortification paid for by further monastic dissolutions.[29]

After 1540 the revival of tension between Habsburgs and Valois took Henry's policy back to more familiar courses and onwards into a confrontation of unprecedented scale with both the French and the Scots. Tetchy talks with James V led in summer 1542 to large-scale but aimless war. An English setback at Hadden Rigg in August was matched by the defeat of James's army in an ambush at Solway Moss in November. The stakes changed when James, allegedly stricken by the humiliation of his men, suddenly died, leaving a six-day-old daughter as queen. Henry grasped the opportunity this offered, negotiating with the nobles captured at Solway Moss for Mary, queen of Scots, to marry his son Edward and thus unite the British kingdoms, a match agreed by the treaty of Greenwich in July 1543. When, within six months, the Scots reneged on this unpalatable deal, he resolved to enforce compliance by war, while loudly reasserting claims to sovereignty over Scotland bolstered by historical research of the sort recently deployed in his campaign for ecclesiastical supremacy. Constant border raiding was joined to larger expeditions. One, backed by ships, burned Edinburgh in 1544, another Kelso and Jedburgh in 1545, but in the latter year a large English raiding force was defeated at Ancrum Moor.[30]

Meanwhile Henry joined Charles V in war against France, seeking to renew the conquests of his youth with the resources gathered in rapacious middle age. In 1543 he sent auxiliaries to the siege of Landrecies and began raids on French shipping, but his great enterprise was held over for 1544. One English army mounted a forlorn siege of Montreuil together with Habsburg forces, but their mission was mainly to distract the French from Henry's favoured prize, Boulogne, which surrendered to the king in person on 14 September after weeks of battering. Within a week Charles made a separate peace, leaving Henry to defend his conquest alone. He did so for nearly two years, fortifying and garrisoning Boulogne, raiding France by land and sea, and defending England against French invasion in 1545, when a large fleet entered the Solent and landed troops on the Isle of Wight. Peace was finally agreed in June 1546. It permitted Henry to keep Boulogne for eight years, after which the French would have to buy it back. It also restored the pensions from the French to the English crown which had featured in every peace since 1475, and which Henry chose to regard as rent for his kingdom of France. And it offered peace to the Scots, but only on ambiguous terms that might compel them to accept the treaty of Greenwich.[31]

At Henry's death in 1547 the leading captain of this last war, Edward Seymour, earl of Hertford and now duke of Somerset, took control of government on behalf of the young Edward VI. Weaker, as lord protector, than an adult monarch, yet inclining to autocracy rather than collaborative rule, and bent on a disruptive extension of Henry's Reformation in religion, he had neither the political strength to consolidate Henry's military gains nor the political strength to abandon them with confidence. He won a crushing victory over the Scots at Pinkie in September 1547 and used it to install English garrisons across southern Scotland and even on the coast north of the Firth of Forth, aiming to support the assured Scots, those who backed the marriage treaty, against their countrymen who opposed it. But he was outmanoeuvred. In summer 1548 Mary was betrothed to the dauphin and taken to France and over the next eighteen months French troops helped the Scots eliminate the English strongholds one by one, some, such as Haddington, after epic sieges. In 1549 opposition to religious change and discontent at social and economic problems sparked revolt in almost every English county, and in the South-West and East Anglia full-scale military campaigns and pitched battles were necessary to suppress the rebels. Henry II of France now saw his chance to recover Boulogne and overran its outlying forts. Those who ousted Somerset in an aristocratic coup in autumn 1549 cut their losses in March 1550 so they might 'lyve in peace tyll our master come to a more age', returning Boulogne to France, effectively giving up on the pensions paid since 1475, and paving the way for a settlement with the Scots in 1551.[32]

Henry's gains and the attempts to retain them came at astonishing cost and it was no wonder that retrenchment marked the regime led by John Dudley, duke of Northumberland, which governed after Seymour's fall. Military charges between 1539 and 1552 totalled some £3.5 million, around £1 million of it spent on campaigns in Scotland and more than £1.3 million on getting and keeping Boulogne. Direct taxation provided about £1.2 million of this. About a quarter of the sum came in subsidies levied on the clergy in addition to the annual tenths introduced in 1534–5, or in the reliefs on goods granted under Edward VI, but three-quarters of it was raised in a fierce six-year burst of taxation on the laity beginning in 1541. Here Henry combined all the exactions devised in his own reign with those of his predecessors. Seven subsidy collections, including the largest of the century so far, were topped off by three grants of the older fixed-yield fifteenth and tenth. A large

The King's Wars 9

forced loan in 1542, never repaid, was followed by another in 1544. A benevolence was raised in 1545 and a 'loving contribution' from richer taxpayers in 1546. All that still left a vast gap between income and expenditure. Perhaps £0.9 million came from sales of land, confiscated both from the monasteries and from the chantries, threatened with dissolution in 1545 and actually dissolved in 1547. The largest contribution, nearly £1.3 million, came from a debasement of the coinage that reduced its silver content from 92.5 per cent to 25 per cent, stoking inflation and causing damaging fluctuations in exchange rates and export trade. And most of what this bought was temporary—forts abandoned to the enemy, troops recruited in much larger numbers than ever before on the general European mercenary market, food eaten by soldiers or left to rot—though Henry's coastal fortifications were solid enough, and there was at least a steady campaign of naval building and administrative consolidation which made a powerful fleet an established part of the English state apparatus.[33]

Edward died young in 1553 and this led to more domestic mobilization, first in a brief succession crisis and then to confront Sir Thomas Wyatt's rebellion in 1554, mounted to oppose Queen Mary's marriage to Charles V's son Philip and the queen's restoration of Catholicism. Though the marriage treaty stipulated that England need not join in the war then in progress between Habsburgs and Valois, once Philip had succeeded his father as king of Spain and lord of the Low Countries he pressed for English engagement against France, and in 1557 he secured it. English troops helped him take Saint-Quentin and the English navy fought the French in the Channel, but the French troops of the regent Mary of Guise opened a second front from Scotland and early in 1558 the French surprised Calais. Heavy subsidies were levied, larger in annual yield at face value even than those of the 1540s, forced loans were taken, crown lands were sold, customs rates were increased, and English crown debt, which had been largely cleared after Henry VIII's borrowing spree on the money markets of Antwerp, began to mount again. All this came after several dire harvests and during a devastating outbreak of influenza. Even so Philip thought that his English subjects were not straining themselves as hard as they might, and after Mary's death he felt little obligation to help them achieve more than a face-saving mention of the possible return of Calais in the general peace of 1559.[34]

Mary's successor Elizabeth soon faced new challenges, as political and religious dissension afflicted each of her neighbours in turn. In 1560, after understandable hesitation, she intervened in Scotland to help a band of Protestant lords take control of the government from the queen mother Mary of Guise and expel her French troops. In 1562, again urged on by councillors and captains concerned with the fate of international Protestantism, she accepted an offer from the hard-pressed French Huguenots to occupy Le Havre as a guarantee for loans she had made them. This initiative ended much less successfully, as Catholic and Protestant French patched up their differences in 1563 to expel the English, who made peace in 1564, renouncing any prospect of the recovery of Calais, for which the queen had hoped. Her navy, steadily reinforced, played a significant part in both these campaigns, but its costs contributed to the alarming bill of some £0.75 million for what were meant to be limited ventures. Parliamentary subsidies, including that with the highest yield at face value of the entire century, covered two-thirds of this, and increasing customs duties some of the rest, but international loans were still necessary and these costs left the queen with a lasting aversion to the expense of war.[35]

For the next dozen years Elizabeth engaged in the French Wars of Religion and in the revolt against Spanish rule which took shape in the Low Countries from 1566 by more indirect means. She lent money and weaponry to the Huguenots and the Dutch patriots and encouraged cooperation between them. She turned a blind eye to attacks on Spanish shipping or illegal trading with the Spanish colonies by her own subjects and by Dutch and French privateers who used her ports. She did not stop some of her leading noblemen and veteran captains working with London merchants and French and Dutch exiles to recruit companies of volunteers, hundreds strong, to join the rebel armies. In 1568–9 she confiscated money on its way by sea to the Low Countries to pay the Spanish army of the duke of Alba and brought on a threat of invasion by the duke and his men. Open war in alliance with the Dutch did not come until 1585 and English troops did not return to France until 1589, but forces were sent to Scotland to back the Protestant regency regime there in 1572–3 and from 1570 a new class of faster, more nimble but heavily-gunned 'race built' warships was added to the navy. For all the rhetoric of Elizabeth's peaceful rule, martial activity of different sorts and the prospect of war were constant in her reign.[36]

Elizabeth's own realms, moreover, were not immune to the troubles of the times. In England the last great revolt of the sixteenth century broke out in the North in 1569, as popular anger at the imposition of reformed religion blended with uncertainty over the succession, stirred by the flight to England of Mary, queen of Scots, and the frustration of great northern lords edged out of regional power by southern courtiers and ambitious local gentlemen. Forces more than twice the size of the rebel host were marched north to suppress the rising. Meanwhile the English military establishment in Ireland continued to grow, as it had done ever since the Kildare revolt of 1534, encouraged by the proclamation of Henry's title as king— rather than merely lord—of Ireland in 1541 and the associated aspiration to exercise effective rule over the entire island. At first this was done largely by persuading Gaelic lords of the benefits of submission to Henry and assimilation to the social and political elite of the new kingdom, but in the later 1540s the army expanded through the establishment of garrisons like those in Scotland. From the 1550s there ensued a policy of plantation, whereby uncooperative Gaelic clans saw their land confiscated and given to English settlers in militarized colonies likened with increasing frequency to those of the Romans. By the late 1560s these changes, together with attempts to enforce the Reformation, produced a new kind of Irish revolt, one mixing Gaelic resistance to plantation with Old English resentment at the power of New English settlers and opposition to religious change. The government's response was an unstable mixture of private-enterprise colonialism and the use of regional captains deploying punitive expeditions and martial law, a solution which left subsidies from English revenues to Irish military expenditure increasing, despite the insistence of a succession of governors that they could make Ireland pay for itself.[37]

As this narrative suggests, the age of Henry VIII was certainly an age of war. Slightly fewer than half the years between 1475 and 1575 saw English military activity against France or Scotland or in the Low Countries, a figure that rises past half when major domestic revolts are added in and reaches nearly three-quarters when we consider the sustained effort in Ireland from 1534 onwards. Some of these wars were more freely chosen by England's rulers than others. Henry's three wars with France, for example, were entered to fulfil ideals of royal honour, live up to the record of his ancestors, or compete with his royal contemporaries, but he could have avoided them had he wished. Somerset's war with Scotland was risked because the prize on offer was too temptingly significant to resist. Other wars— Henry VII's intervention in Brittany, Henry VIII's war with the Low Countries, or Elizabeth's early intervention in Scotland—seem to have been undertaken more reluctantly, as the best means available to meet a wider aim. Sometimes war was forced on English rulers, as in James IV's invasion of 1513 or the French attack on Boulogne in 1549.

Yet such distinctions are less clear than they might look. The lure of honourable conquest on the model of the past may have driven Henry VII more than we think.[38] There may have been more policy in Henry VIII's wars than at first sight appears, first aiming to draw the nobility together under his rule after the divisions of the Wars of the Roses and the oppression of his father's rule, then trying to pacify the quarrels unleashed by his Reformation by uniting his people against the French.[39] Because of the frequency with which taxation featured as a cause of revolt, finally, campaigns to repress revolt, which rulers would certainly have wished to avoid, were often the indirect result of other decisions to wage war; just as were, for example, Scottish invasions of England in response to English invasions of France. As Henry VII's councillor Edmund Dudley warned Henry VIII at the start of his reign, war is 'a greate consumer of treasure and riches' and there 'are mayny waies to enter into yt, and the begyning semeth a greate pleasure, but the waie is verie narroo to come honorablely owt therof'.[40]

The age of Henry VIII was an age of war, yet these wars have not loomed as large as they might in historical writing on the period. It would be wildly unfair to suggest that they have not been studied. Biographers of Henry such as J. J. Scarisbrick, Lacey Baldwin Smith, David Starkey, and Lucy Wooding have stressed his engagement with war: as the most recent of them put it, 'military achievement and military defence were perhaps the most weighty preoccupations consistently sustained by Henry throughout his reign'.[41] Individual campaigns and whole wars have been analysed in their political and diplomatic contexts by a long succession of scholars, prominent among them Charles Cruickshank, Marcus Merriman, David Potter, John Currin, and Paul Hammer. Particular practices and institutions have been masterfully investigated: taxation by Roger Schofield, George Bernard, and Richard Hoyle, recruitment by Jeremy Goring, food supply by Cliff Davies, the navy by David Loades and Nicholas Rodger, and the Calais garrison by David Grummitt.[42] Henry's noblemen's military careers have been charted by Helen Miller, those of his most experienced captains by Luke MacMahon, those of Elizabethan captains in Ireland by Rory Rapple, and those of Elizabethan volunteers in the French Wars of Religion and the Dutch Revolt by David Trim.[43] English adaptation to the tactical and technical innovations of continental warfare has been tested by Gervase Phillips, David Eltis, Mark Fissel, and James Raymond.[44] In what follows I shall draw gratefully upon all this sterling work. Yet apart from two pioneering studies by Cliff Davies, the wider impact of war has been neglected.[45] Certainly there is nothing like the academic industry surrounding the Hundred Years War or the British Civil Wars.

There are many reasons for this comparative neglect. Insofar as the history of war has been left to military historians, they have not found much to excite them. There are no recognizably great generals or sensational battles. Our period lies between the age of Edward III and Henry V, of Crécy, Poitiers, and Agincourt, and that of Cromwell and Marlborough, of Marston Moor, Dunbar, and Blenheim. Its military history has all too often been told not in the epic mode, but in that of tragicomedy: Henry VIII at the comic end, in his bulbous armour with its 54-inch waistline (see Fig. 1.1), hoisted onto his horse from his 'table...to lift one on horsbacke'; Sir Edward Howard at the tragic, plunging to his watery death.[46] There are no definitively new weapon-systems or tactics or strategies to evaluate. In the first

Fig. 1.1. King Henry VIII's armour of 1540 (Royal Collection Trust / © Her Majesty Queen Elizabeth II 2017).

Fig. 1.2. St Mawes Castle, Cornwall. Photograph by the author.

great age of pike and shot and *trace italienne* artillery fortification, the English seemed to prefer bills to pikes, bows to shot, and Henry's old-fashioned coastal forts, as rounded as his armours (see Fig. 1.2), to the beguiling geometry of the new continental bastions.[47] What victories there were have been hard to work into our island story: Flodden and Pinkie a bloody embarrassment to a United Kingdom, Sampford Courtenay and Dussindale an inglorious slaughter of peasant protesters. Those in search of swashbuckling glamour have hurried past to Elizabeth's reign, to Drake and Grenville and the Armada war, a climax to which Henry provides a prelude of questionable value summed up by the fate of the *Mary Rose*, toppling, overweighted like her master, into the waters of the Solent.

Henry's England has also been peripheral to the debate on the military revolution. Historians and historical sociologists have been asking for more than fifty years how important the need for fiscal and military institutions to defend subject populations and compete with other states was as a cause of the development of the powers of the modern state, compared with, for example, the extractive ambitions of the dominant classes, the demand from subjects for justice, or the princely duty to impose the godly discipline of the Reformation and Counter-Reformation.[48] A generation of debate suggests that while war often made a significant contribution to political development elsewhere, its effects on Tudor England were underwhelming. Henry dramatically drove up state revenue per head of population, but this was more by his plunder of the church and reckless debasement than by his innovations in direct taxation.[49] After Henry, as price inflation complicated the government's problems, total revenue contracted drastically in real terms. Only in the first half of Edward's reign and the early years of Elizabeth's did it reach more than half of what Henry had raised in 1543–6, and thereafter it fell below one-third of that level for the rest of the century apart from a blip in the Armada crisis.[50]

Henry had solved his financial problems by short-term means, so much so that historians of the seventeenth century have argued that Henry's wartime spending and the alienation of monastic lands that funded it deprived the Stuarts of the resources they needed to govern England effectively and thus led to the civil wars.[51] Because Henry had not tried to develop long-term sources of revenue, England emerged from the sixteenth century with no regular system of direct taxation or of domestic indirect taxation. And even when parliamentary subsidies were voted in the early seventeenth century they had declined into farcical under-assessment. The slide began as soon as Henry died and probably before. Several peers lowered their declared wealth between the 1546 and 1547 payments of the subsidy voted by parliament in 1545, in 1558 the queen had to point out to subsidy commissioners that everyone knew they had assessed their own wealth at a level 'farre under the some of that they all knowe you have', and by 1566 the Lord Treasurer himself would admit only to an income two-thirds of that he had enjoyed in 1559. By the 1560s, subsidy assessments, when they can be compared with probate assessments of the wealth of the same individuals, were tapping just over a fifth of real wealth, where they had in the 1520s reached nearly half. Already by 1545–6, as Henry made intensive use of the subsidy, individual assessments were down to a third of wealth as assessed for probate and there was a significant increase, compared with the 1520s, in the number of taxpayers who defaulted irretrievably on payment. At least in the North, vigorous assessment, probably over-assessment, of individual wealth in 1540–1 fell back as early as in 1543–4.[52] Meanwhile there was little growth in bureaucracy to administer what revenues there were.

Developments in military institutions were equally unimpressive. From the last years of Henry's reign there was a shift in emphasis in raising troops from what Jeremy Goring called a 'quasi-feudal' to a 'national' basis, changing the emphases between the two systems of recruitment inherited by Henry from the thirteenth and fourteenth centuries. Armies composed of contingents recruited by individual noblemen and gentlemen from their servants, tenants, and friends were superseded from the 1540s by forces made up of county contingents levied by commissioners informed by regular musters of men of military age from every parish.[53] But of the standing armies whose rise was central to the idea of the military revolution there was no sign, except in the small Irish establishment, the even smaller Calais and Berwick garrisons, the tiny ordnance team based at the Tower of London, and the court guards of yeomen and gentlemen pensioners.[54] The one attempt at standing companies of heavy cavalrymen of the sort maintained by the French, Burgundians, Venetians, and others since the mid-fifteenth century lasted only two years until the money for them ran out in 1552.[55] Henry's efforts did generate a substantial standing navy and his successors maintained it, but after its Elizabethan glories it readily fell prey to corruption and decay.[56] If we ask a rather different set of questions from those usual in the military revolution debate, we can see that engagement in war shaped the political development of Henry's England, in relations between towns and central government, for example, or the articulation of noble power.[57] But by the standards of ascending Brandenburg-Prussia, or *grand siècle* France, or even the market-driven, stakeholder-negotiated Dutch Republic, the state formation induced by Tudor England's wars was feeble.[58] It would take the civil wars and those of William III and Marlborough to make England, then Britain, a fiscal-military state.[59]

This was a reality of which mid-Tudor statesmen were uncomfortably aware. William, Lord Paget and William Cecil, Lord Burghley stated it repeatedly in letters and memoranda.[60] For Paget in February 1549, the English government had 'no money at all to speake of in a kinges case' and to 'have yt of the subjectes' was impractical, since disruption to trade would limit what could be had from merchants, clothiers, and wool-farmers and, while any true subject would 'helpe with all that he hath for defence of the realme', not every man was 'throughly wise and able to understand and waye his duetie'. Two months later he added to these fiscal weaknesses two military defects: England had 'great scarsitie of cheiftaynes to conducte the warres' and 'great scarsitie of men and those that be are not most willing to serve in the warre but disobedient and slouthfull'.[61] Twenty years later, Cecil reiterated the 'lack of captens, of soldiers exercised and trayned, of marryners for the navy, of stores of municion, and of treasure to maintain armyes by land or sea', concluding that 'it wer a fearfull thing to imagyn, if the enemyes war at hand to assayle the realme, of what force the resistance wold be'.[62]

The frustration of those charged with the management of English policy is clear, and it has been well used by historians studying the interaction of fiscal power and international strategy to explain why Mary and Elizabeth acted so much more cautiously than their father.[63] What is less certain is what the frustration represents. Were Paget, Cecil, and their colleagues looking at a country bled dry of money and men to feed over-ambitious military strategies by efficient systems of taxation and conscription, or at a society which had successfully fended off most efforts to tap its wealth and manpower, leaving those in government fuming but impotent? Here comparisons may be helpful. These statesmen had to make their assessments in comparative terms, weighing their resources against those of rival states. Sir Nicholas Bacon, for example, pointed out in 1559 that France was four times the size of England and had four times the money and men, and that its king enjoyed, if anything, larger powers than the English monarch to draw on those resources.[64] In the concluding chapter we shall seek to set the effects of Henry's wars on his people in the context of what the debate on the military revolution and other scholarship has taught us about war, state, and society across early modern Europe.

If Henry's wars have not looked sufficiently important to historians of war or historians of the military-fiscal state, most historians have found other things in Henry's times more seductive or significant and have focused attention on those. The history of foreign relations has concentrated on a newly institutionalized diplomacy of resident ambassadors and reflective state papers and on the practice of competitive display: the Field of Cloth of Gold makes much more of a splash than the battle of the Spurs. The recovery of the crown's strength after the Wars of the Roses and the destructive politics of Henry's court have stimulated analysis of political change at the centre and in the regions, as has the debate over a putative Tudor Revolution in Government. Economic and social historians have seen the period as the opening of a phase of significant change, whether of the transition from feudalism to capitalism with the atrophy of serfdom, the enclosure of common land and open fields, and the rise of the cloth industry, or with the beginnings of sustained population recovery after the fifteenth-century slump. Change in all these areas has seemed more important than the paltry shifts evident in warfare. Yet one of the great lessons of the twentieth-century expansion of social and cultural history is that something does not have to be new to be important, that *l'histoire immobile* is just as central to the lives of those who live through it as *l'histoire événementielle*.[65] If this is true of feast and famine, drought and flood, birth and death, why should it not be true of war and peace, as martial decades alternated with and differed from peaceful ones?

Above all Henry's wars have been eclipsed by his Reformation. There is no doubt the Reformation is important, but we only know how important because we have been arguing about it so intensely for so long. Sixty years ago we did not have a locally, socially, and culturally contextualized history of the English Reformation. Then three or four waves of scholars went into the archives and through the cultural world of sixteenth- and early seventeenth-century England and gave us one. Today we have only small parts of a locally, socially, and culturally contextualized history of the Tudors' wars. The same archives and the same contexts can be examined to remedy that.

The spread of Reformation ideas has been tracked through means of transmission oral, written, and printed, and in Chapter 2 we shall look for engagement with war in the media and the minds of Henry's England. The Reformation has been considered in terms of its impact on communities of different sorts and in Chapter 3 we shall examine the impact of war on towns and villages across England. The Reformation has been tested for its effects on different social groups—clergy, gentry, yeomanry—and in Chapter 4 we shall concentrate on the caste most closely associated with war, the nobility and gentry. The Reformation has been seen as a contributor to economic and social change on many levels, from the redistribution of land at the dissolution of the monasteries to the birth of the ethic of capitalism. In Chapter 5 we shall consider the impact of war on trade, industry, and agriculture. Much has been written about the psychological influences of the Reformation, from changing religious experience to individualism and companionate marriage. In Chapter 6 we shall see what we can of the physical and emotional effects of war on individuals and groups. And lastly the Reformation has been given a central role in the consolidation of the English state and English national identity, bonfire night and all. In Chapter 7 we shall consider the role of war in the relationship between the king and his subjects and in the making of Englishness. It seems to me that what we need is a history of war in the age of Henry VIII that will have some of the range, richness, and subtlety of the present historiography of the Reformation. I could not construct that history in six lectures or in a comparatively short book. I cannot do it at all in the way the subject deserves. But let us at least think constructively together about how such a history might look.

2

Wars and Rumours of Wars

The age of Henry VIII may well have been an age of wars, but how much did those wars engage his subjects, whether as combatants or watchers from the home front? It is tempting to think that wars before the age of Louis XIV, or of Napoleon, or even of Lloyd George, mobilized only a small proportion of the population and were too feeble to affect non-combatants in more than passing ways. Try telling that, it is tempting to respond, to the French peasants burnt out of their homes by the Black Prince or Henry V. But we are right to ask whether Henry's wars were neither as intrusive as those of the twentieth century nor as thoroughly reported as those of the twenty-first.

Certainly Henry's armies and navies drew in ever more of his subjects. From 1475 until the 1540s, the forces involved in the campaigns mounted by English monarchs grew ever larger and at a rate much faster than the population was increasing (see Fig. 2.1). In 1475 Edward IV took 13,451 men to France and in 1492 Henry VII took a similar number; both armies were larger than those Henry V led on the Agincourt campaign and the conquest of Normandy.[1] Henry VIII presided over a leap upwards in size as he tried to compete with the larger forces available to his Valois and Habsburg rivals. In 1513 he led probably more than 28,000 Englishmen to France, joining to them 7,000 or more troops hired from Germany and the Low Countries, while more than 26,000 marched north to meet the Scots at Flodden.[2] In 1544 the English levies in France totalled over 32,000, while several thousand more faced the Scots even after the force of some 15,000 that had burnt Edinburgh that summer was withdrawn.[3] Armies sent out of the country were smaller thereafter, but nonetheless substantial: some 21,500 invaded Scotland in 1547, nearly 15,000 in 1548; just over 7,000 campaigned against France in 1557 and in Scotland in 1560; and up to 6,000 occupied Le Havre in 1562.[4] Meanwhile fleets manned by two or three thousand men were set out in parallel with most of these campaigns.[5]

Direct threats to Henry's security produced greater efforts still. To face the Pilgrimage of Grace in 1536 he envisaged an army of 100,000 men, though his lieutenants mustered only a third of that number and led perhaps 16,000 to face the 30,000 or more rebels.[6] At the climax of Henry's military exertions, as England faced war against the French and Scots in the summer of 1545, three great armies were prepared to meet a French invasion. They were never fully mobilized, though the Worcestershire contingent, for example, marched three days towards Portsmouth when Oxfordshire mistakenly signalled news of a landing; the Kent men marched all night into Sussex before being countermanded; 1,500 Londoners

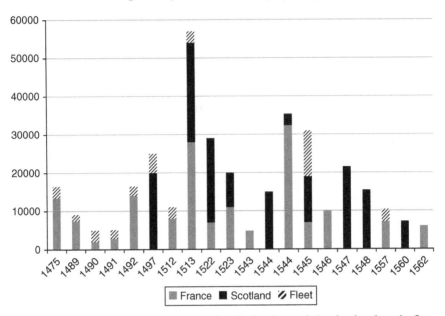

Fig. 2.1. English soldiers sent to France and to the borders with Scotland and on the fleet, 1475–1562.

summoned to Portsmouth made it to Farnham before they were sent back; and even the Glamorgan captains got as far as planning their victualling for a concentration on Severnside. The armies totalled 90,131 men drawn from Wales and England south of the Trent, over and above 12,000 on the fleet, 5,000 sent to Boulogne, and others fighting the Scots. In all more than 110,000 adult men stood ready to fight, out of perhaps 600,000 living in southern and south midland England and Wales at the time: more than one in six adult males, or, to judge from muster returns, one in three of those fit for action.[7] By the same token, perhaps one in twelve of the smaller adult male population of 1513 marched either to Flodden or to Tournai. Henry's wars, then, certainly mobilized his subjects, or at least a good number of the grown men among them. Even in 1513 most people must have known someone who served.

A significant proportion of Henry's subjects in all his realms took part in his wars, then, but by no means the majority. That might not matter so much if their compatriots were feeling the effects of war or concerning themselves with war. It is hard to know what people were thinking about in the past, in an age before even diaries, let alone social media. Yet we can ask what they were reading about and writing to each other about and perhaps what they were talking about. Let us begin with the most widespread reading matter of the age, almanacs. Ephemeral, mostly cheap, but compelling and potentially useful in avoiding disease, farming efficiently, and preparing for national calamities, almanacs were published in their hundreds and read by anyone who could read, from husbandmen and artisans to academics and peers of the realm.[8] Their style was familiar enough to be readily satirized. During Henry's last war with France, some wag produced *A Mery Prognosticacion for the Yere of Chrystes Incarnacyon A Thousande Fyve Hundred Fortye and Foure*, a spoof almanac in verse featuring, in the time-honoured tradition of English comedy, a twelve-line joke about breaking wind. The author caught the flavour of astrological prediction perfectly with the couplet

> Saturne and Mars sheweth it playne
> The eyght day of Apryl it may chaunce to rayne.[9]

Yet satire could not stop devotees devouring the product. Sir Edward Don, a Buckinghamshire knight, was one such. His household accounts show that between March 1518 and March 1551 he bought twenty-nine prognostications and almanacs, mostly for a penny each, sometimes two or three at a time.[10] That he managed to buy nine between 1518 and 1524, years for which only nine editions printed for the English market now survive, must suggest either his obsessiveness, or the numbers we have lost.[11] Less prominent readers, meanwhile, English and Welsh, left notes of their ownership on various surviving copies.[12]

Almanacs predicted political events as well as storms and epidemics and some authors felt surprisingly free to comment on the great and the good. One edition for 1517 speculated, not unreasonably but perhaps rather cheekily, that while Henry VIII was under the influence of Venus he would be likely to 'passe the tyme in honour amonge fair ladyes in most noble maner'.[13] More dangerously, one for 1539 suggested that the set of the stars in the early part of the year 'shall a lyttel greve hym and shall let hym in causys of maryages'.[14] When dealing with popular rebels like those in the South-West in 1497, the allusions to current affairs could be more direct still. One writer for 1498 predicted that 'the kyngis and prynces shall subdue theyr adversaryes as sayd the last yere in my pronostycacions, wherby Cornyshmen yf they had ben wyse myght have ben ware'.[15] Keen to prove the accuracy of his predictions, another author counted off in his 1544 edition nine of his predictions for 1543 that had been proved correct, such as the suggestion that the alliance between the king of France and the duke of Cleves would not remain 'fast nor durable'.[16]

Of a sample of ninety-three almanacs presenting prognostications for particular years published in England, or on the continent but in English, between 1498 and 1569, twenty-eight, nearly one in three, made some specific reference to war, whether to its presence or absence. This might seem an unimpressive proportion, but twenty-one are so fragmentary that it is hard to tell what they covered and indeed others have headings for sections on peace and war, or on the prospects for individual rulers, of which no detail survives. 'Of peace and war' was a regular section heading for Gaspar Laet of Borgloon, commended by one translator as an author 'knowen of olde for an expert maister in that science', whose predictions, often, it was claimed, proved right by events, were published in English regularly between 1517 and 1530, for members of his family who followed him, and for other later writers.[17]

Buyers could choose between reassuringly local observers of the heavens— Anthony Askham at York, William Bourne at Gravesend, William Kenningham at

Norwich, Leonard Digges in Kent, Lewes Vaughan at Gloucester, Henry Low and John Securis at Salisbury—and more exotic experts such as Antonius de Montulmo or Achilles Pirmin Gasser.[18] More exotic still was Nostradamus, whose predictions appeared in English from 1559. It is hard to say what readers were to make of cryptic lines like 'in the peace shalbe mortal warre', and one wonders how books fared on the English market that promised so consistently 'to Fraunce supreme victory', 'Fraunce to be greatly augmented, to triumphe, to magnifie', and 'the enemies of Fraunce in ruine and in subjection to the monarkes of France'.[19] Yet his publishers persevered, with at least eleven English editions between 1559 and 1568.[20] If Nostradamus was unnerving but vague, some authors were much more specific about events. Gaspar Laet foresaw that Henry VIII would be 'enclyned to warr' in 1523 and would spend much on it; that year's parliament voted unprecedented subsidies for an army that marched to within striking distance of Paris.[21] In 1534 Gaspar Laet junior predicted that Charles V would 'wynne townes'; he was wrong, but only by a few months, for in June 1535 the emperor spent the plundered gold of the Incas on the conquest of Tunis.[22]

Other writers made general forecasts which were at least clear, such as that the conjunctions of 1548 between Saturn and Mars and Jupiter and Mars signified 'battell, and warre, and much contrariousnes', or suggested helpful principles, such as that a year when Christmas Day fell on a Saturday would see 'great warre in many countreys'; sunshine on the twelfth day after Christmas, wind on Twelfth Night, or red clouds on the morning of New Year's Day were equally indicators of conflict.[23] Others again tied their comments on war to professional or temperamental groups subject to different astrological influences. Achilles Pirmin Gasser told those subject to Mars, including soldiers, captains of war, butchers, hangmen, and Turks, that they might go on a journey or make war profitably in spring 1546 'yf thei bee not diseased in the shoulders and legges'.[24] For some the identification of influential planets with vengeful pagan deities sounded more than incidental. William Kenningham warned that in winter 1563–4, as Elizabeth's first ill-fated intervention in the French Wars of Religion dragged towards a peace treaty, 'Mars anguler in the house of regall poure and imperie thursteth to bath his sworde in blode'.[25] For some readers the predictions of woe were alarmingly immediate. One, probably from the Chorley family of Lancashire, copied out of the peace and war section of an almanac for 1544, now apparently lost, the warning that 'pryncipally in owr realme her' there would be 'waryans and open war' in which 'many men' would be 'spowled and slayne howses castelles and cetyes shalbe taken brent and destrowed' and 'the peple shalbe withowt merce or pyte'.[26]

For the almanacs' readers their predictions perhaps supplanted those of an older brand of prophecy. Prophecies attributed to Merlin, Bede, Thomas the Rhymer, John of Bridlington, and other soothsayers were much discussed at all social levels in the 1530s and their circulation forbidden by statute in 1542, 1550, and 1563.[27] Much of their power rested in the way they tied historic wars to doom-laden readings of the future, generally couched in terms of heraldic animal imagery. The 'grett battelles in Engeland' of the Wars of the Roses, pitting 'the son ageynst the father', the battle of Bosworth where the blue boar of the earl of Oxford and hart's head of the Stanleys slew the white boar of Richard III, followed by Flodden where the white lion of the Howards overcame the red lion of Scotland, set the scene for cataclysmic wars between North and South, East and West, featuring invasions from France, Flanders, Denmark, Norway, and Ireland, thousands slain, one king killed in battle and another beheaded, before the victor set off for conquests in France and the Holy Land.[28]

Not just English history, but international events of the 1520s were keyed into these predictions to increase their immediacy: the wars between England, France, and the Habsburgs, the Ottoman invasions, and the sack of Rome.[29] The prophecies were formulaic, but insistent on the troubles war would bring: 'many a comly knyght shalbe cast under fete', 'many a wyfe and mayde in morenyng be browght', the streets of London will run with 'stremes blody', 'the more parte off the worlde shalbe distroyed'.[30] For greater insight, if not reassurance, some readers triangulated astrological science with older predictions. One added to a French printed prognostication of 1568 notes in English of a prophecy 400 years old foretelling 'The wrothe of god opon us' for 1573 and 'A gret battell' for 1575.[31] More upbeat prophecies were available. A long treatise of the 1510s, full of practical suggestions for the reform of Irish government, digressed suddenly onto an old prophecy that the English king who brought Ireland to order would proceed to subdue France, rescue the Greeks from the Turks, liberate the Holy Land, and die Emperor of Rome.[32] But this vision was in the minority.

If the predominant tone of the prophets and astrologers was pessimistic, at least some of the latter offered a remedy. Lewes Vaughan promised for 1559 'warre, contention, stryfe, manslaughter, commotions and tumultes' for winter; 'great preparation and going forth to warre' for spring, when 'many shall come to theyr ende by the swoorde'; and 'mortall warre, contentions, and bloudshed' for summer. No wonder he ended thus: 'Therefore let us pray unto God the auctour of peace, to tourne, converte and chaunge, discensions, discordes, commocions and warre, in to peace and concorde, for all thinges is in the hands of God.'[33] Peace and war did indeed feature regularly in the prayers of his contemporaries. From Cranmer's first English prayer book of 1549 onwards, ministers and congregations used the collects for peace at every matins and evensong and prayed at matins

> Geve peace in our time, O Lorde
> Because there is none other that fyghteth for us, but only thou, O God.[34]

For centuries before that the Sarum rite had included a Latin prayer for peace in our time in the canon of the mass and English instructions at the bidding of the beads to pray for 'the unitye and peace of all chrysten realmes, and in especyal for the good state, peace and tranquillite of this realme of Englande', and for 'peace, bothe on lande and on water', sometimes even 'For the pees of thes landes Ynglond and Fraunce, that God make perpetual pees bytwix hem'.[35]

In their reading and their prayers, then, Henry's subjects had plenty of opportunity to think about war. When all this worrying gave way to real conflict, English kings and princes since Edward III had sent out official newsletters to tell the realm of their doings.[36] Henry VII did so regularly. In 1489 he sent out at least two different letters about the progress of his army in Brittany and the flight of the French before them, one of which was passed on to the Pastons and the other to the town of Colchester.[37] In 1492 he wrote to the authorities at York, explaining how he had besieged Boulogne, well garrisoned and fortified with 'bulwarks, fauce brayes and othre subtilties', for sixteen days and done great damage, before accepting highly generous peace terms from the French to avoid further losses among his men or further costs to his kingdom, 'for the wele of our subgietts is oon of the things next our owne suertie we tender moost'.[38] In 1497, knowing that the Londoners would be 'desirous to undirstand the certaynte of such ffeat and exploytis of the warre as owir army hath doon', Henry wrote to the mayor, explaining how James IV of Scots had first 'shameffully ffled' at the approach of the force sent under the earl of Surrey to relieve the siege of Norham, and then 'ffled shamefully and sodeynly' when Surrey entered Scotland to offer him battle. Interestingly, while crowing over the Scots, Henry did not bury bad news, admitting that his troops had returned home sooner than expected despite the great efforts he had made to provision them, and vowing to investigate the causes of this premature end to the campaign, which had been 'full gretly' to his 'dyspleasure'.[39] By the 1520s news was deployed to chivvy taxpayers, details of the successes of Suffolk's army in France in 1523 sent out with requests for early payment of the subsidies to sustain its progress.[40] And already in that decade England's neighbours were trying to flavour the news circulating among her political and economic elites, Charles V's ambassadors sending their servant to the mayor and aldermen of London to tell them of the emperor's capture of Tournai and Milan.[41]

Other royal letters recounted the defeat of rebellion with carefully nuanced detail. Henry VII told the bishop of Bath and Wells how Perkin Warbeck had been repulsed from the walls of Exeter and now faced 'the final conclusion of the matter' in confrontation with the king and his 'host royal'. A month later he painted a picture for the mayor and citizens of Waterford of Perkin's capture and the dramatic 'punition of this great rebellion', as the commons of Devon and Cornwall presented themselves before the king and his commissioners with halters round their necks, begging 'full humbly with lamentable cries for our grace and remission'.[42] Mary told the gentry of Shropshire how she had 'discomfited' Wyatt's rebels despite their march on London. She named the captured captains and revealed that interrogation showed how their true aim was not to oppose her foreign marriage, but 'to destroy our person and deprive us of our estate and dignity royal'.[43]

Some documents surviving in private archives may be partial copies of royal letters of this sort. One that reached the Mores of Loseley lists the destruction wrought on the coast of Brittany by the naval raid of summer 1558: twenty-three townships burnt together with many gentlemen's houses—one of them 'as fayer a howse as any in Bryttaine and was phynyshed but on yere agoo'—and fifty-seven ships burnt in the harbour at Conquet.[44] Lists of the composition of royal armies also circulated. The abbot of Burton copied one detailing the size of retinues for the 1492 campaign into the abbey's register, next to a prognostication of English conquests in France attributed to the Great Turk's personal astrologer.[45] Lists of captains with their badges and banners, like those for 1475 and 1513, were passed between heralds and other aficionados.[46] In 1557 the earl of Bath procured two copies of a breakdown of King Philip's forces in the Netherlands, capturing the international flavour of his army with its awkwardly Anglicized terms—6,000 'swartrutters horsemen' or *schwarze Reiter*, German cavalrymen, and 2,000 'lawnceknyghtes of allmayne' or German landsknecht infantry—and reflecting the optimism of Habsburg planning with its assurance that there was provision for sixth months of campaigning 'for the hole armye in all things'.[47] Notes of the terms of treaties too might be added to private papers, as Sir Thomas Cawarden or Sir William More did with the treaty of Câteau-Cambrésis in 1559 or the earl of Bath with the treaty of Edinburgh of 1560.[48]

Into this world of official standardized manuscript news entered printed news pamphlets. Their rise was not as rapid in England as in France, Germany, or the Netherlands, but by fits and starts they gained ground and they were certainly read.[49] In 1513 two printers produced accounts of Flodden and each now survives in a handwritten transcript, suggesting their circulation and concentrated consumption. One caused uproar at Norwich in 1515, when a Lancashire priest defaced it in protest at local insistence that his countrymen had fled the battle, leaving the East Anglians to win it.[50] By the 1540s government control and private newsgathering were blending to produce more substantial productions. In 1544 inaccurate pamphlets about the earl of Hertford's devastating invasion of Scotland had to be called in for destruction before its events were narrated in an approved 32-page text that began life as a letter to Lord Russell.[51] When it came to the Pinkie campaign of 1547, William Patten, who had accompanied the army, produced an account of over 300 pages, illustrated with maps of the action (see Fig. 2.2).[52] The survival of a copy in at least one gentry family collection suggests that it did circulate, and another copy is marked with the substantial but not extravagant price of 12*d*, half that of its near contemporary the *Book of Common Prayer*.[53] A printed bird's eye view of the battle was also produced, the first to depict a battlefield in the British Isles (see Fig. 2.3).[54] The Northern Rising in 1569–70 generated a slew of pamphlets, and, as we shall see, they had been anticipated by a steady run of publications about the French Wars of Religion.[55]

As the printing of the letter to Russell suggests, news about war was also included in private letters. Those on campaign wrote home to their families, friends, and colleagues as they had done during the Hundred Years War and those letters were then passed on to others.[56] From 1475 we have Thomas Stonor's cheery letter from the camp at Guînes, recounting the comeuppance of an arrogant Frenchman and speculating that 'I suppose the kyng wyll go the next way to Pares', and Sir John Paston's more downbeat account of the end of the campaign.[57] From 1513 we have one detailed letter sent to a Worcester merchant from the siege of Thérouanne and passed on by him to the prior of Worcester, and another to the earl of Devon from Guinegatte, listing the French prisoners from the battle of the Spurs, describing Henry's conquest of Thérouanne and repeatedly thanking God and St George for the king's successes and his 'moost amiable and loving' relationship with his ally the Emperor Maximilian.[58] In 1557 Francis, earl of Bedford sent several reports

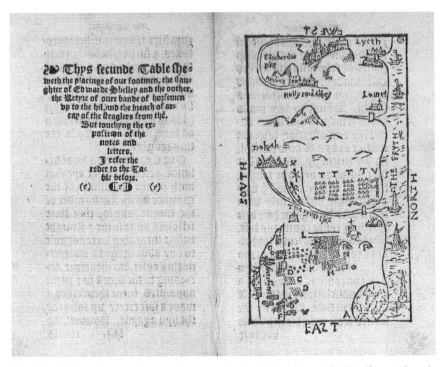

Fig. 2.2. William Patten, *The expedicion into Scotlande* (London, 1548) (Bodleian Library).

from the Saint-Quentin campaign to Sir William Cecil, and in between their arrival the countess kept Cecil informed of her husband's latest news.[59]

Those at great towns and other information hubs passed on wartime news as it arrived. In the 1490s John Marney, a law student in London at Furnival's Inn, sent word to his 'most reverentt and worschypffull ffadyr'—yes, he was asking for money—that Berwick had narrowly escaped capture in a plot orchestrated by a Scottish friar.[60] Some fifty years later John Puleston reported to his father at Wrexham that 'the Frenche king is gone from Bullen with no more harm doing then I have writin to you in my last leter' and Christopher Barker, Garter King of Arms, sent the earl of Shrewsbury news of the warfare around Guînes.[61] In the 1470s and 1480s the Cely family and their friends sent news of international politics and the prospects for war and peace backwards and forwards between London, Calais, and Bruges: in summer 1482 they were sharing the latest about the English campaign in Scotland, with forty-four towns and villages burnt, many lords taken or slain, and the duke of Albany, dissident brother to the king of Scots, accompanying the English army, 'Jhesu be his good spede'.[62] In the 1540s the Johnson family, trading at Calais like the Celys, wrote about the English siege, capture, and defence of Boulogne and the French fleet sent against England, wishing 'God send them small power and worse fortune'.[63] Great noble households also served as centres of news. William Paston wrote to Sir John Paston from

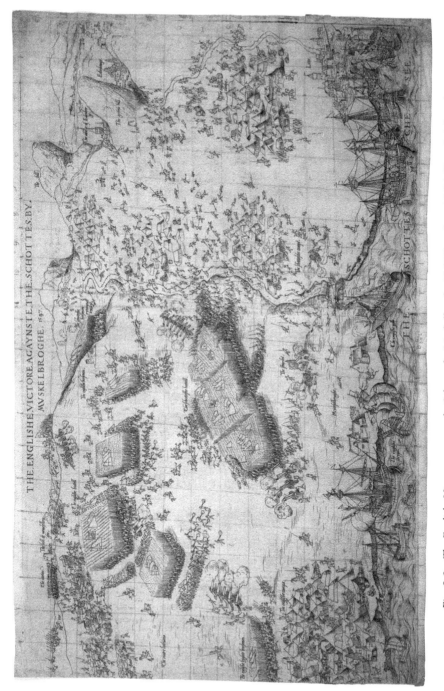

Fig. 2.3. *The Englishe Victore agaynste the Schottes by Muskelbroghe 1547* (London, 1548) (British Library).

their lord the earl of Oxford's castle at Hedingham in 1488 about the English intervention in Brittany and the family exchanged news about the campaign thereafter.[64] News in letters might easily be combined with other sources of wartime information, administrative or predictive. Adam Ralegh wrote from London in July 1545 to Sir Richard Edgecombe at Stonehouse by Plymouth with news of the English and French fleets and of events in Scotland. He enclosed a proclamation about privateering and a prognostication taken from an almanac.[65]

Those in command of English forces in different theatres naturally needed news of events elsewhere and received it both by official communications and by letters from friends. In autumn 1523 Cardinal Wolsey and Brian Tuke sent the earl of Surrey at Newcastle news of the progress of the duke of Suffolk's campaign in France. Surrey was to pass it on both to his subordinates and to the Scots, to serve not only as 'a comforte unto al those that wold favour the kinges desire, but also an abashment and grete discorage to al those that be of the Frenche faccion'.[66] In the same way in 1543 Sir John Wallop, serving on the borders of France, was fed news of English raids from the Calais Pale and captures of French ships, so that he might use it to encourage his Burgundian allies.[67] In September 1544 Francis, earl of Shrewsbury, royal lieutenant in the North, was told of Henry's capture of Boulogne, and in August 1557 the privy council and his friends at court and in the army wrote to him about the victory of Saint-Quentin and its aftermath; he spread each instalment of news around the northern counties.[68]

When invasion threatened, news spread fast, and oral transmission mixed with written. William Rowcleffe wrote to his master John Trevelyan, probably in 1545, of how he had heard that Sir George Carew had come down to Devon post-haste to warn of 1,500 ships at sea, 'Fryngemen and other', who had 'ponted to land in devers places withyn the Rame before Sent Gorge day nexte comyng'.[69] The number of ships had perhaps grown in the telling. Sometimes correspondents, mindful of this risk, qualified their news. Christopher Playter told the earl of Bath in June 1558 as 'newis' that 'my Lord of Northumberland gothe northward with all speed', but distanced himself a little from his next two items: 'the talke also went here that the Frenche king never had suche number in the felld so redie in arms as he hathe at this present. The lyke preparacion the talke gothe shalbe here.'[70] Chroniclers such as Robert Fabyan had to make the same calculations about hearsay. At London in 1512 it was known that English troops were taking ship on the south coast bound for the continent, but the details were foggy. When the first and second contingents left, there was 'no certaynte...where they shuld land'. There was a rumour—'a ffame ran'—that they were going to help the pope against the king of France, which after a fashion they were, for Henry fought his first war with France as a loyal son of Julius II. In practice they were, as Fabyan then realized, 'upon the bordour of Fraunce and of Spayn'. He gave a dramatic narrative of a successful Anglo-Spanish siege of Bayonne almost marred by a Spanish massacre of the inhabitants, an atrocity fortunately averted by the 'strength and polityque meanys of the Inglysh men'. Shortly afterwards he wrote in the margin 'All this mater of the wynnyng of this toun...ys untrewe'.[71]

Most of our examples of written news come from the aristocracy, gentry, higher clergy, and merchant classes. Given their personal engagement in diplomacy, politics, trade, and the affairs of the wider church, perhaps it should not surprise us that the tidings they exchanged spread beyond England's wars to those of Europe and the Near East. We find discussion of the treaty of London of 1518 with its promise of 'an universall peax to be establishide emonges all Christen princes' and of the Ottoman–Safavid wars; of the battle of Mohács and the Colonnas' raid on Rome in 1526; of the likely outbreak of war between France and the Habsburgs in 1551 and its relationship to Ottoman attacks; of how Mary's impending marriage to Philip meant that 'We are lyke to fall owtt with the French'.[72] Such correspondence suggests a lively appetite to understand England's place in European politics and the context for Henry's wars. Interest was intensified further by the sharpening religious polarization of the 1560s and 1570s. Just as printers aimed a run of publications at that section of the English public concerned about the 'ministers of the gospel' and 'defenders of the trueth' and their supporters in France and the Netherlands and outraged by the 'unnaturalnesse, cruelte and murder' perpetrated by their persecutors, so Sir William More collected manuscript documents illustrating the French crisis of 1562, and the Bacon family and their friends sent one another news of the iniquities of Charles IX, '*rex incristianissimus*'—the most unchristian king—and of Sir Humphrey Gilbert's expedition to Flushing in aid of the Dutch rebels.[73]

Oral news spreading among humbler subjects may have been more confined in its interests, or less sophisticated in its understanding—though it has been found by historians of the immediately succeeding period to be 'surprisingly well informed'—but it could feed off written correspondence and printed news, and it certainly encompassed warfare.[74] Laurence Taylor was arrested in Essex in around 1490 for travelling through East Anglia telling people he had been shipped back to Great Yarmouth after his capture in Brittany, where he had witnessed the death or imprisonment of most of the king's forces.[75] John Browne, tinker, exactly the kind of travelling tradesman often found at the centre of later news networks, was in trouble at Hereford in 1514. He had claimed that, while the English had killed the Scots' king at 'the Shotyse fylde', Flodden, they had not really won the battle, having lost their guns, so that the Scots would soon invade again.[76] By 1569 the Thames watermen were passing on to their passengers titbits about the interplay of the Scots, the duke of Alba, and the northern rebels.[77]

Such news might stimulate unhealthy debate. There were repeated fears of this at London, but it was not just a metropolitan issue.[78] In January 1546, in a winter of high food prices following the poor harvest of 1545, William Rye and Anthony Sprowston were riding across north-east Norfolk from North Walsham to Holt. Rye said—or at least so he told the Norwich magistrates when questioned—that it was 'an hard worlde for poor folks' and prayed to God 'yf yt war His pleasure to send a peace'. Sprowston agreed that 'if yt wer not pease shortely yt should make a bare Ynglond'. Rye opined loyally that it would be even worse for realms such as France and Scotland, 'which wer in warre as wele as Inglond', but 'which the kyng's most noble grace has moste vyctoriously and noblely...overcome'. Sprowston was not convinced. 'I praye you', he asked, 'what ded the Inglyshe men in Skoteland but cam in on a Sundaye in the morning when some wer in bedde and some at chyrche, and by a false traytor of Edinborow cam in to Edinborow and ther did but robbe and stele'?[79]

Oral news sometimes spread ahead of official correspondence. In Ireland in September 1542 the deputy had to send to court for confirmation of the rumour that there was 'open warre' with France and Scotland, and in July 1544 the commanders on the northern borders were hearing 'sondry tales and newes...of the kinges majestes journey and royall voyage into Fraunce and also of my lorde of Norffolkes procedinges and doinges in Fraunce' and had to ask their colleagues in the South for reliable updates.[80] Oral discussion of military events at times came close to the world of prophecy. In March 1554 Barnard Saunderson overtook John Harrison on the road from Colney to Norwich. They discussed the price of horses, news of musters, and rumours that the French and Scots would invade between Easter and Whitsun. Harrison claimed to have asserted patriotically that if they did invade 'they shall come to as hard a breakfast as ever they came to, by the grace of God', but Saunderson heard him say something much more in the vein of Thomas the Rhymer, how there would be three battles in the coming months and 'we shall see the king of France in Norwich by Midsummer'.[81] In similar vein, as the treaty of Câteau-Cambrésis was under negotiation, Nicholas Colman dreamt that Scotsmen, Frenchmen, and others were about to pass through England disguised as beggars, setting towns on fire.[82]

Those who fought also recorded information in more systematic ways. Campaign diaries were numerous by comparison with the few surviving from the Hundred Years War.[83] For the 1513 campaign in France we have a Latin work by John Taylor, royal chaplain and clerk of the parliaments. It is detailed, down to the numbers of men killed in various skirmishes, and personal, commenting on some things Taylor himself saw. It is admiring both of the king and of his army, and it has literary pretensions, with allusions to Neptune and reflections on the fall of James IV of Scots.[84] Very different and more typical is a list in English from the same year of 'the progress of the vauntgard into Fraunce', noting the dates when camp was pitched at different places and key events in the campaign.[85] For the invasion of France in 1523 a similar but more idiosyncratic work survives. It too records the progress of the army day by day, but gives a strong impression of what it felt like to be inside it, noting what 'our men' or 'our gonners' did and commenting on noteworthy or sensational events of all sorts: Sir William Skevington shot through his shoe but unharmed, Lord Leonard Grey taking a position from two hundred Frenchmen with just twenty English, the capture of Bray-sur-Somme 'which was the kay of all Fraunce and was never wone before'.[86]

From Boulogne in 1544 we have at least two pieces in the same vein. One recounts the entire campaign from the king's departure from Westminster to the French counter-attacks of October. It concentrates on the actions of 'the most victorious King Henry the Eight', but still speaks of 'our hacquebutiers', 'our artillerye', and 'our men'.[87] The other records the progress of 'our soldyeres', 'our Englyssemen', from Calais to Boulogne before the king arrived, the 'vere hotte' skirmishes with the French as the siege was set, and the development of the siege, breaking off before the fall of the town. Like the 1523 diary it celebrates the deeds of valiant captains and gives the view from within the army, referring to events mysterious to the majority, such as the arrival of a French trumpeter 'the cause of whose comyng' was 'not comonly declaryd' and the appearance of ships off the coast, the origin of which was 'not yet perfectly knowen but it is tought that be of the Spanysh fleit'.[88] A similar account of Hertford's invasion of Scotland that year also survives, again talking in terms of 'our men' and admitting that the author could not name all the villages they had burnt.[89] Hertford's next invasion was chronicled by Bartholomew Butler, York herald, who noted, in amongst the relentless burning, his formal summons to Kelso Abbey before it was captured.[90]

Further texts of this sort must have circulated, because they underlie the accounts of campaigns in printed chronicles. Edward Hall incorporated into his account of Henry's reign a detailed day-by-day narrative of the 1523 campaign different from that surviving in manuscript, but similarly giving an inside view of the campaign, from men 'muche encoraged' by news of their ally the duke of Bourbon, but glad of a rest after two months' marching, 'for they had travailed sore, and the wether was wette and colde', and suffering 'great grefe' when frostbite made their fingernails fall off.[91] Hall seems to have had access to narratives in the same form for Sir Edward Poynings' expedition to Guelders in 1511, the earl of Surrey's campaign in Picardy in 1522, and perhaps other episodes.[92] His successors who assembled the first edition of Holinshed's *Chronicles* in 1577 apparently deployed similarly detailed daily material in their accounts of the Scottish campaign of 1560 and the Le Havre expedition two years later.[93] In putting together their accounts of the fighting on the border with Scotland in 1557–9, they explicitly acknowledged their consultation of five named captains and others who were 'eye witnesses themselves of suche enterpryses and exploytes as chanced in the same warres'.[94]

Henry's wars and those that followed may have been widely discussed and recorded, but did they breed a more general acquaintance with the cosmopolitan ways of Renaissance warfare? The literary and visual culture of the 1550s and 1560s suggests that they may have done, at least at higher social levels. William Baldwin's morality play of 1556, *Love and Life*, looks like a triumph of ingenuity over discretion. It lasted three hours and featured sixty-two characters, each of whose names began with the letter L. Among them were 'Landgrave van Luxenburgh Lieutenant of an army', 'Lodovico de S. Lukerseco, an Italian horseman', 'Lammarkin a Lanceknight', and the wonderfully onomatopoeic drummer 'Lamphadirizumph'.[95] Under Philip and Mary court revels featured Albanian warriors—familiar in western European armies as stradiot light cavalrymen—as well as Irish kerne.[96] For the first Shrove Sunday of Elizabeth's reign there followed a masque of 'swart-rutters' in their distinctive black armour. To complete the picture they were equipped with their characteristic weapons, 'dagges', short firearms that could be used from horseback, and 'pertisauntes' or broad-headed spears.[97]

The garish appeal of continental military dress can be seen in the sketch of a landsknecht drummer, fifer, gunner, and standard bearer tucked into the initial of a dissolution survey of the lands of Glastonbury Abbey; in the similar figures in an overmantel dated 1556 from Newstead Abbey, Nottinghamshire; or, in cruder form, in the carvings from the 1560s on the gatehouse of Little Moreton Hall in Cheshire.[98] The technical terminology of continental warfare spread too. The commander of a large unit of infantry was known to the French and Italians as a *coronel* or *colonello* and to the Spanish as a *maestre de campo*, while the coordinator of infantry drill was a *sergent-major* or *sargento mayor*. It might not surprise us that the English used the terms when hiring mercenaries or inside the army they sent to join the Habsburg war effort in 1557, where Lord Clinton was 'coronell of the fotemen', Edward Chamberlain 'coronell of the pioners', and Sir Thomas Finche 'master of the campe', but it is a little startling to find the churchwardens of Cratfield in Suffolk recording the dinner they laid on in 1553–4 'whan my lord collonell tooke the muster here', and by 1559–60 the English budgeted for a 'serjaunte major' in the army sent towards Scotland.[99]

Soon military fashion bred moral panic. The baggy *Pluderhosen*, slashed and stuffed with expensive fabrics, had allegedly been invented at the siege of Magdeburg in 1550. They were popularized by landsknecht mercenaries and then subjected to scathing denunciation by German Lutheran preachers. In the early 1560s they were accused of bringing the English nation into disrepute for its self-indulgence and driving to crime those who aspired to wear them, but could not afford to do so. Tailors were bound over at London, Chippenham, Winchelsea, and on the Isle of Wight to use no more than one and three-quarter yards of cloth for any pair of hose; London appointed 'sad and discreet personages' as watchers to detect outrageously great hose; and one Richard Walweyn, arrested for wearing 'a very monsterous and outraygous greate payre of hose' saw them put on public display to shame him for his 'extreme folye'.[100] Sometimes even real soldiers got into trouble: at York in 1562 John Webbe, a gentleman of the Berwick garrison, was fined for wearing great hose garnished with silk lace, a shirt with double ruffs, and a dagger more than a foot long.[101]

Henry's wars, then, did engage his subjects, as combatants, as fearful bystanders, as followers of the news and the martial fashions. But the majority of people never went to war, there was by no means always a war on, and what wars there were generally took place at a safe distance from the heartlands of rural and urban England, from villages that had never seen an army and comfortable cities, like Salisbury, that did not even bother to build themselves walls.[102] Was war just a matter of the occasional adventure and some glamorous or alarming gossip, or did it reach deep into the communities of Henry's realm?

3

Towns and Villages

In the course of the sixteenth century, successive English regimes tried with more or less vigour to persuade their subjects to take up a series of practices and beliefs first forged elsewhere in Europe. Some subjects ran ahead of the king or queen and some at least responded with enthusiasm, while others met change with reluctance or even resistance. The new ideas sometimes confronted, sometimes built upon, sometimes blended with pre-existent English traditions. The process worked unevenly in different regions, in town and countryside, or under the sway of different local leaders. The result was a variegated pattern of hybrids, not quite the same anywhere in England or Wales or amongst the English in Ireland, and nowhere quite like the European archetypes. It is probably most fruitfully investigated one or two communities at a time, to see how a village in Devon might differ from the metropolis of London, or a coastal town in Yorkshire from one inland.[1]

This might pass as an account of the Reformation. But my aim here is to see how well it fits the adoption by English communities of the military norms of Renaissance Europe. For the gospel, read gunpowder; for Lollardy, read the longbow; for metrical psalters and books of common prayer, read arquebuses and almain rivets. For London as the power-house of preaching and Protestant printing, read London as the centre of arms imports and the stage for showpiece musters. For the Elizabethan Church of England, demonstrably ramshackle, yet surprisingly successful in creating 'a Protestant nation' if not 'a nation of Protestants', then tested to destruction by Laudianism and puritan revolt, read the Elizabethan military-fiscal system, demonstrably ramshackle, yet surprisingly successful in fighting off Spain and subduing Ireland, then tested to destruction by the Thirty Years War and the Scottish Revolution.[2]

To focus on communities is particularly appropriate, because the primary structures of English military organization were, as we have seen, in transition in the mid-sixteenth century from a system based on the retinues of noblemen and gentlemen to one based on contingents drafted from county militias. Under both systems individuals were required to possess and use arms and armour appropriate to their wealth, but where under the first system individual holdings were supplemented by those of recruiting captains, under the second system 'township arms', those supplied by parishes, became increasingly important. And while the transition from one system to the other was a messy one, as lords continued to be called upon to raise retinues for expeditions for some years after the first dispatch of county levies for overseas service, it also left towns of any size and degree of administrative independence in an anomalous position. In the older system they were treated like lords, asked to raise and equip contingents appropriate to their size; in the newer system they struggled to be treated like counties, to muster their own men at the command of central government without the interference of county commissioners drawn from the neighbouring gentry. Looking at parishes and towns, then, should give us an instructive picture of military change in the England of Henry and his children.[3]

The first question to ask is how much military demands registered in local affairs. Let us examine a sample of 153 sets of churchwardens' accounts taken from all but five English counties.[4] They represent of course only a small portion of the 9,000 or so parishes in England, but they range between quarters of great cities such as London, York, and Bristol, prosperous small towns like Ashburton in Devon or Melton Mowbray in Leicestershire, where the churchwardens might spend £20 or £30 a year, and small villages such as Great Packington in Warwickshire, where the church's annual income was around £1.[5] Until the 1540s few of them spent much on warfare, especially if we exclude marginal military expenses like repair of the local archery butts or the purchase of military material for peaceful purposes: bowstrings to work the church clock, armour for plays, or gunpowder to spice up morris dancing.[6] Although each 'village and hamlet' was supposed, according to a proclamation of 1509, to equip at common expense at least one able man to serve the king, communal arms were not mentioned in orders for musters between 1492 and 1532, and the military surveys of 1522 recorded them rarely, more often for small towns like Dudley or Newport Pagnell than for villages.[7]

By the musters of 1539 things were changing, as commissioners began to command townships to obtain communal equipment for one or more soldiers. Yorkshire was ahead of the game, half the parishes in Claro wapentake already boasting common harness by 1535. The Herefordshire commissioners of 1539 appreciated those who had done their bit, Ledbury who 'have in commyn syx pair of harnes', or Eastnor who 'have iiii peire of harness in aredines in the churche'. Bedfordshire was tougher, with fines of £2 for each parish that did not get its armour by Easter.[8] By the next round of general musters in 1542, townships in some counties were routinely kitting out soldiers to serve in the retinues of local lords. In Shropshire, for example, Patton, Middleton, and Little Wenlock had equipped men to serve with the earl of Shrewsbury, Whittingslow to serve with the earl of Arundel, and Tugford with Sir John Talbot.[9]

In the 1540s the proportion of parishes recording military payments rose from below one in thirteen to just over a quarter. This is a minimum figure, as accounts often do not survive or do not contain sufficient detail for every year, and because, as debates between historians of the later medieval parish have shown us, parish finances worked in such complex ways that it is hard to use churchwardens' accounts to show the totality of corporate expenditure.[10] The change reached down to quite small communities, such as Marston, then two miles outside Oxford, and Great Hallingbury, some twenty miles north of the Revd James Ford's parish of Navestock, Essex.[11] The incidence of military spending increased further from the 1550s to the 1570s, especially if we disregard the parishes situated in the hundred largest towns, where expenditure was often coordinated through the more elaborate structures of civic government. By the 1560s parishes like Tilney All Saints in Norfolk and Weyhill in Hampshire, which had never done so before, were buying armour and sending out soldiers, and nearly 30 per cent of non-urban parishes were recording such payments.[12] Parish stocks of arms appeared with increasing frequency in the muster lists of the 1540s and regularly in those of 1569.[13]

Parishes found different means to meet the new demands placed upon them. First they spent their cash reserves. In the 1540s Bardwell in Suffolk slid deep into deficit before a narrow recovery and Horley in Surrey suffered a gentler, but equally clear, erosion (see Fig. 3.1).[14] Next, many diverted income previously intended for what were coming to be seen as superstitious purposes. At Chagford on Dartmoor the store of St Catherine the Virgin was used to subsidize purchases of armour from 1542–3, and in the hard-pressed years that followed St Michael's store and Our Lady's store, run by its female wardens, also paid military costs.[15] The most illustrious endowments were not safe: at Luton the Fraternity of the Holy and Undivided Trinity and Blessed Virgin Mary, which had numbered among its members Edward IV, Henry VII, and Henry VIII himself, had to produce 9s 6d for armour and 2s 6d cash in hand for a soldier in 1545–6.[16] And the Marian restoration could not put the clock back. At Leverington in Cambridgeshire in 1557, £1 6s 8d had to be taken out of the plough-light money for setting forth soldiers.[17]

When such expedients did not suffice, parishes had to sell their goods or find new income. Sales were an attractive option at a time when Henry might well confiscate parochial wealth, as the first Edwardian inventories of church goods, taken in 1547, show. Of 144 Suffolk churches for which returns survive, sixty-eight,

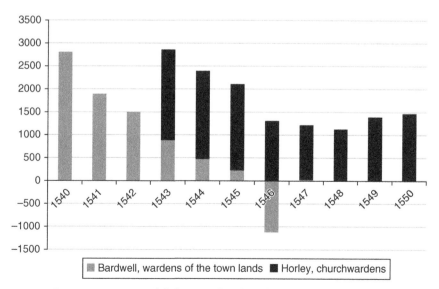

Fig. 3.1. Reserves and deficits on churchwardens' accounts (in pence).

nearly half, had in the past four years sold crosses, copes, chalices, censers, candlesticks, basins, pyxes, and paxes to meet military expenses great or small.[18] The records for Essex and Norfolk are less comprehensive, but show that parishes there—twenty-eight of them in Norfolk alone—were making similar decisions.[19] Counties inland seem to have felt less pressure, but a dozen Surrey, Somerset, Cambridgeshire, Lincolnshire, and Yorkshire parishes show that turning pyxes into pikestaffs was not merely an East Anglian habit.[20] In Cornwall, similarly, churches sold or pawned their plate or bells to pay for the wages, food, drink, and horses of the men they sent to confront the uprising of 1548 in the far west of the county.[21]

An alternative to sales was to broaden the remit of the funds held in some parishes since the 1470s to help poorer residents pay their share of parliamentary taxes.[22] The fifteen penny land, used at Eltham in Kent to cover the costs of cleaning parish armour, sounds like such a fund, and lands enfeoffed to the town's use at Burton-on-Trent, Bury St Edmunds, and Melton Mowbray and a salt-cote maintained by the Lincolnshire fenland villages of Gedney and Moulton were similarly used to cover military charges.[23] From this it was a short step to levying local military rates. In Lancashire it was already established practice in the 1540s for townships to choose four honest men to assess a rate on their neighbours to equip soldiers or pioneers sent to the borders and to enforce payment by distraining animals, while on some duchy of Lancaster manors elsewhere constables levied similar rates.[24] Rates came in in 1557–8 at Morebath in Devon and Yatton in Somerset, and by the end of the 1560s Chagford, Crediton, and many London parishes had joined them.[25]

Boroughs had been coping with military expenditure and administration for a lot longer than parishes. In our period, we should remind ourselves, a number—Exeter, London, Norwich, York—faced the ultimate test of a rebel siege. But it was not just front-line towns that spent on war. A sample of borough accounts or order books drawn from sixty towns located in twenty-eight English and Welsh counties shows that all of them incurred military expenses at some point in our period, and many of them throughout it.[26] They included not only large, rich towns—fourteen of the sixty might be reckoned among the largest twenty in England, sixteen more in the largest hundred, and three others in the hundred richest if not the hundred largest—but also places with a few hundred inhabitants like Bridport, Chippenham, and New Romney, and even such minnows as Fordwich.[27]

Though the range of military costs boroughs had to meet was wider than that of parishes, most of their expenditure also went to clothe and equip soldiers, whether to serve on land or on board ships.[28] They had levied men for royal armies through the Wars of the Roses and were then built into Henry VII's national retinue system, by which he licensed towns, like individual noblemen and gentlemen, to retain men to serve him. Colchester, Coventry, Henley, and Winchester all prepared men under this scheme and other towns designated large contingents to serve under councillors trusted by the king.[29] In successive wars different towns faced different demands. It was all very well for a place like Henley, which seems always to have been asked for four men.[30] Larger towns felt constantly under pressure to find too many soldiers too often. Cambridge and Canterbury were specific, sending men to court to 'gett releffe of viij archers parcell of xx charged for the towne', or to 'labour . . . for the discharge of x of the seid sowdyers that shoulde have gone out of the citie at their charge in to the kynges warres'.[31] York was eloquent, complaining that under pressure of the garrison war in Scotland it was being asked for soldiers 'muche above the nombre that the said citie in auncyent tyme was wonted to fynd when that it was a citie in great ryches and prosperytie'.[32] Others were practical. Dover bought dinner for John Copledike, deputy to the Lord Warden of the Cinque Ports, 'to be gode frende to the towne to ease us that we were not moche charged to find soldiours'.[33] York paid Sir Oswald Wilstrop £10 in gold for help 'in easing the importable chardges that is like to happen in setting forth of men'.[34] Hull was more devious still, leaving out half the men who appeared at its 1539 musters when it certified its military strength to the crown.[35]

None the less, civic pride wished soldiers to represent their towns well. Some care was taken in choosing men and London put badges of swords on the jackets of its troops, Leicester cinquefoils, Shrewsbury leopard's faces, and Canterbury, where James Ford was born and went to school, Cornish choughs.[36] York's men marched out under a banner of white silk with gold leopards and smaller places imitated such grandeur: Faversham spent nearly £3 on an ensign to flutter at the head of its company in 1558.[37] Farewell breakfasts, meals, and drinks were commonplace and Ludlow even bought its soldiers, countermanded from the attempt to rescue Calais in 1558, drinks at Stretton on the way home 'bycause it rayned'.[38] Equally practically, in 1544 Maldon bought its soldiers a nightcap each and gave them all a short haircut before they set out.[39] Some believed in an even bigger send-off. Shrewsbury hired players to entertain its men before they left in 1547–8.[40]

Norwich and York were more sententiously inclined. In 1497 the mayor of Norwich addressed the town contingent as they sat on horseback, ready to depart. 'Sers, ye that be soldeours', he began, 'I charge you in the kingys our sovereign lordys name, that ye kepe governauns amongs you by the weye. And that ye be ruled and governour'd by Thomas Large, your capteyne assigned unto you, he being present chaumberleyn of this cite.' He went on to tell Large to imprison and replace any man who made 'ony frayes, styrres, or variaunces with his feloship'. They did at least then get a drink at the Guildhall door and 2*s* each in spending money.[41] At York in 1542 the mayor gathered the troops at the Magdalen Chapel, on the city boundary. He told their captains 'well and trewly to serve the kings majestie in that journay . . . and luffyngly to entrete all the said soulgers and trewly to pay them ther wags'. So far so good, but he also pointed out that the men were 'not to departe withoute especiall lycence by writing upon payn of the lawe the whiche is dethe'. Perhaps a little shaken, they too got extra money 'in reward to comfort them at ther departing'.[42]

Towns needed to hold musters to know what men they could raise and had long been doing so. Dover, Rye, and York held them periodically under Henry VII and on into the 1520s, a muster book from 1457 survives for Bridport, and Lydd was holding them back in the 1430s.[43] In the 1540s and 1550s ports like Southampton and Great Yarmouth compiled muster books with detailed provisions showing how the men of the town would be organized to resist attack.[44] Yet the quickening national pace of musters did affect them. The great effort of 1539 prompted Guildford to sort out its provision of armour and Winchester to clean its armour, re-head its arrows, and compile a substantial book recording its soldiers.[45] Really big musters were spectacles that stuck in the memory. What one livery company called 'the grate muster made by the cittizens of London' in 1539 was such a sight that business was postponed in the House of Lords so the peers could watch.[46] Town accounts show the frequency of musters, especially at times of crisis—three times in 1557–8 at Faversham, every year between 1544 and 1547 at Ludlow— and sometimes reveal the practicalities.[47] At Cambridge there was much copying out of instructions and articles, 'fourmes tables and tressells' had to be carried out onto Jesus Green or St Thomas's Leys, and the mayor and aldermen treated them- selves to dinner at The Dolphin or the mayor's house afterwards.[48]

Whether equipped by parishes or boroughs, soldiers had to have appropriate gear. At the start of our period the standard equipment of English infantrymen consisted of a helmet, usually a sallet, some body armour, either a stuffed leather jack or a more expensive brigandine of fabric sewn with metal plates, a sword and

Fig. 3.2. Brigandine, mail sleeves, gauntlets, bevor, and sallet (Royal Armouries III.47) © Royal Armouries.

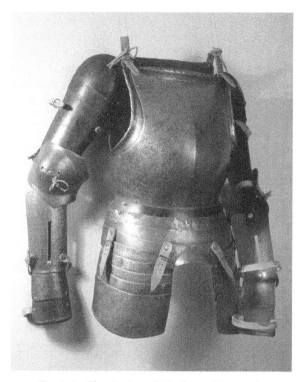

Fig. 3.3. Almain rivets (Winchester Museum).

dagger, sometimes a buckler, a small round shield, and either a bow or a bill, a pole-weapon with a point, a spike, and a sharp blade. When Henley sent its men to serve Henry VII they had a characteristic mixture of bows, bills, jacks, brigandines, sallets, and bits and pieces of mail armour (see Fig. 3.2).[49] In 1513 the constables at Ramsey in Huntingdonshire had two jacks, two breastplates, two sallets, two bucklers, two bills, two swords, one dagger, and assorted mail and plate armour for the body and arms: standards, gussets, sleeves, splints, and a mail apron.[50] Such equipment remained commonplace into the 1540s and sometimes beyond, but new weapons and stronger and more standardized defences steadily penetrated local stores.

New in Henry's first French war were almain rivets, mass-produced South German plate body armours (see Fig. 3.3). The king himself ordered 2,000 of them in 1512 and his subjects soon began to catch up.[51] At Exeter most of the armour produced by individuals and then added to the city's stores in 1512–13 consisted of brigandines, sallets, and splints, but John Calwodley, schoolmaster, produced 'a pere of allemeynrevettes' and the landlord of The Bear also had a set.[52] In the 1520s and 1530s almain rivets appeared in other large southern towns and by the 1540s they were at Barnstaple, Wilton, and York.[53] By the 1550s even the churchwardens at Marston were stocking up with them, but just as they did so, best practice was moving on.[54] In the 1560s pikemen were expected to have the heavier and more expensive corslets. They duly appeared, and much faster than almain rivets had done: at Bury St Edmunds, Cambridge, Lyme Regis, and Winchester by 1564 for example, by 1570 even at Cratfield, Louth, and Ludlow, and by that time they easily outnumbered the older armours at a well-set-up southern town like Faversham.[55] With corslets came the new helmet styles of the mid-century, burgonets, headpieces, and morions.[56]

Armour was expensive—6s to 13s 4d for a set of almain rivets in the 1520s or 1530s, up to £1 13s 4d for a corslet in the 1560s—and needed looking after.[57] As York's councillors put it in 1561, it 'cannot but decaye without diligent skowryng and reparellyng', and parish and borough accounts are full of payments for scouring armour with sand and oiling it to prevent rust, and renewing the harness nails, leather straps, and cloth points with which it was held together.[58] The London pewterers invested in a 'greate block with fete to scowr harneys' and many other companies, parishes, and boroughs set up frames, hooks, or nails to hang their armour on, presses or chests to keep it in, or dedicated armoury chambers, grander or lesser versions of the remarkable survival at Mendlesham in Suffolk.[59]

Keeping armour in good condition was all very well, but sending troops out with it ran the risk that it might never come back, particularly because of the convention that in the event of 'a foughten field... it is allowed to the souldiour by the lawe of armes'.[60] In Denbighshire it was claimed in 1539 that most of the local harness had disappeared to Ireland with the steward of the lordship of Denbigh, John Salusbury, in 1534–5, and never been seen again.[61] Local authorities took steps to avoid such outcomes. In 1542 York instructed its returning soldiers to hand their equipment in to their parish constable or pay compensation.[62] In 1545 Eye had to ask Sir Thomas Tyrrell 'to be good master for our harneys or eles it had ben gon'.[63] In 1554 and 1569 the London cloth-workers issued careful instructions that their men could keep any clothes bought for them to serve in, but must hand in their armour.[64] Perhaps more effectively, the skinners in 1554 paid 9s to seven men 'that broght home their harness'.[65] The ultimate fear was that the community might not be able to defend itself. York worried in 1548 that the crown's demands were so insistent that they might leave the city 'dysolaite of armour for defence of the same'.[66] Dover ordered in 1523 that no one who owned armour or weapons should sell them to anyone outside the town, so that they might remain in Dover 'for the defence of the towne and the realme'.[67] What they feared was the situation Foulsham in Norfolk bemoaned in 1547, that 'by occasyon off the kynges maiestyes warrs we have forborne owght off our... towne xx mens harnessys so that we remayne att thys tyme destytute not only for the maynteynyng off hys gracys warrs but also for the defence off oure owne persons'.[68]

Soldiers needed weapons as well as armour. From the rise of the Swiss infantry and their landsknecht opponents in the 1470s and 1480s, pikes were the characteristic weapon of massed infantry formations on European battlefields. The pike came into England rapidly enough—the *Oxford English Dictionary* has a mention in 1487—but took a lot longer to displace the bill. Pikes were being imported in hundreds by the mid-1510s and were in use by 1519 in London's summer marching watches, when the livery company members paraded through the city in arms; they were prominent at the great London muster of 1539, and for a London muster before the queen in 1558 the livery companies were expected to provide four pikemen for every bill.[69] It was easy for the Londoners: the Tower of London held stocks of modern equipment bought in bulk by the crown, and the companies, like the churchwardens of Westminster, could buy or hire from there.[70] Elsewhere pikes spread at a very uneven rate. Dover had them in the 1520s and Plymouth in the 1540s, but not until the 1550s did they appear at Marston, Rye, Southampton, and Worcester.[71] Central government urged local authorities on, but their calls fell on deaf ears. In 1548 the York muster commissioners were told to look for men 'mete to handle the pyke', but they returned only billmen and archers then and throughout the 1550s, catching up with the pike, like most other places, only in the 1560s.[72]

With pikes went shot. Effective hand-held firearms first appeared in Europe in the later fifteenth century and made a significant impact on the battlefield from the 1520s. In England the government stockpiled them from Edward IV's reign at Calais and in the Tower, but at first they spread only as far as the larger towns, Dover and London in the 1520s, Winchester, Worcester, and Great Yarmouth by the 1550s.[73] Elsewhere the government had to set itself a training mission. York, which had returned only eight 'gonners with harquebutts and handgonnes' at its February 1548 musters, was asked that October to find fifty men 'suche as be unmarried and willing to lerne to shute in a hagbutte', and was repeatedly asked for handgunners thereafter.[74] By 1564 the city had absorbed the message sufficiently well that it created a forerunner of the trained bands system envisaged in the 1570s, just as towns developed poor relief systems ahead of the national provision made by the poor laws, naming pikemen, arquebusiers, and billmen or halberdiers who were to have 'quarterly mustering and teachyng... to use their said weapons' at the Old Baile in the city and Toft Green outside it.[75] By Elizabeth's reign many other towns were fielding arquebuses, ports like Boston or Liverpool, and inland towns like Bury St Edmunds and Cambridge.[76] Yet now the government, annoying as ever, was moving beyond the arquebus to demand more modern weapons such as the sophisticated caliver, the long-barrelled currier, and the short-barrelled dag. After 1560 curriers and dags appeared at Winchester, Faversham, and Cambridge, but the caliver was commonest, reaching not just London, but Ashburton, Barnstaple, Cambridge, Louth, and Southampton by 1572.[77] By that time, too, gunpowder weapons were at last spreading to rural parish armouries.[78]

To defend themselves effectively, large towns also needed bigger guns. Across our period these were changing in manufacture and deployment. Early on most were of forged-iron construction, loaded at the breech with removable chambers, and were fired from fixed positions. Wheeled guns came in from the mid-fifteenth century and cast guns of bronze, without chambers, rather later, as in the famous train with which the French invaded Italy in 1494. Around 1500 many larger English towns had guns, but they were not at the forefront of technological advance. In the 1480s and 1490s Rye had various guns with chambers that could serve equally well on ship or on land, attached to posts seated in holes in the ground, priced in shillings rather than pounds.[79] York's guns in 1511 were smallish pieces with chambers, assigned two or three to each city gate.[80] By then coastal towns were more ambitious. Plymouth, Dover, and Rye all built up their stocks of guns over Henry VII's reign and into the next, and each had what they called great guns, usually on wheels, by 1512, as did Newcastle upon Tyne.[81] Southampton even had a gun with a name as great princes did, 'Thomas with the Beerd' (though he was getting aged, in service since at least 1468 and perhaps 1434), plus a long serpentine, a short serpentine, guns on carts, and 'orgons', guns with multiple barrels.[82] How big a great gun was is of course hard to say, but the chamber for Thomas with the Beard weighed 200 lb, so the whole gun might have weighed 600 to 1,000 lb, the size of a large serpentine, and in 1512 Great Yarmouth was aiming to make guns 9 feet long and able to shoot a mile, though still with chambers.[83]

Cast bronze guns came in from the 1510s for ambitious or exposed places like Norwich, Southampton, and Plymouth, but the prices were painful: £5 each for wheeled slings at Norwich, up to £7 10s each at Southampton, more than £50 for six bronze falconets at Norwich in 1545.[84] Given the cost, it is no surprise that the change to cast guns was slow. Many of Plymouth's, Southampton's, and Great Yarmouth's guns had chambers into the 1540s, and Dover had guns with chambers on its bulwarks as late as 1555.[85] Meanwhile projectiles were gradually developing from stone to metal. In 1482–3 Southampton invested in 'pekkyng hamers for gonnestones' and two tons of stone to use them on, and it went on using gunstones into the 1520s.[86] Plymouth still made shot from stone from Staddon, on the moors south of the town, in the 1510s. It had begun to make lead and iron shot in the 1480s, but only in the 1540s did iron completely win out.[87] Small anti-personnel guns, meanwhile, fired lead pellets, like those Southampton bought in 1483–4, or iron pellets or dice, like those Dover, Plymouth, and Southampton were making in the 1510s and 1520s.[88]

On the coast much smaller communities kept up with firearm technology. After the French landing of 1545, the captain of the Isle of Wight ordered each parish to procure a modern 'falconet of bronze and iron' and keep it in a gun-house attached to the parish church. The guns made for Carisbrooke and Brading still survive, dated 1549 and inscribed with the names of the makers, John and Robert Owen, the king's gun-makers, and the name of the parish for which each was made (see Fig. 3.4), while some of the gun-houses lasted into the nineteenth century.[89] In the 1540s Eastbourne too was buying cast iron guns, two sakers and three robinets, while Suffolk coastal parishes from north to south—Lowestoft, Kirkley, Kessingland, North Hales, Easton Bavents, Southwold, Walberswick, Leiston, and Aldeburgh—spent money on guns and ammunition.[90] Harwich's response to the succession crisis of 1553 shows the locals' ready familiarity with guns, both iron and bronze, and the technique for making hailshot sewn up in canvas pokes with a sail needle.[91] Ports also made increasing administrative provision for their guns. Rye had a gun garden and Great Yarmouth appointed four townsmen as masters of its ordnance in 1543 and turned its hospital into a gunnery store in 1551.[92]

Fig. 3.4. Carisbrooke parish gun (Carisbrooke Castle Museum). Photograph by the author.

Guns needed powder, and everywhere purchases mounted. Plymouth worked its way up from 39 lb in 1496–7 to a massive 1,009 lb, ten barrels, in 1544, and Southampton's purchases expanded at a similar rate (see Fig. 3.5).[93] The spread of handguns meant that even those merely equipping infantrymen needed powder. By 1569 a single London company, the drapers, were laying in 60 lb at a time.[94] Powder was hard to keep in good condition and needed restoration if it decayed or absorbed water. In 1486–7 Dover had to dry its gunpowder and in 1501–2 Plymouth bought 3 lb of saltpetre and 3*d* worth of vinegar 'to mend the gun powder'.[95] London's solution was more drastic, ordering its gunpowder sold off when peace came in 1514 'forsomoche as the seyd pouder dayly asketh grete charge in the kepyng therof'.[96]

Guns needed gunners, and York employed one by the 1470s, Plymouth by the 1490s, Southampton by the 1510s, and Rye by the 1520s.[97] All these were in the top fifty towns, but by the 1550s Poole had a gunner and by that time Dover was employing them for individual bulwarks.[98] At a time of technological change England suffered a skills shortage. It was met with the time-honoured expedient of selective immigration. Southampton had 'John Ducheman' and 'John Vandersson' working on gunpowder and gunstones in the 1470s and 1480s, Dover paid two Dutchmen for 'mendyng' its gunpowder in 1495–6, and by 1512–14 Southampton had a whole team of foreign gunners. 'Derike Gunner' and 'Baltazar Gonner' were presumably Dutch or German and 'Conrede Smythe', 'Jonker Shaf', 'Christofer van Gratis', and 'Markes Stroyzborow' were Swiss.[99] Only from the 1520s did Southampton manage to recruit more local-sounding gunners like Roger Cobley,

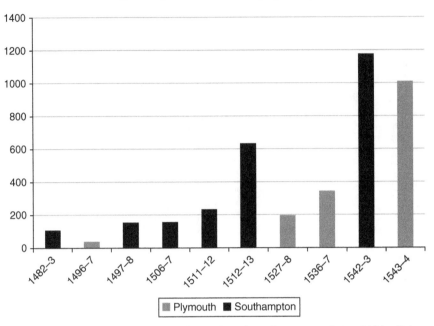

Fig. 3.5. Gunpowder purchases at Plymouth and Southampton, 1482–1544 (in lbs).

Richard Netley, and John Norton.[100] Whatever their origins, gunners needed to practise. At Plymouth in the 1540s empty barrels were used as buoys to shoot at in the harbour, and Southampton may have done something similar when they experimented 'to see how farr our gonnes wold shute'.[101]

However hard they tried, it was difficult for towns to keep up with the growing sophistication and expense of top-of-the range artillery. Fortunately the crown, which had no desire to see the French or Spanish occupy a major port, offered a solution by loaning guns from the royal stores. In 1545 Great Yarmouth took delivery of a powerful suite of bronze guns, mounted on wheeled carriages and firing iron shot: two demi-cannons, one culverin, and two sakers.[102] By 1547 Poole had a demi-culverin and an iron saker from the royal stores at Portsmouth and a bronze culverin from the Tower of London.[103] In 1569, Rye acknowledged receipt of a major stock of guns from the ordnance office: one demi-cannon, two culverins, eleven sakers, three minions, four falcons, three port pieces, and four fowlers.[104] In the process, the masters of the ordnance office became from the 1520s important contacts for towns concerned to keep their guns up to scratch: Sir William Skevington and Sir Christopher Morris for Dover and Hull, Sir Thomas Seymour at Great Yarmouth.[105]

There was less help for communities equipping troops to meet the intensifying demands of the crown for more standardized and modern equipment. They were left at the mercy of captains or commissioners who might reject the armour or weapons with which they supplied their men. Sheffield turned out a motley collection of bows, bills, jacks, splints, skulls, and sallets to confront the northern earls in 1569, until the queen's commissioners ordered substantial payments to equip one man with a corslet and pike and another with an arquebus and morion.[106] All too often the captain judging the equipment turned out to be conveniently able to supply replacements at a price that suited him. Sir Robert Constable wanted £33 6s 8d from York in 1548 to arm their fifty trainee hackbutters to his satisfaction.[107] Between 1558 and 1562 Ludlow spent nearly a quarter of the costs of setting forth eight men on buying equipment from the captain; Bury St Edmunds paid the captain of their men several shillings more than the going rate for a corslet and two arquebuses; and the London carpenters paid more than a third of the costs of the men they sent to Le Havre to Captain Vaughan for armour, jerkins, and weapons.[108]

Other requirements were easier and perhaps more enjoyable to meet. Effective pike and shot warfare required soldiers to march in formation, and the best help to that was the beat of a drum (see Fig. 3.6). Drumming was a practice closely associated with the landsknechts—in his English–French dictionary of 1530 John Palsgrave included the definition 'dromslade, suche as almayns use in warre'—and was adopted from them by English troops as early as 1514.[109] The London drapers' company had six drummers in the marching watch in 1526, in the great city muster of 1539 the Londoners marched with 'drounslates playing a fore them alle the way', and for the marching watch in 1541, the drapers hired pikes and guns, drummers and flute players, eight experts to brandish two-handed swords, and one 'Nynyan Saunderson to play with a flag', while the company captains were decked out in 'dubletts sloppys and hose after the Alman fasshion'.[110] The Londoners, though amateurs, wanted to do things in style, and the mercers and goldsmiths soon joined in.[111] From London drumming spread ever onwards, as drums were bought, repaired, repainted, and played at musters. By 1558 they had reached Bridport, Canterbury, Faversham, Plymouth, and Southampton, by 1573 Bodmin and even little Fordwich.[112]

Large-scale warfare placed various other demands on towns. Especially earlier in the period, the crown often asked for horses to carry soldiers even if they were to fight on foot, a demand that persisted longest in the North where 'well horsed' men were best 'able to make exploytes against the kings enymyes'.[113] A horse cost more than a set of infantry armour, around £1 in the 1530s, up to £2 in the 1540s.[114] Occasionally towns were even asked to equip light horsemen, more expensive than infantry, or to provide horses to draw wheeled cannon.[115] Siege warfare demanded large labour forces and from the 1540s towns and parishes were asked to levy pioneers or workmen as well as troops.[116] Carts were needed for munitions and victuals and Melton Mowbray, Beverley, and York supplied carts, horses, and carters for the Scottish wars of the 1540s and 1550s.[117] Ports were called upon for ships, the Cinque Ports in particular performing ship service whenever the king or his army needed transporting to France.[118]

Everywhere in Europe new fortifications, better proof against siege artillery and better able to harness the defensive potential of guns large and small, were the sign of the gunpowder revolution, replacing or supplementing the high, thin medieval walls still kept in repair by many English towns.[119] In England the new style was

Fig. 3.6. Drummer and flag-bearer from the frontispiece of Niccolò Machiavelli, *The arte of warre* (London, 1562) (Bodleian Library).

Fig. 3.7. The fortifications of Berwick (1558–70). Photograph by the author.

most obvious in Henry's large concentric coastal forts, built in stone, paid for by the crown, often with the profits of the dissolution of the monasteries, and much criticized since for their use of rounded walls rather than the angled bastions of the *trace italienne*, which would shortly become the European norm and would be implemented at Berwick in 1558–70 (see Fig. 3.7). But just as evident to contemporaries were smaller and less solid fortifications, common enough that Thomas Lever could use 'blockehouses and bulwarkes made and kepte of the kynges fayth-ful subjectes for the savegarde of thys realme' as an illustration in a sermon of 1550 for the offices in church and state which, like the blockhouses, should be manned by faithful men.[120]

Invasion scares like those of 1539, 1545, 1556–8, and 1569 prompted the crown to send commissioners round the coast inspecting fortifications. Those most in the front line had started to fortify themselves long before. From the 1470s to the 1520s Plymouth, Southampton, Dover, and Poole were building bulwarks, blockhouses, and gun platforms of earth and timber and sometimes of brick and stone.[121] But the projects of the 1540s to 1560s were different in scale, because of the large quantities of earth that needed to be moved for the style of cannon-proof fortifications the English were building at the same time at sites across southern Scotland.[122] The solution was forced labour by the citizens. In 1539 the townsfolk of Harwich built new trenches and bulwarks and the commissioners noted approv-ingly that women and children joined in the digging.[123] In 1545 Great Yarmouth, which already had three bulwarks, built an earth rampart half a mile long behind its medieval walls.[124] That time the workforce was provided by the town councillors each sending one or two men, but in January 1558, with the shock of the fall of Calais, the entire population was ordered to work on the ramparts with shovels, baskets, and barrows on Mondays, Wednesdays, and Fridays.[125] In 1569 the towns-folk set to again, constructing an earth artillery platform 222 feet long and 32 feet wide. The future town clerk and civic historian Henry Manship recalled that he was 'with other the then grammar scholars of Yarmouth, by the space of three days, a young labourer, or rather loiterer, amongst them, more willing to help to carry a maund of earth in my hand than a satchel of books on my shoulder'.[126] Rye in 1545 and Dover in 1557 similarly set their inhabitants to work to improve their fortifications.[127]

Coastal bulwarks were a more general charge. Commissioners were instructed in 1544 to view the coast and 'cause th'olde trenches, bulwarks of erthe and suche like defences to be preparyd or to be mayde newe with thelpe of the countre'.[128] In Norfolk, Weybourne Hope was seen as a prime invasion site, with easy access from deep water. It was defended by a bulwark to which parishes up to ten miles inland contributed.[129] Similar contributions were levied across Suffolk, Devon, and Lincolnshire, so that in 1545–6 Plymouth, for example, received £13 6s 8d in 'ready money geven by the country towards the maintenance of our bulwarks and ordynance', while Morebath paid towards bulwarks at Seaton, some forty miles away.[130]

Warning beacons were even more widespread than bulwarks, twenty-three sets of churchwardens in eight counties contributing to them. They had long existed, but both the structures themselves and the plans for their use needed to be kept in shape.[131] The network, much admired by the French ambassador in 1539, allowed news of invasion to be spread along sight-lines drawn for Kent by William Lambarde in his *Perambulation* of 1596 (see Fig. 3.8). There were beacons along the coast, funded both by ports and by inland parishes, and on high ground all across the country, including the far North, where the system was used to warn of major incursions by the Scots.[132] Instructions issued in 1546 and again ten years later required that 'wyse and vigillaunte' persons or 'honest householders' be appointed to tend the beacons. They prescribed signalling routines for firing one, two, or three beacons at different points for dangers of different severity and appro-priate responses to the sight of the beacons on fire, suggesting the gentry and other 'honest and sober men' should be ready to take charge so that 'the people shold not wander up and downe amazed'.[133]

Different locations called forth different practicalities. At Plymouth and Launceston the beacons burnt furze, whereas Dover's signal fires used wood.[134] York's Bilborough beacon used an iron 'brandreth' or three-legged brazier, and tar barrels, apparently on a wooden structure which needed an 'expert carpenter' to keep it in repair.[135] Watching the beacons must have been cold work and shelters were built for the watchmen. Launceston put up a 'bekyn howse' in 1542–3 and at Cockayne Hatley in Bedfordshire in February 1556 a beggar girl slept the night in 'the beacon howse'.[136] The beacon watch was only the most prominent part of a gamut of wartime watching. Ports watched the sea for suspicious shipping,

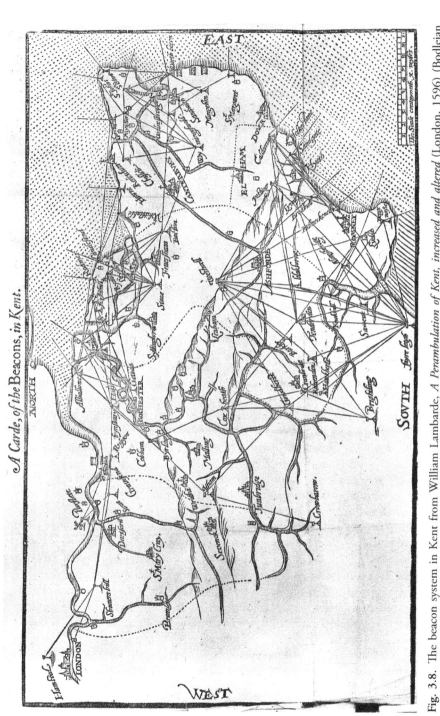

Fig. 3.8. The beacon system in Kent from William Lambarde, *A Perambulation of Kent, increased and altered* (London, 1596) (Bodleian Library).

sometimes with paid watchmen or rotas of townsfolk posted at coastal vantage points—Rame Head, Flamborough, Bridlington Quay—sometimes by sending out boats as far as the French coast.[137] In the commotion time of 1549 there was watching in the most unlikely places: Cambridge sent out Edward Loft as a 'scout watch' to Thetford.[138]

English and Welsh towns generally did not have to put up with large garrisons, but when they did, the experience could be stressful. The townsfolk of Beaumaris complained that Sir Roland Vielleville's soldiers sometimes sallied out from the castle to attack them and once trained the castle's loaded guns on the town.[139] Hull too had its troubles, but the worst problems came at Portsmouth. As its importance as a naval base grew it was given large wartime garrisons, more than 500 men in autumn 1513, but it was Sir Adrian Poynings, its governor in the 1560s, who let things get out of hand. His men, sometimes acting in armed bands forty strong, repeatedly arrested and imprisoned civic officers as they tried to go about their business, freed malefactors from custody, and expelled townsfolk from their houses. One soldier, asked by the mayor to return a prisoner, 'made a fflippe with his finger and thume saying Tushe for him'. One ex-mayor stated in his will that he went 'in fear of my life from Sir Adrian Poynings, captain of Portsmouth, and his servants'.[140]

Other encounters were more fleeting, but equally awkward. Southampton put guards on its gates to keep the soldiers out when the army came home in 1475, York and Rye had to lend soldiers money or buy them drinks to pacify them in 1481–2, and one Dover parish paid 8*d* in Edward VI's reign for watching the church when the soldiers were in town.[141] In the 1560s the authorities at Bristol and Liverpool were hard put to pacify brawling between their citizens and soldiers bound for Ireland.[142] There might be extra difficulties when the troops were foreign. York had to set prices carefully to avoid trouble when Germans passed through in the 1540s, and one party were to be kept away from the local nightlife, expected 'to goo to ther beds and rest at ix of the clok at nyght'.[143] Sheer numbers were problem enough: with more than 3,000 soldiers in the city to face the Northern Rising in 1569, York had to resort to price-setting again.[144]

When added to more usual charges, local military expenditure could have a serious impact on the finances of boroughs as of parishes, especially at a time of heavy national taxation to pay for war. As Ian Archer's calculations for London show, in the 1540s and 1550s national and local levies combined to place a greater burden on urban society in real terms than at any other point in the century (see Fig. 3.9).[145] At a front-line town like Rye we can see even more vividly the importance of military expenditure in the town's budget and the way the burden increased in the 1540s and 1550s (see Fig. 3.10).[146] As in parishes, cash reserves went first. Poole's borough finances took hit after hit from the 1490s to the 1540s, building up reserves in peacetime only to empty away in war (see Fig. 3.11).[147] At London two years of war from 1544 to 1546 took the blacksmiths' company from 17*s* 6*d* in hand to £7 18*s* in debt.[148]

Burdens had to be passed on to the citizenry, but towns chose to do it in different ways. Some pushed them downwards onto wards, parishes, or trade guilds.[149] Some

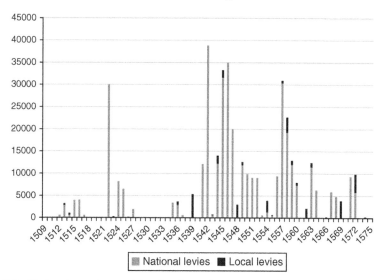

Fig. 3.9. National taxation and local military levies at London, 1509–75 (source: Ian Archer, 'The Burden of Taxation on Sixteenth-Century London', *Historical Journal* 44 (2001), table 3).

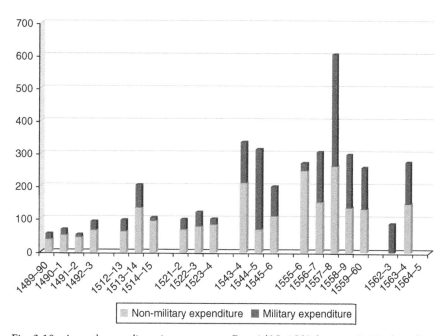

Fig. 3.10. Annual expenditure in war years at Rye, 1485–1559 (source: G. Mayhew, 'Rye and the Defence of the Narrow Seas: A Sixteenth Century Town at War', *Sussex Archaeological Collections* 127 (1984), table 2).

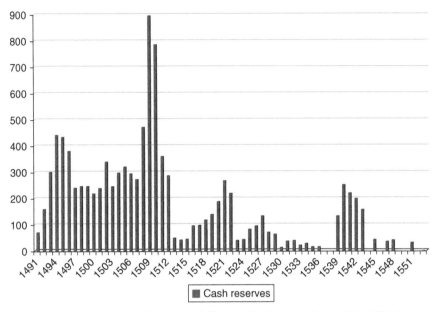

Fig. 3.11. Cash reserves (to the nearest shilling) in Poole town chest, 1491–1553 (source: Dorset HC, DC/PL/CLA23).

organized things centrally, but preferred individuals to contribute in kind. In 1522 Faversham resolved that the mayor should always have three sets of armour in his house, each jurat two, and each of the twenty-four, the larger town council, one.[150] In 1548 Norwich even insisted that each widow of a city justice of the peace should keep armour for two men and each widow of an alderman one.[151] Contributions might be more multifarious. At Exeter in 1512–14 citizens were allowed to pay money or contribute arms, armour, or services: the making up of six or eight coats, six bows from a bowyer, six swords from a furbisher, ten hats from a hatmaker.[152]

Under pressure boroughs dug deep, often at the expense of their churches in a microcosm of the king's Reformation. In the 1540s Plymouth sold church plate and King's Lynn church bells to buy munitions and Great Yarmouth spent the wealth of its Guild of Our Lady over the Haven on the town's defences.[153] In 1548 the mayor and borough of Wilton recorded their unanimous assent that as 'the inhabitantes of the same borough er pore and not able to beare the charges', 'the mony of the church box of every church within the same borough shall to the sum of vi^li xiij^s iiij^d in the hole go towerdes the maintenance of the kynges wares' and Leicester did the same.[154] When such expedients ran out, general rating was the only answer and at least eighteen of our towns introduced it. Some costs had to be met in cash—Poole's charges for the upkeep and manning of Brownsea Castle, for example—and regular rating made sense.[155] Others mixed rates with demands on individuals or, like Leicester, began by rating town councillors and turned at length to a general rate.[156]

Several historians have seen the sixteenth century as an important period in the development of the structures and practices of government in English parishes and boroughs and of their integration into a more effective English state, but in their analyses the wars of Henry VIII have not loomed large. While Beat Kümin and Robert Tittler assert the importance of the period from the 1530s to the 1560s as what Kümin calls 'an absolutely crucial stage in the absorption of the parish into the wider…Tudor state' and Tittler 'a turning point in the history of English urban society', it is the changes of the Reformation that they emphasize.[157] For Steve Hindle it was the Elizabethan poor laws above all that made the parish 'to an unprecedented extent a local expression of state power', though he gives a supporting role to the militia act of 1558.[158] Of course the Reformation and the poor laws were important, but it is striking how many of the changes noted by these scholars were paralleled or even anticipated by the steps taken in response to the military demands of Henry and his successors. This was true not just of rating systems and the expropriation of church wealth, but also in questions of identity, bureaucracy, and the distribution of power.

Most towns dressing troops or warding off county muster commissioners asserted a corporate identity already well formed, but the terminology used by those making up church accounts betrays the ambiguities of institutional developments at parish level. Was it in fact the ecclesiastical parish that was becoming the primary unit of military organization in Henry's England, believably so as Henry made himself supreme head and seemed set to merge church and state, or was it something else? At St Michael Cornhill the accounts made clear that while the churchwardens, sexton, and beadle took care of the armour kept in the church steeple under the guidance of the vestrymen, it was the armour 'belonging to the warde', to the city of London's Cornhill Ward.[159] Elsewhere contemporaries were reaching for something like the later concept of the civil parish, but where in the South-West and much of the South communities spoke of their church or parish armour, in Hampshire it was the tithing armour, and from Essex to Lincolnshire and across to Leicestershire it was the town's or township's armour, even when, as at Melton Mowbray, it was kept in a locked press in the church vestry.[160]

The roles taken by different officers suggest similar ambiguities. Often it was the parish constable or constables, or the tithingman, agents of the parish or township in its judicial and fiscal functions, who took charge of military funds and equipment, or oversaw the setting out of soldiers.[161] In some places, specialists seem to have emerged, John Newcomb acting as 'conductor' of Chagford's soldiers to their muster points several years running and William at Tynwell accounting repeatedly for military costs at Morebath.[162] Elsewhere it was the churchwardens, even the clergy, who took an active part. At St Michael Spurriergate in York Sir Thomas Worrall, the stipendiary priest who conducted much of the parish's business, handed over an assortment of arms and armour to four past and present churchwardens in 1546.[163] At Ashburton the constable and tithingman escorted the soldiers to musters, but many other leading parishioners, including the churchwardens, took part in military preparations.[164]

Warfare also generated paperwork. Large boroughs had the administrative resources to cope with military organization, though there was still a fluster at times: in 1536 the London coopers' company paid two men for seven days' work 'running and going about at the wardens' commandment' to get everything organized.[165] Smaller towns and parishes found that mustering men, rating taxpayers, and buying armour meant, just like Reformation and Counter-Reformation, writing multiple bills, books, and indentures. In 1557–8 alone, Yatton paid 6*d* for 'the booke to gather to sette forthe sodwdyars' and 4*d* for a muster bill, while by 1568–9 Crediton was making three copies of its 'boucke for rating of armor and artilery'.[166]

As decisions had to be taken, so political power became concentrated in parish elites, just as urban oligarchies tightened to face new challenges. Hindle has written of a 'contraction of participation in parochial governance', in which what contemporaries called 'the best sort of the inhabitants' rose by the early seventeenth century to dominate affairs in many parishes.[167] In some places this trend to oligarchy might be traced back to the later fifteenth century and perhaps linked to the response of village and small town notables to the economic and social strains of renewed population growth, but in others it accelerated in our period.[168] Parish authorities making controversial moves to fund warfare in the 1540s were keen to stress that they acted with the consent of the parish or the whole township, or the assent of the parishioners, keeping alive the validating power of the ideal parish community.[169] Yet in some places distinctions were evident. Money was lent by a churchwarden to equip soldiers at St Michael Spurriergate 'as all oure masters doith knowe'.[170] Large sales of plate to fund military expenditure were made at Woodbridge in Suffolk 'with the consente of diverse and sundrie of the honestie of the same towne'.[171] Banningham in Norfolk sold its goods and set forth soldiers 'with the consent of the beste of the parisshe'.[172] War was shaping the parish and the borough alongside Reformation and social change.

Here we have mostly considered Henry's subjects in groups, but they also met the challenges of his wars as individuals. As we shall see in Chapter 6, this was true for every man, but never more so than for noblemen and gentlemen. For them war offered unparalleled opportunities for glory, reward, and promotion, but also that fate worse than death, dishonour. In January 1546, as the churchwardens of Suffolk were selling off their plate to buy armour for his men, Henry Howard, earl of Surrey, was stumbling off the battlefield at Saint-Etienne outside Boulogne, his best captains slain and his men in flight, allegedly begging the gentlemen around him to run him through 'and make him forget the day'.[173] Next we shall follow him and his kind into the king's wars.

4

Noblemen and Gentlemen

Sir Edward Don, whom we have met as a collector of almanacs, made a habit of copying moral tags into his household account book. In March 1533 he noted his resolution 'no longer to lyve then to serve my naturel soveryne lorde in defendyng hym and hys realme in batayle as a man'.[1] The sentiments were typical of his class and generation. Lord Berners expected that reading Froissart's *Chronicles* in his English translation 'exciteth, moveth and stereth the strong hardy warriours, for the great laude that they have after they ben deed, promptly to go in hande with great and harde parels, in defence of their countre'.[2] Charles Blount, Lord Mountjoy, composed this improving epitaph 'for a monument to my children, to continue and keep themselves worthy of so much honour as to be called hereafter to die for their master and country':

> Willingly have I sought, and willingly have I found,
> The fatall end that wrought me hither as dutie bound:
> Discharged I am of that I ought to my cuntry by honest wound,
> My soule departed Christ hath bought, the end of man is ground.[3]

But were these just loyal platitudes? And were they, in any case, passing away with the generations forged in the Hundred Years War and dangerously re-heated in the Wars of the Roses? Some contemporaries certainly thought so. In the 1470s William Worcester was already complaining that rather than cultivating the 'disciplines, doctrine and usage of scole of armes', young gentlemen were setting themselves to learn 'the practique of law, or custome of lande, or of civil matier, and so wastyn gretlie theire tyme' in holding courts and similar business.[4] By the 1540s it was apparently accountancy rather than law that had become the route to a comfortable life, but Elis Gruffudd of the Calais garrison was equally scathing. The latest captains, he thought, were 'a lot of feckless boys who were sent to school to learn to count money and become auditors rather than soldiers'.[5]

These complaints do not fit well with the fact that the leaders of gentle society, the parliamentary peerage, kept up a strong record of military service. In 1492 three-quarters either joined Henry VII's French campaign or sent their eldest sons, and more than half the rest were northerners who served against the Scots.[6] In 1513 again the numbers not serving either in France, at sea, or at Flodden were tiny.[7] In 1544 half the adult peers were in France with the king and nearly a quarter fighting the Scots.[8] These figures look even more impressive when we realize that William Worcester's golden age was not quite as golden as he thought. Half the peers in the Hundred Years War were occasional soldiers at best, and only one in six a relentless campaigner.[9]

If we widen our enquiry to look at members of the House of Commons, we start to understand Worcester's concerns. Apparently fewer than a quarter of all MPs between 1509 and 1558 campaigned on land or sea, and the proportion involved in war at all, for example by mustering or victualling troops, barely reached a quarter. These are minimum figures, but they still give pause for thought. They come better into focus when we separate out the burgesses representing towns from the knights of the shire, generally senior landed gentry, well over half of whom went to war.[10] This did mark a decline, for in some fourteenth-century parliaments as many as 69 per cent of the knights of the shire were campaigners, but it also perpetuated a distinction, for most burgesses had no military experience even in the fourteenth century.[11]

The demilitarization of the landed elite was a long process and one shaped by strategic circumstance. Fifteenth-century knights of the shire were much less likely to have extensive military experience than their fourteenth-century predecessors, because the Lancastrian war of steady conquest and standing garrisons was harder to combine with domestic political and social life than Edward III's raiding campaigns had been. The result was an increasing differentiation between a social elite who could fight, but rarely did, and an expert set of whole-hearted captains.[12] To be fair to William Worcester, it was precisely these experts that he had in mind when he lamented his lost heroes. Perhaps he would not have been disappointed to meet William, Lord Grey de Wilton, 'that honorable baron, and right famous captayne in his dayes', and Henry VIII's other generals.[13] Worcester could not reflect, as we can, that demilitarization followed not a timeless age of ancestral heroism, but a century of militarization of the English elite from Edward I's reign to Edward III's, followed by a fifteenth century in which only perhaps a quarter or a fifth of the gentry in many counties served overseas.[14] He also did not stop to ask whether peers whose homes lay in different parts of the realm had to take different attitudes to campaigning. The lords of the English Pale in Ireland campaigned as regularly throughout our period as those of the northernmost counties of England.[15] Further strategic change, moreover, might bring re-militarization of the sort Roger Manning has identified among the English peerage and gentry faced with the confessional wars and standing armies of the seventeenth century.[16]

Apparent demilitarization also sprang from a change in the composition of the top strata of society. Ideas of gentility were mutating, as heraldry, for example, became a mark of gentle descent rather than of military distinction, and new groups were entering the gentry and the peerage.[17] Some of the peers who did not serve in 1544 were lawyers or administrators, and many of our non-combatant MPs were similar. Elis Gruffudd, in his idiosyncratic way, noticed the change: most of the gentry round London by the 1540s, he thought, 'were the children of clothiers, others of farmers, some even of lawyers and butchers and carters if they had money enough to buy the lands of the monasteries or take them on lease'.[18] William Paget, the low-born royal secretary knighted in 1544 and ennobled in 1549, saw things clearly, telling Francis I in 1542 and Charles V in 1544 that he was 'no man of warre', just as the French captain of Boulogne, Oudart du Biez, explained to Paget that he was only obeying orders when he detained him in 1543, being 'no counsaillour...but...a man of warre, as you see'.[19] A similar awareness of the diversifying nature of social elites across western Europe was evident in the wry entertainment derived by the French court from the spectacle of the London alderman Richard Reed, sent by Henry to fight under 'the sharp discipline militar of the northern wars' because he would not pay the benevolence of 1545, and subsequently captured by the Scots.[20]

With diversification went specialization. Just as being a lawyer or an auditor was a professional skill that marked one out among the gentry, so was being a captain, a trend marked by the spread of the title 'captain' in the 1550s and 1560s. It first came patchily into use at Calais and Boulogne and on the Scottish border, then in 1557 the accounts of the army in France used it wholesale, and soon it was everywhere.[21] In the early 1560s Ludlow mentioned 'Capten Hacklete' passing through and the Londoners sent their men off with 'Captayn Vawghan' and 'Captain Leyton'.[22] The typical captain was a younger son or bastard of landowning stock, like many who had made careers in arms in the past.[23] Before 1558 the Calais and Boulogne garrisons provided opportunities for men like the bastard sons of Lords Berners and Cobham or those of Sir Edward Poynings, of whom Thomas, judged worthy of promotion as one 'longest acquaynted in the warres with the Frenchmen uppon the frontyers', became deputy of Boulogne, Edward captain of the guard at Boulogne, and Adrian captain of the citadel at Boulogne and eventually captain of Portsmouth.[24] In the wars either side of 1558 there were careers for the younger brothers of the earls of Rutland and Worcester and those of Lords Darcy and Zouche.[25] Thereafter, Ireland was the place. Some thought it axiomatic that English captains there be recruited among 'younger brethern of good discresion' and of the leading garrison captains of the 1560s and 1570s, Sir Nicholas Bagenal, Francis Cosby, and Sir Henry Radcliffe were second sons, Sir Richard Bingham, Sir George Bourchier, and Sir William Drury third sons.[26]

Leading troops into battle was only one part of the military role of the nobility and gentry. The deployment of their social authority was also fundamental in assembling armies. In the century after 1475 five different ways of raising troops, all inherited from the past, interacted in what Jeremy Goring, as we have seen, has called a shift from a 'quasi-feudal' to a 'national' system of recruitment.[27] The first and oldest mechanism remained in the background much of the time, but came into its own from the 1540s. This was the levy of all able men between sixteen and sixty for national defence under commissions of array. Secondly, for overseas expeditions in the Hundred Years War, kings raised armies under contracts with the captains of individual companies. Thirdly, to assist in assembling such contingents, but also for wider political and administrative purposes, lords recruited retinues of men sworn to their service. Fourthly, around this core of retainers, lords could call on a wider following of servants, tenants, and friends who accepted their protection and would serve them as part of what the Victorians dubbed bastard feudalism. Kings needed these third and fourth mechanisms to work if they were to recruit armies effectively; but they were also worried at the potential they gave for violent disorder and judicial corruption in private disputes. Their response was to legislate against retaining, but then license those whom they trusted to retain.[28]

Henry VII did this so systematically that he produced what we might think of as a fifth mechanism, a national retinue scheme under which trusted peers, councillors, household men, and towns recruited large retinues sworn to the king's service under licence, returning their names to the king's secretary. The result was impressive: one Burgundian observer recorded that Henry held 40,000 fine and strong men ready in their homes and that the French much feared what he might do with them.[29] Traces of the scheme remain in the archives of the king's mother, who sent messengers round Lincolnshire in 1508 'to calle in her reteyned servauntes... to doe the kynges grace service', of Sir Henry Willoughby, who preserved his licence to retain, with its characteristic advertisement of the king's 'grete studie, labour and policie' in securing peace, and of Sir Thomas Lovell, whose list survives of 1,365 retainers from thirteen counties.[30] Henry's scheme died with him, but its aspirations persisted.[31] The general proscription or military survey of spring 1522, a remarkable attempt to record the names, wealth, and military equipment of every adult male in England together, crucially, with the relationships of tenure and service that would channel his recruitment for war, may have marked a final effort to generalize it.[32]

In the absence of such a scheme, kings were dependent on some combination of indentures, private retinues, and wider affinities to harness the recruiting powers of the nobility and gentry. Indentures were used in 1492 and 1512, but thereafter replaced by letters requiring lords to raise a number of men from among their tenants, servants, and those under their rule and offices.[33] We shall explore each of these categories of recruits in turn, but we should note that these letters never mentioned retainers. This was odd, because as J. P. Cooper pointed out many years ago, retaining was alive and well into the 1580s and 1590s.[34] Henry VII's attitude towards it had been calculatedly divisive. Those he trusted were encouraged to retain on a large scale, those he did not trust were spectacularly punished, in George, Lord Bergavenny's case with a massive fine and the extraction of a promise not to go to the counties where his estates lay without the king's permission.[35]

Succeeding regimes tried unsuccessfully to alternate between permissive policies in wartime and restrictive policies in peacetime. The war of 1512–14 was bookended by proclamations revoking all licences to retain and followed by high-profile prosecutions of peers and their retainers.[36] Then, in 1522, retainers were reported in large numbers to the commissioners for the general proscription. Some came in handfuls, but Thomas, marquess of Dorset, one of those prosecuted in 1516, had seventy-seven retainers in Worcestershire alone.[37] Some of the retainers of 1522 were explicitly retained by fees, livery coats, or 'placardes', but others must have done service in a previous campaign and continued to regard themselves as retained.[38] When Sir William Gruffudd, chamberlain of North Wales, was accused in 1519 of maintaining an illegal retinue more than a hundred strong, he insisted that he had retained men with his badge only in wartime; as witnesses pointed out, this did not stop men continuing to wear his badge if they thought that 'suche as did were his cognysaunce he wold favour, and suche as did not he wold be extreme unto theym'.[39] From the 1540s regular warfare and popular disorder revived the granting of licences to retain to peers, councillors, and courtiers.[40] Under Edward, trusted councillors were even given standing companies of men-at-arms paid by the king, though spending cuts soon put a stop to that.[41]

At least half a dozen of Sir William Gruffudd's retainers were also his estate tenants.[42] This should not surprise us, for muster lists show us that the tenantry were central to the process of recruitment. In 1492, for example, Lord Latimer's retinue included Miles Bayne, archer, and Christopher Johnson and Thomas Pereson, billmen, his tenants at Snape and Well.[43] In 1508 Lovell's retainers included the tenants of his brother-in-law Lord Roos, whose estates were in his keeping.[44] In 1542 the countess of Rutland sent two or three men from each of the family's manors in Leicestershire and Lincolnshire to join her husband on the Scottish border.[45] Even when individuals cannot be matched in this way, the role of the tenantry can be confirmed by the matches between the surnames of those serving in retinues and the tenants recorded in the general proscription or in estate records.[46] And at a broader level still the destinations to which returning soldiers were paid conduct money match time and again the distribution of their captains' estates. This was true in 1513 for peers such as the duke of Buckingham, the earl of Essex, and Lord Bergavenny, in 1523 for Lords Conyers, Clifford, and others.[47] It was still true in 1557, when many of the earl of Pembroke's men went to Wilton, the earl of Rutland's to Helmsley, the earl of Bedford's to Tavistock, and Sir John Perrot's to Haverfordwest.[48] Such recruiting was facilitated by lordly record-keeping. Walter Strickland's book recording 279 tenants from seven different estates in Westmorland able to serve as bowmen or billmen, on horse or on foot, still survives.[49]

Yet tenant recruitment was on the slide. The 1540s saw a number of lawsuits between lords and tenants who simply refused to serve, and a statute of 1550 permitting landlords to evict the recalcitrant could not stem the tide.[50] Had the tenants changed, or had the wars changed? Probably both: a system designed for quick campaigns in civil wars or brief expeditions to France was ill-suited to the relentless garrison warfare of Boulogne, Haddington, or Le Havre, while the spread of leasing and rise in rents in an expanding agricultural market produced a new breed of assertive large-scale farmers.[51] Not even Henry VIII could beat both the military revolution and the rise of agrarian capitalism. In Mary's reign one estate surveyor, William Homberston, already looked back to the good old days when there was 'suche a knott of collaterall amytie between the lordes and the tenaunts' that 'if the lord were at any tyme commaunded to serve the king's majestie, the tenaunts woulde leave wife, chylderne, and substaunce, and follow ther lord, and adventure ther lyves with hym most willinglye'. Indeed, he continued, beginning to strain credulity, they 'had no care of ther lyves', remembering that 'if ther chance were to be left in the feilde' their widow should have their lands to provide for their children.[52]

As tenants began to doubt such certainties, lords dealt with them in three different ways, confrontational, cajoling, or contractual. In the short term confrontation might appear to work. On 31 August 1557 William Anne of Aylesbury, tenant to

Sir Thomas Pakington, was committed to the Fleet prison by the privy council 'for his stubburne behaviour towardes the said Sir Thomas and refusall to come to his musters'. Subsequently Anne was ordered to submit himself 'with promise from hensfourthe to behave himself as a tenant ought to do, and to exhorte as moche as lye in him the rest of the tenantes to do the like'.[53] The earl of Bath's estate officers preferred the carrot to the stick. In that same trying year of war and disease Humphrey Colles, trying to muster the earl's tenants, thought the earl should write to thank those who had 'extended there benevolence unto' him so that he might 'fynde them more willinge upon semblable occasion'.[54] Sir Anthony Browne's servants, similarly, were told 'gentlie to intreat' his tenants to be ready when he should send for them, assuring them that 'thus doenge they do my master greate pleasur'.[55]

In the longer term the contractual approach won out. Agreements binding tenants to serve when called upon or forfeit their holding can be found as early as 1486.[56] From the 1510s leases began to carry the more elaborate formula that the tenant would serve in person, find a sufficient substitute, or pay to find one. At first this happened where there was special need: on the Isle of Wight, for example, or for lords who held captaincies at Calais.[57] But from the 1530s to the 1550s many greater and lesser landowning families introduced such clauses. Some of their tenants even passed on the resulting costs to their sub-tenants, stipulating that a few shillings were payable in addition to the rent 'at everye time when' the lessee 'shall furnishe enye men to the warres for . . . his lande lorde'.[58] Military service was becoming commodified and the prosperous tenant could pay for someone else to risk his life; except, ironically, in the northernmost counties, where 'tenant right' tenures, strong on military obligations but favourable in other ways, were consolidated just as Anglo-Scottish relations took a turn towards friendship and union.[59]

The centrality of the tenantry gave estate officers a prime role not only in recruitment, but also in military service. In the 1520s and 1530s the Percies' stewards, bailiffs, and park keepers took charge of leading the earl of Northumberland's tenants to war.[60] In 1492 one of Sir Henry Willoughby's demi-lances, a horseman well equipped though lacking the full armour of the man-at-arms or spear, was Arnold Gee, his bailiff of Sutton-on-Trent, one of Lord Latimer's was Thomas Morley, his bailiff of Snape, and Sir Ralph Longford and the earls of Oxford and Shrewsbury also numbered estate officers in their retinues.[61] The commissioners of 1522 noted the bailiffs and park keepers of various landlords, generally men with military equipment for themselves and sometimes even for others.[62] Greater lords with larger retinues needed the service of more senior officers. In 1533 the earl of Derby was insistent that his steward Sir Robert Bellingham should lead men under him, rather than serve at the command of Lord Dacre.[63]

Captains' own tenants were joined by the tenants of the king or of other lords, religious houses in particular, whom the recruiter served as estate steward. Heads of religious houses who came under pressure from one neighbouring gentleman to let him recruit their tenants could respond that until the steward had decided which men to levy, the other applicant 'colde have none'.[64] The large expansions in the crown's landholdings under Henry VII and again at the dissolution of the monasteries made this source of manpower particularly important. Repeated statutes, proclamations, and letters to stewards asserted the king's unique right to call on the service of his tenants and lawsuits show stewards' attempts to enforce it.[65] In Sir Thomas Lovell's licensed retinue about one-third of the men were recruited through crown stewardships and another fifth through his offices on monastic and episcopal estates.[66] In 1513 Sir Henry Marney raised nine times as many men through his offices in the duchies of Cornwall and Lancaster as from his own Essex lands.[67] This trend also amplified the military role of the royal household, though not in the same way as in continental monarchies, where guards units proliferated.[68] Henry never had more than a few hundred yeomen of the guard and around fifty king's spears or gentlemen pensioners, but the stewardships held by courtiers gave them the power to recruit.[69] Even lords with large landholdings drew on stewardships. The marquess of Dorset retained at least thirty-five men at Droitwich, where he was steward for the queen, the stewardships of Furness and Whalley were important to the earl of Derby's recruitment, and the duke of Norfolk drew on Bury St Edmunds Abbey and the University of Cambridge.[70]

Household servants were less numerous than tenants in most retinues, but of central importance.[71] The 1492 musters hint at this, recording recruits such as 'John of the Pantre' or 'George of the Chamber'.[72] County musters show that peers could arm very large numbers of servants: in Sussex in 1539 Lord Lawarr produced fifty-seven fully equipped for war, the earl of Arundel 123, and William Fitzwilliam, earl of Southampton, 183.[73] Servants were expected to be supremely loyal to their masters, hence the emphasis on arming them to confront rebels.[74] Long service must have played a part in that. Five or six of the earl of Oxford's spears or demi-lances from 1492, nine archers, seven billmen, a custrel or lightly armed horseman, and a page were still his household servants sixteen years later.[75] When Lovell died in 1524, he rewarded his old servants William Kerkby and Robinet Water, who had been his archers in France thirty-two years before.[76] Loyalty was reciprocated. John, Lord Latimer set out in his will that any of his servants 'notably hurt or maimed' when following him to war should be compensated with a year's wages, and Sir Giles Strangways that each servant accompanying him should have his horse and harness.[77] Servants may have been well prepared to fight if other households were like that of Sir David Owen, whose servants behaved like the Three Musketeers in quiet Midhurst in March 1505, fighting among themselves in the street with swords, staffs, and bows and arrows, with fatal effects for a yeoman who came out of his house at the wrong moment.[78] Yet as retinues gave way to county contingents, household service became a draft-dodging measure. In 1556 one Hampshire man was casting around for a master, worried that 'if any going forthe be, he is a man likely to be one, onles he be retained into some service'.[79]

As in the Hundred Years War, captains looked to bolster their retinues by sub-contracting.[80] In 1492 the marquess of Dorset asked the help of Sir John Trevelyan to 'pourvey me of iii or fore good archers, or mo'.[81] In 1523, Sir Edward Guildford, expected to raise 500 'of the best and of the tallest persones apparayled in every thing for the war', wrote anxiously to his local subordinates to 'take payne...with diligens as my very trust is in youe'. They were to speak with Thomas Aldy and Guildford's other 'frendes' and ask them 'to appoint me the tallest men that be in that parties . . . so that ye may have theire names that I may be in a suertie of them'; they were to ask Aldy himself 'that he be in my compeny in this journey . . . as my trust is that he wylbe assone with me as with any other man'.[82] Such networks bridged the gap between the huge indentured retinues, geared to military recruitment, of a John of Gaunt or a William Lord Hastings, and the military clienteles of the earls of Leicester in the 1580s and Essex in the 1590s.[83]

Finally captains amplified their retinues by asking friendly towns to contribute men. When the recruiter held a relevant office—Sir Edward Poynings as Warden of the Cinque Ports, or William, Lord Sandys as steward of Andover—requests were readily met, though they fitted into wider calculations of patronage, protection, and gift-exchange.[84] With larger and more independent-minded boroughs, matters were more fluid. The dukes of Norfolk drew men from Norwich, the earls of Huntingdon from Leicester, but such relationships were under constant negotiation.[85] The bailiffs of Shrewsbury told the earl of Shrewsbury in 1492 that, while the townsfolk were willing to serve him in domestic campaigns as they had served his ancestors, they could 'in noe wyse' be persuaded to join him overseas.[86]

Lords also had to be able to equip the men they raised. They provided their coats and claimed the money back later from the crown.[87] Sir Richard Gresham, the London merchant who had just bought the Fountains Abbey estate, received itemized accounts showing how £6 10*s* had been spent in autumn 1542 on forty white coats with red crosses for his men, made up by a tailor and his servants who came to his manor house at Brimham.[88] Some recruits had arms and armour, some lords raised money from their wider tenantry to buy it, but most often lords armed men from their own stocks.[89] These were both larger and more modern than the town and village armouries we have already examined. Sir Reynold Bray had six handguns as early as 1503, for example, and Thomas Cromwell 272 in 1540.[90] Knights and esquires often produced equipment for half a dozen men or more at musters and some of the Cornish gentry in 1569 could equip whole companies in the latest style: Sir John Arundell of Lanherne had twenty corslets, forty almain rivets, ten handguns, ten bows, twenty pikes, forty bills, and equipment for two lightly and two heavily armed horsemen.[91] Several peers went further still, with calivers, dags, and cannon.[92] Even the lawyers and auditors that so worried William Worcester and Elis Gruffudd packed a punch. John Smith, serjeant at law, left his son in the 'armoury or gallery' at Smiths Hall in Blackmore, Essex in 1543 a complete harness for the upper body and eight sets of almain rivets.[93] Thomas Burgoyn, auditor of the duchy of Lancaster, left his sons in 1546 a similar selection of almain rivets—was it his auditor's instincts that made him specify each set was 'able and sufficient and complete'?—with other armour and weapons.[94] Everywhere peers and gentlemen either employed armourers full-time to keep their equipment in good repair, or called them in for days or weeks at a time to scour, and oil, and mend it.[95]

Horses were also important, so important that successive acts of parliament ordered wealthy men to keep brood mares and great horses and permitted the confiscation of under-sized stallions roaming common pastures and begetting offspring too puny for the defence of the realm.[96] In 1547 and 1565 instructions went out to local authorities to check that gentlemen were keeping great horses and the 1569 muster commissioners carefully noted mares in parks.[97] Thomas Blundeville, author on horsemanship, urged constant vigilance, for the lack of 'great horses, and gueldinges meete for service' would, 'if any invasion shuld chaunce' 'quickly appere (I feare me) to the great perill and danger of this her highnes realme'.[98] The leading generals at least seem to have done their bit. Lord Grey de Wilton lost seventy-two great horses and a hundred geldings in an attempt to relieve Haddington, the earl of Arundel sent sixty great horses 'out of his owne stable' against Wyatt, and the most expensive horse to cause a victim's death in a sixteenth-century coroner's inquest, worth £20 when most horses were worth a pound or two, belonged to the earl of Pembroke.[99] While the earls of Kildare before their downfall had allegedly kept a stud large enough to supply all of English Ireland with horses fit for war, others' establishments were notable for sheer quality. Blundeville singled out Sir Nicholas Arnold, formerly captain at Boulogne and governor of Ireland, for his 'industry and diligence' in breeding fine Neapolitan horses in Gloucestershire.[100]

Horses were not the only expense of campaigning. Captains had to equip them-selves and their retinues in suitable style and stockpile cash for unanticipated expenses in the field, not least because the exercise of lordly command demanded conspicuous consumption. Sir Rhys ap Thomas reportedly took £3,000 in gold and silver on the 1513 campaign and Sir Edward Guildford gave one servant £90 in a casket to cover 'necessaries consernyng the seyd Sir Edward during the kynges warres'.[101] All manner of expedients were necessary to raise cash. The duke of Norfolk in 1475 and Thomas, Lord Scrope of Masham in 1492 mortgaged lands, Sir John Arundell of Lanherne in 1513 sold plate, Sir Edward Burgh in 1492 took loans at allegedly usurious rates from the London alderman Sir William Capel, and John Grenfeld in 1557 borrowed money at high interest and lost the manor on which he had secured it.[102] Several captains sold land, sometimes at knock-down prices, and the marquess of Dorset in 1512 made perpetual leases at fixed rents, presumably in exchange for large fines.[103] Fortunate were courtiers who could ask the king for cash advances—£7 to John Carr to buy himself armour in 1492, £133 6s 8d to Sir Thomas Knyvet 'to furnysshe himself and his company' in 1512—or those with rich kinsmen, like Arthur Plantagenet, Viscount Lisle, who borrowed more than £200 from the earl of Arundel.[104] More common were complaints of the great costs of serving the king in war, convenient in fending off other creditors, it is true, but sometimes heartfelt and convincing.[105] The earl of Bedford, ordering the sale of timber to meet his costs in 1557, was engagingly straightforward: 'my charges…this jornaye hathe ben moche greatter then I dyd accownt apon'.[106]

Costs worsened in the event of mishap. When Sir John Carew died on his burning ship in 1512, he lost much of the plate and cash bequeathed to his wife by her first husband, as well as the clothing and armour he had bought with her money.[107] Capture was almost worse, for its repercussions could last for gener-ations. Grey de Wilton had to borrow £8,000 from the crown and sell lands to pay the ransom charged him after the fall of Guînes in 1558, with the risk his family might be 'utterly undone for ever'; matters were compounded by his nobly generous help in paying the equally exorbitant ransom of one of his subordinates.[108] His case was exceptional, but capture was an occupational hazard for those who served at Calais and Boulogne, befell some on shorter campaigns or in Ireland, and called for ransoms running to hundreds of pounds or more.[109] The wise made what provision they could, for example in marriage settlements permitting the diversion of revenues in the event of capture.[110]

Death and capture were not the only risks. In war, as the marquess of Dorset reminded the Willoughby family in pressing them to settle his sister's jointure, 'ther ys as you knowe myche daunger and casualtye'.[111] Wounds were readily incurred on the way to battle: a horse kick broke Marney's leg in 1513 and in 1558 the earl of Rutland's leg was 'hurte in the shippe' as he tried to rescue Calais.[112] Wounds were worse in combat or under bombardment, while disease redoubled the danger. At Le Havre half a dozen English captains were wounded, half a dozen killed outright, three drowned in a Channel shipwreck, and a dozen died of plague.[113] Even those who survived might lose those dear to them. Sir Thomas Cheyne and Sir Giles Strangways lost sons who accompanied them to Montreuil and Boulogne.[114]

Yet war was compelling. Some found it exhilarating, reporting breathlessly how they had chased the enemy from the field, or speaking of it with studied casualness as 'sporte'.[115] The discomforts of war were a badge of honour. 'I meane nothing lesse than the sparing of my pore body in anything wherin I maye do his majestie service' avowed John Dudley, Lord Lisle, and Lord Leonard Grey, brother to the marquess of Dorset, tore a strip off William Body, a self-important royal commissioner, when he complained about his lodgings on campaign: 'I saide, I was sure he sholde never be so good, as the dukes of Norfoke, and Suffolke, and my lorde my brother, whom I had seen lodged wors'.[116] Yet war needed to be done nobly. In Ireland the gentry of the English Pale were horrified when Grey confiscated the horses, armour, and weapons of Lords Delvin and Gormanston and made them walk home when they failed to follow him in fording a river in the face of the enemy.[117]

Others, admittedly, found war wearisome. By 1557, the earl of Bath complained, he had been sent to keep order in Devon because of the 'unquiet state' of the county three years running, it had cost him more than £1,300, he was sure he could not go again because it was too painful to ride, and he had never been given £2 a day to serve as lieutenant there as the earl of Bedford had.[118] War was a serious business, but that did not preclude a sharp, dark sense of humour. On embassy in Spain in 1518 Lord Berners topped the joke cracked by the French ambassador as the court watched the Spanish martial art of cane play, with its stylized recreation of the light cavalry warfare of the Moorish frontier. As the men wheeled their horses the Frenchman said it seemed a good way to teach them to flee their enemies. Berners retorted that the French had already learnt that at the battle of the Spurs.[119] Sir Thomas Wharton was equally sardonic after a successful raid on the Scottish borders had brought in a large haul of livestock. Since the laird of Buccleuch was boasting of the large sums in gold he had received from Cardinal Beaton to secure his allegiance to the anti-English party in Scotland, Wharton suggested to the duke of Suffolk, 'he might the better forgo part of his sheipe'.[120]

The qualities expected of commanders were demanding. In 1557 the earl of Pembroke was appointed captain general for his 'wisdome, dexteritye, activitye, valiantnes and experience in the warre'.[121] Experience, vigilance, diligence, or 'pain-fulness', the preparedness to take pains to make sure things were done properly, were often commended, as was activeness, the quality displayed by Lord Leonard Grey, 'a stirrer abroode, and no sleaper in the morning'.[122] Hardiness, boldness, was good, though best when tempered with discretion, circumspection, or 'sad' advice, and worst when tending to rashness.[123] There were differences, though, between paternalist and coercive styles of command. Elis Gruffudd drew a contrast, no doubt overblown, between Lord Clinton and the earl of Surrey. Clinton, 'greatly beloved among all ranks', 'played his part like a brave and noble captain by risking his life among his soldiers...courteously thanking and rewarding generously those soldiers who did any brave deeds...while courteously rebuking those who were to blame'. Surrey and his captains, rather than 'comfort the soldiers with kindly, tender, godly words', used to 'call on the soldiers with vain contemptuous words... beating and shoving the common soldiers forward'.[124] As captain of the castle at Broughty Crag in Scotland, Sir Andrew Dudley, brave but haughty, impressed but alienated his men, whereas his successor, Sir John Luttrell, pleaded their cause affectionately with his superiors and shared in their privations, even working alongside them to dig fortifications, as inspirational commanders from Protector Somerset downwards made a point of doing.[125]

Captains reflected on command through military literature. Sir Richard Morison claimed, when introducing his translation of Frontinus in 1539, that 'the noble capitaynes of England, have oft declared, that they lytell nede any instructions, any bokes, to teach them to towse their enemies', but this was humanist exagger-ation.[126] While the English do not seem to have pursued literal reproduction of Roman weapons, institutions, and tactics with the same enthusiasm as the Italians, the French, or, later, the Dutch, they were well aware of the value of classical mili-tary wisdom.[127] Fifteenth-century English captains read translations of Vegetius and the fifth earl of Northumberland's papers included 'a draw3th off order and apparel off a prince when he goeth to warr'.[128] Classical and contemporary writ-ings on war were translated for noblemen: Sallust and Onosander for the second and fourth dukes of Norfolk, a life of Scipio for the earl of Pembroke, Vegetius for the earl of Bedford, an account of the Schmalkaldic War for the earl of Derby.[129] In the 1540s Edward Seymour and John Dudley apparently used recently composed military treatises and booklets of military diagrams of the sort also owned by Richard Worsley, captain of the Isle of Wight, while in the next generation several of the first wave of Elizabethan military works were dedicated to Dudley's sons, Ambrose, earl of Warwick, and Robert, earl of Leicester.[130] Some captains even wrote handbooks. Thomas Audley and Henry Barrett were long-serving soldiers of comparatively low birth, but Sir Ralph Bulmer seems to have been the author of a work on 'the maner and fashion of levying of armes in this our nation of England' presented to his fellow Yorkshire knight Sir Oswald Wilstrop.[131]

War could advance a gentleman's social standing, for military campaigns were major opportunities to acquire knighthood (see Fig. 4.1). War could also make or

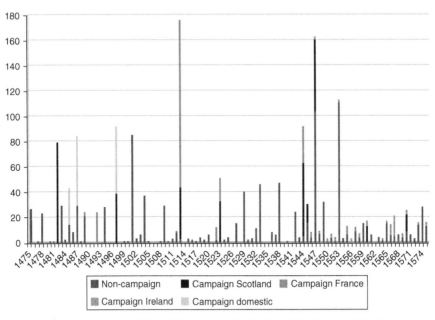

Fig. 4.1. Knights created, 1475–1575 (source: W. A. Shaw, *The Knights of England*, 2 vols (London, 1906), i. 136–53, ii. 17–77).

break a reputation. Wounds might announce honour: it was said of Sir William Godolphin that the wounds he got at Boulogne were 'no less to the beautifying of his fame, than the disfiguring of his face'.[132] Failures might equip enemies to traduce. Sir John Brydges was incensed when his neighbour John Warneford 'in many honorable and worshipfull assembles companyes and conferences' defamed him as 'a croke nosed knave and also a very coward and that he was so provyd at Bolleyn'. Warneford was condemned in Star Chamber to admit on his knees in open court that he had untruly slandered Brydges and ask his forgiveness. The charge may have had so much bite because Brydges had been with the earl of Surrey on the fateful day their troops fled from the French at Saint-Etienne.[133] Thomas Temys was less secure in his gentility than Brydges, but charged with worse failings. No wonder he denied a neighbour's accusation that when the French attacked the Isle of Wight 'I stood in the king's garrison like a man when thou as a traitor and coward fleddest out of said Isle with thy wife and conveyest then all thy plate and thy money with thee as the king's untrue subject.'[134] Such reputation might become the topic of very public debate. Lord Wentworth, in command at Calais when it fell, was ventriloquized in a ballad of 1559 bewailing his fate in the most banal of verse.[135]

  Martial reputation inhered in families as well as individuals. Heraldry might blazon real deeds as well as haunt prophetic imaginations. Sir Edward Guildford, marshal of Calais, punned on his firebrand badge in answer to a French challenge, and burnt the nearby countryside.[136] Sir Edward Stanley was made Lord Monteagle for his deeds at Flodden, holding a 'hill or mounte ageinst the Scottes' under his family's eagle crest.[137] When heralds toured the country recording coats of arms they noted the deeds, the deaths, and the military offices of members of gentle families from the Hundred Years War to the recent past: Robert Clere of Ormsby, 'slaine at Musselborough', Percies, Eures, and Bowes who served at Berwick and Norham, Bourchiers and Wingfields who served at Calais.[138] John Leland heard similar stories, of Oliver St John 'that died at Fonterabye in Spayne when the late marquise of Dorset was there', of the two Fitzwilliam brothers 'slayn at the felde of Floddoun of the Scots'.[139] Survivors took such tales to heart. Sir William Fitzwilliam pledged to 'do the Scots some displeasure' in revenge for his brothers.[140]

Tombs formed a link between individual identity and the lasting local power of families. It was normal to commemorate gentlemen substantial enough to be man- orial lords with effigies or brasses depicting them in armour whether or not they had notable military careers, but a special emphasis on military achievement could be added.[141] Repeated service to a great age was a theme in the epitaphs for Sir Marmaduke Constable, who made it from France in 1475 to Flodden in 1513, and for Sir George Beeston, who lasted from Boulogne to the Armada.[142] The second duke of Norfolk's long epitaph recited his services from Barnet to Flodden.[143] Sir John Clerk's epitaph at Thame recalled his capture of the duke of Longueville at the battle of the Spurs and Sir Ralph Sadler's tomb carried the Scottish banner he captured at Pinkie.[144] Funerals too might go out of their way to emphasize prowess. The second duke of Norfolk's mourners were treated, in between his various funeral masses, to an hour-long sermon on the text 'Behold, the lion of the tribe of Judah triumphs'.[145] By the time Grey de Wilton died in 1562 the service was very different, morning prayer and communion with psalms 'of prayse and thanksgevinge for the departure of the deade in the faythe of Christe', but the sermon 'much comendyd his worthye servyce...as well in Fraunce as in Scotland'.[146]

Fame came in many forms. One was membership in the historic companionship of English chivalry, the order of the Garter, a distinction that still recognized mar- tial prowess as well as royal favour.[147] Another was the naming of fortifications built or commanded by the captain, a recognizably modern recognition strategy. Calais had Lovell's bulwark, Guînes had Whetehill's bulwark. The Calais marsh had a set of bulwarks named for their captains, and Ambleteuse outside Boulogne had bastions called Berkeley's Mount, Bourcher's Mount, and Stourton's Mount.[148] Most redolent of the need to urge men to build defences under fire were the bul- warks of Haddington, named for their captains, Bowes, Tailor, and Wilford, while at the next incursion into Scotland the forts built to besiege Leith were named Mount Pelham and Somerset's Mount.[149]

Objects large and small might also testify to martial experience. Thomas Hardres added the iron-bound gates of Boulogne to his house in Kent, Giles Alington a bell from Boulogne to Horseheath in Cambridgeshire.[150] Books were marked with inscriptions that showed where they had been plundered: a shepherd's calendar from Morlaix, Cicero's letters from Boulogne, a history of Scotland, a canon law collection, and a Latin bible from Edinburgh.[151] Weapons were especially eloquent. Edward Lord Windsor, one of the first Englishmen over the walls of Saint-Quentin in 1557, kept in his armoury a 'case of dagges with black stockes which came from Saynt Quyntynes'.[152]

More deliberate commemorations were also popular. Guests of John Dudley at his London house would have seen maps of his campaigns in Scotland and Norfolk, guests of the earl of Pembroke his 'trencher of estate curiously wrought with the siege of St Quentin', guests of Clement Paston his jewel representing the capture of a French galley.[153] Sir John Fulford had a large painting of the battle of Gravelines and, most spectacularly, William Fitzwilliam and his half-brother Sir Anthony Browne commissioned ten panel paintings and a five-part mural for their house at Cowdray in Sussex depicting the great events of their careers, from the Guyenne expedition of 1512 to the invasion of France in 1544 and the defence of Portsmouth in 1545 (see Figs. 4.2 and 7.1).[154] More bizarrely, Sir Richard Bulkeley apparently had the ash trees at Baron Hill on Anglesey planted in the formation taken up by the English army at Pinkie.[155]

An armoured portrait did not necessarily denote a devoted warrior: for Sir Richard Bingham, who fought in Scotland, France, the Netherlands, and the Mediterranean and ended as president of Connacht, it probably did, whereas for John, first Lord Mordaunt (see Fig. 6.2), who did not even serve in 1544, it surely did not.[156] But some portraits represented the sitter at moments of particular glory or self-sacrifice, like the striking depictions of Edwardian captains by Hans Eworth featuring Pinkie, Haddington, and a battle at sea (see Fig. 4.3).[157] Sir William Drury accompanied his portrait by a plan of Edinburgh Castle, which he had won by bombardment in 1573, surrounded by the heraldry of sixteen brothers-in-arms.[158] One group of captains in particular revelled in praise for their martial achievements, the Welsh gentry. Sir Rhys ap Thomas of Dinefwr and Carew, Sir Rhys Mawnsel of Oxwich, the Salusburys of Lleweni, the Gruffudds of Penrhyn, and many more were lauded for their deeds at Thérouanne, Tournai, Boulogne, and Saint-Quentin, at Bosworth, Blackheath, and Mousehold, at Edinburgh and in Ireland, in the praise poems and elegies of Tudur Aled, Lewys Môn, Lewys Morgannwg, Siôn Tudur, and other touring bards. Assertions of their importance in each victory flowed with cheerful abandon and comparisons with Arthur and Lancelot, Charlemagne and Roland came readily to hand.[159]

Military experience also had more practical benefits. It justified noblemen's counsel to the king as experts on the problems of Ireland or the North. Archbishop Lee of York, for example, argued that the social benefit of Hexham Priory 'in tyme of warr', might be testified by 'manye of the noble men of this realme, that hath done the kinge's highnes service in Scotland'.[160] War also built regional and local power, as those who led armies consolidated their bonds with those who served under them. Knights and gentlemen making wills sometimes mentioned that they were going to war under 'the most noble captain' the earl of Shrewsbury, or were to 'wayte uppon the right noble prynce Charles duke of Suffolk into the partiez of Fraunce, ther to warre upon the French men'.[161] Once on campaign, commanders recommended those serving under them for reward and knighted those who had done well.[162] The second, third, and fourth dukes of Norfolk managed to confer 136 knighthoods between them, and the speedy Edward Seymour 123 in

THE ENCAMPMENT OF KING HENRY VIII AT MARQUISON, JULY MDXLIV.

ENGRAVED FROM A COEVAL PAINTING AT COWDRAY IN SUSSEX, THE SEAT OF LORD VISCOUNT MONTAGUE.

Fig. 4.2. James Basire, 'The encampment of King Henry VIII at Marquison, July 1544, from a coeval painting at Cowdray' (British Library).

three and a half years.[163] Such practices reinforced the ties of kinship, friendship, and clientage that animated armies on campaign, whether led by great lords like Norfolk or Suffolk, or veteran captains like Sir Edward Poynings.[164]

The experience of fighting together then fed back into the relationships that made local politics and local government work, all the more so when local noblemen

Fig. 4.3. Hans Eworth, Thomas Wyndham with arquebus and powder flask. © The Earl of Radnor, Longford Castle.

coordinated local defence. This was true of the Fitzgerald earls of Kildare, for example, the Percy earls of Northumberland, or the Lords Dacre of Gilsland, border magnates whose castles, households, and wider followings were more important to national defence than those of any other noblemen, but whose careers rested more precariously on their success in military leadership and regional governance than did those of their less exposed colleagues.[165] Only when military responsibilities were completely out of alignment with local politics did the pain outweigh the gain. The earl of Bath, with estates in Devon and Suffolk, somehow ended up as captain of Beaumaris Castle on Anglesey. Its towers were collapsing, his deputy

Sir Richard Bulkeley resigned on finding that the locals would not come to defend it, and the messenger the earl sent to London found his 'tragicall sute' for help batted backwards and forwards between the majority of the privy council, who insisted that no one ever attacked Anglesey anyway, and Lord Paget, who 'knewe of dyvers attemptes made to that ile', but was unavailable for comment, as he and his wife were leaving to take the waters at Bath.[166]

As the leaders of landed society and the gentry below them campaigned less often, war came to shape local politics in different ways. The huge armies required by Henry in 1544–5 tested the retinue system to breaking point and commissions of array came into more general use to levy contingents of men county by county, a procedure repeated for the wars of Edward, Mary, and Elizabeth in Scotland and France.[167] To face the threat of invasion in 1545, counties were grouped under the dukes of Norfolk and Suffolk and Lord Russell, who were charged with raising men and overseeing coastal defences, just as various peers had been in 1539.[168] From these experiments was born the lord lieutenancy. From 1550 every county was put under one or more peer, privy councillor, or trusted knight, charged not only with mustering and levying men, but also with a more general 'speciall care of good ordre to be had in the countre'.[169] Mary tried to revoke the scheme, but was forced by war and rebellion to revive it; Elizabeth maintained it, though not with any permanency until 1585.

In many cases the appointment merely confirmed a local supremacy either long established or newly won—the earl of Shrewsbury in Derbyshire, the earl of Pembroke in Wiltshire—but in others it sought to arrogate power to men trusted at the centre: John Dudley put William Parr, marquess of Northampton, in charge of six counties, while Elizabeth gave Oxfordshire to her vice-chamberlain Sir Francis Knollys.[170] Certainly the post was worth having. In 1556 the earl of Derby wrote to Sir Edward Hastings asking him to move the queen to renew his commission as lieutenant of Lancashire and Cheshire and not to include the counties in the earl of Shrewsbury's remit. He felt strongly about the matter. 'I thinke my service no lesse acceptable than myself hable and of power equall with hym to serve her majestie in th'office of leuetenant of the same countiez', he wrote, 'wher my servantes tenantes offices and frendes for the most parte do remayne. And not to serve as an objecte under hym remembering both our services heretofore.' His wish was to serve the queen 'with honour and not as a meane subjecte, wherebie the cuntrey might speake evill and thinke that her grace hade withdrawen summe parte of her good wille from me'.[171] When Shrewsbury was nonetheless appointed over him, he wrote to his rival to ask that he should have the leading of the men raised in Lancashire and Cheshire and the right to name their captains.[172] Personal honour and private lordship were as much bound up with the lord lieutenancy as they had been with the command of Henry's armies.

The power of the lieutenants worked through and alongside that of other land-owners. Though the appointment of deputy lieutenants was not systematized until the 1560s, the commissions of 1550–1 permitted it and the system's begetter John Dudley duly named three deputies in Warwickshire.[173] In June 1559 the marquess of Northampton's deputies for Northamptonshire, George Lord Zouche, Sir John Spencer, and Sir Robert Lane, met at Kettering to divide up the county between them, taking half a dozen hundreds each, and to plan what to do about musters, law enforcement, invasion, or rebellion.[174] Thus the lieutenancy shared in a broader reconfiguration of the landed elite's participation in war. The intensive taxation, mustering, and defensive measures of the mid-century drew them repeatedly into action as commissioners and that action shaped their relationships with their neighbours and their sense of responsibility for local and national government.

Already in the 1520s the accounts of magistrates like Sir Henry Willoughby show them touring their county sitting as muster commissioners, and the muster returns of the 1530s, 1540s, and 1560s show knights, esquires, and peers hard at work: Lords Mordaunt and Bray in Bedfordshire and Lord Stafford in Staffordshire in 1539, Viscount Bindon in Dorset in 1569.[175] In wartime they had to find drafts of men, Spencer, for example, 300 from Northamptonshire in August 1557: it was hard, because some landowners had been asked for individual contingents, others were away on the Saint-Quentin campaign, few men could handle a pike or an arquebus, even the archers were not 'sutche as wee would wysshe' and, in the midst of an epidemic, there were 'veray many weake sicke and dead'.[176] It was even busier on the coast. In spring 1557 Sir Henry Bedingfield and two neighbours were commissioned to fortify Norfolk against the French and erect warning beacons there.[177] In August that year the earls of Bath and Oxford and Lords Rich and Darcy were doing the same for Suffolk and Essex.[178] As activities multiplied, so did their fiscal implications, and commissioners began to levy rates to pay for soldiers' coats and conduct money, or for arms and armour for the militia.[179] Communities responded by making friends with the commissioners, Melton Mowbray giving the marquess of Northampton a gallon of wine at the musters, Louth sending its churchwardens armed with sack and sugar to 'speake with Mr Tyrwhit and Mr Captayne Coopledike for order of the towne harnes', Bridport wining and dining the earl of Bedford and other muster commissioners.[180]

Those implementing policy at county level were under constant pressure from above, to carry out requests well and monitor local responses. Spencer, raising men for the relief of Calais, was told to report 'who youe shall fynde towardlye and who do shewe theym selfes otherwise in this servyce'.[181] The earl of Bath, charged by the duke of Norfolk to raise 100 Suffolk men for the fleet in 1558, was reminded to make sure 'that these menne nowe to be set forthe may be chosen and piked as my trust ys in yowr lordship'.[182] They were equally under pressure from besides and below for moderation or favour. Sir Henry Bedingfield, raising troops in Norfolk, got a letter from Sir Richard Southwell asking that one of his servants be excused from overseas service.[183] Lord North was diverted from pressing Cambridge University for men in 1569 by a timely letter from Sir William Cecil.[184] Such demands were doubtless irritating, but they were also the currency of influence. They called for particular finesse in the transitional period from the 1540s to the 1560s, as lieutenants and commissioners had to balance instructions to raise troops from whole counties against the expectation of lords that their men would be exempted from the 'comon mostrewes'.[185]

William Worcester, then, was right, the gentry and even the peerage were on average spending more of their time holding courts and less of their time leading troops in the field, but this was part of a wider integration into the service of the commonwealth. The metamorphosis was evident in the praise poetry directed to the Welsh gentry, who were increasingly described not just as well-bred warriors and generous patrons, but as prudent magistrates, esteemed statesmen, governors of the country.[186] Various aspects of the relationship between the Tudor monarchs and the landed elite, particularly the peerage, were awkward: tightening royal control of local justice and violent disorder, a narrowing of royal counsels and the rise of new men; but periodic opportunities for military command for those so inclined and a wider set of functions in what some were coming to call by the 1570s 'the defence of the state' helped ease these tensions in a mutually satisfactory way.[187]

Already by 1557–8 the peers were not turning out en masse to campaign across the Channel, but we should not draw from that the same pessimistic conclusion that William Worcester might have done. Of fifty-four adult English peers in those years, only six fought at Saint-Quentin and seven against the Scots, but two served in the navy, three at Calais, and one in Ireland, and one sent his eldest son to France. Six stood ready to defend the North against invasion, six to defend the South, and eight others mustered troops. Four joined the army raised to relieve Calais and one the commission to investigate its loss. Only eleven took no explicit part in war, and several of them were managing the crown's central financial machinery or had had military careers earlier in life.[188] The variety of their commitments shows how they could play their part in a new breadth of military activity and continue to serve king, queen, and commonwealth.

Peter Betham, translator of Jacopo di Porcia's military treatise for English consumption, understood this. He realized that some might think it strange that he did not dedicate his work to 'some actyve and valyaunt capitayne, whose prowesse is wytnessed by his martiall affayres, and bolde enterprises'. Some people thought, he admitted, that such captains ought 'to have the patronage of all those thynges that appertayne to knyghthode and chivalry'. Yet in a preface written in December 1543 he defended his choice of patron, Thomas, Lord Audley, the Lord Chancellor, on the grounds that 'there be amonge noble men, that be worthye to have the praysefull name of a capytayne, not for theyr brode shoulders, out sette brestes, and knyghtlye feates', but rather for their 'wysedome, conveyaunce, and watchefull foreseinge of all suche thynges, whych by any meanes maye anoie or overwhelme the state of the common wealth'. Audley, imitator of the 'dilygente carefulnesse and swete orations' by which Cicero led the Romans to victory over Catiline and of the wisdom that enabled Ulysses to overthrow the Trojans and Hannibal to shake Rome, was such a man. Thus, argued Betham, he was a worthy dedicatee, one who had gained 'great renoume' and 'honour' because it was by his 'advyse and counsayle' that the realm's enemies had been 'on everye parte subdued'.[189] Audley stood for a social elite who continued to lead the nation in war and consolidate their status in doing so, even if some of them did it not from horseback, but from the council table or the counting house.

Some of the men we have met in this chapter, like Nicholas Bagenal or Francis Cosby, made their fortunes in war. A few, like Grey de Wilton, lost them. But war is inherently destructive and its overall effects on the economy of Henry's England were surely negative. How negative, and how universally negative, we shall next have to ask.

5

Trade and Tillage

In 1513 Peter Collys wrote two letters to his master, John Empson, brother of the more famous and recently executed Sir Richard Empson, to explain why he was having trouble collecting his rents and selling his timber. He painted a grim picture: 'the world ys ded and herd to cum by mone as ever hit was yn any mannys days a lyve'. The problem was 'this besy world of warre that settith mennys hartys awey clene so that hit makyth the world as dede as ever hit was for selling of eny thing except hit be that thing that must be had of very pure nede'.[1] War made money short firstly because taxation was drawing money out of local society: as Collys explained, 'thies paymentes that be payed to the kyng all redy have made men so bare'. Collys, perhaps because he was not writing from a major manufacturing region, did not mention a second reason why war might slow the economy, the disruption it caused to England's exports. But he did mention a third effect of war, that people were spending on 'harnessyng of men', buying arms and armour. Might the economic effects of war have been not merely depressive, but also distorting and even in some ways stimulating?

The question has been asked of many different wars and has always proved hard to answer, spawning titanic but inconclusive debates. To Werner Sombart's argument, pronounced ominously from the Germany of 1913, that the development of large armies and navies deploying firearms and powerful warships had stimulated technical innovation, industrial enterprise, greater organization in the supply of food and clothing, and capital concentration, thus assisting in the birth of capitalism, John Nef answered that, while the arsenals and naval shipyards of the early modern age were indeed impressive, so were the peaceable ventures of the era in mining, fishing, cloth-making, trade, and urban food supply, and that the European economy that advanced fastest in the later sixteenth and earlier seventeenth century was that of England, a country whose people 'farmed, mined, manufactured, and traded peacefully' while France, Germany, and the southern Low Countries were devastated by the Wars of Religion and the Thirty Years War.[2]

Twenty years after Nef wrote, battle was joined between M. M. Postan and K. B. McFarlane over the effects on England of the Hundred Years War. For McFarlane the English maintained manageably small armies for intermittent campaigns, funded by taxes often borne by overseas customers for English wool, and used them to plunder France wholesale while the English countryside remained inviolate. For Postan, in contrast, the diversion of manpower, shipping, and production, the burden of taxation, and the interruption to commerce, especially at a time of labour shortage induced by plague, were all substantial, were not demonstrably compensated by the spoil of France, and generated no significant economic gains. In the course of the debate Postan even abandoned his earlier attraction to Sombart's idea that war might at least have moved capital out of the hands of hidebound landlords and peasants into those of more innovative investors.[3]

Subsequent commentators have criticized these controversialists from various angles, for considering the deployment of resources or the boundaries of a national economy in ways that would have made no sense to contemporaries, for instance; for collapsing the very different phases of the Hundred Years War into a single unit; for failing to compare expenditure on warfare with that on other major medieval enterprises such as religion; or for isolating war artificially from the wider economic climate, expanding on Nef's admission that 'war cannot properly be considered, as we have been doing, as an independent factor', or Postan's judgement that 'in the machinery of social change the war was not so much the mainspring as a make-weight'.[4] These critics have also reflected that in such matters it is impossible to satisfy those who are 'consumed by a passion for calculating things' since, as all four of the original participants noted at different points, they were beset by 'the intractability of the financial evidence', or 'the small numerical data that we possess', and thus faced 'a hopeless statistical task', for 'statistics are not available to settle the matter'.[5]

For Henry's wars too we do not have reliable statistics, or any statistics at all, for many of the trends we would need to measure to make a full audit of the economic effects of war, of the sort that can be more credibly attempted for periods from the late seventeenth century on.[6] Yet we may take encouragement from another trend in the debates that followed McFarlane and Postan, an inclination to make enlightening distinctions or comparisons between the wartime experience of different regions, social groups, or commercial sectors. In the Hundred Years War, for example, while England's eastern ports lost ships in royal service and found their herring and wine trades disrupted, south-western ports seem to have done well from shipbuilding, privateering, government investment, and a growth in political voice that enabled them to advance their own economic interests.[7]

Peter Collys's impressions are easiest to relate to these historical debates when we consider taxation. The direct tax policies of Henry VIII were remarkably successful (see Fig. 5.1). When the money supply was around a million pounds, only half of it in the silver used for everyday transactions, taking more than £100,000 in cash out of the economy in 1512–13, more than £400,000 in 1522–4 and again in 1541–3, then more than £700,000 in 1544–6, must have caused problems.[8] Already in 1475 the Pastons had had trouble selling timber because of the weight of war taxation, and George Bernard, examining the widespread refusal to pay the amicable grant in 1525, and Richard Hoyle, analysing the deeper economic crisis of the later 1540s, have each shown how taxation pulled money out of circulation, producing, as Hoyle has put it, 'a collapse of trade and a sharp deflation', especially as parliamentary subsidies taxed wealth held in goods and capital harder than income from land.[9] Meanwhile pressure on individuals amplified pressure on communities, as church goods were sold in the 1540s to pay 'the taske for ease of the poore people'.[10]

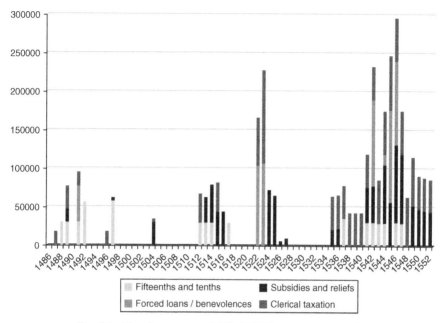

Fig. 5.1. Taxation revenue, 1485–1552 (sources: see note 8).

In contrast to the large impact of taxation, the direct damage done by war to most of Henry's lands was small compared to the devastation wrought by huge armies or constant raiding where the great European powers of his day clashed. Florence, Rome, Milan, Metz, and Magdeburg faced full-scale sieges by the armies of Charles V; Milan, Naples, Perpignan, and Luxembourg by those of Francis I; Belgrade, Buda, and Vienna by those of Süleyman the Magnificent. In this context, Sir Thomas Wyatt's brief occupation of Southwark looks tame.[11] Some places were more vulnerable than others. It was not just the Isle of Wight in 1545 that faced French raids: Weymouth, Wyke Regis, and Portland in 1491, Brighton in 1514 and Marazion around the same time, Kingsteignton rather later, Dover in 1544, Brighton, Newhaven, and Seaford in 1545.[12] Poor Edward Spencer of Hunstanton, Norfolk, probably in 1475, was 'take owte of his howse by Frenchemen upon the see coost' and ransomed for £100.[13] The Scilly Isles and the Channel Isles were more permanently exposed, Sark at one point under French occupation for four years.[14] But none of the mainland coasts suffered like the land borders with Scotland and Gaelic Ireland.

Two centuries of warfare had made the Scottish borders perilous. The monks of Holme Cultram, some twenty miles from Gretna Green, complained to the pope in 1508 that the Scots had destroyed their buildings and possessions and they had had to take refuge in Wolsty Castle.[15] In the quavering peace of the early 1540s individual Englishmen were killed by the Scots when out farming, one 'slaye at his oune plughe', another 'upon the daye light, labouring at his husbandrye'.[16] Yet even in the far North destruction was for the most part narrowly confined. Upper

Weardale, fifty miles from the border, was hit by occasional Scottish raids, but suffered more from lawless English neighbours.[17] St Bees Priory lay on the coast a similar distance inside England. In 1523 the prior panicked at news of a Franco-Scottish fleet, worried that 'this country shalbe utterly destroyed for ever' since 'this poure coste and country...is not acustomed with such weres'.[18] Careful examination of estate and tithe accounts for the parishes south of Berwick has shown that wartime raids from the 1480s to the 1520s wasted whole farms and depressed production, but the effects were localized and production recovered fast when peace was re-established.[19]

Even in the 1540s, while the Scots could take livestock, goods, and prisoners or burn houses up to ten miles inside England at Kyloe or Wooler, they struck mostly the border dales, in the upland areas unprotected by the chain of fortified houses making up the 'plenished ring of the border', or the villages nearest the Tweed like Ord, Heaton, Twizell, Tillmouth, and Wark.[20] And when raids were expected, English commanders had grain stores threshed for storage further inland.[21] Insecurity spread much further in Ireland and was less constrained by the rhythms of diplomatic relations between kings. Gaelic lords sometimes raided English areas for weeks at a time, in 1533 one party of O'Byrnes even broke into Dublin Castle and took away plunder and prisoners, and as late as 1566 the O'Byrnes' and O'Tooles' depredations stopped only four miles short of the city. But even in Ireland the Pale was becoming more secure as English governance revived under the leadership of the Fitzgerald earls of Kildare and successive English deputies.[22]

To humble the Scots in the 1540s Henry's men planned not just 'divastacion and spoyle of the countrey' but that 'there fyshinge may be lettede, and ther fysher bootes destroyde', and that 'the Scottis shuld have no maner of vente or uttring of theyr wullis and salmon...whiche is the oonly commoditie of Scotland'.[23] How far did England suffer from such wider economic warfare? War clearly interfered with international trade, as dips in customs revenue attest (see Fig. 5.2). Its two main effects, arrests of merchants and attacks on shipping, were illustrated by the sad experience of William Johnson, citizen and skinner of London, in 1522. He was trading at Bordeaux when war broke out, whereupon most of his goods 'amountyng to grete sommez of money were then attached and takyn by Frenchmen wythyn the sayd town of Burdeux and he robbyd and dyspoylyd of the most parte of all his goodes and utterly undon'. Somehow he took ship for London, but 'yn hys retournyng upon the see' he 'not only was by dyverce Frenchmen takyn prisoner but also all such goodes as he then had wer also robbyd spoylyd and taken from hym', so that he was even more 'utterly undon'.[24]

In wartime Anglo-French trade was frozen by reciprocal arrests of merchants and, while this affected English exports such as tin, it hit the wine trade particularly hard, depressing imports and driving up prices until peace returned (see Fig. 5.3).[25] In 1525 a letter-writer noted excitedly that with peace announced, English consumers 'schorttle schalle have goode cheype merchaundyes', specifying corn, linen cloth, and 'all maner wynes', red, white, claret, white malmsey, rumney, bastard, camplete, tyre, muscadel, alicant, and hollock.[26] Safe-conducts or import

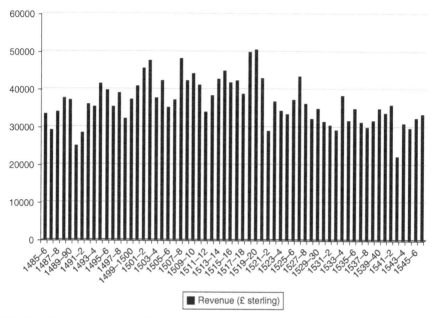

Fig. 5.2. Customs revenue, 1485–1547 (source: G. Schanz, *Englische Handelspolitik gegen Ende des Mittelalters*, 2 vols (Leipzig, 1881), ii. 37–59).

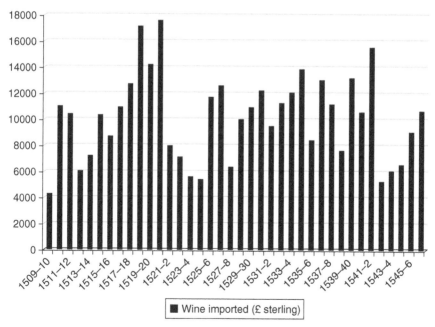

Fig. 5.3. Wine imports, 1509–47 (source: G. Schanz, *Englische Handelspolitik gegen Ende des Mittelalters*, 2 vols (Leipzig, 1881), ii. 148).

licences for trade of all sorts, sometimes using neutral or allied ships, were available at a price in open war or at times of tension, but they were all too often revoked or ignored.[27] Wartime stagnation made merchants cautious. Before the wars of 1542–7, the merchants of Bristol were registering on average fourteen apprentices a year, afterwards twenty a year, but in wartime the average dropped below ten and at worst it fell to four.[28]

Once at sea wartime trade was made hazardous by privateers, an anachronistic term, but the best we have for those who preyed on enemy shipping with some kind of government licence. French ships from Dieppe, Honfleur, Boulogne, and the Breton ports hunted the narrow seas, others the coasts of Brittany, the mouth of the Garonne, the Bay of Biscay, and even the coasts of Ireland.[29] The Scots, both in royal ships and in those owned by individual captains, operated not only in the North Sea, but also off Calais, Normandy, Brittany, and Gascony, around the Isle of Wight, and in western waters from Dumbarton and Ayr.[30] In 1532, one Londoner on his way to Bordeaux found himself pinned in at Fowey amid swirling news of Scots in the Channel, in the Scillies, off Land's End: they had taken fourteen English ships and driven nine or ten into Brest.[31] Shipping was not safe even when England was at peace with her neighbours, as Danes, Spaniards, and Bretons scoured the seas, joined at times by Dunkirkers, Hollanders, and Zeelanders set off by turmoil in the Low Countries.[32] But wartime was worse, and losses could be spectacular. It was said in London that three ships taken with 'riche merchandise' on their way back from Antwerp in 1558 were worth more than £20,000.[33] Even such threats might have positive side-effects for some, however: war in the 1540s was a fillip to Bristol's Iberian trade, which benefited from the fact that the Bristol Channel was safer from French attacks than the English Channel.[34]

Though less well recorded than international commerce, coastal trade was vital in distributing food, fuel, and other commodities around England, exchanging, for example, Norfolk grain for Newcastle coal.[35] Local accounts like those for Poole (see Fig. 5.4), which included the quayage levied on all incoming ships, or those for the tonnage levied at Plymouth (see Fig. 5.5), suggest that war hit coastal trade as much as international, as do lawsuits and letters about ships from Newcastle or the Norfolk ports taken off Yorkshire or Lincolnshire loaded with grain, malt, or coal.[36] The small size and small crews of the crayers and other ships in which coastal trade was carried made it vulnerable to daring raiders. In the winter of 1543–4 the Scots took ships along the Norfolk coast and in 1549 the French scooped up coastal traders off Sussex.[37] In autumn 1544 the depredations of Scottish ships off Scarborough, Whitby, and Hartlepool, 'hovering upp and downe uppon thiese costes', were such that 'the kynges majestes subjectes can not well use any trade on the sees in thes partes without daungier'; as powder for shore artillery ran low there were even worries that the Scots would 'burne the shipps and the botes in the harbores and peres hereaboute'.[38] Simultaneously Newcastle found its coastal trade dried up as many of its ships were stuck in other harbours, 'driven in by men of warr'.[39]

Fishing boats were particularly vulnerable, spending long hours at sea with small crews, whether close inshore going after flat-fish or pilchards, further out at sea for

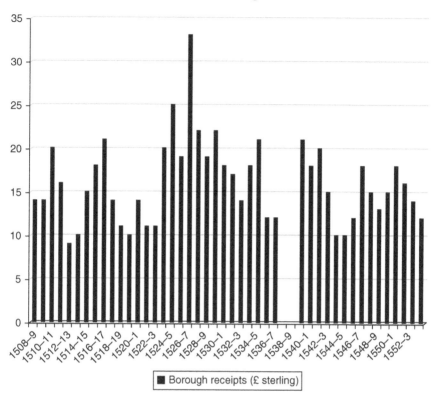

Fig. 5.4. Poole borough receipts including quayage, 1509–54 (source: Dorset HC, DC/PL/CLA 23).

herring, hake, or sprats, or on the way back from the distant Norway, Iceland, or Newfoundland fisheries for cod or ling.[40] The North Sea and Channel coasts were equally unsafe. In the 1540s, the Scots took Southwold fishers on their way back from Iceland, and the French raided off Devon and Dorset, Yorkshire and Durham.[41] The effects were inhibiting. In 1524 representatives of Norfolk and Suffolk told Wolsey and the king they dare not fish because French men of war cruised off their shores.[42] The king told Dover in 1544 that all their boats should be sent out to fish, but they replied that 'sithen the tyme of warre they in no wise ar able to perfourme the same'.[43] At Yarmouth in 1564 the risks were pooled in a scheme whereby all those fishing from the town would collectively ransom any captured boat.[44] We should reserve our special sympathy for John Byrcham, Robert Saumon, Bartholomew Storme, and Robert Wyndell of Whitby, who went out fishing in the early 1520s in a 25-ton ship owned by William, prior of Bridlington and Elizabeth Dodys, widow. On their way back to port they were met by 'a ship of war of Fraunce', which took them captive, but agreed to ransom ship, crew, and catch for £22 6s 8d. Byrcham was sent in to Whitby and on to Bridlington, where the owners agreed to cover the cost. The French were paid off and the ship

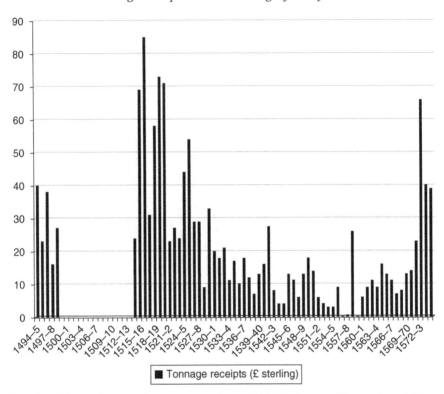

Fig. 5.5. Plymouth borough tonnage receipts, 1514–75 (source: Plymouth and West Devon RO, 1/129, fos. 86v–159v).

and crew were released, only to be captured immediately by Scots. John Byrcham sued the owners for the ransom money, which they had refused to pay because they had not got their ship back; at least he had a good lawyer, a certain Thomas Cromwell.[45]

Many English seamen ended up as prisoners in France or Scotland. The customary ransom for a mariner was £1 and a master £2, but merchants were seen as richer pickings, even though many of those captured were young apprentices or factors. Their ransoms ran up to £30, though the expenses of a long imprisonment might add £50 or more, and groups of merchants could yield a rich haul: £372 from one party captured by Scots between Calais and London in the 1490s.[46] Charitable contributions from boroughs, livery companies, or parishes helped meet ransom demands, as did alms collected under royal licence.[47] In the 1540s the churchwardens of Leigh-on-Sea in Essex spent £17 10s redeeming local men from France and those at North Hales in Suffolk £13 freeing prisoners in Scotland.[48] Without such help, prisoners and their friends had to put together complex ransom packages which readily went wrong.[49] At the peace of 1564 local officials investigated what English prisoners remained in France, to avoid agonies like the five-year captivity endured by the Norwich apprentice merchant Godfrey Sharles in the 1470s, during which time he went deaf.[50]

The dangers war posed to trade and fishing were evident in the precaution taken against them: wafting, the provision of armed ships as convoy escorts or fisheries protection vessels. Wafting could be bought from private contractors, but was costly. In the early 1490s, when the Flemish rebels based at Sluis were blockading Antwerp, a group of London merchants hired a Genoese carrack, the *Santa Maria*, with 150 men, to protect them, apparently at a cost of £400. That got them as far as Veere in Zeeland, where they had to hire smaller boats with local soldiers to escort them through the channels to Antwerp.[51] More moderate, but still signifi- cant, was the going rate at Middelburg for escorts to London in the 1510s, 2*d* in the shilling or one-sixth the value of the freight to be protected.[52] Much better were communal solutions, preferably with an admixture of royal coordination and resources. As the navy grew, so the crown became more ambitious in the protection it would offer, but it never guaranteed to replace self-help. As Henry VII pointed out in 1491, while his 'grete armee reamaigneth on the see for the better defense of our subgietts haunting the same', 'Frenshe pirats and thieves lieing in awaite for there avauntagies and prayes' might still attack fishermen when 'our seid armee is ferr of from thaym'.[53]

Overseas traders turned readily to the king's protection, albeit at a price and sometimes with impatience that the escorts did not arrive at the time they wanted them.[54] Royal help in getting the wool fleets of the Merchants of the Staple from Hull to Calais and the cloth fleets of the Merchant Adventurers from London to Zeeland grew steadily from the 1480s to the 1550s.[55] Naval protection for the long-distance fishermen of the Iceland fleet, who paid towards the costs in propor- tion to the size of their ships, increased over the same period, and by the 1510s even the East Anglian herring fleet was expensively protected by the king's ships, though safety was not guaranteed: in 1524 seven Iceland boats and one wafter were overcome by the Scots.[56] Meanwhile Henry was understandably concerned to guard the ships that carried supplies to his armies and brought back expensive arms shipments from the continent.[57] His ships also cruised the Channel, and one lucky English factor, William Myldenhall, was taken by the French with his cargo of Spanish wine but 'rescued by an Englisshe ship being a capitayne of the kinges warres' two days later.[58]

Yet the navy could not do everything, as Henry's councillors pointed out in a rather petulant tone in November 1544. They told Newcastle merchants who complained of Scottish depredations that it would be 'over burdenous and allmost impossible thatt the kinges majeste shuld sett to the sees, shippes to defende all partes of the realme'; they should therefore set out ships 'for defence of their own goodes and trafique' as other ports had done.[59] Hull had indeed put out three ships, only to see them dispersed by storms and Scottish attacks, but York and Scarborough pleaded incapacity.[60] Norfolk and Suffolk, the northerners were told, had done better, wafting their fishermen 'during all this hering tyme'.[61] Great Yarmouth had well-established mechanisms for fisheries protection. In 1557, for example, the town assembly hired two ships with guns to protect the fishers and in 1563 it set up Thomas Bettes's ship the *Elizabeth George* to do the same.[62] Yarmouth's instinct for self-defence was particularly strong. On Sunday 30 November 1544 the townsmen rushed out of church to rescue two crayers laden with wheat for Boulogne taken by the French and took six French prisoners in the process; fourteen months later a ship and thirty boats, supported by the town's guns, took two Dieppe raiders in the Yarmouth roads and sank a third.[63] The Cinque Ports too could look after themselves: they fitted out two barks to protect their herring fleet in 1563, while Rye launched boats to recue its inshore fishermen in 1564.[64] By 1559 the Newcastle Merchant Adventurers had learned their lesson; they levied over £50 on their members to pay for the queen's ship *Falcon* to escort their vessels to Flanders and man the *Marye Flour* to join her.[65]

War clearly interfered with various sectors of the economy, but did it substitute alternative economic activities for those it inhibited? Cloth exports dipped in wartime, though not too badly, because the Low Countries, the major export market for cloth, was usually an ally, and because governments shaken by the disorders of the 1520s in clothing districts affected by interruptions to trade made efforts to keep exports flowing and workers employed.[66] In 1525 export troubles apparently exacerbated the slow-down caused by the taxation of mercantile capital, and from the late 1520s governments tried to prevent export interruptions causing unemployment and domestic unrest. By drawing money out of the economy, war presumably also depressed the domestic demand for cloth. Yet war also stimulated that domestic demand because so many coats were made for soldiers and sailors.[67] Christopher Dyer has estimated the total cloth production of England in the 1520s at 200,000–240,000 cloths, of which 80–90,000 were exported, and John Oldland put the total for the early 1540s at some 320,000, 130,000 of them for export.[68] The difference between wartime and peacetime exports was of the order of 8,000 cloths a year. Coats for 40,000 men in the army and navy in 1544, at eight coats per 24-yard broadcloth or six coats per 18-yard kersey, would have absorbed perhaps 6,000 of those missing cloths, and in the invasion summer of 1545 purchases may have been wider still, as people reportedly equipped themselves 'willinglie of their owne minde and of their own costes and charges' with white soldiers' coats.[69] It seems unlikely, though possible, that these coats merely replaced other clothes that taxpayers or soldiers would have bought anyway. Soldiers' coats were not expected to wear well: in 1542 coats that had had a couple of weeks' wear were regarded as unfit for future use, 'the most parte of the same' being 'all worne out with harneys'.[70] Occasionally towns kept coats in store along with their armour, but more commonly they were sold off cheaply after a campaign, or left with the soldiers who had worn them.[71]

Some of the cloth used in wartime would have been imported, certainly the fustian used for the arming doublets worn under plate armour, and probably the linen cloth and canvas used to line helmets or back mail, but most was made in England. Until the 1550s it was mostly white or undyed—hence the standard Scottish name for English soldiers, whitecoats—and its dressing, if any, was the minimal cottoning, while small amounts of red cloth were bought to apply red crosses for identification.[72] From the 1540s the cloth was sometimes dyed, starting with the elaborate blue, black, white, red, and yellow combinations needed to make coats in the livery colours of the duke of Norfolk, Lord Russell, and others for the spectacular Boulogne campaign of 1544, but thereafter the dye, if any, tended to be blue, which was cheap.[73] The cloth came from all over England. At various times Londoners used Hampshire kersey, blue Suffolk cloth, light blue northern kersey, and Peniston white, while Cambridge bought Bridgwater red and Liverpool got blue watchet from Yorkshire.[74] It was mostly of low quality, friezes, kerseys, or kelters rather than more expensive varieties, but it still made work for weavers, spinners, wool-growers, clothiers, and, latterly, dyers.[75] Provincial drapers too did well: the Willoughbys of Wollaton bought cloth for soldiers at Coventry, Lichfield, and Drayton Bassett, while Sir Richard Gresham's officers at Fountains Abbey bought it at Ripon.[76] Coats and breeches needed tailors too, and towns often employed three or four in parallel to make them up fast.[77] Shoes, boots, hats, tents, whatever was bought for soldiers made work for someone, and sometimes in bulk orders.[78] Coat money and the conduct money spent by soldiers on their way to fight represented taxation channelled rapidly back into the manu- facturing and hospitality sectors, and the sums involved were significant, some 7 per cent of direct taxes between 1539 and 1552.[79]

Other resources were redirected into war in ways that distorted but maintained economic activity. Grain, meat, fish, and cheese were bought up in large quantities in the East Riding of Yorkshire and the Midlands for Scottish campaigns, Hampshire for France, East Anglia for both. Official prices were fair, but payment could be slow and local purchasing was often done by large-scale grain merchants or butchers who made a tidy profit. In this respect warfare against France had a subtly different effect on the home economy from that generated by warfare against Scotland, but then again, even when wars against the two old enemies did not run in parallel they alternated in fairly quick succession, as in the 1470s and 1480s or early 1560s.[80] By the 1560s feeding the navy was a well-organized but challenging operation in which purveyors bought staple supplies from different counties on a quota system.[81] Occasionally the provisioning operations of whole towns were requisitioned, Sandwich and Dover to feed men and horses crossing the Channel, Stamford to host 10,000 men at five days' notice as the king marched against the Yorkshire rebels in 1489, the bakers of York, Durham, Newcastle, or London to bake bread or biscuit for armies or navies.[82] Some claimed that the purchase of supplies caused inflation, tripling the price of beef because so many oxen—428 of them—were salted for the Guyenne campaign of 1512, or creating 'scarsytie of victualls' in London in 1563 in supplying Le Havre.[83] It is not clear that military demand did significantly increase prices, but it must have helped to keep markets moving, and Liverpool was cheered by the large amounts the queen's victualler spent on supplies to fight Shane O'Neill in 1566.[84] Elaborate supply services and brutal regulations for punishing prostitution apparently left little room for the female camp followers who often sold supplies and processed plunder in other European armies of the day; yet a scattering of women with baskets and jars appeared in depictions of Henry's army in 1544, women in ports certainly played a role in receiving the goods taken by pirates and privateers, and Calais and Boulogne in the 1540s were, if we believe Elis Gruffudd, overrun with prostitutes, to the delight of their godless garrisons.[85]

Those with horses to sell also did well in wartime and some of the prices paid by churchwardens or borough treasurers look alarmingly high.[86] The London livery companies had a torrid time in 1536–7 and 1549. As the crown first issued and then countermanded orders to raise mounted men, they bought horses on a seller's market and then sold them for much less than they had paid for them, or gave them away in payment for the food they had eaten in the meantime.[87] On the northern border in the 1540s affordable horses were in short supply, and at York in 1557 the horses ridden by its troops had to be 'priced by iiij honest men indifferently'.[88] Commissioners were charged to buy up carts and wagons and draught horses and oxen, but could rarely find enough, especially in the North, and even in the Midlands in 1569 arrangements were chaotic. Thirteen out of ninety-two carts pressed in Leicestershire to supply the army were abandoned by their carters, two were taken and sold by the mayor of Doncaster to pay for the hay consumed by the cart horses, and when it was decided to auction the rest locally and compensate their owners in cash, three men travelled up from Melton Mowbray to make sure they were not defrauded.[89] Such commandeering must have disrupted inland trade, just as the confiscation of his horse by soldiers marching against the Pilgrimage of Grace in October 1536 stopped John Jane delivering his master's kerseys from Torbryan to Exeter, but it did not happen often enough to have a major impact, except perhaps in the North during wars with the Scots.[90]

Henry's wars caused another major diversion of activity in the building industry. As parish church building stalled, work on monastic sites was reduced to demolition or conversion, and the Elizabethan country house boom and the yeomanry's great rebuilding of rural England had not yet got underway, Henry's fortifications energized construction. Between 1539 and 1570, when country houses from Little Saxham Hall to Gorhambury House cost a few thousand pounds each, the government spent nearly £700,000 building fortifications, more than half on England's coasts and borders and the rest in France and Scotland.[91] Where country houses employed fifty or sixty men at a time, half a dozen of these projects peaked at 1,000 men or more and smaller ventures made it past 500.[92] Royal powers of impressment and steady wages pulled in workers from Somerset and Gloucestershire to Sandgate in Kent, from Kent, Suffolk, and Worcestershire to Berwick.[93] Brickmakers and tilers went from Shrewsbury to Ireland, to build Fort Protector and Fort Governor—tactfully renamed after 1553 Maryborough and Philipstown— while Irish masons worked at Berwick, spending their money on clothes at Liverpool on the way home.[94] Building supplies—stone, timber, ironwork—were sourced on an appropriately gargantuan scale, and sometimes at significant distances: timber for the forts on the Scilly Isles was felled in Monmouthshire.[95] Henry's works were exceptional, but others built too. At Norham Castle, Bishops Fox and Ruthal made significant changes to cope with artillery, including the construction of a casemate that has been characterized as an 'embryo bastion'. In 1510–11 up to sixty-one labourers worked on the site, some all year, and there were twenty masons, some from as far away as Yorkshire, four quarrymen, two smiths, and several lime burners. Bulky materials were shipped from Gateshead or Newcastle to Berwick and local men carried supplies in on packhorses, including coal from the pits at Tweedmouth, Scremerston, and Ford, eight miles away. Substantial works continued in subsequent years, especially in the wake of the Flodden campaign.[96]

Ships were also diverted for warfare, pressed by royal commissioners to expand the navy's fighting forces or to carry supplies to the king's armies.[97] Even foreign vessels in English ports were often taken up, their owners compensated at a higher rate than Englishmen.[98] Henry VII had to send messengers round the coast to see what ships they could find, but by the start of Elizabeth's reign the government was systematically estimating availability.[99] Sailors were more of a problem, especially as the navy expanded. When there were perhaps 20–30,000 experienced mariners in England, taking up several thousand to man the navy was no easy task. By the 1560s a well-developed system rested on the issue of commissions to ships' masters and others, which they would present to local authorities in port towns asking them to call seamen before them for selection.[100] The offer of dependable pay and conduct money seems usually to have been enough to man the royal ships, but in wartime things got tight.[101] Newcastle and Whitby claimed in 1544 that most of their mariners were in royal service and sailors sent home sick from the king's ships at Portsmouth in 1513 came from all around the southern coasts, from Barnstaple, Plymouth, and Dartmouth to London, Great Yarmouth, and Lynn.[102] Early in Elizabeth's reign the net was cast wider still, as ships at Gillingham and Chatham were crewed by men from a dozen counties, from Norfolk and Suffolk to Monmouthshire and Carmarthenshire.[103]

The coincidence of warfare and fishing in late summer was a particular problem. In August 1545 women were going out fishing from the south-western ports because most of the fishermen had been taken up for the navy, in September 1556 it was suggested that pressed fishermen be allowed a few days' leave to fish, and in July 1559 the Cinque Ports could find no herring fishers to sit on a jury because so many were 'taken up to the queene's warres'.[104] The watermen of London claimed immunity from impressment to serve in the queen's rowbarges, but this was overridden by statute in 1555 and thereafter they were drafted together with river boatmen from Windsor, Marlow, and Henley-on-Thames.[105] In busy years foreign sailors were taken up like foreign ships, for dental evidence suggests that up to a quarter of the crew of the *Mary Rose* may have been southern Europeans.[106]

The shortage of crews was exacerbated by the attraction of privateering. Letters of marque allowing individual merchants to take compensation for their losses from compatriots of those who had robbed them were issued throughout the period and led to attacks at sea as well as confiscations of goods in England.[107] But wartime brought a more general invitation. From 1544 proclamations encouraged owners and captains to set out ships 'for the annoyance of his majesty's enemies', permitting them to keep any 'ships, vessels, munitions, merchandises, wares, victuals and goods' they could take.[108] The king's ships sometimes took prizes in wartime worth hundreds of pounds, but with privateering larger profits beckoned.[109]

In twelve months one Kingswear captain backed by an Exeter merchant made nine voyages and took £11,000 worth of grain, wine, and fish for an initial outlay of some £450; another captain took 70,000 fish from just one French ship on its way back from Newfoundland.[110] The south-western coast—Dartmouth, Fowey, Plymouth—always generated enthusiastic privateers, but other ports were not left behind: Hull, Grimsby, King's Lynn, and Great Yarmouth; Liverpool and Bristol; Lyme Regis, Southampton, and Rye.[111] Rye, which preyed on fishermen off the Norman coast as well as French traders, made enough from the goods its ships captured and a head tax levied on hundreds of prisoners to offset much of the cost of its fortifications.[112] At London in 1544 the disused Grey Friars, Austin Friars, and Black Friars were filled with wine and fish taken off French ships and by the war of 1562–4 there were reckoned to be 400 English privateering ships in action.[113]

Privateering was attractive to the crown, since it harmed the enemy at minimal cost, but it was also problematic. When the king needed ships and sailors he might find they were gone. Lord Russell complained in 1545 that many western ships had set off 'to their owne adventures', having 'hollie given themselves to pillage and robberie', which was perhaps a bit rich coming from the owner of the *Mawdelyn Russell*, which had taken a neutral Spanish ship earlier that year and sold its cargo at Plymouth, just as the Lord Admiral had his own ship the *Fowecon Lisle* operating out of Falmouth.[114] In 1558 the problem recurred and Mary's government tried to recall all privateers to man the navy.[115] Moreover, to allow English ships to waylay neutral vessels and remove enemy goods, as Henry explicitly did, was to invite the undiscriminating to attack any ship and work out the details later.[116] German and Flemish ships were vulnerable, but the biggest problems came with the Spaniards. Robert Reneger of Southampton's capture of the *San Salvador*, loaded with American gold, off Cape St Vincent in March 1545, prompted the arrest of English merchants in Spain and, in reaction, a free-for-all assault on Spanish shipping which brought in exotic booty but took three years of diplomacy to unravel. Similar events unfolded in 1563–4, showing how thin the line was between privateering and outright piracy; indeed, the 1540s and 1560s seem to have formed key stages in the rise of a set of effectively professional English pirate captains and crews.[117]

Henry VII had taken stern action for the reformation of those 'lieing upon the see as comyn pyrates robbyng and dispoilling as well our soubgiettes as oure frendes', but the problem was intractable and the depredations of English pirates cropped up in law courts domestic and foreign throughout our period.[118] If English ports became too hot, there were always those in France, where exiles in Mary's reign based themselves, or in Ireland, which was, according to the earl of Surrey in 1521, 'the very land of refuge that Englysh pyrattes resort moost unto'.[119] Ports also succoured 'skymers of the see of dyvers nacyons', or got drawn into contests between foreign vessels in the expectation of reward.[120] Religious politics soon coloured such collaboration. In the 1560s and 1570s English pirates cheerfully cooperated with French and Dutch Protestant privateers, operating first from Le Havre, and then out of Irish ports and quiet harbours such as Helford and Milford Haven under the patronage of vice-admirals such as Sir John Killigrew and Sir John Perrot.[121] Elizabeth issued numerous proclamations against piracy and inappropriate privateering; her navy swept the seas for pirates; she even named specific pirates for arrest, among them Martin Frobisher, whom she then sent out to catch other raiders.[122] Some thought she ought to do more: at Worcester in 1575 the queen was told that she, having 'so mighty a navye as never any of your noble progenytours earst had the like', might 'very easly daunte and represse thes robbers that your subjectes may with safetye sayle and use their trafyque'.[123] Some looked after themselves, Southampton taking the sixty-ton *Edward of Hampton* in 1565 and executing its crew, Great Yarmouth sinking an English pirate ship operating under letters of marque from the Huguenot Admiral Coligny in 1569.[124] But the pirates survived, and when the time came to annoy the king of Spain they were useful.[125]

Privateering had its equivalent on land. On the border with Scotland the wars of the 1540s developed a large-scale plunder economy, its prime commodities livestock, prisoners, and household goods. The results were reported to the king— who had ordered that Scottish raids be requited 'thre hurtes for one'—with a statistical fetishism reminiscent of the 1960s Pentagon.[126] In eight raids on the West March between 1 and 8 November 1542, for example, usually by smallish parties operating at night, 278 cattle, sixty sheep, thirty-nine horses, and nineteen prisoners were taken, while on the East March there were 159 raids in the two years from June 1544.[127] On return the plunder was carefully divided up by each party's leaders, and it was valuable: Lord Wharton reckoned the 1,300 high-quality sheep taken on one raid into Ettrick Forest was worth more than £100.[128] In total 1,296 horses, 10,386 cattle, and 12,492 sheep were taken in five months in 1544 across all three marches. The numbers of sheep were comparable to those of the great East Anglian sheepmasters of the day, who rarely ran more than 15,000 each.[129]

Yet the prisoners may have been worth more than anything else. By 'all the lawe of armes that ever have bene', as the duke of Suffolk put it rather exasperatedly in settling a dispute, each prisoner belonged to his individual captor, 'who ventured his lif in taking of him'.[130] The captor might exact whatever ransom he could, but generally took one year's revenue for the landed, £80 for a lesser laird, £600 for a peer.[131] Lists show how well individuals might do. In June 1544, on the way back from burning Jedburgh, English troops met Scots returning from a raid over the Tweed and took 229 of them. In the English party were the militarized border clans of Tynedale and Redesdale, their names familiar to followers of north-eastern football. The Charltons, four of them, scored fifteen prisoners, five Milburns bagged twenty-one, and Henry Robson five. These were all ordinary Scots, but the gentlemen of the garrisons took their social equals: the Cockburn laird of Langton, the laird of Ayton's brother, Lord Home's nephew and his secretary.[132] We cannot price the 1,654 Scots taken on the East Marches in 1544–6, but they must have been valuable, though sometimes that value lay in exchange for an Englishman taken at Hadden Rig or elsewhere.[133] Even at Pinkie the borderers made very sure to take plenty of prisoners, in some cases before the battle was won to the satisfaction of their southerner comrades in arms.[134] So regular was the trade in prisoners that when the Scottish government banned its subjects from visiting

Berwick it had to make exception 'to borrowe presoners, or to paye thair ransomes in money'.[135]

In other theatres pickings were slimmer. The economies of the Gaelic lordships in Ireland were poorer than that of Scotland, though raids that struck lucky might take hundreds of cattle and horses.[136] France was richer, but much of the warfare there was static. Around the English garrisons at Calais, Tournai, and Boulogne and the siege camps of 1544, some raids culled large hauls of livestock or the wares on sale at a country fair, but generally profit came from handfuls of prisoners.[137] When the English did break across the Somme in 1523 they found that their Burgundian colleagues were more expert plunderers than they.[138] There were celebrity prisoners, the chevalier Bayard and the duc de Longueville in 1513, the baron de Saint-Blancard, captured aboard his galley, in 1546, but not enough to start an industry.[139]

Even at home the urge to liberate property in wartime was strong. Some soldiers on the way to France or Scotland were tempted to 'take their neyghboures cattyle and vittayle' without payment, and English troops in Ireland too readily plundered their hosts in the Pale, sometimes on the excuse that they were really rebels.[140] In England some rebels plundered, but so did those serving the king, undeterred by royal prohibitions or encouraged by captains who thought plunder 'a terror to the refractory' and 'a great incuragement to those who should fight against them'.[141] In the Western Rising in 1549 a proclamation allowed any loyal subject to lay hands on the lands and goods of any active rebel, but things got out of hand. Several Exeter churches had their plate or books plundered by the king's army, or by rebels from whom loyalists then took them, while the attempt by the king's commander Lord Russell to systematize confiscation and reward as the revolt subsided bred squabbling and injustice. Thomas Knill in Devon and John Bealburye in Cornwall found their goods and ransoms disputed by multiple grant-ees, Alice Harrys had to buy back her dead husband's goods and leases for £66 13s 4d, and John Furse of Crediton faced a demand for £140 to free his 'body and goods' despite the fact he had been ill in bed throughout the revolt.[142]

If much economic activity was hindered or distorted by war, some was acceler-ated, above all the trade in armaments. Large imports stocked the crown's stores and enabled merchants to supply individuals or institutions. The highest quality arms and armour were to be bought abroad and individuals who could shop in Flanders, or, later, ship large orders direct from Hamburg, did so.[143] But most English consumers were dependent on imports to London or other ports such as Hull or Newcastle.[144] Bowstaves came in by tens of thousands, supplied mainly by merchants from Cologne and the Baltic who had access to the mountainous and northerly regions where yew trees grew stronger than they did in England.[145] In the 1480s Hanse merchants and other foreigners were bringing into London bar-rels full of armour, large amounts of gunpowder, and thousands of gunstones.[146] For a while the Italians who dealt with the Tudors in international trade and bank-ing, the Cavalcanti, Frescobaldi, Portinari, della Fava, and others, were important for guns, armour, powder, saltpetre, and naval stores, and in the 1540s Henry had to negotiate directly with the Venetian Republic for Brescian handguns.[147] Then

Hanse merchants came to the fore again, Danzigers for saltpetre, Cologne men for armour and guns: Gerhard Grevrath imported 1,400 handguns in 1549–50 and the international arms magnate Philipp Palm 1,682 armours in 1561–2.[148]

Londoners played their part too, importing bowstaves, gunpowder, or Milanese armours from the 1480s, paving the way for the Greshams, who dealt in armaments and naval supplies from the 1510s.[149] The scale of their operations was impressive—John Gresham could lend his colleagues in the mercers' company eighty-six corslets to wear at musters in 1558—and early in Elizabeth's reign Thomas Gresham became the crown's principal agent in buying continental arms, armour, and gunpowder.[150] The Greshams were not the only domestic importers in their generation. London haberdashers, grocers, and armourers brought in pikes, sword blades, halberd heads, gunpowder, saltpetre, and match, mostly from Antwerp.[151] Others did well out of the navy. In the 1560s Christopher Draper and Thomas Allen each did thousands of pounds' worth of business with the Admiralty, mostly in imported Baltic ropes and tar.[152]

War boosted the retail trade in arms and armour, allegedly doubling prices as 'covetous persons' took advantage of shortages and prompting several attempts at royal price control.[153] Equally peace brought prices down. William Paston pointed out in 1493 that 'now the werres be done, ye shall have harneyse every daye better chepe than other'.[154] When the rebels were 'dispersed in the North' in 1569, similarly, Sir Nicholas Bacon told his servant not to buy any dags yet, for 'I shalbe provided at easyer pryses and of good also'.[155] London was the great centre of the retail trade, though not even Londoners necessarily knew their way around it: in 1558 the founders' company had to pay a penny to 'a man that brought us wher the jackes wer sold'.[156] London armourers carried large stocks of armour, sufficient to sell twenty almain rivets at a time or hire out armour at 5 or 10 per cent of the purchase price for use in marching watches or musters.[157] No wonder it was the armourers who made 'earnest sute' for the revival of the marching watch in the 1560s.[158] They also stocked guns, while the London cutlers did a good trade in swords, pikes, and bills, and other traders, such as drapers and hatmakers, sold armour on a smaller scale.[159]

Most customers bought their arms and armour at London, but they were also available in provincial towns like Durham, Lincoln, Norwich, Ludlow, and Shrewsbury, at fairs and, second-hand, even in villages.[160] Newcastle was a big retail centre for the northern borders. In 1514–15 John Brandling, one of the city's richest merchants, supplied Norham Castle with bows, arrows, halberds, guns, and powder.[161] Ports bought guns and powder in from abroad and Plymouth bought guns direct from Spanish manufacturers, paying them in cloth or hake and sending three cheeses as an extra reward.[162] But in the long run the crown's stores became the most important source of supply. In 1545 it was suggested that the men of the northern garrisons should be 'furnisshed with weapons of the kinges store at Newcastell and Barwycke at reasonable prices' and in the 1560s there were sales from the stocks bought up by Gresham.[163]

War brought work for military craftsmen; indeed an interlude of 1560 claimed that 'the armurer, the fletcher, and the bowyer' were undone by peace.[164] They served on campaign—the army in France in 1523 had fourteen bowyers, five fletchers, five stringers, and five gunpowder makers—and worked at home in manufacture or maintenance, but changing technology might threaten liveli-hoods.[165] Those who complained most about the decay of their trade were bowyers and fletchers.[166] They worked in big cities, medium-sized towns like Birmingham, Marlborough, and Leeds, and even some villages, but everywhere they fell into difficulties.[167] At London the crown spread orders for thousands of bows around half a dozen bowyers in the 1510s and 1520s, but by the 1550s the emphasis was on pikes and guns and the livery companies were ordering just a dozen or two bows at a time.[168] Twenty London bowyers made wills between 1500 and 1569, but none after that date.[169] At York the bowyers and fletchers were fading by the mid-century (see Fig. 5.6), and it was the same at Bristol and King's Lynn.[170] At Norwich, three bowyers and six fletchers became freemen under Henry VIII, one of each under Edward VI, and none thereafter. The census of the poor in 1570 included an octogenarian fletcher 'that hath lytle work' and a fifty-year-old unemployed bowyer.[171]

Henry was not content to import luxury armour, but brought in the armourers themselves, setting up first Milanese, then Flemish and German experts in a royal workshop at Greenwich, making strong, fashionable armour for himself and his courtiers.[172] They followed a previous generation of foreign armourers working in London, Vincent Tytler of Hainaut with his dozen foreign workmen making armours for 'diverse lords of this noble royaume', Ralph of Ponthieu, royal brig-andine maker, and others.[173] There were English armourers too, and they kept

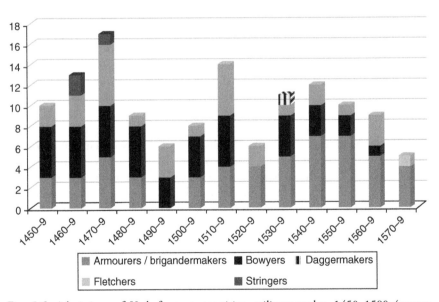

Fig. 5.6. Admissions of York freemen practising military trades, 1450–1580 (source: *Register of the Freemen of the City of York*, ed. F. Collins, 2 vols, SS 96, 102 (Durham, 1897–1900)).

going better than the bowyers and fletchers, not only at London, where their livery company managed by the 1570s to absorb the bladesmiths and secure powers to inspect all arms on sale in the city, but also at York (see Fig. 5.6) and other towns, from Bodmin and Truro through Ludlow, Oxford, Cambridge, and Walsingham to Durham.[174] Yet their work seems to have consisted increasingly in selling and servicing foreign products, or making up uncomplicated brigandines or coats of plates.[175] William Gurre made armour for a hundred footmen for the king in 1512, but after the war secured a contract worth nearly twice as much for cleaning and repairing thousands of items.[176] At least the insistence that towns and parishes, noblemen and gentlemen maintain stocks of armour made work for armourers, furbishers, or cutlers to keep them in trim, paid at a daily rate, or sometimes retained by the year, and sometimes in a long-term relationship: St Martin in the Fields used William Waters every year from 1555 to 1567, St James's Louth Richard Rygges from 1560 to 1572.[177] Guns, both handguns and larger pieces, seem primarily to have been looked after by smiths or locksmiths, but armourers and bowyers also took a hand and specialists steadily emerged, first at the Tower, then in London, where migrant gunsmiths from the sophisticated but troubled Low Countries and France set up in ever larger numbers from the 1540s to the 1570s.[178] Handgun-making might indeed be cited as an industry in which immigrant expertise brought domestic manufactures up to a sufficient standard to compete with imports, but when compared with the new draperies in cloth-making or even the development of domestic metalwares the economic weight of such enterprises looks small.[179]

Henry's wars produced some strange dead-ends in weapons development, like his breech-loading gun-shields (see Fig. 5.7). Despite their alarming recoil and hot gas emissions, and their odd resemblance to a lethal dustbin lid, they were sent into action, for example on the *Mary Rose*.[180] But his campaigns also stimulated the development of famous regional arms industries. In 1514 the king's fletcher took delivery of over 180,000 arrow heads from one Sheffield hardwareman, for example, and Birmingham bills could be bought in the 1520s.[181] Still more celebrated at the time was the casting of iron cannon in the Weald. The leading gunfounders of the 1520s and 1530s were Italians and Frenchmen such as Francesco Arcana and Pierre Baude, joined from the 1530s by Robert, John, and Thomas Owen.[182] They worked in bronze at London, but in 1543, the blast furnaces of Sussex, which had been making shot since the 1490s, began to produce cast iron guns, apparently on the initiative of William Levett, rector of Buxted, and Francesco Arcana's son Arcangelo. By 1553 the ordnance office had bought more than 250 Sussex cannon and the industry developed strongly through Elizabeth's reign, stimulating a wider boom in Wealden iron.[183]

Gunpowder-making was another field for foreign expertise. Henry VIII kept a succession of powder makers busy at the Tower from Hans Wolf to Anthony of Naples, though English master gunners worked alongside them.[184] The search for domestic saltpetre supplies was a haphazard and stressful affair, as Henry licensed saltpetre men to dig up his subjects' lands and buildings. By the 1540s they were causing trouble in towns from Shrewsbury and Ludlow to London and Poole.[185]

Fig. 5.7. Gun-shield, *c.*1545 (The Walters Art Museum, Baltimore MD).

Elizabeth's government gave blessing to a sequence of entrepreneurs who undertook to supply saltpetre either manufactured by controlled chemical processes—
which never worked very well—or at least dug up and boiled over wood fires with
'less annoyance' than usual. The effects were unimpressive, yielding by the 1570s
only about a tenth of the government's needs, and prompting elaborate evasion. In
1571 Sir Henry Jerningham wrote to his friend Thomas Kytson for help, 'for that
I understand you can by art make a salt peter man so blynd that although he pas-
seth by your great woodes yet he shal not be able to see or vew them to tak of them
for the making of salt peter'.[186]

   Shipbuilding must also have been stimulated by war, for new ships for the navy
or privateering and repairs to battle damage. Shipyards were widely distributed
around the English coast, and sail-makers, ropers, blacksmiths, plumbers, and others
joined shipwrights in plying their trades there.[187] The Tudors made only patchy
use of the earlier system by which private shipowners constructing vessels large
enough for naval use were paid a cash bounty or remitted customs dues, relying
instead on the profitability of long-distance trade to incentivize the construction of
large ships.[188] Meanwhile permanent royal dockyard facilities at Portsmouth,
Deptford, Chatham, and elsewhere gradually increased in scale of expenditure and
employment. In 1559 there were 524 craftsmen and labourers at work on twenty-two

ships and in 1570, in peacetime, there were more than 400.[189] Specialist artisans did well out of the navy. In 1562–3 alone Richard Stevens, compass-maker of Tower Hill, supplied 156 standard compasses and four great compasses at a cost of £22.[190] But he was no doubt also selling to trading ships and it is hard to know how far to push an analysis of industries related to war, particularly when so much of military expenditure was on food for men and horses and when unlikely objects had military uses. The cutting of marshland reeds was of vital importance to the navy, as thousands of sheaves of them were burnt to soften the pitch on the hulls of ships for breaming, scraping off detritus.[191] Goose-farming was in its way part of the military-industrial complex, as the flight feathers of geese were also the best flight feathers for arrows: in 1555 Cuthbert Fletcher was sent on a nine-day trip over the Pennines from Norham Castle to Appleby and Brough to buy 8,000 of them to fletch the arrows of the castle garrison, a task which then took him and his servant eighty-four days.[192]

Wars also tend to generate an illicit economy and Henry's were no exception. Supplies were stolen from quays as they were being loaded, soldiers sold off their horses, armour, and weapons, and there were opportunities for profit for those buying, distributing, and selling off supplies of food and drink for armies and navies.[193] More systematic fraud was practised by those who pretended to have royal commissions to purvey horses—sometimes just so people would pay them to go away—or those who took money at musters to allow some men to stay at home. The last was a regular problem from the 1540s and so serious by Mary's reign that point five of the nine-point instructions issued to those raising troops in 1558 was that no money should be taken to spare anyone.[194] John Vaughan in 1562 seems to have combined two kinds of racket, taking money from parishes on the pretext of providing armour for their men and then taking money from soldiers to exempt them from service.[195] Captains in garrisons developed corrupt routines for over-charging the crown, the 'polling and pilling' and 'abomynable robberie' against which the duke of Norfolk railed in 1560, that spread to the 'country captains' of newly levied troops, if they had not already worked out such tricks for themselves.[196] For those handling the king's money in wartime there was a constant temptation to help themselves, but contemporaries were intolerant of those who went too far and it was said snidely of one English official in Ireland that the size of his luggage betrayed the scale of his corruption: 'he came hythir with a smale male, but he comythe whom with his trussyng coffers'.[197]

Governments central and local tried to punish such abuses and deal with wider problems caused by war. Proclamations to hold food prices down were issued in almost every year of conflict.[198] Musters were countermanded in 1560 so as not to hinder the harvest.[199] Between 1546 and 1560 Guildford and Hereford questioned vagabonds who had served in the Boulogne garrison, York was told to implement the vagabondage statutes against ex-soldiers prone to 'loter', and the Kent towns were warned to make sure that no discharged soldiers 'be suffred to lyve oute of serves or withoute his occupacion or idely or suspeciously' or to 'cary aboute with theym handgonnes or dagges', so that the country might be spared 'notable fellonys and burglaries'.[200] Abingdon common council worried in 1561 that if townsmen went off to serve in other towns' contingents, their wives and children would be left a charge on Abingdon's poor rates, just as one Southwark parish found itself paying out to the wives of those serving at Le Havre.[201] Policy on enclosure had to address the fear that depopulation was causing 'a lack of people to defend us against our enemies', as John Hales put it, and the reality that some enclosure disputes involved the obstruction of archery practice in open fields and others the responsibility of different users of the land for providing soldiers to serve the king.[202] Policy on the fishing industry aimed to keep ships afloat and sailors employed: as Cecil put it, 'it is necessary for the restoring of the navye of England to have more fish eaten'.[203] Policy on horse-breeding and timber-growing aimed to keep armies and dockyards supplied.[204]

War, then, harmed the economy, but also in various ways and in various places diverted or even stimulated it. Some people did well: privateer captains, arms importers, horse dealers; and others did badly: wine merchants, fishermen, farmers by the Tweed. It is as hard to draw up a balance sheet for Henry's wars as Postan and McFarlane found it to agree on the costs and benefits for England of the Hundred Years War. In Henry's day there were fewer of the factors McFarlane thought brought profit: plunder from France, famous prisoners, king's ransoms; but the much larger size of armies and navies in proportion to the population and the lesser significance of domestic labour shortages as the population grew make calculations about the recycling of wealth within the economy more significant but equally intractable. It is at least clear that the debasement of the coinage to fund Henry's and Edward's wars had dire effects, causing inflation and problems with exchange rates and exports, and taxation may have been almost as bad, as repeated levies diminished capital and broke credit, hitting hardest large-scale traders and those in capital-intensive industries.[205] In general terms Nef's argument that the immunity of most of England to large-scale campaigning favoured its economic health must be true, though the careers of grain merchants who did well from provisioning contracts, or of traders who bankrolled privateering, suggest the legitimacy of Sombart's suggestions about capital formation, even if the shipbuilding or iron-founding industries were not really large enough to support his idea of a military-industrial revolution.[206] On the largest scale we should also remind ourselves that population growth, the incidence of disease, the climate, and the quality of the harvest had more profound effects on economic development and individual life chances than any of Henry's wars.

As for the more direct impact of war, it seems hard to see how Edward IV's claim that it would bring 'encrese of riches and prosperite' could ever have made sense, except in terms of a plunder of France even more complete than that achieved under Edward III, or a re-conquest of Gascony and Normandy which would make comfortable careers for English garrison captains and bring back both the fourteenth-century wine trade and peaceful Lancastrian commerce across an English-dominated Channel.[207] In the age of a resurgent French monarchy these prospects were small. The Edwardian and Elizabethan statesmen who promoted military industries did so not in the interests of prosperity, but in the quest for security, and for import substitution to lessen the impact of arms supplies on the balance of payments.[208] That fitted with the view expressed by a string of councillors around 1560—Bacon, Cecil, Mason, Paget—that England had been exhausted by wars beyond her capacity, as Thomas Barnabe told Cecil in 1552, that the English had 'spent out al our riches, and destroyed a great number of subjects, and left al our mony in Flanders, Heynou, and Artous, to the utter destruction of our realm'.[209] No contemporaries seem to have thought realistically that war bred more wealth than it consumed. But did it really involve the destruction of 'a great number of subjects'? So far we have talked about war for half a book and hardly anyone has got hurt: next we shall have to turn to killing and dying.

6

Killing and Dying

The history of war and society, as it has been practised in the last fifty years or so, grew out of a desire to write more than just traditional military history, a history of strategy, and tactics, and weapons systems. Yet it has in turn been criticized for studying everything but killing and dying, of discreetly averting its gaze from the blood, sweat, and terror of battle.[1] The challenge to write a more experiential history of war has been most persuasively met by historians of the twentieth century. They are endowed with appropriate sources—memoirs, interviews, psychiatric surveys—generated after a romantic watershed which made reflection on individual experience a more acceptable activity for the novel-reading classes. They are also dealing with armies conscripted from among the civilian population, who had to be prepared en masse to confront the alien face of war.[2] Yet Henry VIII's forces too were full of men pulled suddenly away from the plough and the loom and the fishing boat. We do not have even the correspondence and biographical material available for noblemen and gentlemen to gauge the attitudes to war of those outside the social elite. But we can still ask how ready they were for warfare, what kind of soldiers they became, and whether their experience of war was most likely to be a death sentence or an adventurous career break.

Englishmen were supposed to own weapons appropriate to their social rank and their enemies thought they knew how to use them. The French ambassador Charles de Marillac told the governor of Picardy in 1541, 'you will understand well enough that all Englishmen are skilled in war after a fashion'.[3] But governments worried that 'after a fashion' might not be good enough and held musters with increasing regularity from the 1520s at which all adult men were supposed to present their weapons for view. Muster returns can be combined with wills and inventories to trace the private ownership of arms and armour, but each present problems. Muster returns, even those for the ambitious general proscription of 1522, are highly variable in the detail they record and whether they noted what people brought to musters or what they should have brought, a point on which the government changed its mind part way through the 1522 survey.[4] At least for 1522 we have a tabulation of the returns for twenty-seven counties, suggesting that there were enough bows and bills to equip 98 per cent of the 128,250 able men who appeared at musters, but that there was armour for only a quarter of them.[5] This figure of something over 30,000 able and equipped men matches fairly well the total numbers of troops put into the field in 1513 and the ratio of armour to able men persisted into the musters of 1539 and beyond.[6]

Wills and inventories are of less statistical use, telling us mostly about the older and richer parts of the population, and perhaps not enumerating weapons even when testators possessed them. What they can do is give us a sense of the variety of arms and what they meant to their owners. Richard Thornton, alderman of York, had no ordinary brigandines, but brigandines covered with tawny satin and gilt nails; John Brodocke, apothecary of Southampton, had no mere handgun, but a dag, a currier, and a stylish 'hande gone layde with bone'.[7] Some testators bequeathed lovingly enumerated items to their sons, or brothers, or nephews, or godsons, or brothers-in-law, or cousins, or apprentices, or friends, in a way that suggests their attachment to them and sometimes their own memory of receiving them as gifts.[8] Others alluded to their habit of using their arms and armour. William Robynson, citizen and cloth-worker of London, left his brother in 1541 his 'wacchynge harness', worn on city watch duty, and Tristram Bolling of Chellow, Yorkshire, left for his mortuary payment in 1502 his best horse, jack, sallet, bow and arrows, sword and buckler, all used together 'as I went to the werr'.[9]

The patterns of ownership and trajectories of change these sources reveal are roughly parallel with the development of communal and lordly armouries, though with some surprises, like the frequent ownership of bows and other weapons by clergymen, caught uneasily between a canon law that forbade them to shed blood and the demands of masculinity, personal safety, and national defence: one rector of St Aldates, Oxford, had two sallets, a breastplate, a pair of splints, and a halberd.[10] The ownership of arms and armour generally correlated with wealth. In 1522 at Coventry armour holdings were concentrated in the richer residential districts, while in the Cornish hundred of West in the same year 99 per cent of households with goods worth £20 or more could present at least one full set of armour at musters, 81 per cent of households with goods worth between £10 and £20, 47 per cent of households with goods worth between £3 and £10, but only 14 per cent of households with goods worth less than £3.[11] A comparison of muster and subsidy returns for Herefordshire in the 1540s, where these survive in sufficient detail, shows that the wealthy were both more likely to own armour and weapons and more likely than their poorer neighbours to be judged not fit enough to use them (see Fig. 6.1).[12]

Bows, swords, and daggers were the commonest weapons, especially if we leave on one side bills or staffs which might have been for martial or for agricultural use. Bows were mentioned more often than swords at musters, but both appear frequently in wills and inventories and swords featured regularly in lists of stolen goods.[13] As for armour, at least until the 1540s almain rivets were outnumbered by older or more miscellaneous harness. Port towns kept up best with change. At Southampton almain rivets were frequent from the 1550s and by the 1570s some testators had corslets and morions, whereas the best Oxfordshire could show before 1575 were the almain rivets of a Great Milton husbandman and a Banbury shoemaker.[14] It was the same with weaponry. At Southampton thirteen pikes were produced at musters in 1556, 109 in 1561, and they appear in inventories too.[15] Handguns, infinitesimally few until the 1530s, spread, first in towns, from the

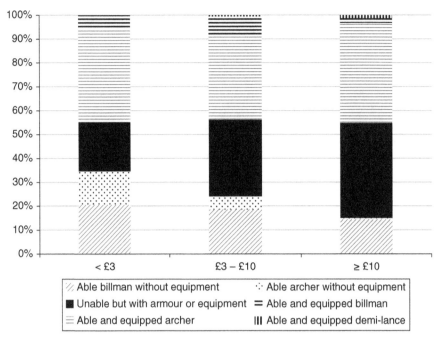

Fig. 6.1. Herefordshire musters 1542 and subsidy assessments 1544: military equipment, ability, and wealth in forty-five townships (sources: see note 12).

1540s, and were becoming common by the musters of 1569. In Cornwall there were twenty-two at Bodmin, twenty at Saltash, fifteen each at Truro and Fowey, but guns were also scattered through the countryside, particularly in the richer parts, and accidents reflect their growing diffusion.[16] Some regions had specialities. In West Cornwall and perhaps in Portland they brought slings to musters, in South Wales long spears, in North Wales clubs.[17] And the proportion of horsed and armed able men was twice as high in Cumberland or the North Riding of Yorkshire as in the South or Midlands.[18]

Inventories show that people lived with weapons all over their houses. They were most often found in the hall, followed by galleries for those who had them, but there were swords and bows in bedchambers, handguns in parlours, poleaxes in counting houses, and brigandines in the children's chamber; one man kept his sallet and splints in the kitchen cupboard and another kept his in the cheese chamber.[19] The social distribution of the ownership of arms and armour might lead us to ask whether their possession was aspirational. In high society it surely was: the customers of Henry's luxury Greenwich armourers included the poets Wyatt and Surrey, the northern peers Lord Neville and the earl of Cumberland, and the captains of Calais and Boulogne, Lords Maltravers and Poynings.[20] One level down from them, the London mercer Vincent Randall, ordering armour from Antwerp in 1551, was equally picky. He told his servant Thomas Cranfield that he wanted a mail coat 'after the moost best fazion and the essyest to bowthe to

Fig. 6.2. John, Lord Mordaunt, *c.*1550, in blackened and gilded Greenwich armour (Royal Armouries I.55) © Royal Armouries.

goo or ryde in and to tacke of and an', together with a steel cap 'as ys most ussyd and occupied of the best sortte and fazion and coveryd over with sylcke'.[21] Further down still, did village notables buy arms and armour out of a dull sense of obligation, or, if a Greenwich armour had the same sexy glint as a sports car (see Fig. 6.2), did a well-made set of almain rivets have the allure of a Ford Capri or an Audi Quattro? The jurors explaining an accident at Bridgwater in 1517 cannot have been entirely tongue-in-cheek when they said it started with two men wanting to show each other the beauty of their swords.[22]

Armour had its peacetime uses in making a brave show at a riot or in the courtroom, but guns were much more versatile and they became the must-have purchase of the mid-century.[23] Their attraction was enhanced by the fact that, like luxury clothing, their ownership was limited by statute to those of a certain wealth, with the aim of deterring poaching and rebellion and encouraging archery. The statutes were taken sufficiently seriously that individuals secured licences to breach them and the complaints of those who thought the rules were not enforced hard enough—gentlemen fond of hawking, for example, who saw their prey blasted out of the sky by plebs with guns before they had the chance to hunt it—suggest that the cachet conferred by the laws made guns all the more desirable.[24] Guns were useful not only for game shooting and pest control but, as the gun control statutes admitted, as a superior alternative to crossbows for defence of the home. They were a risky deterrent against burglars—a Lincolnshire yeoman in 1555 and the servant of a Worcestershire widow in 1544 were killed when guns kept for domestic defence went off accidentally—but an effective one. John Herte, leader of a gang that terrorized the family of Thomas Cheswiss, yeoman, of Mickley, Cheshire, in spring 1557 with a technique more familiar in the Low Countries, threatening to burn the house down with gunpowder and matches in the dead of night if not paid off, was shot by Cheswiss's servant Ralph Caldway when he broke into the house and died of his wounds under arrest in Chester Castle ten days later.[25]

Kings wanted subjects not just to possess weapons, but to know how to use them. By the 1560s musters involved training delivered by muster masters, but long before that muster commissioners checked the ability to fight.[26] They counted half or more of the adult male population too immature, too old, too insecure and transient, or, as some commissioners explicitly stated, too sick or lame when the musters were taken, to fight at all.[27] Even among the able distinctions were made between those more suitable to be archers or to be billmen, and between the 'mean' or 'indifferent', 'the seconde sorte' or 'thirde sorte', and the 'good' or 'best' or 'choyce menne', those who, as archers, 'canne shoote a good strong shoote', or those who 'can shote in handgons qualivers etc'.[28] The logical next step after identifying who owned equipment and who was fit to fight was to reallocate arms and armour from the richer and perhaps older men who owned them, men like Christopher Farbeke at Newcastle in 1539, 'an agyde man hym selffe and past the warrys', but in possession of two jacks, splints, steel bonnets, and bills, to the younger, fitter, and perhaps more expendable, like Christopher's neighbours who were 'able to do the kynge goode service in hys warrys, but they lake harnes and be not able to by ytt'.[29] In 1522–3 such redistribution was clearly attempted, at some 1539 musters individuals were told whose equipment they were to use—admittedly, often their father's or their master's—and in 1553 there were explicit instructions to 'taike the harneise from the insuffycyent and delyver the sayme to the suffycyent'.[30]

Yet rich old men in village and town elites did not always put their armour on poor young men and send them off to die. On the contrary, the 'better sort' were sometimes happy to be counted 'choice men'.[31] In Yorkshire in the 1530s the list of able archers, horsed and harnessed, for each township, was often headed by gentlemen or even esquires: Michael Rawdon of Rawdon, Laurence Keighley of Newall, John Gascoigne of Barwick in Elmet, John Myddelton of Kirkstall.[32] In Wiltshire in 1539, yeomen rich enough to own armour and horse were listed as able archers in one village after another.[33] In Devon in 1569 we know the names not only of those who owned equipment and those able to fight, but also of the village notables who supplied the information and did not shirk from their duties. The position of first-named able archer seems to have been a particular mark of standing, manliness, and skill. In a string of villages from Blackawton and Bratton Clovelly to Washford Pyne and Zeal Monachorum it was occupied not just by the richest farmers, but by presenters who nominated themselves.[34]

How did men learn to use weapons? Any physical activity was in one sense preparation for war. Ploughmen in particular were thought to have the muscles needed for archery, unlike feeble shepherds; wrestling, coroners' inquests show us, was a popular recreation and a test of virility, in which at least one contestant told his fellows he would prove to them he was a 'manly man'; for the gentry, hunting encouraged bold riding, risk-taking, and bloodshed.[35] But some weapons clearly demanded special practice, above all archery, particularly archery with bows of the heavy pull-weight needed for armour-piercing arrows. Regular practice was enjoined by statute and proclamation. In some places at least, towns like Fordwich and Ludlow, it was enforced by fines on defaulters, in others, above all London, encouraged by shooting matches with prizes and pageantry. Coroners' inquests show dozens of fatalities at practice right across England, as gentlemen and yeomen, butchers, weavers and shoemakers, husbandmen, labourers, and boys honed their skills.[36] Archery practice shaped men's bodies, as skeletons from the battle of Towton and the *Mary Rose* show.[37] It also shaped the way they judged distance: in recording his journeys around England and Wales, John Leland expressed distances three dozen times in flight shots, arrow shots, bow shots, or butt shots, and others did the same.[38] Accident statistics suggest the decline of archery practice over the century, as bows became more expensive, less demanded by governments at war, and less exciting than guns. Meanwhile as handguns spread, with hesitant encouragement from above, so did the ability to shoot them, from handfuls of urban residents in the 1520s and 1530s, many of them foreigners, to hundreds per county in 1569: 314 in Oxfordshire, 492 in Cornwall.[39] Firing larger guns was a skilled trade and one in demand, its secrets, contained in manuscript manuals or learnt by apprenticeship, steadily mastered by the English and Welsh until foreign expertise was no longer at such a premium as it had been until the 1520s and natives furnished all the master gunners of the early Elizabethan navy, except perhaps one.[40]

As for hand-to-hand combat, fighting with swords or swords and bucklers, small round shields for parrying blows, sometimes friendly, sometimes more confrontational, was popular, and among all social ranks, as accidents, Star Chamber cases, bequests in wills, and even penances imposed on sword-fighting priests suggest.[41] Learning started young for those who could afford it. In 1558 the earl of Rutland paid to have his sons, aged about 7 and 9, taught 'to playe with weapons'.[42] Some communities offered prizes for buckler playing, but London, concerned for public safety in a crowded city, tried to ban it from the 'open stretes and lanes' and to shut down sword-fighting schools, while other towns forbade the wearing of swords, at least by hot-headed young men.[43] From the 1550s matters were complicated by the rise of the rapier with its deadly point and sharp cutting edges, well designed for 'murder and evident death', and the masters of defence who toured the country to teach its use.[44] Such masters also gave instruction in the bill, but this was comparatively uncomplicated, as it was related to agricultural tools and using it in combat drew on the skills of quarterstaff fighting, an activity which crops up in coroners' inquests and in Star Chamber cases.[45] Other staff weapons such as the partisan or halberd, accidents suggest, may have demanded more practice than the bill to get used to the weight of the head on the staff.[46]

Fighting from horseback demanded considerable control of one's horse and Thomas Blundeville set out a rigorous programme of warhorse training, including the firing of guns and a routine to accustom horses to advance against armed men on foot. Noisy servants with staffs, he recommended, should stand threateningly in the horse's path, but conveniently retreat as the horse nerved itself to charge them, taking care not to hit the horse, 'least you utterlye discourage him for ever'.[47] Jousting at court or at Calais gave gentlemen practice in fighting with the lance, but different types required different techniques. There were complaints when northern horsemen, used to lances which were 'rownd and lyght', were supplied with excessively 'greatt and bostowes' spears from the ordnance office.[48] With the equipment they owned and were used to, Devon gentlemen and esquires in 1569 comfortably passed muster as able light horsemen, but before real fighting started on the northern border in 1560 it was thought that newly raised cavalry would need to be 'taught to use there lances and there pistolettes'.[49]

Even putting on armour was a complex act and took strength and practice. The Knight in Sir Thomas Smith's *Discourse of the Commonweal* worried that his servants were not strong enough to wear 'any heavy armor in time of war' and Hugh Latimer remembered as a boy helping his father buckle on his armour as he set off to the battle of Blackheath.[50] The London livery companies paid armourers to help their men get dressed for marching watches and musters, occasions which must have got men there and in other large towns used to wearing armour and carrying weapons, one of Henry Barrett's training priorities in his captain's handbook of 1562.[51] Though marching watches were dented by the Reformation, some towns strove to maintain or revive them in the 1550s and 1560s, or merged them with increasingly elaborate musters.[52] Meanwhile it became fashionable to put on more lifelike displays, perhaps even with fake casualties, to demonstrate familiarity with the modern wars of firearms and sieges.[53] At York on Shrove Tuesday 1555, the young men showed the mayor, aldermen, and commons 'honest and pleasant pastyme, one sort in defending a fort and th'other in makyng th'assaults'.[54] On New Year's Day 1557 Trinity College, Cambridge put on 'a show...of the wynninge of an holde and taking of prisoners, with waytes, trumpettes, gonnes, and squybbes'.[55] When Elizabeth visited Bristol in 1574, she watched from a timber scaffold as 300 arquebusiers and 100 pikemen assaulted two forts in the marsh.[56]

Yet being able to use a weapon was not the same as being a soldier. As Henry Barrett put it with regard to handgunners, 'althoughe to other uses they can right well use the same', they were 'oftetymes in warelyke poyntes ignorant'.[57] Thomas Audley, who wrote a military treatise towards the end of Henry's reign, reckoned that a captain might make a recruit 'a man of warre mete to serve within a fortnight though he never saw warres before'. But this was a 'good captaine...taking a little paynes' and Audley thought that under an incompetent captain men might 'goe iiij or v years in the warres and in the ende never the wyser'.[58] It is hard to find evidence of deliberate training of new recruits, but not impossible: in 1560, with the queen's encouragement, the duke of Norfolk sent orders to the captains of the men placed in garrisons across Northumberland 'to see them trayned and taught to use their weapons so as they may be the more apte for service'.[59] Even earlier than that wise captains and veterans alike must have taken some pains to prepare newcomers for combat, if only to avoid the risk to themselves if their new colleagues turned and ran.

What material did captains have to work on? It is much harder to identify those sent to fight among drafts from the county militia than among those recruited in the retinues of lords and gentlemen, but town records can help. Throughout the period urban authorities put some effort into picking the 'good, sad and hable men' requested by the crown.[60] From the 1480s to the 1510s those who served in urban contingents were often craftsmen. For Scotland in 1481, for instance, Coventry found seven tailors, four shearmen, four shoemakers, three smiths, two cappers, two dyers, two wiredrawers, two butchers, two yeomen, and fifteen other artisans, ranging from a locksmith to a haberdasher.[61] Into the 1540s, 1550s, and 1560s towns like York, Guildford, Liverpool, and Worcester included such men in their companies, respectable guildsmen, minor office-holders, and taxpayers, but there seems to have been a steady decline in status summed up by Wilton, which sent a future mayor to Bosworth in 1485 and a future constable to Boulogne in 1546.[62] In the countryside, similarly, the 1530s, 1540s, and 1550s still saw complaints from yeomen and husbandmen pressed for service abroad about the fate of their farms, complaints of a sort which would be hard to find later in the century, but the habit was already spreading of paying someone else to serve in one's place, £1 apparently being the going rate in 1549.[63] Within months of Henry's death, meanwhile, the instructions reaching local society from above were becoming ambiguous, the earl of Shrewsbury instructing the counties in his charge to send against the Scots 'good and able' men, including arquebusiers 'of the most lively and meet men to serve', but also reminding them of the benefits of choosing 'such idle men and others as the country may best spare'.[64] Thus the path was set towards the pattern of the 1590s. By then requests for solid, able men were met by drafts of very mixed quality. At best they blended old soldiers and the rootless poor with labourers, servants, husbandmen, and artisans, numbers of the more substantial of whom managed to get themselves replaced before they reached actual combat. At worst the counties sent out rogues and vagabonds in an act of 'social cleansing'.[65]

The process by which the burden of military service shifted down the social ladder over the century was clearest at London, where the livery companies apparently operated a sliding scale by which company members served in the defence of the city and were sometimes sent against rebels elsewhere in England, but were seldom dispatched overseas.[66] Even when the younger members of the company were nominated to serve abroad, they were increasingly allowed to find substitutes.[67] The results could be dire. The carpenters, drapers, pewterers, and skinners each found that men they had got ready to serve in the 1540s, 1550s, or 1560s ran away before they could be sent off, and in 1560 the drapers averted this only by keeping their two recruits in the city counter prison overnight.[68] The distinction made in London looks much like that developing in towns in the Netherlands between the *schutters*, solid burghers who served in militias for the defence of the town and the maintenance of public order, and poorer men or country folk recruited to serve on campaign.[69] Desperation might overcome this distinction. For the relief of Calais in 1558 the Londoners did send out company members, both those bound apprentices in 1549–50 and with settled if undistinguished careers ahead of them, and those who had been freemen since the mid-1540s and had watched the walls of London against Wyatt.[70] But for the most part Elizabethan citizens with any stake in society exercised their military duty, whether conceptualized as that of the stout Roman citizen-soldier or that of the valiant servant of the Lord of Hosts, in civic watches and trained band musters rather than on distant campaigns.[71]

Amateur soldiers, or those who began as amateurs, were important because there were so few professionals. As is often pointed out, England had no standing army like the French *compagnies de l'ordonnance* or the Spanish *tercios*. At court there were a few hundred guards, the standing naval establishment was small, the garrisons of Calais and its satellite fortresses totalled between 700 and 900 men, Berwick less than a hundred, Carlisle fewer still; the occupations of Tournai and Boulogne demanded larger garrisons, but were short-lived.[72] In Ireland English armies of between 200 and 700 served successive governors until the revolt of 1534 brought a permanent establishment ranging from 1,000 to 2,500.[73] Around the English coasts Henry's fortifications held garrisons totalling some 300 men, around half of them gunners, while some two dozen gunners worked at the Tower of London.[74]

The professional military establishment of mid-Tudor England, then, numbered a few thousand at best. Yet they were disproportionately important. Calais, Boulogne, and later Ireland provided a reservoir of expertise for other expeditions and nurtured those two great spokesmen for the hard-done-by Tudor soldier, Elis Gruffudd and Thomas Churchyard.[75] The border fortresses were nurseries of militancy: William Paget likened garrison captains to 'fishes of the see, for as th'one desyreth nothing but water, so th'other desyreth nothing but warre'.[76] Yeomen of the guard, king's spears, gentlemen pensioners, and full-time gunners stiffened English armies, navies, and garrisons.[77] And the handbook authors Audley and Barrett were a Calais veteran and a yeoman of the guard respectively.[78] Again the young duke of Norfolk in 1560 made the situation clear, explaining that the men of the Berwick garrison would have to play a central part in any expedition into Scotland because 'they be well trayned and for the moste part olde souldiours and as I understand so skillfull, specially for the harquebuserie and for the pike also, as ther be no better'.[79]

Beyond this core was a penumbra of semi-professionals. Armourers often had fighting skills: six men identified as armourers or surnamed Armourer served in retinues in 1492, and two in the companies mustered at Canterbury in May 1514.[80] Park-keepers and foresters were expected to be good archers, and the foresters of Sherwood Forest supplied fifteen archers for Sir Thomas Lovell's retinue in 1508, five of whom had served him in 1492.[81] The gentlemen of the northern borders and their household servants directly retained by the king as the traditional arrangements for the wardenships of the marches broke down from the 1530s must have been experienced enough warriors to bolster the defences of the border.[82] More alarming for contemporary moralists were what John Hooper, bishop of

Gloucester, called 'such as are every man's men for money; as these runagates and lance-knights are, that sell both body and soul to such as will hire them, they care not whether the cause be wrong or right'.[83] England was not an exporter of mercenaries on the scale of Switzerland, or Germany, or Albania, but, as a Venetian observer put it in 1557, 'like other nations' the English 'go abroad and take part in one war and the other'.[84] In the troubled Netherlands of the 1470s, 1480s, and 1490s, hundreds served the Valois and Habsburg dukes of Burgundy under famous captains like Sir Thomas Everingham and Sir John Middleton, while others were hired by the dukes' rivals the Flemish cities, under less well-known contemporaries like John Edward, Englishman, whose local wife, Jehanne van Lierde, collected the wages of his company of archers at Ghent in 1488.[85] From then until the 1540s Englishmen fought in smaller numbers, the adventurous, the desperate, or young gentlemen looking for military education.[86] Then in the 1550s, as the dissolution of the English garrisons in Scotland and at Boulogne sharply diminished opportunities in royal service, hundreds served on each side in the wars between France and the Habsburgs, footmen, light horsemen, and expert miners, among them the future Elizabethan captains Richard Bingham, William Drury, Nicholas Malby, and William Pelham, and the colourful adventurer Thomas Stukeley.[87]

These mercenaries had specific skills. Often they were expert archers, their fire falling 'as thick as snow', but the English were not stuck in the past.[88] The light horsemen were adaptable enough to fight with pistols and boar spears by the 1550s, like the Albanians and Germans alongside them.[89] Many may have trained among the adventurers—runaway apprentices or soldiers dismissed for drunkenness, said some contemporaries—who served for plunder, rather than pay, on the fringe of English armies in campaign after campaign, from 1492 to 1562, and 'dayly learned feates of warre'.[90] Mercenaries and adventurers alike had a reputation for pillage—one party was ambushed by the French as they returned to the Habsburg garrison at Saint-Omer in 1486 singing for joy because they had so much plunder— and for ruthless burning of the enemy countryside.[91] As the count of Roeulx, Habsburg governor of Flanders, put it, 'when it comes to burning it is necessary to use the English'.[92] Such behaviour invited reprisals. Some Englishmen were burnt alive in 1485 in the town hall of Hulst where they had barricaded themselves after the inhabitants turned on them.[93] In 1524 a party of adventurers cattle-rustling out of Guînes found themselves hopelessly surrounded by French troops from the Boulogne garrison and surrendered. Their captors sold them to the peasants of the village they had been raiding, who massacred them. In revenge their colleagues burned the village down two days later, killed thirty-six prisoners, and sent the one survivor to Boulogne as a warning.[94]

When it came to getting more ordinary recruits to fight, recruiters and captains recognized the importance of morale. Audley saw that captains needed 'chieflie to know' 'what good will' their men 'have to fight', for when soldiers 'determyne themselves...for to abide the fight and to give the manlie onset...one man is worth two men'.[95] When preparing to assault Boulogne, Henry's commanders wanted the captains to 'feale the disposytion of their souldyours'.[96] Fatigue was also seen to dent capability: as Audley put it, 'weried men if thei be assailed in tyme of his weriness is halfe overcome all readie by the reason of his weriness'.[97] Desertion must have indicated either unwillingness to fight or disillusionment and seems to have been a steady trickle, not only in dire straits—Lord Ferrers' men going back to Herefordshire in 1513 rather than mount a new raid on the French coast where they had suffered heavy losses, or the earl of Rutland's in 1549 slipping away from the beleaguered, under-fed, and plague-ridden English garrisons in Scotland—but also at the outset of campaigns.[98] The inappropriately named John Bull, a yeoman of Sprowston in Suffolk, indicted for mustering in Sir Richard Lee's company at Ipswich on 1 August 1557 and sliding home two weeks later, must stand for many of his colleagues.[99]

Mutinies were recurrent when soldiers or sailors felt their interests threatened by interruptions to pay or by dangerous strategic choices.[100] At Guînes in 1558 Lord Grey de Wilton's men urged him to surrender after a bloody siege. At first they asked him to 'have consideration of theyr lyves, which as long as any hoape remayned they wyllyngly had ventured'. When he refused the French terms as insufficiently honourable and urged 'lett us end then as honestie, dutie, and fame doothe wyll us', they 'in a mutenie flatly answered, that they for his vainglorie woulde not sell their lyves' and he had to concede.[101] Mutinies might split armies. In 1523 one body of troops chanting 'Home, Home' was confronted by another chanting 'Hang, Hang' and in 1536 Lord Deputy Grey had to arm himself and his followers and turn his guns against the mutinous sections of his army in Ireland.[102] It may well be that the change in recruitment from the retinue system to the more impersonal system of county drafts made it harder to hold armies together and inspired the move to fiercer and more regularized disciplinary procedures evident from the 1540s.[103] In the heated atmosphere of 1549 mere withdrawal from musters could result in proclamation as a rebel and the confiscation of goods.[104] In rebellions of course desertion might actually mean changing sides, as people did in 1554 both from the queen's forces to Wyatt's and from the rebels to the queen.[105] On the other hand, the practice of granting leave must have meant that soldiers were trusted to return to duty. Garrison captains granted written licences to return home which could be presented to local officials.[106] Sometimes leaves for a week or even a month were given for specific purposes, to buy replacement horses, recover health, or settle financial affairs.[107] In 1546 Henry allowed many of his garrison troops to return home 'uppon theyr long absence out of theyr natural cuntreys, havyng desired to se theyr wiefes and childern for a tyme'.[108]

In combat fear and disorder, men falling into 'a shake' like the Scots at Solway Moss, readily led to flight.[109] Those who survived the experience powerfully evoked its mixture of rational self-preservation and irrational panic. At Ancrum Moor the English suffered 'a gret disorder amonges our men at the joynīng of the bataile', and at Hadden Rigg part of the ambushed English raiding force made off with its booty, while another part 'began to trot, and schortlye fell in tyll gallapyne, and thane the most part of all the ost brak reulle and fled'.[110] At Edinburgh the English troops, under cannon fire from the castle, 'fell into such a soden rage and feare' that 'with suche exclamacion and cryenges out upon no ground or cause, they began to flee so fast out of the towne, as by reason of the streight passage at the gate, the thrang and presse was so gret, that one of theym was like to distroye an other'.[111] At Saint-Etienne, when 'our furst rancke and the second were come to the pusshe of the pike, ther grewe a disorder in our men, and withoute cause fledd', a result explicable only by 'a humour that sometyme raigneth in Englisshe men'. Thereafter 'the furye of their flight was such, that it boted litell the travaile that was taken upon everye straycte to staye them'.[112] In such episodes good captains tried to stem the rush. Some dismounted to steady their men: as Thomas, Lord Wharton put it, 'seyng mysorder ther, I alighttid of my horse with my bowe'.[113] They could be surrounded and captured if the rest of the army melted away, as it did at Hadden Rigg, or 'slayne in the furst rancke', as a dozen captains were at Saint-Etienne.[114] But sometimes their efforts made all the difference. At the gates of Edinburgh the defensive fire was such that the English attackers 'beganne to shrynke and retiere', but then 'the gentlemen...gave the onsett and made so sharpe assaulte' that the attack pressed on.[115]

In explaining how ordinary men could be brought to stand and fight and kill in war, we have to reckon with the association between authoritative manliness and physical force in sixteenth-century society. A generation of debate has established that while late medieval and early modern England saw higher rates of homicide than the present, partly because many assaults that now end in hospital emergency wards then ended in death from wounds or infection, neither was a hotbed of random violence; violence, even assault in response to verbal insult, was purposive and expected to be proportionate. The king claimed the right to exercise legitimate violence in the punishment of crime and in war, a right he delegated to his judges and to his soldiers. But those soldiers, if mature men, were also used to exercising legitimate violence of their own, as parish constables dragging offenders to the stocks, as husbands, fathers, and masters disciplining members of their house-holds.[116] New soldiers, then, were attuned to the targeted use of manly force, though not to senseless slaughter. In situations of confrontation they were also used to a heightened language of dispute that threatened to maim or stab one's opponent even when all that usually resulted was a shove or a trip or a beard-pull. In such confrontations neighbours or servants held back the assailant so that his honour was vindicated without his doing extreme harm to his rival.[117] In war there were no restraining friends.

The idea that the king's wars or the defence of the commonweal were just and therefore it was morally legitimate to use force in them was widely circulated. Preachers told their hearers that 'to fight against the king's enemies, being called unto it by the magistrates, it is God's service', that they might go into battle 'as charitable persons...in the name of God...not in their own cause, but for the conservation of the public weal'; they even told other preachers to exhort the soldiery 'manfully to fight, when time requireth, and shew them how honest and godly a thing it is to jeopard their life for the wealth of their country'.[118] Audley's model speech to the army before battle duly made repeated references to the king's rights and honour as the cause for which men were fighting. But it was much more passionate about the need for soldiers to 'bere yourselves manfullie and nobly this daye', for the 'hope and likelyhod of victorie' lay 'in the manly harts of men, whiche will ever shewe their faces with courage of lyons towards their ennemyes', and not 'wretchedly turn thir faces and shewe thir weake backs to their enemies'.[119] In the same way, John Dudley told his troops at Pinkie to 'Pluck up their hearts! And show themselves men!', and Sir Maurice Dennis exhorted his 'to play the men, showing thereby the assurance of victory'.[120] While there were links in the muscles between wrestling, archery practice, and battle, manliness was the connection between them in the mind, heart, and stomach. Writing in 1548, William Forrest was worried that the deteriorating diet of Englishmen would prevent them from the manly feats of wrestling and shooting and thus from defending their country. His recommendation was clear:

> Geeve Englische men meate after their olde usage,
> beeif, mutton, veale, to cheare their courage;
> and then I dare to this byll sett my hande:
> they shall defende this owre noble Englande.[121]

Manly, manful, and manhood are terms that recur endlessly to commend valour in combat.[122] It was the manliness of fighting that gave the entertaining world-turned-upside-down kick to stories like that of Long Meg of Westminster, a heroine of pamphlets, ballads, and plays apparently based on a brothel-keeper of the 1550s and 1560s, who had allegedly stood in for a soldier at Boulogne and beaten a Frenchman in single combat.[123]

Manliness, reassuringly, was not recklessness. The self-control and discretion that were features of ideal masculinity were also prized by military theorists. William Worcester made the distinction between 'the hardy man' who suddenly and without discretion 'avauncyth hym yn the felde to be halde courageouse', and the 'manly man' who 'wille so discretely avaunce hym that he wille entend to hafe the ovyr hand of hys adversarye, and safe hymsylf and hys felyshyp'.[124] Barrett, similarly, thought that 'hardie and valiant courage' was best deployed with 'circumspection' and when 'perill ys pondered'.[125] Hardiness was praised when a fierce charge or heroic resistance was tactically useful, but it was not the supreme military virtue.[126] This analysis applied even to the famous. One chronicler attributed the death of Sir Edward Howard to his 'to muche hardinesse', while some blamed the defeat at Ancrum Moor on the 'over moch courage' of Sir Ralph Eure, warden of the Middle Marches.[127]

Particularly admired was the kind of steadfast conduct that has won medals in more recent wars. At Diksmuide in 1489 John Pereson, a baker from Coventry, had his foot shot off by a gun but kept firing arrows, kneeling or even sitting down, until the enemy fled.[128] Between Calais and Boulogne in 1543, a soldier called Kelleway, fighting on foot, killed or wounded seven French horses and one man before he was overpowered, a display that his superiors thought 'shal put the Frenchemen all this yere in greater feare of us'.[129] At Pinkie, Grey de Wilton, leading a cavalry charge, was struck in the mouth by a pike which broke a tooth, went through his tongue and passed three fingers deep into the roof of his mouth. Yet he pressed on after the retreating Scots until, overcome by heat and loss of blood, he had to be revived with a firkin of ale.[130] At Le Havre the identical twins Nicholas and Andrew Tremayne of Collacombe, Devon, fought inseparably and when one was killed, the other stepped fatally into his place.[131]

Peer pressure must have been important in making men fight. As their ships sat off the Spanish coast, William Bery, master of the *John of Kingswear*, was reluctant to join other English captains in sailing into a neutral Spanish port to attack the ships there in search of French goods, contrary to his instructions from the ship's owners. The others told him it was 'more meter for hym to kepe shepe than to be master of any shippe of warre'.[132] More soberly Barrett recognized the value of 'the politike and wise perswasions of auncient soldiers' in convincing the 'ignorante' to fight 'whiche else mighte wishe to flee'.[133] Audley built peer pressure into his tactical recommendations, suggesting that two or three ranks of the most experienced pikemen at the back of a square would 'kepe in your men behind from flying'.[134]

Self-preservation also triggered violence. Alexander Schawe, rector of Colby in Norfolk, served Thomas, Lord Howard as a shipboard chaplain in 1511. When it came to hand-to-hand fighting with Scottish pirates, as he told the papal curia when petitioning for absolution, if he had not fought against those 'despoilers and slayers of men ... it is credible that he could not have escaped death'.[135] A group of adventurers cut off by the French in 1524 made a similar calculation: 'if any thing save our lives, it must be God and our hardines'. 'If you se me begin to flie, slaie me out of hande', said their captain. They cried God for mercy, kissed the earth, shook hands, and fought to the death.[136] Such small group loyalty, often stressed by historians of modern wars, must have been particularly strong in retinues raised among neighbours and kinsmen. In 1492, for example, the earl of Oxford's retinue contained two or three men each with the surnames Amberley, Boteler, Bray, Brereley, Bulle, Canon, Davy, Fere, London, Phelyppe, Tedder, Throughton, Warden, and Youle.[137]

Clearly some took to violence with an enthusiasm that unnerved those around them. This might be temporary and attributable to an overheating imbalance of the bodily humours that were thought to govern the temperament. English borderers revenged themselves on Scottish raiders 'in the heate of their blood' and one captain explained why he had to be restrained from fighting an insolent subordinate: 'I was at heyt with hym as he with me, wiche I awght nott to have beyn ... butt a extreym fooym will make ony man forget hym self'.[138] For some, excess was more habitual. When Sir Ralph Eure's body was identified after Ancrum Moor, the earl of Arran exclaimed 'God have mercy on him ... for he was a fell cruell man, and over cruell, which many a man and fatherles barne might rew'.[139] Where reports of others' raids are full of sheep and cattle, Eure's recount his five-hour assault on Moss Tower, Eckford, where thirty-seven Scots were killed and eighty taken prisoner, 'nott a man of them unhurtt'.[140]

Eure, it seems, had crossed the line drawn by Audley, who wished 'all good souldiers to be no more blooddie than the lawe of armes doth require'.[141] Eure's savagery outlived him, as his death and those of his companions two years earlier served as justification for the lack of mercy shown by the border horsemen to the Scots who fled before them at Pinkie and were struck down in large numbers. Some riders broke three or four swords as they hacked at the heads and necks of those running away from them, a contest sufficiently unequal that the official chronicler of the victory felt the need to explain that the relentless killing did not spring merely from 'cruelty...or delight in slaughter'.[142] But even Eure had his limits. In November 1542 he and Ralph Bulmer attacked Coldstream Priory, which they had heard was full of local Scots and their goods. They hoped to summon it, storm it, and 'by the lawe of armes put all to the sake', taking revenge 'with slawghtter' for the recent killing of an English herald. But all the Scottish layfolk had gone and they were met at the priory gates by the prioress and clergy in their vestments with a cross; and 'thus', they admitted, 'wer we disapontid to do ony slawter onless we shuld owttrely have shaymed our selfes for ever'. They contented themselves with burning down the buildings while the nuns knelt outside, singing psalms.[143] Grey de Wilton seems to have rivalled Eure's ferocity, though again he bound himself by the law of arms. In taking a fortified church from the French in 1557 he refused a surrender offered too late, citing the law of arms, and saw the entire garrison killed.[144] Such predispositions ran in families. Eure's brother Henry was described by Ralph Bulmer as 'a verry fre bornner' and Grey's admiring son was an enthusiast for brutal conquest in Elizabethan Ireland.[145]

Sometimes it was heavy losses that drove men into atrocities. At Diksmuide the English, sent to fight the Flemish rebels and their French allies, lost some 500 men, including Henry Lovel, Lord Morley, in a frontal attack down a narrow road against a fortified position. When they broke through, there was not only much killing among the Flemings, 2,000 or more, but also a deliberate massacre of the French. Five or six hundred of them took refuge in a building, reportedly crying out 'Ransom! Ransom! We're just soldiers, we don't care about these Flemings', but the English, pretending not to understand, put all but fifty to the sword.[146] When the French tried to retake Boulogne by night in October 1544, the English, outraged at the killing of several hundred unarmed pioneers when the attackers broke into the town, slew the French as they expelled them rather than take prisoners.[147] The perilous storming of a town could unleash the same bloodlust. At Saint-Quentin in 1557 it was said that the English had killed thirty-four women and children in one house on the marketplace.[148] The claustrophobic world of shipboard combat drove some in the same direction, especially when torture might discover the hiding place or ownership of goods. One English privateering crew of the 1540s tormented their captives by tightening bowstrings round their hands and 'prevy members' and another in the 1570s hanged the master of a Dutch ship till he was half dead; once he revealed where his money-bags were, they weighted him with stones and threw him into the sea.[149] Though not much discussed, rape was the foul accompaniment to plunder on such occasions as the surrender of Boulogne.[150]

Did soldiers who returned to England bring such behaviour with them? Social commentators worried that they might, that soldiers, beginning with 'excessious drynkynge' and 'abhominable sweryng' and seducing women to 'ungodlye livinge', might end with worse.[151] Certainly some were uncouth. Portsmouth's master gunner allegedly pleaded with the town council until they made him a burgess, but then told the mayor that the honour was worthless: 'if it had ben worthe a turde...he shold not have had yt'.[152] Soldiers did sometimes commit robberies, steal horses, fight murderously among themselves, or carry out killings in family feuds.[153] But men who were not soldiers also did such things, and perhaps men inclined to violence were more likely to become or remain soldiers. Recruitment in the Hundred Years War clearly linked service to pardon for violent crime, hence perhaps Edward IV's repeated assertion that the best means for 'justice to be set up and sur peas to be kept inwardes' was 'a notable and a mighty were outewardes'.[154] In 1480, 1545, and 1563 men were recruited straight from prison and it was at least suggested in other years.[155] Some soldiers were arrested as vagrants on their way to join up and some families dumped their problems on the army: in 1514 Lord Darcy told the treasurer of Berwick to take his cousin's bastard son, Percival Wortley, into the garrison 'however unthrifty and drunken ye shall find him'.[156] Perhaps contemporaries got the balance right when they thought of the restless, drawn to soldiering, 'beyng indeyd suche maner of men as were sumwhat unruly before they were sent', returning 'not unlike nowe to be further owte of frame', likely to 'take boldenesse to offend' the king's subjects.[157] The problem was always likely to get worse as recruitment patterns changed: the shiftless, the rootless, the poor, and the desperate drafted into Elizabeth's armies had less to come home to than the yeoman tenants and household servants of the gentry and nobility and the urban craftsmen of Henry VII's day.

Did many soldiers come home anyway? We know some did, as they were paid when they handed their equipment back in or taken to court if they refused to do so, though it is not clear whether most of those had made it out of England.[158] Some retired in middle age, like Robert Parker, who settled down at Carlisle with his wife and children in the 1530s, after twelve years' service 'in hys youthe being strong and lusty and mette for the north borders'.[159] Some, as we have seen, came back to their towns to continue careers ending in major or minor civic office. Others did not come back, as they made wills, 'beinge in the kinges warfare', hurriedly providing for their families as best they could.[160] Death rates are hard to calculate, but they seem often to have been surprisingly low. Flodden and Pinkie were bloody encounters, but English losses were far less than Scottish, perhaps 1,500 at Flodden, something over 5 per cent of the English force, and half that number, a rather lower proportion, at Pinkie.[161] Failed assaults on fortifications could be murderous, that on Leith in 1560 costing 500 lives, but were rare.[162] On northern border raids, those slain in combat were counted in handfuls and even in major encounters English losses came in tens and twenties, Ancrum Moor worst with hundreds killed.[163] Again and again English commanders filed reports like Wharton's of 14 February 1544, 'We brought all the kynges majesties subjectes home without losse of any.'[164] Nor did the English on raids slay many Scots, for the incentives lay not with killing the enemy, but with capturing him for ransom or driving him away while taking his livestock and goods. Coastal raids and those mounted from Calais seem to have been similar, a dozen, a score, exceptionally fifty men lost out of parties of up to a thousand or more.[165]

Even large expeditions might not be too costly. In a four-month campaign involving three sieges in the Netherlands in 1511, Sir Edward Poynings lost fewer than 100 out of 1,500 men.[166] In 1513, most companies apparently came home almost complete, though there is some suspicion that payment was claimed for absentees.[167] In September 1557, after two months of campaigning and the storming of Saint-Quentin, the English army counted fewer than 2 per cent of its men dead and a handful taken prisoner.[168] Naval engagements when whole ships burnt up or went down with their crews—the *Regent* in 1512, the *Mary Rose* in 1545—or when boarding parties lost more than half their strength were terrible, but sufficiently rare to be notorious, while naval gunnery was not yet sufficiently fierce to produce the storms of timber splinters that made the Restoration navy such an apocalyptic place to fight.[169]

Some theatres were more deadly than others. In Ireland tens or scores were killed in quite small encounters, and recurrent rebellions and early plantation schemes exacerbated the tendency to treat all enemies as rebels and hang or behead those not killed in combat.[170] Around Boulogne the intensive fighting of 1544–6 and 1549–50 made clashes between soldiers and peasants frequent and desperate, while hundreds died each time the English garrison fought a major encounter with their French besiegers.[171] Losses were similarly heavy in domestic rebellions. Perhaps a hundred of the marquess of Northampton's men were killed in their expulsion from Norwich in 1549, a proportion comparable to that of the English losses at Flodden, while the Norfolk rebels may have lost one in six of their strength at Norwich and Dussindale, a proportion three or four times higher than Flodden, and the south-western rebels at Fenny Bridges, Clyst St Mary, and Sampford Courtenay many more, nearly half their total force.[172] No wonder Grey de Wilton said that he had never been in such murderous fighting as that outside Exeter.[173] As in Ireland, though more often with some kind of trial, executions followed fast on rebel defeats.[174]

When armies returned home much smaller than they started, the cause was usually disease. In September 1557 only 74 per cent of the English troops in Picardy were fit to fight because, beside the 2 per cent who had died, 5 per cent had been sent home as too sick or disabled to continue—most of them among the pioneers—and 19 per cent were sick or hurt, but still in the camp, the sick out-numbering the wounded by five to one. Seven weeks later, when the army crossed from Calais, only 53 per cent of the men in companies that can be traced through-out the campaign were still under arms, but how many of the sick and wounded had died and how many been sent home we cannot tell.[175] Probably many were like Sir William Courtenay, who survived the fighting unscathed, but made his will when 'visited with bodily sickness' and died on 29 September.[176] The army in the North at the same time was suffering the same problems, with many captains dead or incapacitated by illness.[177] This was a year of dire epidemics, probably influenza, at home and abroad, but the figures were not unusual in comparison with those for Elizabethan armies or indeed those in the Napoleonic Wars and the Crimea.[178] In Ireland too disease was a major factor. Of 220 yeomen of the guard who accom-panied the earl of Surrey there in 1520, eighteen were dead within four months, probably of the plague, and a year later he had lost perhaps a quarter of his army to the plague and the flux.[179]

Sometimes the grip of sickness on an army shocked even its commanders and made it a lethal carrier of infection. At Le Havre in June 1563 plague was taking 500 soldiers, about a tenth of the garrison, each week, and when the troops were evacuated to Portsmouth the parish registers show what happened: eighteen people were buried from April to June, 222 from July to September, some soldiers, but also many townsfolk once the sickness spread to them.[180] The same coincidence of war and disease worried local authorities in 1558. York cancelled its Corpus Christi plays as the time was 'bothe trowblesomne with warres and also contagiouse with sykeness' and muster commissioners were told to avoid 'calling to many people to one place, lest the infeccon of this common syknes be therby occasioned further to sprede'.[181] Joining an army was dangerous, then, but not necessarily more danger-ous than moving to a city: a quarter of Londoners died in the plague year of 1563 and at Norwich some epidemics were worse than that.[182]

In armies death rates from infected wounds must have been high, as they were in everyday accidents, but wounds were certainly not left untreated. Barrett recom-mended each company should have a surgeon able to extract bullets and salve inflammation.[183] Named surgeons featured in retinues in 1492, 1508, and 1513 and Sir John Gage, who had fought in Scotland and France in the 1540s, had among his campaign gear 'a little teynt for a surgion'.[184] Thomas Gale, surgeon at Montreuil and Saint-Quentin and author of a treatise on gunshot wounds designed to help the army at Le Havre, claimed to have found seventy-two surgeons at London to serve on land and sea in a single year and the fleet recruited at least fifteen surgeons at London in 1562–3.[185] The professional pride and practical skill of some surgeons are evident from the finds belonging to the barber-surgeon of the *Mary Rose*.[186] Yet the sudden demand in wartime let in all manner of unsuitable candidates. Gale complained that at Montreuil he found men being treated by sow-gelders and cobblers, whose abilities, beyond cutting and sewing, must have left something to be desired.[187]

Captains, parishes, towns, and livery companies provided medical care or at least relief for their wounded, sometimes at substantial cost.[188] Christopher Coo, captain of the *John Baptist* in 1522–4, spent £6 18s on care for sixteen men burnt at the capture of a French ship, and at Norwich in 1549 Captain Thomas Drury paid a local surgeon £1 13s 4d for treating his wounded men.[189] Southampton spent 1s 4d in 1543 sending for 'a surgene callyd a bone setter' when John Ynglett broke his arm tackling French ships off the Isle of Wight, 3s 4d to the setter for his services, and 4d to Sir Hector for saying mass for John, though whether the mass was for the success of his treatment or for the relief of his soul after its failure is not clear.[190] Medical discharge was also available. In winter 1513, thirty-six sailors who 'were seke and colde no longer do servyse' were sent home from the fleet at Portsmouth, those who fell sick on the campaign of 1523 were allowed to go home on passports, in 1544 the duke of Norfolk was sending so many men home sick from Calais that he had to appoint a four-man committee to weed out malingerers, and in the 1560s the navy issued standard-form passes for sick sailors.[191] One indi-vidual we can track is David Howe of Hunsdon in Hertfordshire, who came home to his brother's house after he was wounded at Le Havre in April 1563 with a bullet in the thigh. On 20 May he joined his brother on a cart trip to Ware, perhaps desperate after a month on his sickbed, but his wounded leg was further crushed by falling wood when his brother drove too fast, and he died on 2 June.[192] Spiritual health was also a concern. Barrett thought each company should have a minister to lead prayers, preach, give communion, and exhort the sick, wounded, and those 'in extremitie' to godliness. Chaplains were regularly present, from the friar who accompanied York's troops in 1482 to the five priests serving with the companies at Canterbury in 1514 and beyond, while even in the absence of chaplains ships' companies made their own provisions for religious practice.[193]

Those permanently incapacitated might become dependent on charity or reward. Henry VIII gave the constableship of Tenby Castle to a man 'sore hurt and maimed' at Blackheath and a pension to a gunner blinded at Morlaix.[194] He also made provision in the new cathedrals he set up in the wake of the dissolution of the monasteries for up to 124 men 'decayde' or 'maimed' in 'the kinges warres', to pray and help with cleaning and bell-ringing if they could; the life was comfortable enough that some of them survived for years. Occasionally letters of recommendation or appointment recited their services: Henry Skarrett had been six or seven years a soldier in Ireland before he was incapacitated in storming a castle in the O'Donnell lordship; John Watson had served Henry, Edward, Mary, and Elizabeth in wars in France and Scotland and been maimed in the left hand before he joined Peterborough cathedral in 1571.[195] Henry gave places in his father's almshouse at Westminster to veterans like John Long, who lost his leg at Boulogne, and Mary planned to establish a well-funded hospital in London for 'pore, impotent and aged souldiers' in 'extreme poverty...or...hurt or maym'd in the warres of this realme'.[196] But royal provision can never have sufficed. Before the Reformation bishops issued indulgences for alms-collecting to individuals like Ralph Pudsey, disfigured by a wound that destroyed his upper jaw in Henry's first wars, but still alive in 1521, and hospitals and almshouses occasionally provided for maimed soldiers, as they did more explicitly by the 1560s.[197] Alms payments to soldiers, whether wounded or just in poverty, appear in the household accounts of the aristocracy and gentry, in churchwardens' accounts, and in guild or borough accounts.[198] Captains paid alms to those who had served under them and livery companies paid pensions to the widows of those they had recruited.[199]

As the poor laws tightened restrictions on begging, special provision had to be made. Robert Copland's treatise of the 1530s, *The hye way to the spyttell hous*, showed some sympathy to soldiers out of wages, who should be found work, but complained about vagabonds begging in soldiers' clothing.[200] In 1546 disbanded soldiers in London were given licences to beg to avoid the sort of scene glimpsed at Norwich in December 1561, when Edmund Abbott was hauled before the court of aldermen for begging on the city's streets.[201] Abbott asked a passer-by 'to be good and friendly to a poor man that hath been hurt and maimed in the queen's affairs, maimed in my arm as your mastership may well perceive'. Asked about the circumstances in general terms, he replied that he was 'hurt with a piece of ordnance', but his questioner wanted to know where he served. 'I served in one of the queen's galleys called *Speedwell* and was hurt being on the Narrow Seas' answered

Abbott, but the potential donor wanted to know when. Satisfied on that score, he asked the name of the galley's captain, and was told that it was Captain Holden. 'In what conflict were you hurt?' came next, to which Abbott elaborated 'I was hurt between Portsmouth and the Isle of Wight being matched and coupled with one of the French king's ships.' Reading the exhaustive exchange one begins to suspect that Abbott had latched onto a reader of the rogue pamphlets that warned of the elaborate lengths to which vagrants would go to sham respectable poverty. The *Speedwell* was a real galley, and there had been squadrons sweeping the Narrow Seas and the Solent, so his story is plausible, but that is the most we can say.[202]

War caused emotional trauma as well as physical, though our sources rarely allow us to describe it. Military service might cause homesickness—Cynfrig Hanmer wrote a poem from France about how he missed Llaneurgain—or family concern.[203] Margaret Paston told her eldest son Sir John in 1475 to keep an eye on his brothers, as they were 'but yonge sawgeres', and little knew what soldiering meant.[204] Lady Jane Dormer refused to wear her jewels all the while her son was in French captivity after being taken at the siege of Montreuil in 1544.[205] Sometimes the problem was not what went on at the wars but what went on at home. Thomas Delaryver of Brandsby, Yorkshire, claimed that while he was away for three years on the borders, John Barton came frequently to his house and successfully urged his wife Anne 'to accomplysshe his unlawfull, voluptuous and carnall appetite and desier with her'. To be fair, Barton claimed that Delaryver invented the story because his wife reproved him for 'abhomynably usyng hymselffe with one Jane Wildon', but the tale of wartime adultery must have been believable.[206]

Henry made intense efforts to militarize his subjects, mustering them, ordering them to equip themselves, drafting them into his ever larger armies. But did these efforts in the end demilitarize them? Sending the yeoman farmers who had turned out for Blackheath on long campaigns in France soon cooled their ardour. Elis Gruffudd complained of the 'many wealthy farmers' from Essex and Suffolk, those who 'were thinking of their wives and children and husbandry', who mutinied rather than prolong the campaign of 1523 into the biting winter. Henry's large armies could be raised only by including men like this, who were not what Gruffudd called 'those men of the common soldiers who had set their mind on being men of war', but repeated attempts to conscript them made them more likely to avoid service.[207]

These yeomen and substantial urban craftsmen were the men who owned arms and armour, but now the government was telling them to make that equipment available to others rather than to use it themselves, or to contribute to township arms of the latest model. They were the men who had honed their archery skills by hours at the butts, but now the government was telling them that while archery practice was a good thing, it was guns that won wars. They were the men, as churchwardens, aldermen, parish constables, and the 'better sort' of parishioners, who had to manage the new systems and send their younger, poorer, less secure neighbours to an uncertain fate in Elizabeth's wars, in large numbers in total, it is true, but only a few thousand at a time. They kept their armour to the musters of 1569 and beyond, but if they used it at all it was in the trained bands, a force designed, like the retinues their grandfathers had joined, to win a short civil war, throw back an invasion, or put down a revolt, rather than to rot in the siege trenches of the Netherlands, Ireland, or France.[208] To use Gruffudd's distinction, they were men, who might certainly be expected to fight, but they were not men of war, whose business was fighting, just as gentlemen might be gentlemen, but not captains. As Henry's children curtailed his military ventures the men of war grumbled, but his other male subjects may not have been so sorry, and the smaller military ventures of the next ninety years seem to have consolidated the distinction between those who might have to fight and those who were fighters.[209] It is possible that an adult male successor bent on driving onwards Henry's plans might have succeeded in creating a nation of dedicated and skilful modern warriors, but given how often soldiers mutinied and deserted even under Henry, and how fast the social level of recruits fell and the search for substitutes accelerated after his death, it seems unlikely.

There are parallels with other aspects of Henry's rule. As we have seen, his pressure for wartime taxation raised unprecedented sums, but encouraged the slide into local under-assessment that crippled the tax system from Elizabeth's reign to the Civil Wars. Henry's reforms in the Church, meanwhile, led for many of his subjects not to enlightened faith, but to bewilderment and perhaps apathy or disenchantment, and here even Henry himself seemed to realize by his last years that he had brought confusion and division rather than general godliness.[210] It would be charitable to assume that Henry lacked the foresight to appreciate these consequences, but some of those around him—one thinks of Sir Thomas More's comment that 'if my head could win him a castle in France it should not fail to go'—suspected that, as long as his honour and his appetite were satisfied in conquest, whether of his worldly or his spiritual enemies, he did not care.[211] To these wider relationships between kings, peoples, governance, and commonweal, we shall now turn our attention.

7

Kings and Peoples

In his military treatise Thomas Audley suggested that kings or their captains facing battle should inspire their troops with an elaborate model speech. This began with the king's 'right...honour and...wealth', and promised his men reward if they did well, but continued in much wider vein. They were to consider 'your worshipp and perpetuall fame to your countrie, which hathe so many yeares contynued in honor without slander of cowardice by the valiant actes done by th'andes of your noble progenitors whiche hathe had to do with those nacions with whome by the grace of God you shall have to do withall this daie'.[1] We have reflected on how the English people in the age of Henry VIII thought about war, prepared for war, served in war, lost or gained from war, and killed or died in war. But how did all these activities shape their identity as the English people and their relationship with Henry and his government?

Of the elements in Audley's speech, we can perhaps take reward for granted—certainly those who thought they had served well petitioned for grants or pardons throughout the period—and national glory we shall come to later, but what of the king's rights with which he began?[2] They loomed large in contemporary explanations of war. The phrase 'the king's wars' was used in every imaginable context, in wills, in leases, in lawsuits, in muster rolls, in financial accounts.[3] Conventional expositions of just war theory placed great stress on the need for just war to be authorized by legitimate political authority and for that authority to be acting on just cause.[4] The English king's title to lands in France unjustly detained, indeed to the crown of France, served as such a cause. The king's 'verray right and true title' to Normandy and the French crown, from which he had been 'put out wrongfullie' loomed large for William Worcester in the 1470s, looking back to his late master Sir John Fastolf and to Fastolf's late master John, duke of Bedford, regent of Lancastrian France until his death in 1435.[5] But interest in the crown's claims persisted much longer. In 1491 Shrewsbury borough council wrote of Henry VII's 'gret viage into Fraunce to chalenge his ri3t and to obteigne his enheritaunce there'.[6] In 1512 Gascon noblemen swore loyalty to Henry VIII as king of France and in 1523 Suffolk's army on the Somme collected similar oaths.[7] As late as 1563 the occupation of Le Havre aimed to defeat 'the Franchemens intentones...to deteyne Calles and the terrytories frome the crowne contrary to all right'.[8]

How seriously did subjects take these claims? J. S. Brewer presumably intended no irony in his comment of 1867 that sixteenth-century Englishmen 'believed as fully in the right and title of their kings to France as we believe in our title to India or Ireland', but he seems to have been right.[9] In May 1553 at Norwich Thomas

Aldersey told a Frenchman who said he had seen the king of France twenty times at Paris, 'Fellow, talk not of such things, for thou speakest thou wottest not what, for the king our master is king of France.'[10] Perhaps he was picking a fight, but others agreed. Early in Henry's reign an anonymous customs official, probably from Ipswich, composed a manuscript defence of the king's title to the French throne countering the arguments of printed French treatises, and in 1549 John Coke, secretary to the English Merchant Adventurers at Antwerp, penned an answer to a French text in which two heralds debated the respective merits of England and France, again asserting the English claim.[11] Even Arthur Golding, the English translator of Caesar's *Gallic War*, explained in 1565 that since Edward III's time 'our Englishe nation' had 'sore afflicted' the French in contention for 'the substance of the crowne and possession of the whole realme, descended to our kinges by ryghte of inheritance...the right remaynyng styl to the crowne of England'.[12] Claims to English pre-eminence over Scotland seem to have had narrower purchase, though in the heady reign of Edward VI they merged with visions of British Protestant unity to inspire some: one astrological writer anticipated the ambitions of James VI and I by calling Edward the 'mooste noble emperoure of great Bryttayne'.[13]

The second great motivation for just war was the defence of one's country. Already in William Worcester's generation, and with increasing insistence in that of Sir Richard Morison, Edward Walshe, and Thomas Becon, Roman notions of devotion to 'res publica'—which had already fed into scholastic and canonist thought on the just war—made commonplace the argument that 'like as a man recevethe his lyving in a region or in a countree, so is he of naturall reason bounde to defende it', indeed that 'among all transitory thinges we are principally bounde to our native countreye'.[14] Kings duly stressed the defensive purposes of their wars. Henry VII insisted that he was resisting the 'hurt and annoyance' plotted by the French against his 'reame and subgiettes' and the 'grete cruelte' of the King of Scots so that his people might 'lyve in rest and peas for many yeres to come'.[15] In 1513 warnings of 'the manyfest daunger' posed to the realm by French and Scots who planned 'to brenne, slee, robbe, and distroy' in various quarters were taken on board by one reader, who underlined 'the manyfest daunger' in his copy of the printed statutes of war.[16] In 1539 Morison explained that Henry was preparing against enemies who 'seke our bloude,...covet our destruction'.[17] The diplomatic isolation brought on by the break with Rome made such arguments more compelling and the great invasion scare of 1545 even more so, perhaps explaining why the enormously heavy taxes of 1545–6 were paid with scarcely a grumble.[18] Scottish raids made the defensive argument yet more immediate in the North than in the South. York was told repeatedly that the king fought not just for his own rights and honour but 'for the defence of this his realme', for its 'suretie', 'saulfty', and 'honour', what was summed up by the 1540s as 'the common welth of our realme and subjects'.[19]

Henry's martial activity was presented as demonstrating both his wisdom and his care for his people. Morison stressed the king's determination to 'diligentely watche, that we maye safely slepe', fortifying the 'ruinous places of the see quostes, by whiche our enemies might sodeynly invade us' such that soon 'England wol than be moch liker a castel, than a realme', and a few years later Becon echoed his message.[20] The theme ran through government correspondence. The king ordered defensive preparations 'lyke a most noble, prudent and corragious prince, mynding the defence and preservacon of all his loving subjects'.[21] The subsidy act of 1545 waxed especially lyrical: despite enemy assaults

> wee the people of this his realme have for the most part of us lived under his majesties sure protection, and do yet so live out of all feare and danger as if there were no warre at all, even as the small fishes of the sea in the most tempestuous and stormie weather do lie quietely under the rocke or banke side

(the metaphor continues beyond the patience of modern, and perhaps even of contemporary, readers).[22] Subjects must surely respond in grateful cooperation, paying their taxes to support the king's charges 'for the defence and preservacion of them theire wiefes and children', charges for which he was spending his treasure, selling his lands, and daily enduring 'manifolde paines and labore of body' and 'travell and care of mynde'.[23] Henry seems to have convinced himself that even his conquest of Boulogne offered such 'great commoditie' for his kingdom that, if he thought of handing it back, his commanders 'and all the rest of our realme' would rather advise him 'of freshe t'employe all our forces to the defence of it'.[24] Elizabeth's tone was less grandiose, but she too had her parliamentary spokesmen emphasize that rather than spend on 'superfluous and sumptuous buildeinges of delighte' she was investing 'in necessarie defence of her people', in 'the common wealth and surety' of the realm, in the navy, for example, 'one of the chiefest defence for the preservation of us and our realm against the malice of any foreign potentate'.[25]

A third justification for legitimate violence was the defence of the ruler's God-given authority against rebels. This was sometimes strengthened by emphasizing the rebels' collaboration with the realm's 'auncient enemies in forreyn partes', but commanders found it rickety.[26] In 1525 the men recruited to confront the amicable grant rebels were unwilling to fight against their 'kindred and companions', their 'neighbors'.[27] In 1549 it was thought that Somerset and Dorset men, despite exhortation to be as 'redie to fight against those rank rebells and papists of Devon as be cometh good subjects', would 'most fayntly fight agaynst the Devonshyre men, theyr neighbors'.[28] Troops from more distant shires—Welshmen in the South-West, Midlanders in East Anglia—seem, together with foreign mercenaries, to have borne the brunt of the fighting in 1549, just as southerners were mobilized against the North in 1536 and 1569.[29]

In Ireland the sense of fighting against rebels was more ingrained, and the Kildare rebellion and subsequent proclamation of Henry's kingship strengthened it further. Already in the 1530s it became quite acceptable to capture fortifications and simply execute all inside, and hard to stop captains and soldiers 'shamefully murdering Irishmen', even those 'beeing at peas and conversant famylierly with theym'; yet also necessary to compromise, for example by letting the townsfolk of Limerick trade with those who were technically rebels, 'though peradventure the same is not all justifiable by extremytie of the kinges lawes'.[30] From the 1550s flexibility and terror were facilitated, in a way done only rarely and with circumspection in English revolts, by the wide use of commissions of martial law under which suspected rebels might be summarily tried and put to death.[31] Here, by the end of our period, ruthless conquest was further justified by neo-Roman ideas of subjecting, or, if needs be, eliminating barbarous natives in the project to construct the colonies of a superior civilization, an approach anticipated in the instructions given to the English forces at Boulogne in 1544 and after to devastate and clear the surrounding area ready for colonial occupation.[32]

Meanwhile a fourth justification, the defence of true religion, was mutating. In the late fifteenth century Englishmen in ones and twos still took the cross to fight the infidel, while the English branch of the Knights Hospitallers survived in some vigour to its dissolution in 1540 and revived under Mary.[33] But already for Morison in the 1530s fighting in defence of Henry's Reformation made Englishmen's enemies, 'not so moche oures, as Goddes ennemies'.[34] Some English Protestant writers, while stopping short of Anabaptist pacifism, may have sought to argue that even wars for religion were immoral and best avoided.[35] But the message did not get through. In 1549 young King Edward VI wrote in his homework that it was glorious to fight for true religion 'as often happens in contemporary wars'.[36] By the 1560s some felt sure that when defending Elizabethan England they were defending the gospel, and that Elizabethan England should do more to defend the gospel elsewhere. In his sermon at the opening of parliament in 1563, Alexander Nowell, dean of St Paul's, explained that Elizabeth's 'most holy wars' in Scotland and France had been made 'without ambition', not only for 'the surety of this our realm' but also 'for conscience' sake', to defend those whom her enemies of their 'devilish pretensed purpose' planned to destroy.[37] By the end of her reign the duty to crush rebels and civilize the Gaelic natives in Ireland and the duty to resist popery in brotherhood with the Huguenots and the Dutch came together under the banner of national defence to ward off successive Spanish armadas and subdue Irish lords in league with Spain. In this context the militia trained bands, under the control of a lieutenancy loyal not just to Queen Elizabeth but to the vision of her reign held by the inner ring of her council, became the citizen army of a Protestant monarchical republic.[38]

A different but historically persuasive justification for international war was as an antidote to civil war, for, as Giovanni Botero would put it in 1589, 'military enterprises are the most effective means of keeping a people occupied'.[39] In preparation for his French campaign of 1475 Edward IV argued that 'a notable and a mighty werre outewardes' was the best remedy for 'the long continued troubeles and divisions of this our reame of England'; indeed that 'it is nat wele possible, nor hath ben seene since the Conquest, that justice, peax, and prosperite hath continued any while in this lande in any king's dayes but in suche as have made were outward'.[40] Henry VIII did not put things quite so explicitly, but he did insist repeatedly that his royal house had rescued the country from disputed succession and dire civil conflict and that rebellion might revive such division.[41] In 1536, as rebellion spread across the North, Sir Richard Morison asked 'Is there any in Englande, that hathe not harde of Palme Sonday filde, Blacke hethe felde, and many other... These two feldes how many wydowes made they, howe many fatherles chylderne, what bloode they coste us.'[42]

Palm Sunday field, Towton, bloodiest battle of the Wars of the Roses, loomed large in historical memory. Chronicles reckoned there were 20,000 or more slain and John Leland noted that it took five pits, still visible seventy years later, to bury them.[43] As England faced invasion in 1539, Morison structured much of his *Exhortation to styrre all Englyshe men to the defence of theyr countreye* around the antithesis between the rebellions of 1536–7, which it seemed 'wold have done excedynge moche hurt to England', and the glorious external wars of Edward III, Henry V, and Henry VIII.[44] It was also recognized that civil war had weakened England against her external enemies. Jean Berteville, a French mercenary captain serving Edward VI, must have picked up from his English colleagues if he had not already worked out for himself the general if not strictly accurate principle that English losses—Normandy, Guyenne, Roxburgh—had always taken place in time of civil dissension.[45]

The printed historical literature of the age enshrined the same contrast. The simplest, smallest, and most numerous historical works were the *Short cronycle, Cronicle of yeares,* and *Breviat cronicle* texts printed at London and Canterbury in a score of editions between 1540 and 1561.[46] For these histories St Albans, Northampton, Wakefield, Towton, Edgecote, Barnet, and Tewkesbury were each 'a cruell battayle' or 'a cruell fight', five of them killing 10,000 men or more, 36,700 at Towton 'and all Englyshemen'.[47] In contrast Edward III and the Lancastrian captains did 'noble prowes' in 'feates of armes', 'noble feates', and 'valyaunt actes', and Agincourt sometimes occupied almost a page by itself.[48] Henry's own wars also loomed large. Early expeditions and the campaigns of the 1520s framed fulsome rehearsal of the triumphs of 1513, as Henry 'dyscomfyted the power of Fraunce' and took Théroaunne and Tournai, while 100,000 Scots were defeated and their king slain at Flodden, and of the 1540s, Edinburgh destroyed and Boulogne so 'victoryouslye conquered' that it 'woulde have comforted all true Englishe men's hartes to have hard and sene the vyctorye and conquest'.[49] In the editions of the 1550s and 1560s, Henry's last French war occupied as much space as the reigns of Edward V, Richard III, and Henry VII put together.[50] Longer texts from the 1530s to the 1560s, Fabyan's, Cooper's, Grafton's, and Stow's Chronicles, told the same story of 'terrible and cruell' civil wars and great victories over France and Scotland, and it was not just the kings who were heroes.[51] Pinkie was won by the wisdom, policy, and valour of the English captains 'and the good stomake of our souldiours'; even the siege of Le Havre showed the 'valiaunt harts and stout courages of al our countrey men', who fought on although the 'streates lay full of the stinking corpses not hable to be buried for the multitude of them that died' from the 'dreadfull plague'.[52]

There was more to read on England's glorious martial past and present. Caxton urged lovers of chivalry to reflect on the deeds not only of Arthur's knights but of Edward I, Edward III, and Henry V and their companions: to find out about Sir Robert Knolles, Sir John Chandos, and the rest, he urged, 'rede Froissart'.[53] Leland, Fabyan, Coke, the *Breviat cronicle*, and Morison all referenced Froissart, as did one reader annotating Cooper's Chronicle, while Nicholas Wotton, on embassy at the imperial court in 1544, used Froissart's work together with printed Scottish histories to explain to doubters why the capture of Edinburgh was so significant.[54] Access was facilitated by Lord Berners' massive translation of Froissart, published at the king's command in 1523–5 and reprinted in the 1540s and 1560s, such that Stow could call Froissart in 1570 'common in men's handes of the translation of the noble J. Bourcher out of the French into Englishe'.[55]

A long poem about the Agincourt campaign was printed in 1536, there were new English and Latin lives of Henry V, and young Elizabethans collected brief Latin verses on his victories.[56] The contemporary work that did most to place Henry VIII's wars in this framework was Hall's Chronicle, in which nearly half the history of England since 1399 was taken up by Henry's 'triumphant reigne'. It was a large book, but marketable, with three editions between 1548 and 1560.[57] In 1550 the countess of Rutland bought a copy, in 1559 the earl of Bath's London agent was trying to get him one along with a picture of the new queen (price 26s 8d), and other chronicles in print and manuscript soon began to refer to it.[58] The final piece in the jigsaw was placed by the news publications we considered in Chapter 2. Hall's treatment of Henry's last war against Scotland incorporated the text of the king's declaration of war, while printed chronicles referred for details of Pinkie to Patten's 'expedicon in to Scotland'.[59]

It is hard to know how readers responded to this material, but some early users did mark or annotate passages on Anglo-Scottish or Anglo-French relations in printed English or Latin chronicles, reaching from Edward I and Edward III through Agincourt to Thérouanne, Tournai, Flodden, Boulogne, Pinkie, and Saint-Quentin.[60] At least four had an unhealthy taste for totting up the numbers of Scots killed in battles.[61] Some showed their thoughtful engagement by writing different names for battles in the margin, 'Scotishe fielde' for Flodden, 'Muscleborough fielde' for Pinkie, or marking turning points: 'Cherburge the last towne that was lost in Normandy'.[62] Others commented on politics—'cause wherefore [En]gland clames the [cro]wne of Franse'—or strategy—'the cause why France was lost'—or tactics: one wrote 'archers' next to Crécy, another 'archers of those dayes' next to Agincourt, adding by their use of stakes 'stratagema sagittariorum'.[63] One early sixteenth-century reader annotated both the Hundred Years War from beginning to end and the major events of the Wars of the Roses, including the marriage between 'Owen a welche man of low degre' and 'a quen' by whom he had 'yssew', without apparently realizing that this was a reference to the Tudor ancestry of Henry VIII.[64] William Paget and Thomas Audley, presumably on the basis of such reading of chronicles, made similar historical reflections to these annotators. Paget thought the English might still use the 'old policyes of England' to defeat French cavalry and Audley proposed that one should put well-armoured pikemen in the front rank, 'which in old tymes was called men at armes on foote, for that thei were better armyd and also were men of more force and experience than th'other were'.[65]

The printed chronicles mostly derived from a tradition of manuscript chronicle writing which persisted in its own right. Loquacious memoirists like Charles

Wriothesley, Henry Machyn, and the Greyfriars chronicler retailed military news as it came into London.[66] Much briefer chronicles kept at Ashridge, Canterbury, London, Newcastle, Tenterden, and Worcester all noted the capture of Boulogne and sometimes other events.[67] Those writing at Calais, Plymouth, and Butley Priory picked out local wartime news, genealogical compilers mentioned Henry's victories of 1513, and those adding stanzas on his reign to historical poems stressed his 'martiall actes' as 'a conqueror...a prince invictissimus'.[68]

The landscape too could be read as a historical catechism. Memorial chapels marked the site of internecine slaughter: outside Shrewsbury, on what locals still called 'the heathe called the battell field'; at Saxton, near Towton; at Barnet; at Tewkesbury, where Edward Prince of Wales was venerated; at Dadlington for the dead of Bosworth.[69] Where there were no chapels there were crosses, at Hedgeley Moor, at Northampton, at Wakefield, where people still talked in Leland's time about the sad death of the young earl of Rutland.[70] In his travels Leland heard tell of many ancestors struck down or houses defaced in the late 'civile warre' and Bosworth, Nibley Green, and other encounters were commemorated in long-lasting oral traditions.[71] The blessings of 'our long peace and quietness within the realm' since the civil wars, conversely, were evident in the building of fine houses rather than castles, or so Thomas Smith argued in 1549.[72]

Sites and monuments spoke equally of the successes of foreign war. Leland noted churches and castles built by the heroes of the Hundred Years War, Trinity College, Pontefract, and Bunbury College, Cheshire, by Sir Robert Knolles and Sir Hugh Calveley, 'companions and great menne of warre'; Ampthill Castle, Beverston Castle, Stourton Castle, and Sudeley Castle, all 'by spoyles goten in Fraunce'; Hampton Court, Herefordshire, and parts of Farleigh Hungerford Castle, based on the profits of French prisoners.[73] Leland did note those killed or ransomed in France, or ports burned in French raids, but his general impression was positive.[74] Battles against the Scots could be pin-pointed in the northern landscape but were most visible at Durham, where the banner of David II, captured at Neville's Cross, hung in the cathedral, a wooden cross marked the site of the victory, and an explanatory table gave details of the battle and its heroes.[75] After Flodden, Heaton Castle remained visibly beaten by the Scots, but the captured standards joined the trophies at Durham.[76] As he toured the coasts, finally, Leland saw king and subjects working together in his own time to defend the realm: blockhouses and bulwarks made by towns, by gentlemen, 'by the contery', and castles 'late begon by the king'.[77] In Ireland, as ever, the dynamic was rather different: Lord Leonard Grey left one sliver of a battered and captured castle of the O'Connors standing, 'to that entent, that Irishmen moght see to what purpose the keping of ther castels servithe'.[78]

Henry's subjects knew how to fit his campaigns into these histories. Nicholas West, dean of Windsor, wished in a letter of 1513 that the king might return from campaign 'with as grett honour as ever had any off his predecessors in Frawnce'.[79] In the wake of 1513, petitioners referred to Henry's 'noble and victorioux warres' or requested his signature with his 'most victorious hand'; from the late 1530s, his men in Ireland fell over each other to wish him 'moche victory', 'contynuall victory over your ennimyes', 'the full establishement of your moste glorious commenced vyctories'; but it was above all after the capture of Boulogne that 'victorious' was the epithet Henry wanted to hear.[80] Henry Parker, Lord Morley duly dedicated the 'Lyfe of Thesius' he gave the king at New Year 1545 to his 'most victoryus' monarch.[81] Ordinary subjects joined in. In November 1544, Edmund Kene of Deane, Hampshire, dated his will in 'the most noble and victorious' reign of Henry VIII.[82] And it did not stop with Henry. Edward's councillors had him write to York in 1548 that he needed troops to fight the Scots to preserve the gains won by 'our victories upon them in these our tender yeres'.[83] In November 1557, perhaps flushed with news of Saint-Quentin, John Greene of Marske, Yorkshire, dated his will in the 'moist victorius renes' of Philip and Mary.[84]

It was possible to ponder history more analytically. Some still found success, comparing the submission of the Irish to Henry to that achieved at greater cost by Richard II, or judging in summer 1543, after the treaty of Greenwich and the proclamation of Irish kingship, that 'never prynce hath had so gret and noble a conquest of Irland and Scotland, as the kinges majeste our master hath at the present'.[85] Some posed challenges, the marquess of Winchester telling Exeter corporation as Calais tottered in 1558 that the king, queen, and realm 'had never suche an injury offered unto them syns Edward the thirds tyme'.[86] Some raised questions. Would Henry have to begin a new conquest of Ireland like Henry II, put in as much effort there as Edward I had to subdue Wales, fight off Scottish intervention in Ulster as in the days of Edward Bruce?[87] Thomas Barnabe worried in 1552 that 'we should not fynd the realm of Fraunce after the sort that we did for sixscore yeres agone, when we did conquere yt. For...then the duke of Normandy, and the duke of Brytayne, and the duke of Burgoigne, were al three agaynst the French king, and now yt is knytt al to one realm.'[88] Whether consciously or not, he was both echoing the analysis of those expert observers of the balance of power Machiavelli and the Venetian diplomatic service, and picking up Edward IV's line of argument from the 1470s that the promise of alliance with the dukes of Brittany and Burgundy, being 'two the myghtyest prynces of Fraunce', made a unique opportunity for Edward to 'entre and challenge the right that to hym appartegneth in Fraunce' and to 'acheve th'entent of his conquest'.[89]

For some, the trophies of past triumph and stories of civil strife were very personal. Sir David Owen, who lived until 1535 and led 103 men in the rearward of Henry's army in 1513, had tapestries showing Henry V, Henry VI, the dukes of Clarence, Bedford, and Gloucester, and 'diverse other great men'. He was the bastard son of Owen Tudor, who had fought for Henry V, married his widow, and been executed after Mortimer's Cross, that 'Owen a welche man of low degre' our chronicle reader did not recognize.[90] Oral memory too keyed battles into personal histories. In Yorkshire, Lancashire, and Gloucestershire, deponents in court cases used Flodden as a point of reference in Elizabeth's reign and beyond. The historic weight of Flodden was evident in anticipation from the wills made by those going to 'the felde agaynste the Scottes', 'to do battle against the king of Scotland for the defence of the realm of England', and in retrospect from the epitaph of Sir Marmaduke Constable, one of its three verses entirely devoted to the battle.[91] In the marches Blore Heath had something of the same significance and in 1543 the vicar of Much Wenlock buried John Trussingham, 'an aged lame man' from the local almshouse, who claimed to have been there.[92] In a different way the alliterative qualities of 'the warres of Turwine and Turneie' bore them forward through mid-Tudor diplomatic letters and court cases into Elizabethan drama and historical writing.[93] Some events stuck because of their horror: in a court case of 1551 Christopher Leynam recalled how he had been at the burning of the 'Carrick of France and the Regent of England'.[94] Others were of obvious significance: the great storm that prevented the relief of Calais became proverbial as 'the wind that blew awaie Calis', 'the great tempest that happened at the losse of Calice'.[95] Ballads may have helped enshrine certain encounters in popular memory, Bosworth and Flodden above all, Pinkie and the Howards' chase after Andrew Barton, the loss of Calais and English efforts against 'the cruel tyranny of the Guise'.[96]

Written records tied the king's wars into institutional histories. The London livery companies recorded in their accounts every time they went out to welcome Edward IV or Henry VII back from battle.[97] Merton College, Oxford noted Henry VII's campaigns domestic and international into the College Register and York put a substantial account of Flodden in the civic records.[98] At Lincoln's Inn they registered Solway Moss, won 'by the polycye of th'enlishmen, being not the tenth part in nombre to the Skottes' and the capture of Boulogne, 'which was never before gotten by any kyng of England'. The scribe got quite carried away, noting that 'There mought be moche more laudes and worthier thynges herin spoken of the kynges grace then my wyt or my pen can set forth; for, as I there hard say, he sayde himself he wolde never departe thens tyll the towne were goten.'[99] Dating formulae responded to triumph or humiliation. At Heathfield in Somerset in 1513 Richard Hadley started his new account book 'after the wynnynge of Tirwyn and Turnay in Picardi'.[100] At Worcester Roger Warde, surveyor of the suppressed priories purchased for the city, dated his accounts 'after the geting of Boleyn the furste yere'.[101] At Bridgwater a military assessment was recorded dourly in February 1558, 'yn which yere Calyes by the French was takyin'.[102]

It was in the king's interest to channel this sense of historic English war-making into the will to fight specific enemies. This might be done by blurring the lines, as William Worcester did, between the great deeds of great kings and those of the 'Englisshe nacion', done to the 'gret renomme and worship of this reaume'; he pointed out that 'the famous king and mighty prince king Edward the thrid' and 'the prince of blissid memorie King Harry the v^the' achieved what they did only by the 'valiauntnes of Englishe men'.[103] John Dudley at Pinkie seems to have taken this line, echoing Audley's model speech in reminding the English troops of the honour passed on to them by their predecessors, who were more accustomed to victory than defeat.[104] Another technique was to tell the English that foreigners thought they had declined from their ancestral valour. Morison claimed to have heard a foreign gentleman remark that 'Th'actyvitie of Englyshmen hath ben greate, if histories be true', but 'it is nothynge so nowe...they have ben of good hartes, couragyouse, bolde, valiant in marciall feates: But those Englyshe men are deade'.[105] Foreigners from Wilwolt von Schaumburg in 1492 to the duke of Aarschot in 1543 did indeed evaluate the English soldiers they met on campaign in the light of those they had read about in chronicles.[106] The decline of archery may have posed a problem here. At least until the 1550s foreigners, whether planning crusading campaigns or merely reporting on their visits to England, associated English military prowess inextricably with the bow, and its decline may have left Englishmen wondering where their talents lay.[107]

A third technique was to speak regularly of the king's and the realm's ancient enemies. Government correspondence referred to the Scots from Edward IV's time to Mary's as the king's 'ancient enemys', his 'auncient adversariez', or, remembering claims to English overlordship, his 'enemys and rebells', though with the more complex relationships of Elizabeth's reign language was moderated.[108] The French king was the king's 'auncient enemy', the French, with their 'perverse and most cruell purpose', the 'auncyent enemyes' of the realm.[109] The repetition of these formulae by local authorities, urban and noble, and even more so by individuals or their clerks in wills or lawsuits, suggests that these ideas were absorbed.[110] So do the comments of foreign observers. A Spanish merchant reported that 'the best word an Englishman can find to say of a Frenchman is "French dog"', a Flemish captain that 'Englyshe menne' habitually 'fyght wythe a good harte agaynste Frenche menne'.[111] The Venetian diplomat Giovanni Michiel, more coolly analytical, spoke of Anglo-Scottish relations in terms of 'the hatred which neighbouring nations generally entertain one towards another, which is increased, in this instance, by constant wars, old quarrels, and disputes about confines'.[112]

War became a credibly national effort because of the way armies were composed. In Henry's wars the boys from the Mersey and the Thames and the Tyne came together, at Flodden where Howard followers from East Anglia and Sussex joined the levies of Lancashire, Cheshire, and Yorkshire to back up the borderers, at Thérouanne and Tournai where retinues from all over southern and Midland England were afforced by contingents from Cumberland, Northumberland, Yorkshire, and Cheshire, and large companies from North and South Wales.[113] The first response to invasion, it is true, was to call upon the North to resist the Scots and the South to resist the French, but for larger operations more complex arrangements came into place. The homes of the retinue leaders in the vanguard of the army sent against Scotland in 1497 showed the wide distribution one would expect from its dependence on the king's household men, spread across the realm from the West Country to Yorkshire and from Carmarthenshire to Kent as a royal affinity to secure political control.[114] The homes of those levied to fight as soldiers in France in 1557 again suggest a national effort, with large contingents from Yorkshire and Wales as well as southern England and a range from Devon to Cumberland and Northumberland. Some surprising omissions—Essex, Cornwall— disappear when we add in those levied as pioneers or miners. When we compare this recruitment pattern as best we can with the manpower available as indicated by musters, it appears that some areas, Norfolk for example, were lightly burdened for no apparent reason, while the North-West, North-East, and north Midlands were held in reserve for war with the Scots. When it came a few months later they were indeed called to reinforce the borders.[115]

Those who organized military effort at local level were likewise drawn together into what they sometimes called 'the defence of the realme', as borough officers and churchwardens recorded with increasing frequency where their soldiers were sent.[116] Just as civil war in the fifteenth century had raised southern fears of pillaging northerners, so account books sometimes showed the divisive effects of civil conflict: in 1483 when the 'Kentish men' rose and the 'Northern men' came to defend the king, in 1536 'when the insurrection was in Lincolnshire', or soldiers went 'ayenst the northen men'.[117] In contrast, as Morison repeatedly stressed, the needs of national defence rose above the divisions evident in the revolts of 1536–7.[118] For these purposes soldiers went to Portsmouth or Berwick, or to Boulogne, Saint-Quentin, or Le Havre, to Guelders, Scotland, or Ireland.[119] Sometimes the significance and immediacy were palpable. Faversham sent its men to Dover in 1558 'at what tyme Calice was besyged', spending £2 8*s* 8*d* on meat and drink for the town's men 'lyinge longe at Dover at the besiege of Callyce'.[120]

Those who stayed at home were expected to pray for the king's success. The muster commissioners for Herefordshire in 1539 identified those fit to fight, those unfit but possessing arms and armour, and other 'pore subjects...not mete for the warre and being of no abilitie to have abilamentes of warre', whom they left out of the muster book, 'referryng them to pray to all mighty Godde for your moste roiall estate long tyme prosperously and joyously t'endere'.[121] Local authorities organized such prayers to 'the gret God of batells'.[122] At London in 1523, on the anniversary of Agincourt, the bishop, judges, mayor, and aldermen led a general procession to pray for the army in the North, where a battle with the Scots was thought to be imminent.[123] Communities were also told to celebrate victories, to show that 'the kynges highness and his people be glad and joious'. Bonfires, bell-ringing, and beer in the streets combined to make what contemporaries called a 'triumph'. Battle after battle, conquest after conquest was greeted in this way: Berwick, Thérouanne, Tournai, Flodden, Pavia, Edinburgh, Boulogne, Pinkie, Saint-Quentin. The external successes, Boulogne above all, attracted much more fuss than the defeat of rebels. They also roused more excitement than peace treaties, the opposite of the situation in the Low Countries, where peace, with its renewal of trade and removal of ravaging armies, caused hearty festivity. The only rivals for attention in England were the births of princes that promised a secure succession and with it domestic peace. Prince Edward's birth was the only celebration of Henry's reign that outshone the bonfires and bells for Boulogne.[124]

The effects of Henry's wars extended beyond the English. They enabled the Welsh to serve the crown while celebrating their Welshness, sometimes in rivalry with their neighbours. Tudur Aled thought Sir Rhys ap Thomas's victories evoked the envy of England and Lewys Daron praised Huw ap Sion ap Madog for capturing Thérouanne when the English could not, while Elis Gruffudd's Welshness coursed through his career, from his outrage at the suggestion that it was the Welsh who mutinied on the campaign of 1523 to his outrage at the suggestion that it was a Welsh soldier who tried to betray Boulogne in 1545.[125] The Welsh in Ireland, who served in large numbers proportionate to their share of the total English and Welsh population, defined themselves by difference from the Irish, in tune with the way the English in Ireland celebrated Wales as a model of the civility to which the Irish should aspire. Lewys Morgannwg praised Sir Rhys Mawnsel for his victories over the wild Irish and Siôn Salbri of Denbigh for the ruthless way he killed them.[126] For those whose ancestors had been longer resident in Ireland, the effects were more ambivalent. Gaelic lords tempted by the offer of assimilation in Henry's Irish kingdom might show their loyalty by raising a company of native kerne for service in Scotland or France, while peasants in the Pale were berated for their degeneracy as they gave up archery, and Old English lords and gentry were alienated from the crown and its New English agents by the conversion of their obligation to military service into a heavy and unparliamentary tax, the cess.[127]

In England identities were reinforced by the way that war made people differentiate themselves from the foreigners in their midst, as orders went out to arrest enemy aliens, confiscate their goods, and, on the borders with Scotland, replace them with English tenants.[128] In 1480–4 and 1496 Scots were arrested at London and Hereford, and in 1513 official returns of Scots and Frenchmen were compiled by local authorities and their goods sold for the king.[129] In 1522 the aldermen of London searched their wards for Frenchmen and then sat with royal councillors to assess their goods, the bailiff of Shrewsbury travelled to Westminster to certify the number of Frenchmen in the town, and at Dover seventeen Scots were listed with their places of birth, marital and employment status, children, and wealth: John Watson, shoemaker, was worth £8 8s 5½d.[130] In 1542 Norwich carefully listed its seventeen Frenchmen, including two embroiderers who worked for Sir Richard Southwell and Sir Thomas Lestrange, and took sureties for their good behaviour, while at Chichester in 1543 Frenchmen were arrested and then exchanged for Englishmen arrested in France.[131] From York, Hull, and Stamford, to Norwich, Oxford, Dover, and Exeter, those born near the borders or at Calais rushed in wartime to prove they were not Scots or French, producing certificates from their local clergy or other reputable witnesses.[132]

Coastal towns, worried about fifth columnists, resorted to making all Frenchmen wear a white cross on their left arm, or expelled them entirely, as Calais did.[133] In the nervous wake of the fall of Calais even those Frenchmen who had denizen status were investigated, for fear they might 'compass imagine and procure sundrye mischeifes and damage to be doone by the Frenche nation to this realme'.[134] York's two smiths, a crossbow-maker, and a surgeon were all well behaved, but an Oxford bookbinder had to find sureties to prove that he was not a spy.[135] In time religious polarities complicated national enmities, and in 1562 refugee French Protestants in the Kent ports were encouraged to move inland rather than thrown into gaol.[136] None the less, those who concealed their identity might be punished, a servant at London whipped in 1563 for not admitting he was French.[137]

At musters foreigners were pointed out and noted down. In 1522, for instance, there were many Bretons in Cornwall and Galyon Hone, the Dutch glass painter reckoned an able billman, at Eton, while at the Northumberland musters in 1539 the commissioners counted 231 Scots.[138] Tensions might escalate when troops were being recruited. At London a Scottish member of the drapers' company refused to be sent to the defence of Portsmouth in 1545 and in 1560 one pewterer had to be fined for telling another that he 'played the Scotes part and had a Scottes hart'.[139] The goldsmiths imprisoned a Frenchman who refused to contribute in cash to their preparations to save Calais but offered a pound of candles instead, a suggestion they evidently regarded as a piece of Gallic sarcasm.[140]

Foreign mercenary soldiers were by no means as common a sight in England as in most continental countries, but they did appear. There were Germans and Swiss under Henry VII, Germans at Portsmouth and on the Isle of Wight in 1512–13, and the garrison warfare of the 1540s around Boulogne, Calais, and the English strongholds in Scotland drew in many more.[141] Nicander Nucius accompanied a Greek captain to the North in 1545–6 and found Englishmen generally well-disposed to foreigners.[142] Matters were tenser at Calais, where Elis Gruffudd denounced the over-paid, over-fed 'depraved, brutish soldiers from all nations under the sun' who served alongside him.[143] The most prolonged exposure of the English to foreign soldiers came during the risings of 1549, and the results were ugly. The western rebels reportedly 'abhored' those sent against them and slew many, while Kett's rebels captured an Italian captain, rejected ransom offers, stripped him of his splendid clothes and armour, and hanged him.[144] Looking back on the risings, one Marian observer claimed that the mercenaries fled the fighting and went off to plunder, until 'afterwards most of them were killed by the peasants', an account that finds unusual confirmation in a coroner's report showing a murderous assault at Huntingdon by a landsknecht, perhaps from the garrisons in Scotland or the army that had beaten Kett's rebels three weeks earlier, who seems subsequently to have been lynched.[145] On campaign abroad there was often trouble between English and German troops. They fell out at Dordrecht in 1481, outside Thérouanne in 1513, near Le Quesnoy in 1543, and at Saint-Quentin in 1557.[146] Conversely when Englishmen in French and imperial pay encountered one another in the 1550s, they tried to avoid fighting and guaranteed one another's ransoms.[147]

One further sign of English martial identity was devotion to St George. His was a royal cult, focused at Windsor and in the order of the Garter, but others joined in. When Henry VII visited Cambridge in 1506, the parishioners of Holy Trinity pounced on him and his lords on St George's Day and extracted contributions of £1 15s 4d towards a statue of St George for the church, more than a quarter of the total cost.[148] He presided over all Englishmen at war, York wishing Richard duke of Gloucester in 1482 'God and Saynt George to be your gude gyde' against the Scots, Sir Thomas Everingham hoping to God, Our Lady, and St George that a relative would do good service in the defence of Flanders in 1479.[149] His cult was an inevitable, though rather belated, victim of the Reformation, St George's Day declared not to be a holiday by a statute of 1552.[150] Already in 1550 the firebrand bishop John Hooper denounced the way in which 'in time past' 'the Englishman' used to call 'upon Saint George, the Frenchman upon Saint Denys, the Scot upon Saint Andrew', making them 'strange gods'. 'But', he continued, 'praised be the mercy of God! I hear say, and believe it, that Englishmen hath resigned Saint George's usurped title to the living God, the God of battle.'[151] If so it may have contributed further to the blending of national war and holy war consummated under Elizabeth.

Warfare cultivated loyalty to the crown as it displayed royal magnificence. We think first of palaces, pageantry, and progresses when we consider how the Tudors showed their subjects the greatness that commanded obedience, but the king at war was a splendid sight. Henry VII in 1492 wore a jewel-encrusted helmet, left London 'wyth honourable tryumph', and crossed to France with a gilded crown at the masthead of his flagship.[152] Henry VIII in 1513 wore gilded and engraved armour and, when he expected battle, ordered all his rich tents put up, topped by royal heraldic beasts.[153] Something of this grandeur was present even when the monarch was not. For his campaign in Guelders in 1511 Sir Edward Poynings was equipped with a silken standard of the cross of St George, seventeen feet long, and twelve eight-foot pennons of the same design, and in the following year the earl of Surrey was issued with a green and white standard six yards long, bearing the red dragon with flames, and the marquess of Dorset with banners of the arms of the duchy of Guyenne and a picture of St George.[154]

For those at sea or in port the navy was also an impressive sight (see Fig. 7.1). Great ships, painted with the royal arms and flying flags of St George, bore names redolent of royal power and dynastic identity.[155] Under Henry VII there were the *Regent* and the *Sovereign*, under Henry VIII the *Henry Grace à Dieu*, the *Mary Imperial*, the *Falcon in the Fetterlock*, *Portcullis*, and *Peter Pomegranate*, in honour of the Yorkist, Beaufort, and Aragonese badges. Under Edward and Mary came the *Double Rose* and the *Philip and Mary*, and under Elizabeth the *Elizabeth Jonas*, named to commemorate the queen's rescue from her enemies, as miraculous as that of Jonah from the whale.[156] Fortifications similarly were garnished with royal arms (see Fig. 7.2), badges, and loyal inscriptions, 'God save King Henry' and 'God save Prince Edward' carved in wood at St Mawes and more elaborate Latin invocations in the stonework, composed by John Leland.[157] Individual soldiers got to play their part in the dynastic pageant when their towns—Norwich and Plymouth in 1497, London in 1513, York in 1523—chose to dress them in green and white, the Tudor livery colours.[158] The effects of all this were amplified by the dissemination of texts and images. Hall's Chronicle was relentless in its depiction of the magnificence of Henry's wars and, while English printers were not yet capable of showing the king at war, the more sophisticated entrepreneurs of Antwerp obliged with images which must have been available on the English market given the lively London–Antwerp trade (see Fig. 7.3).[159]

The idea that Henry's wars were glorious, as a manifestation of magnificence, as a perpetuation of the Hundred Years War, and as a prophylactic against civil unrest, was not unquestioned. Erasmus, his English friends, and some of their Protestant successors combined classical and biblical ideas to argue that war was irrational, ignoble, and unchristian.[160] More had his Utopians pity their enemies, for they knew that subjects 'don't go to war of their own volition but are thrust into it by the madness of princes', and in his epitaph he spent as many lines on his role in the peace of Cambrai of 1529 as on his whole public career up to that point.[161] Some of those who opposed the amicable grant in 1525 thought that rather than spend on war, Henry would have done better to imitate his father, 'which lakked no riches or wisdom to wynne the kingdome of Fraunce if he had thought it

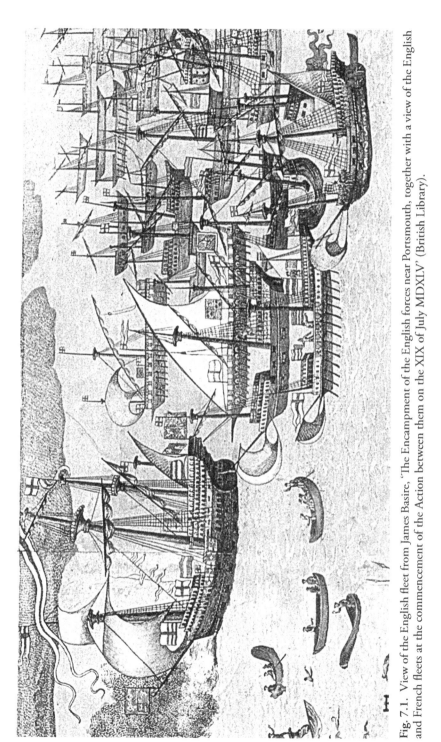

Fig. 7.1. View of the English fleet from James Basire, 'The Encampment of the English forces near Portsmouth, together with a view of the English and French fleets at the commencement of the Action between them on the XIX of July MDXLV' (British Library).

Fig. 7.2. Royal arms over the entrance to St Mawes Castle, Cornwall. Photograph by the author.

expedient'.[162] But such unequivocal opinions seem always to have been in a minority and while mid-Tudor policy-makers adopted some of the Erasmian analysis of war and peace, they also made much more pragmatic calculations about national interests and capacities.[163]

Many ingredients contributed to English identity in the sixteenth century: a shared history and legal culture reaching back to Anglo-Saxon times, an increasingly flexible vernacular language, Renaissance ideas of citizenship, and Reformation ideas of religious destiny.[164] But within that wide framework Henry's wars marked his England, especially in their dialogue with a Hundred Years War that remained, it has been argued, 'fundamental' to the sixteenth century's 'fraught constructions of linguistic and national identity'.[165] His wars killed more people and built more buildings than his Reformation and filled more space in contemporary historical writing, and they did as much as the Reformation to shape the reigns of his successors. Under those successors three very different intellectuals expressed overlapping views on how the late king's wars fitted into English history and shaped the relationship between the king and his people. They were William Thomas, who served as clerk to Edward's privy council but was executed by Mary, Sir Thomas Chaloner, a diplomat for Edward, Mary, and Elizabeth, and the anonymous author of a Machiavellian treatise on the government of England presented to Philip II.

For William Thomas, Henry's wars had aimed to defend the peaceable English in Ireland against the barbarous Irish and, having done so, to bring the Irish by conciliation 'to the state of civil, reasonable, patient, humble, and well-governed Christians'; to turn the ancient contention between English and Scots to one 'perpetual united people, and peace' by the marriage of Edward to Mary; and to

Fig. 7.3. Portrait print of Henry VIII by Hans Liefrinck of Antwerp, 1538–44 (Rijksmuseum, Amsterdam).

claim reasonable compensation by the conquest first of Thérouanne and Tournai, then of Boulogne, for the tribute owed by the French kings to the English in right of their claim to the throne of France.[166] Chaloner agreed that Henry's wars were not fought for 'greedy ambition', but thought he aimed to keep the balance between his neighbours the Habsburgs and Valois, each driven by a 'destructive lust for empire', to reprove the French for their barbarous alliance with the Ottomans and the Scots for their treaty-breaking, and to defend his subjects against the great danger of invasion, thus 'preserving the homeland for the people and the people for the homeland'.[167] He came close to modern analysts of state formation in arguing that 'Henry was compelled to levy taxes greater than those of his predecessors because the power of neighbouring kings had grown exceedingly.'[168] The Machiavellian treatise took for granted that rulers made war, but argued that Henry had quickly remedied the weakness of the kingdom, which he found 'without trained soldiers and without an experienced commander'.[169]

When it came to Henry's achievements, all three authors concurred. Though capturing Boulogne and burning Edinburgh were impressive, Henry's annus mirabilis was 1513, as he achieved 'glorious victory...as much by the conquest of Thérouanne and Tournai and the ignominious flight of the French as by the rout of the Scots'.[170] They all caught too the ambiguities of Henry's military machine. His fortress-building was picked out by Thomas and by Chaloner, who also stressed his collection of cannon, his encouragement of the breeding of war-horses, and his construction of 'a handsome and mighty fleet' of 'ships, built much larger than others by new methods'.[171] Yet the Machiavellian treatise stressed that while in 1513 he had armed tens of thousands of his subjects, 'when the war was over they returned to cultivating the land and to their usual activities without tumult or the thought of it, which came from the prudence of the prince, who knew how to train them and make use of them in war and how to use his authority to order them back to their trades in peacetime'.[172] Chaloner too noted this ability to mobilize and demobilize and argued that Henry's subjects accepted this, 'confident that he undertook nothing in vain'.[173]

It was precisely this dependence of Henry's war-making on subjects who were at best part-time soldiers, indeed part-time taxpayers, that tied his wars so closely into his people's conceptions of national history and national identity. They gave war a place in the memories of families, and not just the gentry, the Clervaux of Croft in Yorkshire who lost John Clervaux 'in the kynges service at the Scottisfelde' or the Cleres of Ormsby in Norfolk who lost Thomas Clere after service at Montreuil, his nephew Robert at Pinkie, and his brother Sir John in a raid on the Orkneys in 1557.[174] John Astley, bottle-maker of Coventry, left £2 in 1564 to the son of his brother who had been killed at Saint-Quentin seven years earlier.[175] Decades later, Archbishop Sancroft learnt the story of his grandfather's great-uncle, drowned on the way to Boulogne in 1544 when the rolling guns in his ship overturned it.[176] England's military arrangements also made it fit better than many of its neighbours the classical ideal of a citizenry mobilized to fight in defence of the common weal. Already in the 1510s it could be argued, admittedly by an author comparing the English with the Irish rather than the Swiss, that 'the kinges armye in Ingland is the comyns', that no 'comen folke in all this worlde is soo mightty, and soo strong in the fylde, as the comyns of England', and that this was why no 'comen folke in all this worlde maye compare with the comyns of Ingland, in ryches, in fredom, in lyberty, welfare, and in all prosperytie'.[177] It was of course ironic that such formulations reached an ever more classical perfection just as recruiting practices in the real world made an ever clearer distinction between a respectable citizenry organized for self-defence, a small and sometimes disgruntled set of men bent on military careers, and a class of often unwilling recruits sent to join them in their campaigns.

It is often said that generals fight the last war, but Henry took the army of the last war, the Wars of the Roses, used it to refight the war before that, the Hundred Years War, and left his son to refight the war before that, Edward I's failed conquest of Scotland. That sounds like a recipe for failure, yet Henry made conquests, as he knew great kings did: not just in France where he clung so hard to Boulogne, but also in Scotland, where he died still hoping that Edward's marriage to Mary might unite the realms, and in Ireland, where his ablest, or perhaps most optimistic, subordinates combined armed force with political dexterity to raise the prospect of a united and obedient kingdom. Henry's wars left his subjects both traumatized and inspired: there was perhaps more than he intended in W. G. Hoskins's characterization of Henry as 'the Stalin of Tudor England'.[178] Henry's heavy taxation and debasement of the coinage warped the mid-Tudor economy, his assault on France, ambitions in Ireland, and bid to control Scotland overstretched mid-Tudor strategy, and his naval expansion gave his successors both a tool for maritime ambition and a lump in the royal budget. He left to serve his children a generation of captains on land who looked back plaintively to his reign as a time when 'chivalry . . . soldiers . . . and manhood' were 'so much esteemed that he was thought happy and most valiant that sought credit by the exercises of arms' and a generation of captains at sea accustomed to help themselves liberally to the profits of foreign shipping.[179] He left them a body of subjects allergic to painful taxation and recruitment and yet admiring of his victories and his fortifications; a nation prone to congratulate Elizabeth on her measures of rearmament while grudging her the resources to pursue them.[180] He left them the nation that Chaloner, Thomas, and the author of the Machiavellian treatise were appraising. But he also left them the nation that Cecil, Paget, and Bacon were trying, sometimes in despair, to govern.

8

This Busy World of War

Henry fought his wars in a Europe scarred by war. In the East the Ottoman and Muscovite empires were expanding by conquest. The Ottomans took Belgrade in 1521, Rhodes in 1522, and Buda in 1541, not to mention Damascus in 1516, Cairo in 1517, and Baghdad in 1534; the Muscovites Pskov in 1510, Smolensk in 1514, Kazan in 1552, and Astrakhan in 1556. In the South Italy was devastated by two generations of conflict between 1494 and 1559, as the Valois kings of France, the Trastámara, then Habsburg, kings of Spain, and the Habsburg Holy Roman Emperors invaded repeatedly, while Venice, Florence, and the papacy strove to preserve their independence. Valois and Habsburgs clashed further west too, along the Pyrenees, in Provence and Savoy, and all along the borders of the Low Countries, from Luxembourg to Flanders.

At the centre of it all stood the Emperor Charles V, whom Henry met in 1520 and 1522. Charles, or his lieutenants, overran Tournai and Cambrai, Utrecht and Groningen, Milan and Tunis, even Mexico and Peru. They captured Francis I of France at the battle of Pavia in 1525, held off the Ottomans from Vienna in 1529 and 1532, and crushed the German Protestant princes at the battle of Mühlberg in 1547. Yet Charles could get no rest. As he wrote in 1524, already weary more than thirty years before he abdicated his realms in a state of depressed exhaustion, 'Peace is beautiful to talk of but difficult to have, for as everyone knows it cannot be had without the enemy's consent.'[1] His ultimate aim may have been universal monarchy, religious peace in Christendom, or simply good rule and defence of the territories God had given him, but his ultimate means was necessarily to make himself an 'impresario of war'.[2]

Henry's people talked about war, campaigned in force, mustered regularly, and paid plenty of taxes. As we have seen, this shaped the powers and responsibilities of boroughs, parishes, and landed elites and their lines of communication with the crown; it steered government intervention in the economy and invited entrepreneurial responses; it sent individuals to death or adventure; it moulded attitudes to king, nation, and history. But how far were Henry and his realms just being towed along in a wave of general European development in all this—as they were, perhaps, in the growth of global trade, or the quest to recover the values of the classical world, or the urge to spiritual regeneration—and how far was their experience of the world of war idiosyncratic?

It was not only in England that war made the news. All over Europe the calculations of merchants, the interests of war-making monarchs, and the fears of peaceable subjects drove the spread of information about the ups and downs of conflict. Many kings kept their noble commanders or the leading citizens of their towns informed of the progress of war on other fronts and some passed on such tidings.[3] From the 1530s printed news pamphlets flooded Germany, France, and the Low Countries and war was often their main focus. Pictures and maps of towns under siege spread widely in the same period. Printed or hand-written government announcements about victory and peace, the size of armies, and the reasons for taxes had preceded them in most of these markets, as they did in England. For the illiterate there were tidings of war, sometimes subversive or satirical, in the rumours of the marketplace and the ballads of the street singers.[4] Spanish soldiers kept accounts of their campaigns, as English soldiers did, and they were similarly used by contemporary chroniclers.[5]

At Paris and Ghent, as at London, printed news, contemporary histories, public announcements, and private correspondence interacted to produce an understanding of events written down in personal chronicles which might express dismay as well as admiration at the effects of royal policy.[6] Meanwhile prophetic and astrological warnings about war were even more widely spread in Italy than in England, multiplied in cheap print and popular song, and keyed into the events of the early Italian Wars.[7] In France, where the Norman gentleman Gilles de Gouberville bought almanacs with almost as much enthusiasm as Sir Edward Don, prognostications, portents, and prophecies harped on recurrent wars and plagues to build a climate of 'eschatological anguish'.[8] Everyone, it seems, talked and worried about war. Perhaps the English did so less urgently than those more exposed to invasion, but they certainly did so.

English rates of mobilization for war were comparatively high. Attempts to calculate the proportion of national populations under arms at any point before the modern age are sketchy, but they suggest that while most Englishmen who served as soldiers in our period did so only occasionally, perhaps on a single campaign like those of 1513 or 1544, a much higher proportion of Englishmen than Frenchmen or Spaniards served as soldiers at some point.[9] No early modern society could mobilize all its men for war at the same time, however much it adhered to the principle that all must fight together to defend the common good. Even the famously martial Swiss never turned out more than half their equipped men and tried, sometimes ineffectually, to arrange service in rotation.[10] The Spanish militia ordinances of 1495–6 counted on mobilizing only one man between the ages of 20 and 45 in every twelve.[11] The Ottoman sipahi cavalry, supported by land grants, were in theory all available to join in campaigns, but in practice no more than three-quarters of them ever served at one time, and of course they were supported by large numbers of non-combatant peasants.[12] Such limitations were overcome only in besieged towns. When there was sufficient political will to resist, bolstered by the threat of sack if the town fell, everyone who could take part in the defence did: at Pavia in 1524–5, at Florence in 1529–30, at La Rochelle in 1573, for example.[13]

England's high mobilization rates reflect the fact that it was unusual among major states in depending so largely and so consistently for armed force on the military obligations of individual subjects and the communities in which they lived. But this placed it at one end of a spectrum rather than in a wholly unique position. Various polities retained or revived systems by which towns and villages raised troops not only for local defence, sometimes elastically interpreted, but also for more distant expeditions—the Tyrol, Bavaria, Savoy, Tuscany, Naples, Sicily, the Venetian mainland territories, and so on—while Dutch and German towns held regular musters of their inhabitants to check their military preparedness.[14] These arrangements might of course be adapted to their own purposes by rebels, as they were in the Pilgrimage of Grace or the German Peasant War, and in civil wars even comparatively demilitarized areas such as the Rouergue in the 1560s soon bred urban and village militias under freebooting captains of rival confessional allegiances drawn from, or aspiring to join, the local nobility.[15]

The most striking parallel to the English model, and one equally mixed in its effectiveness, was Sweden, in which an infantry militia of peasant conscripts, slowly trained in the use of modern weapons, was developed from the 1540s alongside cavalry raised by the nobility, artillery bought by the king, and a few foreign mercenaries.[16] The most obvious contrast to the English model—beyond the Ottomans with their sipahi cavalry and their tax-funded standing army of janissary infantry, household cavalry, and artillerymen—was France. Observers agreed that the French monarchs kept their common people unarmed to enhance their own control and depended on their standing companies of noble cavalry and the hire of foreign mercenary infantry. Yet in practice there were repeated, though never wholly successful, experiments with conscripted native infantry, from the francs-archers of Charles VII to the legions of Francis I, while volunteers served in large numbers, coming by the 1540s to form long-serving regular companies.[17]

Communities elsewhere were expected to support military effort as English towns and parishes were, though the details varied. The equipment for the French francs-archers was to be provided at parish expense, and in the 1520s the armour and weaponry prescribed were modernized from the original model of the 1440s.[18] French towns and the surrounding villages had to provide food for the royal troops garrisoned on them even in peacetime, and in wartime those near the borders might be asked for huge contributions to feed the king's camps, while horses, carts, and pioneers were called for to move the king's artillery.[19] Matters were similar across the border in the Low Countries.[20] Warning systems were another communal responsibility, hilltop beacons or church bells among the Swiss and the Tyroleans, trumpets from watchtowers followed by frantic bell-ringing in French towns.[21] Warfare remained a communal and an emotive activity even in the heartlands of commercialized mercenary recruitment. In the Vorarlberg, to the east of Lake Constance, villagers raised money to ransom 250 of their neighbours captured serving as landsknechts far away on the frontier of Hungary in 1552.[22]

Towns everywhere were primarily responsible for maintaining their own fortifications, but found rulers ready to intervene to tell them to spend more or to take over the provision of defences at a cost in money and political freedom. The result was that the latest styles in fortification, especially when fully built in stone or brick, spread very unevenly even in areas much more exposed to invasion than England. Italian and Dutch townsfolk laboured hurriedly to build earth fortifications just as

English townsfolk did, and it was only strategic circumstances that meant that some such efforts were put to the test and others were not.[23] In the same way most towns bought large guns, but there could be tension over the degree to which towns should be equipped to exercise independent military force. In the comparatively centralized English and French monarchies, towns increasingly received artillery from the king to supplement their defences as some compensation for their corralling into royal and national strategies.[24] German towns, in contrast, had considerable freedom to arm and fortify themselves as they thought best, but found the costs of fortification and troop hire prohibitive.[25] Towns in the Low Countries fell awkwardly between these two poles. They kept major stocks of weaponry including cannon, handguns, gunpowder, and shot, and they were more likely to find rulers requesting the loan of their artillery than offering them guns, but they were also likely to be forcibly disarmed or punitively fined if things went wrong in their relationship with the prince.[26] Everywhere haggling over the scale of commitments—even in Switzerland smaller communities tried to reduce the size of contingents demanded of them—mixed with the pride that put civic arms on cannon and tents and commemorated local victories.[27]

Patterns of strategy determined what kinds of burdens communities carried and in some ways English towns and villages got off lightly. English towns were less troubled by garrisons than many in Italy and the Low Countries, and not at all by the citadels constructed from Rome and Florence to Ghent and Antwerp to compel the obedience of restless townsfolk.[28] Similarly the fact that no enemy force tried to land at Weybourne in Norfolk meant that the landscape alterations recommended by the marquess of Northampton in the 1540s, a dike and sluice to flood the town marsh and create an obstacle 'gretly noyous to our said enemyes yf they should chaunce at any tyme hereafter to londe therein', never came into action, unlike the flooding deliberately used to block the Spanish conquest of Holland in 1573–4.[29] War put urban finances under strain everywhere, but no English town faced the massive impact of military expenditure seen in front-line towns like Ghent between 1477 and 1492 and 's-Hertogenbosch in 1506–8.[30]

Complaints that noblemen were abandoning the martial ways of their ancestors could be heard from France and Spain to Italy and reflected there, as in England, both the rise of alternative styles of service and routes to power and the rival attractions of peace.[31] Such participation rates as can be calculated bear out the grumbling: it has been estimated that only some 15 per cent of French noblemen fought in the French Wars of Religion.[32] Where nobles did flock to the colours, so that they made up for example about 15 per cent of the membership of Spanish infantry companies, they came from regions where the nobility was a broad caste with many members far less prosperous than the English gentry.[33] Yet everywhere, even among the Swiss, military leadership remained overwhelmingly a matter for noblemen.[34] French and Spanish captains consumed military treatises just as avidly as their English counterparts and authored them more prolifically.[35]

Among French nobles the language of honourable and self-sacrificial service to the king in war, marked out by courageous acts and often performed in perpetuation of family traditions, was widespread.[36] Indeed, it has been suggested that the ability of French noblemen to identify their sufferings in war with those of Christ on the cross was an important part of their psychology.[37] Noble German landsknecht captains who raised mercenary companies on commission were commemorated with elaborate funerals and tombs in family chapels draped with captured banners, just as much as aristocrats from England, France, and the Low Countries who served in more traditional military roles.[38] Honourable mementoes of great encounters graced their homes—Georg von Frundsberg had Francis I's rich sword from Pavia, Maximiliaan van Egmond-Buren the cup Charles V gave him to commemorate his crossing of the Rhine in the Schmalkaldic War—and fortress bastions immortalized their names.[39] Yet noblemen were not sole masters of their own reputations and public debate could charge a Constable Montmorency with cowardice in France or a duke of Alba with tyranny in the Low Countries.[40]

No English nobleman could match the independent military power of a minor German or Italian prince or even of the Campbell earls of Argyll, with their thousands of clansmen, galley fleet, and artillery train, yet their role in raising troops was important.[41] Many other polities deployed the social influence of the greater and lesser nobility in constituting their armies, but not quite in the same ways as in England. The composition of the companies of heavy cavalry led by noblemen in the standing forces of France and the Low Countries was closely bound up with the running of their households and the construction of their local affinities, and they used the same connections of clientage to recruit infantry and additional cavalry companies when the need arose, arming them from their private arsenals of pikes, handguns, and cannon.[42] When recruiting cavalry some German captains exploited feudal ties, while Flemish, Italian, and, most often, German noblemen, like those in successive generations of the Sittich von Ems family, signed up their villagers, even their serfs, as infantry.[43] Even military entrepreneurs operating on a free market needed trusted subordinates, from muster-clerks and judges to captains, to organize and lead their forces, and these were often drawn from their neighbours, while great noblemen leading armies developed and exploited clientage relationships with mercenary recruiting captains.[44]

Noblemen had to campaign on the basis of their personal credit not only as mercenary enterprisers on land or sea but also as commanders-in-chief. Before the battle of Pavia, Antonio de Leyva, inside the besieged town, had to melt down his plate to pay his men, and Charles de Lannoy had to pawn his plate to keep together the army marching to Leyva's relief.[45] In this sense English noblemen, their men's pay and even coat and conduct money guaranteed by the comparatively effective fiscal machinery of the English state, had things easy. The more personal costs of high-status campaigning, a fine equipage and generous entertainment for subordinates and colleagues, were the same everywhere, as was the occupational hazard of a high ransom if captured.[46] Death rates were higher for some continental nobilities than for the English, especially in civil war: more than one in five of the captains of the French king's heavy cavalry serving in 1562–3 had been killed in action or assassinated by the end of the French Wars of Religion.[47] Private fortresses were of more importance to the defence of territories more threatened by invasion such as the Low Countries than they were in England, but the English were not the only ones to think that the rolling acres of the aristocracy should be put to use in breeding horses for war.[48]

In other countries as in England, successful command brought financial profit for some and high office for others; indeed good management could make serious money even in a losing war, as Sebastian Schertlin did in the Schmalkaldic War.[49] Military competence generally had to be combined with landed wealth to win the provincial governorships and similar offices which in most polities conferred even more power than the English lord lieutenancy. Governorships were central to the coordination of provincial defence in France and in the Low Countries and vice-royalties in the Spanish monarchy, of Milan, Naples, or Sicily for example, more powerful yet.[50] Occasionally military success outweighed ancestry and landed power in such appointments, as when Frundsberg was named chief captain of the Tyrol.[51] In general successful military contracting brought more informal kinds of local influence: in 1567 it was reported that all the lords of Saxony followed the lead of the renowned enterprisers Hilmar von Münchhausen and Georg von Holle.[52] Whatever the formal structure of office-holding, in most border regions, where Scotland met England, for example, where the Habsburg Low Countries met Guelders and France, or where Croatia met Ottoman Bosnia, networks of lordship, kinship, and clientage among the local nobility were vital in the coordin-ation of defence.[53] Noble leadership in war, then, was the norm everywhere, but varied in its operation according to political and social structures. In monarchies, in France and the Low Countries as much as in England, command was expected to be decisive and yet consultative and submitted to the direction of the ruler.[54] In some republics, notably the Swiss city-state of Zürich, harsh political struggles had to be fought to establish the right of the authorities to prevent local nobles acting as military entrepreneurs for foreign rulers.[55]

The economies of many areas of Europe were more severely affected by war than that of England. First Lombardy and then Piedmont were devastated by repeated campaigns in the Italian Wars, just as tracts of Norway and Sweden were laid waste in the Northern Seven Years War, and Livonia ravaged again and again, causing severe and long-term loss of population.[56] Particularly hard hit in the short term were regions, such as Flanders and Brabant in the 1480s, where armies both dis-rupted the rural economy by raiding and choked urban manufacturing by cutting off its trade outlets.[57] On and behind the front lines, plundering or extortion by supposedly friendly troops, sometimes justified by the argument that whoever was supposed to be paying them had failed to do so, but they could not simply go away and leave civilians exposed to enemy attack, was a recurrent problem in Germany and Switzerland, Italy, France, and the Low Countries.[58] In some regions, such as Hainaut, repeated assaults by both hostile and supposedly friendly troops had the long-term effect of moving population away from border areas to safer villages at the other end of the province.[59] Probably the most transformative attacks were those on the areas bordering the Ottoman Empire, which relied on relentless raiding to soften up the targets of its invasion plans.[60]

While it was a commonplace everywhere that food prices were driven up by wars, however elaborate the efforts made by governments to supply their armies, the greater intensity of warfare and the greater scale of trade—worth perhaps five times more per head of population—interacted to give war a stronger role in shaping the commerce of the Low Countries, for example, than that of England. It eliminated the once flourishing grain trade between France and Holland, concentrated control of wine imports in the hands of the minority of rich merchants who could bid the highest prices for safe-conducts, and favoured Haarlem's innovative and high-quality cloth industry over Leiden's less flexible manufactures as traditional trade routes came under wartime stress.[61] Charles V's wars disrupted trade in another way in Spain by his requisitioning of shipping, native and foreign, all around the coasts for longer-range expeditions than Henry's, like those to Tunis in 1535 and Algiers in 1541.[62] Meanwhile some other areas of Europe faced more serious attacks on their local trade than did England. The fact that foreign armies never came near the great internal trade arteries of England by road or river meant that interruptions to inland trade like those on the Meuse in 1554 were never a problem, and England's fisheries and coastal populations got off lightly compared with those of Spain and Italy, facing the bases of the North African corsairs who raided for slaves as well as plunder.[63]

Government action to address such ill-effects was patchy everywhere. Urban, provincial, and princely authorities in the Low Countries naturally put great efforts into trade convoys and fisheries protection and also into fishery truces and the provision of safe-conducts. Differences between the economic interests of different provinces and between the strategic interests of some provinces and of the Habsburg dynasty made it hard to coordinate policy, however, while the English with their simpler political structures, smaller fishing fleets, and shorter trading routes made wafting look comparatively easy.[64] Meanwhile the Spanish, stung by attacks on their Atlantic trade, began to organize convoys between the 1520s and 1560s, first near home and then from the Caribbean.[65] Princes and their ministers found the need to source military supplies more urgent than that to heal the wounds of war. In France, for example, the quest for saltpetre elicited considerable government effort and culminated in monopoly control.[66] In the Low Countries legislation seemed to control illicit exports of horses and armaments with more effect than it did the ravages of an ill-disciplined soldiery.[67]

By modern standards few sixteenth-century governments were successful in taxing the wealth of their subjects. Per capita taxes in real terms fell in Spain from the 1520s to the 1550s, French tax revenues also failed to keep up with inflation after the 1520s, and in both it was only in the late sixteenth and seventeenth centuries that taxes on individuals, so far as they can be calculated, rose in real terms.[68] English monarchs, then, were not alone in struggling to make their taxes work, yet taxes were capable of dangerous economic effects. In other polities where taxation was in general less efficient but much more regular than in England, it had the potential to cause fewer sharp crises but more long-term distortion. Taxation for expansionist warfare depressed the French economy under Louis XI and, far more drastically, the Russian economy under Ivan the Terrible, prompting many peasants to flee their lands and join the Cossacks.[69] Fiscal policies proved economically distorting in more subtle ways in the Venetian mainland territories, where the manufactures of subject cities were constricted by taxation imposed to support the republic's war effort, and in Naples, where the issue of government bonds offering up to 20 per cent interest to fund warfare sucked capital out of trade, industry, and agriculture.[70] Taxation proved temporarily but perennially socially disruptive where it sparked rebellion, in Guyenne in 1542 and 1548 for example, or in the Low Countries, where the duke of Alba's Tenth Penny fatally exacerbated the Dutch Revolt.[71]

It is hard to prove that military demand gave a decisive stimulus to agricultural or industrial production anywhere in early modern Europe, except perhaps in specialized arms industries like those of Liège.[72] The iron-masters of Burgundy, the Gatinais, and the Ardennes did steady business in shot for the French king's artillery, but there, as in England, iron had many other uses.[73] The Venetian state, funded mainly by taxes on trade and consumption, devoted 38 per cent of its expenditure to war in 1555, 58 per cent in 1574, and this redistributed income to those who could supply the right materials or perform the necessary labour for building fortresses, maintaining galleys, or feeding and housing soldiers, but the effects were diffuse.[74] Elsewhere similar factors to those in England came into play. Flemish towns bought up cloth in large quantities to kit out their civic militias and this must have balanced wartime disruption of trade to some extent.[75] Large-scale arms traders did well as armies got bigger and weapons more sophisticated, but they generally traded in other goods too.[76] Different parts of the Spanish realms were established suppliers of different foodstuffs to royal armies and fleets, wheat and wine from Andalusia, salted meat from Galicia, chickpeas from Sicily, cheese from Sardinia; big expeditions made so much work for the bakers and coopers of Malaga that others had to be called in from other towns, but big expeditions were exceptional.[77] The best-known entrepreneurial venture in response to the demand for modernized fortifications was that of Gilbert van Schoonbeke. He brought together bricks from Brabant, lime from Namur, timber from Flanders, and turf from Utrecht to build nine bastions, five gates, and six kilometres of walls at Antwerp in 1549–52 in return for a mighty profit and the right to develop a whole new commercial, industrial, and residential zone of the city. But his career, and the city he fortified, the greatest trading centre in northern Europe, were extraordinary.[78]

In general plunder, corruption, and banking were the economic activities most likely to reap a profit from war. The plundering of goods and taking of prisoners for ransom were important motivations for most troops and helped drive local economies as merchants followed Swiss armies, for example, buying up booty for cash.[79] Wherever war persisted, plunder became an important part of the local commercial landscape just as it did on the Anglo-Scottish border: at Tournai, for example, a French enclave surrounded by Habsburg lands; or in southern France in the Wars of Religion, where Catholic and Protestant communities raided one another; not to mention in the Mediterranean, where slaving and plunder raids criss-crossed the sea, or the Adriatic, where the Uskok port of Senj maintained itself almost entirely by piracy.[80] In France and the Low Countries authorities tried to exploit the profit motive of privateers and pirates to cause harm to their enemies while regulating their activities to limit the damage they did to international relations. Towns such as Dunkirk, Flushing, and La Rochelle did very well out of these arrangements and they formed the basis for successful privateering campaigns by the Huguenots in the French Wars of Religion and the patriots in the Dutch Revolt.[81] Corrupt practices crept into most institutions where money was collected and spent and military systems were no exception.[82] More unusual in comparison to England, whose exposure to large-scale banking in support of state expenditure was limited to unhappy experiments in the 1540s, was the profitable symbiosis between Genoese banking and the Spanish war effort under Charles V and Philip II.[83]

There was little questioning anywhere in Europe that wars might be just. Popes regularly prosecuted wars, Martin Luther eased the consciences of captains, Julius II and Huldrych Zwingli campaigned in person, many humanists glorified generals though others denounced warmongers, and even among the Anabaptists not all communities rejected violence.[84] When the legitimacy of a war rested on the legitimacy of the authority declaring it, the psychological burden of killing was apparently lessened by the sense that war was on the king's conscience not the soldier's, at least until the unsettling fluctuations of royal policy in the French Wars of Religion left commanders to take the blame for slaughter disowned by the king.[85] Whether all men were equally expected to fight in wars was another matter. Across Europe from the mid-fifteenth century, as armies of permanently retained soldiers or regularly hired mercenaries grew and Roman models of military service to the commonweal were adapted to fit current developments, distinctions were hardening between men, who might certainly be expected to fight, but might in practice take steps to avoid unpleasantly active military service, and men of war, whose business was fighting.[86]

In the deployment of their citizens for war, South German towns and those in the Low Countries passed through the same evolution as those in England, but rather earlier. Around 1500, sometimes as late as the 1520s, many were sending out on campaign companies with a high proportion of artisan citizens, sometimes drawn from the widespread urban guilds of archers, crossbowmen, and handgunners. Yet the numbers within urban contingents of neighbouring peasants and substitutes drawn from the urban poor steadily increased, and so did the temptation to hire in whole companies from military enterprisers. By the mid-sixteenth century, respectable civic militiamen stayed home to guard the walls and keep the peace, rather than marching off to war.[87] French town militias and shooting confraternities had gone through the same transition rather earlier, ceasing to campaign perhaps as early as the 1420s, but playing a full part in the defence of towns like Marseilles in 1524.[88] Among the Swiss even in their golden age the hiring of substitutes was routine, so that the young, the rootless, and the rural stood in for the middle-aged, the established, and the urban; the captains sometimes complained, as they did in England, that the lazy and unwarlike were sent for the wrong reasons and the best men stayed at home.[89]

Defiantly exaggerated manliness was part of the flamboyant, costly dress and transgressive behaviour of the landsknechts, fascinating and alarming in equal measure to more settled society as torrents of condemnation and wide sales of military prints suggest.[90] Tall, strong, adult men, some able to show wounds won at battles ten or twenty years ago, were the backbone of the French king's army in the 1560s, but in civil war conditions they used their strength to extort whatever they needed from an intimidated population.[91] Yet adult manhood, patriarchal discipline, and the obligations of citizenship and peace-keeping were bound up with the possession and use of arms in much more stabilizing ways in the traditions of German towns, as they seem to have been among the English militia.[92] French noblemen, like English, recognized that 'the hot passion and ardour of courage' had to be tempered by self-control and obedience to commands, and indeed the whole systematization of tactics and drill can be seen as part of the humanist project of education and social discipline.[93]

Drill could do little to stop massacres, which were recurrent in the sort of situations that brought the English to them: heavy losses, stormed cities, social or ethnic hatreds. The Swiss did have a particular reputation for not taking prisoners, born of their realization that their mass assault tactics would be neutralized if individuals turned aside to secure captives, and fearsomely driven home when men from Lucerne and Zug struck down hundreds of their confederates from Bern when they caught them plundering corpses before the fighting was over at Dornach in 1499, but bloodlust or 'forward panic' could sweep any fighting men away.[94] Extreme violence was also used to obtain ransoms or information from prisoners.[95] The horror of battle, while not a theme for memoirists in the way it would later become, was reflected in landsknecht songs that spoke of wading through blood at Pavia, Italian ballads that told how the corpses on the battlefield at Ghiaradadda fed the dogs for thirty days, and accounts of panics like that sparked by a surprise attack at Schwaderloh, when Count Wolfgang von Fürstenberg stood shouting 'Turn round!' at his men, but they would not listen.[96]

In self-confident military communities ideas of martial honour were readily shared between noble captains and their men, though landsknecht honour blended knightly conceptions of an order dedicated to war, whose wounds were tokens of courage, with those of peasants and urban guildsmen, stressing for example the importance of pay as rightful tribute to skill.[97] Georg von Frundsberg was celebrated in landsknecht songs for such gestures as his preparedness to fight at Creazzo in 1513 rather than accept humiliating terms from the Venetians—'Many enemies, much honour' was his slogan—but also for trying to get his men their just deserts.[98] Such community of interest was more easily cultivated by captains—Sebastian Schertlin was another—who visibly tried to preserve their men's lives and welfare.[99] Protector Somerset was not alone in taking up the spade to inspire his men to dig in: Charles de Lannoy, Emmanuel Philibert of Savoy, and William of Orange did the same.[100]

Towns expected their citizens and guildsmen to own the arms and armour necessary for civic self-defence and inventories and muster lists from Germany and the Low Countries show that they generally did so at a level commensurate with their wealth, age, and social standing and at a technological level ahead of their English counterparts: more than one in six householders in Nördlingen had a gun in 1488, one in four by 1581.[101] In the countryside too weapons were widespread but by no means universal. With adjustments for local traditions and the precocity of German gunnery, the roll-call of armed peasants at Oettingen-Wallerstein in 1525 would not have looked out of place in an English muster return, one in three carrying a pike or halberd, one in four wearing some armour, one in ten with a gun.[102]

The English may have been uncommonly attached to their bows and bills, but authorities all over Europe struggled to persuade their subjects to take up the rulers' weapons of choice. Italian mercenary infantry characteristically used more firearms than the Spanish, French, or Germans, so much so that employers had to force more of them to carry the pike.[103] Even among the Swiss many individuals preferred to wield the halberd or short pike—better for self-preservation if it came to a close fight—rather than the long pike for which the confederates became famous, while those who owned armour had to be encouraged to lend it to those who were actually going off on campaign, and there was a shortage of handgunners when compared with their rivals: only one in twenty of the Bern contingent for the Italian campaign of 1512.[104] For the Swiss with their pike charge and hand-to-hand combat, as for the English with their archery, the attachment to traditional weapons and traditional tactics was a matter not just of inertia, but of emotive self-definition. In his song about the bloody defeat of the Swiss at Bicocca, Niklaus Manuel despised the way their entrenched enemies had hidden in the ground like animals to shoot down the manly onrushing pikemen.[105] To meet specific skills gaps in the use of advanced weaponry, however, even the Swiss would bring in foreign expertise. They hired German artillerymen as the French did, just as those in need of military engineers in France and the Low Countries generally turned to Italians.[106]

Meanwhile modernizers everywhere plodded on with surveys and exhortations. The town of Biberach found in 1540 that about half of its subject peasants had body armour, but only one in six a firearm, and most of those were antiquated.[107] At Ueckermünde in Pomerania in 1543 the ducal authorities did more than complain about ill-equipped subjects turning up to musters, ordering fifteen of the richer townsfolk to buy new armour and weapons more appropriate to their station, just as Henry's muster commissioners would have done.[108] Even landsknechts and others hired on the open market could be made more effective by the supply of plentiful and standardized weaponry from government stores of the sort both the French and the Habsburgs assembled, or, later in the sixteenth century, from stocks bought up by recruiting captains.[109] It was, ironically for rulers, in communities determined to preserve some freedom from princely control that military modernization proceeded to best effect, the towns of Flanders turning out companies with pikes, crossbows, and handguns in the fifteenth century for their revolts against the Valois and Habsburg counts just as for defence against French invasion, and facing repeated, and at length final, disarmament as punishment for revolt.[110] This was not the only situation in which authorities tried to control, rather than promote, the ownership of arms. Many villagers saw their weaponry confiscated after the German Peasant War and rural gun ownership, as in England, was discouraged at both imperial and territorial level to inhibit poaching and robbery.[111]

Before the age of the Elizabethan trained bands and the many contemporary German select militia schemes, formal training is hard to find anywhere except in the occasional musters of ordinance-bound standing armies, but other troops seem at least to have had their fitness to fight checked when they were signed up and where possible militias selected able young men for mobilization.[112] Landsknecht companies and those in the Spanish *tercios* mixed new recruits into small groups with more experienced soldiers who must have been expected to show them the ropes when companies formed up and who took a lead in battle.[113] Fighting together seems to have bound French nobles into 'armed communities', German foot soldiers into 'communities of violence', and Spanish infantrymen into 'a tight warrior society', whether or not they were recruited wholesale from particular towns and villages, as some landsknechts were, or deliberately mixed up by regional origin, as were companies raised in Spain.[114]

Such solidarities did not of course always make bodies of troops amenable to command. Mutinies among German and Spanish troops were regular and organized affairs, much more organized than among the English because of their companies' longer terms of service and stronger internal organization.[115] The janissaries, although technically the slaves of the sultan, were quite happy to mutiny over wage arrears or strategic disagreements.[116] Successful captains had to be good at negotiating with mutineers, though even the greatest might prove powerless before overwhelming discontent, like Georg von Frundsberg before the sack of Rome, and some captains were killed or maimed by their men.[117] Desertion was a problem for many armies, the feared Swiss and Germans included.[118]

The social origins and motivations of recruits seem everywhere to have been mixed. Landsknechts serving in the ranks ranged from urban and rural labourers through cottagers and artisans—some of them skilled builders and masons—to the sons of patricians and lesser noblemen. The Spanish infantry were equally diverse and in both cases, while financial need at a time of population pressure and falling real wages was a prime reason to enlist, a desire for adventure or the need to escape personal difficulties also came into play.[119] At one end of the scale of voluntary service, adventurers who served for plunder rather than pay hovered around the landsknechts, apparently served Flemish towns in the wars of 1477–92, and operated in large numbers on the margins of Swiss armies, some of their raids apparently carnivalesque ventures by young men around Christmas time or before Lent.[120] At the opposite end of the scale, many regimes conscripted prisoners on occasion or offered pardons to bandits like those of Corsica or Catalonia for entering army service, but such characters only ever formed a small proportion of any force.[121]

Death rates seem to have been as variable in other armies as they were in the English. Some detailed pay records, like those for the Spanish army in Naples in 1500–1, suggest very moderate losses on campaigns without major battles or, presumably, major epidemics.[122] In contrast disease regularly cut back armies and on occasion devastated them. In the occupation of Rome in 1527 and the long march into and out of Provence in 1536 the Spaniards may have lost a third of their effectives and in four months besieging Naples in summer 1528 the French lost some two-thirds of theirs.[123] Battles where both sides stood and fought for a long time, like Marignano, could produce heavy casualties, but so could those, like Schwaderloh, where one side fled and pursuit was cruelly easy.[124] It was this that made the ability to steady panicky men, or to rein in those who might make themselves vulnerable to counter-attack and dispersal, such a key skill for com- manders: to stand on foot in the ranks as Frundsberg did at Bicocca or Dudley did at Pinkie, to kneel together after battle and give thanks for preservation, were key gestures.[125] Immediate surgical attention and some longer-term medical care was a feature of many armies, but death was ever-present and it was no wonder spirit- ual care was also thought necessary: Zwingli felt it his duty as a parish priest to accompany his neighbours on their mercenary service.[126] Charitable provision for those maimed in war or those widowed by it was as patchy in other countries as in England. In France it was a matter of occasional royal grants and some access to general charitable provision by religious or urban institutions, while plans for military hospitals there never quite got off the ground.[127] Venice, admittedly, seems to have been more organized, providing pensions for invalid soldiers or assistance to the families of those killed on active service from the 1440s.[128]

The reintegration of former soldiers into society was a problem everywhere. Some demobilized landsknechts settled back into their home areas—easiest of course for young nobles, urban patricians, or students returning from an inter- lude of adventure—or found new work as castle guards, foresters, or noble henchmen, but others begged or stole.[129] Swiss mercenary service generated a class of deracinated and violent veterans whose best option was to look for the next opportunity to sign on for service whether the local authorities approved or not.[130] The most alarming prospect for local governors was that bands of unemployed soldiers might stay together and live off the land, as Swiss, German, and French infantry companies often did, resisting even collective action by princes and cities like that attempted in northern Germany in 1546. This explains contemporaries' admiration for the comparatively peaceful expansion and contraction of Henry's armies.[131]

The combination of royal rights and national defence served to justify war in other countries as it did in England. The king's rights and titles and his rivalries with his unreasonably ambitious enemies loomed large in French justifications of war and appeals to troops before battle.[132] Classical models were drawn in there as elsewhere to blend duty to king with duty to country. Pierre Ronsard assured the French army in 1558 that 'it is a holy war to die for one's prince and defend one's land', just as Charles V's councillors told the towns of Spain in 1522 that natural law and divine law had written in the heart of every man that 'each is obliged to defend his king and his country against those who wish to attack it'.[133] The claim to reserve the right of individual subjects' service for the defence of the homeland was an important aspect of the establishment of sovereignty, for example in Zürich, where men still broke the ban on mercenary enrolment half a century after its con- ception, but by then rarely pleaded ignorance of it or offended repeatedly.[134] Loyalty to king and country was never absolute, but it does seem to have been stronger in old established kingdoms such as England and France than in polities more recently and confrontationally drawn together. Englishmen were occasionally executed for spying for the enemy, but such incidents were far commoner in the Low Countries.[135]

Many nations or regions felt they possessed a historic military reputation that might be burnished or betrayed: not just the English, the Swiss, and the Italians, but the Namurois, the Gascons, the Basques, and so on.[136] For some it was tied to specific sites, for the French, who began soon after the peace of 1559 to visit the battlefields of Italy to ponder on the wars gone by, or the Spaniards, who avoided Metz and its 'wide surrounding countryside whitened by Spanish bones' on their way from Italy to the Low Countries in 1567.[137] In some places its relationship with royal policy was much more complex than in England. The Habsburgs from Maximilian's time on wanted to shape the landsknechts as a German infantry in imperial service, but their success was mixed. Imperial bans on service to other powers were far from effective, yet men recruited for the Habsburgs might massacre those serving their enemies as traitors rather than recognize them as fellow Germans or fellow military workmen. Captains who had cheerfully served Francis I in earlier campaigns swung back towards the Habsburgs in 1543–4 because of their concerns that French power had expanded too far into Germany. Even assertions of the freedom to serve other rulers familiarized Germans with the idea of duty to 'the German nation of the Holy Empire and the beloved fatherland'.[138]

The effects of war on relations between rulers and subjects were also complicated. Machiavelli thought that sufferings at the hands of a ruler's enemies, so long as the ruler was not hated in the first place, might make subjects 'identify themselves even more with their prince'.[139] In the Low Countries it seems that subjects mostly accepted their rulers' explanation that the trials of war were to be attributed to the trouble-making French kings and their allies the dukes of Guelders, but that criticism for mishandled campaigns, excessive taxation, and relentless plundering sometimes reached beyond corrupt ministers and self-interested captains to the Habsburg regents and the rulers themselves.[140] In France, conversely, Charles V functioned as a convenient bogeyman, blamed in government announcements, printed histories, propagandistic verse, fictional allegories, and private chronicles alike for the ambition and trickery that compelled Francis I and Henry II to fight him so often in pursuit of their natural duty to preserve the greatness of their kingdom.[141] Charles himself found contrasting success in his major realms in his efforts to tie his personal glory and dynastic strategy to the perceived interests and historic identity of the political nation. Only in Castile did he secure the commitment needed to underpin his grandest schemes and, at length, those of his son Philip II. Here was a country shaped by the *Reconquista* of territory from the Moors, completed at Granada in 1492; one whose soldiers fought for 'the glory of the king, the triumph of the faith, honour and worldly goods' and readily saw themselves as legionaries of a neo-Roman empire; one whose armies were led by a nobility happy to operate all over a monarchy stretching from Sicily to the Low Countries and out across the Atlantic, while also bargaining for concessions to their freedom of action at home. In Italy and the Low Countries, even in the Iberian territories of the crown of Aragon, matters were less straightforward.[142]

The idea that foreign wars might defuse internal conflicts was widespread. Machiavelli detected it, for example, behind the policy of Ferdinand of Aragon.[143] Admiral Coligny advocated it in promoting French intervention in the Low Countries in 1569–72: he argued that to turn the rival armies in France against the king's enemies abroad would serve to put out the fire that was consuming the realm and return the kingdom to its 'pristine estate, honour and dignity'.[144] His analysis is an indication that in the years after 1559 France and the Low Countries were passing through the sort of explosion of internal tensions no longer contained by external effort that England had suffered from 1450 and that Henry VIII's generation looked back on with horror.

Such arguments fitted the way in which the coordination of military effort consolidated national identities and demonized foreign enemies. The Germans, for example, were drawn together, despite their many divisions, against the tyrannous French-speaking Burgundians in the wars of 1474–7, then against the German-hating Hungarians in 1477–91, then against the cow-loving peasant Swiss in the Swabian War of 1499.[145] The French found walk-on parts in narrating their wars for wicked Englishmen, deceptive and half-Moorish Spaniards, hostile Hainaulters, and unreliable Italians.[146] The different provinces in the Low Countries were more integrated into a single fatherland by their common effort over many decades against the French and their allies than they were pulled apart by divergent strategic priorities, though the balance was mixed. And, crucially, the more the Low Countries drew together, the more they were able to identify and defend their common interests against those of the other elements in the Habsburgs' composite monarchy, generating parallel problems to those the Tudors found in using English and Welsh officials and troops to control an Ireland—or perhaps two Irelands, Gaelic and Old English—increasingly aware of difference from its neighbours.[147]

Specific phenomena sharpened these effects by making individuals identify those with whom they shared an identity and those with whom they did not. Some developments ran along the lines set by princely policy. Arrests of enemy subjects and their goods as wars broke out, for example, were the norm in France and the Low Countries, as in England.[148] Other trends operated at a more obtuse angle to official strategy. Troops from different nations fell out regularly in polyglot armies, particularly those more used to fighting against each other than to cooperating, such as the landsknechts and the Swiss, while troops of the same nationality might decline to fight one another although ostensibly on different sides.[149] While civilians found most soldiers sent to defend them a burden, the foreignness of Albanians in France or Spaniards in the Low Countries does seem to have exacerbated matters and alienated subjects from the rulers who employed them.[150] More broadly it seems that concepts of Italian identity and Italian ideas of different foreign identities were sharpened by contact with invading armies and long-term garrisons from all over Europe.[151]

When domestic discontent led to revolt, the behaviour of native troops facing rebels varied in other countries as much as in England and Ireland. Sometimes soldiers would mutiny rather than attack peasants whom they characterized as their friends.[152] Many European rulers and elites therefore thought that mercenaries from distant parts would be more dependable than locals in putting down revolt or banditry: from Bohemia, the Grisons, or the Balkans in Germany in 1525, from Germany at Ghent in 1540, from Spain in the Low Countries in 1567, from Greece and Croatia in the Venetian mainland territories.[153] Yet when native soldiers did meet rebels in battle, extreme violence could ensue. There were massacres in the Brabantine civil war of 1488–9 and in the German Peasant War at Frankenhausen, Saverne, and elsewhere, just as there were in East Anglia and the South-West in 1549, and the lure of plunder or fat ransoms could overcome any fellow-feeling soldiers may have felt for the peasants.[154]

In religious civil wars the punishment of rebels came together with the defence of true faith to generate bloody warfare, though this could not always align simply with loyalties to rulers or nations, as the careers of the dukes of Guise in France show.[155] Religious motivations elsewhere were equally complex. Spanish soldiers seem to have thought of themselves as fighting for the faith when they faced heretics or infidels, yet they desecrated churches and humiliated cardinals with glee in the sack of Rome.[156] In the Ottoman Empire sultans legitimated warfare by the need to conquer infidel lands or rebuke schismatic rivals, but their armies, while drawn together by evening prayers and religious banners, were peopled by adherents of many varieties of Islam and none.[157] For others war and politics could be still more readily compartmentalized from religion. Eric II of Brunswick-Lüneburg, prince of Calenberg-Göttingen, who raised and led troops for Charles V and Philip II for thirty years and bargained very hard for payment of his wages, left his territories Lutheran despite a personal conversion back to Rome, and Duke Adolf of Holstein saw no contradiction between his own evangelical faith and the provision of thousands of cavalry for, and receipt of large pensions from, Philip II.[158]

Everywhere prayer petitioned for victory and public festivities gave thanks for it. The young Francesco Gonzaga, marquis of Mantua, called for prayers and masses from the Mantuan clergy as he marched to the battle of Fornovo, just as French kings and rulers of the Low Countries regularly ordered both intercession before battle and celebration, generally involving bonfires, afterwards.[159] These rather diffuse wartime reinforcements of the bonds between rulers and subjects were accompanied by more specific efforts to make war proclaim royal magnificence. The Ottoman sultan Süleyman I commissioned illustrated histories of his campaigns just as the Emperor Maximilian and Louis XII of France did, while Charles V commemorated his enterprises not only in manuscripts but also in luxurious series of tapestries.[160] Fortifications in France, Spain, and the Low Countries bore emblems of princely greatness and it has even been suggested that Francis I, like Henry, built his fortifications for much of his reign high and round rather than low and angled because like that they constituted a more visible sign of royal power.[161] As angle-bastioned fortress towns became the accepted way to consolidate frontiers, so these new foundations were named to commemorate their founders— Mariembourg and Vitry-le-François, Charlemont and Philippeville, Cosmopoli on Elba and Frederikstad on the Skagerrak—and their impact was magnified by such advertisements as the medals and frescoes that depicted Cosmopoli or the print of a planned 'Carlo Quinto Borgo' to replace devastated Hesdin.[162]

The busy world of war, then, was one in which Henry's subjects shared with many other Europeans. Yet their geographical situation, their rulers' strategic choices, their political and military traditions, and their economic means of subsistence meant that while they passed through the same changes as most of their neighbours, they did so rather more slowly and with some local peculiarities. They did not have armies fighting in Italy, after all, that great storm centre of military confrontation, innovation, and exchange in the decades following 1494. Their first significant exposure to the combination of shock troops, skirmishers, firearms, and fortifications forged there came in the warfare of 1542–6. English ambassadors and captains wrote home in those years about the 'horssemen and footemen of all nations' who served Charles V, about Hungarian hussars, Albanian light horse, and armoured German horsemen with spears and guns (the early *Reiter*), and about the landsknecht with 'his cappe full of fethers, his dubblette and hosen cutte and jaggidde, his swerde by his syde, an arcabowse yn his necke'. They mastered the latest styles of fortification perfected by 'engeners', explaining first that these were 'maisters of workes' for fortresses, and the best ways to attack and defend these forts, putting this, like their other new capacities, to work in the Scottish wars of 1547–50.[163] They learnt the Italianate terminology of the new warfare, with its colonels, and infantry, and the title captain, and they learnt the Germanic style of companies of footmen marching to the beat of drums, but they learnt them a decade or two after the French.[164] And their adaptation was all the slower because the English nobility were comparatively isolated from the world of European war and politics, without for example the military and personal links to Germany of French landsknecht commanders like the d'Aussy family, or Dutch generals with German wives like the count of Egmond, or indeed of German princes serving as generals in the Low Countries like Engelbrecht or Hendrik of Nassau, William of Orange, or Peter-Ernst of Mansfeld.[165]

This balance between engagement and detachment was one caught by contemporary observers. Petrus Nannius, a Louvain professor, published a dialogue in 1543 apparently inspired by discussions between noblemen in the Low Countries who had served as ambassadors to England and military commanders. In it he summed up English military ways as placing 'more trust in civilian forces than in the outside soldier, and more trust in arrows than in guns'. He endorsed the English use of a militia with proper humanist enthusiasm, but stood back from the obsession with archery that harked back to the glories of the Hundred Years War, his military expert concluding that 'those extremely skilful people' should 'add new armaments to the old'.[166] In 1557 Giovanni Michiel, the Venetian ambassador, reckoned that the English could raise tens of thousands of 'men of deeds who would voluntarily and without compulsion come forward to serve as soldiers within the kingdom and abroad' and equip them with armour and weapons, including those from the impressive stores of the nobility, but that there 'would be few among them who would know how to move under arms, and to handle the pike, harquebuse, or other sort of weapon, it not being the custom in that kingdom for the inhabitants to perform any sort of exercise with similar arms' because of their singular confidence in the bow and the bill, 'contrary ... to the judgment of the captains and soldiers of other nations'.[167]

The pressures of intensive involvement with modern warfare from the 1540s to the 1560s, first as the centre of Habsburg–Valois conflict moved from Italy to the borders of France and the Low Countries, then with the outbreak of the French Wars of Religion and Dutch Revolt, affected England in diverse ways. In some areas change in English practice accelerated. Corslets and calivers became standard equipment in English towns and villages faster than almain rivets and arquebuses had done, and drums spread fast to go with them. Heavy cast bronze guns arrived in ports in larger numbers and more standardized format than the older forged iron pieces. The navy steadily modernized its ships until they were among the best in Europe. In other ways—the ways that worried Cecil and Paget—England's military capacities were eroded. Tax assessments lost touch with economic realities and the willingness of those other than the very rich and politically ambitious or the very poor to serve in expeditions overseas declined.

The result, as in England's Reformation, was that some things changed thoroughly and fast—think of the dissolution of the monasteries—and others—think of the establishment of a preaching ministry—changed slowly and may have had different effects to those intended. As in the Reformation, the impact of change varied by region. In war it was ports and the North that in different ways, for modernity and commitment, put the inland South to shame, whereas in religious change it was London, the South-East, and East Anglia that forced the pace. And always, in war and religion, it was Ireland that posed different and challenging questions. On the other hand, as in the Reformation, the fact that England was a comparatively centralized state, whose monarchs possessed considerable inherited tools of political control, made standardizing change and administrative development in some ways easier to achieve than in more fragmented polities and thus less dependent on the compelling force of war. If Tudor England did not have as much of a military revolution as her neighbours, it was not only because she could manage her defences with fewer bastioned fortifications or well-drilled musketeers, but also because her rulers faced fewer obstacles of aristocratic, urban, and provincial independent-mindedness that could be overcome only by the irresistible logic of military necessity.

It also seems that the fluctuations between war and peace were more sharply felt in England than in other polities. Henry accelerated in each of his major wars from a level of military expenditure well below that of his neighbours, who had to maintain their larger peacetime military establishments, to a level similar to theirs, despite the smaller size of the population and the lesser wealth of the trading centres under his control; then he decelerated again.[168] While rapid mobilization and demobilization characterized the armies of all European powers, England was an extreme example, expanding minimal standing forces into armies and navies deploying a high proportion of the population.

Foreign commentators testified to the strains that this generated in a way that helps explain the gap between Cecil and Paget with their sense of the exhaustion of the kingdom's resources and Chaloner and Thomas with their upbeat assessments of Henry's war-making. In February 1559 the Danish and Spanish ambassadors agreed about the country's dire state, 'how greatly this realm has been despoiled of its resources', for 'the country has no money, and it is very difficult to be got out of the people ... There is nobody in the country fit for war' and thus the English were unable to 'stand alone against the French'.[169] Yet two and a half years later, in autumn 1561, England looked to the Venetian diplomat Michiel Surian like 'the most wealthy and powerful of all the kingdoms of the north', with its 'number of warlike men', its strong fleet, its wartime subsidies 'paid within two months without any complaint or the slightest tumult' and 'the advantage of its natural position, which is easy to defend and difficult to attack'; and a year after that, as Elizabeth intervened in the French Wars of Religion, even the Spanish admitted that she had 'excellent' ships 'well armed' with which she was 'determined to make herself queen of the seas', thousands of men, indeed 'as many infantry men ... as they want', and 'artillery and arms ... which are good and abundant', and that her ministers showed 'diligence in obtaining money ... in all possible ways'.[170]

War, then, marked the lives of Henry's subjects and changed English society and the English state, not in the same ways as in other European polities, not perhaps as deeply as in some of them, but still in significant ways and in ways similar to those in much of Europe. War, of course, was not the only thing that Henry's subjects thought about. Work and play, eating and drinking, love and marriage and children, sickness and health, heaven and hell loomed larger for many of them much of the time. But at many moments in many places, war touched and shaped their lives, and if we forget that, then our understanding of their England, their king, and their way of life will not have the depth it deserves.

Notes

PREFACE

1. P. Young and R. Holmes, *The English Civil War: A Military History of the Three Civil Wars 1642–1651* (London, 1974), 53.
2. J. Keegan, *The Face of Battle: A Study of Agincourt, Waterloo and the Somme* (London, 1991 edn), 318.
3. L. Stone, 'Interpersonal Violence in English Society 1300–1980', *PP* 101 (1983), 22–33.
4. 27 Henry VIII c. 26, s. 1, 17.

CHAPTER 1

1. *StP*, v. 88.
2. *StP*, x. 730.
3. P. Tudor-Craig, 'Henry VIII and King David', in D. Williams (ed.), *Early Tudor England: Proceedings of the 1987 Harlaxton Symposium* (Woodbridge, 1989), 183–205; 1 Samuel 17:45–51, 18:7; 1 Kings 5:3.
4. W. M. Ormrod, 'England in the Middle Ages', in R. Bonney (ed.), *The Rise of the Fiscal State in Europe c.1200–1815* (Oxford, 1999), 19–52.
5. M. Prestwich, *Armies and Warfare in the Middle Ages: The English Experience* (New Haven CT and London, 1996), 88–96, 121–5.
6. S. J. Gunn, 'The French Wars of Henry VIII', in J. Black (ed.), *The Origins of War in Early Modern Europe* (Edinburgh, 1987), 28–51.
7. G. Croenen, 'The Reception of Froissart's Writings in England: The Evidence of the Manuscripts', in J. Wogan-Browne (ed.), *Language and Culture in Medieval Britain: The French of England, c.1100–c.1500* (Woodbridge, 2009), 414–19; J. Bellis, *The Hundred Years War in Literature, 1337–1600* (Woodbridge, 2016), 51–163, 193–4.
8. C. Allmand, *The Hundred Years War* (Cambridge, 1988), 136–41; J. Watts, 'Polemic and Politics in the 1450s', in M. L. Kekewich et al. (eds), *The Politics of Fifteenth-Century England: John Vale's Book* (Stroud, 1995), 7–18.
9. J. R. Lander, 'The Hundred Years War and Edward IV's 1475 Campaign in France', in his *Crown and Nobility, 1450–1509* (London, 1976), 238–9; M. J. Tucker, *The Life of Thomas Howard, Earl of Surrey and Second Duke of Norfolk, 1443–1524* (London, 1964); R. Virgoe, 'Sir John Risley (1443–1512), Courtier and Councillor', *NA* 38 (1981–3), 140–8.
10. J. Ross, *John de Vere, Thirteenth Earl of Oxford (1442–1513): 'The Foremost Man of the Kingdom'* (Woodbridge, 2011), 65–8, 83–5, 147–8; *The Complete Peerage*, ed. V. Gibbs et al., 13 vols (London, 1910–59), x. 131; *LP*, I, ii. 1661(3).
11. W. T. MacCaffrey, 'Radcliffe, Thomas, third earl of Sussex (1526/7–1583), lord lieutenant of Ireland and courtier', A. Duffin, 'Clinton, Edward Fiennes de, first earl of Lincoln (1512–1585)', *ODNB*.
12. A. Lyall, 'Arnold, Sir Nicholas (c.1509–1580), lord justice of Ireland', C. Lennon, 'Bagenal [Bagnal], Sir Nicholas (d. 1590/91), soldier', S. G. Ellis, 'Croft, Sir James (c.1518–1590), lord deputy of Ireland and conspirator', S. Kelsey, 'Drury, Sir William (1527–1579), soldier and lord justice of Ireland', *ODNB*.

13. D. M. Loades, *The Life and Career of William Paulet (c.1475–1572), Lord Treasurer and First Marquis of Winchester* (Aldershot, 2008), 11, 63–74, 129–35, 140–53.
14. Lander, 'Edward IV's Campaign', 220–41; M. Jurkowski, 'Parliamentary and Prerogative Taxation in the Reign of Edward IV', *Parliamentary History* 18 (1999), 271–90; C. Richmond, '1485 and All That, or What Was Going On at the Battle of Bosworth', in P. W. Hammond (ed.), *Richard III: Loyalty, Lordship and Law* (London, 1986), 186–91, 203–6.
15. A. Grant, 'Foreign Affairs under Richard III', in J. Gillingham (ed.), *Richard III: A Medieval Kingship* (London, 1993), 113–32.
16. J. M. Currin, 'England's International Relations 1485–1509: Continuities amidst Change', in S. Doran and G. Richardson (eds), *Tudor England and its Neighbours* (Basingstoke, 2005), 14–43; J. M. Currin, ' "The King's Army into the Partes of Bretaigne": Henry VII and the Breton Wars, 1489–1491', *War in History* 7 (2000), 379–412; J. M. Currin, ' "To Traffic with War?" Henry VII and the French Campaign of 1492', in D. Grummitt (ed.), *The English Experience in France c.1450–1558: War, Diplomacy and Cultural Exchange* (Aldershot, 2002), 106–31; M. L. Bush, 'Tax Reform and Rebellion in Early Tudor England', *History* 76 (1991), 382–5; R. W. Hoyle, 'Resistance and Manipulation in Early Tudor Taxation: Some Evidence from the North', *Archives* 20 (1993), 161–2; M. Bennett, 'Henry VII and the Northern Rising of 1489', *EHR* 105 (1990), 34–59.
17. S. G. Ellis, 'Henry VII and Ireland, 1491–1496', in J. F. Lydon (ed.), *England and Ireland in the Later Middle Ages* (Blackrock, 1981), 237–43; I. Arthurson, 'The King's Voyage into Scotland: The War that Never Was', in D. Williams (ed.), *England in the Fifteenth Century* (Woodbridge, 1987), 1–22; I. Arthurson, *The Perkin Warbeck Conspiracy 1491–1499* (Stroud, 1994), 100–88; Bush, 'Tax Reform and Rebellion', 386–9.
18. S. Cunningham, *Henry VII* (Abingdon, 2007), 131–45, 209–23, 253–63.
19. N. Murphy, 'Henry VIII's First Invasion of France: The Gascon Expedition of 1512', *EHR* 130 (2015), 25–56; D. M. Loades, *The Tudor Navy: An Administrative, Political and Military History* (Aldershot, 1992), 54–73; C. G. Cruickshank, *Army Royal: Henry VIII's Invasion of France 1513* (Oxford, 1969); Prestwich, *Armies and Warfare*, 117–18; G. Phillips, *The Anglo-Scots Wars 1513–50* (Woodbridge, 1999), 111–33.
20. C. G. Cruickshank, *The English Occupation of Tournai 1513–1519* (Oxford, 1971); R. W. Hoyle, 'War and Public Finance', in D. N. J. MacCulloch (ed.), *The Reign of Henry VIII: Politics, Policy and Piety* (Basingstoke, 1995), 84–6; M. R. Horowitz, 'Henry Tudor's Treasure', *HR* 82 (2009), 560–79; S. J. Gunn, 'The Act of Resumption of 1515', in D. T. Williams (ed.), *Early Tudor England: Proceedings of the Fourth Harlaxton Symposium* (Woodbridge, 1989), 87–106.
21. S. G. Ellis, *Ireland in the Age of the Tudors: English Expansion and the End of Gaelic Rule* (London, 1998), 119–26.
22. Loades, *Tudor Navy*, 104–12; Phillips, *Anglo-Scots Wars*, 138–45; S. J. Gunn, 'The Duke of Suffolk's March on Paris in 1523', *EHR* 101 (1986), 596–634.
23. Hoyle, 'War and Public Finance', 86–91.
24. G. W. Bernard, *War, Taxation and Rebellion in Tudor England: Henry VIII, Wolsey and the Amicable Grant of 1525* (Brighton, 1985); G. W. Bernard and R. W. Hoyle, 'The Instructions for the Levying of the Amicable Grant, March 1525', *HR* 67 (1994), 190–202.
25. S. J. Gunn, 'Wolsey's Foreign Policy and the Domestic Crisis of 1527–8', in S. J. Gunn and P. G. Lindley (eds), *Cardinal Wolsey: Church, State and Art* (Cambridge, 1991), 149–77.

26. Phillips, *Anglo-Scots Wars*, 146–7; S. E. Lehmberg, *The Reformation Parliament, 1529–1636* (Cambridge, 1970), 133, 147–8, 157–8.
27. Ellis, *Ireland in the Age of the Tudors*, 134–43.
28. R. W. Hoyle, *The Pilgrimage of Grace and the Politics of the 1530s* (Oxford, 2001); R. W. Hoyle, 'The Origins of the Dissolution of the Monasteries Reconsidered', *HJ* 38 (1995), 275–305; M. L. Bush, '"Enhancements and Importunate Charges": An Analysis of the Tax Complaints of October 1536', *Albion* 22 (1990), 403–19.
29. J. Youings, *The Dissolution of the Monasteries* (London, 1971), 78–90; *HKW*, iv. 374–5.
30. Phillips, *Anglo-Scots Wars*, 148–77; M. H. Merriman, *The Rough Wooings: Mary Queen of Scots 1542–1551* (East Linton, 2000), 58–221.
31. D. L. Potter, *Henry VIII and Francis I: The Final Conflict, 1540–47* (Leiden and Boston MA, 2011); D. L. Potter, 'Foreign Policy', in MacCulloch (ed.), *Reign of Henry VIII*, 125–8; Loades, *Tudor Navy*, 124–38; Merriman, *Rough Wooings*, 195–205.
32. Phillips, *Anglo-Scots Wars*, 178–255; Merriman, *Rough Wooings*, 221–348; M. L. Bush, *The Government Policy of Protector Somerset* (London, 1975); D. L. Potter, 'The Treaty of Boulogne and European Diplomacy, 1549–50', *HR* 55 (1982), 50–65.
33. Hoyle, 'War and Public Finance', 90–9; G. J. Millar, *Tudor Mercenaries and Auxiliaries 1485–1547* (Charlottesville VA, 1980); Loades, *Tudor Navy*, 74–102, 139–59.
34. D. M. Loades, *The Reign of Mary Tudor*, 2nd edn (London, 1991), 16–21, 49–51, 304–61; Loades, *Tudor Navy*, 157–77; R. Schofield, 'Taxation and the Political Limits of the Tudor State', in C. Cross et al. (eds), *Law and Government under the Tudors: Essays presented to Sir Geoffrey Elton on his Retirement* (Cambridge, 1988), 232.
35. P. Hammer, *Elizabeth's Wars: War, Government and Society in Tudor England, 1544–1604* (Basingstoke, 2003), 54–70; D. Trim, 'Seeking a Protestant Alliance and Liberty of Conscience on the Continent, 1558–85', in Doran and Richardson (eds), *Tudor England and its Neighbours*, 139–52; Loades, *The Tudor Navy*, 178–217; Schofield, 'Taxation', 232.
36. Trim, 'Seeking a Protestant Alliance', 152–77; D. Trim, 'The "Foundation-Stone of the British Army"? The Normandy Campaign of 1562', *Journal of the Society for Army Historical Research* 77 (1999), 71–87; Loades, *The Tudor Navy*, 217–31; Hammer, *Elizabeth's Wars*, 81–104.
37. K. J. Kesselring, *The Northern Rebellion of 1569: Faith, Politics, and Protest in Elizabethan England* (Basingstoke, 2007); Ellis, *Ireland in the Age of the Tudors*, 184–9, 265–310, 345.
38. J. M. Currin, 'Henry VII and the Treaty of Redon (1489): Plantagenet Ambitions and Early Tudor Foreign Policy', *History* 81 (1996), 343–58.
39. Gunn, 'French Wars of Henry VIII', 28–47.
40. Edmund Dudley, *The Tree of Commonwealth*, ed. D. M. Brodie (Cambridge, 1948), 50.
41. J. J. Scarisbrick, *Henry VIII* (Harmondsworth, 1971 edn), 40–64, 551–606; L. B. Smith, *Henry VIII: The Mask of Royalty* (London, 1971), 201–23; D. R. Starkey, *Henry: Virtuous Prince* (London, 2008), 20–1; L. Wooding, *Henry VIII* (Abingdon, 2009), 66.
42. In addition to works cited below, see: J. J. Goring, 'Social Change and Military Decline in Mid-Tudor England', *History* 60 (1975), 185–97; C. S. L. Davies, 'Provisions for Armies, 1509–50: A Study in the Effectiveness of Early Tudor Government', *EcHR* n.s. 17 (1964–5), 234–48; N. A. M. Rodger, *The Safeguard of the Sea: A Naval History of Britain, volume 1, 660–1649* (London, 1997); D. Grummitt, *The Calais Garrison: War and Military Service in England, 1436–1558* (Woodbridge, 2008).
43. H. Miller, *Henry VIII and the English Nobility* (Oxford, 1986); L. MacMahon, 'Chivalry, Military Professionalism and the Early Tudor Army in Renaissance Europe:

A Reassessment', in D. Trim (ed.), *The Chivalric Ethos and the Development of Military Professionalism* (Leiden, 2003), 183–212; R. Rapple, *Martial Power and Elizabethan Political Culture: Military Men in England and Ireland, 1558–1594* (Cambridge, 2009); D. Trim, 'Fighting "Jacob's warres": English and Welsh Mercenaries in the European Wars of Religion: France and the Netherlands, 1562–1610', King's College London Ph.D. Thesis (2003).

44. Phillips, *Anglo-Scots Wars*, 42–103; D. Eltis, *The Military Revolution in Sixteenth-Century Europe* (London, 1995); M. C. Fissel, *English Warfare, 1511–1642* (London and New York, 2001), 1–49; J. Raymond, *Henry VIII's Military Revolution: The Armies of Sixteenth-Century Britain and Europe* (London and New York, 2007).

45. C. S. L. Davies, 'The English People and War in the Early Sixteenth Century', in A. C. Duke and C. A. Tamse (eds), *Britain and the Netherlands, vi* (The Hague, 1977), 1–18; C. S. L. Davies, 'England and the French War, 1557–1559', in J. Loach and R. Tittler (eds), *The Mid-Tudor Polity c.1540–1560* (London, 1980), 159–85.

46. E. Hurren, 'Cultures of the Body, Medical Regimen, and Physic at the Court of Henry VIII', in T. Betteridge and S. Lipscombe (eds), *Henry VIII and the Court: Art, Politics and Performance* (Farnham, 2013), 67; *The Inventory of King Henry VIII*, ed. A. Hawkyard, M. Hayward, P. Ward, and D. R. Starkey, 2 vols to date (London, 1998–), i, no. 1922; D. M. Loades, 'Howard, Sir Edward', *ODNB*.

47. T. F. Arnold, *The Renaissance at War* (London, 2001); G. Parker, *The Military Revolution: Military Innovation and the Rise of the West, 1500–1800* (Cambridge, 1988), 26–8; C. G. Cruickshank, *Elizabeth's Army*, 2nd edn (Oxford, 1966), 1–2, 102–18.

48. A vast literature includes M. Roberts, 'The Military Revolution, 1560–1660', in his *Essays in Swedish History* (London, 1967), 195–225; Parker, *The Military Revolution*; C. J. Rogers (ed.), *The Military Revolution Debate: Readings on the Military Transformation of Early Modern Europe* (Boulder CO, 1995); J. Glete, *War and the State in Early Modern Europe: Spain, the Dutch Republic and Sweden as Fiscal-Military States, 1500–1660* (London, 2002); S. Gunn, D. Grummitt, and H. Cools, 'War and the State in Early Modern Europe: Widening the Debate', *War in History* 15 (2008), 371–88; F. Tallett and D. J. B. Trim (eds), *European Warfare, 1350–1750* (Cambridge, 2010).

49. P. K. O'Brien and P. A. Hunt, 'The Rise of a Fiscal State in England, 1485–1815', *HR* 66 (1993), 148–63.

50. Hammer, *Elizabeth's Wars*, 27–42.

51. L. Stone, *The Causes of the English Revolution* (London, 1972), 59–61; C. S. R. Russell, 'Parliament and the King's Finances', in C. S. R. Russell (ed.), *The Origins of the English Civil War* (London, 1973), 94–6.

52. H. Miller, 'Subsidy Assessments of the Peerage in the Sixteenth Century', *Bulletin of the Institute of Historical Research* 28 (1955), 21–2; Schofield, 'Taxation', 239, 242–55; Hoyle, 'Resistance and Manipulation', 170–1; R. Schofield, *Taxation under the Early Tudors 1485–1547* (Oxford, 2004), 126–7, 176.

53. Goring, 'Social Change', 188–95.

54. C. Brady, 'The Captains' Games: Army and Society in Elizabethan Ireland', in T. Bartlett and K. Jeffery (eds), *A Military History of Ireland* (Cambridge, 1996), 136–59; Grummitt, *Calais Garrison*, 49–56; Raymond, *Henry VIII's Military Revolution*, 145, 153–4, 163–79; A. Hewerdine, *The Yeomen of the Guard and the Early Tudors: The Formation of a Royal Bodyguard* (London, 2012).

55. M. M. Norris, 'The 2nd Earl of Rutland's Band of Men-at-Arms, 1551–2', *HR* 68 (1995), 100–16.

56. Rodger, *Safeguard of the Sea*, 364–78.

57. S. Gunn, D., Grummitt, and H. Cools, *War, State, and Society in England and the Netherlands, 1477–1559* (Oxford, 2007).

58. Glete, *War and the State*, 28–9, 140–73.

59. J. S. Wheeler, *The Making of a World Power: War and the Military Revolution in Seventeenth-Century England* (Stroud, 1999); M. J. Braddick, *State Formation in Early Modern England c.1550–1700* (Cambridge, 2000), 177–285; J. Brewer, *The Sinews of Power: War, Money and the English State, 1688–1783* (London, 1989).

60. D. L. Potter, 'Mid-Tudor Foreign Policy and Diplomacy: 1547–63', in Doran and Richardson (eds), *Tudor England and its Neighbours*, 107–9, 112–14, 117–19, 121–2; Hammer, *Elizabeth's Wars*, 54–70.

61. 'The Letters of William, Lord Paget of Beaudesert, 1547–1563', ed. B. L. Beer and S. M. Jack, *The Camden Miscellany* xxv, CS 4th ser. 13 (1974), 23, 31.

62. *A Collection of State Papers, relating to affairs in the reigns of King Henry VIII, King Edward VI, Queen Mary, and Queen Elizabeth, transcribed from original letters and other authentick memorials, left by William Cecill Lord Burghley*, ed. S. Haynes and W. Murdin, 2 vols (London, 1740–59), i. 582, 585.

63. Potter, 'Mid-Tudor Foreign Policy', 106–9; Hammer, *Elizabeth's Wars*, 236–44.

64. 'Letters of William, Lord Paget', 77; Potter, 'Mid-Tudor Foreign Policy', 108.

65. P. Burke, *The French Historical Revolution: The Annales School 1929–89* (Oxford, 1990), 32–42, 61–4, 113–14.

CHAPTER 2

1. J. R. Lander, 'The Hundred Years War and Edward IV's 1475 Campaign in France', in his *Crown and Nobility, 1450–1509* (London, 1976), 237; J. M. Currin, '"To Traffic with War?" Henry VII and the French Campaign of 1492', in D. Grummitt (ed.), *The English Experience in France c.1450–1558: War, Diplomacy and Cultural Exchange* (Aldershot, 2002), 126; A. Curry, 'English Armies in the Fifteenth Century', in A. Curry and M. Hughes (eds), *Arms, Armies and Fortifications in the Hundred Years War* (Woodbridge, 1994), 45.

2. C. G. Cruickshank, *Army Royal: Henry VIII's Invasion of France 1513* (Oxford, 1969), 28–9; G. J. Millar, *Tudor Mercenaries and Auxiliaries, 1485–1547* (Charlottesville VA, 1980), 44–5; G. Phillips, *The Anglo-Scots Wars 1513–1550* (Woodbridge, 1999), 116.

3. D. L. Potter, *Henry VIII and Francis I: The Final Conflict, 1540–47* (Leiden and Boston MA, 2011), 226; *LP*, XIX, ii. 33, 625.

4. Phillips, *Anglo-Scots Wars*, 183; C. S. L. Davies, 'England and the French War, 1557–1559', in J. Loach and R. Tittler (eds), *The Mid-Tudor Polity c.1540–1560* (London, 1980), 166; P. Hammer, *Elizabeth's Wars: War, Government and Society in Tudor England, 1544–1604* (Basingstoke, 2003), 60, 64–5.

5. J. M. Currin, '"The King's Army into the Partes of Bretaigne": Henry VII and the Breton Wars, 1489–1491', *War in History* 7 (2000), 383–410; I. Arthurson, 'The King's Voyage into Scotland: The War that Never Was', in D. Williams (ed.), *England in the Fifteenth Century* (Woodbridge, 1987), 7; D. M. Loades, *The Tudor Navy: An Administrative, Political and Military History* (Aldershot, 1992), 57–8, 66–7, 131, 134, 170.

6. *LP*, XI. 700; R. W. Hoyle, *The Pilgrimage of Grace and the Politics of the 1530s* (Oxford, 2001), 171, 173, 175, 293.

7. PRO, SP1/203, fos. 13–14 (*LP*, XX, i. 1078); *LP*, XX, i. 833, 958, 1105; Potter, *Henry VIII and Francis I*, 373–4; *A Chronicle of England by Charles Wriothesley*, ed.

W. D. Hamilton, 2 vols, CS n.s. 11 (1875), i. 158; H. T. White, 'The Beacon System in Kent', *Archaeologia Cantiana* 46 (1934), 85. Of the militarily able national adult male population mustered for the militia in 1573, the proportion living in those counties detailed to resist the French in 1545 was 61%, a figure we might adjust to some 66% to take into account Wales and London, absent from the tabulated Elizabethan figures. This proportion of the adult male part of the estimated population in 1546, given the high proportion of the population under 15, would amount to some 600,000: E. E. Rich, 'The Population of Elizabethan England', *EcHR*, n.s. 2 (1950), 247–65; E. A. Wrigley and R. Schofield, *The Population History of England, 1541–1871: A Reconstruction* (London, 1981), 208, 528, 566, 568. On muster returns, see Chapter 6.

8. B. S. Capp, *Astrology and the Popular Press: English Almanacs, 1500–1800* (London, 1979), 25–30, 59–66; A. Smyth, 'Almanacs and Ideas of Popularity', in A. Kesson, E. Smith, A. Smyth, and J. Daybell, *The Elizabethan Top Ten: Defining Print Popularity in Early Modern England* (Farnham, 2013), 125–33.

9. *A Mery Prognosticacion for the Yere of Chrystes Incarnacyon A Thousande Fyve Hundred Fortye and Foure* (London, 1543?), A2v.

10. *The Household Book (1510–1551) of Sir Edward Don: An Anglo-Welsh Knight and his Circle*, ed. R. A. Griffiths, Buckinghamshire RS 33 (Aylesbury, 2004), 5, 34, 54, 79, 105, 175, 180, 240, 242, 243, 267, 301, 313, 322, 377, 404, 412, 414, 420, 442, 453.

11. *STC* 388, 389, 406.7, 470.4, 470.5, 470.6, 470.7, 470.8; BL, Harl. 5937 (1521).

12. HL 131401:17: Adrian Velthoven, *The pronostication of maister Adrian of arte and medicine doctour moost expert maister and excellent in astronomy* (London, 1520); University of Illinois copy of Simon Heuring, *An almanacke and prognosticatyon, for the yeare of our Lorde, M.D.LI.* (Worcester, 1551), reproduced in Early English Books Online.

13. Capp, *Astrology*, 67–70; Gaspar Laet, *[Prognostication for the year] M.CCCCC.xvij. translate in the famous cite of Andwerpe* (Antwerp, 1517), A3v.

14. *A Prognostication* (London?, 1539?), B1r.

15. *A Prognostication for 1498* (Westminster, 1498), fo. 1r.

16. Gaspar Laet, *Pronostication of Jaspar Laet doctor of phisicke and astronomy for the yere of our Lorde God M.vc.xliiii* (London, 1544).

17. Gaspar Laet, *The pnostication of Maister Jasp Laet, practised in the towne of Antuerpe, for the yere of Our Lorde, M.D.XX.* (London?, 1520), A1r; *STC* 432, 447.5, 470.3, 470.5, 470.7, 470.9, 471.5, 482.3, 510, 510.3, 511, 511.3, 520, 18054; Capp, *Astrology*, 367–8.

18. *STC* 410, 417, 432, 435.37, 482, 482.3, 482.7, 482.9, 510.5, 511, 511.3, 521.5.

19. Michael Nostradamus, *The prognostication of maister Michael Nostredamus, doctour in phisick* (Antwerp, 1559), B1v, C5r, C6v, F1v, F4v.

20. *STC* 492, 492.2, 492.3, 492.7, 492.9, 492.10, 492.11, 493, 493.3, 493.7, 18694.

21. Gaspar Laet, *Prognostication for the year M.v.C. & xxiii* (London, 1523), A5r; S. J. Gunn, 'The Duke of Suffolk's March on Paris in 1523', *EHR* 101 (1986), 596–634.

22. Gaspar Laet, *An almanack and pronostication of Iaspar Laet for the yere, of our Lord M.D.XXXIV* (Malmö, 1534); J. D. Tracy, *Emperor Charles V, Impresario of War* (Cambridge, 2002), 145–57.

23. Anthony Askham, *A prognosticacion made for the yere of oure Lord Gods thousande fyue hundreth Xlviii* (London, 1548); *The husbandmans practise, or prognostication* (London, 1550?), A5r, A7r–v, A8v.

24. Achilles Pirmin Gasser, *A prognostication for this yere M.D.xlvi* (London, 1546), D5v–6r.

25. William Cuningham, *1564. A new almanach and prognostication, servynge the yere of Christ M.D.L.X.IIII* (London, 1563), A3v.

26. HL, 61635.

27. S. L. Jansen, *Political Protest and Prophecy under Henry VIII* (Woodbridge, 1991), 19–61.

28. Jansen, *Political Protest*, 70–90, 107–9; D. Youngs, *Humphrey Newton (1496–1536), An Early Tudor Gentleman* (Woodbridge, 2008), 162–4.

29. Jansen, *Political Protest*, 128–30, 135–9.

30. Jansen, *Political Protest*, 102, 108, 127.

31. *Predictions des choses plus memorables qui sont a advenir depuis l'an MDLXIII, iusqu'a l'an mil six cens & sept, prise tant des eclipses & grosses Ephemrides de Cyprian Leovitie, que des predictions de Samuel Syderocrate* (n.p., 1568), Lanhydrock House E.1.8.

32. *StP*, ii. 31.

33. Lewes Vaughan, *A new almanacke and prognostication, collected for the yeare of our Lord God. M.D.L.IX* (London, 1559), B8r, C1r.

34. *The First and Second Prayer Books of Edward VI*, ed. E. C. S. Gibson (London, 1910), 26, 29, 354–5, 358.

35. F. E. Brightman, *The English Rite* (2 vols, London, 1915), ii. 1033; *Ceremonies and Processions of the Cathedral Church of Salisbury*, ed. C. Wordsworth (Cambridge, 1901), 22.

36. K. A. Fowler, 'News from the Front: Letters and Despatches of the Fourteenth Century', in P. Contamine, C. Giry-Deloison, and M. H. Keen (eds), *Guerre et société en France, en Angleterre et en Bourgogne xive–xve siècle* (Lille, 1991), 76–81; *The Life and Campaigns of the Black Prince*, ed. R. Barber (Woodbridge, 1986 edn), 20–3, 52–5, 57–9, 83; *Calendar of Letter-Books of the City of London: I: 1400–1422*, ed. R. R. Sharpe (London, 1909), 183, 185, 199, 224, 255; *Letters and Papers illustrative of the Wars of the English in France during the reign of Henry the Sixth, King of England*, ed. J. Stevenson, Rolls Ser. 22, 2 vols in 3 (London, 1861–4), II, ii. 396–400, 409–11.

37. *The Reign of Henry VII from Contemporary Sources*, ed. A. F. Pollard, 3 vols (London, 1915), i. 67–9; *The Red Paper Book of Colchester*, ed. W. G. Benham (Colchester, 1902), 143–4.

38. *YCR*, ii. 94–6.

39. *The Great Chronicle of London*, ed. A. H. Thomas and I. D. Thornley (London, 1938), 278–81.

40. *LP*, III, ii. 3504; Worcestershire Archives, BA2648/9(i), 29–30.

41. LMA, Rep. 4, fo. 104v.

42. *Reign of Henry VII*, i. 168–9, 173–6.

43. *The Manuscripts of the Earl of Westmorland, Captain Stewart, Lord Stafford, Lord Muncaster, and others*, HMC 10th report appendix 4 (1885), 449.

44. SHC, LM1943; Davies, 'England and the French War', 181.

45. *The Manuscripts of Lord Middleton, preserved at Wollaton Hall*, HMC 69 (London, 1911), 263–7.

46. *Edward IV's French expedition of 1475: the Leaders and their Badges being ms. 2. M. 16. College of Arms*, ed. F. P. Barnard (Oxford, 1925); *LP*, I, ii. 2392(i); *A Catalogue of Manuscripts in the College of Arms: Collections*, i, ed. L. Campbell and F. Steer (London, 1988), 59, 185.

47. CUL, Hengrave MS 88(iii), nos. 93, 93B. For dating see J. C. Losada, *San Quintín. El relato vivo y vibrante de las campañas del conde de Egmont en la convulse Europa de Felipe II* (Madrid, 2005), 100–3, 142.

48. SHC, LM1873; CUL, Hengrave MS 88(iii), no. 85.

49. A. Pettegree, *The Invention of News: How the World Came to Know about Itself* (New Haven CT and London, 2014), 71–84.

50. 'A Contemporary Account of the Battle of Floddon, 9th September 1513', ed. D. Laing, *Proceedings of Society of Antiquaries of Scotland* 7 (1870), 141–52; N. Gutierrez and M. Erler, 'Print into Manuscript: A Flodden Field News Pamphlet (British Library Ms Additional 29506)', *Studies in Medieval and Renaissance History* n.s. 8 (1986), 187–230; S. Gunn., D. Grummitt, and H. Cools, *War, State, and Society in England and the Netherlands, 1477–1559* (Oxford, 2007), 208–9.

51. *LP*, XIX, i. 524; *The late expedicion in Scotlande made by the Kynges hyghnys armye, vnder the conduit of the ryght honorable the Erle of Hertforde, the yere of our Lorde God 1544* (London, 1544).

52. William Patten, *The expedicion into Scotlande of the most woorthely fortunate prince Edward, Duke of Soomerset, uncle unto our most noble sovereign lord ye kinges Maiestie Edward the. VI. goovernour of hys hyghnes persone, and protectour of hys graces realmes, dominions and subjectes* (London, 1548).

53. Warwickshire RO, CR1291/666; Bodl. 8° P62 Art Seld.; F. R. Johnson, 'Notes on English Retail Book-Prices, 1550–1640', *The Library* 5th ser. 5 (1950), 89, 105.

54. G. Rimer, T. Richardson, and J. P. D. Cooper (eds), *Henry VIII: Arms and the Man* (Leeds, 2009), 257.

55. K. J. Kesselring, *The Northern Rebellion of 1569: Faith, Politics, and Protest in Elizabethan England* (Basingstoke, 2007), 153–7.

56. *Life and Campaigns of the Black Prince*, 14–20, 23–5, 50–2, 55–6.

57. *Kingsford's Stonor Letters and Papers 1290–1483*, ed. C. Carpenter (Cambridge, 1996), 157–9; *The Paston Letters, 1422–1509 AD*, ed. J. A. Gairdner (4 vols, Edinburgh, 1910), iii. 139.

58. *HMC Westmorland*, 446–7; 'Account of Henry the Eighth's Expedition into France, A.D. 1513', ed. W. C. Trevelyan, *Archaeologia* 26 (1836), 475–8.

59. *Calendar of the Manuscripts of the Most Hon. the Marquis of Salisbury*, 24 vols, HMC 24–47 (London, 1883–1976), i. 142–5.

60. PRO, SC1/52/33.

61. *HMC Sixth Report* (London, 1877), 421; *A Calendar of the Shrewsbury and Talbot Papers in Lambeth Palace Library and the College of Arms*, ed. C. Jamison, E. G. W. Bill, and G. R. Batho, 2 vols, HMC joint publications 6–7 (London, 1966–71), ii. 7.

62. *The Cely Letters 1472–1488*, ed. A. Hanham, EETS 273 (London, 1975), 10–11, 18, 23, 29, 55, 97–101, 103–5, 135–7, 156, 159, 163–5, 168–9, 171, 176, 192–4, 196–7, 200, 203, 209–11, 215–16, 227, 237, 239, 242–6 (quotation at 164).

63. B. Winchester, *Tudor Family Portrait* (London, 1955), 239–65.

64. *Reign of Henry VII*, i. 58–60, 64–5, 89–91.

65. *HMC 2nd Report* (London, 1874), 21.

66. *LP*, III, ii. 3310, 3380, 3398, 3447, 3623; *StP*, iv. 36.

67. *StP*, ix. 488–9.

68. *LP*, XIX, ii. 78, 251, 293, 364. XX, i. 201, ii. 118, 307; *APC*, vi. 150, 348; Nottinghamshire Archives, DD/SR/1/D/10; *YCR*, v. 170–1; *Calendar Shrewsbury and Talbot Papers*, i. 34, ii. 59.

69. *Trevelyan Papers, Part III*, ed. W. C. Trevelyan and C. E. Trevelyan, CS 105 (London, 1872), 15.

70. CUL, Hengrave MS 88(i), no. 90.

71. *Great Chronicle*, 379–80.

72. *Clifford Letters of the Sixteenth Century*, ed. A. G. Dickens, SS 172 (Durham, 1962), 82–3, 107; CUL, Hengrave MS 88(iii), no. 76; *Calendar of the Correspondence of the*

Smyth Family of Ashton Court 1548–1642, ed. J. H. Bettey, Bristol RS 35 (Bristol, 1982), 9.

73. Nicolas des Gallars, *A true report of all the doynges at the assembly concernyng matters of Religion, lately holden at Poyssy in Fraunce* (London, 1562); *The Destruction and sacke cruelly committed by the Duke of Guyse and his company, in the towne of Vassy, the fyrste of Marche, in the year MDLXII* (London, 1562); *STC* 6776, 11263, 11269, 11312, 12507, 15849, 16849.3, 16849.7, 16850, 16851, 16852, 16853; H. Dunthorne, *Britain and the Dutch Revolt 1560–1700* (Cambridge, 2013), 5, 8–10, 30–3, 41; SHC, LM1869/1–7; *Papers of Nathaniel Bacon of Stiffkey*, ed. A. Hassell Smith, 3 vols (Norwich, 1979–90), i. 34, 37–8, 42, 43, 49, 74, 101, 107, 113–14, 123, 156, 161–2, 180; *Calendar Shrewsbury and Talbot Papers*, ii. 88, 90, 133, 357, 362–3.

74. A. Fox, 'Rumour, News and Popular Political Opinion in Elizabethan and Early Stuart England', *HJ* 40 (1997), 597–620.

75. *Red Paper Book of Colchester*, 146–7.

76. Herefordshire Archive and Records Centre, BG11/17/3/1, 1a (*The Manuscripts of Rye and Hereford Corporations*, HMC 13th report 4 (London, 1892), 306); Fox, 'Rumour, News', 602–3.

77. Fox, 'Rumour, News', 604–5.

78. S. J. Gunn, 'Wolsey's Foreign Policy and the Domestic Crisis of 1527–8', in S. J. Gunn and P. G. Lindley (eds), *Cardinal Wolsey: Church, State and Art* (Cambridge, 1991), 169; *Calendar of Letters, Despatches, and State Papers, relating to the Negotiations between England and Spain, Preserved in the Archives at Simancas and Elsewhere*, ed. G. Bergenroth et al., 13 vols (London, 1862–1954), ix. 92, 103, x. 47, 177.

79. W. G. Hoskins, *The Age of Plunder: The England of Henry VIII 1500–47* (London, 1976), 248; *Depositions taken before the Mayor and Aldermen of Norwich, 1549–1567*, ed. W. Rye (Norwich, 1905), 93–4.

80. *StP*, iii. 417; *HP*, ii. 417.

81. *Depositions taken before the Mayor and Aldermen of Norwich*, 59.

82. *Depositions taken before the Mayor and Aldermen of Norwich*, 61–2.

83. *Life and Campaigns of the Black Prince*, 26–40.

84. *LP*, I, ii. 2391.

85. *LP*, I, ii. 2392(ii).

86. BL, Addl. MS 10110, fos. 218–19 (*LP*, III, ii. 3516).

87. *Foedera, Conventiones, Literae et cujuscunque generis Acta Publica*, ed. T. Rymer, 20 vols (London, 1704–35), xv. 52–7.

88. 'A Diary of the Expedition of 1544', ed. W. A. J. Archbold, *EHR* 16 (1901), 503–7.

89. *LP*, XIX, i. 534.

90. 'A Contemporary Account of the Earl of Hertford's Second Expedition to Scotland, and of the Ravages committed by the English Forces in September 1545. From a Manuscript in Trinity College Library, Dublin', ed. D. Laing, *Proceedings of the Society of Antiquaries of Scotland* 1 (1851–4), 271–6.

91. Edward Hall, *Hall's Chronicle* (London, 1809 edn), 661–71.

92. Hall, *Chronicle*, 522–5, 646–8.

93. Raphael Holinshed, *The Chronicles of England, Scotlande, and Irelande*, 4 vols (London, 1577), iv. 1803–14, 1817–33.

94. Holinshed, *Chronicles*, ii. 483–7.

95. *Documents relating to the Revels at Court in the time of King Edward VI and Queen Mary (the Loseley manuscripts)*, ed. A. Feuillerat, Materialien zur Kunde des älteren englischen Dramas 44 (Louvain, 1914), 215–17.

96. *Revels . . . King Edward VI and Queen Mary*, 182–3.

97. *Documents relating to the Office of the Revels in the Time of Queen Elizabeth*, ed. A. Feuillerat, Materialien zur Kunde des älteren englischen Dramas 21 (Louvain, 1908), 41, 94.

98. J. R. Hale, *Artists and Warfare in the Renaissance* (New Haven CT and London, 1990), 263; R. Coope and P. Smith, *Newstead Abbey, A Nottinghamshire Country House: Its Owners and Architectural History 1540–1931*, Thoroton Society Record Ser. 48 (Nottingham, 2010), 13–17; S. Stubbs, *A Souvenir Guide: Little Moreton Hall, Cheshire* (Swindon, 2015), 24, 27.

99. Tracy, *Emperor Charles V*, 31; G. J. Millar, 'Henry VIII's Colonels', *Journal of the Society for Army Historical Research* 57 (1979), 129–36; BL, Stowe MS 571, fos. 120r, 126v, 127r; *Cratfield: a Transcript of the Accounts of the Parish, from A.D. 1490 to A.D. 1642*, ed. J. J. Raven (London, 1895), 83; D. Eltis, *The Military Revolution in Sixteenth-Century Europe* (London, 1995), 103–4, 125; Hatfield House, CP239/8, 239/13a.

100. W. Hooper, 'The Tudor Sumptuary Laws', *EHR* 30 (1915), 439–41; T. Girtin, *The Golden Ram: A Narrative History of the Clothworkers' Company 1528–1958* (London, 1958), 47–8; *Records of Chippenham*, ed. F. H. Goldney (London, 1889), 316–17; *Winchelsea Corporation Records: A Catalogue*, ed. R. F. Dell (Lewes, 1963), 13–14; Isle of Wight RO, OG/UU/4–6; U. Rublack, *Dressing Up: Cultural Identity in Renaissance Europe* (Oxford, 2010), 109–12; D. Miller, *The Landsknechts* (London, 1976), 36.

101. *YCR*, vi. 40.

102. Gunn, Grummitt, and Cools, *War, State, and Society*, 68.

CHAPTER 3

1. E. Duffy, *The Voices of Morebath: Reformation and Rebellion in an English Village* (New Haven CT and London, 2001); S. E. Brigden, *London and the Reformation* (Oxford, 1989); C. Cross, *Urban Magistrates and Ministers: Religion in Hull and Leeds from the Reformation to the Civil War*, Borthwick papers 67 (York, 1985).

2. C. A. Haigh, *English Reformations: Religion, Politics, and Society under the Tudors* (Oxford, 1993), 280; P. Hammer, *Elizabeth's Wars: War, Government and Society in Tudor England, 1544–1604* (Basingstoke, 2003), 253–64; C. S. R. Russell, *The Causes of the English Civil War* (Oxford, 1990), 12–13, 83–130, 161–84.

3. J. Goring, 'The Military Obligations of the English People, 1511–58', London Ph.D. thesis, 1955; J. Goring, 'Social Change and Military Decline in Mid-Tudor England', *History* 60 (1975), 188–97; A. H. Smith, 'Militia Rates and Militia Statutes 1558–1663', in P. Clark, A. G. R. Smith, and N. Tyacke (eds), *The English Commonwealth 1547–1640: Essays in Politics and Society presented to Joel Hurstfield* (Leicester, 1979), 93–100; L. Boynton, *The Elizabethan Militia 1558–1638* (London, 1967), 37–40.

4. Bedfordshire: Northill, Turvey; Berkshire: Abingdon St Helen's, Brightwalton, Reading St Giles, Reading St Lawrence, Reading St Mary, Stanford, Thatcham, Windsor; Bristol: Bristol All Saints, Bristol St Ewens, Bristol St Nicholas; Buckinghamshire: Amersham, Aston Abbots, Wing; Cambridgeshire: Bassingbourn, Cambridge Holy Trinity, Cambridge St Mary the Great, Leverington, Wisbech; Cheshire: Chester Holy Trinity; Cornwall: Stratton; Cumberland: Great Salkeld; Derbyshire: Derby All Saints; Devon: Ashburton, Chagford, Crediton, Dartmouth, Molland, Morebath, Tavistock; Dorset: Sherborne All Hallows, Wimborne Minster; Essex: Bromfield, Dunmow, Great Hallingbury, Harwich, Heybridge, Waltham Abbey, Wivenhoe; Hampshire: Bramley, Crondall, Ellingham, Portsmouth, Stoke Charity, Weyhill,

Winchester St John, Winchester St Peter Chesil, Wootton St Lawrence; Herefordshire: Stoke Edith; Hertfordshire: Ashwell, Baldock, Bishops Stortford; Huntingdonshire: Holywell, Ramsey; Kent: Bethersden, Brenzett, Canterbury St Andrew's, Canterbury St Dunstan's, Dover St Mary, Eltham, Fordwich St Mary, Hawkhurst, Lydd All Hallows, Smarden, Strood; Lancashire: Prescot; Leicestershire: Castle Donington, Leicester St Martin, Melton Mowbray; Lincolnshire: Addlethorpe, Hagworthingham, Leverton, Long Sutton, Louth, Sutterton, Wigtoft; London: All Hallows London Wall, St Andrew Hubbard, St Martin Outwich, St Mary at Hill, St Matthew Friday Street, St Michael Cornhill, St Peter Cheap; Middlesex: St Martin in the Fields, Westminster St Margaret; Norfolk: North Elmham, Tilney All Saints; Northamptonshire: Peterborough; Oxfordshire: Marston, Oxford St Nicholas, Pyrton, South Newington, Spelsbury, Thame; Shropshire: Cheswardine, Ludlow, Worfield; Somerset: Bath St Michael, Chedzoy, Croscombe, Goathurst, Lydeard St Laurence, Nettlecombe, Pilton, Stogursey, Tintinhull, Trull, Yatton, Yeovil; Staffordshire: Walsall; Suffolk: Bardwell, Boxford, Bungay St Mary, Cratfield, Dennington, Metfield, Mildenhall, Walberswick; Surrey: Battersea, Bletchingley, Horley, Kingston-upon-Thames, Lambeth, Wandsworth; Sussex: Arlington, Ashurst, Billinghurst, Cowfold, Lewes St Andrew & St Michael, West Tarring, Worth; Warwickshire: Coventry Holy Trinity, Great Packington, Rowington, Solihull, Warwick St Nicholas; Wiltshire: Calne, Devizes St Mary, Longbridge Deverill, Mere, Salisbury St Edmund, Salisbury St Thomas, Winterslow; Worcestershire: Badsey, Halesowen, Worcester St Michael in Bedwardine; Yorkshire: Hedon St Augustine, Masham, Sheffield, Sheriff Hutton, York St Michael Spurriergate. References for those not cited below are given in the bibliography.

5. *Churchwardens' Accounts of Ashburton, 1479–1580*, ed. A. Hanham, Devon and Cornwall RS n.s. 15 (Exeter, 1970); Leicestershire RO, DG36/140/7–10, 141/1–10, 284/1–10; Warwickshire RO, DR158/19.

6. S. J. Gunn, 'Archery Practice in Early Tudor England', *PP* 209 (2010), 55–7; HL, MS HA Misc Box 8(2); *The Early Churchwardens' Accounts of Bishops Stortford, 1431–1558*, ed. S. G. Doree, Hertfordshire RS 10 (Ware, 1994), 43; Kingston Museum and Heritage Service, KG2/2/1, 100; 'The Churchwardens' Accounts of Mere', ed. T. H. Baker, *Wiltshire Archaeological and Natural History Magazine* 35 (1907–8), 37; *Elizabethan Churchwardens' Accounts*, ed. J. E. Farmiloe and R. Nixseaman, Bedfordshire Historical RS 33 (Streatley, 1953), 7; 'Church Ale-Games and Interludes', ed. G. B. Baker, *The East Anglian* 1 (1864), 334–6.

7. *TRP*, i. 28, 36–7, 61, 69, 89–90, 137; J. J. Goring, 'The General Proscription of 1522', *EHR* 86 (1971), 689–90; *The Certificate of Musters for Buckinghamshire in 1522*, ed. A. C. Chibnall, Buckinghamshire RS 17 (London, 1973), 209, 226, 235, 263, 301, 338, 345, 348–9, 355, 358; *Worcestershire Taxes in the 1520s*, ed. M. A. Faraday, Worcestershire HS n.s. 19 (Worcester, 2003), 1, 10, 19, 35; *The County Community under Henry VIII: The Military Survey, 1522, and Lay Subsidy, 1524–5, for Rutland*, ed. J. Cornwall, Rutland Record Ser. 1 (Oakham, 1980), 20, 23, 27, 33, 42–4, 53, 63, 67; *The 1522 Muster Roll for West Berkshire*, ed. L. Garnish (n.p., 1988), I. 2, 6, 98, 102, 111, 119, 123, 129, 148, 151, II. 72, 73, 78, 90.

8. 'Musters in Claro Wapentake, 1535', ed. W. P. Baildon, *Miscellanea v*, Thoresby Soc. 15 (Leeds, 1909), 111–21; *Bedfordshire Muster Rolls 1539–1831*, ed. N. Lutt, Bedfordshire Historical RS 71 (Bedford, 1992), 7–22, 29; *The Herefordshire Musters of 1539 and 1542*, ed. M. A. Faraday (Walton-on-Thames, 2012), 6–68, 72, 92–116; *The Oxfordshire Muster Rolls, 1539, 1542, 1569*, ed. P. C. Beauchamp, Oxfordshire

RS 60 (Oxford, 1996), xvi, 1–26; *North Wiltshire Musters, anno 30 Henry VIII*, ed. T. Phillipps (London, 1834).

9. *LP*, XVII. 883(M8(2)).

10. C. Burgess, 'Pre-Reformation Churchwardens' Accounts and Parish Government: Lessons from London and Bristol', *EHR* 117 (2002), 306–32; B. A. Kümin, 'Late Medieval Churchwardens' Accounts and Parish Government: Looking beyond London and Bristol', *EHR* 119 (2004) 87–99.

11. *Churchwardens' Accounts of Marston, Spelsbury, Pyrton*, ed. F. W. Weaver and G. N. Clark, Oxfordshire RS 6 (Oxford, 1925); 'Great Hallingbury Churchwardens' Accounts, 1526 to 1634', *Transactions of the Essex Archaeological Society* 23 (1942–5), 110.

12. *The Transcript of the Churchwardens' Accounts of the Parish of Tilney All Saints, Norfolk, 1443 to 1589*, ed. A. D. Stallard (London, 1922), 211; *The Early Churchwardens' Accounts of Hampshire*, ed. J. F. Williams (Winchester, 1913), 160.

13. *Oxfordshire Muster Rolls*, 27–64; *Certificate of Musters in the County of Somerset temp. Eliz. A.D. 1569*, ed. E. Green, Somerset RS 20 (London, 1904); *The Cornwall Muster Roll for 1569*, ed. H. L. Douch (Bristol, 1984); *The Devon Muster Roll for 1569*, ed. A. J. Howard and T. L. Stoate (Bristol, 1977); *The Musters Return for Divers Hundreds in the County of Norfolk, 1569, 1572, 1574 and 1577*, ed. M. A. Farrow, H. L. Bradfer-Lawrence, and P. Millican, 2 vols, Norfolk RS 6–7 (Norwich, 1935–6), i. 25–7; *Surrey Musters (taken from the Loseley MSS)*, Surrey RS 3 (London, 1914–19), 137–60.

14. 'Guild of St Peter in Bardwell', ed. F. E. Warren, *Proceedings of the Suffolk Institute of Archaeology* 11 (1901–3), 131–3; BL, Addl. MS 6173.

15. *The Churchwardens' Accounts of St Michael's Church, Chagford, 1480–1600*, ed. F. M. Osborne (Chagford, 1979), pp. 161, 164, 166–7, 196, 170–1, 203.

16. *The Register of the Fraternity or Guild of the Holy and Undivided Trinity and Blessed Virgin Mary in the Parish Church of Luton, in the County of Bedford, from AD MCCCCLXXV to MVCXLVI*, ed. H. Gough (London, 1906), 17, 48, 52, 232.

17. 'Leverington Parish Accounts', *Fenland Notes and Queries* 7 (1907–9), 250.

18. 'Church Goods in Suffolk, nos. iv–xxiii', ed. J. J. Muskett, *The East Anglian* n.s. 1 (1885–6), 49–51, 67–70, 83–4, 102–4, 114–16, 128–9, 142–3, 159–61, 186–8, 207–9, 223–4, 234–6, 251–3, 274–6, 285–6, 323–4, 342–4, 353–5, 362–3; 'Church Goods in Suffolk, nos. xxiv–xxxix', ed. J. J. Muskett, *The East Anglian* n.s. 2 (1887–8), 3–5, 18–19, 43, 55–6, 70–1, 104–7, 123–4, 135–6, 153–5, 169–70, 189–90, 204–6, 244–6, 283–4, 317–19, 366–7.

19. E. P. Dickin, 'Embezzled Church Goods of Essex', *Transactions of the Essex Archaeological Society*, n.s. 13 (1913–14), 159–60, 169; 'Inventories of Norfolk Church Goods (1552)', ed. H. B. Walters, *NA* 27 (1938–40), 385–413, 28 (1942–5), 11–12, 19, 139–40, 221, 31 (1955–7), 237–53, 266, 287, 33 (1962–5), 480–5.

20. *CSPDE*, 78, 172; *The Edwardian Inventories for Bedfordshire*, ed. F. C. Eeles and J. E. Brown, Alcuin Club Collection 6 (London, 1905); *The Edwardian Inventories for Huntingdonshire*, ed. S. C. Lomas and T. Craib, Alcuin Club Collection 7 (London, 1906); *The Edwardian Inventories for Buckinghamshire*, ed. F. C. Eeles and J. E. Brown, Alcuin Club Collection 9 (London, 1908); *The Chantry Certificates for Oxfordshire and the Edwardian Inventories of Church Goods for Oxfordshire*, ed. R. Graham and T. Craib, Alcuin Club Collection 23 (London, 1920); 'Cambridgeshire Church Goods', ed. J. J. Muskett, *The East Anglian* n.s. 6–9 (1895–1902), *passim*; *Inventories of the Goods and Ornaments in the Churches of Surrey in the reign of King Edward the Sixth*, ed. J. R. Daniel-Thyssen (London, 1869), 24, 33–4, 36–7; *Church Accounts 1457–1559*, ed. R. W. Dunning and M. B. McDermott, Somerset RS 95 (Taunton, 2013), 37,

295–6; P. Thompson, *The History and Antiquities of Boston* (Sleaford, 1997 edn), 164; 'Extracts from the Churchwardens' Accounts of the Parish of Leverton', ed. E. Peacock, *Archaeologia* 41 (1867), 359; *The Inventories of Church Goods for the Counties of York, Durham, and Northumberland*, ed. W. Page, SS 97 (Durham, 1897), 71.

21. *The Edwardian Inventories of Church Goods for Cornwall*, ed. L. S. Snell (Exeter, 1955), 2–5.
22. F. Blomefield, *An Essay towards a Topographical History of the County of Norfolk*, 11 vols (London, 1805–10), iv. 97, 164, 250, 291, v. 134, 200, 337–8, vi. 449–50; *The Visitation of Norfolk in the Year 1563*, ed. G. H. Dashwood and E. Bulwer Lytton, 2 vols (Norwich, 1878–95), ii. 396; PRO, C1/861/62, 1383/60–3; Centre for Buckinghamshire Studies, D-U 1/51/1; R. Schofield, *Taxation under the Early Tudors 1485–1547* (Oxford, 2004), 43–4.
23. 'Eltham Churchwardens' Accounts', ed. A. Vallance, *Archaeologia Cantiana* 48 (1936), 131; 'Select Documents for the Medieval Borough of Burton-upon-Trent', ed. N. J. Tringham, *A Medieval Miscellany*, Collections for the History of Staffordshire, 4th ser. 20 (n.p., 2004), 53; *Accounts of the Feoffees of the Town Lands of Bury St Edmunds, 1569–1622*, ed. M. Statham, Suffolk RS 46 (Woodbridge, 2003), lxi–ii, lxvii, 3, 5, 284; Leicestershire RO, DG36/284/1–10; PRO, C/1371/78–80; D. Thomas, 'Leases of Crown Lands in the Reign of Elizabeth I', in R. W. Hoyle (ed.), *The Estates of the English Crown, 1558–1640* (Cambridge, 1992), 182.
24. PRO, DL1/16/G4, G4a, DL1/27/S13, DL1/28/C8a; DL3/54/L1.
25. *The Accounts of the Wardens of the Parish of Morebath, Devon, 1520–1573*, ed. J. E. Binney (Exeter, 1904), 194–5; *Churchwardens' Accounts of Croscombe, Pilton, Yatton, Tintinhull, Morebath and St Michael's Bath*, ed. E. Hobhouse, Somerset RS 4 (London, 1890), 169; *Churchwardens' Accounts of Chagford*, 198; Devon Heritage Centre, PW1, fo. 107v; *The Church Records of St Andrew Hubbard Eastcheap c.1450–c.1570*, ed. C. Burgess, London RS 34 (London, 1997), 183; *The Accounts of the Churchwardens of the Parish of St Michael, Cornhill, in the City of London, from 1456 to 1608*, ed. W. H. Overall (London, 1871), 160.
26. Abingdon; Andover; Barnstaple; Bedford; Beverley; Boston; Bridgwater; Bridport; Bristol; Bury St Edmunds; Calne; Cambridge; Canterbury; Chichester; Chippenham; Coventry; Dartmouth; Dover; Droitwich; Exeter; Eye; Faversham; Fordwich; Great Yarmouth; Guildford; Haverfordwest; Henley-on-Thames; Hereford; Hull; Launceston; Leicester; Lewes; Liverpool; London; Louth; Ludlow; Lydd; Lyme Regis; Maldon; Newcastle upon Tyne; New Romney; Norwich; Plymouth; Poole; Reading; Rye; Salisbury; Sandwich; Sheffield; Shrewsbury; Southampton; Stratford upon Avon; Wallingford; Warwick; Wilton; Winchester; Windsor; Witney; Worcester; York. References for those not cited below are given in the bibliography.
27. A. Dyer, 'Appendix: Ranking Lists of English Medieval Towns', in D. M. Palliser (ed.), *The Cambridge Urban History of Britain*, i: *600–1540* (Cambridge, 2000), 761–7; P. Clark and J. Hosking, *Population Estimates of English Small Towns 1550–1851* (Leicester, 1993 edn), 41, 77, 79, 159.
28. S. Gunn., D. Grummitt, and H. Cools, *War, State, and Society in England and the Netherlands, 1477–1559* (Oxford, 2007), 51–6; A. Adams, *The History of the Worshipful Company of Blacksmiths from early times until the year 1641* (London, 1937), 29; J. F. Firth, *Coopers Company, London: Historical Memoranda, Charters, Documents, and Extracts, from the Records of the Corporation and the Books of the Company, 1396–1858* (London, 1848), 107; A. H. Johnson, *The History of the Worshipful Company of the Drapers of London*, 5 vols (Oxford, 1914–22), ii. 432; *Wardens' Accounts of the Worshipful Company of Founders of the City of London 1497–1681*, ed. G. Parsloe

(London, 1964), 37; *Memorials of the Goldsmiths' Company*, ed. W. S. Prideaux, 2 vols (London, 1913), i. 56, 69; E. Glover, *A History of the Ironmongers' Company* (London, 1991), 30; C. M. Clode, *Memorials of the Guild of Merchant Taylors of the Fraternity of St John the Baptist in the City of London and of its Associated Charities and Institutions* (London, 1875), 529; C. Welch, *History of the Worshipful Company of Pewterers of the City of London, based upon their own Records*, 2 vols (London, 1902), i. 210; *YCR*, iv. 88.

29. *The Red Paper Book of Colchester*, ed. W. G. Benham (Colchester, 1902), 92–3; *The Coventry Leet Book*, ed. M. D. Harris, 4 vols, EETS 134–5, 138, 146 (London, 1907–13), iii. 608; *Henley Borough Records: Assembly Books i–iv, 1395–1543*, ed. P. M. Briers, Oxfordshire RS 41 (Oxford, 1960), 156; Hampshire RO, W/E1/48, m. 3v; S. J. Gunn, *Henry VII's New Men and the Making of Tudor England* (Oxford, 2016), 103–8, 144–50.

30. *Henley Borough Records*, 94, 103–4, 118, 139, 156, 171.

31. Downing College, Cambridge, MS Bowtell 1, fo. 52r; CCA, CC/FA10, fo. 91r.

32. *YCR*, v. 1–2.

33. BL, Egerton MS 2092, fo. 309r.

34. *YCR*, v. 172.

35. Gunn, Grummitt, and Cools, *War, State, and Society*, 55–6.

36. LMA, Rep. 2, fo. 153r; 'London Chronicle during the reigns of Henry the Seventh and Henry the Eighth', ed. C. Hopper, *Camden Miscellany iv*, CS 73 (1859), 14; J. F. Wadmore, *Some Account of the Worshipful Company of Skinners of London, being the Guild or Fraternity of Corpus Christi* (London, 1902), 87; *Records of the Borough of Leicester*, ed. M. Bateson et al., 7 vols (London, 1899–1974), iii. 92; H. Owen and J. B. Blakeway, *A History of Shrewsbury*, 2 vols (London, 1825), i. 295; *The Manuscripts of Shrewsbury and Coventry Corporations*, HMC 15th report 10 (London, 1899), 35; Gunn, Grummitt, and Cools, *War, State, and Society*, 53–4.

37. *YCR*, iv. 86; KLHC, Fa/Z33, fo. 76r; CCA, CC/FA16, fo. 31v.

38. Shropshire Archives, LB8/1/47/66.

39. Essex RO, D/B3/3/238.

40. *Records of Early English Drama: Shropshire*, ed. J. A. B. Somerset, 2 vols (Toronto, 1994), i. 200–1.

41. Blomefield, *Norfolk*, iii. 175.

42. *YCR*, iv. 84.

43. BL, Egerton MS 2107, fos. 19v, 50v, 2108, fos. 63v, 237–238r; ESRO, Rye 60/4, fos. 32v, 199v, 202r; *YCR*, ii. 125–6, iii. 85; T. Richardson, 'The Bridport Muster Roll of 1457', *Royal Armouries Yearbook* 2 (1997), 46–52; *Records of Lydd*, ed. A. Finn (Ashford, 1911), 24, 58, 62, 64, 177, 186, 198, 269, 315.

44. W. E. Stephens, 'Great Yarmouth under Queen Mary', *NA* 29 (1946), 151–2; Southampton AO, SC5/3/1, fo. 1r; SC13/2/1–3.

45. *Guildford Borough Records 1514–1546*, ed. E. M. Dance, Surrey RS 24 (Frome, 1958), 39–40; Hampshire RO, W/E1/69, m. 1r.

46. Adams, *Blacksmiths*, 16; *Journals of the House of Lords*, 10 vols (London, 1846 edn), i. 106.

47. KLHC, Fa/Z33, fo. 75v; Shropshire Archives, LB8/1/37–40.

48. C. H. Cooper, *Annals of Cambridge*, 5 vols (Cambridge, 1842–1908), ii. 158, 244, 268; KLHC, Fa/Z33, fos. 80r, 108v, 127r.

49. *Henley Borough Records*, 94, 118–19.

50. Huntingdonshire Archives, 2449/25.

51. *LP*, I, i. 1382.

52. Devon Heritage Centre, EAB1/1, fos. 35r–38r, 161r.
53. *Records of Early English Drama: Coventry*, ed. R. W. Ingram (Manchester, 1981), 134; Suffolk RO, Ipswich, EE2/L1/3; Herefordshire Archive and Records Centre, BG11/17/6/5–10/3; Firth, *Coopers*, 103, 107; *Wardens' Accounts Founders*, 79; *Memorials Goldsmiths*, i. 49; Southampton AO, SC5/1/32, fos. 29r–30r; Hampshire RO, W/E1/69, m. 3; *Reprint of the Barnstaple Records*, ed. J. R. Chanter and T. Wainwright, 2 vols (Barnstaple, 1900), ii. 106; *Henley Borough Records*, 230; *Records of Leicester*, iii. 67; Wiltshire and Swindon HC, G25/1/21, fo. 166; Worcestershire Archives, Worcester City Records A14, vol 1, fos. 21v, 26v; *YCR*, iv. 156.
54. *Churchwardens' Accounts of Marston*, 22; Lincolnshire Archives, PAR St James Louth 2, fo. 112r, 3, fo. 6v.
55. Suffolk RO, Bury St Edmunds, C12/13; Cooper, *Annals of Cambridge*, ii. 178; CCA, CC/FA16, fos. 282v, 326v; Clode, *Memorials Merchant Taylors*, 529; Welch, *Pewterers*, i. 229–30; *Records of the Skinners of London, Edward I to James I*, ed. J. J. Lambert (London, 1933), 367; Dorset HC, DC/LR/G1/1, p. 54; Hampshire RO, W/E1/90; *YCR*, vi. 15; *Churchwardens' Accounts of Ashburton*, 165; *Cratfield: A Transcript of the Accounts of the Parish, from AD 1490 to AD 1642*, ed. J. J. Raven (London, 1895), 97; *Church Records of St Andrew Hubbard*, 183; *Accounts of St Michael, Cornhill*, xxv–xxvi; Lincolnshire Archives, PAR St James Louth 3, fos. 63r, 64v; Shropshire Archives, LB8/1/53/74; *Accounts of Morebath*, 228, 238; Southampton AO, SC12/2/3; 'Wandsworth Churchwardens' Accounts from 1558 to 1573', ed. C. T. Davis, *Surrey Archaeological Collections* 17 (1902), 172; Worcestershire Archives, Worcester City Records A14, vol 1, fo. 105v; *YCR*, vi. 15, 28–9; *Faversham Tudor and Stuart Muster Rolls*, ed. P. Hyde and D. Harrington, Faversham Hundred Records 3 (Folkestone, 2000), 3–7.
56. Cooper, *Annals of Cambridge*, ii. 268–9; *Records of the Worshipful Company of Carpenters*, 6 vols (Oxford, 1913–39), iv. 115, 148–9, 233; Firth, *Coopers*, 124; Johnson, *Drapers*, ii. 140; *Wardens' Accounts Founders*, 158, 183–4; Welch, *Pewterers*, i. 230, 262, 266–7; *Records Skinners*, 367; *Weavers*, 168; *The Boston Assembly Minutes 1545–1575*, ed. P. Clark and J. Clark, Lincoln RS 77 (Woodbridge, 1987), 61; *Louth Old Corporation Records*, ed. R. W. Goulding (Lincoln, 1891), 184; Wiltshire and Swindon HC, G25/1/91; *YCR*, vi. 15, 28–9.
57. Hampshire RO, W/E1/69, m. 3; Herefordshire Archive and Records Centre, BG11/17/6/5–10/3, BG11/24/1/11, 13; Suffolk RO, Bury St Edmunds, C12/3; Suffolk RO, Ipswich, EE2/L1/3; Gunn, Grummitt, and Cools, *War, State, and Society*, 63; Southampton AO, SC5/1/32, fos. 29r–30r; *YCR*, vi. 28–9, 60, 156; Welch, *Pewterers*, i. 229; *Records Skinners*, 367; Cooper, *Annals of Cambridge*, ii. 178, 268.
58. *YCR*, vi. 14.
59. R. Tittler, *Architecture and Power: The Town Hall and the English Urban Community c.1500–1640* (Oxford, 1991), 33, 41; *Churchwardens' Accounts of Ashburton*, 136, 161; Cambridgeshire Archives, PB/X71/4; *HMC Ninth Report* (London, 1883), appendix i, 155; *Records Carpenters*, iv. 113, 234; *Memorials Goldsmiths*, i. 75; Clode, *Memorials Merchant Taylors*, 528, 573; Welch, *Pewterers*, i. 137, 168, 260; R. H. Monier-Williams, *The Tallow Chandlers of London*, 4 vols (London, 1970–7), iv. 273; *St Martin-in-the-Fields: The Accounts of the Churchwardens 1525–1603*, ed. J. V. Kitto (London, 1901), 247; *Records of Leicester*, iii. 72; Leicestershire RO, DG36/284/2, fo. 5v; *The Records of the Burgery of Sheffield, commonly called the Town Trust*, ed. J. D. Leader (London, 1897), 34; Boynton, *Elizabethan Militia*, 22–4.
60. CUL, Hengrave MS 88(i), no. 114.

61. *LP*, XIV, i. 654(11); S. T. Bindoff, *History of Parliament: The House of Commons 1509–1558*, 3 vols (London, 1982), iii. 263.
62. *YCR*, iv. 86.
63. Suffolk RO, Ipswich, EE2/L1/4a.
64. T. Girtin, *The Golden Ram: A Narrative History of the Clothworkers' Company* (London, 1958), 34, 57.
65. Wadmore, *Skinners*, 86.
66. *YCR*, iv. 179.
67. BL, Egerton MS 2093, fo. 51r.
68. 'Inventories of Norfolk Church Goods', 28 (1942–5), 11–12.
69. PRO, C1/410/59; A. F. Sutton, *The Mercery of London: Trade, Goods and People, 1130–1578* (Aldershot, 2005), 478; *Records Carpenters*, iv. 95; Johnson, *Drapers*, ii. 276, 411; *Wardens' Accounts Founders*, 142; Clode, *Memorials Merchant Taylors*, 528; *Records Skinners*, 145; 'London Chronicle', 14; Firth, *Coopers*, 97.
70. *Records Carpenters*, iv. 103; Johnson, *Drapers*, ii. 276; *Illustrations of the Manners and Expenses of Antient Times in England*, ed. J. Nichols (London, 1797), 18.
71. BL, Egerton MS 2092, fo. 238r; *Calendar of the Plymouth Municipal Records*, ed. R. N. Worth (Plymouth, 1893), 114; G. Mayhew, 'Rye and the Defence of the Narrow Seas: A Sixteenth Century Town at War', *Sussex Archaeological Collections*, 127 (1984), 115; *Churchwardens' Accounts of Marston*, 22; Southampton AO, SC13/2/2; Worcestershire Archives, Worcester City Records A14, vol 1, fo. 69v.
72. *YCR*, iv. 170–2, v. 15, 144, 153–4, 173, 180, vi. 14–15, 26, 57–8, 60, 81.
73. BL, Egerton MS 2092, fo. 238r; Johnson, *Drapers*, ii. 11, 402–3; 'London Chronicle', 14; Clode, *Memorials of the Guild of Merchant Taylors*, 527; *Illustrations of the Manners and Expenses*, 223–4, 226–8; S. Thrupp, *A Short History of the Worshipful Company of Bakers of London* (London, 1933), 149; *Records Carpenters*, iv. 33, 73; Johnson, *Drapers*, ii. 130, 402–3, 411–12; *Founders*, 142; Welch, *Pewterers*, i. 176, 179, 193, 198, 201, 205; Wadmore, *Skinners*, 86; Hampshire RO, W/E1/85, m. 3; Worcestershire RO, Worcester City Records A14, vol 1, fo. 69v; *HMC Ninth Report*, appendix i, 315.
74. *YCR*, iv. 172, 181–2, v. 4.
75. *YCR*, vi. 81; P. A. Slack, *Poverty and Policy in Tudor and Stuart England* (London, 1988), 73–5, 123, 149–50.
76. Cooper, *Annals of Cambridge*, ii. 268–9; *Liverpool Town Books*, ed. J. A. Twemlow, 2 vols (London 1918–35), i. 338–9; *Boston Assembly Minutes*, 61; Suffolk RO, Bury St Edmunds, C12/3.
77. Hampshire RO, W/E1/90, m. 4d; Cooper, *Annals of Cambridge*, ii. 268–9; *Faversham Tudor and Stuart Muster Rolls*, 1; Hampshire RO, W/E1/90, m. 4d; *Churchwardens' Accounts of Ashburton*, 165; *Reprint of the Barnstaple Records*, ii. 106; Cooper, *Annals of Cambridge*, ii. 268–9; CCA, CC/FA17, fo. 70v; P. E. Jones, *The Butchers of London: A History of the Worshipful Company of Butchers of the City of London* (London, 1976), 178; *Records Carpenters*, iv. 233; Girtin, *Golden Ram*, 57; Firth, *Coopers*, 124; Johnson, *Drapers*, ii. 140; *Founders*, 183–4; *Memorials Goldsmiths*, i. 75; Glover, *Ironmongers*, 40; Welch, *Pewterers*, i. 262, 266–7, 272; *Records Skinners*, 371; Consitt, *Weavers*, 168; *Louth Old Corporation Records*, 184; Southampton AO, SC5/2/1, fo. 63r; Hampshire RO, W/E1/98, m. 4; Worcestershire RO, Worcester City Records A14, vol 1, fo. 105v.
78. 'Molland Accounts', ed. J. B. Phear, *Reports and Transactions of the Devonshire Association* 35 (1903), 230; *Accounts of Morebath*, 240.
79. ESRO, Rye 60/3, fos. 16v, 37r, 38v, 46r, 46v, 47r, 49v, 50r, 76r, 88r, 92v, 93r, 100r, 108v, 113r; Rye 60/4, fos. 55r, 141v, 168r, 170v.

80. *YCR*, ii. 36.

81. *Calendar Plymouth*, 90, 92, 97–8, 100–1; ESRO, Rye 60/3, fos. 88v, 90r; BL, Egerton MS 2107, fos. 4v, 14v, 20r, 36v, 46r, 50r, 61r, 110r, 2092, fos. 71r–72v, 86r–89r; *The Accounts of the Chamberlains of Newcastle Upon Tyne 1508–1511*, ed. C. M. Fraser, Society of Antiquaries of Newcastle Upon Tyne RS 3 (Newcastle Upon Tyne, 1987), xxvi.

82. Southampton AO, SC5/1/15, fos. 26v, 27r, 16, fo. 6r, SC5/1/18, fos. 13v, 14r–v, 19, fos. 46r–v, SC5/1/24A, fo. 3v, SC5/1/26, fos. 38r–39v, SC5/1/27B, fos. 5r, 7r, SC5/1/28, fos. 22v–23r, 27r, 30v, 32v, SC5/1/29, fos. 25r, 30, fos. 38v–40r; R. Moffett, 'Military Equipment in the Town of Southampton during the Fourteenth and Fifteenth Centuries', *Journal of Medieval Military History* 9 (2011), 188. Southampton kept up the habit of naming guns and in 1566–7 they had a port piece called 'made mege' (SC5/1/47, fo. 19v).

83. Southampton AO, SC5/1/18, fo. 14r; *LP* I, i. 1494(57); R. D. Smith and K. DeVries, *The Artillery of the Dukes of Burgundy 1363–1477* (Woodbridge, 2005), app. 1.

84. Southampton AO, SC5/1/27B, fo. 6v, SC5/1/30, fo. 83r–v, SC5/1/31, fo. 22r–v; *Calendar Plymouth*, 107, 109; *Records of the City of Norwich*, ed. W. Hudson and J. C. Tingey, 2 vols (Norwich, 1906–10), ii. 160; W. Rye, 'An Old Cannon at the Great Hospital, Norwich', *NA* 16 (1905–7), 85–90.

85. *Calendar Plymouth*, 103–4, 112, 114, 116, 213; Southampton AO, SC5/1/32, fo. 30r, SC5/1/34, fos. 22v–23r, SC5/1/40, fo. 23v; *Great Yarmouth Assembly Minutes 1538–1545*, ed. P. Rutledge, Norfolk RS 39 (Norwich, 1970), 53; BL, Egerton MS 2094, fo. 140r.

86. Southampton AO, SC5/1/18, fos. 14v, 24v, SC5/1/28, fo. 23r, SC5/1/30, fo. 42v, SC5/1/32, fo. 23r–v.

87. *Calendar Plymouth*, 90, 99–101, 113–14.

88. BL, Egerton MS 2092, fo. 238v; *Calendar Plymouth*, 104; Southampton AO, SC5/1/19, fo. 46v, SC5/1/28, fo. 23r, SC5/1/30, fo. 42r, SC5/1/31, fo. 22v.

89. T. Varley, *Cambridge County Geographies: Isle of Wight* (Cambridge, 1924), 87; *The Victoria History of Hampshire and the Isle of Wight*, ed. H. A. Doubleday and W. Page, 6 vols (London, 1900–14), v. 165, 189, 211, 254.

90. W. Budgen, 'Guns bought for Eastbourne, 1550', *Sussex Notes and Queries* 1 (1926–7), 146–7; 'Church Goods in Suffolk, nos. iv–xxiii', 49, 223, 355, 362, 'Church Goods in Suffolk, nos. xxiv–xxxix', 3, 104, 153, 205; *Walberswick Churchwardens' Accounts AD 1450–1499*, ed. R. W. M. Lewis (London, 1947), 6–7, 11, 14, 54–5, 63–5, 70, 88.

91. Essex RO, T/A122/1, fos. 45r–50r.

92. Mayhew, 'Rye', 115; *Great Yarmouth Assembly Minutes*, 52–3; *HMC Ninth Report*, appendix i, 314.

93. *Calendar Plymouth*, 107, 113; Plymouth and West Devon RO, 1/129, fo. 114r, 1/130, fo. 34r; Southampton AO, SC5/1/18, fo. 26r, SC5/1/24A, fo. 2v, SC5/1/26, fo. 47Br, SC5/1/30, fos. 13r, 35r, SC5/1/40, fo. 30r.

94. Johnson, *Drapers*, ii. 436; Firth, *Coopers*, 95.

95. BL, Egerton MS 2107, fo. 10r; Plymouth and West Devon RO, 1/130, fo. 54v.

96. LMA, Rep. 2, fo. 181r.

97. *York City Chamberlains' Account Rolls 1396–1500*, ed. R. B. Dobson, SS 192 (Gateshead, 1980), 150, 153–4, 167, 171, 184, 188; *YCR*, i. 92; Plymouth and West Devon RO, 1/130, fos. 27v, 35r; *Calendar Plymouth*, 97; Southampton AO, SC5/1/27B, fo. 8v; Mayhew, 'Rye', 115.

98. Dorset HC, DC/PL/CLA51(6); BL, Egerton MS 2094, fo. 172r.

99. Southampton AO, SC5/1/15, fo. 27r, SC5/1/18, fo. 24v, SC5/1/28, fo. 23r, SC5/1/30, fo. 1v, SC5/1/31, fo. 29v SC5/1/32, fo. 23r; BL, Egerton MS 2107, fo. 33r, 2092, fo. 238v.

100. Southampton AO, SC5/1/39, fo. 8r, SC5/1/40, fo. 31v, SC5/1/42, fo. 29v, SC5/1/43, fo. 10v, SC5/1/49, fo. 14v.

101. *Calendar Plymouth*, 114; Southampton AO, SC5/3/1, fo. 86v.

102. *Great Yarmouth Assembly Minutes*, 66–7.

103. H. P. Smith, *The History of the Borough and County of the Town of Poole*, 2 vols (Poole, 1948–51), ii. 119, 122.

104. ESRO, Rye 45/20; Mayhew, 'Rye', 115–16.

105. BL, Egerton MS 2092, fo. 241v, 2094, fo. 140r; *City and County of Kingston Upon Hull: Calendar of the Ancient Deeds, Letters, Miscellaneous Old Documents, &c in the archives of the Corporation*, ed. L. M. Stanewell (Kingston upon Hull, 1951), 315; *Great Yarmouth Assembly Minutes*, 66–7.

106. *Records of the Burgery of Sheffield*, 303–6.

107. *YCR*, v. 12–13, 18; *Records Skinners*, 368; Hampshire RO, W/E1/76, m. 4.

108. Shropshire RO, LB8/1/47/65; Suffolk RO, Bury St Edmunds, C12/3; *Records Carpenters*, iv. 136–7, 148–9; Glover, *Ironmongers*, 41; Welch, *Pewterers*, i. 236; *Records Skinners*, 368.

109. John Palsgrave, *Lesclarcissement de la langue francoyse* (London, 1530), Q6v; PRO, SP1/10, fo. 182r.

110. Johnson, *Drapers*, i. 276–7, ii. 11–12; 'London Chronicle', 14.

111. Sutton, *Mercery*, 478; *Memorials Goldsmiths*, i. 75.

112. *Calendar Plymouth*, 114; Dorset HC, DC/BTB/M7; Southampton RO, SC5/1/42, fos. 15r, 29v, 30r, 43, fo. 10v; KLHC, Fa/Z33, fo. 76r; J. Latimer, *Sixteenth-Century Bristol* (Bristol, 1908), 37–8; *Extracts from Records in the possession of the Municipal Corporation of the Borough of Portsmouth*, ed. R. East (Portsmouth, 1891 edn), 615, 617; *Cornwall Muster Roll 1569*, 58; Hampshire RO, W/E1/98, m. 4, 99, m. 5; CCA, CC/FA16, fos. 31v, 32r; U4/8/37, fo. 10r.

113. *YCR*, iv. 90, 126.

114. *Cratfield*, 49–50, 71; Firth, *Coopers*, 103; Welch, *Pewterers*, i. 137; 'Church Goods in Suffolk, nos. iv–xxiii', 343, 'Church Goods in Suffolk, nos. xxiv–xxxix', 245.

115. *HMC Shrewsbury*, 313; *YCR*, iv. 128, 134, 159, 172, v. 14, 162.

116. Downing College, Cambridge, MS Bowtell 1, fos. 258v–9r; Girtin, *Golden Ram*, 47; *Records of Maidstone, being selections from the documents in the possession of the Corporation* (Maidstone, 1926), 190; *Accounts of Morebath*, 218–19; *Ancient Churchwardens' Accounts of the Parish of North Elmham*, ed. A. G. Legge (Norwich, 1891), 20; *YCR*, iv. 175, v. 52; Worcestershire Archives, Worcester City Records A6, box 4, fo. 48v.

117. Leicestershire RO, DG36/140/1, fo. 3r, DG36/140/3, fo. 2r; *Report on the Manuscripts of the Corporation of Beverley*, HMC 54 (London, 1900), 176; *YCR*, iv. 83–4, v. 17, 20, 163–4.

118. KHLC, NR/FAc3, fos. 104r–6v, 123r–v; ESRO, Rye 60/3, fos. 107r–111v; Mayhew, 'Rye', 117–19; BL, Egerton MS 2107, fos. 19v, 37r, 2092, fos. 10r–13v, 68v–70r, 93r–96r, 99v–101r, 278r, 2093, fos. 2r–3r, 36v, 37v, 213v; CCA, U4/8/26; W. Boys, *Collections for a History of Sandwich* (Canterbury, 1792), 679, 682, 688; Southampton RO, SC5/1/24A, fo. 4r; *YCR*, iv. 99–100, 123–4, v. 168–8; *Report on the Records of the City of Exeter*, HMC (London, 1916), 36–8; Stephens, 'Great Yarmouth', 151.

119. H. L. Turner, *Town Defences in England and Wales: An Architectural and Documentary Study, AD 900–1500* (London, 1970); M. Stoyle, *Circled with Stone: Exeter's City Walls 1485–1660* (Exeter, 2003); Mayhew, 'Rye', 111–14.

120. Thomas Lever, *A sermon preached at Pauls Crosse the xiiii day of December* (London, 1550), A3r.
121. *Calendar Plymouth*, 89, 97–100; Southampton AO, SC5/1/15, fo. 24r, SC5/1/18, fo. 21r, SC5/1/19, fos. 35v–36v, 37v–8r, SC5/1/22, fos. 24r, 28r–v, 32r, SC5/1/28, fo. 31r, SC5/1/30 fos. 2v–6r; SC5/3/1, fos. 3r, 9r, 50v; BL, Egerton MS 2108, fos. 35v, 41r–42r, 69v, 88r, 89r, 92v; Smith, *Poole*, ii. 42; Dorset HC, DC/PL/CLA23, 40.
122. M. H. Merriman, *The Rough Wooings: Mary Queen of Scots 1542–1551* (East Linton, 2000), 250–8.
123. BL, Cotton MS Otho EXI, fos. 302–3.
124. *Great Yarmouth Assembly Minutes*, 16, 57, 60, 63–4.
125. Stephens, 'Great Yarmouth', 152.
126. Henry Manship, *History of Great Yarmouth*, ed. C. J. Palmer (Great Yarmouth, 1854), 46–7.
127. Mayhew, 'Rye', 111–14; ESRO, Rye 45/19; *APC*, i. 190; BL, Egerton MS 2094, fo. 166v.
128. *YCR*, iv. 114.
129. B. Cozens-Hardy, 'Norfolk Coastal Defences in 1588', *NA* 26 (1936–8), 310–14; Blomefield, *Norfolk*, iii. 195; 'Inventories of Norfolk Church Goods', 31 (1955–7), 239, 244–5, 247–8, 251, 253.
130. 'Church Goods in Suffolk, nos. iv–xxiii', 355, 362; 'Church Goods in Suffolk, nos. xxiv–xxxix', 3, 104, 153; *Calendar Plymouth*, 114; *Churchwardens' Accounts of Ashburton*, 116–17; *Churchwardens' Accounts of Chagford*, 166, 170–1; *Accounts of Morebath*, 175, 194–5, 234; John Rylands Library, English MS 220, fo. 50b.
131. KHLC, Sa/FAt20, m. 10; ESRO, Rye 60/3, fo. 61r; *Calendar Plymouth*, 89; *Records of Lydd*, 149–50, 195, 269.
132. William Lambarde, *A Perambulation of Kent, increased and altered* (London, 1596), map facing p. 6; *StP*, iv. 42; Smith, *Poole*, ii. 46; *Calendar Plymouth*, 89, 101, 113; Southampton AO, SC5/1/47, fo. 19v; Stephens, 'Great Yarmouth', 146; 'Inventories of Norfolk Church Goods', 28 (1942–5), 139–40; Lincolnshire Archives, PAR St James Louth 2, fo. 65r; R. Peter and O. B. Peter, *The Histories of Launceston and Dunheved* (Plymouth, 1885), 186–7, 205; C. Kerry, *A History of the Municipal Church of St Lawrence, Reading* (Reading, 1883), 68; 'On the Churchwardens' Accounts of the Parish of Stratton, in the county of Cornwall', ed. E. Peacock, *Archaeologia* 46 (1880), 235; Berkshire RO, WI/FAc1, fo. 54r; *YCR*, iv. 140–3, 152, 158, 176. v. 17, 144–6, 158–9, vi. 74–6; 'Eltham Churchwardens' Accounts', 131; 'Extracts from Metfield Churchwardens' Account Books', ed. N. M. Bower, *Proceedings of the Suffolk Institute of Archaeology* 23 (1939), 146; 'Molland Accounts', 213, 220, 228; *Accounts of Morebath*, 149, 161; *The Churchwardens' Accounts of West Tarring, Sussex*, ed. W. J. Bessey (n.p., 1934), part 3, 244; 'Church Goods in Suffolk, nos. iv–xxiii', 355, 'Church Goods in Suffolk, nos. xxiv–xxxix', 104; 'Inventories of Norfolk Church Goods', 27 (1938–40), 406, 31 (1955–7), 239, 244–5, 247–8, 251; *Ancient Churchwardens' Accounts North Elmham*, 12, 28–9, 36–7, 45, 47, 49, 54, 86; Durham UL, CCB/B/76/13(190054), fo. 5, CCB/B/76/23(190195), m. 2, CCB/B/76/34a(190195), m. 2; *StP*, iv. 638.
133. H. T. White, 'The Beacon System in Kent', *Archaeologia Cantiana* 46 (1934), 77–96; W. Budgen, 'Orders as to Beacons, 1546', *Sussex Notes and Queries* 1 (1926–7), 82–4, 116–18; *YCR*, iv. 140–3, 159, 176, v. 144–6.
134. *Calendar Plymouth*, 89; Peter and Peter, *Launceston*, 205; BL, Egerton MS 2107, fos. 8v, 40v, 47v.
135. *YCR*, v. 158–9, vi. 74–5.
136. Cornwall RO, B/LAUS/172; PRO, KB9/591b/286.

137. HL, MS BA277; BL, Egerton MS 2107, fo. 8v, 2108, fo. 69v, 2093, fo. 38r; KHLC, NR/FAc3, fos. 102v, 105r, 121v, 123r, 132r, 133v; ESRO, Rye 60/3, fos. 37r, 38r, 56r, 61r, 67r, 83v, 91v; Mayhew, 'Rye', 119; Southampton RO, SC5/1/19, fo. 26v; *Winchelsea Corporation Records*, 4; *Calendar Plymouth*, 89, 100–1, 104, 112, 114, 115; *HP*, ii. 462–3.

138. Downing College, Cambridge, MS Bowtell 1, fo. 298r.

139. S. J. Gunn, 'The Regime of Charles, Duke of Suffolk, in North Wales and the Reform of Welsh Government, 1509–25', *Welsh History Review* 12 (1985), 467–9.

140. Gunn, Grummitt, and Cools, *War, State, and Society*, 77–8; Lincolnshire Archives, Monson 7/51, fos. 150v–152v; *Extracts Portsmouth*, 422–34; Bindoff, *Commons*, i. 431.

141. Southampton AO, SC5/1/15, fo. 15v; *YCR*, i. 46–7; ESRO, Rye 60/3, fo. 28v; BL, Egerton MS 1912, fo. 37v.

142. *Adams's Chronicle of Bristol*, ed. F. F. Fox (Bristol, 1910), 108–9; *Liverpool Town Books*, i. 289–91.

143. *YCR*, iv. 133, v. 24.

144. *YCR*, vi. 172–3, 175, 178.

145. I. W. Archer, 'The Burden of Taxation on Sixteenth-Century London', *HJ* 44 (2001), 599–627.

146. Mayhew, 'Rye', 109–11.

147. Dorset HC, DC/PL/CLA23.

148. Adams, *Blacksmiths*, 17.

149. Gunn, Grummitt, and Cools, *War, State, and Society*, 53–4; Shropshire RO, LB8/1/47/66, 97, 99, LB8/1/51/89; Worcestershire RO, Worcester City Records A14, vol 1, fos. 15r–17v, 21r–23v, 26v, 28v–29r, 46v–47v, 69r–71v, 72v, 80r, 105v, 106v.

150. KLHC, Fa/Z 33, fo. 20v.

151. *Records of the City of Norwich*, ii. 174.

152. Devon Heritage Centre, EAB1/1, fos. 35r–38r, 155v.

153. *Calendar Plymouth*, 113; H. J. Hillen, *History of the Borough of King's Lynn*, 2 vols. (Norwich, 1907), ii. 879; *Great Yarmouth Assembly Minutes*, 64.

154. Wiltshire and Swindon HC, G25/1/21, fo. 175; *Records of Leicester*, iii. 55–6.

155. Smith, *Poole*, ii. 118–21.

156. KLHC, Fa/Z 33, fos. 20v, 23r, 37r, 76r; *Henley Borough Records*, 95, 139, 156, 167–8, 192, 215, 230; Wiltshire and Swindon HC, G25/1/21, fos. 48–9, 135–6, 166, 169; *Records of Leicester*, iii. 3, 18, 58, 89–90.

157. B. A. Kümin, *The Shaping of a Community: The Rise and Reformation of the English Parish c.1400–1650* (Aldershot, 1996), 219; R. Tittler, *The Reformation and the Towns in England: Politics and Political Culture, c.1540–1640* (Oxford, 1998), 335.

158. S. Hindle, *The State and Social Change in Early Modern England, 1550–1640* (Basingstoke, 2000), 216.

159. *Accounts of St Michael, Cornhill*, xxv–xxvi, 157, 160, 166, 232.

160. 'On the Churchwardens' Accounts of Stratton', 218, 220; BL, Addl. MS 32,243, fos. 67v, 81r, 88v, 92r; *Churchwardens' Accounts of Ashburton*, 133, 136; *Churchwardens' Accounts of Chagford*, 194; 'Molland Accounts', 214, 230; *Lambeth Churchwardens' Accounts 1504–1645, part i*, ed. C. Drew, Surrey RS 40 (Frome, 1940), 98, 102; J. G. Taylor, *Our Lady of Batersey* (Chelsea, 1925), 342, 349; *St Martin-in-the-Fields*, 139, 149, 157, 178, 222, 234; Devon Heritage Centre, PW1, fo. 86r; 'Eltham Churchwardens' Accounts', 130–1; *Churchwardens' Accounts of St Michael, Spurriergate, York, 1518–1548*, ed. C. C. Webb, 2 vols, Borthwick Texts and Calendars 20 (York, 1997), ii. 326; *Early Churchwardens' Accounts of Hampshire*, 160; *Cratfield*, 82–3; 'Extracts from Metfield', 146; 'Great Hallingbury Churchwardens' Accounts', 110;

'Leverington Parish Accounts', 298; Lincolnshire Archives, PAR St James Louth 3, fos. 28v, 59r, 62r–v, 67v; Huntingdonshire Archives, 2449/25; 'Wandsworth from 1558 to 1573', 172; Leicestershire RO, DG36/284/2, fo. ZZ5v; *Early Churchwardens' Accounts of Hampshire*, 149; 'Church Goods in Suffolk, nos. iv–xxiii', 224; *Oxfordshire Muster Rolls*, 21–64; *Cornwall Muster Roll 1569*, *passim*; *Certificate of Musters in the County of Somerset*, *passim*.

161. 'Church Goods in Suffolk, nos. iv–xxiii', 224; 'Leverington Parish Accounts', 299; *Accounts of Morebath*, 213–14, 216, 238; *Calendar of the Tavistock Parish Records*, ed. R. N. Worth (Plymouth, 1887), 29; Huntingdonshire Archives, 2449/25; Leicestershire RO, DG36/140/3, fos. 2r, 6r; John Rylands Library, English MS 220, fo. 50b; *Churchwardens' Accounts of Marston*, 22; *Churchwardens' Accounts of Croscombe*, 158; *Church Accounts 1457–1559*, 90; *Cratfield*, 76; 'Extracts from Metfield', 146; 'Early Churchwardens' Accounts of Wandsworth, 1545 to 1558', ed. C. T. Davis, *Surrey Archaeological Collections* 15 (1900), 83; *The Churchwardens' Accounts of St Michael's in Bedwardine, Worcester, from 1539 to 1603*, ed. J. Amphlett, Worcestershire HS 6 (Oxford, 1897), 43, 66; J. R. Kent, *The English Village Constable, 1580–1642: A Social and Administrative Study* (Oxford, 1986), 14–23.

162. *Churchwardens' Accounts of Chagford*, 191, 197, 201; *Accounts of Morebath*, 140–219.

163. *Churchwardens' Accounts of St Michael, Spurriergate*, ii. 326n.

164. *Churchwardens' Accounts of Ashburton*, 113–67.

165. Firth, *Coopers*, 104.

166. *Churchwardens' Accounts of Croscombe*, 169–70; *Churchwardens' Accounts of Chagford*, 188, 198; Devon Heritage Centre, PW1, fo. 107v; *Church Records of St Andrew Hubbard*, 183; *Accounts of St Michael, Cornhill*, 160; 'On the Churchwardens' Accounts of Stratton', 220, 221; Essex RO, T/A122/1, fo. 50v; *Churchwardens' Accounts of Ashburton*, 152; *Illustrations of the Manners and Expenses*, 18.

167. Hindle, *State and Social Change*, 215, 216, 228–30.

168. B. A. Kümin, 'The Secular Legacy of the Late Medieval English Parish', in C. Burgess and E. Duffy (eds), *The Parish in Late Medieval England*, Harlaxton Medieval Studies, 14 (Donington, 2006), 109–10; M. K. McIntosh, *Controlling Misbehaviour in England, 1370–1600* (Cambridge, 1998), 23–45, 131–6, 154–62.

169. Kümin, 'Secular Legacy', 99–111; 'Church Goods in Suffolk, nos. iv–xxiii', 143, 276, 362, 'Church Goods in Suffolk, nos. xxiv–xxxix', 55, 70, 105, 123, 136, 153, 169–70, 190, 204, 245; 'Inventories of Norfolk Church Goods', 27 (1939–41), 394, 406, 410, 413, 28 (1942–5), 11, 19, 139, 221, 31 (1955–7), 237, 239–40, 244, 246–8, 251, 266, 287, 33 (1962–5), 480, 482; *Inventories of the Goods and Ornaments in the Churches of Surrey*, 24, 33; *Churchwardens' Accounts of Chagford*, 161; *Edwardian Inventories of Church Goods for Cornwall*, 2–4.

170. *Churchwardens' Accounts of St Michael, Spurriergate*, ii. 324.

171. 'Church Goods in Suffolk, nos. xxiv–xxxix', 317–18.

172. 'Inventories of Norfolk Church Goods', 27 (1939–41), 390.

173. W. A. Sessions, *Henry Howard, the Poet Earl of Surrey: A Life* (Oxford, 1999), 319–24.

CHAPTER 4

1. *The Household Book (1510–1551) of Sir Edward Don: An Anglo-Welsh Knight and his Circle*, ed. R. A. Griffiths, Buckinghamshire RS 33 (Aylesbury, 2004), 246.

2. John Bourchier, Lord, Berners, *Here begynneth the first volum of sir Iohan Froyssart of the cronycles of Englande, Fraunce, Spayne, Portyngale, Scotlande, Bretayne, Flaunders: and other places adioynynge* (London, 1523), A2r.

3. *Testamenta Vetusta*, ed. N. H. Nicolas, 2 vols (London, 1826), ii. 721; John Stow, *A Survey of London*, ed. C. L. Kingsford, 2nd edn, 2 vols (Oxford, 1971), i. 253.

4. William Worcestre, *The Boke of Noblesse addressed to King Edward IV on his Invasion of France in 1475*, ed. J. G. Nichols (London, 1860), 76–7.

5. Elis Gruffudd, 'Boulogne and Calais from 1545 to 1550', ed. M. B. Davies, *Fouad I University Bulletin of Faculty of Arts* 12 (1950), 27.

6. Nottingham UL, Mi/Dc/7, fo. 43r–43v; CA, MS M16bis, fos. 27v–33r, 38r–45r, 48v–60v; Polydore Vergil, *The Anglica Historia of Polydore Vergil A.D. 1485–1537*, ed. D. Hay, CS 3rd ser. 74 (London, 1950), 51–2, 99; *Foedera, Conventiones, Literae et cujuscunque generis Acta Publica*, ed. T. Rymer, 20 vols (London, 1704–35), xii. 494.

7. H. Miller, *Henry VIII and the English Nobility* (Oxford, 1986), 136–7.

8. Miller, *Nobility*, 156–7 and *LP*, XIX, *passim*.

9. A. R. Bell, A. Curry, A. King, and D. Simpkin, *The Soldier in Later Medieval England* (Oxford, 2013), 39–40.

10. S. T. Bindoff, *History of Parliament: The House of Commons 1509–1558*, 3 vols (London, 1982).

11. A. King, ' "What Werre Amounteth": The Military Experience of Knights of the Shire, 1369–1389', *History* 95 (2010), 418–36.

12. Bell et al., *Soldier in Later Medieval England*, 266–7; S. Payling, 'War and Peace: Military and Administrative Service amongst the English Gentry in the Reign of Henry VI', in P. R. Coss and C. Tyerman (eds), *Soldiers, Nobles and Gentlemen: Essays in Honour of Maurice Keen* (Woodbridge, 2009), 240–58.

13. R. Holinshed, *The Chronicles of England, Scotlande, and Irelande*, 4 vols (London, 1577), iv. 1821.

14. A. Ayton, 'Armies and Military Communities in Fourteenth-Century England', in Coss and Tyerman (eds), *Soldiers, Nobles and Gentlemen*, 221–6; J. Ross, 'Essex County Society and the French War in the Fifteenth Century', in L. Clark (ed.), *Conflicts, Consequences and the Crown in the Late Middle Ages*, The Fifteenth Century 7 (Woodbridge, 2007), 53–80.

15. G. Power, *A European Frontier Elite: The Nobility of the English Pale in Ireland, 1496–1566* (Hanover, 2012), 62, 65–6, 79–82, 86–92, 99–100, 109–10, 116–20, 132–4, 144, 150–2, 156, 161–2.

16. R. B. Manning, *Swordsmen: The Martial Ethos in the Three Kingdoms* (Oxford, 2003).

17. M. Keen, *Origins of the English Gentleman: Heraldry, Chivalry and Gentility in Medieval England, c.1300–c.1500* (Stroud, 2002).

18. Gruffudd, 'Boulogne and Calais', 53.

19. *StP*, ix. 115, 334, 690.

20. *StP*, x. 489–90; *LP*, XX, i. 97–8; I. W. Archer, 'The Burden of Taxation on Sixteenth-Century London', *HJ* 44 (2001), 614.

21. *StP*, xi. 4; *APC*, vi. 209, 239, 256, 339, 351, 396, 423, 425, vii. 41, 46, 58, 73, 86, 100; *A Calendar of the Shrewsbury and Talbot Papers in Lambeth Palace Library and the College of Arms*, ed. C. Jamison, E. G. W. Bill, and G. R. Batho, 2 vols, HMC joint publications 6–7 (London, 1966–71), ii. 46, 59, 74; PRO, C1/1278/42; BL, Stowe MS 571, fos. 81r–v, 88r, 90r, 115r, 116r–117v, 119v, 120v, 124r, 131r.

22. Shropshire Archives, LB8/1/48/67; *HMC Ninth Report* (London, 1883), appendix i, 154; *Records of the Worshipful Company of Carpenters*, 6 vols (Oxford, 1913–39), iv. 137, 147–9; T. Girtin, *The Golden Ram: A Narrative History of the Clothworkers' Company* (London, 1958), 47; Holinshed, *Chronicles*, ii. 483–7, iv. 1802, 1807–12, 1818, 1820–33; *APC*, vi. 209; F. Blomefield, *An Essay towards a Topographical History*

of the County of Norfolk, 11 vols (London, 1805–10), iii. 249n; *The Accounts of the Churchwardens of the Parish of St Michael, Cornhill, in the City of London, from 1456 to 1608*, ed. W. H. Overall (London, 1871), 112.

23. Bell et al., *Soldier in Later Medieval England*, 80–4, 93–4.

24. D. Grummitt, *The Calais Garrison: War and Military Service in England, 1436–1558* (Woodbridge, 2008), 110–11; Miller, *Nobility*, 34; *StP*, x. 252; P. W. Hasler, *The House of Commons 1558–1603*, 3 vols (London, 1981), iii. 241–2; *Testamenta Vetusta*, ii. 657–9; *b*, ed. M. St C. Byrne, 6 vols (Chicago IL, 1981), i. 447, 466, 683, 687–8; Gruffudd, 'Boulogne and Calais', 21, 29.

25. Bindoff, *Commons*, iii. 346; Hasler, *Commons*, iii. 9–11; BL, Stowe MS 571, fos. 81v, 89v; Holinshed, *Chronicles*, iv. 1820, 1832–3.

26. *StP*, ii. 413; R. Rapple, *Martial Power and Elizabethan Political Culture: Military Men in England and Ireland, 1558–1594* (Cambridge, 2009), 144–5; R. Morgan, *The Welsh and the Shaping of Early Modern Ireland 1558–1641* (Woodbridge, 2014), 32–50; C. Lennon, 'Bagenal [Bagnal], Sir Nicholas (d. 1590/91), soldier', *ODNB*; B. Cunningham, 'Bingham, Sir Richard (1527/8–1599), soldier and president of Connacht', *ODNB*; G. E. Cokayne, *The Complete Peerage*, ed. V. Gibbs et al., 13 vols (London, 1910–59), ii. 19; C. Lennon, 'Cosby, Francis (d. 1580), soldier and planter in Ireland', *ODNB*; S. Kelsey, 'Drury, Sir William (1527–1579), soldier and lord justice of Ireland', *ODNB*; Hasler, *Commons*, iii. 268–9; M. E. Finch, *The Wealth of Five Northamptonshire Families 1540–1640*, Northamptonshire RS 19 (Oxford, 1956), 111–14.

27. J. J. Goring, 'Social Change and Military Decline in Mid-Tudor England', *History* 60 (1975), 188, 192–4.

28. 8 Edward IV, c. 2; 19 Henry VII, c. 14; M. A. Hicks, 'The 1468 Statute of Livery', *HR* 64 (1991), 15–28; A. Cameron, 'The Giving of Livery and Retaining in Henry VII's Reign', *Renaissance and Modern Studies* 18 (1974), 17–35.

29. *Collection des voyages des souverains des Pays-Bas*, ed. L. P. Gachard, Commission Royale d'Histoire, Collection de chroniques Belges inédits, 4 vols (Brussels, 1876–82), i. 477.

30. M. K. Jones and M. G. Underwood, *The King's Mother: Lady Margaret Beaufort Countess of Richmond and Derby* (Cambridge, 1992), 81, 135–6; *The Manuscripts of Lord Middleton, preserved at Wollaton Hall*, HMC 69 (London, 1911), i. 131–2; *The Manuscripts of His Grace, the Duke of Rutland, G.C.B., preserved at Belvoir Castle*, 4 vols, HMC 24 (London, 1888–1908), iv. 559–66; *The Reign of Henry VII from Contemporary Sources*, ed. A. F. Pollard, 3 vols (London, 1913–14), i. 303. The reference to the statute passed in the late parliament dates this to the years after 1504; it presumably comes from either 1506 or 1508, in both of which years Henry was at Greenwich in late August: L. L. Ford, 'Conciliar Politics and Administration in the Reign of Henry VII', University of St Andrews Ph.D. thesis (2001), 276, 282. For a draft licence probably also associated with the scheme, see W. H. Dunham, *Lord Hastings' Indentured Retainers 1461–83*, Transactions of the Connecticut Academy of Arts and Sciences 39 (New Haven CT, 1955), 96–7.

31. *HMC Middleton*, i. 126–7; Medway Archives, DRb/Ar1/13, fo. 42v; Pierpoint Morgan Library, Rulers of England box 2, no. 22; *A Calendar of the Registers of the Priory of Llanthony by Gloucester 1457–1466, 1501–1525*, ed. J. Rhodes, Gloucestershire RS 15 (Stroud, 2002), 165–6.

32. J. J. Goring, 'The General Proscription of 1522', *EHR* 86 (1971), 681–90, 695–7.

33. PRO, E101/72/3–6; *Descriptive Catalogue of the Charters and Muniments in the Possession of the Rt Hon Lord Fitzhardinge at Berkeley Castle*, ed. I. H. Jeayes (Bristol,

1892), 204, 252; *Report on the Manuscripts of the late Reginald Rawdon Hastings, Esq.*, 4 vols, HMC 78 (London, 1928–47), i. 306; *HMC Middleton*, i. 128; Goring, 'Social Change', 188–9. For examples of, or references to such letters, see (1513) *LP*, I, i. 1804 (28–31); (1525) Longleat House, NMR401–2; (1533) *Correspondence of Edward, third earl of Derby, during the years 24 to 31 Henry VIII*, ed. T. N. Toller, Chetham Society n.s. 19 (Manchester, 1890), 112; (1536) *LP*, XI. 579, 614, 688, 821, 874; (1544) HL, MS HA 6711; 1555: Pierpoint Morgan Library, Rulers of England box 2, Mary I no. 24; (spring 1557) *HMC Tenth Report* (London, 1885), appendix iv, 158; *HMC Third Report* (London, 1872), 239; (summer 1557) *The Manuscripts of His Grace the Duke of Portland, preserved at Welbeck Abbey*, 10 vols, HMC 29 (London, 1891–1931), ii. 10; *Report on the Manuscripts of the Duke of Buccleuch and Queensberry—preserved at Montagu House, Whitehall*, 3 vols, HMC 45 (London, 1899–1926), i. 222; CUL, Hengrave MS 88(iii), no. 77; 1559: *HMC Ninth Report*, appendix ii, 385; *HMC Third Report*, 239.

34. J. P. Cooper, 'Retainers in Tudor England', in his *Land, Men, and Beliefs: Studies in Early-Modern History* (London, 1983), 78–96.

35. A. Dunn, 'Inheritance and Lordship in Pre-Reformation England: George Neville, Lord Bergavenny (c.1470–1535)', *Nottingham Medieval Studies* 48 (2004), 125–7.

36. *TRP*, i. 62, 77; J. A. Guy, *The Cardinal's Court: The Impact of Thomas Wolsey in Star Chamber* (Hassocks, 1977), 31; G. W. Bernard, *The Power of the Early Tudor Nobility: A Study of the Fourth and Fifth Earls of Shrewsbury* (Brighton, 1985), 20; B. J. Harris, *Edward Stafford, Third Duke of Buckingham, 1478–1521* (Stanford CA, 1986), 167, 175.

37. *Coventry and its People in the 1520s*, ed. M. H. M. Hulton, Dugdale Society 38 (Stratford-upon-Avon, 1999), 41; *Worcestershire Taxes in the 1520s*, ed. M. A. Faraday, Worcestershire HS n.s. 19 (Worcester, 2003), xxix, 4, 32, 38, 42, 47, 53, 61; *The 1522 Muster Roll for West Berkshire*, ed. E. A. Garnish (n.p., 1988), I. 6, 11, 48, 50, 53, 57, 139, 164, II. 90; *The Military Survey of Gloucestershire, 1522*, ed. R. W. Hoyle, Gloucestershire RS 6 (Stroud, 1993), 41, 56, 72, 208; *The County Community under Henry VIII: The Military Survey, 1522, and Lay Subsidy, 1524–5, for Rutland*, ed. J. Cornwall, Rutland Record Ser. 1 (Oakham, 1980), 22, 33, 40, 45, 58, 75, 77.

38. *1522 West Berkshire*, I. 6, 11, 139; *Worcestershire Taxes*, 42.

39. S. Gunn, 'The Regime of Charles, Duke of Suffolk, in North Wales and the Reform of Welsh Government, 1509–25', *Welsh History Review* 12 (1985), 475.

40. Cooper, 'Retainers', 85–6; *HMC Seventh Report* (London, 1879), 604; Sussex Archaeological Society, Firle Place MS 326 (NRA Report); 'Calendar of the Marquis of Anglesey's Longdon, Lichfield and other Staffordshire Charters formerly at Beaudesert', ed. I. H. Jeayes, *Collections for a History of Staffordshire*, 3rd series for 1939 (Kendal, 1940), 131; Lincolnshire Archives, 2ANC3/B/22; HL, MS HAP oversize box 4(12).

41. M. M. Norris, 'The 2nd Earl of Rutland's Band of Men-at-Arms, 1551–2', *HR* 68 (1995), 100–16.

42. PRO, STAC2/28/76; Bangor UL, Penrhyn 1608, 1609.

43. CA, MS M16bis, fo. 27v; North Yorkshire RO, ZAL1/1/7, ZAL1/2/6.

44. S. J. Gunn, *Henry VII's New Men and the Making of Tudor England* (Oxford, 2016), 144–5.

45. Cooper, 'Retainers', 85.

46. CA, MS M16bis, fos. 40r–v, 58v; *Military Survey of Gloucestershire*, 73–4, 82–5, 198; Devon Heritage Centre, D1508M/33, 74, 87, 124, 214, 246, 248, 255; DD4163, 4689.

47. Miller, *Nobility*, 139–40, 147.
48. BL, Stowe MS 571, fos. 115v–132r.
49. CUL, Hengrave MS 88(iii), fo. 33r; D. Scott, *The Stricklands of Sizergh Castle* (Kendal, 1908), 101–3; D. Youngs, *Humphrey Newton (1496–1536), An Early Tudor Gentleman* (Woodbridge, 2008), 94.
50. Goring, 'Social Change', 189–90; 3&4 Edward VI, c. 5 s. 8.
51. Goring, 'Social Change', 189–90.
52. 'Survey, temp. Phil. & Mar. of Various Estates late belonging to the Earl of Devon', *Topographer and Genealogist*, 1 (1846), 45; A. Wood, *The Memory of the People: Custom and Popular Senses of the Past in Early Modern England* (Cambridge, 2013), 287–93.
53. *APC*, vi. 163, 167–8.
54. CUL, Hengrave MS 88(i), 104, 125.
55. HL, MS BA35 (1540, 1542, 1551, 1554).
56. *Yorkshire Deeds vol iii*, ed. W. Brown, YASRS 63 (Wakefield, 1922), 150n.
57. J. Goring, 'The Military Obligations of the English People, 1509–1558', University of London Ph.D. Thesis (1955), 93–7, 222–3; Isle of Wight RO, OG/B/35.
58. Cooper, 'Retainers', 91–3; Derbyshire RO, D3287/56/4/3 (NRA report); *Descriptive Catalogue of Derbyshire Charters in Public and Private Libraries and Muniment Rooms*, ed. I. H. Jeayes (London, 1906), 6; Keele UL, Chetwynde Family Papers, CH373; Leicestershire RO, 26D53/202–4, 435–41, 443; Shakespeare Birthplace Trust RO, DR10/750, 773, 776–8, 780–1, 794, 798–9, 817; Sheffield City Libraries, Bagshawe Collection, 1797, 1853 (NRA report).
59. R. W. Hoyle, 'Lords, Tenants and Tenant Right in the Sixteenth Century: Four Studies', *Northern History* 20 (1984), 38–63; R. W. Hoyle, 'An Ancient and Laudable Custom: The Definition and Development of Tenant Right in North-Western England in the Sixteenth Century', *PP* 116 (1987), 24–55; R. W. Hoyle, 'Customary Tenure on the Elizabethan Estates' and '"Shearing the Hog": The Reform of the Estates, c.1598–1640', in R. W. Hoyle (ed.), *The Estates of the English Crown, 1558–1640* (Cambridge, 1992), 196–202, 243–5; J. L. Drury, 'More Stout than Wise: Tenant Right in Weardale in the Tudor Period', in D. Marcombe (ed.), *The Last Principality: Politics, Religion and Society in the Bishopric of Durham 1494–1660* (Nottingham, 1987), 71–100.
60. S. Gunn., D. Grummitt, and H. Cools, *War, State, and Society in England and the Netherlands, 1477–1559* (Oxford, 2007), 139.
61. CA, MS M16bis, fos. 27v, 28r, 39v, 44r; Nottingham UL, Mi5/167/103; North Yorkshire RO, ZAL1/2/6; John Rylands Library, Crutchley 237; Bodl. MS Top. Yorks c34*, fos. 36v, 38r–v; *A Descriptive Catalogue of Sheffield Manorial Records*, ed. T. W. Hall, 2 vols (Sheffield, 1926–8), i. 120–1.
62. *1522 West Berkshire*, II. 32; *Military Survey of Gloucestershire*, 83; *County Community under Henry VIII*, 29, 32, 42, 75.
63. *Correspondence earl of Derby*, 122–3.
64. 'Willoughby Letters of the First Half of the Sixteenth Century', ed. M. A. Welch, *Nottinghamshire Miscellany no. 4*, Thoroton Soc. Record Ser. 24 (Nottingham, 1967), 56–7.
65. J. M. W. Bean, *From Lord to Patron: Lordship in Late Medieval England* (Manchester, 1989), 210–25; Cooper, 'Retainers', 81–4; *HMC Sixth Report* (London, 1877), 444; *StP*, v. 408; PRO, DL1/9/F5c, F5e, F5f, DL1/13/B11, B11a, B11b, B11c, DL1/14/F2, F3, F6, DL21/L19, L19a, L19b, DL1/37/B23.
66. Gunn, *New Men*, 106–7, 144–50.

67. Gunn, *New Men*, 107–8; Miller, *Nobility*, 140–1.
68. P. Contamine, *War in the Middle Ages* (Oxford, 1984), 165–7.
69. A. Hewerdine, *The Yeomen of the Guard and the Early Tudors: The Formation of a Royal Bodyguard* (London, 2012); S. J. Gunn, 'Chivalry and Politics at the Early Tudor Court', in S. Anglo (ed.), *Chivalry in the Renaissance* (Woodbridge, 1990), 116–18; G. Rimer, T. Richardson, and J. P. D. Cooper (eds), *Henry VIII: Arms and the Man* (Leeds, 2009), 324–5; D. R. Starkey, 'Intimacy and Innovation: The Rise of the Privy Chamber, 1485–1547', in D. R. Starkey (ed.), *The English Court from the Wars of the Roses to the Civil War* (London, 1987), 90.
70. *Worcestershire Taxes*, xxix, 61; *Correspondence earl of Derby*, 114–18; Gunn, Grummitt, and Cools, *War, State, and Society*, 213.
71. Goring, 'Social Change', 190–1; Bell et al., *Soldier in Later Medieval England*, 116; *HMC Middleton*, 341, 344, 351, 353, 370–1.
72. CA, MS M16bis, fos. 52v, 55r; *Military Survey of Gloucestershire*, 54; *County Community under Henry VIII*, 63–4, 73; *Worcestershire Taxes*, 8–9.
73. *LP*, XIV, i. 652(M23(2)).
74. *Report on Manuscripts in the Welsh Language*, 2 vols, HMC 48 (London, 1898–1910), i. ii; Longleat House, NMR401.
75. J. Ross, *John de Vere, Thirteenth Earl of Oxford (1442–1513): 'The Foremost Man of the Kingdom'* (Woodbridge, 2011), 82–3, 112, 122, 140–1, 234, 236, 238–9; CA, MS M16 bis, fos. 55v–58r.
76. CA, MS M16 bis, fo. 57*v; PRO, PROB11/23/27.
77. S. E. James, *Kateryn Parr: The Making of a Queen* (Aldershot, 1999), 89; Bindoff, *Commons*, iii. 397.
78. *Sussex Coroners' Inquests 1485–1558*, ed. R. F. Hunnisett, Sussex RS 74 (Lewes, 1985), no. 16.
79. HL, MS STT 1576.
80. Bell et al., *Soldier in Later Medieval England*, 85–6, 130–4.
81. *Trevelyan Papers, Part III*, ed. W. C. Trevelyan and C. E. Trevelyan, CS 105 (London, 1872), 11.
82. BL, Egerton MS 2093, fos. 56v–57r.
83. S. K. Walker, *The Lancastrian Affinity 1361–1399* (Oxford, 1990); M. A. Hicks, 'Lord Hastings' Indentured Retainers?', in his *Richard III and his Rivals: Magnates and their Motives in the Wars of the Roses* (London, 1991), 229–46; S. L. Adams, 'The English Military Clientele, 1542–1618', in C. Giry-Deloison and R. Mettam (eds), *Patronages et clientélismes 1550–1750 (France, Angleterre, Espagne, Italie)* (Villeneuve d'Ascq, 1995), 217–27.
84. Gunn, *New Men*, 107; Hampshire RO, 37M85/4/AC/1, mm. 9–11.
85. Gunn, Grummitt, and Cools, *War, State, and Society*, 208–9; *Records of the Borough of Leicester*, ed. M. Bateson et al., 7 vols (London, 1899–1974), iii. 3, 58–60.
86. H. Owen and J. B. Blakeway, *A History of Shrewsbury*, 2 vols (London, 1825), i. 260.
87. HL, MS HA Misc Box 10(6), m. 2.
88. *Memorials of the Abbey of St Mary of Fountains*, ed. J. R. Walbran, SS 42 (Durham, 1863), 403, 406.
89. HL, MS HA Misc Box 10(6), m. 2.
90. Gunn, *New Men*, 108; Surrey HC, LM59/150, fo. 6r.
91. *Musters for Buckinghamshire*, 222, 224, 225–6; *Military Survey of Gloucestershire*, 1, 49, 96, 195, 212; *The Cornwall Muster Roll 1569*, ed. H. L. Douch (Bristol, 1984), 2, 29.
92. L. Stone, *The Crisis of the Aristocracy 1558–1641* (Oxford, 1965), 218–21.

93. 'Ancient Wills (no. 2)', ed. H. W. King, *Transactions of the Essex Archaeological Society* 3 (1865), 62.

94. *Bedfordshire Wills proved in the Prerogative Court of Canterbury 1383–1548*, ed. M. McGregor, Bedfordshire Historical RS 58 (Bedford, 1979), 172.

95. *HMC Rutland* iv. 283; *Household Book of Sir Edward Don*, 26, 30, 69, 80, 279–81, 287, 289, 305, 360, 366, 369, 391, 394, 402, 451; Longleat House, Devereux Papers 10, fo. 41r; F. G. Emmison, *Tudor Secretary: Sir William Petre at Court and Home* (London, 1961), 52; *Estate Accounts of the Earls of Northumberland 1562–1637*, ed. M. E. James, SS 163 (Durham, 1955), 43.

96. 23 Henry VIII c. 16, 27 Henry VIII c. 6, 32 Henry VIII c. 6, 13, 33 Henry VIII c. 5, 1 Edward VI, c. 5, 1 Elizabeth c. 7, 5 Elizabeth c. 9, 8 Elizabeth c. 8.

97. *YCR*, iv. 154–5, vi. 104–5; *Certificate of Musters in the county of Somerset, temp. Eliz. AD 1569*, ed. E. Green, Somerset RS 20 (London, 1904), 20, 31, 47, 90, 98, 137, 180, 199, 219, 240, 252, 298, 315; *Cornwall Muster Roll 1569*, 144.

98. Thomas Blundeville, *The fower chiefyst offices belongyng to Horsemanshippe* (London, 1566), A3r.

99. *A Commentary of the Services and Charges of William Lord Grey of Wilton*, ed. P. De M. G. Egerton, CS 40 (London, 1847), 16–17; 'Life of the last Fitz-Alan, Earl of Arundel', ed. J. G. Nichols, *Gentleman's Magazine* 104 (1833), 122; PRO, KB9/588a/94.

100. *StP*, iii. 379; Blundeville, *Horsemanshippe*, D2v–3r; Hasler, *Commons*, i. 349–51.

101. PRO, C1/295/37, 513/26; *Yorkshire Star Chamber Proceedings*, ed. W. Brown et al., 4 vols, YASRS 41, 45, 51, 70 (Wakefield, 1909–27), iii. 32–3.

102. *The Parliament Rolls of Medieval England, 1275–1504*, ed. C. Given-Wilson (Woodbridge and London, 2005), vi. 127; *The Register of Thomas Rotherham, Archbishop of York, 1480–1500, vol I*, ed. E. E. Barker, Canterbury and York Soc. 69 (Torquay, 1976), 80; *Cornish Wills 1342–1540*, ed. N. Orme, Devon and Cornwall RS n.s. 50 (Exeter, 2007), 148, 154; PRO, C1/227/45–7, 1429/61–3.

103. C. E. Moreton, *The Townshends and their World: Gentry, Law and Land in Norfolk c.1450–1551* (Oxford, 1992), 119; CUL, Hengrave MS 88(i), no. 137; Devon Heritage Centre, 484M/T1/11; Shropshire Archives, 327/11, 49; PRO, C1/1195/34.

104. PRO, E404/81/1, warrant of 1 March 1492; C1/555/15; Pierpoint Morgan Library, Rulers of England, box 2 no. 9.

105. CUL, Hengrave MS 88(i), no. 29; Bindoff, *Commons*, i. 292; *Testamenta Vetusta*, ii. 734; *HP*, i. 233; PRO, C1/992/49; *Calendar Shrewsbury and Talbot Papers*, ii. 62.

106. Hatfield House, CP152/22.

107. PRO, C1/513/26; R. Halstead, *Succinct Genealogies of the Noble and Ancient Houses of Alno or de Alneto &c* (London, 1685), 70–1.

108. *Commentary Grey of Wilton*, 37; J. Lock, 'Grey, William, thirteenth Baron Grey of Wilton (1508/9–1562)', *ODNB*; Bindoff, *Commons*, ii. 77.

109. Edward Hall, *Hall's Chronicle*, ed. H. Ellis (London, 1809), 651; *LP*, XVIII, ii. 365, 403, XIX, ii. 416, 434, XX, ii. 226, 493; *HP*, ii. 176, 618–19; *StP*, iii. 181; Bindoff, *Commons*, ii. 52, iii. 450.

110. HL, MS HAP oversize box 4(3).

111. 'Willoughby Letters', 76.

112. Gunn, *New Men*, 101; *HMC Rutland*, iv. 381.

113. Holinshed, *Chronicles*, iv. 1820, 1827, 1832–3, 1838–9.

114. Bindoff, *Commons*, i. 636, iii. 396.

115. *HP*, i. 308, ii. 120, 367, 406, 455; *StP*, ii. 234–5, v. 523–4; D. L. Potter, *Henry VIII and Francis I: The Final Conflict, 1540–47* (Leiden and Boston MA, 2011), 389.

116. *HP*, i. 394; *StP*, ii. 399–400.
117. *StP*, iii. 37–8.
118. CUL, Hengrave MS 88(i), nos. 47, 49, 50, 66, 67, 68, 71, 88, 88(iii), no. 95.
119. *LP*, II, ii. 4282.
120. *HP*, ii, 213–14.
121. BL, Stowe MS 571, fo. 78r; HL, MS HAP oversize box 4(10); for an earlier list, see Christine de Pisan, trans. William Caxton, *The Book of Fayttes of Armes and of Chyvalrye*, ed. A. T. P. Byles, EETS 189 (London, 1932), 20–4.
122. *StP*, i. 30, ii. 234, 267, 307, iii. 191–2, 408, 436, 453, x. 446, xi. 58; *HP*, i. 267–8, ii. 384; William Patten, 'The Expedition into Scotland', in *Tudor Tracts*, ed. A. F. Pollard (Westminster, 1903), 122, 130.
123. *StP*, i. 30, 32, iii. 16, 454, x. 618, xi. 4, 17; *HP*, ii. 384; Patten, 'Expedition into Scotland', 59, 130–1.
124. Gruffudd, 'Boulogne and Calais', 41, 69.
125. G. Phillips, 'To Cry "Home! Home!": Mutiny, Morale and Indiscipline in Tudor Armies', *Journal of Military History* 65 (2001), 324–5.
126. Sextus Julius Frontinus, *The strategemes, sleyghtes, and policies of warre, gathered togyther, by S. Iulius Frontinus, and translated into Englyshe, by Rycharde Morysine* (London, 1539), A5r.
127. T. F. Arnold, *The Renaissance at War* (London, 2001), 54–60, 103–5; H. J. Webb, *Elizabethan Military Science: The Books and the Practice* (Madison WI, 1965), 3–50.
128. C. Nall, *Reading and War in Fifteenth-Century England from Lydgate to Malory* (Cambridge, 2012), 11–47; CUL, Hengrave MS 88(iii), fo. 30v.
129. Gunn, Grummitt, and Cools, *War, State, and Society*, 218; Onosander, *Onosandro Platonico, of the generall captaine, and of his office, translated out of Greeke into Italyan, by Fabio Cotta, a Romayne: and out of Italian into Englysh, by Peter Whytehorne* (London, 1563), A2r–4r; Flavius Vegetius, *The foure bookes of Flauius Vegetius Renatus briefelye contayninge a plaine forme, and perfect knowledge of martiall policye, feates of chiualrie, and whatsoeuer pertayneth to warre. Translated out af lattine, into Englishe, by Iohn Sadler* (London, 1572), A2r; the Vegetius translation was first made for Sir Edmund Brudenell, on whose military responsibilities see J. Wake, *The Brudenells of Deene*, 2nd edn (London, 1954), 60–3.
130. J. Raymond, *Henry VIII's Military Revolution: The Armies of Sixteenth-Century Britain and Europe* (London and New York, 2007), 11; J. R. Hale, 'On a Tudor Parade Ground: The Captain's Handbook of Henry Barrett 1562', in his *Renaissance War Studies* (London, 1983), 266; Webb, *Elizabethan Military Science*, 19, 157; Barnaby Rich, *A right exelent and pleasaunt dialogue, betwene Mercury and an English souldier* (London, 1574), A2r; Isle of Wight RO, JER/WA/36/7, m. 19.
131. Raymond, *Henry VIII's Military Revolution*, 9; Hale, 'On a Tudor Parade Ground', 251–2; *HMC Second Report* (London, 1874), 31; M. H. Merriman, *The Rough Wooings: Mary Queen of Scots 1542–1551* (East Linton, 2000), 249.
132. Bindoff, *Commons*, ii. 219.
133. *Star Chamber Suits of John and Thomas Warneford*, ed. F. E. Warneford, Wiltshire RS 48 (Trowbridge, 1993), xvi, 37–9, 45, 57–64; Bindoff, *Commons*, i. 533; Gruffudd, 'Boulogne and Calais', 42.
134. Bindoff, *Commons*, iii. 435.
135. John Marckant, *The purgacion of the ryght honourable lord Wentworth concerning the crime layde to his charge* (London 1559).
136. Hall, *Chronicle*, 641.

137. Miller, *Nobility*, 16–17.

138. *Visitations of the North*, ed. C. H. Hunter Blair and F. W. Dendy, 4 vols, SS 122, 133, 144, 146 (Durham, 1912–32), i. 126, 131, 135, 179, 183, ii. 20, 101–2, iii. 19, 26–8, 121–3, 125, 162; *Heraldic Visitation of the Northern Counties in 1530 by Thomas Tonge, Norroy King of Arms*, ed. W. H. D. Longstaffe, SS 41 (Durham, 1863), 5, 20, 56; *The Visitation of Norfolk in the Year 1563*, ed. G. H. Dashwood and E. Bulwer Lytton, 2 vols (Norwich, 1878–95), ii. 268.

139. John Leland, *The Itinerary of John Leland in or about the Years 1535–1543*, ed. L. T. Smith, 5 vols (London, 1906–10), iv. 87, 128.

140. Bindoff, *Commons*, ii. 143.

141. N. Saul, *English Church Monuments in the Middle Ages* (Oxford, 2009), 201–37; N. Llewellyn, *Funeral Monuments in Post-Reformation England* (Cambridge, 2000), 79, 313–14.

142. P. King, 'Eight English Memento Mori Verses from Cadaver Tombs', *Notes and Queries* n.s. 28 (1981), 495; P. Sherlock, *Monuments and Memory in Early Modern England* (Aldershot, 2008), 151–2.

143. Blomefield, *Norfolk*, ii. 120–5.

144. F. G. Lee, *The History, Description and Antiquities of the Prebendal Church of the Blessed Virgin Mary of Thame* (London, 1883), 95, 99; N. Llewellyn, 'Claims to Status through Visual Codes: Heraldry on Post-Reformation Funeral Monuments', in S. Anglo (ed.), *Chivalry in the Renaissance* (Woodbridge, 1990), 155; J. Weever, *Ancient funerall monuments within the united monarchie of Great Britaine, Ireland, and the islands adiacent* (London, 1631), 593–4.

145. Gunn, Grummitt, and Cools, *War, State, and Society*, 230.

146. *Commentary Grey of Wilton*, 62–3.

147. Gunn, 'Chivalry and Politics', 109–16.

148. *HKW*, iii. 342, 366, 375, 388n, iv. 448, 451, 564, 627, 648–50.

149. *HP*, ii. 598, 603; Holinshed, *Chronicles*, iv. 1808–12.

150. R. G. Jenkins, 'On the Gates of Boulogne, at Hardres Court, in the parish of Upper Hardres', *Archaeologia Cantiana* 4 (1861), 51–3; Bindoff, *Commons*, i. 307.

151. J. Boffey and A. S. G. Edwards, 'Literary Texts', in L. Hellinga and J. B. Trapp (eds), *The Cambridge History of the Book in Britain, volume III, 1400–1557* (Cambridge, 1999), 574; *A Catalogue of the Manuscript Books in the Library of Christ Church, Canterbury*, ed. C. E. Woodruff (Canterbury, 1911), 16; *HMC Third Report*, 184; G. Duff, 'Some Early Scottish Book-Bindings and Collectors', *Scottish Historical Review* 4 (1907), 432–3.

152. Cokayne, *Complete Peerage*, xii. 798; BL, Addl. Roll 74192.

153. D. N. J. MacCulloch, *Tudor Church Militant: Edward VI and the Protestant Reformation* (London, 2000), 55; *Letters and Memorials of State*, ed. A. Collins, 2 vols (London, 1746), i. 27–8; Victoria and Albert Museum, MS L30/1982, fo. 15v (I am grateful to Chris Skidmore for this reference); Thomas Churchyard, *A generall rehearsall of warres, called Churchyardes choise wherein is fiue hundred seuerall seruices of land and sea as seiges, battailes, skirmiches, and encounters* (London, 1579), L3r.

154. R. Polwhele, *The History of Devonshire*, 3 vols (London, 1793–1806), ii. 78–9; Bindoff, *Commons*, ii. 175; C. Lloyd and S. Thurley, *Henry VIII: Images of a Tudor King* (Oxford, 1990), 54–6; W. H. St J. Hope, *Cowdray and Easebourne Priory* (London, 1919), 39–44.

155. Bindoff, *Commons*, i. 538.

156. Rimer et al. (eds), *Henry VIII: Arms and the Man*, 210–11; Miller, *Nobility*, 151, 157; C. S. Knighton, 'Mordaunt, John, first Baron Mordaunt (*c.*1480x85–1562), landowner

and administrator', *ODNB*; M. J. Rodríguez-Salgado (ed.), *Armada 1588–1988* (London, 1988), 266; Cunningham, 'Bingham'.

157. A. Boyle, 'Hans Eworth's Portrait of the Earl of Arundel and the Politics of 1549–50', *EHR* 117 (2002), 31–6.

158. Blomefield, *Norfolk*, i. 280.

159. J. G. Jones, *Beirdd yr Uchelwyr a'r Gymdeithas yng Nghymru c.1536–1640* (Denbigh, 1997), 25–8, 30–2, 67; R. A. Griffiths, *Sir Rhys ap Thomas and his Family: A Study in the Wars of the Roses and Early Tudor Politics* (Cardiff, 1993), 82–5; E. I. Rowlands, 'Terwyn a Thwrnai', *National Library of Wales Journal* 9 (1955–6), 295–300; D. J. Bowen, 'Y canu i deulu'r Penrhyn', *Dwned* 9 (2003), 94–9; R. A. Charles, 'Noddwyr y beirdd yn sir y Fflint', *Llên Cymru* 12–13 (1972–81), 17; *Gwaith Tudur Aled*, ed. T. G. Jones (Cardiff, 1924), nos. VII, XII, XIV, XXXIII; *Gwaith Lewys Daron*, ed. A. C. Lake (Cardiff, 1994), nos. 3, 11; *Gwaith Lewys Môn*, ed. E. I. Rowlands (Cardiff, 1975), nos. VIII, XXXVII, XLVI, LXXVI, LXXIX, LXXXVII, LXXXVIII; *Gwaith Siôn Ceri*, ed. A. C. Lake (Aberystwyth, 1996), no. 50; *Gwaith Syr Dafydd Trefor*, ed. R. Ifans (Aberystwyth, 2005), no. 12; *Gwaith Lewys Morgannwg*, ed. A. C. Lake (Aberystwyth, 2004), nos. 3, 7, 8, 17, 24, 29, 34, 37, 40, 52, 53, 58, 66, 77, 78, 87; *Gwaith Gruffudd Hiraethog*, ed. D. J. Bowen (Cardiff, 1990), nos. 16, 74, 76; *Gwaith Iorwerth Fynglwyd*, ed. H. L. Jones and E. I. Rowlands (Cardiff, 1975), nos. 16, 17, 24.

160. Gunn, Grummitt, and Cools, *War, State, and Society*, 191–2; S. J. Gunn, *Charles Brandon, Duke of Suffolk, c.1484–1545* (Oxford, 1988), 195; *The Priory of Hexham, its Chronicles, Endowments and Annals*, ed. J. Raine, 2 vols, SS 44, 46 (Durham, 1864–5), i, appendix xcv.

161. *Derbyshire wills proved in the Prerogative Court of Canterbury*, ed. D. G. Edwards, 2 vols, Derbyshire RS 26, 31 (Chesterfield, 1998–2003), i. 56, 106; Norfolk RO, NCC Wills 161 Multon; *North Country Wills*, ed. J. W. Clay, 2 vols, SS 116, 212 (Durham, 1908–12), i. 195.

162. Gunn, *Charles Brandon*, 22, 76, 152, 184–6, 192; Gunn, Grummitt, and Cools, *War, State, and Society*, 194, 200–3; S. L. Adams, 'The Dudley Clientele, 1553–1563', in G. W. Bernard (ed.), *The Tudor Nobility* (Manchester, 1992), 245–7.

163. W. A. Shaw, *The Knights of England*, 2 vols (London, 1906), i. 17–21, 31–2, 37–8, 42, 43–6, 52–7, 61–3, 70–7.

164. S. J. Gunn, 'The Duke of Suffolk's March on Paris in 1523', *EHR* 101 (1986), 598–9; Gunn, Grummitt, and Cools, *War, State, and Society*, 140–2; Gunn, *New Men*, 105–6.

165. S. G. Ellis, *Tudor Frontiers and Noble Power: The Making of the British State* (Oxford, 1995), 107–45; Gunn, Grummitt, and Cools, *War, State, and Society*, 201–3.

166. CUL, Hengrave MS 88 (i), nos. 41, 90, 100, 107, 113, 139.

167. Goring, 'Social Change', 190; G. S. Thomson, *Lords Lieutenants in the Sixteenth Century* (London, 1923), 16–18, 22–4; Potter, *Henry VIII and Francis I*, 220–36.

168. Thomson, *Lords Lieutenants*, 18–22.

169. CUL, MS Hengrave 88(iii), no. 84.

170. Thomson, *Lords Lieutenants*, 24–59. For a commission of 1554 in addition to that noted by Thomson, see HL, MS HAP oversize box 4(23).

171. HL, MS HA 12640; Thomson, *Lords Lieutenants*, 37.

172. *Calendar Shrewsbury and Talbot Papers*, ii. 54.

173. Thomson, *Lords Lieutenants*, 60–7; HL, MS HAP oversize box 4(11, 13); Coughton Court, Throckmorton MSS, Box 72, no. 15 (NRA report).

174. BL, Althorp papers A6.

175. *HMC Middleton*, i. 339; *Men at Arms: Musters in Monmouthshire, 1539 and 1601–2*, ed. T. Hopkins, South Wales RS 21 (Cwmbran, 2009), 45, 63; *Bedfordshire Muster*

Rolls 1539–1831, ed. N. Lutt, Bedfordshire Historical RS 71 (Bedford, 1992), 7–8, 24; *1522 West Berkshire*, I. 1; *The Devon Muster Roll for 1569*, ed. A. J. Howard and T. L. Stoate (Bristol, 1977), 1, 246, 249; *Dorset Tudor Muster Rolls, 1539, 1542, 1569*, ed. T. L. Stoate (Bristol, 1978), 1, 23, 26, 47, 56, 82, 90, 117, 127, 165; 'Musters for Northumberland in 1538', ed. J. Hodgson, *Archaeologia Aeliana* 4 (1855), 159, 170, 173, 192; *Certificate of Musters in the County of Somerset*, 15, 326; 'Muster Roll, 1539', *Collections for the History of Staffordshire* n.s. 4 (1901), 216, n.s. 5 (1902), 235, n.s. 6 (1903), 63, 75, 87; *Surrey Musters (taken from the Loseley MSS)*, Surrey RS 3 (London, 1914–19), 137, 175; 'Musters in Skyrack Wapentake, 1539', ed. W. P. Baildon, *Miscellanea ii*, Thoresby Soc. 4 (Leeds, 1893), 245.

176. BL, Althorp papers A6.
177. *HMC Third Report*, 239.
178. CUL, Hengrave MS 88(i), nos. 101, 103.
179. *HMC Seventh Report*, 538; L. Boynton, *The Elizabethan Militia 1558–1638* (London, 1967), 63–4, 69–76; A. H. Smith, 'Militia Rates and Militia Statutes 1558–1663', in P. Clark, A. G. R. Smith, and N. Tyacke (eds), *The English Commonwealth 1547–1640: Essays in Politics and Society presented to Joel Hurstfield* (Leicester, 1979), 96–100.
180. Leicestershire RO, DG36/284/2, fo. 5v; Lincolnshire Archives, PAR St James Louth 3, fo. 28v; Dorset HC, DC/BTB/M7.
181. BL, Althorp papers A6.
182. CUL, Hengrave MS 88(ii), no. 10.
183. A. Weikel, 'The Rise and Fall of a Marian Privy Councillor: Sir Henry Bedingfield 1509/11–1585', *NA* 40 (1987–9), 83.
184. C. H. Cooper, *Annals of Cambridge*, 5 vols (Cambridge, 1842–1908), ii. 248–9.
185. *LP*, XX, i. 100; *HMC Seventh Report*, 538, 613–14; *Yorkshire Deeds vol iii*, 149–50; *Calendar Shrewsbury and Talbot Papers*, ii. 7, 35, 80, 300–1.
186. J. G. Jones, *Concepts of Order and Gentility in Wales, 1540–1640* (Llandysul, 1992).
187. *Proceedings in the Parliaments of Elizabeth I*, ed. T. E. Hartley, 3 vols (Leicester, 1981–95), i. 195.
188. BL, Stowe MS 571; *APC*, vi; *CSPDM*; Cokayne, *Complete Peerage*.
189. Jacopo di Porcia, *The preceptes of warre, setforth by Iames the erle of Purlilia, and translated into englysh by Peter Betham* (London, 1544), A2r–5v.

CHAPTER 5

1. Westminster Abbey Muniments, 16084, 16086; for John Empson see *The Victoria History of the County of Sussex*, ed. W. Page et al., 9 vols in 11 (London, 1905–), iv. 15.
2. W. Sombart, *Krieg und Kapitalismus* (Munich, 1913); J. U. Nef, 'War and Economic Progress 1540–1640', *EcHR* 12 (1942), 13–38.
3. M. M. Postan, 'Some Social Consequences of the Hundred Years War', *EcHR* 12 (1942), 1–12; K. B. McFarlane, 'War, the Economy and Social Change: England and the Hundred Years' War', *PP* 22 (1962), 3–13; M. M. Postan, 'The Costs of the Hundred Years' War', *PP* 27 (1964), 34–53.
4. A. R. Bridbury, 'The Hundred Years War: Costs and Profits', in D. C. Coleman and A. H. John (eds), *Trade, Government and Economy in Pre-Industrial England: Essays presented to F. J. Fisher* (London, 1976), 80–95; W. M. Ormrod, 'The Domestic Response to the Hundred Years War', in A. Curry and M. Hughes (eds), *Arms, Armies and Fortifications in the Hundred Years War* (Woodbridge, 1994), 83–101; Nef, 'War and Economic Progress', 36; Postan, 'Some Social Consequences', 12.

5. Bridbury, 'Hundred Years War', 94; McFarlane, 'War, the Economy and Social Change', 3; Sombart, *Krieg und Kapitalismus*, 103; Postan 'Costs of the Hundred Years' War', 35; Nef, 'War and Economic Progress', 26.

6. D. W. Jones, *War and Economy in the Age of William III and Marlborough* (Oxford, 1988).

7. A. Saul, 'Great Yarmouth and the Hundred Years War in the Fourteenth Century', *Bulletin of the Institute of Historical Research* 52 (1979), 105–15; M. Kowaleski, 'Warfare, Shipping and Crown Patronage: The Impact of the Hundred Years War on the Port Towns of Medieval England', in L. Armstrong, M. M. Elbl, I. Elbl, and L. D. Armstrong (eds), *Money, Markets and Trade in Late Medieval Europe: Essays in Honour of John H. A. Munro* (Leiden and Boston MA, 2007), 233–54.

8. R. Schofield, *Taxation under the Early Tudors 1485–1547* (Oxford, 2004), 170–2; R. W. Hoyle, 'War and Public Finance', in D. MacCulloch (ed.), *The Reign of Henry VIII* (Basingstoke, 1995), 75–99; J. D. Gould, *The Great Debasement: Currency and the Economy in Mid-Tudor England* (Oxford, 1970), 81; C. E. Challis, *The Tudor Coinage* (Manchester, 1978), 233–42; M. Allen, 'The Volume of the English Currency, 1158–1470' *EcHR* n.s. 54 (2001), 607.

9. C. Richmond, *The Paston Family in the Fifteenth Century: Fastolf's Will* (Cambridge, 1996), 24; Hoyle, 'War and Public Finance', 98–9; R. W. Hoyle, 'Taxation and the Mid-Tudor Crisis', *EcHR* n.s. 51 (1998), 653–4, 656–9; G. W. Bernard, *War, Taxation and Rebellion in Early Tudor England: Henry VII, Wolsey and the Amicable Grant of 1525* (Brighton, 1986), 110–30.

10. 'Inventories of Norfolk Church Goods (1552)', ed. H. B. Walters, *NA* 31 (1955–7), 266, 269, 33 (1962–5), 480–2, 486–8.

11. D. M. Loades, *Two Tudor Conspiracies*, 2nd edn (Bangor, 1992), 74–5.

12. D. L. Potter, *Henry VIII and Francis I: The Final Conflict, 1540–47* (Leiden and Boston MA, 2011), 380–1; PRO, E404/81/2; J. Gairdner, 'On a Contemporary Drawing of the Burning of Brighton in the Time of Henry VIII', *TRHS* 3rd ser. 1 (1907), 19–31; A. Anscombe, 'Prégent de Bidoux's Raid in Sussex in 1514 and the Cotton MS. Augustus I(i), 18', *TRHS* 3rd ser. 8 (1914), 103–11; *The Survey of Cornwall by Richard Carew*, ed. J. Chynoweth, N. Orme, and A. Walsham, Devon and Cornwall RS n.s. 47 (Exeter, 2004), fo. 156r; John Leland, *The Itinerary of John Leland in or about the Years 1535–1543*, ed. L. T. Smith, 5 vols (London, 1906–10), i. 225; *StP*, x. 190.

13. PRO, C1/66/365; *Survey of Cornwall*, fo. 131v.

14. E. T. Nicolle, 'The Capture of Sark by the French in 1549 and its Re-Capture in 1553, by a Flemish Corsair', *Bulletin annuel de la Société jersiaise* 10 (1923–7), 157–73; Leland, *Itinerary*, i. 191.

15. *CEPR*, xix. 908.

16. *HP*, i. 134, 142.

17. J. L. Drury, 'More Stout than Wise: Tenant Right in Weardale in the Tudor Period', in D. Marcombe (ed.), *The Last Principality: Politics, Religion and Society in the Bishopric of Durham 1494–1660* (Nottingham, 1987), 73, 89.

18. *The Register of the Priory of St Bees*, ed. J. Wilson, SS 126 (Durham, 1915), 583.

19. R. Lomas, 'The Impact of Border Warfare: The Scots and South Tweedside, c. 1290–c. 1520', *Scottish Historical Review* 75 (1996), 143–67; Durham UL, CCB72/190010, mm. 5–6.

20. *HP*, i. lxxiv, lxxvi, 103, 344, 321, 325, 413, 574, ii. 65, 406, 408; *LP*, XXI, i. 1279; 33 Henry VIII c. 6 s. 18; S. G. Ellis, *Defending English Ground: War and Peace in Meath and Northumberland, 1460–1542* (Oxford, 2015), 35–7, 40–2, 99–103; for the war of 1532–4, see *StP*, iv. 621–2, 625–6, 647.

21. *StP*, iv. 42.

22. *StP*, ii. 168–9; *Calendar of State Papers Ireland, Tudor Period 1566–1567*, ed. B. Cunningham (Dublin, 2009), no. 33; Ellis, *Defending English Ground*, 37–40, 43–52, 65–74, 113–33.

23. *HP*, i. lxvii, 292, ii. 257, 259, 371–2; *Tudor Economic Documents*, ed. R. H. Tawney and E. E. Power, 3 vols (London, 1924), ii. 102.

24. PRO, C1/124/26.

25. *LP*, III, ii. 2497; *HP*, i. 412; *StP*, ix. 295–6, 307–8, 315, 325–6, 335, 338; G. Ramsay, *The City of London in International Trade at the Accession of Elizabeth I* (Manchester, 1975), 132–3; PRO, C1/807/54, 996/11, 1019/33; J. Webb, *Great Tooley of Ipswich: Portrait of an Early Tudor Merchant* (Ipswich, 1962), 31–7.

26. Keele UL, Marquess of Anglesey Papers, General Correspondence, vol 1 no. 1.

27. PRO, C1/51/153, 60/253, 76/105, 322/61; *HP*, ii. 94–5; *The Customs of London, otherwise called Arnold's Chronicle*, ed. F. Douce (London, 1811), 229–30; *Ipswich Borough Archives 1255–1835: A Catalogue*, ed. D. Allen, Suffolk RS 43 (Woodbridge, 2000), 573 (1545); *StP*, iv. 135; *APC*, i. 362, vi. 268–9; CUL, Hengrave MS 88(i), no. 5, 88(iii), no. 72.

28. *Calendar of the Bristol Apprentice Book 1532–1565*, ed. D. Hollis, E. Ralph, and N. M. Hardwick, 3 vols, Bristol RS 14, 33, 43 (Bristol, 1948–92), i. 200, ii. 154.

29. N. A. M. Rodger, 'The Law and Language of Private Naval Warfare', *Mariner's Mirror* 100 (2014), 5–16; *LP*, I, ii. 1871, 2977; *StP*, iii. 465–6, 559, ix. 263–4, 283; PRO, C1/64/722, 143/59, 148/68, 163/82, 390/1, 433/14, 443/29, 455/34, 615/12, 627/38, 645/16, 694/27, 755/24, 1154/8, 1302/33; *Depositions taken before the Mayor and Aldermen of Norwich, 1549–1567*, ed. W. Rye (Norwich, 1905), 54–5.

30. S. Murdoch, *The Terror of the Seas? Scottish Maritime Warfare 1513–1713* (Leiden, 2010), 37–82, 359–61; *StP*, iv. 639, 641–3, ix. 283; *LP*, XVIII, i. 62, XXI, ii. 259; PRO, C1/59/88, 59/92, 196/51, 213/96, 312/26, 461/5, 486/46; *Chronologische lijsten van de Geëxtendeerde Sententiën berustende in het archief van de Grote Raad van Mechelen*, ed. J. Th. de Smidt et al., 6 vols (Brussels and Arnhem, 1966–88), i. 311–12; *Calendar of State Papers, Ireland, Tudor period 1547–1553*, ed. C. Lennon (Dublin, 2015), no. 78.

31. *LP*, V. 906.

32. PRO, C1/60/116, 60/186, 62/419, 64/646, 64/1105, 66/298–9, 66/300, 66/429, 71/1, 146/51, 186/13, 226/41, 526/67, 722/24, 1193/83–5, 1368/33–5; C54/388, m. 16d; *TRP*, i. 291; *Chroniques de Jean Molinet*, ed. G. Doutrepont and O. Jodogne, 3 vols (Brussels, 1935–7), ii. 216–17; *Chronologische lijsten van de Geëxtendeerde Sententiën*, i. 146, 152–3, 163–4, 172, 201–2, 420, 422, 453, iii. 486, iv. 43–4, v. 124, 172, 265–6, 372–3, 386–7, 454, vi. 16; ESRO, Rye 60/3, fo. 67r, Rye 60/4, fo. 29v.

33. 'Two London Chronicles', ed. C. L. Kingsford, *Camden Miscellany XII*, CS 3rd Ser. 18 (London, 1910), 47.

34. E. T. Jones, 'The Bristol Shipping Industry in the Sixteenth Century', University of Edinburgh Ph.D. Thesis (1998), 101–2.

35. N. Williams, *The Maritime Trade of the East Anglian Ports 1550–1590* (Oxford, 1988), 50–68, 138–82.

36. Dorset HC, DC/PL/CLA 23; Plymouth and West Devon RO, 1/129, fos. 86v–159v; PRO, C1/223/41; *StP*, iv. 642; *Acta curiae admirallatus Scotiae 6th Sept. 1557–11th March 1561–2*, ed. T. C. Wade, Stair Soc. 19/2 (Edinburgh, 1937), 22–3, 31, 72, 125. Unfortunately the records of the cobb dues at Lyme Regis, which record individual ships, do not seem to survive in sufficient quantity for effective analysis: Dorset HC, DC/LR/G7/3.

37. *LP*, XIX, i. 7; *CSPDE*, 224.
38. *HP*, ii. 490, 492, 494–6, 500–1.
39. *HP*, ii. 508.
40. W. R. Childs, 'Fishing and Fisheries in the Middle Ages: The Eastern Fisheries', in D. J. Starkey, C. Reid, and N. Ashcroft (eds), *England's Sea Fisheries: The Commercial Fisheries of England and Wales since 1300* (London, 2000), 19–23; M. Kowaleski, 'Fishing and Fisheries in the Middle Ages: The Western Fisheries', ibid. 23–8; E. Jones, 'England's Icelandic Fishery in the Early Modern Period', ibid. 105–9.
41. *HP*, i. 186, 551, 577, 601; *LP*, XX, ii. 190.
42. *StP*, iv. 152.
43. BL, Egerton MS 2093, fo. 213v.
44. *HMC Ninth Report* (London, 1883), appendix i, 315.
45. PRO, C1/469/35.
46. Murdoch, *Terror of the Seas?*, 70–1; *Depositions before the Mayor and Aldermen of Norwich*, 54–5; *LP*, II, i. 354; PRO, C1/59/88, 59/92, 62/312–13, 213/96, 243/23, 457/30, 461/5, 486/46, 922/11; ESRO, Rye 60/3, fo. 39r; *LP*, V. 906; *Calendar of the Plymouth Municipal Records*, ed. R. N. Worth (Plymouth, 1893), 101, 105.
47. Dorset HC, DC/PL/CLA48/3; *Records of the Worshipful Company of Carpenters*, 6 vols (Oxford, 1913–39), iv. 10, 19, 33, 71, 110; *LP*, II, i. 354, IV, ii. 3087; PRO, C1/455/34; M. K. McIntosh, *Poor Relief in England 1350–1600* (Cambridge, 2012), 45–52, 155–6.
48. 'Church Goods in Suffolk, nos. xxiv–xxxix', ed. J. J. Muskett, *The East Anglian* n.s. 2 (1887–8), 104; E. P. Dickin, 'Embezzled Church Goods of Essex', *Transactions of the Essex Archaeological Society*, n.s. 13 (1913–14), 159.
49. PRO, C1/66/342.
50. *HMC Seventh Report* (London, 1879), app. 618; PRO, C1/62/313.
51. A. Crawford, *Yorkist Lord: John Howard, Duke of Norfolk, c.1425–1485* (London, 2010), 172–3; PRO, C1/86/19–22, 163/49.
52. PRO, C1/454/44.
53. *YCR*, ii. 75.
54. *StP*, iv. 249.
55. *British Library Harleian MS 433*, ed. R. Horrox and P. W. Hammond, 4 vols (Gloucester, 1979–83), i. 219, ii. 161; *LP*, I, i. 179(59), 1463(7), 1480, ii. 1812, 2946, III, ii. 2224, 2500, IV, i. 832, V. 717, VII. 48, XVIII, i. 452, XIX, i. 237, XXI, i. 434, 860; PRO, C1/655/2; D. M. Loades, *The Making of the Elizabethan Navy 1540–1590: From the Solent to the Armada* (Woodbridge, 2009), 90.
56. W. R. Childs, 'The Internal and International Fish Trades of Medieval England and Wales: Control, Conflict and International Trade', in *England's Sea Fisheries*, 32; Webb, *Great Tooley of Ipswich*, 80; *LP*, I, i. 438(2 m. 21), 1416, 1480, III, ii. 3071, IV, i. 549, 691, XVIII, i. 447, Addenda i. 873; Loades, *Making of the Elizabethan Navy*, 91.
57. *LP*, I, ii. 1899, 1942, 1976, 3612(75–6), III, ii. 3071, XVIII, i. 675, 729, ii. 408, XIX, i. 95, 237, 238, 595, 981, 1012, ii. 307, 501, 549, 600, 601, 646, 674(xxi), XX, i. 60, 97, 135, 557, ii. 264, XXI, i. 301, 324, 347, 386, 490, 526, 538, 563, 585, 597, 762, ii. 387, 390; Loades, *Making of the Elizabethan Navy*, 95.
58. PRO, C1/427/55; *LP*, IV, ii. 4193.
59. *HP*, ii. 501–2.
60. *YCR*, iv. 118–19; *HP*, ii. 514.
61. *HP*, ii. 501–2.
62. R. Tittler, 'The English Fishing Industry in the Sixteenth Century: The Case of Great Yarmouth', *Albion* 9 (1977), 53–4; W. E. Stephens, 'Great Yarmouth under Queen Mary', *NA* 29 (1946), 151; Williams, *Maritime Trade*, 235–6.

63. H. Manship, *History of Great Yarmouth*, ed. C. J. Palmer (Great Yarmouth, 1854), 108–9.
64. KHLC, NR/JBf8; G. Mayhew, 'Rye and the Defence of the Narrow Seas: A Sixteenth Century Town at War', *Sussex Archaeological Collections* 127 (1984), 124.
65. *Extracts from the Records of the Merchant Adventurers of Newcastle-upon-Tyne*, ii, ed. F. W. Dendy, SS 101 (Durham, 1899), 169–70; Loades, *Making of the Elizabethan Navy*, 111–12.
66. Gould, *The Great Debasement*, 120, 136; Bernard, *War, Taxation and Rebellion*, 136–44; S. J. Gunn, 'Wolsey's Foreign Policy and the Domestic Crisis of 1527–8', in S. J. Gunn and P. G. Lindley (eds), *Cardinal Wolsey: Church, State and Art* (Cambridge, 1991), 172–6; E. Kerridge, *Textile Manufactures in Early Modern England* (Manchester, 1985), 208–9.
67. *A Calendar of the White and Black Books of the Cinque Ports*, ed. F. Hull, Kent Records 19 (London, 1967), 151 for sailors' coats.
68. C. Dyer, *An Age of Transition: Economy and Society in England in the Later Middle Ages* (Oxford, 2005), 148–50; J. Oldland, 'Wool and Cloth Production in Late Medieval and Early Tudor England', *EcHR* n.s. 67 (2014), 29, 38–41.
69. Kerridge, *Textile Manufactures*, 16; PRO, SP1/206, fo. 13r (*LP*, XX, ii. 152).
70. *HP*, i. 220, 225, 236.
71. C. Welch, *History of the Worshipful Company of Pewterers of the City of London, based upon their own Records*, 2 vols (London, 1902), i. 168; F. Consitt, *The London Weavers' Company, volume I, from the Twelfth Century to the close of the Sixteenth Century* (Oxford, 1933), 167; T. Girtin, *The Golden Ram: A Narrative History of the Clothworkers' Company* (London, 1958), 57; *Churchwardens' Accounts of Ashburton, 1479–1580*, ed. A. Hanham, Devon and Cornwall RS n.s. 15 (Exeter, 1970), 142; C. H. Cooper, *Annals of Cambridge*, 5 vols (Cambridge, 1842–1908), ii. 44.
72. Kerridge, *Textile Manufactures*, 14, 17, 19, 23–4; Herefordshire Archive and Records Centre, BG11/17/3/6, BG11/17/6/1, BG11/17/6/3, BG11/17/6/13, BG11/17/6/15, BG11/24/1/11; J. F. Firth, *Coopers Company, London: Historical Memoranda, Charters, Documents, and Extracts, from the Records of the Corporation and the Books of the Company, 1396–1858* (London, 1848), 104–6; *Wardens' Accounts of the Worshipful Company of Founders of the City of London 1497–1681*, ed. G. Parsloe (London, 1964), 99–100; *Cratfield: A Transcript of the Accounts of the Parish, from AD 1490 to AD 1642*, ed. J. J. Raven (London, 1895), 77, 94–5; Welch, *Pewterers*, i. 138, 143, 150; Downing College, Cambridge, MS Bowtell I, fos. 258v–9r; *Records of the Borough of Leicester*, ed. M. Bateson et al., 7 vols (London, 1899–1974), iii. 92; *The Records of the Burgery of Sheffield, commonly called the Town Trust*, ed. J. D. Leader (London, 1897), 304; P. E. Jones, *The Butchers of London: A History of the Worshipful Company of Butchers of the City of London* (London, 1976), 178–9; *Churchwardens' Accounts of Ashburton*, 139, 159; Suffolk RO, Bury St Edmunds, C12/3; *Churchwardens' Accounts of Croscombe, Pilton, Yatton, Tintinhull, Morebath and St Michael's Bath*, ed. E. Hobhouse, Somerset RS 4 (London, 1890), 158, 171; *HP*, i. 157–8, 331–2, 516, ii. 39; *StP*, x. 597; *YCR*, i. 40; LMA, Rep. 2, fo. 153r; C. M. Clode, *Memorials of the Guild of Merchant Taylors of the Fraternity of St John the Baptist in the City of London and of its Associated Charities and Institutions* (London, 1875), 527; Consitt, *Weavers*, 278; *Records Carpenters*, iv. 68; E. Glover, *A History of the Ironmongers' Company* (London, 1991), 27; Shropshire Archives, LB8/1/47/65.
73. Welch, *Pewterers*, i. 149–50, 229; Firth, *Coopers*, 106; *Wardens' Accounts Founders*, 99–100; Cooper, *Annals of Cambridge*, i. 412–13; *Records Carpenters*, iv. 87; Kerridge, *Textile Manufactures*, 163–8.

74. Firth, *Coopers*, 106; Glover, *Ironmongers*, 40; *Records Carpenters*, iv. 95; *Records of the Skinners of London, Edward I to James I*, ed. J. J. Lambert (London, 1933), 367; Cooper, *Annals of Cambridge*, ii. 178; *Liverpool Town Books*, ed. J. A. Twemlow, 2 vols (London 1918–35), i. 338–9.
75. Kerridge, *Textile Manufactures*, 17, 19–20; friezes: Clode, *Memorials Merchant Taylors*, 529; *Churchwardens' Accounts of Ashburton*, 149; *YCR*, vi. 28–9; *Records of the Burgery of Sheffield*, 304; kerseys: Downing College, Cambridge, MS Bowtell I, fos. 258v–9r; Suffolk RO, Bury St Edmunds, C12/3; Firth, *Coopers*, 105; kelter: *Records of the Burgery of Sheffield*, 303–4.
76. *The Manuscripts of Lord Middleton, preserved at Wollaton Hall*, HMC 69 (London, 1911), 345, 351; *Memorials of the Abbey of St Mary of Fountains*, ed. J. R. Walbran, SS 42 (Durham, 1863), 406.
77. Devon Heritage Centre, EAB1/1, fo. 155r; *Churchwardens' Accounts of Ashburton*, 139, 149; *The Churchwardens' Accounts of St Michael's Church, Chagford, 1480–1600*, ed. F. M. Osborne (Chagford, 1979), 201; *Records of the Burgery of Sheffield*, 304–5.
78. *YCR*, v. 183; S. Gunn, D. Grummitt, and H. Cools, *War, State, and Society in England and the Netherlands, 1477–1559* (Oxford, 2007), 83; PRO, C1/1342/34.
79. 'Sir John Daunce's Accounts of Money received from Treasurer of King's Chamber temp. Henry VIII', ed. C. T. Martin, *Archaeologia* 47/2 (1883), 328–9, 335 (totalling £7,941); *CSPDE*, 721; Hoyle, 'War and Public Finance', 89, 93.
80. C. S. L. Davies, 'Provisions for Armies, 1509–50: A Study in the Effectiveness of Early Tudor Government', *EcHR* n.s. 17 (1964–5), 234–42.
81. Loades, *Making of the Elizabethan Navy*, 134–7.
82. *YCR*, i. 42; LMA, Rep. 2, fo. 131r–v; *William Browne's Town: Stamford Hall Book 1465–1492*, ed. A. Rogers (Stamford, 2005), 136; W. Boys, *Collections for a History of Sandwich* (Canterbury, 1792), 681–2; BL, Egerton MS 2092, fos. 507r–12v, 513r–15v.
83. *LP*, I, i. 1183, IV, ii. 3761; Lincolnshire Archives, Monson 7/51, fos. 2r–4v; Edward Hall, *Hall's Chronicle*, ed. H. Ellis (London, 1809), 645; *Three Fifteenth-Century Chronicles*, ed. J. Gairdner, CS n.s. 28 (London, 1880), 122; Elis Gruffudd, 'Boulogne and Calais from 1545 to 1550', ed. M. B. Davies, *Fouad I University Bulletin of Faculty of Arts* 12 (1950), 46; *A Calendar of the Shrewsbury and Talbot Papers in Lambeth Palace Library and the College of Arms*, ed. C. Jamison, E. G. W. Bill, and G. R. Batho, 2 vols, HMC joint publications 6–7 (London, 1966–71), i. 13.
84. C. S. L. Davies, 'Supply Services of the English Armed Forces, 1509–1550', University of Oxford D.Phil. Thesis (1963), 194–200; *Liverpool Town Books*, i. 330.
85. J. A. Lynn, *Women, Armies and Warfare in Early Modern Europe* (Cambridge, 2008); C. Lloyd and S. Thurley, *Henry VIII: Images of a Tudor King* (Oxford, 1990), 74–5, 78–9; J. C. Appleby, *Women and English Piracy, 1540–1720: Partners and Victims of Crime* (Woodbridge, 2013), 54–8, 62–3; C. G. Cruickshank, *Army Royal: Henry VIII's Invasion of France 1513* (Oxford, 1969), 103–4; Gruffudd, 'Boulogne and Calais', 13–14, 27, 40, 74–5, 83–4.
86. *Henley Borough Records: Assembly Books i–iv, 1395–1543*, ed. P. M. Briers, Oxfordshire RS 41 (Oxford, 1960), 94 Herefordshire Archive and Records Centre, BG11/17/6/8; *Cratfield*, 49–50, 71; *YCR*, iv. 83.
87. E. Glover, *Men of Metal: History of the Armourers and Braziers of the City of London* (London, 2008), 46; *Records Carpenters*, iv. 44; Firth, *Coopers*, 104; Welch, *Pewterers*, i. 138–9.
88. *HP*, ii. 564, 735–7; *YCR*, iv. 100, v. 165.

89. Shropshire Archives, LB8/1/7/3; *HMC Seventh Report*, 603; Davies, 'Provisions for Armies', 239; *HP*, i. 279, ii. 258, 267; BL, Althorp papers A6.

90. PRO, C1/947/8–11; C1/1111/61 is similar.

91. M. Airs, *The Tudor and Jacobean Country House: A Building History* (Stroud, 1995), 95–9; *CSPDE*, 721: £151,413 at Calais, £122,696 at Boulogne, £67,113 in Scotland and on the northern border, and £216,409 around the English coasts; *HKW*, iv. 402.

92. Airs, *Tudor and Jacobean Country House*, 72–4; *HKW*, iii. 354, 367, 374, 392; iv. 427, 457, 551, 654; CUL, Hengrave MS 88(iii), no. 67; *HP*, i. 150.

93. *HKW*, iv. 573, 620; *YCR*, iii. 48, vi. 84–5.

94. *The Manuscripts of Shrewsbury and Coventry Corporations*, HMC 15th report 10 (London, 1899), 50; S. G. Ellis, *Ireland in the Age of the Tudors: English Expansion and the End of Gaelic Rule* (London, 1998), 266, 269, 272–3, 291–2; *Liverpool Town Books*, i. 220.

95. PRO, C1/1441/88.

96. A. D. Saunders, 'Norham Castle and Early Artillery Defences', *Fort* 25 (1997), 39–58; Durham UL, CCB/B/72/10(221030A), CCB/B/4/40(189833), m. 8r, CCB/B/4/45(189835), m. 9, CCB/B31c/220204/4, CCB/B/76/12(190042), CCB/B76/14(190055), m. 2, CCB/76/15(190056), fo. 8, CCB/B/76/16(190057), m. 2, CCB/B/76/17(190058), m. 3, CCB/B/76/19(190060), m. 3, CCB/B/77/45, mm. 11r–21r.

97. Jones, 'Bristol Shipping Industry', 106–11; *YCR*, iv. 123–4; Davies, 'Provisions for Armies', 239.

98. ESRO, Rye 60/3, fos. 75r, 100v; PRO, E404/81/1; Loades, *Making of the Elizabethan Navy*, 132–3.

99. Loades, *Making of the Elizabethan Navy*, 101–2, 124.

100. *Reprint of the Barnstaple Records*, ed. J. R. Chanter and T. Wainwright, 2 vols (Barnstaple, 1900), ii. 126; PRO, C1/922/52.

101. Loades, *Making of the Elizabethan Navy*, 131–2.

102. *HP*, ii. 508, 515; *YCR*, v. 19; Mayhew, 'Rye', 111–19; Lincolnshire Archives, Monson 7/51, fos. 159v–60r.

103. *Elizabethan Naval Administration*, ed. C. S. Knighton and D. M. Loades, Navy Records Soc. 160 (Farnham, 2013), 207–12, 436–48.

104. *StP*, i. 827 (*LP*, XX, ii. 190); *CSPDM*, 489; *Calendar White and Black Books of the Cinque Ports*, 258.

105. *Elizabethan Naval Administration*, 441, 473–4.

106. A. J. Stirland, *Raising the Dead: The Skeleton Crew of Henry VIII's Great Ship, the Mary Rose* (Chichester, 2000), 55–6, 149.

107. *The Records of Rye Corporation: A Catalogue*, ed. R. F. Dell (Lewes, 1962), 40; PRO, C1/59/56; *YCR*, i. 13–14.

108. *TRP*, ii. 435–6, 508; *Troubles connected with the Prayer Book of 1549*, ed. N. Pocock, CS n.s. 37 (London, 1884), 46.

109. *LP*, IV, i. 83; *StP*, x. 345; 'Sir John Daunce's Accounts', 312; PRO, C1/1158/14–16.

110. Gunn, Grummitt, and Cools, *War, State, and Society*, 61; *Acta curiae admirallatus Scotiae*, 139, 165, 179–80; for other large profits see PRO, C1/1109/25–7, 1150/41–3, 1435/70.

111. PRO, C1/70/103, 71/75, 73/84, 161, 143/39, 224/27, 228/8, 322/61, 1109/25–7, 1150/41–3, 1435/70; CUL, Hengrave MS 88(i), no. 5; *Calendar Plymouth*, 101–2,

105, 116; *APC*, i. 362; *HMC Ninth Report*, appendix i, 311; *City and County of Kingston Upon Hull: Calendar of the Ancient Deeds, Letters, Miscellaneous Old Documents, &c in the archives of the Corporation*, ed. L. M. Stanewell (Kingston upon Hull, 1951), 92; *StP*, v. 443–4, x. 237, 404; *Liverpool Town Books*, i. 224–5, 284; Jones, 'Bristol Shipping Industry', 111–18; Southampton AO, SC5/1/15, fo. 14v, SC5/1/22, fo. 20v, SC5/1/40, fos. 20v–21r, SC5/3/1, fo. 109r; J. C. Appleby, *Under the Bloody Flag: Pirates of the Tudor Age* (Stroud, 2009), 41–54, 58–9, 73–7, 87–91.

112. Mayhew, 'Rye', 121–4; PRO, C1/321/82; *StP*, ix. 339.

113. *Chronicle of the Grey Friars of London*, ed. J. G. Nicholas, CS 53 (London, 1852), 48; John Stow, *Survey of London*, ed. C. L. Kingsford, 2nd edn, 2 vols (Oxford, 1971), i. 318; *Calendar of State Papers Foreign, Elizabeth, 1558–1589. Vol 7: 1564–1565*, ed. J. Stevenson (London, 1870), 466.

114. PRO, SP1/206, fo. 13r (*LP*, XX, ii. 152); C1/1185/32–3; G. Connell-Smith, *Forerunners of Drake: A Study of English Trade with Spain in the Early Tudor Period* (London, 1954), 134–6, 181–2.

115. *Report on the Records of the City of Exeter*, HMC 73 (London, 1916), 35–6; Mayhew, 'Rye', 121.

116. *LP*, XX, ii. 264.

117. *Calendar Plymouth*, 74; *LP*, XXI, i. 361; Ramsay, *City of London*, 125, 136–9; Connell-Smith, *Forerunners of Drake*, 127–96; PRO, C1/1150/41–3; Appleby, *Under the Bloody Flag*, 14–17.

118. *HMC Exeter*, 14; *City and County of Kingston Upon Hull*, 70; *HMC Ninth Report*, appendix i, 259–60, 273–4; Dorset HC, DC/BTB/N12; 'Dover Documents', ed. J. B. Jones, *Archaeologia Cantiana* 34 (1920), 93–6; KHLC, Fa/CPz 2; ESRO, Rye 60/3, fos. 115r–117v; *The Red Paper Book of Colchester*, ed. W. G. Benham (Colchester, 1902), 71–4; *Select Cases in the Council of Henry VII*, ed. C. G. Bayne and W. H. Dunham, Selden Soc. 75 (London, 1958), 10; HL, MS El 2652, fo. 10r; PRO, C1/59/74, 66/83, 67/172, 71/75, 73/84, 131/9, 640/36, 822/18; *Lettres inédites de Maximilien, duc d'Autriche, roi des Romains et empereur sur les affaires des Pays-Bas, de 1478 à 1508*, ed. L. P. Gachard, 2 vols (Brussels, 1851–2), i. 152–3; *Chronologische lijsten van de Geëxtendeerde Sententiën*, i. 237, v. 171; BL, Egerton MS 2092, fo. 467r; Southampton AO, SC5/1/41, fo. 33r.

119. Loades, *Two Tudor Conspiracies*, 174–8; *StP*, ii. 77; Loades, *Making of the Elizabethan Navy*, 73, 86–7, 109, 159; *Calendar of State Papers, Ireland, 1547–1553*, nos. 27, 29, 31, 38, 59, 79, 112, 187, 189, 371; Appleby, *Under the Bloody Flag*, 59–62, 66–71 and *passim*.

120. PRO, C1/143/73, 651/19–22; *The Manuscripts of Lincoln, Bury St Edmunds, and Great Grimsby Corporations*, HMC 37 (London, 1895), 255; *Yorkshire Star Chamber Proceedings*, ed. W. Brown et al., 4 vols, YASRS 41, 45, 51, 70 (Wakefield, 1909–27), iii. 162–6; *Calendar Plymouth*, 101–2, 106–7; *LP*, XII, i. 528.

121. Connell-Smith, *Forerunners of Drake*, 128–9; Ramsay, *City of London*, 133–6; D. Mathew, 'The Cornish and Welsh Pirates in the Reign of Elizabeth', *EHR* 39 (1924), 337–48; A. L. Rowse, *Tudor Cornwall* (London, 1941), 389–92; G. Williams, *Renewal and Reformation: Wales, c.1415–1642* (Oxford, 1997), 374–9; Hasler, *Commons*, ii. 394–8, iii. 205–7; K. R. Andrews, *Elizabethan Privateering: English Privateering during the Spanish War, 1585–1603* (Cambridge, 1964), 16–18; Loades, *Making of the Elizabethan Navy*, 110; Appleby, *Under the Bloody Flag*, 113–44.

122. *TRP*, ii. 450, 482, 499, 519, 523, 525–6, 553, 562–3, 573, 585, 610; D. M. Loades, *The Tudor Navy: An Administrative, Political and Military History* (Aldershot, 1992),

224–33; Loades, *Making of the Elizabethan Navy*, 79, 87–8, 116–18; Canterbury Cathedral Archives, U4/12/18; J. McDermott, *Martin Frobisher: Elizabethan Privateer* (New Haven CT and London, 2001), 48–78.

123. Worcestershire Archives, Worcester City Records A14, vol 1, fos. 9r–10r.

124. Manship, *Great Yarmouth*, 108; Southampton AO, SC5/3/1, fos. 117r, 119v.

125. Williams, *Maritime Trade*, 233–7; Rowse, *Tudor Cornwall*, 389–92; Andrews, *Elizabethan Privateering*, 81–99, 222–38; Appleby, *Under the Bloody Flag*, 193–246.

126. *HP*, i. 103, 105; M. H. Merriman, *The Rough Wooings: Mary Queen of Scots 1542–1551* (East Linton, 2000), 152–4.

127. Merriman, *Rough Wooings*, 152; *HP*, i. lxviii–lxix, xciii, 313, 574, ii. 42, 65–6, 96–7, 120, 139, 161, 213, 282, 297, 323, 455–6, 465, 560; *LP*, XVII. 1197. For the war of 1532–4, see *StP*, iv. 622, 627–9, 632–4, 640.

128. *HP*, i. xcv, ii. 42, 213, ii. 213.

129. *LP*, XIX, ii. 625; C. E. Moreton, *The Townshends and their World: Gentry, Law and Land in Norfolk c.1450–1551* (Oxford, 1992), 225–6; D. M. Palliser, *The Age of Elizabeth: England under the Later Tudors, 1547–1603*, 2nd edn (London, 1992), 195.

130. *StP*, v. 316–17.

131. *HP*, i. 400, 539, 552, 654–5; *StP*, v. 232–4, 428; *LP*, XVIII, ii. 58.

132. R. Robson, *The English Highland Clans: Tudor Responses to a Medieval Problem* (Edinburgh, 1989); *HP*, ii. 743–5.

133. *HP*, i. 325, 400, 558–9, 646, ii. 437, 444, 485, 587, 591, 618–19; *LP*, XX, i. 377, 381, 658, 867, ii, 945; *The Manuscripts of His Grace, the Duke of Rutland, G.C.B., preserved at Belvoir Castle*, 4 vols, HMC 24 (London, 1888–1908), iv. 194–7.

134. William Patten, 'The Expedition into Scotland', in *Tudor Tracts*, ed. A. F. Pollard (Westminster, 1903), 135.

135. *HP*, i. 335.

136. *StP*, iii. 350, 352; C. Falls, *Elizabeth's Irish Wars* (London, 1950), 88–9, 92.

137. Hall, *Chronicle*, 641, 643–4, 650–1, 659–60, 673–5, 678–82, 685–6, 702; *LP*, XIX, i. 357, 380, ii. 415, XX, i. 957; *CSPFE*, Calais papers 5; *CSPFM*, 695, 702; Louis Brésin, *Chroniques de Flandre et d'Artois: Analyse et extraits pour servir à l'histoire de ces provinces de 1482 à 1560*, ed. E. Mannier (Paris, 1880), 314.

138. S. J. Gunn, 'The Duke of Suffolk's March on Paris in 1523', *EHR* 101 (1986), 618–19.

139. Cruickshank, *Army Royal*, 124–6, 180; *LP*, I, ii. 3018, 3087, 3370, XXI, i. 938, 939, ii. 116, 281, 289, 316, 319, 347, 475(9); Potter, *Henry VII and Francis I*, 389–90.

140. J. R. Hale, 'On a Tudor Parade Ground: The Captain's Handbook of Henry Barrett 1562', in his *Renaissance War Studies* (London, 1983), 250; *StP*, ii. 227, 241, 272, 355, 393, iii. 188, 195, 343.

141. C. E. Moreton, 'Mid-Tudor Trespass: A Break-in at Norwich, 1549', *EHR* 108 (1993), 387–98; PRO, C1/64/188, 66/218; *The Herald's Memoir 1486–1490: Court Ceremony, Royal Progress and Rebellion*, ed. E. Cavell (Donington, 2009), 112; R. W. Hoyle, 'Thomas Master's Narrative of the Pilgrimage of Grace', *Northern History* 21 (1985), 67; *StP*, v. 124.

142. *TRP*, i. 339; *The Edwardian Inventories for the City and County of Exeter*, ed. B. F. Cresswell, Alcuin Club Collections 20 (London, 1916), 18, 21, 23, 66–7, 77, 79, 81, 83; J. Cornwall, *Revolt of the Peasantry 1549* (London, 1977), 190–1, 204–6; *Troubles connected with the Prayer Book of 1549*, 24, 29, 32–3, 41, 68–71; CUL, Hengrave MS 88(i), 13; PRO, C1/1367/82, 1383/2, 1387/14; Plymouth and West Devon RO, 710/7.

143. *The Paston Letters, 1422–1509 AD*, ed. J. A. Gairdner, 4 vols (Edinburgh, 1910), iii. 122–3; *Calendar of the Manuscripts of Major-General Lord Sackville*, 2 vols, HMC 80 (London, 1940–66), i. 2; *Calendar Shrewsbury and Talbot Papers*, i. 42.

144. *The Customs Accounts of Newcastle upon Tyne, 1454–1500*, ed. J. F. Wade, SS 202 (Gateshead, 1995), 132, 145, 148, 150, 230, 262, 273; Durham UL, CCB/B3/29(190288), m. 5; *The Customs Accounts of Hull, 1453–1490*, ed. W. R. Childs, YASRS 144 (Leeds, 1986), 203, 207, 209.

145. S. J. Gunn, 'Archery Practice in Early Tudor England', *PP* 209 (2010), 69–71; *The Overseas Trade of London: Exchequer Customs Accounts 1480–1*, ed. H. S. Cobb, London RS 27 (London, 1990), nos. 15, 16, 32, 77, 156, 169, 170, 197, 200; *The Port and Trade of Elizabethan London: Documents*, ed. B. Dietz, London RS 8 (London, 1972), nos. 33, 147, 733.

146. *Overseas Trade of London*, nos. 15, 24, 37, 46, 59, 60, 58, 82, 83, 85, 89, 93, 94, 96, 97, 102, 103, 106, 114, 117, 121, 129, 130, 134, 136, 139, 156, 159, 168, 173, 176, 177, 180, 181, 183, 187, 196, 200, 205, 208.

147. D. Cressy, *Saltpetre: The Mother of Gunpowder* (Oxford, 2013), 40–2; G. Rimer, T. Richardson, and J. P. D. Cooper (eds), *Henry VIII: Arms and the Man* (Leeds, 2009), 286; Alnwick Castle, Syon MS X.II.I, box 16o; H. L. Blakemore, *A Dictionary of London Gunmakers 1350–1850* (Oxford, 1986), 67, 71, 82, 91, 96; Rimer et al. (eds), *Henry VIII: Arms and the Man*, 296–7.

148. C. Schnurmann, *Kommerz und Klüngel: der Englandhandel Kölner Kaufleute im 16. Jahrhundert* (Göttingen, 1991), 186–202; PRO, C1/410/59, 610/18.

149. PRO, C1/66/373, 67/145, 142/63, 711/28; Gunn, Grummitt, and Cools, *War, State, and Society*, 83; 'Sir John Daunce's Accounts', 309, 332; I. Blanchard, 'Gresham, Sir Richard', *ODNB*; Firth, *Coopers*, 105; *YCR*, iv. 154–5; Hasler, *Commons*, ii. 218.

150. A. F. Sutton, *The Mercery of London: Trade, Goods and People, 1130–1578* (Aldershot, 2005), 478; Ramsay, *City of London*, 116–18; Cressy, *Saltpeter*, 46; *StP*, ix. 418.

151. Clode, *Memorials Merchant Taylors*, 528; A. P. Beaven, *The Aldermen of the City of London: Temp. Henry III—1912*, 2 vols (London, 1908–13), ii. 81; *Port and Trade of Elizabethan London*, nos. 18, 19, 46, 154, 156, 191, 211, 234, 258, 296, 298, 340, 341, 364, 389, 462, 464, 465, 539, 546, 576, 643, 647, 702, 703, 710, 729, 730, 750, 781, 787, 792; Glover, *Men of Metal*, 244.

152. *Elizabethan Naval Administration*, 51, 74, 103–4, 261–2, 279–80, 302–3, 321–2, 325, 398–9.

153. LMA, Rep. 5, fo. 315v; *HP*, i. 172; *YCR*, vi. 172–3; *TRP*, i. 213, 235.

154. *Paston Letters and Papers of the Fifteenth Century*, ed. N. Davis, R. Beadle, and C. Richmond, 3 vols (Oxford, 1971–2005), iii. 25.

155. *Letters from Redgrave Hall: The Bacon Family 1340–1744*, ed. D. MacCulloch, Suffolk RS 60 (Woodbridge, 2007), 35.

156. *Wardens' Accounts Founders*, 142.

157. *Records Carpenters*, ii, 198, iv. 115; *Memorials of the Goldsmiths' Company*, ed. W. S. Prideaux, 2 vols (London, 1913), i. 50; *Records Skinners*, 145; J. F. Wadmore, *Some Account of the Worshipful Company of Skinners of London, being the Guild or Fraternity of Corpus Christi* (London, 1902), 86; Glover, *Men of Metal*, 244; PRO, C1/110/97.

158. Stow, *Survey*, ii. 284.

159. A. H. Johnson, *The History of the Worshipful Company of the Drapers of London*, 5 vols (Oxford, 1914–22), ii. 411; C. Welch, *History of the Cutlers' Company of London*, 2 vols (London, 1916–23), i. 209–10; PRO, C1/165/57, 212/47–8.

160. 'Extracts from the Household and Privy Purse Accounts of the Lestranges of Hunstanton, from A.D. 1519 to A.D. 1578', ed. D. Gurney, *Archaeologia* 25 (1834), 556;

Records of Leicester, iii. 93; *The Household Book (1510–1551) of Sir Edward Don: An Anglo-Welsh Knight and his Circle*, ed. R. A. Griffiths, Buckinghamshire RS 33 (Aylesbury, 2004), 48, 138, 159, 176–7, 200, 235, 255, 359–60, 419; *The Register of Thetford Priory*, ed. D. Dymond, 2 vols, Norfolk RS 59–60 (Norwich, 1995–6), ii. 425, 430; Cooper, *Annals of Cambridge*, ii. 268–9; Lincolnshire Archives, PAR St James Louth 3, fos. 37v, 41v, 63r, 64v; Durham UL, CCB/B3/30, m. 8, CCB/B31c/220204/4, fo. 119r; CUL, EDR/D/5/9; *Ancient Churchwardens' Accounts of the Parish of North Elmham*, ed. A. G. Legge (Norwich, 1891), 46; Shropshire Archives, LB8/1/47/65–7; *HMC Middleton*, 339.

161. Durham UL, CCB/B31c/220204/4, fo. 115v.

162. *Calendar Plymouth*, 97–9, 104, 113–14, 116; Southampton AO, SC5/1/27B, fo. 6v, SC5/1/30, fo. 83r–v, SC5/1/31, fo. 22r–v.

163. *HP*, ii. 588; L. Boynton, *The Elizabethan Militia 1558–1638* (London, 1967), 69–70.

164. Anon., *A newe interlude of impacyente pouerte* (London, 1560), A2r.

165. 'Sir John Daunce's Accounts', 330–1; *Records of the Borough of Northampton*, ed. C. A. Markham and J. C. Cox, 2 vols (London, 1898), i. 204–6, *Calendar of the Patent Rolls, 1494–1509* (London, 1916), 91–2.

166. *HMC Shrewsbury*, 48–9; *LJ*, i. 12–14; B. Megson, *Such Goodly Company: A Glimpse of the Life of the Bowyers of London, 1300–1600* (London, 1993), 61.

167. I. Arthurson, 'The King's Voyage into Scotland: The War that Never Was', in D. Williams (ed.), *England in the Fifteenth Century* (Woodbridge, 1987), 12; Devon HC, EAB1/1, fo. 155v; *HMC Rutland*, iv. 310, 325; B. H. Cunnington, *Some Annals of the Borough of Devizes*, 2 vols (Devizes, 1825), i. 23; 'Testamenta Leodiensia', ed. W. Brigg, *Miscellanea vol ii*, Thoresby Soc. 4 (Leeds, 1892–5), 140; *Early Northampton Wills*, ed. D. Edwards, M. Forrest, J. Minchinton, M. Shaw, B. Tyndall, and P. Wallis, Northamptonshire RS 42 (Northampton, 2005), 237; *St Albans Wills 1471–1500*, ed. S. Flood, Hertfordshire RS 9 (Hitchin, 1993), no. 78; Southampton AO, SC5/1/32, fo. 30r, SC5/3/1, fo. 96v; *Worcestershire Taxes in the 1520s*, ed. M. A. Faraday, Worcestershire HS n.s. 19 (Worcester, 2003), 39; Worcestershire Archives, Registered wills V, fo. 336r.

168. 'Sir John Daunce's Accounts', 310, 332, 335; *Memorials Goldsmiths*, i. 57; Johnson, *Drapers*, ii. 412.

169. PRO, KB9/397/32, 400/67, 454/41; Stow, *Survey*, ii. 79, 370; Megson, *Such Goodly Company*, 63–6.

170. H. Swanson, *Medieval Artisans: An Urban Class in Late Medieval England* (Oxford, 1989), 101–4; *Register of the Freemen of the City of York*, ed. F. Collins, 2 vols, SS 96, 102 (Durham, 1897–1900); *Calendar of the Bristol Apprentice Book*, i. 199–200, ii. 153–4, iii. 17, 52, 78, 85, 95, 99, 103, 109; *A Calendar of the Freemen of Lynn, 1292–1836* (Norwich, 1913), 52, 55, 59, 78, 79, 86, 89, 95, 100, 103, 105, 106.

171. *Calendar of the Freemen of Norwich from 1307 to 1603*, ed. W. Rye (London, 1888); *The Norwich Census of the Poor 1570*, ed. J. F. Pound, Norfolk RS 40 (Norwich, 1971), 34, 87.

172. Rimer et al. (eds), *Henry VIII: Arms and the Man*, 148–54.

173. PRO, C1/61/439, 64/687, 228/50, 272/53; <http://www.englandsimmigrants.com/person/29829> (accessed 2 April 2015); K. E. Lacey, 'The Military Organization of the Reign of Henry VII', in M. Strickland (ed.), *Armies, Chivalry and Warfare in Medieval Britain and France: Proceedings of the 1995 Harlaxton Symposium* (Stamford, 1998), 249–50.

174. Swanson, *Medieval Artisans*, 70–1; *Register of the Freemen of the City of York*; Glover, *Men of Metal*, 34–67; *Cornwall Muster Roll 1569*, ed. H. L. Douch (Bristol, 1984), 2,

58, 61; *Cambridge Borough Documents*, i, ed. W. M. Palmer (Cambridge, 1931), 121; Canterbury RO, U4/12/12; Durham UL, CCB/B3/32, m. 5, CCB/B3/25, m. 5; Shropshire Archives, LB8/1/34/65; *Cartulary of Osney Abbey*, ed. H. E. Salter, 6 vols, Oxford HS 89–91, 97–8, 101 (Oxford, 1929–36), i. 19–20; Southampton AO, SC5/3/1, fo. 27v; *Household Book of Sir Edward Don*, 348–9, 361, 369, 391; Nottingham UL, Mi5/161/5; 'Extracts from the Lestranges', 450.

175. PRO, C1/64/145, 793; *The Durham Household Book*, ed. J. Raine, SS 18 (Durham, 1844), 138–9.

176. Rimer et al. (eds), *Henry VIII: Arms and the Man*, 256; 'Sir John Daunce's Accounts', 310, 332, 334.

177. *St Martin-in-the-Fields: The Accounts of the Churchwardens 1525–1603*, ed. J. V. Kitto (London, 1901), 157, 162, 178, 210, 222, 234; Lincolnshire Archives, PAR St James Louth 3, fos. 6v, 59r, 64v, 67v, 72v; *York City Chamberlains' Account Rolls 1396–1500*, ed. R. B. Dobson, SS 192 (Gateshead, 1980), 156; Cooper, *Annals of Cambridge*, i. 244, 392; Shropshire RO, LB8/1/47/45, LB8/1/47/16A, LB8/1/48/78, LB8/1/51/84, 89, LB8/1/53/75, 77; *Minutes and Accounts of the Corporation of Stratford-upon-Avon and other records 1553–1620*, ed. R. Savage, E. I. Fripp, and L. Fox, 5 vols to date, Dugdale Soc. 1, 3, 5, 10, 35 (Oxford, 1921–), ii. 38; BL, Addl. MS 32243, fos. 41v, 48r, 49r63v, 64v, 67v, 75v, 77r, 80r, 83r, 84v, 86v, 88v, 92r–v, 97r, 100r–v; P. Maryfield, 'Love as Brethren': A Quincentenary History of the Coopers' Company* (London, 2000), 31–2; *Records Carpenters*, iv. 73, 103, 113, 115, 137–8, 183, 233; Firth, *Coopers*, 106; Johnson, *Drapers*, ii. 402–3; *Memorials Goldsmiths*, i. 50; Clode, *Memorials Merchant Taylors*, 522, 528; *Records Skinners*, 145–6; Consitt, *Weavers*, 262; B. J. Heath, *Some Account of the Worshipful Company of Grocers of the City of London*, 3rd edn (London, 1869), 9; Welch, *Pewterers*, i. 273; DHC, EAB1/1, fo. 161r; Boynton, *Elizabethan Militia*, 24; for noblemen and gentlemen, see Chapter 4.

178. *Records Carpenters*, iv. 138, 233; *Records Skinners*, 371; ESRO, Rye 60/3, fos. 16v, 23r, 50r, 88v, 93r; Plymouth and West Devon RO, 1/130, fos. 5r, 6r, 39v; Southampton AO, SC5/1/24, fo. 3v, SC5/1/26, fos. 38r–39v, SC5/1/28, fos. 22v–23r, 32v, SC5/1/30, fos. 38v, 43v, SC5/1/31, fo. 22r, SC5/1/32, fo. 23r–v, SC5/1/47, fo. 19v; Cunnington, *Devizes*, i. 5–6; *Calendar of Nottinghamshire Coroners' Inquests, 1485–1558*, ed. R. F. Hunnisett, Thoroton Soc. Record ser. 25 (Nottingham, 1969), 122–3; PRO, C1/105/51; Johnson, *Drapers*, ii. 412, 434; Blakemore, *Dictionary of London Gunmakers*; H. L. Blakemore, *Gunmakers of London Supplement 1350–1850* (Bloomfield, 1999).

179. Palliser, *Age of Elizabeth*, 25, 66–7, 293, 300–5.

180. Rimer et al. (eds), *Henry VIII: Arms and the Man*, 228–9; A. Hildred (ed.), *Weapons of Warre: The Armaments of the Mary Rose*, 2 vols (Portsmouth, 2011), ii. 553–77.

181. *LP*, I, ii. 2832(49); Herefordshire Archive and Records Centre, BG11/17/6/5.

182. A. B. Caruana, *The History of English Sea Ordnance 1523–1875: Volume 1—The Age of Evolution 1523–1715* (Rotherfield, 1994), 5–22; Rimer et al. (eds), *Henry VIII: Arms and the Man*, 306–7; SHC, LM1086/1–5.

183. Arthurson, 'King's Voyage into Scotland', 9; B. Awty and C. Whittick, 'The Lordship of Canterbury, Iron-Founding at Buxted, and the Continental Antecedents of Cannon-Founding in the Weald', *Sussex Archaeological Collections* 140 (2002), 71–81; B. Awty, 'Iron and Brass Ware in East Sussex in the 1540s', *Sussex Archaeological Collections* 144 (2006), 215–19; Caruana, *English Sea Ordnance*, 33.

184. Southampton AO, SC5/1/15, fo. 27r; Cressy, *Saltpeter*, 42–5; for more on Anthony of Naples, see PRO, C1/861/3–11.

185. Cressy, *Saltpeter*, 43–5; Clode, *Memorials Merchant Taylors*, 522; Shropshire RO, LB8/1/39/19.
186. Cressy, *Saltpeter*, 53–72; CUL, Hengrave MS 88(ii), no. 28.
187. Loades, *Making of the Elizabethan Navy*, 125–7.
188. Loades, *Tudor Navy*, 52–3, 92, 192; Loades, *Making of the Elizabethan Navy*, 132.
189. Loades, *Making of the Elizabethan Navy*, 65–6, 83, 146, 155–6.
190. *Elizabethan Naval Administration*, 41, 99, 202, 266, 281, 307, 398.
191. *Elizabethan Naval Administration*, 40, 56, 106, 140, 158, 347, 385.
192. M. Strickland and R. Hardy, *From Hastings to the Mary Rose: The Great Warbow* (Thrupp, 2005), 42; Durham UL, CCB/B77/47, fo. 10r.
193. Lincolnshire Archives, Monson 7/51, fo. 2v; *YCR*, iv. 134; Johnson, *Drapers*, ii. 110; Davies, 'Supply Services', 183–90.
194. Bodl. Tanner MS 194, fo. 45r; HL, MS El 2652, fos. 8r, 15r, 18v; *APC*, i. 133, vii. 43; CUL, Hengrave MS 88(i), no. 114.
195. *HMC Seventh Report*, app. 617.
196. *A Collection of State Papers, relating to affairs in the reigns of King Henry VIII, King Edward VI, Queen Mary, and Queen Elizabeth, transcribed from original letters and other authentick memorials, left by William Cecill Lord Burghley*, ed. S. Haynes and W. Murdin, 2 vols (London, 1740–59), i. 239, 312, 321, 327; *Yorkshire Star Chamber Proceedings*, ii. 47, 64, iii. 29–30, 61–2.
197. *StP*, ii. 244.
198. Davies, 'Provisions for Armies', 238.
199. HL, MS HA 4137.
200. *Guildford Borough Records 1514–1546*, ed. E. M. Dance, Surrey RS 24 (Frome, 1958), 140; *The Manuscripts of Rye and Hereford Corporations*, HMC 13th report 4 (London, 1892), 318; *YCR*, v. 44; BL, Egerton MS 2094, fo. 195r; *HMC Exeter*, 38.
201. *Selections from the Municipal Chronicles of the Borough of Abingdon*, ed. B. Challenor (Abingdon, 1898), 124–5; St Saviour Southwark records: LMA, P92/SAV/1382 (I owe this reference to Ian Archer).
202. J. J. Goring, 'Social Change and Military Decline in Mid-Tudor England', *History* 60 (1975), 185; Centre for Buckinghamshire Studies, AR16/89 BAS/1/55; Moreton, *Townshends*, 188; *Monastic Chancery Proceedings (Yorkshire)*, ed. J. S. Purvis, YASRS 88 (Wakefield, 1934), 34–6; *Middlesex County Records*, ed. J. C. Jeaffreson, 4 vols (London, 1886–92), i. 38.
203. R. C. L. Sgroi, 'Piscatorial Politics Revisited: The Language of Economic Debate and the Evolution of Fishing Policy in Elizabethan England', *Albion* 35 (2003), 1–15.
204. *LJ*, i. 64, 78, 88, 135, 141–2, 144–5, 149–50, 158, 175, 177–80, 184, 193–4; 33 Henry VIII, c. 5; Loades, *Making of the Elizabethan Navy*, 119.
205. Palliser, *Age of Elizabeth*, 156–63, 168–9, 173–5; Hoyle, 'Taxation', 654–74.
206. Davies, 'Supply Services', 71–96.
207. *The Coventry Leet Book*, ed. M. D. Harris, 4 vols, EETS 134–5, 138, 146 (London, 1907–13), ii. 409; *Literae Cantuarienses*, ed. J. B. Sheppard, 3 vols, Rolls Ser. 85 (London, 1887–9), iii. 281–2.
208. Cressy, *Saltpeter*, 48–75; J. Thirsk, *Economic Policy and Projects: The Development of a Consumer Society in Early Modern England* (Oxford, 1978), 24–34.
209. D. L. Potter, 'Mid-Tudor Foreign Policy and Diplomacy: 1547–63', in S. Doran and G. Richardson (eds), *Tudor England and its Neighbours* (Basingstoke, 2005), 107–9; *Tudor Economic Documents*, ii. 97.

CHAPTER 6

1. R. M. Citino, 'Military Histories Old and New: A Reintroduction', *American Historical Review* 112 (2007), 1070–1.

2. J. Keegan, *The Face of Battle: A Study of Agincourt, Waterloo and the Somme* (London, 1991 edn); J. Bourke, *An Intimate History of Killing: Face-to-Face Killing in Twentieth-Century Warfare* (London, 1999); Y. N. Harari, *The Ultimate Experience: Battlefield Revelations and the Making of Modern War Culture, 1450–2000* (Basingstoke, 2008).

3. D. L. Potter, *Un homme de guerre au temps de la Renaissance: la vie et les lettres d'Oudart du Biez, maréchal de France, gouverneur de Boulogne et de Picardie (vers 1475–1553)* (Arras, 2001), 156.

4. J. J. Goring, 'The General Proscription of 1522', *EHR* 86 (1971), 688–9; J. Cornwall, *Wealth and Society in Early Sixteenth-Century England* (London, 1988), 281–8; *The Certificate of Musters for Buckinghamshire in 1522*, ed. A. C. Chibnall, Buckinghamshire RS 17 (1973), 24; *The Military Survey of Gloucestershire, 1522*, ed. R. W. Hoyle, Gloucestershire RS 6 (1993), xiv–xvii, xxi–xxv; *The Cornwall Military Survey 1522*, ed. T. L. Stoate (Bristol, 1987), 55–6, 59–61, 63–4; *Worcestershire Taxes in the 1520s*, ed. M. A. Faraday, Worcestershire HS n.s. 19 (Worcester, 2003), 1–68. For editions of muster returns not cited in the notes, see the bibliography.

5. *LP*, IV, i. 972; Goring, 'General Proscription', 695n; the proportions in Surrey, not included in the tabulation, were similar: 'Abstract of Original Returns of the Commissioners for Musters and the Loan in Surrey', ed. T. Craib, *Surrey Archaeological Collections* 30 (1917), 15, 17, 28.

6. *LP*, XIV, i. 652, XVII. 882; *YCR*, iv. 170, 172.

7. *TE*, iv. 253, v. 124; *Southampton Probate Inventories, 1447–1575*, ed. E. Roberts and K. Parker, 2 vols, Southampton RS 34–5 (Southampton, 1992), ii. 301, 305. For editions of wills and inventories not cited in the notes, see the bibliography.

8. *Bedfordshire Wills 1484–1533*, ed. P. L. Bell, Bedfordshire Historical RS 76 (Bedford, 1997), 47, 52; *Elizabethan Life: Wills of Essex Gentry and Yeomen preserved in the Essex Record Office*, ed. F. G. Emmison (Chelmsford, 1980), 2, 69, 99, 121; *Elizabethan Life: Wills of Essex Gentry and Merchants proved in the Prerogative Court of Canterbury*, ed. F. G. Emmison (Chelmsford, 1978), 10, 47, 83–4, 107, 113, 184–5, 221, 227; *Lincoln Wills, 1532–1534*, ed. D. Hickman, Lincoln RS 89 (Lincoln, 2001), nos. 40, 193, 260, 324, 368, 468, 550, 578; *London Consistory Court Wills 1492–1547*, ed. I. Darlington, London RS 3 (1967), nos. 108, 117, 177, 192, 193, 228; *St Albans Wills 1471–1500*, ed. S. Flood, Hertfordshire RS 9 (Hitchin, 1993), nos. 86, 123, 160, 275; *TE*, iii. 215, 241–2, 299, iv. 19, 51, 130, 248, 252–3, 334–5, v. 7, 10, 19, 34, 36, 46, 60, 62–3, 75, 109, 148, 164, 167, 176–7, 208, 210, 234, 238, 244–5, 267, 277, vi. 18, 41, 85, 146, 218, 239, 240, 267; *Swaledale Wills and Inventories 1522–1600*, ed. E. K. Berry, YASRS 152 (Leeds, 1998), 60; *North Country Wills*, ed. J. W. Clay, 2 vols, SS 116, 121 (Durham, 1908–12), i. 137–9, 203, 260.

9. *London Consistory Court Wills*, no. 146; *TE*, iv. 204.

10. L. Boynton, *The Elizabethan Militia 1558–1638* (London, 1967), 33–7, 183–6; D. Thiery, 'Plowshares and Swords: Clerical Involvement in Acts of Violence and Peacemaking in Late Medieval England, c. 1400–1536', *Albion* 36 (2004), 203–9; *HMC Seventh Report* (London, 1879), 614; *LP*, XIV, i. 652(M6, M23(5)); *Bedfordshire Wills 1480–1519*, ed. P. L. Bell, Bedfordshire Historical RS 45 (Bedford, 1966), 30; *Bedfordshire Wills 1531–1539*, ed. P. L. Bell and B. Tearle, Bedfordshire Family History Soc. occasional paper 3 (Bedford, 2005), 28; *Bedfordshire Wills 1537–1545*, ed. P. L. Bell and

B. Tearle, Bedfordshire Family History Soc. occasional paper 4 (Bedford, 2010), 17; *Chesterfield Wills and Inventories 1521–1603*, ed. J. M. Bestall and D. V. Fowkes, Derbyshire RS 1 (Matlock, 1977), 25, 91; *Lincoln Wills, 1532–1534*, no. 24; *London Consistory Court Wills*, nos. 2, 56, 58, Bodl. Oxford University Archives, Registrum Cancellarii F, fos. 28v–9r, 68r–v, 104r, 191r, 246v–7r, 248v–9v; *North Country Wills*, i. 184, 204–5; *TE*, iii. 235, 291, iv. 227, 284, 287, vi. 289.

11. *Coventry and its People in the 1520s*, ed. M. H. M. Hulton, Dugdale Soc. 38 (Stratford-upon-Avon, 1999), 40; *Cornwall Military Survey*, 54–78.
12. *The Herefordshire Musters of 1539 and 1542*, ed. M. A. Faraday (Walton-on-Thames, 2012), 129–51; *Herefordshire Taxes in the Reign of Henry VIII*, ed. M. A. Faraday (Hereford, 2005), 168–76, 212–20.
13. *Calendar of Assize Records: Essex Indictments, Elizabeth I*, ed. J. S. Cockburn (London, 1978), nos. 9, 101, 203, 209, 537, 690; *Calendar of Assize Records: Kent Indictments, Elizabeth I*, ed. J. S. Cockburn (London, 1979), nos. 52, 117, 158, 233, 239, 247, 304, 369, 392, 468, 625, 697, 718, 756, 781–2; *Calendar of Assize Records: Surrey Indictments, Elizabeth I*, ed. J. S. Cockburn (London, 1980), nos. 189–91, 363, 398, 403, 501, 509, 554, 565, 646, 654, 736; *Calendar of Assize Records: Sussex Indictments, Elizabeth I*, ed. J. S. Cockburn (London, 1975), nos. 70, 439, 494.
14. *Southampton Probate Inventories*, i. 31, 43, 106, 125, 180, 209–10, 241, ii. 271, 301, 308, 317, 318, 335, 364, 378, 389, 393, 409, 419, 424; *Household and Farm Inventories in Oxfordshire, 1550–1590*, ed. M. A. Havinden, Oxfordshire RS 44 (Oxford, 1965), 50, 60.
15. Southampton AO, SC13/2/2, fo. 11v; SC5/3/1, fo. 1r; SC13/2/3; *Southampton Probate Inventories*, i. 40, 54, 62, 69, 76, 89, 90, 116, 128, 135, 157, 167, 180, 186, 190, 241, ii. 264, 271, 301, 305, 315, 318, 335, 344, 347, 363, 378, 388, 403, 419, 424.
16. *The Cornwall Muster Roll for 1569*, ed. H. L. Douch (Bristol, 1984), 2, 12, 35, 55, 58–61, 76–8, 83–4, 119–20; *Certificate of Musters in the County of Somerset, temp. Eliz. AD 1569*, ed. E. Green, Somerset RS 20 (London, 1904), 138–9, 265–6, 287, 292, 312; S. J. Gunn, 'Archery Practice in Early Tudor England', *PP* 209 (2010), 73–80.
17. *Cornwall Military Survey 1522*, 29–79, 138–82; *Cornwall Muster Roll 1569*, iii, 72–121; John Leland, *The Itinerary of John Leland in or about the Years 1535–1543*, ed. L. T. Smith, 5 vols (London, 1906–10), i. 252; *Dorset Tudor Muster Rolls, 1539, 1542, 1569*, ed. T. L. Stoate (Bristol, 1978), 75–7; *Men at Arms: Musters in Monmouthshire, 1539 and 1601–2*, ed. T. Hopkins, South Wales RS 21 (Cwmbran, 2009), 81–2, 93–4; *LP*, XIV, i. 654(2, 8).
18. M. L. Bush, *The Pilgrimage of Grace: A Study of the Rebel Armies of October 1536* (Manchester, 1996), 418–24; *StP*, v. 435; *CSPDM*, 607.
19. *Southampton Probate Inventories*, i. 43, 54, 62, 69, 76, 82, 87, 102, 103, 106, 113–14, 116, 125, 128, 135, 141, 156–7, 163, 167, 176, 180, 186, 190, 241, ii. 247, 250, 262, 264, 271, 273, 301, 305, 308, 315, 317, 318, 323, 327, 329, 335, 339, 341, 344, 347, 364, 366, 368, 378, 387–9, 393, 403, 409, 411, 419, 420, 421, 424, 427, 428; 'Probate Inventories of Worcester Tradesmen, 1545–1614', ed. A. D. Dyer, *Miscellany II*, Worcestershire HS n.s. 5 (Worcester, 1968), 10, 18–19, 26, 33; PRO, KB9/596/154; BL, Egerton MS 2093, fo. 72r–v; *John Isham, Mercer and Merchant Adventurer*, ed. G. D. Ramsay, Northamptonshire RS 21 (Gateshead, 1962), 157; *Inventories of Worcestershire Landed Gentry 1537–1786*, ed. M. Wanklyn, Worcestershire HS 16 (Worcester, 1998), 8; *The Medieval Records of a London City Church (St Mary at Hill) AD 1420–1559*, ed. H. Littlehales, 2 vols, EETS 125, 128 (London, 1904–5),

i. 38, 43, 45; *A Calendar of Charters and other Documents belonging to the Hospital of William Wyggeston at Leicester*, ed. A. H. Thompson (Leicester, 1933), 40.

20. G. Rimer, T. Richardson, and J. P. D. Cooper (eds), *Henry VIII: Arms and the Man* (Leeds, 2009), 148–54.

21. *Calendar of the Manuscripts of Major-General Lord Sackville*, 2 vols, HMC 80 (London, 1940–66), i. 2; A. P. Beaven, *The Aldermen of the City of London: Temp. Henry III–1912*, 2 vols (London, 1908–13), ii. 35.

22. PRO, KB9/474/47.

23. *HMC Fifth Report* (London, 1876), 434, 455; HL, MS El 2652, fos. 10v, 14v; PRO, KB9/534/7, 545/69; STAC2/21/227; *Select Cases in the Council of Henry VII*, ed. C. G. Bayne and W. H. Dunham, Selden Soc. 75 (London, 1958), cxxxv–cxxxvii; *Select Cases before the King's Council in the Star Chamber*, ii, ed. I. S. Leadam, Selden Soc. 25 (London, 1911), 71, 77; *Lancashire and Cheshire Cases in the Court of Star Chamber*, ed. R. Stewart-Brown, RS for Lancashire and Cheshire 71 (Manchester, 1916), 88; *Yorkshire Star Chamber Proceedings*, ed. W. Brown et al., 4 vols, YASRS 41, 45, 51, 70 (Wakefield, 1909–27), iii. 4, 34, 72, iv. 50, 106, 111–12.

24. 6 Henry VIII c. 13, 14&15 Henry VIII, c. 7, 25 Henry VIII, c. 17; 33 Henry VIII c. 6; M. Hayward, *Rich Apparel: Clothing and the Law in Henry VIII's England* (Farnham, 2009); *LP*, VI. 1631; Lincolnshire Archives, 1PG1/55; HL, MS HA over-size box 14(11a); CUL, Hengrave MS 88(i), no. 126; Gunn, 'Archery Practice', 78–80.

25. 33 Henry VIII c. 6, ss. 4, 7; PRO, C1/655/58; KB9/543/6, 562/71, 602a/63, 625b/324, 626/31, 637/374, 682a/73, 682b/131, 696a/57, 702c/383, 704b/229, 985/84, 1012a/15; CHES24/92/2/unnumbered, 94/4/unnumbered; F. Vanhemelryck, *De criminaliteit in de ammanie van Brussel van de late middeleeuwen tot het einde van het Ancien Régime (1404–1789)*, Verhandelingen van de Koninklijke Academie voor Wetenschappen, Letteren en Schone Kunsten van België, Klasse der Letteren 97 (Brussels, 1981), 218–19.

26. HL, MS HA 4137; *YCR*, vi. 81.

27. E. E. Rich, 'The Population of Elizabethan England', *EcHR*, n.s. 2 (1950), 249–52; *The County Community under Henry VIII: The Military Survey, 1522, and Lay Subsidy, 1524–5, for Rutland*, ed. J. Cornwall, Rutland Record Ser. 1 (1980), 8–9; *Coventry and its People*, 39–40; Cornwall, *Wealth and Society*, 213, 225–30; *Men at Arms*, 11; *Herefordshire Musters*, viii.

28. *YCR*, iv. 90, 100, 105, 125–6, 131, 172, vi. 80; *The Military Survey of 1522 for Babergh Hundred*, ed. J. Pound, Suffolk RS 28 (Woodbridge, 1986); *Certificate of Musters for Buckinghamshire*, 23; *LP*, XIV, i. 652(M12, M20(4)); *Faversham Tudor and Stuart Muster Rolls*, ed. P. Hyde and D. Harrington, Faversham Hundred Records 3 (Folkestone, 2000), xiv, xxii; *The Oxfordshire Muster Rolls, 1539, 1542, 1569*, ed. P. C. Beauchamp, Oxfordshire RS 60 (Oxford, 1996), 65; Boynton, *Elizabethan Militia*, 67; *Surrey Musters (taken from the Loseley MSS)*, Surrey RS 3 (London, 1914–19), 175–8.

29. 'A Muster of the Fencible Inhabitants of Newcastle-upon-Tyne in the year 1539', ed. G. B. Richardson, *Archaeologia Aeliana* 4 (1855), 125, 133.

30. *LP*, IV, i. 972; Goring, 'General Proscription', 697–8; BL, Egerton MS 2093, fo. 56r–v; *Military Survey of Gloucestershire*, xvi; *LP*, XIV, i. 652(M14(2)); *Dorset Tudor Muster Rolls, 1539, 1542, 1569*, ed. T. L. Stoate (Bristol, 1978), 90–1, 93–6, 99, 102, 104–5, 107; *APC*, iv. 300.

31. *Coventry and its People*, 40.

32. 'Musters in Skyrack Wapentake, 1539', ed. W. P. Baildon, *Miscellanea ii*, Thoresby Soc. 4 (Leeds, 1893), 246, 249–51, 253, 256–7; 'Musters in Skyrack Wapentake, 1539,

part ii', ed. W. P. Baildon, *Miscellanea iii*, Thoresby Soc. 9 (Leeds, 1899), 102–3, 107; 'Musters in Skyrack Wapentake, 1539, part iii', ed. W. P. Baildon, ibid. 299, 304.

33. *North Wiltshire Musters, anno 30 Henry VIII*, ed. T. Phillipps (London, 1834), 16–35.

34. *The Devon Muster Roll for 1569*, ed. A. J. Howard and T. L. Stoate (Bristol, 1977), 164–5, 168–9, 109, 112, 171, 173, 183, 189, 202, 213–14, 230, 245.

35. Gunn, 'Archery Practice', 72; William Worcestre, *The Boke of Noblesse addressed to King Edward IV on his Invasion of France in 1475*, ed. J. G. Nichols (London, 1860), 76; PRO, KB 9/445/25, 458/36, 475a/37, 489/63, 495/66, 531/20, 533/167, 539/61, 550/109, 554/93, 556/42, 573/55, 574/103, 574/113, 627b/240, 629b/243, 970/78, 985/133, 1073a/41; *The Chronicle of John Hardyng*, ed. H. Ellis (London, 1812), i; R. B. Manning, *Hunters and Poachers: A Cultural and Social History of Unlawful Hunting in England 1485–1640* (Oxford, 1993), 35–56.

36. Gunn, 'Archery Practice', 53–69; J. Ellis, 'Archery and Social Memory in Sixteenth-Century London', *Huntington Library Quarterly* 79 (2016), 32–4.

37. C. Knüsel, 'Activity-Related Structural Change', in V. Fiorato, A. Boylston, and C. Knüsel (eds), *Blood Red Roses: The Archaeology of a Mass Grave from the Battle of Towton, AD 1461* (Oxford, 2000), 105–9, 115–16; A. J. Stirland, *Raising the Dead: The Skeleton Crew of Henry VIII's Great Ship, the Mary Rose* (Chichester, 2000), 118–34.

38. Leland, *Itinerary*, i. 67, 96, 194, 219, 254, ii. 79, iii. 24, 96, 114, 124, iv. 6, 42, 50, 62, 68, 98, 135, 136, v. 24, 48, 101, 184 (flight shots); i. 207, iii. 75, 85, 91, iv. 134 (bow shots); i. 70, 318, 319, 321, 326, iii. 100, iv. 28, v. 61 (arrow shots); i. 85, 201, iv. 4 (butt shots); William Patten, 'The Expedition into Scotland', in *Tudor Tracts*, ed. A. F. Pollard (Westminster, 1903), 81, 84.

39. Gunn, 'Archery Practice', 73–80; PRO, KB 9/479/89, 504/31; Southampton AO, SC5/3/1, fos. 17r, 50r; *Certificate of Musters for Buckinghamshire*, 212–13; *LP*, XIV, i, 652(M23); 25 Henry VIII, c. 17 ss. 10, 17; 33 Henry VIII c. 6 ss. 6, 18–20; *Military Survey of Gloucestershire*, 209; *Dorset Tudor Muster Rolls*, 75, 102, 104–5, 125; *CSPDM* 607; *Oxfordshire Muster Rolls*, 65; *Cornwall Muster Roll 1569*, 144; *Devon Muster Roll for 1569*, 23, 53, 136, 151, 249.

40. I. Arthurson, 'The King's Voyage into Scotland: The War that Never Was', in D. Williams (ed.), *England in the Fifteenth Century* (Woodbridge, 1987), 8; *StP*, iv. 38, 47–8; *LP*, IV, i. 83, 266, 512, 1715, XX, i. 621(10); Durham CCB31c/220204/4, fo. 118r; *A newe interlude of impacyente pouerte* (London, 1560), A2r; BL, Addl. MS 63649; *Calendar of the Bristol Apprentice Book*, ii. 153, iii. 52; *Elizabethan Naval Administration*, ed. C. S. Knighton and D. M. Loades, Navy Records Soc. 160 (Farnham, 2013), 117–26, 128–38, 142–53, 160–71, 209, 211, 334–41, 348–54, 366–70, 374–82, 390–3, 400–3, 411–21, 425–7, 443–4.

41. *Calendar of Nottinghamshire Coroners' Inquests, 1485–1558*, ed. R. F. Hunnisett, Thoroton Soc. Record Ser. 25 (Nottingham, 1969), no. 39; *Sussex Coroners' Inquests 1485–1558*, ed. R. F. Hunnisett, Sussex RS 74 (Lewes, 1985), no. 16; PRO, KB9/9/452/92, 474/47, 486/46, 619a/130, 9/1014b/203, 965/60, 985/134, 1013b/185; Southampton AO, SC5/3/1, fo. 53r; C. V. Phythian-Adams, 'Rituals of Personal Confrontation in Late Medieval England', *Bulletin of the John Rylands Library* 73 (1991), 78, 83; *Lincoln Wills, 1532–1434*, nos. 40, 193, 578; *London Consistory Court Wills*, nos. 177, 192, 228; *TE*, v. 7, 28, 34–6, 62–3, 114, 118, 176, 208, 238, vi. 18, 41, 85, 230, 239; *Acts of Chapter of the Collegiate Church of SS Peter and Wilfred, Ripon, AD 1452 to AD 1506*, ed. J. T. Fowler, SS 64 (Durham, 1875), 288, 303.

42. *The Manuscripts of His Grace, the Duke of Rutland, G.C.B., preserved at Belvoir Castle*, 4 vols, HMC 24 (London, 1888–1908), iv. 382, 385.

43. *The Accounts of the Wardens of the Parish of Morebath, Devon, 1520–1573*, ed. J. E. Binney (Exeter, 1904), 226; LMA, Rep. 4, fo. 52r; S. Anglo, *The Martial Arts of Renaissance Europe* (New Haven CT and London, 2000), 7–8; Southampton AO, SC5/3/1, fos. 17r, 70r; *Calendar of the Plymouth Municipal Records*, ed. R. N. Worth (Plymouth, 1893), 70; *Minutes and Accounts of the Corporation of Stratford-upon-Avon and other records 1553–1620*, ed. R. Savage, E. I. Fripp, and L. Fox, 5 vols to date, Dugdale Soc. 1, 3, 5, 10, 35 (Oxford, 1921–), i. 72, 82, 84, 100, 126.

44. Anglo, *Martial Arts*, 35–6, 95–112; *TRP*, ii. 432, 493, 542; J. P. Anglin, 'The Schools of Defense in Elizabethan London', *Renaissance Quarterly* 37 (1984), 393–410; *YCR*, vi. 92; *HMC Ninth Report* (London, 1883), appendix i, 249. For early rapier users, see W. Coster, *Kinship and Inheritance in Early Modern England: Three Yorkshire Parishes*, Borthwick papers 83 (York, 1993), 17; *Southampton Probate Inventories*, i. 92, 199, 250, ii. 329, 366, 390; *Derbyshire Wills proved in the Prerogative Court of Canterbury 1393–1574*, ed. D. G. Edwards, Derbyshire RS 26 (Matlock, 1998), 153; PRO, KB9/589/113; J. Hunter, *South Yorkshire*, 2 vols (Wakefield, 1974 edn), ii. 173–6.

45. Anglo, *Martial Arts*, 159–68; PRO, KB8/18b/151, KB9/443/11, 476/96, 484/23, 494/81, 527/77, 556/145, 571/49, 603/33, 606b/237, 619a/130, 631b/166, 970/38, 975/118, 1004/5, 1072/43; *Sussex Coroners' Inquests 1485–1558*, nos. 15, 16; Phythian-Adams, 'Rituals of Personal Confrontation', 74–8, 81–2, 86–8.

46. Anglo, *Martial Arts*, 167–8; PRO, KB 9/588a/94; Rimer et al. (eds), *Henry VIII: Arms and the Man*, 266–7.

47. Thomas Blundeville, *The fower chiefyst offices belongyng to Horsemanshippe: The Arte of Rydynge* (London, 1566), A3v, U3v–4r.

48. *CSPFE*, Calais papers 43, 47; 'Life of the last Fitz-Alan, Earl of Arundel', ed. J. G. Nichols, *Gentleman's Magazine* 104 (1833), 13; *HP*, i. 263; *HMC Third Report* (London, 1872), appendix i, 262.

49. *Devon Muster Roll for 1569*, 70, 86–7, 91, 119; Hatfield House, CP152/42.

50. *A Discourse of the Commonweal of this Realm of England*, ed. M. Dewar (Charlottesville VA, 1969), 83; Hugh Latimer, *Sermons*, ed. G. E. Corrie, 2 vols, Parker Soc. (Cambridge, 1844), ii. 101.

51. C. M. Clode, *Memorials of the Guild of Merchant Taylors of the Fraternity of St John the Baptist in the City of London and of its Associated Charities and Institutions* (London, 1875), 526; *Records of the Worshipful Company of Carpenters*, 6 vols (Oxford, 1913–39), iv. 103; John Stow, *A Survey of London*, ed. C. L. Kingsford, 2nd edn, 2 vols (Oxford, 1971), i. 101–4; *A Calendar of Dramatic Records in the Books of the Livery Companies of London 1485–1640*, ed. J. Robertson and D. J. Gordon, Malone Soc. Collections 3 (Oxford, 1954), 2, 3; Leland, *Itinerary*, i. 131; J. B. Sheppard, 'The Canterbury Marching Watch with its Pageant of St. Thomas', *Archaeologia Cantiana* 12 (1878), 27–46; *Records of the City of Norwich*, ed. W. Hudson and J. C. Tingey, 2 vols (Norwich, 1906–10), ii. 120–1; *Records of Early English Drama: Coventry*, ed. R. W. Ingram (Manchester, 1981), 86, 12, 134, 136, 177, 179, 195–7, 200, 205; J. R. Hale, 'On a Tudor Parade Ground: The Captain's Handbook of Henry Barrett 1562', in his *Renaissance War Studies* (London, 1983), 255–8, 274, 276, 279–80, 284.

52. *Records of Early English Drama: York*, ed. A. F. Johnston and M. Rogerson, 2 vols (Manchester, 1979), i. 263, 285, 297, 300, 302–4, 307–8, 323, 327, 332–3, 341, 355, 356; *Liverpool Town Books*, ed. J. A. Twemlow, 2 vols (London 1918–35), i. 387–8; Stow, *Survey*, ii. 284; *Calendar Plymouth*, 17–18, 105, 121; A. Douglas, 'Midsummer in Salisbury: The Tailors' Guild and Confraternity 1444–1642', *Renaissance and Reformation* 25 (1989), 35–40.

53. Hale, 'On a Tudor Parade Ground', 264n.

54. *YCR*, v. 117.

55. *A Collection of Letters, Statutes, and other documents from the MS Library of Corpus Christi College, illustrative of the History of the University of Cambridge, during the period of the Reformation, from AD MD to AD MDLXXII*, ed. J. Lamb (London, 1838), 196.

56. *Adams's Chronicle of Bristol*, ed. F. F. Fox (Bristol, 1910), 113–14.

57. Hale, 'On a Tudor Parade Ground', 284.

58. Thomas Audley, 'A Treatise on the Art of War', ed. W. St P. Bunbury, *Journal of the Society for Army Historical Research* 6 (1927), 69.

59. Hatfield House, CP138/13; *A Collection of State Papers, relating to affairs in the reigns of King Henry VIII, King Edward VI, Queen Mary, and Queen Elizabeth, transcribed from original letters and other authentick memorials, left by William Cecill Lord Burghley*, ed. S. Haynes and W. Murdin, 2 vols (London, 1740–59), i. 218, 221, 252.

60. B. J. Heath, *Some Account of the Worshipful Company of Grocers of the City of London*, 3rd edn (London, 1869), 10.

61. *The Coventry Leet Book*, ed. M. D. Harris, 4 vols, EETS 134–5, 138, 146 (London, 1907–13), ii. 479–80, iii. 608; *Henley Borough Records: Assembly Books i–iv, 1395–1543*, ed. P. M. Briers, Oxfordshire RS 41 (Oxford, 1960), 171; S. J. Gunn, *Henry VII's New Men and the Making of Tudor England* (Oxford, 2016), 145–7.

62. S. Gunn., D. Grummitt, and H. Cools, *War, State, and Society in England and the Netherlands, 1477–1559* (Oxford, 2007), 53–4; *YCR*, iv. 129, 156; *Guildford Borough Records 1514–1546*, ed. E. M. Dance, Surrey RS 24 (Frome, 1958), 63, 95–6, 101, 105, 110, 117, 119–21, 126, 134–7, 140; *Liverpool Town Books*, i. 93, 157–8, 221–2, 242, 268, 327, 438, 440, 443–4, 450, 479; Worcestershire Archives, Worcester City Records A14, vol 1, fos. 16r–17v, 21v–23r, 25v, 26v, 28v–29r, 42r, 53r, 79r, 82v, 97r; Worcester City Records A6, box 4, fo. 48r; Registered wills VI, fo. 70r; Original wills 1551/72, 1562/108, 1570/41a, 1575/97; Wiltshire and Swindon HC, G25/1/21, pp. 44, 48, 52, 55, 73, 171, 172, 180.

63. PRO, C1/1048/31, 1055/42, 1061/58–9, 1094/12, 1101/43–4, 1103/44, 1155/61, 1186/29–32, 1204/99–101, 1246/24, 1261/34, 1283/24, 1342/23–5, 1466/15; C1/1240/84 for substitutes.

64. *Illustrations of British History*, ed. E. Lodge, 3 vols (London, 1838), i. 142.

65. N. Younger, *War and Politics in the Elizabethan Counties* (Manchester, 2012), 172–6, 183–5; R. Morgan, *The Welsh and the Shaping of Early Modern Ireland 1558–1641* (Woodbridge, 2014), 24–32; J. J. N. McGurk, *The Elizabethan Conquest of Ireland* (Manchester, 1997), 32–4.

66. *Memorials of the Goldsmiths' Company*, ed. W. S. Prideaux, 2 vols (London, 1913), i. 27; *Records Carpenters*, iv. 9, 49, 58, 68–9, 79, 95, 100, 108–12, 115, 123–4, 132, 135, 146, 156, 167, 232, 240, 242; *Wardens' Accounts of the Worshipful Company of Founders of the City of London 1497–1681*, ed. G. Parsloe (London, 1964), 125–7, 133–44; C. Welch, *History of the Worshipful Company of Pewterers of the City of London, based upon their own Records*, 2 vols (London, 1902), i. 176, 179, 183, 194, 197–8, 202–3, 213, 218–19, 267; A. H. Johnson, *The History of the Worshipful Company of the Drapers of London*, 5 vols (Oxford, 1914–22), i. 141, ii. 70; C. M. Clode, *The Early History of the Guild of Merchant Taylors of the Fraternity of St John the Baptist, London* (London, 1888), 250.

67. Johnson, *Drapers*, i. 131, 431; Welch, *Pewterers*, i. 216; *Wardens' Accounts Founders*, 149, 152, 156–9, 160–3, 166; *Memorials Goldsmiths*, i. 58.

68. Welch, *Pewterers*, i. 149–50, 236; Johnson, *Drapers*, ii. 80, 110–12; *Records Carpenters*, iv. 7, 17, 30, 43–4, 87, 116, 137; *Records of the Skinners of London, Edward I to James I*, ed. J. J. Lambert (London, 1933), 368; Welch, *Pewterers*, i. 236.

69. P. Knevel, *Burgers in het geweer: De schutterijen in Holland, 1550–1700* (Hilversum, 1994); Gunn, Grummitt, and Cools, *War, State, and Society*, 56–60.

70. *Wardens' Accounts Founders*, 140, 142, 156; *Records Carpenters*, iii. 187–8, iv. 31, 68–9, 94–6, 110, 115, 123, 190, 239, 110, 155, 178.

71. P. Withington, 'Introduction—Citizens and Soldiers: The Renaissance Context', *Journal of Early Modern History* 15 (2011), 18–27; M. Smuts, 'Organized Violence in the Elizabethan Monarchical Republic', *History* 99 (2014), 418–32.

72. A. Hewerdine, *The Yeomen of the Guard and the Early Tudors* (London, 2012), 29–41; D. M. Loades, *The Tudor Navy: An Administrative, Political and Military History* (Aldershot, 1992), 178–89; D. Grummitt, *The Calais Garrison: War and Military Service in England, 1436–1558* (Woodbridge, 2008), 44–56; C. G. Cruickshank, *The English Occupation of Tournai 1513–1519* (Oxford, 1971), 67–91; G. J. Millar, *Tudor Mercenaries and Auxiliaries 1485–1547* (Charlottesville VA, 1980), 167–9.

73. S. G. Ellis, 'The Tudors and the Origins of the Modern Irish States: A Standing Army', in T. Bartlett and K. Jeffery (eds), *A Military History of Ireland* (Cambridge, 1996), 116–35; C. Brady, 'The Captains' Games: Army and Society in Elizabethan Ireland', ibid. 136–59.

74. *HKW*, iv. 444, 484–5, 530, 537n, 541n, 545n, 549, 555, 556, 558, 569, 586, 598, 603n, 687; *LP*, XV. 323; J. Raymond, *Henry VIII's Military Revolution: The Armies of Sixteenth-Century Britain and Europe* (London and New York, 2007), 163–4.

75. Grummitt, *Calais Garrison*, 15–18, 108–11; William Patten, 'The Expedition into Scotland', in *Tudor Tracts*, ed. A. F. Pollard (Westminster, 1903), 109, 117; S. L. Adams, 'A Puritan Crusade? The Composition of the Earl of Leicester's Expedition to the Netherlands, 1585–1586', in his *Leicester and the Court: Essays on Elizabethan Politics* (Manchester, 2002), 181–2; R. Lyne, 'Churchyard, Thomas (1523?–1604), writer and soldier', *ODNB*; B. F. Roberts, 'Gruffudd, Elis (b. c.1490, d. in or after 1556), copyist and chronicler', *ODNB*.

76. *StP*, ix. 78.

77. Hewerdine, *Yeomen of the Guard*, 81–94; S. J. Gunn, 'Chivalry and Politics at the Early Tudor Court', in S. Anglo (ed.), *Chivalry in the Renaissance* (Woodbridge, 1990), 116–18; D. L. Potter, *Henry VIII and Francis I: The Final Conflict, 1540–47* (Leiden and Boston MA, 2011), 229; Patten, 'Expedition into Scotland', 109, 117, 120; Raymond, *Henry VIII's Military Revolution*, 164–79.

78. Raymond, *Henry VIII's Military Revolution*, 9; Hale, 'On a Tudor Parade Ground', 252–4.

79. Hatfield House, CP138/13.

80. CA, MS M16bis, fos. 27v, 40r, 51v, 55r, 60v; PRO, SP1/10, fos. 181v, 182r; A. R. Bell, A. Curry, A. King, and D. Simpkin, *The Soldier in Later Medieval England* (Oxford, 2013), 149, 153, 188–9, 208.

81. Bell et al., *Soldier in Later Medieval England*, 228; 33 Henry VIII c. 6; Gunn, *New Men*, 147.

82. S. G. Ellis, *Defending English Ground: War and Peace in Meath and Northumberland, 1460–1542* (Oxford, 2015), 156–61.

83. John Hooper, *Early Writings*, ed. S. Carr, Parker Soc. (Cambridge, 1843), 372.

84. *Calendar of State Papers and Manuscripts, Relating to English Affairs, Existing in the Archives and Collections of Venice and other Libraries of Northern Italy, vol VI part ii, 1556–1557*, ed. R. Brown (London, 1881), 1047.

85. A. Sablon du Corail, 'Les étrangers au service de Marie de Bourgogne: de l'armée de Charles le Téméraire à l'armée de Maximilien (1477–1482)', *Revue du Nord* 84 (2002), 389–412; E. L. Meek, 'The Career of Sir Thomas Everingham, "Knight of the North", in the Service of Maximilian, duke of Austria, 1477–81', *HR* 74 (2001), 238–48; Grummitt, *Calais Garrison*, 78, 101; Jean Molinet, *Chroniques de Jean Molinet*, ed. G. Doutrepont and O. Jodogne, 3 vols (Brussels, 1935–7), i. 465–6, 521, ii. 138, 141; 'Chronique d'Adrien de But', in *Chroniques relatives à l'histoire de la Belgique sous la domination des ducs de Bourgogne*, ed. K. de Lettenhove, 3 vols (Brussels, 1870–6), i. 659–60; Louis Brésin, *Chroniques de Flandre et d'Artois: Analyse et extraits pour servir à l'histoire de ces provinces de 1482 à 1560*, ed. E. Mannier (Paris, 1880), 39; *Fragments inédits de Romboudt de Doppere*, ed. H. Dussart (Bruges, 1892), 11, 13, 109; *Inventaire-sommaire des archives départementales antérieures à 1790: Nord*, ed. C. Dehaisnes et al., 10 vols (Lille, 1863–1906), iv. 276–7; Jean Surquet, 'Mémoires en forme de chronique, ou histoire des guerres et troubles de Flandre', in *Corpus chronicorum Flandriae. Vol 4*, ed. J. J. de Smet, CRH (Brussels, 1865), 584–6; Stadsarchief Gent, OA 20/6, fos. 12r–13r, 22v–24r, 63r, 80r; J. Haemers and B. Verbist, 'Het Gentse gemeenteleger in het laatste kwart van de vijtiende eeuw: Een politieke, financiele en militaire analyse van de stadsmilitie', *Handelingen der Maatschappij voor Geschiedenis on Oudheidkunde te Gent* 62 (2008), 315.
86. *LP*, II, ii. 3690, IV, i. 471, 501, 578, 1925, ii. 2531, 4330, X. 969, XI. 428, 436, 439, 471, XII, i, 1181, app. 4, ii. 210, 287, 307, 319, 323, 333, 343, 366, 371, 598, XVII. 1091, 1106, XVIII, i. 99, 113, ii. 64; Edward Hall, *Hall's Chronicle*, ed. H. Ellis (London, 1809), 732, 739; A. Henne, *Histoire du règne de Charles-Quint en Belgique*, 10 vols (Brussels, 1858–60), iv. 367; *Inventaire-sommaire Nord*, iv. 328, viii. 302; ADN, B2316/125847; D. Daniell, *William Tyndale: A Biography* (New Haven CT and London, 1994), 373; R. Polwhele, *The History of Devonshire*, 3 vols (London, 1793–1806), ii. 131n.
87. Thomas Churchyard, *A generall rehearsall of warres, called Churchyardes choise wherein is five hundred severall services of land and sea as seiges, battailes, skirmiches, and encounters* (London, 1579), A1r–D2v; Brésin, *Chroniques*, 207, 217, 234; *CSPFE*, 699; *CSPFM*, 100, 169–70, 174, 307, 559; Jean Thieulaine, 'Un livre de raison en Artois (XVIe siècle). Extraits historiques', ed. X. de Gorguette d'Argoeuves, *Mémoires de la Société des antiquaires de La Morinie* 21 (1881), 144, 179; Pierre-Ernest de Mansfeld, *Journal de captivité du comte Pierre-Ernest de Mansfeld, écrit au donjon de Vincennes 1552–1554*, ed. P.-E. [le prince de] Colloredo-Mannsfeld and J. Massarette (Paris, 1933), 58–9, 75–6; D. M. Loades, *Two Tudor Conspiracies*, 2nd edn (Bangor, 1992), 166–7, 201–3, 219–20, 222–3; Henne, *Histoire*, ix. 281, 284, 343, 346, 348, x. 30–1; *CSPFM* 84, 97, 307, 559, 598, 613; *Inventaire-sommaire Nord*, v. 171–2, 181, 195, 205, viii. 304–7; R. Rapple, *Martial Power and Elizabethan Political Culture: Military Men in England and Ireland, 1558–1594* (Cambridge, 2009), 95–118, 253–4; S. Kelsey, 'Drury, Sir William (1527–1579), soldier and lord justice of Ireland', *ODNB*; R. C. L. Sgroi, 'Piscatorial Politics Revisited: The Language of Economic Debate and the Evolution of Fishing Policy in Elizabethan England', *Albion* 35 (2003), 13n; 'The Travels and Life of Sir Thomas Hoby, Knight', ed. E. Powell, *Camden Miscellany x*, CS 3rd ser. 4 (London, 1902), 94; Emanuele Filiberto, *I diari delle campagne di Fiandra di Emanuele Filiberto, duca di Savoia*, ed. E. Brunelli and P. Egidi, Biblioteca della Società storica subalpina 112 (n.s. 21) (Turin, 1928), 9, 135; J. E. Tazón, *The Life and Times of Thomas Stukeley (c.1525–78)* (Aldershot, 2003), 30, 34–8. On miners, see C. Duffy, *Siege Warfare: The Fortress in the Early Modern World 1494–1660* (London, 1996 edn), 50; ADN, B2521/91338, 91339, 91345; *Inventaire-sommaire Nord*, v. 190, 202, viii. 282; *CSPDM*, 196; 'Dagverhaal

van den veldtogt van keizer Karel V in 1554', ed. [C. A.] R. Macaré, *Kronijk van het Historisch Genootschap Gevestigd te Utrecht* 7 (1851), 295.

88. Molinet, *Chroniques*, i. 243, 264; *LP*, XVII. 1091, 1106; R. R. Sharpe, *London and the Kingdom*, 3 vols (London, 1894–5), i. 480.

89. Churchyard, *Generall Rehearsall*, A3v, A4v, B1r.

90. Molinet, *Chroniques*, ii. 333; Hall, *Chronicle*, 646, 648, 651, 659, 669, 678–80, 686; Hale, 'On a Tudor Parade Ground', 250; BL, Egerton MS 2092, fo. 241v; *LP*, XVIII, ii. 64, XX, i. 504; Sharpe, *London and the Kingdom*, i. 412; R. Holinshed, *The Chronicles of England, Scotlande, and Irelande*, 4 vols (London, 1577), iv. 1820; Johnson, *Drapers*, ii. 231.

91. Molinet, *Chroniques*, i. 356, 523; Brésin, *Chroniques*, 87–8; *Fragments inédits de Romboudt de Doppere*, 41; Churchyard, *Generall Rehearsall*, A2r.

92. Henne, *Histoire*, x. 30–1.

93. ADN, B1703, fos. 95r–6r.

94. Hall, *Chronicle*, 675; for other reprisals see Antoine de Lusy, *Le journal d'un bourgeois de Mons, 1505–1536*, ed. A. Louant (Brussels, 1969), 44–5, 49.

95. Audley, 'Treatise', 77; *YCR*, iv. 103–4.

96. PRO, SP1/192, fo. 69v (*LP*, XIX, ii. 221).

97. Audley, 'Treatise', 74.

98. *LP*, I, i. 1978, 1851, VII. 1141; ESRO, Rye 60/3, fos. 16v, 75r; S. J. Gunn, 'The Duke of Suffolk's March on Paris in 1523', *EHR* 101 (1986), 599; *YCR*, iv. 124, vi. 167; *HMC Rutland*, iv. 193; *APC*, vi. 126, 212, 284, 311–13, 384, vii. 328.

99. PRO, KB9/1005/18.

100. G. Phillips, 'To Cry "Home! Home!"': Mutiny, Morale and Indiscipline in Tudor Armies', *Journal of Military History* 65 (2001), 313–32; J. D. Alsop, 'A Regime at Sea: The Navy and the 1553 Succession Crisis', *Albion* 24 (1992), 577–90.

101. *A Commentary of the Services and Charges of William Lord Grey of Wilton*, ed. P. De M. G. Egerton, CS 40 (London, 1847), 32–7; for another account see Churchyard, *Generall Rehearsall*, I4v–K2r.

102. Gunn, 'Suffolk's March', 623–5; *StP*, ii. 355, 393–4.

103. Phillips, 'Mutiny', 327–9; L. Boynton, 'The Tudor Provost-Marshal', *EHR* 77 (1962), 437–55.

104. *HMC Tenth Report* (London, 1885), appendix iv, 421.

105. Loades, *Two Tudor Conspiracies*, 64–7; *Depositions taken before the Mayor and Aldermen of Norwich, 1549–1567*, ed. W. Rye (Norwich, 1905), 57–8.

106. J. J. Raven, 'Tholdman', *Proceedings of the Suffolk Institute of Archaeology* 10 (1898–1900), 394–8.

107. *YCR*, iv. 110; *StP*, ii. 38, iii. 188, 443; *HP*, ii. 119, 627–8; Herefordshire Archive and Records Centre, BG11/17/6/75.

108. *StP*, xi. 311.

109. *HP*, i. lxxxv.

110. *HP*, i. 158, ii. 565, 567.

111. *HP*, ii. 368.

112. *StP*, xi. 4–5.

113. *HP*, i. 158, ii. 281, 615; Patten, 'Expedition into Scotland', 122.

114. *StP*, xi. 4.

115. *HP*, i. 158, ii. 367.

116. P. C. Maddern, *Violence and Social Order: East Anglia 1422–1442* (Oxford, 1992); S. D. Amussen, 'Punishment, Discipline, and Power: The Social Meanings of Violence

in Early Modern England', *Journal of British Studies* 34 (1995), 1–34; A. Shepard, *Meanings of Manhood in Early Modern England* (Oxford, 2003), 93–113, 127–51.

117. Phythian-Adams, 'Rituals of Personal Confrontation', 78–80, 82–5.

118. Latimer, *Sermons*, i. 416–17; Thomas Becon, *The Early Works of Thomas Becon*, ed. J. Ayre, Parker Soc. (Cambridge, 1843), 251–2.

119. Audley, 'Treatise', 78; for an earlier model see Christine de Pisan, trans. William Caxton, *The Book of Fayttes of Armes and of Chyvalrye*, ed. A. T. P. Byles, EETS 189 (London, 1932), 76–7.

120. Patten, 'Expedition into Scotland', 121–2.

121. *Tudor Economic Documents*, ed. R. H. Tawney and E. E. Power, 3 vols (London, 1924), iii. 41.

122. *Commentary Grey of Wilton*, 21; *StP*, ii. 352, ix. 734, x. 642; Churchyard, *General Rehearsall*, A1r, B1v, B3, C1r–v, G3r–v, G5v–6r, H1v; Hall, *Chronicle*, 336, 345, 395, 419, 434, 441, 457, 459, 479, 481, 525, 532, 538, 551, 555, 601, 629, 638, 651, 659, 667, 673, 681, 683, 704, 726, 737, 856, 860.

123. B. S. Capp, '*Long Meg of Westminster*: A Mystery Solved', *Notes and Queries* 45 (1998), 302–4; Anon., *The Life of Long Meg of Westminster* (London, 1635), 20–3, 25–33.

124. Worcestre, *Boke of Noblesse*, 65.

125. Hale, 'On a Tudor Parade Ground', 281.

126. *StP*, ii. 352, 357, 362, iii. 453–4, ix. 453.

127. Thomas Lanquet, *An epitome of chronicles . . . now finished and continued to the reigne of our soveraine lorde kynge Edwarde the sixt by Thomas Cooper* (London, 1549), Zzz1v–2r; *HP*, ii. 569.

128. *The Herald's Memoir 1486–1490: Court Ceremony, Royal Progress and Rebellion*, ed. E. Cavell (Donington, 2009), 171–2.

129. *StP*, ix. 454.

130. *Commentary Grey of Wilton*, 15; Patten, 'Expedition into Scotland', 120.

131. D. Lysons and S. Lysons, *Magna Brittania, VI, Devonshire* (London, 1822), 307–8.

132. G. Connell-Smith, *Forerunners of Drake: A Study of English Trade with Spain in the Early Tudor Period* (London, 1954), 160–1.

133. Hale, 'On a Tudor Parade Ground', 280.

134. Audley, 'Treatise', 129.

135. *CEPR*, xix. 687.

136. Hall, *Chronicle*, 686.

137. CA, MS M16bis, fos. 55v–58r.

138. *HP*, i. xciii, 117; for fumes see also Hall, *Chronicle*, 458, 549.

139. *HP*, ii. 565.

140. *HP*, ii. 456.

141. Audley, 'Treatise', 133.

142. Patten, 'Expedition into Scotland', 100–1, 125–7.

143. *HP*, i. xciii.

144. *CSPFM*, 689.

145. *HP*, i. xciii; J. Lock, 'Grey, Arthur, fourteenth Baron Grey of Wilton (1536–1593), lord deputy of Ireland and soldier', *ODNB*.

146. Molinet, *Chroniques*, ii. 136–7; Jean Surquet, 'Mémoires en forme de chronique, ou histoire des guerres et troubles de Flandre', in *Corpus chronicorum Flandriae. Vol 4*, ed. J. J. de Smet, CRH (Brussels, 1865), 579; Hall, *Chronicle*, 446.

147. Elis Gruffudd, 'The "Enterprises" of Paris and Boulogne, 1544', ed. M. B. Davies, *Fouad I University Bulletin of Faculty of Arts* 11 (1949), 90–2.

148. 'Dagverhaal 1554', 324.
149. Connell-Smith, *Forerunners of Drake*, 169; N. Williams, *The Maritime Trade of the East Anglian Ports 1550–1590* (Oxford, 1988), 236–7.
150. N. Murphy, 'Violence, Colonisation and Henry VIII's Conquest of France, 1544–46', *PP* 233 (2016), 25–7.
151. Hale, 'On a Tudor Parade Ground', 250; *Discourse of the Commonweal*, 93; J. R. Hale, 'Sixteenth-Century Explanations of War and Violence', *PP* 51 (1971), 10–11.
152. *Extracts from Records in the possession of the Municipal Corporation of the Borough of Portsmouth*, ed. R. East (Portsmouth, 1891 edn), 128.
153. *APC* vi. 124, 127–9; PRO, KB9/579/237, 580/194; *LP*, III, ii. 2415(26), 2994(28), 3670; *Yorkshire Star Chamber Proceedings*, i. 12–13.
154. *Coventry Leet Book*, ii. 409; *Literae Cantuarienses*, ed. J. B. Sheppard, 3 vols, Rolls Ser. 85 (London, 1887–9), iii. 275–6, 278, 284.
155. *Coventry Leet Book*, ii. 426–8; *Oxfordshire Muster Rolls*, xiv; M. C. Fissel, *English Warfare 1511–1642* (London and New York, 2001), 86; K. J. Kesselring, *Mercy and Authority in the Tudor State* (Cambridge, 2003), 84; *A Calendar of the Shrewsbury and Talbot Papers in Lambeth Palace Library and the College of Arms*, ed. C. Jamison, E. G. W. Bill, and G. R. Batho, 2 vols, HMC joint publications 6–7 (London, 1966–71), ii. 79.
156. PRO, C1/66/377; R. E. Horrox, *Richard III: A Study of Service* (Cambridge, 1989), 243–4; *LP*, I, ii. 3030.
157. *YCR*, v. 44.
158. Welch, *Pewterers*, i. 139; Wadmore, *Skinners*, 86; HL, MS BA277; PRO, DL1/16/T3.
159. PRO, C1/870/3.
160. *London Consistory Court Wills*, no. 210; *Oxfordshire Muster Rolls*, 61; Oxfordshire HC, MS Wills Oxon. 179, fos. 319v–320r.
161. G. Phillips, *The Anglo-Scots Wars 1513–50* (Woodbridge, 1999), 116, 132, 186, 199.
162. P. Hammer, *Elizabeth's Wars: War, Government and Society in Tudor England, 1544–1604* (Basingstoke, 2003), 61.
163. *StP*, iv. 47, 628–9, 634, 640; *HP*, i. lxviii–lxix, lxxxv–lxxxvi, 103, 110, 157–8, 308, 310, 344, 574, ii. 96–7, 118, 119–20, 139, 282, 297, 323, 362–3, 367–9, 406, 572, 574, 738–9; Phillips, *Anglo-Scots Wars*, 153. Admittedly, the English may have played down their losses at Ancrum Moor: Phillips, *Anglo-Scots Wars*, 170–1; M. H. Merriman, *The Rough Wooings: Mary Queen of Scots 1542–1551* (East Linton, 2000), 359.
164. *HP*, i. lxix, ii. 282.
165. Hall, *Chronicle*, 659, 660, 661, 702; *CSPFM*, 689, 706, 711.
166. Hall, *Chronicle*, 522–5.
167. H. Miller, *Henry VIII and the English Nobility* (Oxford, 1986), 136–42.
168. BL, Stowe MS 571, fos. 80v–82v, 87v–90r, 97r–132r.
169. Hall, *Chronicle*, 534–5, 863; *LP*, I, ii. 1851; C. Carlton, *This Seat of Mars: War and the British Isles, 1485–1746* (New Haven CT and London, 2011), 210–13.
170. *StP* ii. 80, 129, 168, 234–5, 236–7, 262, 265, 362, 525, iii. 16, 18, 27, 161, 337, 408; *Calendar of State Papers, Ireland, Tudor period 1547–1553*, ed. C. Lennon (Dublin, 2015), nos. 84, 127, 336; *Annals of the Kingdom of Ireland, by the Four Masters, from the earliest period to the year 1616*, ed. J. O'Donovan, 2nd edn, 7 vols (Dublin, 1856), iv. 1211, v. 79, 1307, 1329, 1371, 1409, 1437, 1453, 1473, 1489, 1495–7, 1503, 1521–7, 1537, 1539, 1549, 1581, 1587, 1603, 1647–9; D. Edwards, 'The Escalation of Violence in Sixteenth-Century Ireland', in D. Edwards, P. Lenihan, and C. Tait

(eds), *The Age of Atrocity: Violence and Political Conflict in Early Modern Ireland* (Dublin, 2007), 34–78.

171. Murphy, 'Violence', 24–37; Potter, *Henry VIII and Francis I*, 203–4, 273–6, 281–3, 287–93; Millar, *Tudor Mercenaries and Auxiliaries*, 121–3, 151–8, 164–5.

172. F. Blomefield, *An Essay towards a Topographical History of the County of Norfolk*, 11 vols (London, 1805–10), i. 411; J. Whittle, 'Lords and Tenants in Kett's Rebellion 1549', *PP* 207 (2010), 7–9, 20–2; J. Cornwall, *Revolt of the Peasantry 1549* (London, 1977), 103, 135, 163, 172–3, 180, 184–6, 199–201, 217, 221–3, 234; A. Wood, *The 1549 Rebellions and the Making of Early Modern England* (Cambridge, 2007), 46–7, 68–9; for a recent reassessment of Dussindale informed by landscape analysis, see A. Hodgkins, 'Reconstructing Rebellion: Digital Terrain Analysis of the Battle of Dussindale (1549)', *Internet Archaeology* 38 (2015), <http://dx.doi.org/10.11141/ia.38.3> (accessed 25 September 2015).

173. Cornwall, *Revolt of the Peasantry 1549*, 186.

174. Wood, *The 1549 Rebellions*, 70–7.

175. *A Collection of State Papers*, i. 204; BL, Stowe MS 571, fos. 80v–82v, 87v–90r, 97r–132r.

176. S. T. Bindoff, *History of Parliament: The House of Commons 1509–1558*, 3 vols (London, 1982), i. 719.

177. *Calendar of the Shrewsbury and Talbot Papers*, ii. 70–1.

178. D. Stewart, 'Sickness and Mortality Rates of the English Army in the Sixteenth Century', *Journal of the Royal Army Medical Corps* 91 (1948), 23–35.

179. *LP*, III, ii. app. 15; *StP* ii. 37–8, 84, iii. 193; S. G. Ellis, *Ireland in the Age of the Tudors: English Expansion and the End of Gaelic Rule* (London, 1998), 120.

180. W. T. MacCaffrey, 'The Newhaven Expedition, 1562–63', *HJ* 40 (1997), 17–18; Hammer, *Elizabeth's Wars*, 65; *Extracts Portsmouth*, 609–17.

181. *YCR*, v. 179; *Yorkshire Deeds vol iii*, ed. W. Brown, YASRS 63 (Wakefield, 1922), 149; *YCR*, v. 180, 184–5; BL, Althorp Papers A6.

182. D. M. Palliser, *The Age of Elizabeth: England under the Later Tudors, 1547–1603*, 2nd edn (London, 1992), 60.

183. Hale, 'On a Tudor Parade Ground', 275.

184. CA, MS M16bis, fo. 53v; *HMC Rutland*, iv. 563; Rimer et al. (eds), *Henry VIII: Arms and the Man*, 61; *Cornwall Muster Roll 1569*, 60; Bindoff, *Commons*, ii. 179–82; R. G. Rice, 'The Household Goods, etc, of Sir John Gage of West Firle, Co. Sussex, KG, 1556', *Sussex Archaeological Collections* 45 (1892), 127.

185. Rimer et al. (eds), *Henry VIII: Arms and the Man*, 61; Thomas Gale, *Certaine workes of chirurgerie, newly compiled and published by Thomas Gale, maister in chirurgerie* (London, 1563), A3r, Cc3r; *Elizabethan Naval Administration*, 209–10, 444.

186. J. Gardiner and M. J. Allen (eds), *Before the Mast: Life and Death Aboard the Mary Rose* (Portsmouth, 2005), 171–225.

187. Rimer et al. (eds), *Henry VIII: Arms and the Man*, 61.

188. *Records of Lydd*, ed. A. Finn (Ashford, 1911), 260; *HMC Ninth Report*, appendix i, 177; *Coventry Leet Book*, ii. 532, iii. 582–3; *Ancient Churchwardens' Accounts of the Parish of North Elmham*, ed. A. G. Legge (Norwich, 1891), 58; Johnson, *Drapers*, ii. 160, 432; *Elizabethan Naval Administration*, 222.

189. *LP*, IV, i. 83; Cornwall, *Revolt of the Peasantry 1549*, 217.

190. Southampton AO, SC5/1/40 fos. 20v–21r.

191. Lincolnshire Archives, Monson 7/51, fos. 159v–160r; Hall, *Chronicle*, 662; Phillips, 'Mutiny and Discontent', 321–2; D. Stewart, 'Disposal of the Sick and Wounded of

the English Army during the Sixteenth Century', *Journal of the Royal Army Medical Corps* 90 (1948), 31–2; *StP*, x. 106, 114; *Elizabethan Naval Administration*, 555.

192. PRO, KB9/607b/186.

193. Hale, 'On a Tudor Parade Ground', 275–6; *YCR*, i. 64; CA, MS M16bis, fo. 54r; PRO, SP1/10, fos. 178v–82r (*LP*, II, i. 471); C24/29; Gunn, *New Men*, 106; V. V. Patarino, 'The Religious Shipboard Culture of Sixteenth and Seventeenth-Century English Sailors', in C. A. Fury (ed.), *The Social History of English Seamen, 1485–1649* (Woodbridge, 2012), 145–71.

194. *LP*, I, i. 519(43), V. 220(28), VI. 1625(4), XIV, ii. 781(fo. 67), Addenda, i. 364.

195. N. Orme and M. Webster, *The English Hospital 1070–1570* (New Haven CT and London, 1995), 158–9; *LP*, XX, i. 412; *Peterborough Local Administration: The Last Days of Peterborough Monastery*, ed. W. T. Mellows, Northamptonshire RS 12 (Kettering, 1947), 101, 104–6; *Peterborough Local Administration: The Foundation of Peterborough Cathedral AD 1541*, ed. W. T. Mellows, Northamptonshire RS 13 (Kettering, 1941), lvii, 114; *Records of Bristol Cathedral*, ed. J. Bettey, Bristol RS 59 (Bristol, 2007), 14, 19, 42; *Documents Illustrating Early Education in Worcester 685 to 1700*, ed. A. F. Leach, Worcestershire HS 29 (London, 1913), 118, 150.

196. *LP*, XX, ii. 418 (24, 25); C. M. Fox, 'The Royal Almshouse at Westminster c.1500–c.1600', Royal Holloway University of London Ph.D. Thesis 2013, 217, 295; D. M. Loades, *Mary Tudor: A Life* (Oxford, 1989), 373–4.

197. 'Ely Episcopal Registers', *Ely Diocesan Remembrancer* 305 (1910), 182; Devon HC, Chanter 15, fo. 7v; Orme and Webster, *English Hospital*, 112, 118, 154; W. A. Bewes, *Church Briefs* (London, 1896), 64–5; *Kent Chantries*, ed. A. Hussey, Kent Records 12 (Ashford, 1936), 245.

198. *LP*, IV, i. 771; *The Manuscripts of Lord Middleton, preserved at Wollaton Hall*, HMC 69 (London, 1911), 347–9, 358–9, 361, 364; BL, Harleian MS 2177, fo. 21v; *Memorials Goldsmiths*, i. 63; *Reprint of the Barnstaple Records*, ed. J. R. Chanter and T. Wainwright, 2 vols (Barnstaple, 1900), ii. 127.

199. *Household Accounts and Disbursement Books of Robert Dudley, Earl of Leicester, 1558–1561, 1584–1586*, ed. S. L. Adams, CS 5th ser. 6 (Cambridge, 1995), 105; *HMC Rutland*, iv. 372; T. Girtin, *The Golden Ram: A Narrative History of the Clothworkers' Company* (London, 1958), 47.

200. Robert Copland, *The hye way to the spyttell hous* (London, 1536?), B2r–B3r.

201. Sharpe, *London and the Kingdom*, i. 416; *Records of the City of Norwich*, ii. 180.

202. A. L. Beier, *Masterless Men: The Vagrancy Problem in England 1560–1640* (London, 1985), 7–8; D. M. Loades, *The Making of the Elizabethan Navy 1540–1590: From the Solent to the Armada* (Woodbridge, 2009), 106–7, 160.

203. R. A. Charles, 'Noddwyr y beirdd yn sir y Fflint', *Llên Cymru* 12–13 (1972–81), 17n.

204. *The Paston Letters, 1422–1509 AD*, ed. J. A. Gairdner, 4 vols (Edinburgh, 1910), iii. 135–6.

205. PRO, C1/1421/47.

206. *Yorkshire Star Chamber Proceedings*, ii. 67–73.

207. Elis Gruffudd, 'Suffolk's Expedition to Montidier 1523', ed. M. B. Davies, *Fouad I University Bulletin of Faculty of Arts* 7 (1944), 39–41.

208. Boynton, *Elizabethan Militia*, 175–6; Younger, *War and Politics*, 133–6.

209. Rapple, *Martial Power*, 51–85; K. V. Thomas, *The Ends of Life: Roads to Fulfilment in Early Modern England* (Oxford, 2009), 44–76.

210. L. Wooding, *Henry VIII* (Abingdon, 2009), 240–3, 248–57, 268–70.

211. R. Marius, *Thomas More* (London, 1993 edn), 231.

CHAPTER 7

1. Thomas Audley, 'A Treatise on the Art of War', ed. W. St P. Bunbury, *Journal of the Society for Army Historical Research* 6 (1927), 78; Christine de Pisan, trans. William Caxton, *The Book of Fayttes of Armes and of Chyvalrye*, ed. A. T. P. Byles, EETS 189 (London, 1932), 75–6.

2. *HMC Second Report* (London, 1874), 80; R. W. Hoyle, *The Pilgrimage of Grace and the Politcs of the 1530s* (Oxford, 2001), 403.

3. *The Churchwardens' Book of Bassingbourn, Cambridgeshire 1496–c.1540*, ed. D. Dymond, Cambridgeshire Records Soc. 17 (Cambridge, 2004), 191; Oxon CRO, MS Wills Oxon. 179, fo. 320r; *Derbyshire Wills proved in the Prerogative Court of Canterbury 1393–1574*, ed. D. G. Edwards, Derbyshire RS 26 (Matlock, 1998), 87, 183; *Testamenta Vetusta*, ed. N. H. Nicolas, 2 vols (London, 1826), ii. 713; F. Blomefield, *An Essay towards a Topographical History of the County of Norfolk*, 11 vols (London, 1805–10), ii. 320; Derbyshire RO, D3287/56/4/3 (NRA report); PRO, C1/513/26; 'Muster Roll, 1539', *Collections for the History of Staffordshire* n.s. 5 (1902), 243; 'Inventories of Norfolk Church Goods (1552)', ed. H. B. Walters, *NA* 27 (1938–40), 399, 410–11, 413, 28 (1942–5), 11–12, 19, 221, 31 (1955–7), 237, 244–5, 33 (1962–5), 484–5; *Guild Stewards' Book of the Borough of Calne*, ed. A. W. Mabbs, Wiltshire Archaeological Soc. Records Branch 7 (Devizes, 1953), 4; CCA, CC/FA10, fo. 91r; KLHC, Fa/Z33, fos. 24v, 37v; *Records of the Borough of Leicester*, ed. M. Bateson et al., 7 vols (London, 1899–1974), iii. 89–90; J. F. Firth, *Coopers Company, London: Historical Memoranda, Charters, Documents, and Extracts, from the Records of the Corporation and the Books of the Company, 1396–1858* (London, 1848), 103–5.

4. F. H. Russell, *The Just War in the Middle Ages* (Cambridge, 1975), 297–303.

5. N. Orme, 'Worcester [Botoner], William', *ODNB*; G. L. Harriss, 'Fastolf, Sir John', *ODNB*; William Worcestre, *The Boke of Noblesse addressed to King Edward IV on his Invasion of France in 1475*, ed. J. G. Nichols (London, 1860), 3, 6–7, 15–19, 22–5, 41–2, 44–6.

6. H. Owen and J. B. Blakeway, *A History of Shrewsbury*, 2 vols (London, 1825), i. 259.

7. N. Murphy, 'Henry VIII's First Invasion of France: The Gascon Expedition of 1512', *EHR* 130 (2015), 50; S. J. Gunn, 'The Duke of Suffolk's March on Paris in 1523', *EHR* 101 (1986), 616; *HMC Third Report Appendix iv* (London, 1885), 157.

8. *YCR*, vi. 57–8.

9. *LP*, III, i. cxl.

10. *Depositions taken before the Mayor and Aldermen of Norwich, 1549–1567*, ed. W. Rye (Norwich, 1905), 43.

11. *Debating the Hundred Years War: Pour ce que plusieurs (la loi salique) and a declaracion of the trew and dewe title of Henry VIII*, ed. C. Taylor, CS 5th ser. 29 (Cambridge, 2006), 31–49, 135–270; *Le débat des hérauts d'armes de France et d'Angleterre: suivi de The debate between the heralds of England and France*, ed. L. Pannier (Paris, 1877), 53–125, at p. 120.

12. Julius Caesar, *The eyght books of Caius Iulius Caesar*, trans. Arthur Golding (London, 1565), **2r–v.

13. Arnould Bogaert, trans. John Coke, *A pronostication for diuers yeares ryght vtyle and profytable to al sortes of people* (London, 1553), A1r.

14. Worcestre, *Boke of Noblesse*, 57; Richard Morison, *An Exhortation to styrre all Englyshe men to the defence of theyr countreye* (London, 1539), A3v–4r; Thomas Becon, *The Early Works of Thomas Becon*, ed. J. Ayre, Parker Soc. (Cambridge, 1843), 245, 251; Edward

Walshe, *The office and duety in fightyng for our country* (London, 1545), B3r; Russell, *Just War*, 297–8, 302.

15. *The Manuscripts of His Grace, the Duke of Rutland, G.C.B., preserved at Belvoir Castle*, 4 vols, HMC 24 (London, 1888–1908), i. 13; *Christ Church Letters*, ed. J. B. Sheppard, CS n.s. 19 (London, 1877), 62–3; BL, Addl. MS 70948/1.

16. *Statutes and ordenaunces of warre* (London, 1513), HL, HEH 61101; 3 Henry VIII, c. 22, 4 Henry VIII, cc. 1, 19; *Historia et Cartularium Monasterii Sancti Petri Gloucestriae, vol iii*, ed. W. H. Hart, Rolls Ser. 33 (London, 1867), xxviii.

17. Morison, *Exhortation*, D4r–v.

18. I owe the suggestion about the 1540s to Cliff Davies.

19. *YCR*, i. 35, 40, 58, iv. 90, 126, 171, v. 165, vi. 57–8.

20. Morison, *Exhortation*, D3r–D4r; Sextus Julius Frontinus, *The strategemes, sleyghtes, and policies of warre, gathered togyther, by S. Iulius Frontinus, and translated into Englyshe, by Rycharde Morysine* (London, 1539), A2v–3r; Becon, *Early Works*, 245.

21. BL, Egerton MS 2093, fo. 211r; *YCR*, iv. 111–12, 126.

22. 37 Henry VIII, c. 25.

23. HL, MS HA Correspondence Box 1 HA 13886.

24. *StP*, x. 134.

25. *Proceedings in the Parliaments of Elizabeth I*, ed. T. E. Hartley, 3 vols (Leicester, 1981–95), i. 71–2, 85, 186; *Elizabethan Naval Administration*, ed. C. S. Knighton and D. M. Loades, Navy Records Soc. 160 (Farnham, 2013), 8–9.

26. *Descriptive Catalogue of the Charters and Muniments in the Possession of the Rt Hon Lord Fitzhardinge at Berkeley Castle*, ed. I. H. Jeayes (Bristol, 1892), 321–2.

27. *Report on Manuscripts in the Welsh Language*, 2 vols, HMC 48 (London, 1898–1910), i. ii; Edward Hall, *Hall's Chronicle*, ed. H. Ellis (London, 1809), 700.

28. *Troubles connected with The Prayer Book of 1549*, ed. N. Pocock, CS n.s. 37 (London, 1884), 32, 47.

29. J. Cornwall, *Revolt of the Peasantry 1549* (London, 1977), 132–6, 160–1, 176–86, 193, 197–200, 209–14, 221–3; Hoyle, *Pilgrimage of Grace*, 283–6; K. J. Kesselring, *The Northern Rebellion of 1569: Faith, Politics, and Protest in Elizabethan England* (Basingstoke, 2007), 79, 89.

30. *StP*, ii. 361–2, 440–1, 443, iii. 65, 110, 337, 408.

31. J. M. Collins, *Martial Law and English Laws, c.1500–c.1700* (Cambridge, 2016), 43–75.

32. D. Armitage, *The Ideological Origins of the British Empire* (Cambridge, 2000), 25–6, 48–59; N. Murphy, 'Violence, Colonisation and Henry VIII's Conquest of France, 1544–46', *PP* 233 (2016), 44–51.

33. Borthwick Institute, Bishop's Register 22, fo. 337r; *Historiae Dunelmensis Scriptores Tres*, ed. J. Raine, SS 9 (London, 1839), cccxc–cccxci; *Records of the City of Norwich*, ed. W. Hudson and J. C. Tingey, 2 vols (Norwich, 1906–10), ii. 156–7; *Registra Johannis Whethamstede, Willelmi Albon et Willelmi Walingforde, Abbatum Monasterii Sancti Albani*, ed. H. T. Riley, Rolls Ser. (London, 1873), 191–2; G. O'Malley, *The Knights Hospitallers of the English Langue 1460–1565* (Oxford, 2005).

34. Morison, *Exhortation*, B3v.

35. B. Lowe, 'A War to End All Wars? Protestant Subversions of Henry VII's Final Scottish and French Campaigns (1542–45)', in D. Wolfthal (ed.), *Peace and Negotiation: Strategies for Coexistence in the Middle Ages and the Renaissance* (Turnhout, 2000), 185–94.

36. D. N. J. MacCulloch, *Tudor Church Militant: Edward VI and the Protestant Reformation* (London, 1999), 21.

37. A. Nowell, *A Catechism written in Latin by Alexander Nowell, Dean of St Paul's*, ed. G. E. Corrie, Parker Soc. (Cambridge, 1853), 226–7.

38. N. Younger, *War and Politics in the Elizabethan Counties* (Manchester, 2012), 11–47, 132–6, 142–5; M. Smuts, 'Organized Violence in the Elizabethan Monarchical Republic', *History* 99 (2014), 418–32.

39. J. R. Hale, 'Sixteenth-Century Explanations of War and Violence', *PP* 51 (1971), 21.

40. *The Coventry Leet Book*, ed. M. D. Harris, 4 vols, EETS 134–5, 138, 146 (London, 1907–13), ii. 409; *Literae Cantuarienses*, ed. J. B. Sheppard, 3 vols, Rolls Ser. 85 (London, 1887–9), iii. 282.

41. 3 Henry VIII, c. 5, 25 Henry VIII, c. 22, 28 Henry VIII, c. 24, 32 Henry VIII, c. 25.

42. Richard Morison, *A lamentation in whiche is shewed what ruyne and destruction cometh of seditious rebellion* (London, 1536), B1v.

43. *The Great Chronicle of London*, ed. A. H. Thomas and I. D. Thornley (London, 1938), 196–7; John Leland, *The Itinerary of John Leland in or about the Years 1535–1543*, ed. L. T. Smith, 5 vols (London, 1906–10), i. 43.

44. Morison, *Exhortation*, D1v–2r.

45. Jean Berteville, *Recit de l'expedition en Ecosse l'an M.D. XLVI. et de la battayle de Muscleburgh*, ed. D. Constable (Edinburgh, 1825), 17–18.

46. *STC* 9968–9976, 9985.5–9989.5.

47. *A breuiat cronicle* (London, 1552), H2r, H4v, H5r, H5v, H6r, H8v, I1v, I2v.

48. *A breuiat cronicle* (1552), D3v, F3r–v, G5v, H2r.

49. *A breuiat cronicle* (1552), K3v–4v, K6v–7v, L8r–M2v; *A short cronycle* (London, 1540), B8r–C1v, C3r–C4r; *A Chronicle of yeres* (London, *c.*1558), E1r–7r; compare *The Customs of London, otherwise called Arnold's Chronicle*, ed. F. Douce (London, 1811), xlvii–xlviii.

50. *A breuiat cronicle* (1552), I5v–K2v, L7v–M5r.

51. *STC* 10660–10664.5, 12147–12150, 15217–15220, 23319–23319.5, 23322, 23323.5, 23325–23325.5; Robert Fabyan, *Fabyan's Chronicle* (London, 1533), fos. 204v, 206v, 220r; Thomas Lanquet, *An epitome of chronicles… now finished and continued to the reigne of our soueraine lorde kynge Edwarde the sixt by Thomas Cooper* (London, 1549), Vvv2r, Vvv3v, Vvv4r, Dddd3r; Thomas Lanquet, *An epitome of chronicles* (London, 1559), Dddd3v; Richard Grafton, *An abridgement of the chronicles of England* (London, 1562), fos. 107r, 109r, 112v, 143v; John Stow, *A summarie of Englyshe chronicles* (London, 1565), fos. 117r, 119r–v, 121r–v, 138v–139r, 141v, 150v, 153r–v, 173v–174r, 203r–206r.

52. Lanquet, *Epitome of chronicles* (1549), Zzz1v; Richard Grafton, *An abridgement of the chronicles of England* (London, 1564), fos. 123r, 178v.

53. R. Llull, *The Book of the Ordre of Chyvalry, translated and printed by William Caxton*, ed. A. T. P. Byles, EETS 168 (London, 1926), 122–3.

54. Leland, *Itinerary*, iv. 116; Robert Fabyan, *Prima pars cronecarum* (London, 1516), Ss7r; *Débat des hérauts d'armes*, 69–99; *A breuiat cronicle* (1552), D3v; Morison, *Exhortation*, C3r; New York Public Library, *KC 1559 Lanquet, fo. 241r; *StP*, ix. 677.

55. *STC* 11396, 11396.5, 11396.7, 11397; John Stow, *A summarye of the chronicles of Englande* (London, 1570), a8v.

56. *Here after foloweth ye batayll of Egyngecourte [and] the great sege of Rone by kynge Henry of Monmouthe the fyfthe of the name that wan Gascoyne and Gyenne and Normandye* (London, 1536); J. Bellis, *The Hundred Yars War in Literature, 1337–1600* (Woodbridge, 2016), 160–3; *The First English life of King Henry the Fifth written in 1513 by an*

anonymous author known commonly as the translator of Livius, ed. C. L. Kingsford (Oxford, 1911); 'Vita Henrici Quinti, Roberto Redmanno auctore', in *Memorials of Henry the Fifth, King of England*, ed. C. A. Cole, Rolls Ser. (London, 1858), ix–xxviii, 1–59; R. R. Reid, 'The Date and Authorship of Redmayne's "Life of Henry V"', *EHR* 30 (1915), 691–8; HL, MS 8, fos. 5v, 6v, 24v, 65r, 86r.

57. P. C. Herman, 'Hall, Edward', *ODNB*.

58. *HMC Rutland*, iv. 369; CUL, Hengrave MS 88(i), no. 15; *A breuiat cronicle* (1552), G7v, G5v, H2r; Stow, *Summarie* (1565), fos. 139r, 157r; M.-R. McLaren, *The London Chronicles of the Fifteenth Century: A Revolution in English Writing* (Woodbridge, 2002), 125.

59. Hall, *Chronicle*, 846–56; *Breuiat cronicle* (1552), N1r; *Chronicle of yeres* (c.1558), F2r; Stow, *Summarie* (1565), fo. 209v.

60. Higden: New York Public Library, *KC1482 Higden, fos. 381v, 386v, 391r; *HKW*, iv. 496; Caxton: Bodl. S. Seld d4(1), fos. 124r, 126r, 129r, 129v; St Albans: HL, RB 97027, B1r–C2v; Bodl. F.2.27 Art. Seld, fo. 77r; Bodl. Arch. G d.19, B6v; Arnold: John Rylands Library, R77741, fos. 123r, 125r, 128v, 144v, 145v, 149v, 151r, 152v; Fabyan: Bodl. Auct. QQ Supra II.33, Nn5r; Bodl. Douce F 503, rr3v; HL, RB 93555, 156, 181–2, 207, 217–19, 234, 356–7, 362, 378, 398, 409, 415, 420; Hall: HL, RB 61301, fos. 37v–8r, 39r, 41v, 107r, 153v, 155r, Henry VIII, fo. 36v, table to Henry VIII, A6r; Grafton: Bodl. Wood 144, fos. 123r, 167r, 179r; Bodl. 8° A7 Art, fos. 78v, 79v, 81r; Cooper: New York Public Library, *KC 1559 Lanquet, fos. 232v, 235v–44v, 254v, 273v, 286v, 287r, 291v; BL 195 a19, fos. 237r–8v, 239v, 241v, 243v, 273v; Vergil: Nottingham UL, DA130.V4, 376–7.

61. Caxton: HL RB 59601, K5v, K6r, K7r, L1v, P3r, Q3r, U2r, Y5v; Bodl. Mal. 10, t4r, t5r, y6r, A3v; Fabyan: Bodl. Byw. Adds 10, Hh4r, Hh5v, Hh6v; St Albans: Bodl. Arch. G d.21, u6v, u7v, u8v, A5v.

62. Cooper: HL, RB 316433, fos. 273v, 292r; Vergil: Bodl. CC39 Art, m4v–n2r.

63. Vergil: Bodl. Vet. D1 c. 35, 360; Hall: HL, RB 61301, fo. 153v; Cooper: Canterbury Cathedral Library, H/M-4-33, fo. 241r; Fabyan: RB 59655, ii, fo. 172r.

64. Bodl. Arch. G d.21, A7r–B1r, B6v, B8r, G1r–H2r, H8r, Iiv, K1r, K3v, K5v–7v.

65. *StP*, x. 468; Audley, 'Treatise', 129.

66. McLaren, *London Chronicles*; *A Chronicle of England by Charles Wriothesley*, ed. W. D. Hamilton, 2 vols, CS n.s. 11 (London, 1875), i. 136–8, 142–3, 147–9, 151–3, 156–65, 185–6, ii. 11–12, 20–2, 31, 34–5, 107–11, 138–41; *The Diary of Henry Machyn Citizen and Merchant-Taylor of London (1550–1563)*, ed. J. G. Nichols, CS 42 (London, 1848), 143–7, 150, 152–3, 158, 162–4, 292–3, 295, 298, 302, 311–12; *Chronicle of the Greyfriars of London*, ed. J. G. Nichols, CS 53 (London, 1852), 24–5, 29, 32, 45–52, 61, 66, 86–8.

67. HL, MS El 9/H/15, fo. 117r; *HMC Fifth Report* (London, 1876), 434; *HMC Sixth Report* (London, 1877), 569; 'London Chronicle during the reigns of Henry the Seventh and Henry the Eight', ed. C. Hopper, in *Camden Miscellany iv*, CS 73 (London, 1859), 16–17; *Heraldic Visitation of the Northern Counties in 1530 by Thomas Tonge, Norroy King of Arms*, ed. W. H. D. Longstaffe, SS 41 (Durham, 1863), lxii–lxvii; 'A Bailiff's List and Chronicle from Worcester', ed. D. MacCulloch and P. Hughes, *The Antiquaries Journal* 75 (1995), 241–50.

68. *The Register or Chronicle of Butley Priory*, ed. A. G. Dickens (Winchester, 1951), 43; *Calendar of the Plymouth Municipal Records*, ed. R. N. Worth (Plymouth, 1893), 16; *The Chronicle of Calais*, ed. J. G. Nichols, CS 35 (London, 1846), 1–48; 'Two London Chronicles', ed. C. L. Kingsford, *Camden Miscellany XII*, CS 3rd Ser. 18 (London,

1910), 44–9; S. Anglo, 'The "British History" in Early Tudor Propaganda', *Bulletin of the John Rylands Library* 44 (1961), 48; L. R. Mooney, 'Lydgate's "Kings of England" and Another Verse Chronicle of the Kings', *Viator* 20 (1989), 275–6; Bodl. MS Lat. Th. d 15, fo. 131v; *Here is a lytell shorte cronycle, begynnynge at the. vii. ages of the worlde, w[ith] the comy[n]ge of Brute: and the reygne of all the kynges* (London, 1530), A4r.

69. Leland, *Itinerary*, i. 43, ii. 82–3, iv. 77; PRO, CHES24/93/6/unnumbered; *Great Chronicle*, 217; N. Rogers, 'The Cult of Prince Edward at Tewkesbury', *Transactions of the Bristol and Gloucester Archaeological Society* 101 (1983), 187–9; *LP*, I, i. 857(18); N. Orme, 'Church and Chapel in Medieval England', *TRHS* 6th ser. 6 (1996), 83, 88.

70. N. Pevsner, J. Grundy, and S. Linsley, *The Buildings of England: Northumberland* (London, 1992), 313; Leland, *Itinerary*, i. 8, 41.

71. Leland, *Itinerary*, i. 88, ii. 5, 18, 22, 44, 103, iv. 77, 105, 124–5, 132, 162–3, v. 3, 12, 102, 151, 221, 222; J. Broadway, *'No Historie so Meete': Gentry Culture and the Development of Local History in Elizabethan and Early Stuart England* (Manchester, 2006), 136–7.

72. *A Discourse of the Commonweal of this Realm of England*, ed. M. Dewar (Charlottesville VA, 1969), 82–4.

73. Leland, *Itinerary*, i. 39, 102, 138, ii. 56, 72, iv. 132–3, 141, v. 8, 223.

74. Leland, *Itinerary*, i. 5, 159, 203–4, 221, 250, 265, 276, ii. 14, 17, 21–2, 75, iv. 34, 87, 110, 113–15, 130, v. 147, 149.

75. Leland, *Itinerary*, i. 66, 68, 114, v. 50, 51, 125; *Rites of Durham*, ed. J. T. Fowler, SS 107 (Durham, 1903), 6–7, 29, 95.

76. Leland, *Itinerary*, v. 64, 125.

77. Leland, *Itinerary*, i. 192–3, 196–7, 200, 202–4, 207, 214, 221, 250, 252, 279–83, 305, 323.

78. *StP*, ii. 441.

79. *Report on Manuscripts in Various Collections*, 8 vols, HMC 55 (London, 1901–13), vii. 21.

80. PRO, C1/513/26; R. Halstead, *Succinct Genealogies of the Noble and Ancient Houses of Alno or de Alneto etc* (London, 1685), 71; *StP*, iii, 46, 71, 174, 175, 179, 186, 190, 191, 232, 268, 313, 338, 353, 365, 374, 376, 381, 384, 391, 394, 400, 411, 416, 418, 448, 449, 453, 454, 460, 469, 487, 496, 500, 504, 505–6, 527, 531, 538, 544, 556, 561, 569.

81. J. P. Carley, 'Presentation Manuscripts from the Collection of Henry VIII: The Case of Henry Parker, Lord Morley', in R. C. Alston (ed.), *Order and Connexion* (Cambridge, 1997), 173.

82. Hampshire RO, will B1544/62.

83. *YCR*, iv. 171.

84. *Swaledale Wills and Inventories 1522–1600*, ed. E. K. Berry, YASRS 152 (Leeds, 1998), 103.

85. *StP*, iii. 100, 417, ix. 412.

86. *Report on the Records of the City of Exeter*, HMC 73 (London, 1916), 36.

87. *StP*, ii. 73, 134, 191.

88. *Tudor Economic Documents*, ed. R. H. Tawney and E. E. Power, 3 vols (London, 1924), ii. 97.

89. Niccolò Machiavelli, *Le opere di Niccolò Machiavelli*, ed. P. Fanfani, L. Passerini, and G. Milanesi, 6 vols (Florence, 1873–7), vi. 298, 302; *Relations des ambassadeurs vénitiens sur les affaires de France au XVIe siècle*, ed. N. Tommaseo, 2 vols (Paris, 1838), i. 181, ii. 33, 177; *Literae Cantuarienses*, iii. 280–1.

90. W. H. St J. Hope, *Cowdray and Easebourne Priory* (London, 1919), 113; R. A. Griffiths, 'Tudor, Owen [Owain ap Maredudd ap Tudur] (c.1400–1461), courtier', *ODNB*; *LP*, I, ii. 2053(6ii).

91. A. Wood, *The Memory of the People: Custom and Popular Senses of the Past in Early Modern England* (Cambridge, 2013), 217; Hull History Centre, DDSY/104/16 (NRA report); *TE*, v. 45–6; Borthwick Institute, Probate register 8, fos. 118v–119r; P. King, 'Eight English Memento Mori Verses from Cadaver Tombs', *Notes and Queries* n.s. 28 (1981), 495.

92. Wood, *Memory of the People*, 221; 'The Register of Sir Thomas Botelar, Vicar of Much Wenlock', *Transactions of the Shropshire Archaeological and Natural History Society* 6 (1883), 102.

93. *StP*, ix. 344, 723, x. 391, xi. 116; PRO, SP70/87, fo. 164v; C1/1094/12, 1466/15; Raphael Holinshed, *The First and Second volumes of Chronicles*, 6 vols (London, 1587), vi. 1080; Anon., *The true tragedie of Richard the third* (London, 1594), I1v; Bodl. 8° Rawl. 962, Grafton, *Abridgement* (1564), fo. 123r.

94. PRO C24/29.

95. Holinshed, *First and Second volumes of Chronicles*, vi. 1579; I owe the second reference, from a Kentish lawsuit of the late 1570s, to Kat Byrne.

96. C. H. Firth, 'The Ballad History of the Reigns of Henry VII and Henry VIII', *TRHS* 3rd ser. 2 (1908), 21–30; C. H. Firth, 'The Ballad History of the Reigns of the Later Tudors', *TRHS* 3rd ser. 3 (1909), 53–4, 72–3; D. A. Lawton, 'Scottish Field: Alliterative Verse and Stanley Encomium in the Percy Folio', *Leeds Studies in English* n.s. 10 (1978), 42–57; John Awdelay, *The wonders of England* (London, 1559); William Birch, *A new balade of the worthy seruice of late doen by Maister Strangwige in Fraunce, and of his death* (London, 1562).

97. A. H. Johnson, *The History of the Worshipful Company of the Drapers of London*, 5 vols (Oxford, 1914–22), i. 137, 139; *Memorials of the Goldsmiths' Company*, ed. W. S. Prideaux, 2 vols (London, 1913), i. 27–8, 30; C. Welch, *History of the Worshipful Company of Pewterers of the City of London, based upon their own Records*, 2 vols (London, 1902), i. 45, 65.

98. *Registrum Annalium Collegii Mertonensis 1483–1521*, ed. H. E. Salter, Oxford HS 76 (Oxford, 1923), 72, 98, 122, 167, 202, 208, 214; *YCR*, iii. 41–2.

99. *The Records of the Honourable Society of Lincoln's Inn: The Black Books*, ed. W. P. Baildon and R. Roxburgh, 5 vols (London, 1897–1968), i. 262–3, 266–8.

100. Somerset Heritage Centre, DD/L/P/33/7.

101. Worcestershire Archives, Worcester City Records A10, box 2, vol 1 (unfol.).

102. *HMC Third Report* (London, 1872), 320.

103. Worcestre, *Boke of Noblesse*, 2–4, 9–20, 40–9.

104. Berteville, *Recit de l'expedition en Ecosse*, 14.

105. Morison, *Exhortation*, B3v.

106. Wilwolt von Schaumburg, *Die Geschichten und Taten Wilwolts von Schaumburg*, ed. A. Von Keller, Bibliothek des Litterarischen Vereins in Stuttgart, 50 (Stuttgart, 1859), 123; *StP*, ix. 439, 475.

107. *Calendar of Letters, Despatches, and State Papers, relating to the Negotiations between England and Spain, Preserved in the Archives at Simancas and Elsewhere*, ed. G. Bergenroth et al., 13 vols (London, 1862–1954), i. 552; N. Housley, *Religious Warfare in Europe 1400–1536* (Oxford, 2002), 112; O'Malley, *Knights Hospitaller*, 299; *The Travel Journal of Antonio de Beatis. Germany, Switzerland, the Low Countries, France and Italy, 1517–1518*, ed. J. R. Hale and J. M. A. Lindon, Hakluyt Soc. 2nd ser. 150 (London,

1979), 103–4; R. Barrington, 'A Venetian Secretary in England: An Unpublished Diplomatic Report in the Biblioteca Marciana, Venice', *HR* 70 (1997), 177–8, 181; *Calendar of State Papers and Manuscripts, Relating to English Affairs, Existing in the Archives and Collections of Venice and other Libraries of Northern Italy, vol VI part ii, 1556–1557*, ed. R. Brown (London, 1881), 1047.

108. *YCR*, i. 36, 55, 57, 58, 136, ii. 129, iv. 125–6, 153, 171, v. 163; BL, Egerton MS 2093, fo. 49r; *Household Books of John Duke of Norfolk, and Thomas earl of Surrey; temp 1481–90*, ed. J. P. Collier, Roxburgh Club 61 (London, 1854), 502–3.

109. *YCR*, iv. 112; BL, Egerton MS 2093, fos. 49r, 56r; 4 Henry VIII, c. 1, 37 Henry VIII, c. 25; *The Red Paper Book of Colchester*, ed. W. G. Benham (Colchester, 1902), 28; *Proceedings in the Parliaments of Elizabeth I*, i. 169.

110. *Household Books of John Duke of Norfolk*, 502–3; Nottingham UL, Ga12,750; Norfolk RO, NCC Wills 161 Multon; *Cornish Wills 1342–1540*, ed. N. Orme, Devon and Cornwall RS n.s. 50 (Exeter, 2007), 148; PRO, DL1/21/L19; *TE*, iii. 273.

111. *Chronicle of King Henry VIII of England*, ed. M. A. S. Hume (London, 1889), 120; *StP*, ix. 439.

112. *Calendar of State Papers Venice 1556*–1557, 1050.

113. W. A. Shaw, *The Knights of England*, 2 vols (London, 1906), ii. 36–42; S. Gunn., D. Grummitt, and H. Cools, *War, State, and Society in England and the Netherlands, 1477–1559* (Oxford, 2007), 141; *LP*, I, ii. 2481, 2651, 2652; H. Miller, *Henry VIII and the English Nobility* (Oxford, 1986), 138–41; E. W. Ives, 'Patronage at the Court of Henry VIII: The Case of Sir Ralph Egerton of Ridley', *Bulletin of the John Rylands Library* 52 (1970), 351–6; 'Testamenta Leodiensia', ed. G. D. Lumb, *Miscellanea iii*, Thoresby Soc. 9 (Leeds, 1897–9), 81–2.

114. I. Arthurson, 'The King's Voyage into Scotland: The War that Never Was', in D. Williams (ed.), *England in the Fifteenth Century* (Woodbridge, 1987), 9–10, 16–22.

115. BL Stowe MS 571, fos. 97r–132r; E. E. Rich, 'The Population of Elizabethan England', *EcHR* n.s. 2 (1950), 254; *APC* vi. 24–5, 250, 261.

116. 'Church Goods in Suffolk, nos. iv–xxiii', ed. J. J. Muskett, *The East Anglian* n.s. 1 (1885–6), 49.

117. A. King, 'The Anglo-Scottish Marches and the Perception of "The North" in Fifteenth-Century England', *Northern History* 49 (2012), 37–50; 1483: *Memorials Goldsmiths*, i. 27; 1487: *Henley Borough Records: Assembly Books i–iv, 1395–1543*, ed. P. M. Briers, Oxfordshire RS 41 (Oxford, 1960), 103–4; 1536: A. Crawford, *A History of the Vintners' Company* (London, 1977), 92–3; BL, Egerton MS 2092, fos. 358v, 438r; Firth, *Coopers Company*, 103–4; Berkshire RO, WI//FA1, fo. 39r; 1548 Cornwall: *Calendar Plymouth*, 115; 1549 Norfolk: 'Cambridgeshire Church Goods', ed. J. J. Muskett, *The East Anglian* n.s. 9 (1902), 137; P. Thompson, *The History and Antiquities of Boston* (Sleaford, 1997 edn), 164; 1554: *Records of the Worshipful Company of Carpenters*, 6 vols (Oxford, 1913–39), iv. 64; *Wardens' Accounts of the Worshipful Company of Founders of the City of London 1497–1681*, ed. G. Parsloe (London, 1964), 127; Leicestershire RO, DG36/140/6, fo. B11r.

118. Morison, *Exhortation*, B4r–5r, C5r–v, D3v.

119. Portsmouth: *The Early Churchwardens' Accounts of Hampshire*, ed. J. F. Williams (Winchester, 1913), 37; *Illustrations of the Manners and Expenses of Antient Times in England*, ed. J. Nichols (London, 1797), 15; Berwick: *The Churchwardens' Accounts of St Michael's in Bedwardine, Worcester, from 1539 to 1603*, ed. J. Amphlett, Worcestershire HS 6 (Oxford, 1897), 43; *The Boston Assembly Minutes 1545–1575*, ed. P. Clark and J. Clark, Lincoln RS 77 (Woodbridge, 1987), 32; Boulogne: 'Church Goods in

Suffolk, nos. iv–xxiii', 50; *The Accounts of the Wardens of the Parish of Morebath, Devon, 1520–1573*, ed. J. E. Binney (Exeter, 1904), 176; *Reading Records: Diary of the Corporation*, ed. J. M. Guilding, 4 vols (London, 1892–6), i. 213; Saint-Quentin: *Boston Assembly Minutes*, 23; *Reading Records*, i. 258; Le Havre: *Accounts of Morebath*, 219; *Illustrations of the Manners and Expenses*, 16, 17; *Guild Stewards' Book of the Borough of Calne*, ed. A. W. Mabbs, Wiltshire Archaeological Soc. Records Branch 7 (Devizes, 1953), 6; CCA, CC/FA16, fo. 241r; *Calendar of the Records of the Borough of Haverfordwest 1539–1660*, ed. B. G. Charles, Bulletin of the Board of Celtic Studies History and Law Series 24 (Cardiff, 1967), 174; *Records Carpenters*, iv. 137, 147–9; *Liverpool Town Books*, ed. J. A. Twemlow, 2 vols (London 1918–35), i. 221–2; *The Manuscripts of Shrewsbury and Coventry Corporations*, HMC 15th report 10 (London, 1899), 15; Guelders: BL Egerton MS 2092, fos. 57r, 65r; Scotland: 'Church Goods in Suffolk, nos. xxiv–xxxix', ed. J. J. Muskett, *The East Anglian* n.s. 2 (1887–8), 70–1; 'Extracts from the Churchwardens' Accounts of the Parish of Leverton', ed. E. Peacock, *Archaeologia* 41 (1867), 359, 363; *Churchwardens' Accounts St Michael's in Bedwardine*, 19, 21; *Churchwardens' Accounts of St Michael, Spurriergate, York, 1518–1548*, ed. C. C. Webb, 2 vols, Borthwick Texts and Calendars 20 (York, 1997), ii. 293, 315, 324n; Shropshire Archives, LB8/1/46/103; *HMC Shrewsbury*, 35; Ireland: 'Molland Accounts', ed. J. B. Phear, *Reports and Transactions of the Devonshire Association* 35 (1903), 227; *Accounts of Morebath*, 228; *Calendar of the Tavistock Parish Records*, ed. R. N. Worth (Plymouth, 1887), 30; *Reprint of the Barnstaple Records*, ed. J. R. Chanter and T. Wainwright, 2 vols (Barnstaple, 1900), 121, 143; *HMC Shrewsbury*, 15.

120. KHLC, Fa/Z33, fos. 74v, 75v.

121. *The Herefordshire Musters of 1539 and 1542*, ed. M. A. Faraday (Walton-on-Thames, 2012), 4.

122. *YCR*, ii. 102.

123. LMA, Rep. 4, fo. 163v.

124. S. J. Gunn, 'War, Dynasty and Public Opinion in Early Tudor England', in G. W. Bernard and S. J. Gunn (eds), *Authority and Consent in Tudor England: Essays presented to C. S. L. Davies* (Aldershot, 2002), 131–49; Gunn, Grummitt, and Cools, *War, State, and Society*, 269–72.

125. *Gwaith Lewys Daron*, ed. A. C. Lake (Cardiff, 1994), no. 3, ll. 35–6; *Gwaith Tudur Aled*, ed. T. G. Jones (Cardiff, 1924), no. 12, ll. 75–6; Elis Gruffudd, 'Suffolk's Expedition to Montdidier 1523', ed. M. B. Davies, *Fouad I University Bulletin of Faculty of Arts* 7 (1944), 35–7, 39–40; Elis Gruffudd, 'The "Enterprises" of Paris and Boulogne, 1544', ed. M. B. Davies, ibid. 11 (1949), 71, 84, 87; Elis Gruffudd, 'Boulogne and Calais from 1545 to 1550', ed. M. B. Davies, ibid. 12 (1950), 24, 54, 62, 67–8, 90.

126. R. Morgan, *The Welsh and the Shaping of Early Modern Ireland 1558–1641* (Woodbridge, 2014), 17–23, 134–6; *Gwaith Lewys Morgannwg*, ed. A. C. Lake (Aberystwyth, 2004), nos. 17, 78.

127. D. G. White, 'Henry VIII's Irish Kerne in France and Scotland', *The Irish Sword* 3 (1958), 213–35; *StP*, ii. 12, 24, 163; C. Brady, *The Chief Governors: The Rise and Fall of Reform Government in Tudor Ireland, 1536–1588* (Cambridge, 1994), 209–44.

128. 1513: CCA, CC/FA10, fo. 41r; 1522: BL, Egerton MS 2093, fo. 38v; *HMC Exeter*, 9; *Records of the Borough of Leicester*, iii. 21–2; *HMC Eighth Report* (London, 1881), appendix i(ii), 416a; Southampton AO, SC5/1/32, fo. 22v; 1541: *StP*, v. 192–3; 1549: *Troubles connected with the Prayer Book*, 46; for implementation see KHLC, NR/JBf4; *Chronicle of England by Charles Wriothesley*, ii. 20.

129. PRO, C1/61/347, 483, C1/66/204; LMA, Rep. 1, fos. 5v–6r; KHLC, NR/FAc3, fo. 123r–v; Sa/FAt20, m. 8; Gunn, Grummitt, and Cools, *War, State, and Society*, 309–10; HL, MS BA275.
130. LMA, Rep. 5, fos. 118r, 305v; *HMC Shrewsbury*, 48; BL, Egerton MS 2093, fos. 38v–39r; Berkshire RO, WI/FAc1, fo. 21r.
131. *Records of the City of Norwich*, ii. 170–1; PRO, C1/1109/70, 73–4.
132. *YCR*, i. 17–18, 24, 169, 175–6, ii. 168, iii. 15–16; *A Volume of English Miscellanies illustrating the History and Language of the Northern Counties of England*, ed. J. Raine, SS 85 (Durham, 1890), 35–52; E. Gillett and K. A. MacMahon, *A History of Hull*, 2nd edn (Hull, 1989), 98; PRO, C1/355/93, 731/29; *Records of the City of Norwich*, ii. 105; BL, Egerton MS 2093, fos. 106v, 179r, 2092, fo. 518v; *Epistolae Academicae 1508–1596*, ed. W. T. Mitchell, Oxford HS, n.s. 26 (Oxford, 1980), 141–2.
133. KHLC, NR/FAc3, fo. 123r; Southampton AO, SC5/1/29, fo. 24v; *Calendar Plymouth*, 112; *LP*, XVIII, ii. 204.
134. *HMC Exeter*, 9; 4 & 5 Philip & Mary, c. 6.
135. *YCR*, v. 187–8; C. H. Cooper, *Annals of Cambridge*, 5 vols (Cambridge, 1842–1908), ii. 144; *Selections from the Records of City of Oxford*, ed. W. H. Turner (Oxford, 1880), 274–5.
136. KHLC, NR/JBf8.
137. P. Griffiths, *Lost Londons: Change, Crime and Control in the Capital City, 1550–1660* (Cambridge, 2008), 322.
138. *The Cornwall Military Survey 1522*, ed. T. L. Stoate (Bristol, 1987); *The Certificate of Musters for Buckinghamshire in 1522*, ed. A. C. Chibnall, Buckinghamshire RS 17 (1973), 225; *HKW*, iii. 34–5; 'Musters for Northumberland in 1538', ed. J. Hodgson, *Archaeologia Aeliana* 4 (1855), 201.
139. Johnson, *Drapers*, ii. 80; Welch, *Pewterers*, i. 213.
140. *Memorials Goldsmiths*, i. 58.
141. Arthurson, 'King's Voyage into Scotland', 8–9; *Memorials of King Henry the Seventh*, ed. J. Gairdner, Rolls Ser. 10 (London, 1858), 127; Lincolnshire Archives, Monson 7/51, fos. 118v–22v; *LP*, I, ii. 2657; G. J. Millar, *Tudor Mercenaries and Auxiliaries 1485–1547* (Charlottesville VA, 1980), 65–180.
142. *The Second Book of the Travels of Nicander Nucius, of Corcyra*, ed. J. A. Cramer, CS 17 (London, 1841), 14, 89–95.
143. Gruffudd, 'Boulogne and Calais', 14–18, 22, 24–7, 37, 41, 74.
144. J. Vowell, alias Hooker, *Description of the Citie of Excester*, 3 parts, Devon and Cornwall RS 12 (Exeter, 1919–47), ii. 96; Cornwall, *Revolt of the Peasantry*, 171.
145. PRO, KB8/18/119.
146. Jean de Dadizeele, *Mémoires de Jean de Dadizeele, souverain bailli de Flandre*, ed. K. de Lettenhove, Société d'émulation de Bruges. Recueil de chroniques, chartes et autres documents concernant l'histoire et les antiquités de Flandre, 3e série (Bruges, 1850), 24; C. G. Cruickshank, *Army Royal: Henry VIII's Invasion of France 1513* (Oxford, 1969), 102–3; *LP*, XVIII, ii. 92; 'Dagverhaal van den veldtogt van keizer Karel V in 1554', ed. [C. A.] R. Macaré, *Kronik van het Historisch Genootschap Gevestigd te Utrecht* 7 (1851), 324–5.
147. Thomas Churchyard, *A generall rehearsall of warres, called Churchyardes choise wherein is fiue hundred seuerall seruices of land and sea as seiges, battailes, skirmiches, and encounters* (London, 1579), B4v, C1r.
148. Cambridgeshire Archives, P/22/5/1, fo. 17r; J. Good, *The Cult of St George in Medieval England* (Woodbridge, 2009), 52–126.

149. *YCR*, i. 55; Dadizeele, *Mémoires*, 91–2.
150. 5 & 6 Edward VI, c. 3; *Chronicle of the Greyfriars*, 74.
151. John Hooper, *Early Writings*, ed. S. Carr, Parker Soc. (Cambridge, 1843), 312–14.
152. PRO, E36/285, fo. 79r; E404/81/1, unnumbered warrant of 8/2/1492; *Great Chronicle*, 247.
153. Hall, *Chronicle*, 543, 549–50, 552.
154. *The Great Wardrobe Accounts of Henry VII and Henry VIII*, ed. M. Hayward, London RS 47 (Woodbridge, 2012), 133; BL, Egerton MS 3025, fos. 37v, 40v.
155. *Elizabethan Naval Administration*, 76, 99, 104–5, 173, 231, 263, 281, 307, 324, 383, 463.
156. D. M. Loades, *The Tudor Navy: An Administrative, Political and Military History* (Aldershot, 1992), *passim*; *The Navy of Edward VI and Mary I*, ed. C. S. Knighton and D. M. Loades, Navy Records Soc. 157 (Farnham, 2011), 474–5, 477, 478, 501–2, 503.
157. J. P. D. Cooper, *Propaganda and the Tudor State: Political Culture in the Westcountry* (Oxford, 2003), 44, 130, 176–8, 260; Leland, *Intinerary*, i. 248.
158. Blomefield, *Norfolk*, iii. 175; *Calendar Plymouth*, 94; LMA, Rep. 2, fo. 153r; *YCR*, iii. 89.
159. D. de Hoop Scheffer and A. J. Klant-Vlielander Hein, *Vorstenportretten uit de eerste helft vande 16de eeuw: Houtsneden als propaganda* (Amsterdam, 1972), 39–41; for sale of pictures of Henry at Bergen op Zoom see *LP*, VI. 518.
160. R. P. Adams, *The Better Part of Valor: More, Erasmus, Colet and Vives on Humanism, War and Peace, 1496–1535* (Seattle WA, 1962); B. Lowe, *Imagining Peace: A History of Early English Pacifist Ideas, 1340–1560* (University Park PA, 1997), 147–245.
161. Thomas More, *Utopia*, ed. D. Baker-Smith (London, 2012), 101; Nicholas Harpsfield, *The Life and Death of Sir Tomas Moore, Knight, sometimes Lord High Chancellor of England*, EETS 186 (London, 1932), 279–80.
162. G. W. Bernard, *War, Taxation and Rebellion in Tudor England: Henry VIII, Wolsey and the Amicable Grant of 1525* (Brighton, 1985), 3–4.
163. Lowe, *Imagining Peace*, 246–309; D. L. Potter, 'Mid-Tudor Foreign Policy and Diplomacy: 1547–63', in S. Doran and G. Richardson (eds), *Tudor England and its Neighbours* (Basingstoke, 2005), 108–22.
164. R. Helgerson, *Forms of Nationhood: The Elizabethan Writing of England* (Chicago IL, 1992); C. Shrank, *Writing the Nation in Reformation England, 1530–1580* (Oxford, 2004).
165. J. Bellis, *The Hundred Years War in Literature, 1337–1600* (Woodbridge, 2016), 187.
166. William Thomas, *The Pilgrim: A Dialogue on the Life and Actions of King Henry the Eighth*, ed. J. A. Froude (London, 1861), 66–70.
167. Thomas Chaloner, *Thomas Chaloner's In Laudem Henrici Octavi (Latin Edition and English Translation)*, ed. J. B. Gabel and C. C. Schlam (Lawrence, KS, 1979), 11–12, 37, 39, 42–5, 68–9, 72–3.
168. Chaloner, In Laudem Henrici Octavi, 66–7.
169. *A Machiavellian Treatise by Stephen Gardiner*, ed. P. S. Donaldson (Cambridge, 1975), 121.
170. Chaloner, In Laudem Henrici Octavi, 39–41, 44–7; Thomas, *The Pilgrim*, 79; *Machiavellian Treatise*, 121.
171. Thomas, *The Pilgrim*, 78; Chaloner, In Laudem Henrici Octavi, 70–1.
172. *Machiavellian Treatise*, 121.
173. Chaloner, In Laudem Henrici Octavi, 50–1.

174. PRO, C1/453/64; W. A. Sessions, *Henry Howard, the Poet Earl of Surrey: A Life* (Oxford, 1999), 301–4; *The Visitation of Norfolk in the Year 1563*, ed. G. H. Dashwood and E. Bulwer Lytton, 2 vols (Norwich, 1878–95), ii. 268.

175. Lichfield RO, B/C/11 (John Astley 1563). I owe this reference to Thomas Carter.

176. J. J. Raven, 'Tholdman', *Proceedings of the Suffolk Institute of Archaeology* 10 (1898–1900), 398.

177. *StP*, ii. 10.

178. W. G. Hoskins, *The Age of Plunder: The England of Henry VIII 1500–1547* (London, 1976), 232.

179. R. Rapple, *Martial Power and Elizabethan Political Culture: Military Men in England and Ireland, 1558–1594* (Cambridge, 2009), 20 and *passim*; G. Connell-Smith, *Forerunners of Drake: A Study of English Trade with Spain in the Early Tudor Period* (London, 1954), 127–203.

180. R. Holinshed, *The Chronicles of England, Scotlande, and Irelande*, 4 vols (London, 1577), i. 86–8; W. T. MacCaffrey, 'Parliament and Foreign Policy' and J. D. Alsop, 'Parliament and Taxation', both in D. M. Dean and N. L. Jones (eds), *The Parliaments of Elizabethan England* (Oxford, 1990), 65–90, 91–116; R. Schofield, 'Taxation and the Political Limits of the Tudor State', in C. Cross et al. (eds), *Law and Government under the Tudors: Essays presented to Sir Geoffrey Elton on his Retirement* (Cambridge, 1988), 239–41, 252–5.

CHAPTER 8

1. K. Brandi, *The Emperor Charles V* (London, 1965 edn), 219.

2. J. D. Tracy, *Emperor Charles V, Impresario of War* (Cambridge, 2002).

3. D. L. Potter, *Renaissance France at War: Armies, Culture and Society c.1480–1560* (Woodbridge, 2008), 57–8, 258–63; S. Gunn, D. Grummitt, and H. Cools, *War, State, and Society in England and the Netherlands, 1477–1559* (Oxford, 2007), 258, 262.

4. A. Pettegree, *The Invention of News: How the World Came to Know about Itself* (New Haven CT and London, 2014), 40–57, 70–88, 117–34, 139–51; Potter, *Renaissance France at War*, 63–5, 259–71, 305–6; R. V. Tooley, 'Maps in Italian Atlases of the Sixteenth Century', *Imago Mundi* 3 (1939), 12–47; E. Pognon, 'Les plus anciens plans des villes gravés et les événements militaires', *Imago Mundi* 22 (1968), 13–19.

5. M. Martínez, *Front Lines: Soldiers' Writing in the Early Modern Hispanic World* (Philadelphia, 2016), 23–8.

6. Potter, *Renaissance France at War*, 274–80, 328–31; A.-L. van Bruaene, *De Gentse memorieboeken als spiegel van stedelijk historisch bewustzijn (14de tot 16 de eeuw)*, Verhandelingen van de Maatschappij voor Geschiedenis en Oudheidkunde te Gent 22 (Ghent, 1998).

7. O. Niccoli, *Prophecy and People in Renaissance Italy* (Princeton NJ, 1990), 3–29, 50–1, 61–88, 175–7.

8. D. Crouzet, *Les guerriers de Dieu: la violence au temps des troubles de religion, vers 1525–vers 1610*, 2 vols (Seyssel, 1990), i. 101–53.

9. R. Bean, 'War and the Birth of the Nation State', *Journal of Economic History* 33 (1973), 210–12; C. Tilly, *Coercion, Capital and European States, AD 990–1990* (Oxford, 1990), 79; I. Sherer, *Warriors for a Living: The Experience of the Spanish Infantry during the Italian Wars* (Leiden, 2017), 29.

10. W. Schaufelberger, *Der Alte Schweizer und sein Krieg. Studien zur Kriegsführung vornehmlich im 15. Jahrhundert*, 2nd edn (Zürich, 1966), 67–71, 141–6.

11. R. Quatrefages, 'Etat et armée en Espagne au début des temps modernes', *Mélanges de la Casa de Velázquez* 17 (1981), 88–90.

12. R. Murphey, *Ottoman Warfare 1500–1700* (London, 1999), 36–43.

13. J.-M. Le Gall, 'Les combattants de Pavie, Octobre 1524–24 février 1525', *Revue histo-rique* 671 (2014), 579–80; J. M. Najemy, *A History of Florence 1200–1575* (Oxford, 2006), 454–61; J. de Pablo, 'Contribution à l'étude de l'histoire des institutions militaires huguenotes, II. L'armée huguenote entre 1562 et 1573', *Archiv für Reformationsgeschichte* 48 (1957), 196–7.

14. R. Baumann, *Georg von Frundsberg, der Vater der Landsknechte und Feldhauptmann von Tirol: Eine gesellschaftsgeschichtliche Biographie* (Munich, 1984), 118; R. Baumann, *Das Söldnerwesen im 16. Jahrhundert im bayerischen und süddeutschen Beispiel. Eine gesells-chaftsgeschichtliche Untersuchung*, Miscellanea Bavarica Monacensia 79 (Munich, 1978), 267–71; G. Hanlon, *The Twilight of a Military Tradition: Italian Aristocrats and European Conflicts, 1560–1800* (London, 1998), 51–2, 62, 68; S. Pepper, 'Warfare and Operational Art: Communications, Cannon and Small War', in F. Tallett and D. Trim (eds), *European Warfare 1350–1750* (Cambridge, 2010), 198–9; Gunn, Grummitt, and Cools, *War, State, and Society*, 98; B. A. Tlusty, *The Martial Ethic in Early Modern Germany: Civic Duty and the Right of Arms* (Basingstoke, 2011), 20–1.

15. Gunn, Grummitt, and Cools, *War, State, and Society*, 319–20; Baumann, *Georg von Frundsberg*, 233, 236–7, 240–2; S. Desachy-Delclos, 'Les élites militaires en Rouergue au XVIe siècle', *Annales du Midi* 108 (1996), 9–27.

16. J. Glete, *War and the State in Early Modern Europe: Spain, the Dutch Republic and Sweden as Fiscal-Military States, 1500–1660* (London, 2002), 202–3; R. I. Frost, *The Northern Wars: War, State and Society in Northeastern Europe, 1558–1721* (Harlow, 2000), 33–6.

17. Murphey, *Ottoman Warfare*, 43–5; Potter, *Renaissance France at War*, 95–123, 324–7; Niccolò Machiavelli, *Art of War*, ed. C. Lynch (Chicago IL, 2003), 23, 25; *Relations des ambassadeurs vénitiens sur les affaires de France au XVIe siècle*, ed. N. Tommaseo, 2 vols (Paris, 1838), i. 185–7, 305, 397, 491, 495–7, ii. 11, 149.

18. Potter, *Renaissance France at War*, 102–5.

19. P. Contamine, 'L'artillerie royale française à la veille des guerres d'Italie', *Annales de Bretagne* 71 (1964), 229–31, 238–40; Potter, *Renaissance France at War*, 236–48.

20. Gunn, Grummitt, and Cools, *War, State, and Society*, 81–2.

21. Schaufelberger, *Der Alte Schweizer*, 57–61; E. von Frauenholz, *Entwicklungsgeschichte des Deutschen Heerwesens*, 2 vols in 3 (Munich, 1935–7), II, ii. 27–8; B. Chevalier, *Les bonnes villes de France du XIVe au XVIe siècle* (Paris, 1982), 123–4.

22. R. Baumann, *Landsknechte. Ihre Geschichte und Kultur vom späten Mittelalter bis zum Dreißigjährigen Krieg* (Munich, 1994), 199–200.

23. Potter, *Renaissance France at War*, 185–6; Gunn, Grummitt, and Cools, *War, State, and Society*, 70–3, 100–1; M. E. Mallett and C. Shaw, *The Italian Wars 1494–1559* (Harlow, 2012), 185.

24. P. Contamine, 'Les industries de guerre dans la France de la Renaissance: l'exemple de l'artillerie', *Revue historique* 271 (1984), 270, 276–7.

25. D. Eltis, 'Towns and Defence in Later Medieval Germany', *Nottingham Medieval Studies* 33 (1989), 91–103.

26. P. Stabel, 'Militaire organisatie, bewapening en wapenbezit in het laatmiddeleeuwse Brugge', *Revue belge de philologie et d'histoire* 89 (2011), 1065–9; J. Haemers and B. Verbist, 'Het Gentse gemeenteleger in het laatste kwart van de vijftiende eeuw. Een politieke, financiële en militaire analyse van de stadsmilitie', *Handelingen van de Maatschappij voor Geschiedenis en Oudheidkunde te Gent* 62 (2008), 314–15; Gunn,

Grummitt, and Cools, *War, State, and Society*, 73, 103–4; J. Decavele and P. van Peteghem, 'Ghent "Absolutely" Broken', in J. Decavele (ed.), *Ghent: In Defence of a Rebellious City* (Antwerp, 1989), 107–12.

27. Schaufelberger, *Der Alte Schweizer*, 74–6; Quatrefages, 'Etat et armée en Espagne', 95–7, 103; Gunn, Grummitt, and Cools, *War, State, and Society*, 65–7, 99.

28. S. Pepper and N. Adams, *Firearms and Fortifications: Military Architecture and Siege Warfare in Sixteenth-Century Siena* (Chicago IL, 1986), 27–8, 59–72, 158; Sherer, *Warriors for a Living*, 78–82; Gunn, Grummitt, and Cools, *War, State, and Society*, 73, 75–8, 304.

29. 'Inventories of Norfolk Church Goods (1552)', ed. H. B. Walters, *NA* 31 (1955–7), 253; G. Parker, *The Grand Strategy of Philip II* (New Haven CT and London, 1998), 129–34.

30. Haemers and Verbist, 'Gentse gemeenteleger', 296–9; Gunn, Grummitt, and Cools, *War, State, and Society*, 92–5.

31. J. R. Hale, *War and Society in Renaissance Europe, 1450–1620* (London, 1985), 91–9.

32. J. M. Constant, 'The Protestant Nobility in France during the Wars of Religion: A Leaven of Innovation in a Traditional World', in P. Benedict, G. Marnef, H. Van Nierop, and M. Venard (eds), *Reformation, Revolt and Civil War in France and the Netherlands 1555–1585* (Amsterdam, 1999), 76.

33. Sherer, *Warriors for a Living*, 21–2.

34. D. Parrott, *The Business of War: Military Enterprise and Military Revolution in Early Modern Europe* (Cambridge, 2012), 49–50.

35. Potter, *Renaissance France at War*, 190–7; F. González de León, ' "Doctors of the Military Discipline": Technical Expertise and the Paradigm of the Spanish Soldier in the Early Modern Period', *Sixteenth Century Journal* 27 (1996), 61–85.

36. Potter, *Renaissance France at War*, 88–94; B. Sandberg, *Warrior Pursuits: Noble Culture and Civil Conflict in Early Modern France* (Baltimore MD, 2010), 43–6, 143–9, 164–7, 175–8.

37. Symphorien Champier, *Les gestes ensemble la vie du preulx Chevalier Bayard*, ed. D. Crouzet (Paris, 1992), 14–55.

38. Baumann, *Georg von Frundsberg*, 29–32, 100, 106, 302–4, 311–13; Potter, *Renaissance France at War*, 300–1; Gunn, Grummitt, and Cools, *War, State, and Society*, 229–31.

39. Baumann, *Georg von Frundsberg*, 217–18; Potter, *Renaissance France at War*, 171–2, 177; Gunn, Grummitt, and Cools, *War, State, and Society*, 227–8, 305.

40. *Relations des ambassadeurs vénitiens sur les affaires de France*, i. 379; A. C. Sawyer, 'The Tyranny of Alva: The Creation and Development of a Dutch Patriotic Image', *De zeventiende eeuw* 19 (2003), 186–203.

41. J. E. A. Dawson, *The Politics of Religion in the Age of Mary, Queen of Scots: The Earl of Argyll and the Struggle for Britain and Ireland* (Cambridge, 2002), 51–6.

42. Potter, *Renaissance France at War*, 70–85, 114; T. Rentet, 'Network Mapping: Ties of Fidelity and Dependency among the Major Domestic Officers of Anne de Montmorency', *French History* 17 (2011), 115–17; K. B. Neuschel, *Word of Honor: Interpreting Noble Culture in Sixteenth-Century France* (Ithaca NY and London, 1989), 61–3, 173–9; S. Carroll, *Noble Power during the Wars of Religion: The Guise Affinity and the Catholic Cause in Normandy* (Cambridge, 1998), 69–76; Gunn, Grummitt, and Cools, *War, State, and Society*, 142–6, 151; Contamine, 'Les industries de guerre', 269–70.

43. B. Bei der Wieden, 'Niederdeutsche Söldner vor dem Dreißigjährigen Krieg. Geistige und mentale Grenzen eines sozialen Raums', in B. R. Kroener and R. Pröve (eds), *Krieg und Frieden. Militär und Gesellschaft in der Frühen Neuzeit* (Paderborn, 1996),

98; Gunn, Grummitt, and Cools, *War, State, and Society*, 145; Mallett and Shaw, *Italian Wars*, 160, 277; Baumann, *Landsknechte*, 64.

44. Baumann, *Georg von Frundsberg*, 121, 128–9, 212, 262, 307–8; Baumann, *Landsknechte*, 56–7, 173–6; M. Arfaioli, *The Black Bands of Giovanni: Infantry and Diplomacy during the Italian Wars* (Pisa, 2005), 63–4, 70–5, 89; Gunn, Grummitt, and Cools, *War, State, and Society*, 147–8.

45. Parrott, *Business of War*, 45, 53, 78–83, 90–1; Baumann, *Georg von Frundsberg*, 256–63; Le Gall, 'Combattants de Pavie', 571.

46. Gunn, Grummitt, and Cools, *War, State, and Society*, 165–6, 178–80; Potter, *Renaissance France at War*, 47; Schaufelberger, *Der Alte Schweizer*, 181; Baumann, *Georg von Frundsberg*, 102.

47. J. B. Wood, *The King's Army: Warfare, Soldiers and Society during the Wars of Religion in France, 1562–1576* (Cambridge, 1996), 147, 270–1.

48. Gunn, Grummitt, and Cools, *War, State, and Society*, 152–3; Machiavelli, *Art of War*, 160.

49. Baumann, *Landsknechte*, 180–2; F. Redlich, *The German Military Enterpriser and his Work Force: A Study in European Economic and Social History*, 2 vols (Wiesbaden, 1964–5), i. 83–4; Gunn, Grummitt, and Cools, *War, State, and Society*, 179–80, 182–4, 186–90; C. Michon (ed.), *Les conseillers de François Ier* (Rennes, 2011), 131–43, 155–61, 163–70, 265–72, 443–54, 463–506.

50. D. L. Potter, *War and Government in the French Provinces: Picardy 1470–1560* (Cambridge, 1993), 65–112; P. Rosenfeld, 'The Provincial Governors from the Minority of Charles V to the Revolt', *Anciens Pays et Assemblées d'Etats* 17 (1959), 3–63; Tracy, *Emperor Charles V*, 274–88; H. G. Koenigsberger, *The Government of Sicily under Philip II of Spain: A Study in the Practice of Empire* (London, 1951), 171–95.

51. Baumann, *Georg von Frundsberg*, 110, 190.

52. Bei der Wieden, 'Niederdeutsche Söldner', 96–7.

53. J. W. Armstrong, 'Local Society and the Defence of the English Frontier in Fifteenth-Century Scotland: The War Measures of 1482', *Florilegium* 25 (2008), 140–4; Gunn, Grummitt, and Cools, *War, State, and Society*, 203–7; J. D. Tracy, *Balkan Wars: Habsburg Croatia, Ottoman Bosnia, and Venetian Dalmatia, 1499–1617* (Lanham MD, 2016), 69–78, 116–26, 165–77, 221–5, 276–9.

54. Potter, *Renaissance France at War*, 48–57; Gunn, Grummitt, and Cools, *War, State, and Society*, 166–7.

55. H. Romer, *Herrschaft, Reislauf und Verbotspolitik. Beobachtungen zum rechtlichen Alltag der zürcher Solddienstbekämpfung im 16. Jahrhundert* (Zürich, 1995), 37–65, 218–38.

56. Mallett and Shaw, *Italian Wars*, 290–2; Frost, *Northern Wars*, 75–80.

57. A. Sablon du Corail, 'L'État princier à l'épreuve. Financer et conduire la guerre pendant la crise de l'État bourguignon (1477–1493)', *Revue historique* 679 (2016), 559–60.

58. S. Xenakis, *Gewalt und Gemeinschaft: Kriegsknechte um 1500* (Paderborn, 2015), 292–6, 317–20; Schaufelberger, *Der Alte Schweizer*, 116–27; Sherer, *Warriors for a Living*, 84–92, 132–5; Potter, *War and Government*, 203–4, 217–20; Potter, *Renaissance France at War*, 85, 103, 109, 122–3, 130, 132, 134, 144, 232, 248–53; Sablon du Corail, 'L'État princier à l'épreuve', 566–73; Gunn, Grummitt, and Cools, *War, State, and Society*, 273–6.

59. *Les dénombrements de foyers dans le comté de Hainaut (XIVe–XVIe siècles)*, ed. M. A. Arnould (Brussels, 1956), 189–96, 283–6, 604–16, 618.

60. Tracy, *Balkan Wars*, 36–41, 43–4, 52–3, 57–8, 61–4, 71–2, 169–72, 203–7, 256–8, 260–2, 279.

61. Schaufelberger, *Der Alte Schweizer*, 81–109; F. Tallett, *War and Society in Early Modern Europe, 1495–1715* (London, 1992), 159–60; C. Lesger, *Handel in Amsterdam ten tijde van de Opstand: Kooplieden, commerciële expansie en verandering in de ruimtelijke economie van de Nederlanden ca.1550–ca.1630* (Hilversum, 2001), 31; M. van Tielhof, *De Hollandse graanhandel, 1470–1570: Koren op de Amsterdamse molen* (The Hague, 1995), 11–33; J. Craeybeckx, *Un grand commerce d'importation: Les Vins de France aux anciens Pays-Bas (XIIIe–XVIe siècles)* (Paris, 1958), 207–49; H. Kaptein, *De Hollandse textielnijverheid 1350–1600: Conjunctuur en continuïteit* (Hilversum, 1998), 84–167.

62. R. Quatrefages, 'La Proveeduría des Armadas: de l'expédition de Tunis (1535) à celle d'Alger (1541)', *Mélanges de la Casa de Velázquez* 14 (1978), 225–35.

63. C. Baes, 'Un épisode de la querelle Habsburg-Valois: la campagne de Henri II aux Pays-Bas en 1554', *Revue belge de Philologie et d'Histoire* 73 (1995), 338–9; M. J. Rodríguez-Salgado, *The Changing Face of Empire: Charles V, Philip II and Habsburg Authority, 1551–1559* (Cambridge, 1988), 220–3, 260–6, 285–6.

64. L. Sicking, *Neptune and the Netherlands: State, Economy, and War at Sea in the Renaissance* (Leiden, 2006), 132–288.

65. J. Glete, *Warfare at Sea, 1500–1650: Maritime Conflicts and the Transformation of Europe* (London, 2000), 149.

66. Contamine, 'Les industries de guerre', 263–8, 279–80.

67. Gunn, Grummitt, and Cools, *War, State, and Society*, 273–5, 278–9, 290–1.

68. I. A. A. Thompson, '"Money, Money and Yet More Money!" Finance, the Fiscal-State, and the Military Revolution: Spain 1500–1650', in C. J. Rogers (ed.), *The Military Revolution Debate: Readings on the Military Transformation of Early Modern Europe* (Boulder CO, 1995), 286; J. B. Collins, *Fiscal Limits of Absolutism: Direct Taxation in Early Seventeenth-Century France* (Berkeley CA, 1988), 55; J. Gelabert, 'The Fiscal Burden', in R. Bonney (ed.), *Economic Systems and State Finance* (Oxford, 1995), 558–71.

69. M. Le Mené, 'L'économie angevine sous Louis XI', in B. Chevalier and P. Contamine (eds), *La France de la fin du xve siècle: renouveau et apogée* (Paris, 1985), 58–60; Frost, *Northern Wars*, 85–7.

70. Mallett and Shaw, *Italian Wars*, 294; A. Calabria, *The Cost of Empire: The Finances of the Kingdom of Naples in the Time of Spanish Rule* (Cambridge, 1991), 104–29.

71. R. J. Knecht, *Renaissance Warrior and Patron: The Reign of Francis I* (Cambridge, 1994), 480–3; J. Powis, 'Guyenne 1548: The Crown, the Province and Social Order', *European Studies Review* 12 (1982), 1–15; F. H. M. Grapperhaus, *Alva en de tiende penning*, 2nd edn (Deventer, 1984), 185–314.

72. Tallett, *War and Society*, 216–32; B. Roosens, 'Het arsenaal van Mechelen en de wapenhandel (1551–1567)', *Bijdragen tot de geschiedenis* 60 (1977), 239–42.

73. Contamine, 'Les industries de guerre', 260–2.

74. J.-C. Hocquet, 'Venice', in R. Bonney (ed.), *The Rise of the Fiscal State in Europe c.1200–1815* (Oxford, 1999), 384–5.

75. Stabel, 'Militaire organisatie', 1065; Haemers and Verbist, 'Gentse gemeenteleger', 303.

76. Gunn, Grummitt, and Cools, *War, State, and Society*, 286–7.

77. Quatrefages, 'La Proveeduría des Armadas', 236–46.

78. H. Soly, *Urbanisme en kapitalisme te Antwerpen in de 16de eeuw: de stedebouwkundige en industriële ondernemingen van Gilbert van Schoonbeke* (Brussels, 1977).

79. Schaufelberger, *Der Alte Schweizer*, 168–89; Baumann, *Landsknechte*, 90–1; Xenakis, *Gewalt und Gemeinschaft*, 265–326; Le Gall, 'Combattants de Pavie', 574.

80. Gunn, Grummitt, and Cools, *War, State, and Society*, 79; Desachy-Delclos, 'Élites militaires', 21–3; F. Braudel, *The Mediterranean and the Mediterranean World in the Age*

of Philip II, 2 vols (London, 1973), ii. 865–91; C. W. Bracewell, *The Uskoks of Senj: Piracy, Banditry, and Holy War in the Sixteenth-Century Adriatic* (Ithaca NY, 1992), 45–50, 89–117.

81. Sicking, *Neptune and the Netherlands*, 420–80; Glete, *Warfare at Sea*, 134–55.

82. Baumann, *Landsknechte*, 76–9; Potter, *Renaissance France at War*, 229–31; Gunn, Grummitt, and Cools, *War, State, and Society*, 26, 72, 279; Sherer, *Warriors for a Living*, 45–6.

83. R. B. Outhwaite, 'The Trials of Foreign Borrowing: The English Crown and the Antwerp Money Market in the Mid-Sixteenth Century', *EcHR* n.s. 19 (1966), 289–305; Mallett and Shaw, *Italian Wars*, 292–3.

84. D. S. Chambers, *Popes, Cardinals and War: The Military Church in Renaissance and Early Modern Europe* (London, 2006); Bei der Wieden, 'Niederdeutsche Söldner', 86–8; G. R. Potter, *Zwingli* (Cambridge, 1976), 369–70, 409–14; J. M. Stayer, *Anabaptists and the Sword* (Lawrence KS, 1972).

85. H. Drévillon, *L'individu et la guerre. Du Chevalier Bayard au Soldat Inconnu* (Paris, 2013), 83–6.

86. C. Allmand, *The* De Re Militari *of Vegetius: The Reception, Transmission and Legacy of a Roman Text in the Middle Ages* (Cambridge, 2011), 128–37, 251–348.

87. Baumann, *Söldnerwesen*, 50–65; Tlusty, *Martial Ethic*, 191–200; Stabel, 'Militaire organisatie', 1057–60; Haemers and Verbist, 'Gentse gemeenteleger', 295–318; L. Crombie, *Archery and Crossbow Guilds in Medieval Flanders, 1300–1500* (Woodbridge, 2016), 37–50; Gunn, Grummitt, and Cools, *War, State, and Society*, 56–9; P. Knevel, *Burgers in het geweer: De schutterijen in Holland, 1550–1700* (Hilversum, 1994), 44–53, 66–111.

88. Chevalier, *Les bonnes villes*, 121–3, 127–8; P. Contamine, *Guerre, état et société à la fin du moyen âge. Études sur les armées des rois de France, 1337–1494* (Paris, 1972), 215–17, 335–6.

89. Schaufelberger, *Der Alte Schweizer*, 70–1, 76–8.

90. Parrott, *Business of War*, 67; M. Rogg, '"Zerhauen und zerschnitten, nach adelichen Sitten"? Herkunft, Entwicklung und Funktion soldatischer Tracht des 16. Jahrhunderts im Spiegel zeitgenössischer Kunst', in Kroener and Pröve (eds), *Krieg und Frieden*, 109–35.

91. J. B. Wood, *The King's Army: Warfare, Soldiers and Society during the Wars of Religion in France, 1562–1576* (Cambridge, 1996), 92–6, 116–18, 226–9.

92. Tlusty, *Martial Ethic*, 11–45, 58–60, 133–45, 265–9.

93. Potter, *Renaissance France at War*, 94; Drévillon, *L'individu et la guerre*, 22–9.

94. Mallett and Shaw, *Italian Wars*, 19–21, 25, 105, 124, 170, 195, 241, 266, 276; Schaufelberger, *Der Alte Schweizer*, 137, 178–83; Xenakis, *Gewalt und Gemeinschaft*, 241–63; Sherer, *Warriors for a Living*, 145–60, 210–18.

95. Xenakis, *Gewalt und Gemeinschaft*, 281–3; Sherer, *Warriors for a Living*, 160–70.

96. Baumann, *Georg von Frundsberg*, 218; M. Rospocher, 'Songs of War: Historical and Literary Narratives of the "Horrendous Italian Wars" (1494–1559)', in M. Mondini and M. Rospocher (eds), *Narrating War: Early Modern and Contemporary Perspectives* (Bologna, 2013), 89; Xenakis, *Gewalt und Gemeinschaft*, 238–41.

97. Baumann, *Landsknechte*, 112–19; Xenakis, *Gewalt und Gemeinschaft*, 70–88, 111–18, 184, 212.

98. Baumann, *Georg von Frundsberg*, 105, 107, 131–5, 140–1, 218, 309.

99. Baumann, *Georg von Frundsberg*, 308–9; Baumann, *Söldnerwesen*, 262–3.

100. Le Gall, 'Combattants de Pavie', 592; 'Dagverhaal van den veldtogt van keizer Karel V in 1554', ed. [C. A.] R. Macaré, *Kronijk van het Historisch Genootschap Gevestigd te Utrecht* 7 (1851), 296–7.

101. Stabel, 'Militaire organisatie', 1060–5; Tlusty, *Martial Ethic*, 134–45.

102. Tlusty, *Martial Ethic*, 171.

103. Arfaioli, *Black Bands*, 14–20, 67, 65–7.

104. Schaufelberger, *Der Alte Schweizer*, 18–24; W. Schaufelberger, *Marignano: Strukturelle Grenzen eidgenössischer Militärmacht zwischen Mittelalter und Neuzeit* (Zürich, 1993), 79.

105. Schaufelberger, *Marignano*, 80–1, 121–6.

106. Contamine, 'L'artillerie royale', 227; Schaufelberger, *Marignano*, 79; Potter, *Renaissance France at War*, 180–2; C. van den Heuvel, *'Papiere Bolwercken': De introductie van de Italiaanse stede-en vestingbouw in de Nederlanden (1540–1609) en het gebruik van tekeningen* (Alphen aan den Rijn, 1991), 23–129.

107. Baumann, *Söldnerwesen*, 270–1.

108. H. Schnitter, *Volk und Landesdefension. Volksaufgebote, Defensionswerke, Landmilizien in den deutschen Territorien vom 15. bis zum 18. Jahrhundert* (Berlin, 1977), 44.

109. Baumann, *Georg von Frundsberg*, 212; Baumann, *Landsknechte*, 64, 170; Contamine, 'Les industries de guerre', 251–2.

110. Stabel, 'Militaire organisatie', 1049–73; Haemers and Verbist, 'Gentse gemeenteleger', 291–325.

111. Tlusty, *Martial Ethic*, 72, 81–7, 171.

112. Schaufelberger, *Der Alte Schweizer*, 43–55; Mallett and Shaw, *Italian Wars*, 189; Baumann, *Landsknechte*, 76; Schnitter, *Volk und Landesdefension*, 45–6, 71–132.

113. Xenakis, *Gewalt und Gemeinschaft*, 129–38; Sherer, *Warriors for a Living*, 33–5, 92–3, 187–8, 243–4.

114. Sandberg, *Warrior Pursuits*, 268–73; Xenakis, *Gewalt und Gemeinschaft*, 327–46; Baumann, *Landsknechte*, 70–1; Sherer, *Warriors for a Living*, 33–5, 241.

115. Xenakis, *Gewalt und Gemeinschaft*, 120–9, 141–230; Sherer, *Warriors for a Living*, 102–41; G. Parker, *The Army of Flanders and the Spanish Road 1567–1659* (Cambridge, 1972), 185–206.

116. Murphey, *Ottoman Warfare*, 134–5.

117. Baumann, *Georg von Frundsberg*, 122–7, 269–76; P. Burschel, *Söldner im Nordwestdeutschland des 16. und 17. Jahrhunderts: Sozialgeschichtliche Studien*, Veröffentlichungen des Max-Planck-Instituts für Geschichte, 113 (Göttingen, 1994), 197; Sherer, *Warriors for a Living*, 115–16, 124–32, 138–40.

118. Schaufelberger, *Der Alte Schweizer*, 138–46; Xenakis, *Gewalt und Gemeinschaft*, 174–5, 180, 210.

119. Baumann, *Landsknechte*, 62–71; Xenakis, *Gewalt und Gemeinschaft*, 47–53; Sherer, *Warriors for a Living*, 16–26.

120. Schaufelberger, *Der Alte Schweizer*, 152–68; Xenakis, *Gewalt und Gemeinschaft*, 139–40; Haemers and Verbist, 'Gentse gemeenteleger', 317–18.

121. Tallett, *War and Society*, 86.

122. R. Quatrefages, 'A la naissance de l'armée moderne', *Mélanges de la Casa de Velázquez* 13 (1977), 512–19.

123. Mallett and Shaw, *Italian Wars*, 150, 167–8, 170, 194–5, 233; Sherer, *Warriors for a Living*, 64–5, 71–2; Baumann, *Landsknechte*, 129–30.

124. Mallett and Shaw, *Italian Wars*, 86, 100, 108, 129–30.

125. Baumann, *Georg von Frundsberg*, 189–93, 199–200; Jean Berteville, *Recit de l'expedition en Ecosse l'an M.D. XLVI. et de la battayle de Muscleburgh*, ed. D. Constable (Edinburgh, 1825), 14.

126. Mallett and Shaw, *Italian Wars*, 196; Sherer, *Warriors for a Living*, 75–7, 233–5, 247–8; Potter, *Zwingli*, 34–9.

127. Potter, *Renaissance France at War*, 210–11.

128. M. E. Mallett and J. R. Hale, *The Military Organisation of a Renaissance State: Venice, c.1400 to 1617* (Cambridge, 1984), 195–6.

129. Bei der Wieden, 'Niederdeutsche Söldner', 99–102; Baumann, *Landsknechte*, 131–4, 141–5; Burschel, *Söldner*, 274–80, 291–303.

130. Parrott, *Business of War*, 50–3.

131. Mallett and Shaw, *Italian Wars*, 98, 104, 199; Baumann, *Landsknechte*, 136–41; Potter, *Renaissance France at War*, 253–4; Bei der Wieden, 'Niederdeutsche Söldner', 102–5.

132. Potter, *Renaissance France at War*, 15–26, 201–3.

133. Quatrefages, 'Etat et armée en Espagne', 94; Potter, *Renaissance France at War*, 313.

134. Romer, *Herrschaft*, 20, 283–327.

135. William Patten, 'The Expedition into Scotland', in *Tudor Tracts*, ed. A. F. Pollard (Westminster, 1903), 139; Gunn, Grummitt, and Cools, *War, State, and Society*, 255–6.

136. Mallett and Shaw, *Italian Wars*, 64, 94; Le Gall, 'Combattants de Pavie', 575–7; Gunn, Grummitt, and Cools, *War, State, and Society*, 296–7; Potter, *Renaissance France at War*, 97–8, 109–10, 113–14, 187; Sherer, *Warriors for a Living*, 17, 244–5, 249.

137. Martínez, *Front Lines*, 45–8.

138. Baumann, *Landsknechte*, 58–62; Baumann, *Georg von Frundsberg*, 136–7, 215; J. V. Wagner, *Graf Wilhelm von Fürstenberg (1491–1549) und die politisch-geistigen Mächte seiner Zeit* (Stuttgart, 1966), 246–7; Frauenholz, *Entwicklungsgeschichte*, II, ii. 17.

139. Niccolò Machiavelli, *The Prince*, ed. G. Bull (Harmondsworth, 1961), 73.

140. Gunn, Grummitt, and Cools, *War, State, and Society*, 283–5.

141. Potter, *Renaissance France at War*, 15–26, 274–84, 309–31.

142. Tracy, *Emperor Charles V*, 108, 200, 289–303, 310–11; Parker, *Grand Strategy*, 92–109, 151; R. Puddu, *El soldado gentilhombre* (Barcelona, 1984), 10, 109–11, 244–5; Rodríguez-Salgado, *Changing Face of Empire*, 129–30, 288–96.

143. Machiavelli, *The Prince*, 120.

144. N. M. Sutherland, *The Huguenot Struggle for Recognition* (New Haven CT, 1980), 183–210; J. Delaborde, *Gaspard de Coligny, Amiral de France*, 3 vols (Paris, 1879–82), iii. 560–5.

145. C. Sieber-Lehmann, *Spätmittelalterlicher Nationalismus: die Burgunderkriege am Oberrhein und in der Eidgenossenschaft* (Göttingen, 1995); A. Schröcker, *Die deutsche Nation: Beobachtungen zur politischen Propaganda des ausgehenden 15. Jahrhunderts* (Lübeck, 1974), 33–41; Xenakis, *Gewalt und Gemeinschaft*, 97–101; T. A. Brady, *Turning Swiss: Cities and Empire 1450–1550* (Cambridge, 1985), 57–72; *In Helvetios—wider die Kuhschweizer: Fremd- und Feindbilder von den Schweizern in antieidgenössischen Texten aus der Zeit von 1386 bis 1532*, ed. C. Sieber-Lehmann and T. Wilhelmi (Bern, 1998), 7–20, 85–122, 130–9, 221–2, 227–40.

146. Potter, *Renaissance France at War*, 25, 276–7, 280, 282, 312, 316–17, 320.

147. Gunn, Grummitt, and Cools, *War, State, and Society*, 297–8, 308, 312–17.

148. Potter, *Renaissance France at War*, 41; Gunn, Grummitt, and Cools, *War, State, and Society*, 310–12.

149. Mallett and Shaw, *Italian Wars*, 52, 95, 111, 133; Baumann, *Landsknechte*, 114–15, 127; Xenakis, *Gewalt und Gemeinschaft*, 97–101, 109–10, 259–63; Le Gall, 'Combattants de Pavie', 573.

150. J. Garrisson, *Protestants du Midi 1559–1598* (Toulouse, 1980), 165; Gunn, Grummitt, and Cools, *War, State, and Society*, 299–302.

151. Mallett and Shaw, *Italian Wars*, 301–3.

152. Xenakis, *Gewalt und Gemeinschaft*, 191–212.

153. Baumann, *Landsknechte*, 189–90; Xenakis, *Gewalt und Gemeinschaft*, 192; Gunn, Grummitt, and Cools, *War, State, and Society*, 301; Parker, *Grand Strategy*, 121–2; Mallett and Hale, *Military Organisation of a Renaissance State*, 377.

154. B. Willems, 'Militaire organisatie en staatsvorming aan de vooravond van de Nieuwe Tijd: Een analyse van het conflict tussen Brabant en Maximiliaan van Oostenrijk (1488–1489)', *Jaarboek voor Middeleeuwse Geschiedenis* 1 (1998), 277–8; *The German Peasant's War: A History in Documents*, ed. T. Scott and R. W. Scribner (Atlantic Highlands NJ, 1991), 289–308; Baumann, *Landsknechte*, 189–92.

155. S. Carroll, *Martyrs and Murderers: The Guise Family and the Making of Europe* (Oxford, 2009).

156. Sherer, *Warriors for a Living*, 163–4, 169, 246–8.

157. Murphey, *Ottoman Warfare*, 25–6, 141–57; Tracy, *Balkan Wars*, 38, 53, 95, 316.

158. F. Edelmayer, *Söldner und Pensionäre: das Netzwerk Phillipps II. im Heiligen Römischen Reich* (Vienna, 2002), 174–5, 187–202, 215.

159. D. Chambers, 'Francesco II Gonzaga, marquis of Mantua, "Liberator of Italy"', in D. Abulafia (ed.), *The French Descent into Renaissance Italy 1494–95: Antecedents and Effects* (Aldershot, 1995), 223; Potter, *Renaissance France at War*, 259, 263, 267, 271–3; Gunn, Grummitt, and Cools, *War, State, and Society*, 267, 270–2.

160. Murphey, *Ottoman Warfare*, 6; J. R. Hale, *Artists and Warfare in the Renaissance* (New Haven CT and London, 1990), 97–105, 250–2; Potter, *Renaissance France at War*, 299–300; F. Checa Cremades, *Carlos V: La imagen del poder en el renacimiento* (Madrid, 1999), 105–6, 144, 215–16, 226–34, 250.

161. Potter, *Renaissance France at War*, 161–2; Checa Cremades, *Carlos V*, 217–20; Gunn, Grummitt, and Cools, *War, State, and Society*, 303–5.

162. Gunn, Grummitt, and Cools, *War, State, and Society*, 305; C. Duffy, *Siege Warfare: The Fortress in the Early Modern World 1494–1660* (London, 1996 edn), 49, 165; G. M. Battaglini, *Cosmopolis: Portoferraio medicea, storia urbana, 1548–1737* (Rome, 1978), 15–50; Van den Heuvel, *'Papiere Bolwercken'*, 98, 104.

163. *StP*, ix. 108, 186, 339–40, 465, 524, 552, 598; G. Phillips, *The Anglo-Scots Wars 1513–50* (Woodbridge, 1999), 92–3, 256–7.

164. Potter, *Renaissance France at War*, 95, 120–2, 287–8.

165. Constant, 'Protestant Nobility', 74; P. B. De Troeyer, *Lamoraal van Egmont: Een critische studie over zijn rol in de jaren 1559–64 in verband met het schuldvraagstuk*, Verhandelingen van de Koninklijke Academie voor Wetenschappen, Letteren en Schone Kunsten van België, Klasse der Letteren 40 (Brussels, 1961), xxv, 50; F. Rachfahl, *Wilhelm van Oranien und der niederländische Aufstand*, 3 vols (The Hague, 1906–24), i. 34–238, ii. 85–128, 347–93, 625–7, 686–7, 801–2, 842–50, 886–8, 896–901, iii. 213–44, 316–604; J. Massarette, *La vie martiale et fastueuse de Pierre-Ernest de Mansfeld (1517–1604)*, 2 vols (Paris, 1930), i. 1–258.

166. A. Vos, 'The Humanism of Toxophilus: A New Source', *English Literary Renaissance* 6 (1976), 198–200.

167. *Calendar of State Papers and Manuscripts, Relating to English Affairs, Existing in the Archives and Collections of Venice and other Libraries of Northern Italy, vol VI part ii, 1556–1557*, ed. R. Brown (London, 1881), 1046–7.

168. Mallett and Shaw, *Italian Wars*, 213–16; Potter, *Henry VIII and Francis I*, 432.

169. S. L. Adams and D. S. Gehring, 'Elizabeth I's Former Tutor Reports on the Parliament of 1559: Johannes Spithovius to the Chancellor of Denmark, 27 February 1559',

EHR 128 (2013), 52; *Calendar of Letters and State Papers relating to English Affairs, preserved principally in the Archives of Simancas, vol I, 1558–1567*, ed. M. A. S. Hume (London, 1892), 34.

170. *Calendar of State Papers Relating to English Affairs in the Archives of Venice, vol VII, 1558–1580*, ed. R. Brown and G. C. Bentinck (London, 1890), 328; *Calendar of Letters Simancas 1558–1567*, 256, 260, 262, 265–6, 268, 271, 273, 294, 299, 302, 336, 340–1.

Bibliography

MANUSCRIPT SOURCES

Belgium

Ghent: Stadsarchief Gent
OA Oud archief

England and Wales

Alnwick: Alnwick Castle
Syon MSS

Aylesbury: Centre for Buckinghamshire Studies
AR16/89 BAS Buckinghamshire Archaeological Society collection
D-U Uthwatt of Great Linford and Andrewes of Lathbury collection
PR 234/5/1 Churchwardens' accounts of Wing

Bangor: Bangor University Library
Penrhyn collection

Bedford: Bedfordshire and Luton Archives and Records Service
Bor BD6/10 Bedford borough accounts

Bristol: Bristol Record Office
04026/1–5 Bristol great audit books

Bury St Edmunds: Suffolk Record Office
C12 Bury St Edmunds borough records, bills 1560

Cambridge: Cambridge University Library (CUL)
EDR Ely Diocesan Records
Hengrave MSS

Cambridge: Cambridgeshire Archives
P/22/5/1 Churchwardens' accounts of Holy Trinity, Cambridge
PB/X71/1–10 Cambridge borough accounts

Cambridge: Downing College
MS Bowtell 1 Cambridge borough accounts

Canterbury: Cathedral Archives (CCA)
CC/FA2, 5–17 Canterbury chamberlains' accounts
U4 Fordwich borough records
U4/8/4a–37 Fordwich mayor's accounts
U4/25 Churchwardens' accounts of St Mary's, Fordwich

Chelmsford: Essex Record Office
D/B3/3/226–42 Maldon chamberlains' accounts
D/P248/5/1 Churchwardens' accounts of Bromfield
T/A122/1 Churchwardens' accounts of Harwich

Chichester: West Sussex Record Office
Chichester City Records AE/1–2 Borough accounts
MP245 Churchwardens' accounts of Billinghurst
Par11/9/1 Churchwardens' accounts of Ashurst
Par516/9/1 Churchwardens' accounts of Worth

Chippenham: Wiltshire and Swindon History Centre
189/1 Churchwardens' accounts of St Mary, Devizes
1020/25 Churchwardens' accounts of Longbridge Deverill
G25/1/21 Wilton borough general entry book

Coughton Court
Throckmorton MSS (NRA report)

Dorchester: Dorset History Centre
DC/BTB Bridport borough records
DC/LR/G1/1 Lyme Regis mayor's accounts
DC/LR/G7/3 Lyme Regis cobb dues accounts
DC/PL/CLA 23, 26 Poole borough old record books
DC/PL/CLA 46(1), 48 (3), 49(4), 50(5), 51(6), 52(7) Poole borough accounts
PE/WM/CW1/40 Churchwardens' accounts of Wimborne Minster

Durham: Durham University Library
CCB Bishopric of Durham records

Exeter: Devon Heritage Centre
484M Mamhead collection
Chanter Records of the diocese of Exeter
D1508M Courtenay of Powderham collection
DD Deposited deeds
EAB1/1–2 Exeter borough act books
PW1 Churchwardens' accounts of Crediton

Hatfield: Hatfield House
CP Cecil Papers

Hereford: Herefordshire Archive and Records Centre
BG11/17, 24 Hereford borough accounts and documents
J72/8 Churchwardens' accounts of Stoke Edith

Hull: Hull History Centre
U DDSY Sykes of Sledmere collection (NRA report)

Huntingdon: Huntingdonshire Archives
2280/28 Churchwardens' accounts of Holywell cum Needingworth
2449/25 Churchwardens' accounts of Ramsey

Ipswich: Suffolk Record Office, Ipswich branch
EE2/L1/3–4 Eye borough chamberlains' accounts

Keele: Keele University Library
Chetwynde Family Papers
Marquess of Anglesey papers

Kingston-upon-Thames: Kingston Museum and Heritage Service
KG2/2/1–2 Churchwardens' accounts of Kingston-upon-Thames

Lanhydrock: Lanhydrock House
Early printed books

Leicester: Leicestershire Record Office
DG36/140/1–10, 284/1–10 Churchwardens' and town lands wardens' accounts of Melton
    Mowbray
26D53 Shirley family collection

Lewes: East Sussex Record Office (ESRO)
Rye 45/19, 20 Rye letters and indentures
Rye 60/3–4 Rye chamberlains' accounts

Lewes: Sussex Archaeological Society
Firle Place MSS (NRA report)

Lichfield: Lichfield Record Office
B/C/11 wills

Lincoln: Lincolnshire Archives
ANC Ancaster collection
Monson collection
PAR Addlethorpe 10 Churchwardens' accounts of Addlethorpe
PAR St James Louth 7/2, 7/3 Churchwardens' accounts of Louth
PAR Sutton St Mary 9 Churchwardens' accounts of Long Sutton
1PG Pearson-Gregory collection

London: The British Library (BL)
Additional MSS
Additional MS 6173 Churchwardens' accounts of Horley
Additional MS 32243 Churchwardens' accounts of Stratton
Additional MS 33192 Churchwardens' accounts of Arlington
Additional Rolls
Althorp papers

Cotton MSS
Egerton MS 1912 Churchwardens' accounts of St Mary's Dover
Egerton MSS 2092–4, 2107–8, Dover borough accounts and documents
Harleian MS 2177 Churchwardens' accounts of Holy Trinity, Chester
Stowe MSS

London: The College of Arms (CA)
M series manuscripts

London: London Metropolitan Archives (LMA)
P92/SAV St Saviour Southwark records
Rep. London Repertories

London: The National Archives: Public Record Office (PRO)
C1 Chancery: Early Chancery Proceedings
C 24 Chancery: Examiners' Office: Town Depositions
C54 Chancery and Supreme Court of Judicature: Close Rolls
CHES24 Palatinate of Chester: Chester County Court and Court of Great Sessions of
    Chester, and Flint Justice's Sessions: Files
DL1 Duchy of Lancaster: Court of Duchy Chamber: Pleadings
E36 Exchequer: Treasury of Receipt: Miscellaneous Books
E101 Exchequer: King's Remembrancer: Various Accounts
E404 Exchequer of Receipt: Warrants for Issue
KB8 Court of King's Bench: Crown Side: Baga de Secretis
KB9 Court of King's Bench: Crown Side: Indictments Files, Oyer and Terminer Files and
    Informations Files
PROB11 Prerogative Court of Canterbury and related Probate Jurisdictions: Will
    Registers
SC1 Special Collections: Ancient Correspondence of the Chancery and the Exchequer
SP1 State Papers Henry VIII: General Series
STAC2 Court of Star Chamber: Proceedings, Henry VIII

London: Victoria and Albert Museum
MS L30/1982 Inventory of William Herbert, earl of Pembroke

Longleat: Longleat House
Devereux papers
Miscellaneous volumes
NMR North Muniment Room collection

Maidstone: Kent History and Library Centre (KHLC)
Fa Faversham borough records
NR New Romney borough records
P46/5/1 Churchwardens' accounts of Brenzett
Sa/FAt9–22 Sandwich treasurers' accounts

Manchester: John Rylands Library
Crutchley collection
English MS 220 Churchwardens' accounts of Leverton
Early printed books

Matlock: Derbyshire Record Office
D3287 Gell family of Hopton collection (NRA report)

Newport: Isle of Wight Record Office
JER/WA Worsley of Appuldurcombe collection
OG Oglander collection

Northallerton: North Yorkshire Record Office
PR/MAS3/1/1 Churchwardens' accounts of Masham
ZAL Milbank collection

Norwich: Norfolk Record Office
NCC Wills

Nottingham: Nottinghamshire Archives
DD/SR Savile of Rufford collection

Nottingham: Nottingham University Library
Ga Galway collection
Mi Middleton collection
Early printed books

Oxford: Bodleian Library
Oxford University Archives
Rawlinson Manuscripts
Tanner Manuscripts
MSS Lat. Th.
MSS Top. Yorks
Early printed books

Oxford: Oxfordshire History Centre
MS Wills Oxon. Oxfordshire wills

Plymouth: Plymouth and West Devon Record Office
1 Plymouth borough records
710 Woolcombe of Hemerdon collection

Reading: Berkshire Record Office
D/P24/5/1 Churchwardens' accounts of Brightwalton
D/XP149/1 Churchwardens' accounts of New Windsor
W/JBc Wallingford borough court rolls
WI/FAc1 Windsor borough chamberlains' accounts

Sheffield: Sheffield City Libraries
Bagshawe Collection (NRA report)

Shrewsbury: Shropshire Archives
327 Corbet of Adderley collection
LB8/1 Ludlow bailiffs' accounts
P58/B/1/1/1 Churchwardens' accounts of Cheswardine

Southampton: Southampton Archives Office
SC5/1 Southampton stewards' accounts
SC5/3 Southampton mayors' accounts
SC13/2/1–3 Southampton muster books

Stratford upon Avon: Shakespeare Birthplace Trust Record Office
DR10 Gregory of Stivichall collection

Strood: Medway Archives
DRb Bishopric of Rochester records

Taunton: Somerset Heritage Centre
D/B/bw1830 Bridgwater bailiffs' accounts
DD/L/P Luttrell of Dunster

Truro: Cornwall Record Office
B/LAUS/172 Launceston borough stewards' accounts

Warwick: Warwickshire Record Office
CR1291 Greswold of Malvern Hall collection
CR1618/WA1/1 Warwick chief burgess's accounts
DR64/63 Churchwardens' accounts of Solihull
DR87/1 Churchwardens' accounts of St Nicholas', Warwick
DR158/19 Churchwardens' accounts of Great Packington
DR581/45 Churchwardens' accounts of Holy Trinity, Coventry

Westminster: Westminster Abbey
WAM Westminster Abbey Muniments

Winchester: Hampshire Record Office
37M85/4/AC/1 Andover borough accounts
W/E1 Winchester borough chamberlains' accounts
Wills

Woking: Surrey History Centre (SHC)
LM Loseley papers

Worcester: Worcestershire Archives
BA1006/31b–32a Droitwich borough records
BA2648/9 Worcester episcopal registers
Original wills
Registered wills
Worcester City Records A6, box 4 Worcester borough miscellaneous volume
Worcester City Records A10, box 2, vol 1 Worcester borough accounts audit
Worcester City Records A14, vol 1 Worcester borough chamber order book

York: Borthwick Institute of Historical Research
Bishops' Registers
Probate Registers

France

Lille: Archives Départementales du Nord (ADN)
B series

USA

New York: New York Public Library
Early printed books

New York: Pierpoint Morgan Library
Rulers of England box 2

San Marino, CA: Huntington Library (HL)
MSS BA Battle Abbey collection
MSS El Ellesmere collection
MSS HA, HAP Hastings Manuscripts
MS HA Misc Box 8(2) Churchwardens' accounts of Castle Donington
MSS STT Temple of Stowe collection
Early printed books

SIXTEENTH-CENTURY PRINTED WORKS

Anon., *A newe interlude of impacyente pouerte* (London, 1560).
Anon., *The true tragedie of Richard the third* (London, 1594).
Askham, Anthony, *A prognosticacion made for the yere of oure Lord Gods thousande fyue hundreth Xlviii* (London, 1548).
Awdelay, John, *The wonders of England* (London, 1559).
Birch, William, *A new balade of the worthy seruice of late doen by Maister Strangwige in Fraunce, and of his death* (London, 1562).
Blundeville, Thomas, *The fower chiefyst offices belongyng to Horsemanshippe* (London, 1566).
Bogaert, Arnould, trans. John Coke, *A pronostication for diuers yeares ryght vtyle and pro-fytable to al sortes of people* (London, 1553).
Bourchier, John, Lord, Berners, *Here begynneth the first volum of sir Iohan Froyssart of the cronycles of Englande, Fraunce, Spayne, Portyngale, Scotlande, Bretayne, Flaunders: and other places adioynynge* (London, 1523).
A breuiat cronicle (London, 1552).
Caesar, Julius, *The eyght books of Caius Iulius Caesar*, trans. Arthur Golding (London, 1565).
A Chronicle of yeres (London, c.1558).
Churchyard, Thomas, *A generall rehearsall of warres, called Churchyardes choise wherein is fiue hundred seuerall seruices of land and sea as seiges, battailes, skirmiches, and encounters* (London, 1579).
Copland, Robert, *The hye way to the spyttell hous* (London, 1536?).
Cuningham, William, *1564. A new almanach and prognostication, seruynge the yere of Christ M.D.L.X.IIII* (London, 1563).
The Destruction and sacke cruelly committed by the Duke of Guyse and his company, in the towne of Vassy, the fyrste of Marche, in the year MDLXII (London, 1562).
Fabyan, Robert, *Prima pars cronecarum* (London, 1516).
Fabyan, Robert, *Fabyan's Chronicle* (London, 1533).

Frontinus, Sextus Julius, *The strategemes, sleyghtes, and policies of warre, gathered togyther, by S. Iulius Frontinus, and translated into Englyshe, by Rycharde Morysine* (London, 1539).

Gale, Thomas, *Certaine workes of chirurgerie, newly compiled and published by Thomas Gale, maister in chirurgerie* (London, 1563).

Gallars, Nicolas des, *A true report of all the doynges at the assembly concernyng matters of Religion, lately holden at Poyssy in Fraunce* (London, 1562).

Gasser, Achilles Pirmin, *A prognostication for this yere M.D.xlvi* (London, 1546).

Grafton, Richard, *An abridgement of the chronicles of England* (London, 1562).

Grafton, Richard, *An abridgement of the chronicles of England* (London, 1564).

Here after foloweth ye batayll of Egyngecourte [and] the great sege of Rone by kynge Henry of Monmouthe the fyfthe of the name that wan Gascoyne and Gyenne and Normandye (London, 1536).

Here is a lytell shorte cronycle, begynnynge at the. vii. ages of the worlde, w[ith] the comy[n]ge of Brute: and the reygne of all the kynges (London, 1530).

Heuring, Simon, *An almanacke and prognosticatyon, for the yeare of our Lorde, M.D.LI.* (Worcester, 1551).

Holinshed, Raphael, *The Chronicles of England, Scotlande, and Irelande*, 4 vols (London, 1577).

Holinshed, Raphael, *The First and Second volumes of Chronicles*, 6 vols (London, 1587).

The husbandmans practise, or prognostication (London, 1550?).

Laet, Gaspar, *[Prognostication for the year] M.CCCCC.xvij. translate in the famous cite of Andwerpe* (Antwerp, 1517).

Laet, Gaspar, *The pnostication of Maister Jasp Laet, practised in the towne of Antuerpe, for the yere of Our Lorde, M.D.XX.* (London?, 1520).

Laet, Gaspar, *Prognostication for the year M.v.C. & xxiii* (London, 1523).

Laet, Gaspar, *An almanack and pronostication of Iaspar Laet for the yere, of our Lord M.D.XXXIV* (Malmö, 1534).

Laet, Gaspar, *Pronostication of Jaspar Laet doctor of phisicke and astronomy for the yere of our Lorde God M.vc.xliiii* (London, 1544).

Lambarde, William, *A Perambulation of Kent, increased and altered* (London, 1596).

Lanquet, Thomas, *An epitome of chronicles . . . now finished and continued to the reigne of our soveraine lorde kynge Edwarde the sixt by Thomas Cooper* (London, 1549).

Lanquet, Thomas, *An epitome of chronicles* (London, 1559).

The late expedicion in Scotlande made by the Kynges hyghnys armye, vnder the conduit of the ryght honorable the Erle of Hertforde, the yere of our Lorde God 1544 (London, 1544).

Lever, Thomas, *A sermon preached at Pauls Crosse the xiiii day of December* (London, 1550).

Marckant, John, *The purgacion of the ryght honourable lord Wentworth concerning the crime layde to his charge* (London 1559).

Morison, Richard, *A lamentation in whiche is shewed what ruyne and destruction cometh of seditious rebellion* (London, 1536).

Morison, Richard, *An exhortation to styrre all Englyshe men to the defence of theyr countreye* (London, 1539).

Nostradamus, Michael, *The prognostication of maister Michael Nostredamus, doctour in phisick* (Antwerp, 1559).

Onosander, *Onosandro Platonico, of the generall captaine, and of his office, translated out of Greeke into Italyan, by Fabio Cotta, a Romayne: and out of Italian into Englysh, by Peter Whytehorne* (London, 1563).

Palsgrave, John, *Lesclarcissement de la langue francoyse* (London, 1530).

Patten, William, *The expedicion into Scotlande of the most woorthely fortunate prince Edward, Duke of Soomerset, uncle unto our most noble sovereign lord ye kinges Maiestie Edward the.*

VI. goovernour of hys hyghnes persone, and protectour of hys graces realmes, dominions and subjectes (London, 1548).

Porcia, Jacopo di, *The precepts of warre, setforth by Iames the erle of Purlilia, and translated into englysh by Peter Betham* (London, 1544).

Predictions des choses plus memorables qui sont a advenir depuis l'an MDLXIII, iusqu'a l'an mil six cens & sept, prise tant des eclipses & grosses Ephemrides de Cyprian Leovitie, que des predictions de Samuel Syderocrate (n.p., 1568).

A Prognostication for 1498 (Westminster, 1498).

A Prognostication (London?, 1539?).

Rich, Barnaby, *A right exelent and pleasaunt dialogue, betwene Mercury and an English souldier* (London, 1574).

A short cronycle (London, 1540).

Statutes and ordenaunces of warre (London, 1513).

Stow, John, *A summarie of Englyshe chronicles* (London, 1565).

Stow, John, *A summarye of the chronicles of Englande* (London, 1570).

Vaughan, Lewes, *A new almanacke and prognostication, collected for the yeare of our Lord God. M.D.L.IX* (London, 1559).

Vegetius, Flavius, *The foure bookes of Flauius Vegetius Renatus briefelye contayninge a plaine forme, and perfect knowledge of martiall policye, feates of chiualrie, and whatsoeuer pertayneth to warre. Translated out af [sic] lattine, into Englishe, by Iohn Sadler* (London, 1572).

Velthoven, Adrian, *The pronostication of maister Adrian of arte and medicine doctour moost expert maister and excellent in astronomy* (London, 1520).

Walshe, Edward, *The office and duety in fightyng for our country* (London, 1545).

PRINTED PRIMARY SOURCES

The 1522 Muster Roll for West Berkshire, ed. E. A. Garnish (n.p., 1988).

'Abstract of Original Returns of the Commissioners for Musters and the Loan in Surrey', ed. T. Craib, *Surrey Archaeological Collections* 30 (1917), 13–30.

'Account of Henry the Eighth's Expedition into France, A.D. 1513', ed. W. C. Trevelyan, *Archaeologia* 26 (1836), 475–8.

The Accounts of the Chamberlains of Newcastle Upon Tyne 1508–1511, ed. C. M. Fraser, Soc. of Antiquaries of Newcastle Upon Tyne RS 3 (Newcastle Upon Tyne, 1987).

The Accounts of the Churchwardens of the Parish of St Michael, Cornhill, in the City of London, from 1456 to 1608, ed. W. H. Overall (London, 1871).

Accounts of the Feoffees of the Town Lands of Bury St Edmunds, 1569–1622, ed. M. Statham, Suffolk RS 46 (Woodbridge, 2003).

The Accounts of the Wardens of the Parish of Morebath, Devon, 1520–1573, ed. J. E. Binney (Exeter, 1904).

Acta curiae admirallatus Scotiae 6th Sept. 1557–11th March 1561–2, ed. T. C. Wade, Stair Soc. 19/2 (Edinburgh, 1937).

Acts of Chapter of the Collegiate Church of SS Peter and Wilfred, Ripon, AD 1452 to AD 1506, ed. J. T. Fowler, SS 64 (Durham, 1875).

Acts of the Privy Council of England, ed. J. Dasent, 2nd ser., vols i–vi, *A.D. 1542–1558* (London, 1890–3).

Adams's Chronicle of Bristol, ed. F. F. Fox (Bristol, 1910).

'All Hallows' Church Accounts, Sherborne', ed. J. Fowler, *Notes and Queries for Somerset and Dorset* 23–6 (1939–54).

'Amersham Parish Accounts', ed. F. G. Lee, *Records of Buckinghamshire* 7 (1892–6), 43–51.

Ancient Churchwardens' Accounts of the Parish of North Elmham, ed. A. G. Legge (Norwich, 1891).

'Ancient Wills (no. 2)', ed. H. W. King, *Transactions of the Essex Archaeological Society* 3 (1865), 53–63.

Annals of the Kingdom of Ireland, by the Four Masters, from the earliest period to the year 1616, ed. J. O'Donovan, 2nd edn, 7 vols (Dublin, 1856).

Anon., *The Life of Long Meg of Westminster* (London, 1635).

'Aston Abbotts: Parish Account Book', ed. W. Bradbrook, *Records of Buckinghamshire* 10 (1910–16), 34–50.

Audley, Thomas, 'A Treatise on the Art of War', ed. W. St P. Bunbury, *Journal of the Society for Army Historical Research* 6 (1927), 65–78, 129–33.

'A Bailiff's List and Chronicle from Worcester', ed. D. MacCulloch and P. Hughes, *The Antiquaries Journal* 75 (1995), 235–53.

Becon, Thomas, *The Early Works of Thomas Becon*, ed. J. Ayre, Parker Soc. (Cambridge, 1843).

Bedfordshire Muster Rolls 1539–1831, ed. N. Lutt, Bedfordshire Historical RS 71 (Bedford, 1992).

Bedfordshire Wills 1480–1519, ed. P. L. Bell, Bedfordshire Historical RS 45 (Bedford, 1966).

Bedfordshire Wills 1484–1533, ed. P. L. Bell, Bedfordshire Historical RS 76 (Bedford, 1997).

Bedfordshire Wills 1531–1539, ed. P. L. Bell and B. Tearle, Bedfordshire Family History Soc. occasional paper 3 (Bedford, 2005).

Bedfordshire Wills 1537–1545, ed. P. L. Bell and B. Tearle, Bedfordshire Family History Soc. occasional paper 4 (Bedford, 2010).

Bedfordshire Wills 1543–1547, ed. P. L. Bell and B. Tearle, Bedfordshire Family History Soc. occasional paper 5 (Bedford, 2012).

Bedfordshire Wills proved in the Prerogative Court of Canterbury 1383–1548, ed. M. McGregor, Bedfordshire Historical RS 58 (Bedford, 1979).

Berteville, Jean, *Recit de l'expedition en Ecosse l'an M.D. XLVI. et de la battayle de Muscleburgh*, ed. D. Constable (Edinburgh, 1825).

'Bletchingley Churchwarden's Accounts, 1546–1552', ed. T. Craik, *Surrey Archaeological Collections* 29 (1916), 25–33.

The Boston Assembly Minutes 1545–1575, ed. P. Clark and J. Clark, Lincoln RS 77 (Woodbridge, 1987).

Boxford Churchwardens' Accounts 1530–1561, ed. P. Northeast, Suffolk Records Soc. 23 (Woodbridge, 1982).

Brésin, Louis, *Chroniques de Flandre et d'Artois: Analyse et extraits pour servir à l'histoire de ces provinces de 1482 à 1560*, ed. E. Mannier (Paris, 1880).

British Library Harleian MS 433, ed. R. Horrox and P. W. Hammond, 4 vols (Gloucester, 1979–83).

Calendar of Assize Records: Essex Indictments, Elizabeth I, ed. J. S. Cockburn (London, 1978).

Calendar of Assize Records: Kent Indictments, Elizabeth I, ed. J. S. Cockburn (London, 1979).

Calendar of Assize Records: Surrey Indictments, Elizabeth I, ed. J. S. Cockburn (London, 1980).

Calendar of Assize Records: Sussex Indictments, Elizabeth I, ed. J. S. Cockburn (London, 1975).

Calendar of the Bristol Apprentice Book 1532–1565, ed. D. Hollis, E. Ralph, and N. M. Hardwick, 3 vols, Bristol RS 14, 33, 43 (Bristol, 1948–92).

A Calendar of Charters and other Documents belonging to the Hospital of William Wyggeston at Leicester, ed. A. H. Thompson (Leicester, 1933).

Calendar of the Correspondence of the Smyth Family of Ashton Court 1548–1642, ed. J. H. Bettey, Bristol RS 35 (Bristol, 1982).

Calendar of the Court Books of the Borough of Witney 1538–1610, ed. J. L. Bolton and M. M. Maslen, Oxfordshire RS 54 (Gloucester, 1985).

A Calendar of Dramatic Records in the Books of the Livery Companies of London 1485–1640, ed. J. Robertson and D. J. Gordon, Malone Soc. Collections 3 (Oxford, 1954).

Calendar of Entries in the Papal Registers relating to Great Britain and Ireland, ed. W. H. Bliss et al., 19 vols to date (London and Dublin, 1893–).

A Calendar of the Freemen of Lynn, 1292–1836 (Norwich, 1913).

Calendar of the Freemen of Norwich from 1307 to 1603, ed. W. Rye (London, 1888).

Calendar of Letter-Books of the City of London: I: 1400–1422, ed. R. R. Sharpe (London, 1909).

Calendar of Letters, Despatches, and State Papers, relating to the Negotiations between England and Spain, Preserved in the Archives at Simancas and Elsewhere, ed. G. Bergenroth et al., 13 vols (London, 1862–1954).

Calendar of Letters and State Papers relating to English Affairs, preserved principally in the Archives of Simancas, vol I, 1558–1567, ed. M. A. S. Hume (London, 1892).

Calendar of the Manuscripts of Major-General Lord Sackville, 2 vols, HMC 80 (London, 1940–66).

Calendar of the Manuscripts of the Most Hon. the Marquis of Salisbury, 24 vols, HMC (London, 1883–1976).

'Calendar of the Marquis of Anglesey's Longdon, Lichfield and other Staffordshire Charters formerly at Beaudesert', ed. I. H. Jeayes, *Collections for a History of Staffordshire*, 3rd series for 1939 (Kendal, 1940), 71–158.

Calendar of Nottinghamshire Coroners' Inquests, 1485–1558, ed. R. F. Hunnisett, Thoroton Soc. Record ser. 25 (Nottingham, 1969).

Calendar of the Patent Rolls, 1494–1509 (London, 1916).

Calendar of the Plymouth Municipal Records, ed. R. N. Worth (Plymouth, 1893).

Calendar of the Records of the Borough of Haverfordwest 1539–1660, ed. B. G. Charles, Bulletin of the Board of Celtic Studies History and Law Series 24 (Cardiff, 1967).

A Calendar of the Registers of the Priory of Llanthony by Gloucester 1457–1466, 1501–1525, ed. J. Rhodes, Gloucestershire RS 15 (Stroud, 2002).

A Calendar of the Shrewsbury and Talbot Papers in Lambeth Palace Library and the College of Arms, ed. C. Jamison, E. G. W. Bill, and G. R. Batho, 2 vols, HMC joint publications 6–7 (London, 1966–71).

Calendar of State Papers, Domestic Series, of the Reign of Edward VI 1547–1553 preserved in the PRO, rev. edn, ed. C. S. Knighton (London, 1992).

Calendar of State Papers, Domestic Series, of the Reign of Mary, 1553–1558, ed. C. S. Knighton (Chippenham, 1998).

Calendar of State Papers, Foreign, Elizabeth, 1558–1589. Vol 7: 1564–1565, ed. J. Stevenson (London, 1870).

Calendar of State Papers, Foreign Series, of the Reign of Edward VI, 1547–1553, ed. W. B. Turnbull (London, 1861).

Calendar of State Papers, Foreign Series, of the Reign of Mary, 1553–1558, ed. W. B. Turnbull (London, 1861).

Calendar of State Papers, Ireland, Tudor Period 1547–1553, ed. C. Lennon (Dublin, 2015).

Calendar of State Papers, Ireland, Tudor Period 1566–1567, ed. B. Cunningham (Dublin, 2009).

Calendar of State Papers and Manuscripts, Relating to English Affairs, Existing in the Archives and Collections of Venice and other Libraries of Northern Italy, vol VI part ii, 1556–1557, ed. R. Brown (London, 1881).

Calendar of State Papers Relating to English Affairs in the Archives of Venice, vol VII, 1558–1580, ed. R. Brown and G. C. Bentinck (London, 1890).

Calendar of the Tavistock Parish Records, ed. R. N. Worth (Plymouth, 1887).

A Calendar of the White and Black Books of the Cinque Ports, ed. F. Hull, Kent Records 19 (London, 1967).

Cambridge Borough Documents, i, ed. W. M. Palmer (Cambridge, 1931).

'Cambridgeshire Church Goods', ed. J. J. Muskett, *The East Anglian* n.s. 6 (1895–6), 145–9, 199–203, 225–8, 241–3, 7 (1897–8), 33–7, 49–52, 97–9, 171–7, 209–12, 359–62, 8 (1899–1900), 1–4, 33–4, 58–60, 90–1, 129–31, 162–5, 184–5, 197–8, 211–12, 229–30, 252–4, 265–7, 281–4, 298–300, 310–11, 339–40, 360–1, 376–8, 9 (1901–2), 6–9, 23–5, 42–3, 49–50, 73–5, 94–6, 105–8, 117–20, 136–8, 236–8, 248–50, 262–5, 282–3, 301–3, 348–9.

Cartulary of Osney Abbey, ed. H. E. Salter, 6 vols, Oxford HS 89–91, 97–98, 101 (Oxford, 1929–36).

A Catalogue of the Manuscript Books in the Library of Christ Church, Canterbury, ed. C. E. Woodruff (Canterbury, 1911).

The Cely Letters 1472–1488, ed. A. Hanham, EETS 273 (London, 1975).

Ceremonies and Processions of the Cathedral Church of Salisbury, ed. C. Wordsworth (Cambridge, 1901).

The Certificate of Musters for Buckinghamshire in 1522, ed. A. C. Chibnall, Buckinghamshire RS 17 (London, 1973).

Certificate of Musters in the County of Somerset, temp. Eliz. AD 1569, ed. E. Green, Somerset RS 20 (London, 1904).

Chaloner, Thomas, *Thomas Chaloner's* In Laudem Henrici Octavi *(Latin Edition and English Translation)*, ed. J. B. Gabel and C. C. Schlam (Lawrence, KS, 1979).

Champier, Symphorien, *Les gestes ensemble la vie du preulx Chevalier Bayard*, ed. D. Crouzet (Paris, 1992).

The Chantry Certificates for Oxfordshire and the Edwardian Inventories of Church Goods for Oxfordshire, ed. R. Graham and T. Craib, Alcuin Club Collection 23 (London, 1920).

Chesterfield Wills and Inventories 1521–1603, ed. J. M. Bestall and D. V. Fowkes, Derbyshire RS 1 (Matlock, 1977).

Christ Church Letters, ed. J. B. Sheppard, CS n.s. 19 (London, 1877).

The Chronicle of Calais, ed. J. G. Nichols, CS 35 (London, 1846).

A Chronicle of England by Charles Wriothesley, ed. W. D. Hamilton, 2 vols, CS n.s. 11 (London, 1875).

Chronicle of the Grey Friars of London, ed. J. G. Nichols, CS 53 (London, 1852).

The Chronicle of John Hardyng, ed. H. Ellis (London, 1812).

Chronicle of King Henry VIII of England, ed. M. A. S. Hume (London, 1889).

'Chronique d'Adrien de But', in *Chroniques relatives à l'histoire de la Belgique sous la domination des ducs de Bourgogne*, ed. K. de Lettenhove, 3 vols (Brussels, 1870–6).

Chronologische lijsten van de Geëxtendeerde Sententiën berustende in het archief van de Grote Raad van Mechelen, ed. J. Th. de Smidt et al., 6 vols (Brussels and Arnhem, 1966–88).

Church Accounts 1457–1559, ed. R. W. Dunning and M. B. McDermott, Somerset RS 95 (Taunton, 2013).

'Church Ale-Games and Interludes', ed. G. B. Baker, *The East Anglian* 1 (1864), 334–6.

The Church Book of St Ewen's, Bristol, 1454–1584, ed. B. R. Masters and E. Ralph, Bristol and Gloucestershire Archaeological Soc., records section 6 (Bristol, 1967).

'Church Goods in Suffolk, nos. iv–xxiii', ed. J. J. Muskett, *The East Anglian* n.s. 1 (1885–6), 49–51, 67–70, 83–4, 102–4, 114–16, 128–9, 142–3, 159–61, 186–8, 207–9, 223–4, 234–6, 251–3, 274–6, 285–6, 323–4, 342–4, 353–5, 362–3.

'Church Goods in Suffolk, nos. xxiv–xxxix', ed. J. J. Muskett, *The East Anglian* n.s. 2 (1887–8), 3–5, 18–19, 43, 55–6, 70–1, 104–7, 123–4, 135–6, 153–5, 169–70, 189–90, 204–6, 244–6, 283–4, 317–19, 366–7.

The Church Records of St Andrew Hubbard Eastcheap c.1450–c.1570, ed. C. Burgess, London RS 34 (London, 1997).

The Churchwardens' Account Book for the Parish of St Giles, Reading, ed. W. L. Nash (Reading, 1881).

'Churchwardens' Accounts All Saints' Church Walsall 1462–1531', ed. G. P. Mander, *Collections for a History of Staffordshire* 3rd series for 1928 (Kendal, 1930).

Churchwardens' Accounts of Ashburton, 1479–1580, ed. A. Hanham, Devon and Cornwall RS n.s. 15 (Exeter, 1970).

Churchwardens' Accounts at Betrysden 1515–1573, ed. F. R. Mercer, Kent Records 5/3 (Ashford, 1928).

'The Churchwardens' Accounts of the Church and Parish of St Michael without the North Gate, Bath', ed. C. B. Pearson, *Somersetshire Archaeological and Natural History Society Proceedings* 23–6 (1878–81).

Churchwardens' Accounts of Croscombe, Pilton, Yatton, Tintinhull, Morebath and St Michael's Bath, ed. E. Hobhouse, Somerset RS 4 (London, 1890).

Churchwardens' Accounts of Marston, Spelsbury, Pyrton, ed. F. W. Weaver and G. N. Clark, Oxfordshire RS 6 (Oxford, 1925).

'The Churchwardens' Accounts of Mere', ed. T. H. Baker, *Wiltshire Archaeological and Natural History Magazine* 35 (1907–8), 23–92.

The Churchwardens' Accounts of the Parish of Allhallows, London Wall, ed. C. Welch (London, 1912).

Churchwardens' Accounts of the Parish of Badsey, with Addington, in Worcestershire, from 1525 to 1571, ed. W. H. Price and E. A. B. Barnard (Hampstead, 1913).

'Churchwardens' Accounts of the Parish of Cowfold in the time of King Edward IV', ed. W. B. Otter, *Sussex Archaeological Collections* 2 (1849), 316–25.

'The Churchwardens' Accounts of the Parish of Great Salkeld', ed. C. M. L. Bouch, *Transactions of the Cumberland and Westmorland Antiquarian and Archaeological Society*, n.s. 49 (1950), 134–41.

'Churchwardens' Accounts of the Parish of St Andrew, Canterbury, from AD 1485 to AD 1625', ed. C. Cotton, *Archaeologia Cantiana* 32–5 (1917–21).

'The Churchwardens' Accounts of the Parish of St Mary, Thame', ed. W. P. Ellis, *Berks, Bucks and Oxon Archaeological Journal*, 7–20 (1901–15).

The Churchwardens' Accounts of the Parish of St Mary's, Reading, Berks, 1550–1662, ed. F. N. A. Garry and A. G. Garry (Reading, 1893).

'The Churchwardens' Accounts of the Parish of Worfield', ed. H. B. Walters, *Transactions of the Shropshire Archaeological and Natural History Society*, 3rd series 3–9 (1903–9).

The Churchwardens' Accounts of Prescot, Lancashire, 1523–1607, ed. F. A. Bailey, RS of Lancashire and Cheshire 104 (Preston, 1953).

'The Churchwardens' Accounts of St Andrew's and St Michael's, Lewes from 1522 to 1601', ed. H. M. Whitley, *Sussex Archaeological Collections*, 45 (1902), 40–61.

'Churchwardens' Accounts of St Dunstan's, Canterbury', ed. J. M. Cowper, *Archaeologia Cantiana* 16 (1886), 289–321, 17 (1887), 77–149.

Churchwardens' Accounts of S. Edmund and S. Thomas, Sarum, 1443–1702, ed. H. J. F Swayne (Salisbury, 1896).

Churchwardens' Accounts of St Mary the Great Cambridge from 1504 to 1635, ed. J. E. Foster, Cambridge Antiquarian Soc., 8o series 35 (Cambridge, 1905).

'Churchwardens' Accounts of Saint Mary's, Sutterton', *Archaeological Journal* 39 (1882), 53–63.

Churchwardens' Accounts of St Michael, Spurriergate, York, 1518–1548, ed. C. C. Webb, 2 vols, Borthwick Texts and Calendars 20 (York, 1997).

The Churchwardens' Accounts of St Michael's in Bedwardine, Worcester, from 1539 to 1603, ed. J. Amphlett, Worcestershire HS 6 (Oxford, 1897).

The Churchwardens' Accounts of St Michael's Church, Chagford, 1480–1600, ed. F. M. Osborne (Chagford, 1979).

'The Churchwardens' Accounts of St Michael's Church, Oxford', ed. H. E. Salter, *Transactions of the Oxfordshire Archaeological Society* 78 (1933).

The Churchwardens' Accounts of St Nicholas, Strood, ed. H. R. Plomer, 2 vols, Kent Records 5/1–2 (Ashford, 1915–27).

Churchwardens' Accounts of the Town of Ludlow, in Shropshire, from 1540 to the end of the reign of Queen Elizabeth, ed. T. Wright, CS 102 (London, 1869).

The Churchwardens' Accounts of West Tarring, Sussex, ed. W. J. Bessey (n.p., 1934).

The Churchwardens' Book of Bassingbourn, Cambridgeshire 1496–c.1540, ed. D. Dymond, Cambridgeshire Records Soc. 17 (Cambridge, 2004).

'The Churchwardens' Book of Sheriff Hutton, AD 1524–1568', ed. J. S. Purvis, *Yorkshire Archaeological Journal* 36 (1944–7), 178–89.

City Chamberlains' Accounts in the Sixteenth and Seventeenth Centuries, ed. D. M. Livock, Bristol RS 24 (Bristol, 1966).

City and County of Kingston Upon Hull: Calendar of the Ancient Deeds, Letters, Miscellaneous Old Documents, &c in the archives of the Corporation, ed. L. M. Stanewell (Kingston upon Hull, 1951).

Clifford Letters of the Sixteenth Century, ed. A. G. Dickens, SS 172 (Durham, 1962).

Collection des voyages des souverains des Pays-Bas, ed. L. P. Gachard, Commission Royale d'Histoire, Collection de chroniques Belges inédits, 4 vols (Brussels, 1876–82).

A Collection of Letters, Statutes, and other documents from the MS Library of Corpus Christi College, illustrative of the History of the University of Cambridge, during the period of the Reformation, from AD MD to AD MDLXXII, ed. J. Lamb (London, 1838).

A Collection of State Papers, relating to affairs in the reigns of King Henry VIII, King Edward VI, Queen Mary, and Queen Elizabeth, transcribed from original letters and other authentick memorials, left by William Cecill Lord Burghley, ed. S. Haynes and W. Murdin, 2 vols (London, 1740–59).

A Commentary of the Services and Charges of William Lord Grey of Wilton, ed. P. De M. G. Egerton, CS 40 (London, 1847).

'A Contemporary Account of the Battle of Floddon, 9th September 1513', ed. D. Laing, *Proceedings of the Society of Antiquaries of Scotland* 7 (1870), 141–52.

'A Contemporary Account of the Earl of Hertford's Second Expedition to Scotland, and of the Ravages committed by the English Forces in September 1545. From a Manuscript in Trinity College Library, Dublin', ed. D. Laing, *Proceedings of the Society of Antiquaries of Scotland* 1 (1851–4), 271–6.

Cornish Wills 1342–1540, ed. N. Orme, Devon and Cornwall RS n.s. 50 (Exeter, 2007).

The Cornwall Military Survey 1522, ed. T. L. Stoate (Bristol, 1987).

The Cornwall Muster Roll for 1569, ed. H. L. Douch (Bristol, 1984).

Correspondence of Edward, third earl of Derby, during the years 24 to 31 Henry VIII, ed. T. N. Toller, Chetham Soc. n.s. 19 (Manchester, 1890).

The County Community under Henry VIII: The Military Survey, 1522, and Lay Subsidy, 1524–5, for Rutland, ed. J. Cornwall, Rutland Record Ser. 1 (Oakham, 1980).

The Coventry Leet Book, ed. M. D. Harris, 4 vols, EETS 134–5, 138, 146 (London, 1907–13).

Coventry and its People in the 1520s, ed. M. H. M. Hulton, Dugdale Soc. 38 (Stratford-upon-Avon, 1999).

Cratfield: A Transcript of the Accounts of the Parish, from AD 1490 to AD 1642, ed. J. J. Raven (London, 1895).

The Customs Accounts of Hull, 1453–1490, ed. W. R. Childs, YASRS 144 (Leeds, 1986).

The Customs Accounts of Newcastle upon Tyne, 1454–1500, ed. J. F. Wade, SS 202 (Gateshead, 1995).

The Customs of London, otherwise called Arnold's Chronicle, ed. F. Douce (London, 1811).

Dadizeele, Jean de, *Mémoires de Jean de Dadizeele, souverain bailli de Flandre*, ed. K. de Lettenhove, Société d'émulation de Bruges. Recueil de chroniques, chartes et autres documents concernant l'histoire et les antiquités de Flandre, 3ᵉ série (Bruges, 1850).

'Dagverhaal van den veldtogt van keizer Karel V in 1554', ed. [C. A]. R. Macaré, *Kronijk van het Historisch Genootschap Gevestigd te Utrecht* 7 (1851), 280–308.

Le débat des hérauts d'armes de France et d'Angleterre: suivi de The debate between the heralds of England and France, ed. L. Pannier (Paris, 1877).

Debating the Hundred Years War: Pour ce que plusieurs (la loi salique) and a declaracion of the trew and dewe title of Henry VIII, ed. C. Taylor, CS 5th ser. 29 (Cambridge, 2006).

'Dennington Notes', ed. C. Raven, *Proceedings of the Suffolk Institute of Archaeology* 7 (1889–91), 120–3.

Les dénombrements de foyers dans le comté de Hainaut (XIVe–XVIe siècles), ed. M. A. Arnould (Brussels, 1956).

Depositions taken before the Mayor and Aldermen of Norwich, 1549–1567, ed. W. Rye (Norwich, 1905).

Derbyshire Wills proved in the Prerogative Court of Canterbury 1393–1574, ed. D. G. Edwards, Derbyshire RS 26 (Matlock, 1998).

Descriptive Catalogue of the Charters and Muniments in the Possession of the Rt Hon Lord Fitzhardinge at Berkeley Castle, ed. I. H. Jeayes (Bristol, 1892).

Descriptive Catalogue of Derbyshire Charters in Public and Private Libraries and Muniment Rooms, ed. I. H. Jeayes (London, 1906).

A Descriptive Catalogue of Sheffield Manorial Records, ed. T. W. Hall, 2 vols (Sheffield, 1926–8).

Despatches of Michele Suriano and Marc' Antonio Barbaro, Venetian Ambassadors at the Court of France 1560–1563, ed. A. H. Layard, Publications of the Huguenot Society of London 6 (Lymington, 1891).

The Devon Muster Roll for 1569, ed. A. J. Howard and T. L. Stoate (Bristol, 1977).

'A Diary of the Expedition of 1544', ed. W. A. J. Archbold, *EHR* 16 (1901), 503–7.

The Diary of Henry Machyn Citizen and Merchant-Taylor of London (1550–1563), ed. J. G. Nichols, CS 42 (London, 1848).

A Discourse of the Commonweal of this Realm of England, ed. M. Dewar (Charlottesville VA, 1969).

Documents Illustrating Early Education in Worcester 685 to 1700, ed. A. F. Leach, Worcestershire HS 29 (London, 1913).

Documents relating to the Office of the Revels in the Time of Queen Elizabeth, ed. A. Feuillerat, Materialien zur Kunde des älteren englischen Dramas 21 (Louvain, 1908).

Documents relating to the Revels at Court in the time of King Edward VI and Queen Mary (the Loseley manuscripts), ed. A. Feuillerat, Materialien zur Kunde des älteren englischen Dramas 44 (Louvain, 1914).

Dorset Tudor Muster Rolls, 1539, 1542, 1569, ed. T. L. Stoate (Bristol, 1978).

'Dover Documents', ed. J. B. Jones, *Archaeologia Cantiana* 34 (1920), 93–100.

Dudley, Edmund, *The Tree of Commonwealth*, ed. D. M. Brodie (Cambridge, 1948).

'The Dunmow Parish Accounts', ed. L. A. Majendie, *Transactions of the Essex Archaeological Society* 2 (1863), 229–37.

The Durham Household Book, ed. J. Raine, SS 18 (Durham, 1844).

The Early Churchwardens' Accounts of Bishops Stortford, 1431–1558, ed. S. G. Doree, Hertfordshire RS 10 (Ware, 1994).

The Early Churchwardens' Accounts of Hampshire, ed. J. F. Williams (Winchester, 1913).

'Early Churchwardens' Accounts of Wandsworth, 1545 to 1558', ed. C. T. Davis, *Surrey Archaeological Collections* 15 (1900), 80–127.

Early Northampton Wills, ed. D. Edwards, M. Forrest, J. Minchinton, M. Shaw, B. Tyndall, and P. Wallis, Northamptonshire RS 42 (Northampton, 2005).

Edward IV's French expedition of 1475: the Leaders and their Badges being ms. 2. M. 16. College of Arms, ed. F. P. Barnard (Oxford, 1925).

The Edwardian Inventories for Bedfordshire, ed. F. C. Eeles and J. E. Brown, Alcuin Club Collection 6 (London, 1905).

The Edwardian Inventories for Buckinghamshire, ed. F. C. Eeles and J. E. Brown, Alcuin Club Collection 9 (London, 1908).

The Edwardian Inventories of Church Goods for Cornwall, ed. L. S. Snell (Exeter, 1955).

The Edwardian Inventories for the City and County of Exeter, ed. B. F. Cresswell, Alcuin Club Collections 20 (London, 1916).

The Edwardian Inventories for Huntingdonshire, ed. S. C. Lomas and T. Craib, Alcuin Club Collection 7 (London, 1906).

Elizabethan Churchwardens' Accounts, ed. J. E. Farmiloe and R. Nixseaman, Bedfordshire Historical RS 33 (Streatley, 1953).

Elizabethan Life: Wills of Essex Gentry and Merchants proved in the Prerogative Court of Canterbury, ed. F. G. Emmison (Chelmsford, 1978).

Elizabethan Life: Wills of Essex Gentry and Yeomen preserved in the Essex Record Office, ed. F. G. Emmison (Chelmsford, 1980).

Elizabethan Naval Administration, ed. C. S. Knighton and D. M. Loades, Navy Records Soc. 160 (Farnham, 2013).

'Eltham Churchwardens' Accounts', ed. A. Vallance, *Archaeologia Cantiana* 47 (1935), 71–102, 48 (1936), 120–50.

'Ely Episcopal Registers', *Ely Diocesan Remembrancer* 305 (1910), 180–2.

Emanuele Filiberto, *I diari delle campagne di Fiandra di Emanuele Filiberto, duca di Savoia*, ed. E. Brunelli and P. Egidi, Biblioteca della Società storica subalpina 112 (n.s. 21) (Turin, 1928).

Epistolae Academicae 1508–1596, ed. W. T. Mitchell, Oxford HS n.s. 26 (Oxford, 1980).

Estate Accounts of the Earls of Northumberland 1562–1637, ed. M. E. James, SS 163 (Durham, 1955).

'Extracts from the Church-wardens Accompts of the Parish of St Helen's, in Abingdon, Berkshire', ed. J. Ward, *Archaeologia* 1 (1770), 12–23.

'Extracts from the Churchwardens' Accounts of the Parish of Leverton', ed. E. Peacock, *Archaeologia* 41 (1867), 333–70.

'Extracts from Churchwardens' Books', *The East Anglian* 1–3 (1864–9).

'Extracts from the Household and Privy Purse Accounts of the Lestranges of Hunstanton, from A.D. 1519 to A.D. 1578', ed. D. Gurney, *Archaeologia* 25 (1834), 411–569.

'Extracts from Metfield Churchwardens' Account Books', ed. N. M. Bower, *Proceedings of the Suffolk Institute of Archaeology* 23 (1939), 128–47.

Extracts from the Records of the Merchant Adventurers of Newcastle-upon-Tyne, ii, ed. F. W. Dendy, SS 101 (Durham, 1899).

Extracts from Records in the possession of the Municipal Corporation of the Borough of Portsmouth, ed. R. East (Portsmouth, 1891 edn).

Faversham Tudor and Stuart Muster Rolls, ed. P. Hyde and D. Harrington, Faversham Hundred Records 3 (Folkestone, 2000).

The First and Second Prayer Books of Edward VI, ed. E. C. S. Gibson (London, 1910).

The First Book of the Churchwardens' Accounts of Heybridge, Essex (c.1509–1532), ed. W. J. Pressey (n.p., 1938).

The First Churchwardens' Book of Louth 1500–1524, ed. R. C. Dudding (Oxford, 1941).

The First English life of King Henry the Fifth written in 1513 by an anonymous author known commonly as the translator of Livius, ed. C. L. Kingsford (Oxford, 1911).

Foedera, Conventiones, Literae et cujuscunque generis Acta Publica, ed. T. Rymer, 20 vols (London, 1704–35).

Fragments inédits de Romboudt de Doppere, ed. H. Dussart (Bruges, 1892).

The German Peasant's War: A History in Documents, ed. T. Scott and R. W. Scribner (Atlantic Highlands NJ, 1991).

The Great Chronicle of London, ed. A. H. Thomas and I. D. Thornley (London, 1938).

'Great Hallingbury Churchwardens' Accounts, 1526 to 1634', *Transactions of the Essex Archaeological Society* 23 (1942–5), 98–115.

The Great Wardrobe Accounts of Henry VII and Henry VIII, ed. M. Hayward, London RS 47 (Woodbridge, 2012).

Great Yarmouth Assembly Minutes 1538–1545, ed. P. Rutledge, Norfolk RS 39 (Norwich, 1970).

Gruffudd, Elis, 'Suffolk's Expedition to Montdider 1523', ed. M. B. Davies, *Fouad I University Bulletin of Faculty of Arts* 7 (1944), 33–43.

Gruffudd, Elis, 'The "Enterprises" of Paris and Boulogne, 1544', ed. M. B. Davies, *Fouad I University Bulletin of Faculty of Arts* 11 (1949), 37–95.

Gruffudd, Elis, 'Boulogne and Calais from 1545 to 1550', ed. M. B. Davies, *Fouad I University Bulletin of Faculty of Arts* 12 (1950), 1–90.

'Guild of St Peter in Bardwell', ed. F. E. Warren, *Proceedings of the Suffolk Institute of Archaeology* 11 (1901–3), 81–133.

Guild Stewards' Book of the Borough of Calne, ed. A. W. Mabbs, Wiltshire Archaeological Soc. Records Branch 7 (Devizes, 1953).

Guildford Borough Records 1514–1546, ed. E. M. Dance, Surrey RS 24 (Frome, 1958).

Gwaith Gruffudd Hiraethog, ed. D. J. Bowen (Cardiff, 1990).

Gwaith Iorwerth Fynglwyd, ed. H. L. Jones and E. I. Rowlands (Cardiff, 1975).

Gwaith Lewys Daron, ed. A. C. Lake (Cardiff, 1994).

Gwaith Lewys Môn, ed. E. I. Rowlands (Cardiff, 1975).

Gwaith Lewys Morgannwg, ed. A. C. Lake (Aberystwyth, 2004).

Gwaith Siôn Ceri, ed. A. C. Lake (Aberystwyth, 1996).

Gwaith Syr Dafydd Trefor, ed. R. Ifans (Aberystwyth, 2005).

Gwaith Tudur Aled, ed. T. G. Jones (Cardiff, 1924).

'Hagworthingham Church Book', *Lincolnshire Notes and Queries* 1 (1888–9), 5–9.

Halesowen Churchwardens' Accounts (1487–1582), ed. F. Somers, Worcestershire HS 40 (London, 1952–7).

Hall, Edward, *Hall's Chronicle*, ed. H. Ellis (London, 1809).

Hamilton Papers, ed. J. Bain, 2 vols (Edinburgh, 1890–2).

Harpsfield, Nicholas, *The Life and Death of Sir Tomas Moore, Knight, sometimes Lord High Chancellor of England*, EETS 186 (London, 1932).

Henley Borough Records: Assembly Books i–iv, 1395–1543, ed. P. M. Briers, Oxfordshire RS 41 (Oxford, 1960).

Heraldic Visitation of the Northern Counties in 1530 by Thomas Tonge, Norroy King of Arms, ed. W. H. D. Longstaffe, SS 41 (Durham, 1863).

The Herald's Memoir 1486–1490: Court Ceremony, Royal Progress and Rebellion, ed. E. Cavell (Donington, 2009).

The Herefordshire Musters of 1539 and 1542, ed. M. A. Faraday (Walton-on-Thames, 2012).

Herefordshire Taxes in the Reign of Henry VIII, ed. M. A. Faraday (Hereford, 2005).

Historia et Cartularium Monasterii Sancti Petri Gloucestriae, vol iii, ed. W. H. Hart, Rolls Ser. 33 (London, 1867).

Historiae Dunelmensis Scriptores Tres, ed. J. Raine, SS 9 (London, 1839).

HMC Second Report (London, 1874).

HMC Third Report (London, 1872).

HMC Third Report Appendix iv (London, 1885).

HMC Fifth Report (London, 1876).

HMC Sixth Report (London, 1877).

HMC Seventh Report (London, 1879).

HMC Eighth Report (London, 1881).

HMC Ninth Report (London, 1883).

HMC Tenth Report (London, 1885).

Hooper, John, *Early Writings*, ed. S. Carr, Parker Soc. (Cambridge, 1843).

Household Accounts and Disbursement Books of Robert Dudley, Earl of Leicester, 1558–1561, 1584–1586, ed. S. L. Adams, CS 5th ser. 6 (Cambridge, 1995).

The Household Book (1510–1551) of Sir Edward Don: An Anglo-Welsh Knight and his Circle, ed. R. A. Griffiths, Buckinghamshire RS 33 (Aylesbury, 2004).

Household Books of John Duke of Norfolk, and Thomas earl of Surrey; temp 1481–90, ed. J. P. Collier, Roxburgh Club 61 (London, 1854).

Household and Farm Inventories in Oxfordshire, 1550–1590, ed. M. A. Havinden, Oxfordshire RS 44 (Oxford, 1965).

Illustrations of British History, ed. E. Lodge, 3 vols (London, 1838).

Illustrations of the Manners and Expenses of Antient Times in England, ed. J. Nichols (London, 1797).

In Helvetios—wider die Kuhschweizer: Fremd- und Feindbilder von den Schweizern in anti-eidgenössischen Texten aus der Zeit von 1386 bis 1532, ed. C. Sieber-Lehmann and T. Wilhelmi (Bern, 1998).

Inventaire-sommaire des archives départementales antérieures à 1790: Nord, ed. C. Dehaisnes et al., 10 vols (Lille, 1863–1906).

The Inventories of Church Goods for the Counties of York, Durham, and Northumberland, ed. W. Page, SS 97 (Durham, 1897).

Inventories of the Goods and Ornaments in the Churches of Surrey in the reign of King Edward the Sixth, ed. J. R. Daniel-Thyssen (London, 1869).

'Inventories of Norfolk Church Goods (1552)', ed. H. B. Walters, *NA* 26 (1935–7), 245–70, 27 (1938–40), 97–144, 263–89, 28 (1942–5), 89–106, 133–80, 30 (1947–52), 75–87, 160–7, 213–19, 370–8, 31 (1955–7), 200–9, 233–98, 33 (1962–5), 480–90.

Inventories of Worcestershire Landed Gentry 1537–1786, ed. M. Wanklyn, Worcestershire HS 16 (Worcester, 1998).

The Inventory of King Henry VIII, ed. A. Hawkyard, M. Hayward, P. Ward, and D. R. Starkey, 2 vols to date (London, 1998–).

Ipswich Borough Archives 1255–1835: A Catalogue, ed. D. Allen, Suffolk RS 43 (Woodbridge, 2000).

John Isham, Mercer and Merchant Adventurer, ed. G. D. Ramsay, Northamptonshire RS 21 (Gateshead, 1962).

Journals of the House of Lords, 10 vols (London, 1846 edn).

Kent Chantries, ed. A. Hussey, Kent Records 12 (Ashford, 1936).

Kingsford's Stonor Letters and Papers 1290–1483, ed. C. Carpenter (Cambridge, 1996).

Lambeth Churchwardens' Accounts 1504–1645, part i, ed. C. Drew, Surrey RS 40 (Frome, 1940).

Lancashire and Cheshire Cases in the Court of Star Chamber, ed. R. Stewart-Brown, RS for Lancashire and Cheshire 71 (Manchester, 1916).

Latimer, Hugh, *Sermons*, ed. G. E. Corrie, 2 vols, Parker Soc. (Cambridge, 1844).

Leland, John, *The Itinerary of John Leland in or about the Years 1535–1543*, ed. L. T. Smith, 5 vols (London, 1906–10).

Letters and Memorials of State, ed. A. Collins, 2 vols (London, 1746).

Letters and Papers illustrative of the Wars of the English in France during the reign of Henry the Sixth, King of England, ed. J. Stevenson, Rolls Ser. 22, 2 vols in 3 (London, 1861–4).

Letters and Papers, Foreign and Domestic, of the Reign of Henry VIII, ed. J. S. Brewer et al., 23 vols in 38 (London, 1862–1932).

Letters from Redgrave Hall: The Bacon Family 1340–1744, ed. D. MacCulloch, Suffolk RS 60 (Woodbridge, 2007).

'The Letters of William, Lord Paget of Beaudesert, 1547–1563', ed. B. L. Beer and S. M. Jack, *The Camden Miscellany* xxv, CS 4th ser. 13 (1974), 1–141.

Lettres inédites de Maximilien, duc d'Autriche, roi des Romains et empereur sur les affaires des Pays-Bas, de 1478 à 1508, ed. L. P. Gachard, 2 vols (Brussels, 1851–2).

'Leverington Parish Accounts', *Fenland Notes and Queries* 7 (1907–9), 184–90, 203–7, 247–51, 271–5, 297–302, 329–34.

The Life and Campaigns of the Black Prince, ed. R. Barber (Woodbridge, 1986 edn).

'Life of the last Fitz-Alan, Earl of Arundel', ed. J. G. Nichols, *Gentleman's Magazine* 104 (1833), 10–18, 118–24, 209–15.

Lincoln Wills, 1532–1534, ed. D. Hickman, Lincoln RS 89 (Lincoln, 2001).

The Lisle Letters, ed. M. St C. Byrne, 6 vols (Chicago IL, 1981).

Literae Cantuarienses, ed. J. B. Sheppard, 3 vols, Rolls Ser. 85 (London, 1887–9).

Liverpool Town Books, ed. J. A. Twemlow, 2 vols (London 1918–35).

Llull, R., *The Book of the Ordre of Chyvalry, translated and printed by William Caxton*, ed. A. T. P. Byles, EETS 168 (London, 1926).

'London Chronicle during the reigns of Henry the Seventh and Henry the Eighth', ed. C. Hopper, *Camden Miscellany iv*, CS 73 (1859).

London Consistory Court Wills 1492–1547, ed. I. Darlington, London RS 3 (1967).

Louth Old Corporation Records, ed. R. W. Goulding (Lincoln, 1891).

Lusy, Antoine de, *Le journal d'un bourgeois de Mons, 1505–1536*, ed. A. Louant (Brussels, 1969).

Machiavelli, Niccolò, *Le opere di Niccolò Machiavelli*, ed. P. Fanfani, L. Passerini, and G. Milanesi, 6 vols (Florence, 1873–7).

Machiavelli, Niccolò, *The Prince*, ed. G. Bull (Harmondsworth, 1961).

Machiavelli, Niccolò, *Art of War*, ed. C. Lynch (Chicago IL, 2003).

A Machiavellian Treatise by Stephen Gardiner, ed. P. S. Donaldson (Cambridge, 1975).

Mansfeld, Pierre-Ernest de, *Journal de captivité du comte Pierre-Ernest de Mansfeld, écrit au donjon de Vincennes 1552–1554*, ed. P.-E. [le prince de] Colloredo-Mannsfeld and J. Massarette (Paris, 1933).

Manship, Henry, *History of Great Yarmouth*, ed. C. J. Palmer (Great Yarmouth, 1854).

The Manuscripts of the Earl of Westmorland, Captain Stewart, Lord Stafford, Lord Muncaster, and others, HMC 10th report appendix 4 (1885).

The Manuscripts of His Grace the Duke of Portland, preserved at Welbeck Abbey, 10 vols, HMC 29 (London, 1891–1931).

The Manuscripts of His Grace, the Duke of Rutland, G.C.B., preserved at Belvoir Castle, 4 vols, HMC 24 (London, 1888–1908).

The Manuscripts of Lincoln, Bury St Edmunds, and Great Grimsby Corporations, HMC 37 (London, 1895).

The Manuscripts of Lord Middleton, preserved at Wollaton Hall, HMC 69 (London, 1911).

The Manuscripts of Rye and Hereford Corporations, HMC 13th report 4 (London, 1892).

The Manuscripts of Shrewsbury and Coventry Corporations, HMC 15th report 10 (London, 1899).

The Medieval Records of a London City Church (St Mary at Hill) AD 1420–1559, ed. H. Littlehales, 2 vols, EETS 125, 128 (London, 1904–5).

Memorials of the Abbey of St Mary of Fountains, ed. J. R. Walbran, SS 42 (Durham, 1863).

Memorials of the Goldsmiths' Company, ed. W. S. Prideaux, 2 vols (London, 1913).

Memorials of Henry the Fifth, King of England, ed. C. A. Cole, Rolls Ser. (London, 1858).

Memorials of King Henry VII, ed. J. Gairdner, Rolls Ser. 10 (London, 1858).

Men at Arms: Musters in Monmouthshire, 1539 and 1601–2, ed. T. Hopkins, South Wales RS 21 (Cwmbran, 2009).

Middlesex County Records, ed. J. C. Jeaffreson, 4 vols (London, 1886–92).

The Military Survey of 1522 for Babergh Hundred, ed. J. Pound, Suffolk RS 28 (Woodbridge, 1986).

The Military Survey of Gloucestershire, 1522, ed. R. W. Hoyle, Gloucestershire RS 6 (Stroud, 1993).

Minutes and Accounts of the Corporation of Stratford-upon-Avon and other records 1553–1620, ed. R. Savage, E. I. Fripp, and L. Fox, 5 vols to date, Dugdale Soc. 1, 3, 5, 10, 35 (Oxford, 1921–).

Molinet, Jean, *Chroniques de Jean Molinet*, ed. G. Doutrepont and O. Jodogne, 3 vols (Brussels, 1935–7).

'Molland Accounts', ed. J. B. Phear, *Reports and Transactions of the Devonshire Association* 35 (1903), 198–238.

Monastic Chancery Proceedings (Yorkshire), ed. J. S. Purvis, YASRS 88 (Wakefield, 1934).

More, Thomas, *Utopia*, ed. D. Baker-Smith (London, 2012).

'A Muster of the Fencible Inhabitants of Newcastle-upon-Tyne in the year 1539', ed. G. B. Richardson, *Archaeologia Aeliana* 4 (1855),119–40.

'Muster Roll, 1539', *Collections for the History of Staffordshire* n.s. 4 (1901), 214–57, n.s. 5 (1902), 233–324, n.s. 6 (1903), 61–88.

'Musters in Claro Wapentake, 1535', ed. W. P. Baildon, *Miscellanea v*, Thoresby Soc. 15 (Leeds, 1909), 111–21.

'Musters for Northumberland in 1538', ed. J. Hodgson, *Archaeologia Aeliana* 4 (1855), 157–206.

'Musters in Skyrack Wapentake, 1539', ed. W. P. Baildon, *Miscellanea ii*, Thoresby Soc. 4 (Leeds, 1893), 245–60.

'Musters in Skyrack Wapentake, 1539, parts ii and iii', ed. W. P. Baildon, *Miscellanea iii*, Thoresby Soc. 9 (Leeds, 1899), 99–111, 299–310.

The Musters Return for Divers Hundreds in the County of Norfolk, 1569, 1572, 1574 and 1577, ed. M. A. Farrow, H. L. Bradfer-Lawrence, and P. Millican, 2 vols, Norfolk RS 6–7 (Norwich, 1935–6).

The Navy of Edward VI and Mary I, ed. C. S. Knighton and D. M. Loades, Navy Records Soc. 157 (Farnham, 2011).

North Country Wills, ed. J. W. Clay, 2 vols, SS 116, 121 (Durham, 1908–12).

North Wiltshire Musters, anno 30 Henry VIII, ed. T. Phillipps (London, 1834).

The Norwich Census of the Poor 1570, ed. J. F. Pound, Norfolk RS 40 (Norwich, 1971).

'Notes from the Records of Hawkhurst Church', ed. W. J. Lightfoot, *Archaeologia Cantiana* 5 (1863), 55–86.

'Notes from the Records of Smarden Church', ed. F. Haslewood, *Archaeologia Cantiana* 9 (1874), 224–35.

Nowell, A., *A Catechism written in Latin by Alexander Nowell, Dean of St Paul's*, ed. G. E. Corrie, Parker Soc. (Cambridge, 1853).

'On the Churchwardens' Accounts of the Parish of Stratton, in the county of Cornwall', ed. E. Peacock, *Archaeologia* 46 (1880), 195–236.

'On the Medieval Parish Records of the Church of St Nicholas, Bristol', ed. E. G. C. F. Atchley, *Transactions of the St Paul's Ecclesiological Society* 6 (190-6-10), 35–67.

'On the parish of St Peter Cheap, in the city of London, from 1392 to 1633', ed. W. S. Simpson, *Journal of the Archaeological Association* 24 (1868), 248–68.

The Overseas Trade of London: Exchequer Customs Accounts 1480–1, ed. H. S. Cobb, London RS 27 (London, 1990).

The Oxfordshire Muster Rolls, 1539, 1542, 1569, ed. P. C. Beauchamp, Oxfordshire RS 60 (Oxford, 1996).

Papers of Nathaniel Bacon of Stiffkey, ed. A. Hassell Smith, 3 vols (Norwich, 1979–90).

The Parliament Rolls of Medieval England, 1275–1504, ed. C. Given-Wilson (Woodbridge and London, 2005).

The Paston Letters, 1422–1509 AD, ed. J. A. Gairdner, 4 vols (Edinburgh, 1910).

Paston Letters and Papers of the Fifteenth Century, ed. N. Davis, R. Beadle, and C. Richmond, 3 vols (Oxford, 1971–2005).

Patten, William, 'The Expedition into Scotland', in *Tudor Tracts*, ed. A. F. Pollard (Westminster, 1903), 53–157.

Peterborough Local Administration… Churchwardens' Accounts 1467–1573, ed. W. T. Mellows, Northamptonshire RS 9 (Kettering, 1939).

Peterborough Local Administration: The Foundation of Peterborough Cathedral AD 1541, ed. W. T. Mellows, Northamptonshire RS 13 (Kettering, 1941).

Peterborough Local Administration: The Last Days of Peterborough Monastery, ed. W. T. Mellows, Northamptonshire RS 12 (Kettering, 1947).

Pisan, Christine de, trans. William Caxton, *The Book of Fayttes of Armes and of Chyvalrye*, ed. A. T. P. Byles, EETS 189 (London, 1932).

The Port and Trade of Elizabethan London: Documents, ed. B. Dietz, London RS 8 (London, 1972).

The Pre-Reformation Records of All Saints' Bristol, ed. C. Burgess, 3 vols, Bristol RS 46, 53, 56 (Bristol, 1995–2004).

The Priory of Hexham, its Chronicles, Endowments and Annals, ed. J. Raine, 2 vols, SS 44, 46 (Durham, 1864–5).

'Probate Inventories of Worcester Tradesmen, 1545–1614', ed. A. D. Dyer, *Miscellany II*, Worcestershire HS n.s. 5 (Worcester, 1968).

Proceedings in the Parliaments of Elizabeth I, ed. T. E. Hartley, 3 vols (Leicester, 1981–95).

Reading Records: Diary of the Corporation, ed. J. M. Guilding, 4 vols (London, 1892–6).

Records of the Borough of Leicester, ed. M. Bateson et al., 7 vols (London, 1899–1974).

Records of the Borough of Northampton, ed. C. A. Markham and J. C. Cox, 2 vols (London, 1898).

Records of Bristol Cathedral, ed. J. Bettey, Bristol RS 59 (Bristol, 2007).

The Records of the Burgery of Sheffield, commonly called the Town Trust, ed. J. D. Leader (London, 1897).

Records of Chippenham, ed. F. H. Goldney (London, 1889).

Records of the City of Norwich, ed. W. Hudson and J. C. Tingey, 2 vols (Norwich, 1906–10).

Records of Early English Drama: Coventry, ed. R. W. Ingram (Manchester, 1981).

Records of Early English Drama: Shropshire, ed. J. A. B. Somerset, 2 vols (Toronto, 1994).

Records of Early English Drama: York, ed. A. F. Johnston and M. Rogerson, 2 vols (Manchester, 1979).

The Records of the Honourable Society of Lincoln's Inn: The Black Books, ed. W. P. Baildon and R. Roxburgh, 5 vols (London, 1897–1968).

Records of Lydd, ed. A. Finn (Ashford, 1911).

Records of Maidstone, being selections from the documents in the possession of the Corporation (Maidstone, 1926).

Records of Rowington, volume ii, ed. J. W. Ryland (Oxford, 1922).

The Records of Rye Corporation: A Catalogue, ed. R. F. Dell (Lewes, 1962).

Records of the Skinners of London, Edward I to James I, ed. J. J. Lambert (London, 1933).

Records of the Worshipful Company of Carpenters, 6 vols (Oxford, 1913–39).

The Red Paper Book of Colchester, ed. W. G. Benham (Colchester, 1902).

The Register or Chronicle of Butley Priory, ed. A. G. Dickens (Winchester, 1951).

The Register of the Fraternity or Guild of the Holy and Undivided Trinity and Blessed Virgin Mary in the Parish Church of Luton, in the County of Bedford, from AD MCCCCLXXV to MVCXLVI, ed. H. Gough (London, 1906).

Register of the Freemen of the City of York, ed. F. Collins, 2 vols, SS 96, 102 (Durham, 1897–1900).

The Register of the Priory of St Bees, ed. J. Wilson, SS 126 (Durham, 1915).

'The Register of Sir Thomas Botelar, Vicar of Much Wenlock', *Transactions of the Shropshire Archaeological and Natural History Society* 6 (1883), 93–132.

The Register of Thetford Priory, ed. D. Dymond, 2 vols, Norfolk RS 59–60 (Norwich, 1995–6).

The Register of Thomas Rotherham, Archbishop of York, 1480–1500, vol I, ed. E. E. Barker, Canterbury and York Soc. 69 (Torquay, 1976).

Registra Johannis Whethamstede, Willelmi Albon et Willelmi Walingforde, Abbatum Monasterii Sancti Albani, ed. H. T. Riley, Rolls Ser. (London, 1873).

Registrum Annalium Collegii Mertonensis 1483–1521, ed. H. E. Salter, Oxford HS 76 (Oxford, 1923).

The Reign of Henry VII from Contemporary Sources, ed. A. F. Pollard, 3 vols (London, 1915).

Relations des ambassadeurs vénitiens sur les affaires de France au XVIe siècle, ed. N. Tommaseo, 2 vols (Paris, 1838).

Report on Manuscripts in Various Collections, 8 vols, HMC 55 (London, 1901–13).

Report on Manuscripts in the Welsh Language, 2 vols, HMC 48 (London, 1898–1910).

Report on the Manuscripts of the Corporation of Beverley, HMC 54 (London, 1900).

Report on the Manuscripts of the Duke of Buccleuch and Queensberry...preserved at Montagu House, Whitehall, 3 vols, HMC 45 (London, 1899–1926).

Report on the Manuscripts of the late Reginald Rawdon Hastings, Esq., 4 vols, HMC 78 (London, 1928–47).

Report on the Records of the City of Exeter, HMC 73 (London, 1916).

Reprint of the Barnstaple Records, ed. J. R. Chanter and T. Wainwright, 2 vols (Barnstaple, 1900).

Rites of Durham, ed. J. T. Fowler, SS 107 (Durham, 1903).

St Albans Wills 1471–1500, ed. S. Flood, Hertfordshire RS 9 (Hitchin, 1993).

St Martin-in-the-Fields: The Accounts of the Churchwardens 1525–1603, ed. J. V. Kitto (London, 1901).

Schaumburg, Wilwolt von, *Die Geschichten und Taten Wilwolts von Schaumburg*, ed. A. Von Keller, Bibliothek des Litterarischen Vereins in Stuttgart, 50 (Stuttgart, 1859).

The Second Book of the Churchwardens' Accounts of Heybridge, Essex, ed. W. J. Pressey (n.p., 1936).

The Second Book of the Travels of Nicander Nucius, of Corcyra, ed. J. A. Cramer, CS 17 (London, 1841).

Select Cases before the King's Council in the Star Chamber, ii, ed. I. S. Leadam, Selden Soc. 25 (London, 1911).

Select Cases in the Council of Henry VII, ed. C. G. Bayne and W. H. Dunham, Selden Soc. 75 (London, 1958).

'Select Documents for the Medieval Borough of Burton-upon-Trent', ed. N. J. Tringham, *A Medieval Miscellany*, Collections for the History of Staffordshire, 4th ser. 20 (n.p., 2004).

Selections from the Municipal Chronicles of the Borough of Abingdon, ed. B. Challenor (Abingdon, 1898).

Selections from the Records of City of Oxford, ed. W. H. Turner (Oxford, 1880).

'Sir John Daunce's Accounts of Money received from Treasurer of King's Chamber temp. Henry VIII', ed. C. T. Martin, *Archaeologia* 47/2 (1883), 295–336.

Somerset Wills, ed. M. Siraut, Somerset RS 89 (Taunton, 2003).

Somerset Wills II, ed. A. J. Webb, Somerset RS 94 (Taunton, 2008).

South Newington Churchwardens' Accounts 1553–1684, ed. E. R. C. Brinkworth, Banbury HS 6 (Banbury, 1964).

Southampton Probate Inventories, 1447–1575, ed. E. Roberts and K. Parker, 2 vols, Southampton RS 34–5 (Southampton, 1992).

'Stanford Churchwardens' Accounts (1552–1602)', ed. W. Haines, *The Antiquary* 17 (1888), 70–2, 117–20, 168–72.

Star Chamber Suits of John and Thomas Warneford, ed. F. E. Warneford, Wiltshire RS 48 (Trowbridge, 1993).

State Papers, King Henry the Eighth, 5 vols in 11 (London, 1830–52).

Stow, John, *A Survey of London*, ed. C. L. Kingsford, 2nd edn, 2 vols (Oxford, 1971).

Stratford-upon-Avon Inventories I, 1538–1625, ed. J. Jones, Dugdale Soc. 39 (Stratford-upon-Avon, 2002).

Surquet, Jean, 'Mémoires en forme de chronique, ou histoire des guerres et troubles de Flandre', in *Corpus chronicorum Flandriae. Vol 4*, ed. J. J. de Smet, CRH (Brussels, 1865).

Surrey Musters (taken from the Loseley MSS), Surrey RS 3 (London, 1914–19).

The Survey of Cornwall by Richard Carew, ed. J. Chynoweth, N. Orme, and A. Walsham, Devon and Cornwall RS n.s. 47 (Exeter, 2004).

'Survey, temp. Phil. & Mar. of Various estates late belonging to the Earl of Devon', *Topographer and Genealogist*, 1 (1846), 43–58.

Sussex Coroners' Inquests 1485–1558, ed. R. F. Hunnisett, Sussex RS 74 (Lewes, 1985).

Swaledale Wills and Inventories 1522–1600, ed. E. K. Berry, YASRS 152 (Leeds, 1998).

Testamenta Eboracensia, ed. J. Raine and J. W. Clay, 6 vols, SS 4, 30, 45, 53, 79, 106 (London, 1836–1902).

'Testamenta Leodiensia', ed. W. Brigg, *Miscellanea ii*, Thoresby Soc. 4 (Leeds, 1892–5).

'Testamenta Leodiensia', ed. G. D. Lumb, *Miscellanea iii*, Thoresby Soc. 9 (Leeds, 1897–9).

Testamenta Vetusta, ed. N. H. Nicolas, 2 vols (London, 1826).

Thieulaine, Jean, 'Un livre de raison en Artois (XVIe siècle). Extraits historiques', ed. X. de Gorguette d'Argoeuves, *Mémoires de la Société des antiquaires de La Morinie* 21 (1881), 141–99.

Thomas, William, *The Pilgrim: A Dialogue on the Life and Actions of King Henry the Eighth*, ed. J. A. Froude (London, 1861).

Three Fifteenth-Century Chronicles, ed. J. Gairdner, CS n.s. 28 (London, 1880).

The Town Book of Lewes, 1542–1701, ed. L. F. Salzman, Sussex RS 48 (Lewes, 1946).

The Transcript of the Churchwardens' Accounts of the Parish of Tilney All Saints, Norfolk, 1443 to 1589, ed. A. D. Stallard (London, 1922).

The Travel Journal of Antonio de Beatis. Germany, Switzerland, the Low Countries, France and Italy, 1517–1518, ed. J. R. Hale and J. M. A. Lindon, Hakluyt Soc. 2nd ser. 150 (London, 1979).

'The Travels and Life of Sir Thomas Hoby, Knight', ed. E. Powell, *Camden Miscellany x*, CS 3rd ser. 4 (1902).

Trevelyan Papers, Part III, ed. W. C. Trevelyan and C. E. Trevelyan, CS 105 (London, 1872).

Troubles connected with the Prayer Book of 1549, ed. N. Pocock, CS n.s. 37 (London, 1884).

Tudor Churchwardens' Accounts, ed. A. Palmer, Hertfordshire RS 1 (Braughing, 1985).

Tudor Economic Documents, ed. R. H. Tawney and E. E. Power, 3 vols (London, 1924).

Tudor Royal Proclamations, ed. P. L. Hughes and J. F. Larkin, 3 vols (New Haven CT and London, 1964).

'Turvey Churchwarden's Accounts, 1551–1552', in *Hundreds, Manors, Parishes and the Church*, ed. J. S. Thomson, Bedfordshire Historical RS 69 (Bedford, 1990), 170–4.

'Two London Chronicles', ed. C. L. Kingsford, *Camden Miscellany XII*, CS 3rd ser. 18 (London, 1910).

Vergil, Polydore, *The Anglica Historia of Polydore Vergil A.D. 1485–1537*, ed. D. Hay, CS 3rd ser. 74 (London, 1950).

The Visitation of Norfolk in the Year 1563, ed. G. H. Dashwood and E. Bulwer Lytton, 2 vols (Norwich, 1878–95).

Visitations of the North, ed. C. H. Hunter Blair and F. W. Dendy, 4 vols, SS 122, 133, 144, 146 (Durham, 1912–32).

A Volume of English Miscellanies illustrating the History and Language of the Northern Counties of England, ed. J. Raine, SS 85 (Durham, 1890).

Vowell, alias Hooker, J., *Description of the Citie of Excester*, 3 parts, Devon and Cornwall RS 12 (Exeter, 1919–47).

Walberswick Churchwardens' Accounts AD 1450–1499, ed. R. W. M. Lewis (London, 1947).

'Wandsworth Churchwardens' Accounts from 1558 to 1573', ed. C. T. Davis, *Surrey Archaeological Collections* 17 (1902), 135–75.

Wardens' Accounts of the Worshipful Company of Founders of the City of London 1497–1681, ed. G. Parsloe (London, 1964).

William Browne's Town: Stamford Hall Book 1465–1492, ed. A. Rogers (Stamford, 2005).

'Willoughby Letters of the First Half of the Sixteenth Century', ed. M. A. Welch, *Nottinghamshire Miscellany no. 4*, Thoroton Soc. Record Ser. 24 (Nottingham, 1967).

Winchelsea Corporation Records: A Catalogue, ed. R. F. Dell (Lewes, 1963).

'Winterslow Church Reckonings, 1542–1661', ed. W. Symonds, *Wiltshire Archaeological and Natural History Magazine* 36 (1909–10), 27–49.

'Wivenhoe Records', ed. G. M. Benton, *Essex Review* 37 (1928), 156–69.

Worcestershire Taxes in the 1520s, ed. M. A. Faraday, Worcestershire HS n.s. 19 (Worcester, 2003).

Worcestre, William, *The Boke of Noblesse addressed to King Edward IV on his Invasion of France in 1475*, ed. J. G. Nichols (London, 1860).

York City Chamberlains' Account Rolls 1396–1500, ed. R. B. Dobson, SS 192 (Gateshead, 1980).

York Civic Records, ed. A. Raine, 8 vols, YASRS, 98, 103, 106, 108, 110, 112, 115, 119 (Wakefield, 1939–53).

Yorkshire Deeds vol iii, ed. W. Brown, YASRS 63 (Wakefield, 1922).

Yorkshire Star Chamber Proceedings, ed. W. Brown et al., 4 vols, YASRS 41, 45, 51, 70 (Wakefield, 1909–27).

SECONDARY SOURCES

Adams, A., *The History of the Worshipful Company of Blacksmiths from early times until the year 1641* (London, 1937).

Adams, R. P., *The Better Part of Valor: More, Erasmus, Colet and Vives on Humanism, War and Peace, 1496–1535* (Seattle WA, 1962).

Adams, S. L., 'The Dudley Clientele, 1553–1563', in G. W. Bernard (ed.), *The Tudor Nobility* (Manchester, 1992), 241–65.

Adams, S. L., 'The English Military Clientele, 1542–1618', in C. Giry-Deloison and R. Mettam (eds), *Patronages et clientélismes 1550–1750 (France, Angleterre, Espagne, Italie)* (Villeneuve d'Ascq, 1995), 217–27.

Adams, S. L., 'A Puritan Crusade? The Composition of the Earl of Leicester's Expedition to the Netherlands, 1585–1586', in his *Leicester and the Court: Essays on Elizabethan Politics* (Manchester, 2002), 176–95.

Adams, S. L. and Gehring, D. S., 'Elizabeth I's Former Tutor Reports on the Parliament of 1559: Johannes Spithovius to the Chancellor of Denmark, 27 February 1559', *EHR* 128 (2013), 35–54.

Airs, M., *The Tudor and Jacobean Country House: A Building History* (Stroud, 1995).

Allen, M., 'The Volume of the English Currency, 1158–1470', *EcHR* n.s. 54 (2001), 595–611.

Allmand, C., *The Hundred Years War* (Cambridge, 1988).

Allmand, C., *The De Re Militari of Vegetius: The Reception, Transmission and Legacy of a Roman Text in the Middle Ages* (Cambridge, 2011).

Alsop, J. D., 'Parliament and Taxation', in D. M. Dean and N. L. Jones (eds), *The Parliaments of Elizabethan England* (Oxford, 1990), 91–116.

Alsop, J. D., 'A Regime at Sea: The Navy and the 1553 Succession Crisis', *Albion* 24 (1992), 577–90.

Amussen, S. D., 'Punishment, Discipline, and Power: The Social Meanings of Violence in Early Modern England', *Journal of British Studies* 34 (1995), 1–34.

Andrews, K. R., *Elizabethan Privateering: English Privateering during the Spanish War, 1585–1603* (Cambridge, 1964).

Anglin, J. P., 'The Schools of Defense in Elizabethan London', *Renaissance Quarterly* 37 (1984), 393–410.

Anglo, S., 'The "British History" in Early Tudor Propaganda', *Bulletin of the John Rylands Library* 44 (1961), 17–48.

Anglo, S., *The Martial Arts of Renaissance Europe* (New Haven CT and London, 2000).

Anscombe, A., 'Prégent de Bidoux's Raid in Sussex in 1514 and the Cotton MS. Augustus I(i), 18', *TRHS* 3rd ser. 8 (1914), 103–11.

Appleby, J. C., *Under the Bloody Flag: Pirates of the Tudor Age* (Stroud, 2009).

Appleby, J. C., *Women and English Piracy, 1540–1720: Partners and Victims of Crime* (Woodbridge, 2013).

Archer, I. W., 'The Burden of Taxation on Sixteenth-Century London', *HJ* 44 (2001), 599–627.

Arfaioli, M., *The Black Bands of Giovanni: Infantry and Diplomacy during the Italian Wars* (Pisa, 2005).

Armitage, D., *The Ideological Origins of the British Empire* (Cambridge, 2000).

Armstrong, J. W., 'Local Society and the Defence of the English Frontier in Fifteenth-Century Scotland: The War Measures of 1482', *Florilegium* 25 (2008), 127–49.

Arnold, T. F., *The Renaissance at War* (London, 2001).

Arthurson, I., 'The King's Voyage into Scotland: The War that Never Was', in D. Williams (ed.), *England in the Fifteenth Century* (Woodbridge, 1987), 1–22.

Arthurson, I., *The Perkin Warbeck Conspiracy 1491–1499* (Stroud, 1994).

Awty, B., 'Iron and Brass Ware in East Sussex in the 1540s', *Sussex Archaeological Collections* 144 (2006), 215–19.

Awty, B. and Whittick, C., 'The Lordship of Canterbury, Iron-Founding at Buxted, and the Continental Antecedents of Cannon-Founding in the Weald', *Sussex Archaeological Collections* 140 (2002), 71–81.

Ayton, A., 'Armies and Military Communities in Fourteenth-Century England', in P. R. Coss and C. Tyerman (eds), *Soldiers, Nobles and Gentlemen: Essays in Honour of Maurice Keen* (Woodbridge, 2009), 215–39.

Baes, C., 'Un épisode de la querelle Habsburg-Valois: la campagne de Henri II aux Pays-Bas en 1554', *Revue belge de Philologie et d'Histoire* 73 (1995), 319–41.

Barfield, S., *Thatcham, Berks, and its Manors*, 2 vols (Oxford and London, 1901).

Barrington, R., 'A Venetian Secretary in England: An Unpublished Diplomatic Report in the Biblioteca Marciana, Venice', *HR* 70 (1997), 170–81.

Baumann, R., *Das Söldnerwesen im 16. Jahrhundert im bayerischen und süddeutschen Beispiel. Eine gesellschaftsgeschichtliche Untersuchung*, Miscellanea Bavarica Monacensia 79 (Munich, 1978).

Baumann, R., *Georg von Frundsberg, der Vater der Landsknechte und Feldhauptmann von Tirol: Eine gesellschaftsgeschichtliche Biographie* (Munich, 1984).

Baumann, R., *Landsknechte. Ihre Geschichte und Kultur vom späten Mittelalter bis zum Dreißigjährigen Krieg* (Munich, 1994).

Bean, J. M. W., *From Lord to Patron: Lordship in Late Medieval England* (Manchester, 1989).

Bean, R., 'War and the Birth of the Nation State', *Journal of Economic History* 33 (1973), 203–21.

Beaven, A. P., *The Aldermen of the City of London: Temp. Henry III—1912*, 2 vols (London, 1908–13).

Bei der Wieden, B., 'Niederdeutsche Söldner vor dem Dreißigjährigen Krieg. Geistige und mentale Grenzen eines sozialen Raums', in B. R. Kroener and R. Pröve (eds), *Krieg und Frieden. Militär und Gesellschaft in der Frühen Neuzeit* (Paderborn, 1996), 85–107.

Beier, A. L., *Masterless Men: The Vagrancy Problem in England 1560–1640* (London, 1985).

Bell, A. R., Curry, A., King, A., and Simpkin, D., *The Soldier in Later Medieval England* (Oxford, 2013).

Bellis, J., *The Hundred Years War in Literature, 1337–1600* (Woodbridge, 2016).

Bennett, M., 'Henry VII and the Northern Rising of 1489', *EHR* 105 (1990), 34–59.

Bernard, G. W., *The Power of the Early Tudor Nobility: A Study of the Fourth and Fifth Earls of Shrewsbury* (Brighton, 1985).

Bernard, G. W., *War, Taxation and Rebellion in Tudor England: Henry VIII, Wolsey and the Amicable Grant of 1525* (Brighton, 1985).

Bernard, G. W. and Hoyle, R. W., 'The Instructions for the Levying of the Amicable Grant, March 1525', *HR* 67 (1994), 190–202.

Bewes, W. A., *Church Briefs* (London, 1896).

Bindoff, S. T., *History of Parliament: The House of Commons 1509–1558*, 3 vols (London, 1982).

Blakemore, H. L., *A Dictionary of London Gunmakers 1350–1850* (Oxford, 1986).

Blakemore, H. L., *Gunmakers of London Supplement 1350–1850* (Bloomfield, 1999).

Blomefield, F., *An Essay towards a Topographical History of the County of Norfolk*, 11 vols (London, 1805–10).

Boffey J. and Edwards, A. S. G., 'Literary Texts', in L. Hellinga and J. B. Trapp (eds), *The Cambridge History of the Book in Britain, volume III, 1400–1557* (Cambridge, 1999), 555–75.

Bourke, J., *An Intimate History of Killing: Face-to-Face Killing in Twentieth-Century Warfare* (London, 1999).

Bowen, D. J., 'Y canu i deulu'r Penrhyn', *Dwned* 9 (2003), 94–9.

Boyle, A., 'Hans Eworth's Portrait of the Earl of Arundel and the Politics of 1549–50', *EHR* 117 (2002), 25–47.

Boyle, J. R., *The Early History of the Town and Port of Hedon* (Hull, York, and London, 1895).

Boynton, L., 'The Tudor Provost-Marshal', *EHR* 77 (1962), 437–55.

Boynton, L., *The Elizabethan Militia 1558–1638* (London, 1967).

Boys, W., *Collections for a History of Sandwich* (Canterbury, 1792).

Bracewell, C. W., *The Uskoks of Senj: Piracy, Banditry, and Holy War in the Sixteenth-Century Adriatic* (Ithaca NY, 1992).

Braddick, M. J., *State Formation in Early Modern England c.1550–1700* (Cambridge, 2000).

Brady, C., *The Chief Governors: The Rise and Fall of Reform Government in Tudor Ireland, 1536–1588* (Cambridge, 1994).

Brady, C., 'The Captains' Games: Army and Society in Elizabethan Ireland', in T. Bartlett and K. Jeffery (eds), *A Military History of Ireland* (Cambridge, 1996), 136–59.

Brady, T. A., *Turning Swiss: Cities and Empire 1450–1550* (Cambridge, 1985).

Brandi, K., *The Emperor Charles V* (London, 1965 edn).

Braudel, F., *The Mediterranean and the Mediterranean World in the Age of Philip II*, 2 vols (London, 1973).

Brewer, J., *The Sinews of Power: War, Money and the English State, 1688–1783* (London, 1989).

Bridbury, A. R., 'The Hundred Years War: Costs and Profits', in D. C. Coleman and A. H. John (eds), *Trade, Government and Economy in Pre-Industrial England: Essays presented to F. J. Fisher* (London, 1976), 80–95.

Brigden, S. E., *London and the Reformation* (Oxford, 1989).

Brightman, F. E., *The English Rite*, 2 vols (London, 1915).

Broadway, J., 'No Historie so Meete': Gentry Culture and the Development of Local History in Elizabethan and Early Stuart England* (Manchester, 2006).

Bruaene, A.-L. van, *De Gentse memorieboeken als spiegel van stedelijk historisch bewustzijn (14de tot 16 de eeuw)*, Verhandelingen van de Maatschappij voor Geschiedenis en Oudheidkunde te Gent 22 (Ghent, 1998).

Budgen, W., 'Guns bought for Eastbourne, 1550', *Sussex Notes and Queries* 1 (1926–7), 146–7.

Budgen, W., 'Orders as to Beacons, 1546', *Sussex Notes and Queries* 1 (1926–7), 82–4, 116–18.

Burgess, C., 'Pre-Reformation Churchwardens' Accounts and Parish Government: Lessons from London and Bristol', *EHR* 117 (2002), 306–32.

Burke, P., *The French Historical Revolution: The Annales School 1929–89* (Oxford, 1990).

Burschel, P., *Söldner im Nordwestdeutschland des 16. und 17. Jahrhunderts: Sozialgeschichtliche Studien*, Veröffentlichungen des Max-Planck-Instituts für Geschichte, 113 (Göttingen, 1994).

Bush, M. L., *The Government Policy of Protector Somerset* (London, 1975).

Bush, M. L., '"Enhancements and Importunate Charges": An Analysis of the Tax Complaints of October 1536', *Albion* 22 (1990), 403–19.

Bush, M. L., 'Tax Reform and Rebellion in Early Tudor England', *History* 76 (1991), 379–400.

Bush, M. L., *The Pilgrimage of Grace: A Study of the Rebel Armies of October 1536* (Manchester, 1996).

Calabria, A., *The Cost of Empire: The Finances of the Kingdom of Naples in the Time of Spanish Rule* (Cambridge, 1991).

Cameron, A., 'The Giving of Livery and Retaining in Henry VII's Reign', *Renaissance and Modern Studies* 18 (1974), 17–35.

Capp, B. S., *Astrology and the Popular Press: English Almanacs, 1500–1800* (London, 1979).

Capp, B. S., 'Long Meg of Westminster: A Mystery Solved', *Notes and Queries* 45 (1998), 302–4.

Carley, J. P., 'Presentation Manuscripts from the Collection of Henry VIII: The Case of Henry Parker, Lord Morley', in R. C. Alston (ed.), *Order and Connexion* (Cambridge, 1997), 159–76.

Carlton, C., *This Seat of Mars: War and the British Isles, 1485–1746* (New Haven CT and London, 2011).

Carroll, S., *Noble Power during the Wars of Religion: The Guise Affinity and the Catholic Cause in Normandy* (Cambridge, 1998).

Caruana, A. B., *The History of English Sea Ordnance 1523–1875: Volume 1—The Age of Evolution 1523–1715* (Rotherfield, 1994).

A Catalogue of Manuscripts in the College of Arms: Collections, i, ed. L. Campbell and F. Steer (London, 1988).

Challis, C. E., *The Tudor Coinage* (Manchester, 1978).

Chambers, D. S., 'Francesco II Gonzaga, marquis of Mantua, "Liberator of Italy"', in D. Abulafia (ed.), *The French Descent into Renaissance Italy 1494–95: Antecedents and Effects* (Aldershot, 1995), 217–29.

Chambers, D. S., *Popes, Cardinals and War: The Military Church in Renaissance and Early Modern Europe* (London, 2006).

Charles, R. A., 'Noddwyr y beirdd yn sir y Fflint', *Llên Cymru* 12–13 (1972–81), 3–44.

Checa Cremades, F., *Carlos V: La imagen del poder en el renacimiento* (Madrid, 1999).

Chevalier, B., *Les bonnes villes de France du XIVe au XVIe siècle* (Paris, 1982).

Childs, W. R., 'Fishing and Fisheries in the Middle Ages: The Eastern Fisheries', in D. J. Starkey, C. Reid, and N. Ashcroft (eds), *England's Sea Fisheries: The Commercial Fisheries of England and Wales since 1300* (London, 2000), 19–23.

Childs, W. R., 'The Internal and International Fish Trades of Medieval England and Wales: Control, Conflict and International Trade', in D. J. Starkey, C. Reid, and N. Ashcroft (eds), *England's Sea Fisheries: The Commercial Fisheries of England and Wales since 1300* (London, 2000), 32–5.

Citino, R. M., 'Military Histories Old and New: A Reintroduction', *American Historical Review* 112 (2007), 1070–90.

Clark, P. and Hosking, J., *Population Estimates of English Small Towns 1550–1851* (Leicester, 1993 edn).

Clode, C. M., *Memorials of the Guild of Merchant Taylors of the Fraternity of St John the Baptist in the City of London and of its Associated Charities and Institutions* (London, 1875).

Clode, C. M., *The Early History of the Guild of Merchant Taylors of the Fraternity of St John the Baptist, London* (London, 1888).

Cokayne, G. E., *The Complete Peerage*, ed. V. Gibbs et al., 13 vols (London, 1910–59).

Collins, J. B., *Fiscal Limits of Absolutism: Direct Taxation in Early Seventeenth-Century France* (Berkeley CA, 1988).

Collins, J. M., *Martial Law and English Laws, c.1500–c.1700* (Cambridge, 2016).

Colvin, H. M. (ed.), *The History of the King's Works*, 6 vols (London, 1963–82).

Connell-Smith, G., *Forerunners of Drake: A Study of English Trade with Spain in the Early Tudor Period* (London, 1954).

Consitt, F., *The London Weavers' Company, volume I, from the Twelfth Century to the close of the Sixteenth Century* (Oxford, 1933).

Constant, J. M., 'The Protestant Nobility in France during the Wars of Religion: A Leaven of Innovation in a Traditional World', in P. Benedict, G. Marnef, H. Van Nierop, and M. Venard (eds), *Reformation, Revolt and Civil War in France and the Netherlands 1555–1585* (Amsterdam, 1999), 69–82.

Contamine, P., 'L'artillerie royale française à la veille des guerres d'Italie', *Annales de Bretagne* 71 (1964), 221–61.

Contamine, P., *Guerre, état et société à la fin du moyen âge. Études sur les armées des rois de France, 1337–1494* (Paris, 1972).

Contamine, P., 'Les industries de guerre dans la France de la Renaissance: l'exemple de l'artillerie', *Revue historique* 271 (1984), 249–80.

Contamine, P., *War in the Middle Ages* (Oxford, 1984).

Coope, R. and Smith, P., *Newstead Abbey, A Nottinghamshire Country House: Its Owners and Architectural History 1540–1931*, Thoroton Soc. Record Ser. 48 (Nottingham, 2010).

Cooper, C. H., *Annals of Cambridge*, 5 vols (Cambridge, 1842–1908).

Cooper, J. P., 'Retainers in Tudor England', in his *Land, Men, and Beliefs: Studies in Early-Modern History* (London, 1983), 78–96.

Cooper, J. P. D., *Propaganda and the Tudor State: Political Culture in the Westcountry* (Oxford, 2003).

Cornwall, J., *Revolt of the Peasantry 1549* (London, 1977).

Cornwall, J., *Wealth and Society in Early Sixteenth-Century England* (London, 1988).

Coster, W., *Kinship and Inheritance in Early Modern England: Three Yorkshire Parishes*, Borthwick papers 83 (York, 1993).

Cox, J. C. and Hope, W. H. St J., *The Chronicles of the Collegiate Church or Free Chapel of All Saints' Derby* (London, 1881).

Cozens-Hardy, B., 'Norfolk Coastal Defences in 1588', *NA* 26 (1936–8), 310–14.

Craeybeckx, J., *Un grand commerce d'importation: Les Vins de France aux anciens Pays-Bas (XIIIe–XVIe siècles)* (Paris, 1958).

Crawford, A., *A History of the Vintners' Company* (London, 1977).

Crawford, A., *Yorkist Lord: John Howard, Duke of Norfolk, c.1425–1485* (London, 2010).

Cressy, D., *Saltpeter: The Mother of Gunpowder* (Oxford, 2013).

Croenen, G., 'The Reception of Froissart's Writings in England: The Evidence of the Manuscripts', in J. Wogan-Browne (ed.), *Language and Culture in Medieval Britain: The French of England, c.1100–c1500* (Woodbridge, 2009), 409–19.

Crombie, L., *Archery and Crossbow Guilds in Medieval Flanders, 1300–1500* (Woodbridge, 2016).

Cross, C., *Urban Magistrates and Ministers: Religion in Hull and Leeds from the Reformation to the Civil War*, Borthwick papers 67 (York, 1985).

Crouzet, D., *Les guerriers de Dieu: la violence au temps des troubles de religion, vers 1525–vers 1610*, 2 vols (Seyssel, 1990).

Cruickshank, C. G., *Elizabeth's Army*, 2nd edn (Oxford, 1966).

Cruickshank, C. G., *Army Royal: Henry VIII's Invasion of France 1513* (Oxford, 1969).

Cruickshank, C. G., *The English Occupation of Tournai 1513–1519* (Oxford, 1971).

Cunningham, S., *Henry VII* (Abingdon, 2007).

Cunnington, B. H., *Some Annals of the Borough of Devizes*, 2 vols (Devizes, 1825).

Currin, J. M., 'Henry VII and the Treaty of Redon (1489): Plantagenet Ambitions and Early Tudor Foreign Policy', *History* 81 (1996), 343–58.

Currin, J. M., '"The King's Army into the Partes of Bretaigne": Henry VII and the Breton Wars, 1489–1491', *War in History* 7 (2000), 379–412.

Currin, J. M., '"To Traffic with War?" Henry VII and the French Campaign of 1492', in D. Grummitt (ed.), *The English Experience in France c.1450–1558: War, Diplomacy and Cultural Exchange* (Aldershot, 2002), 106–31.

Currin, J. M., 'England's International Relations 1485–1509: Continuities amidst Change', in S. Doran and G. Richardson (eds), *Tudor England and its Neighbours* (Basingstoke, 2005), 14–43.

Curry, A., 'English Armies in the Fifteenth Century', in A. Curry and M. Hughes (eds), *Arms, Armies and Fortifications in the Hundred Years War* (Woodbridge, 1994), 39–68.

Daniell, D., *William Tyndale: A Biography* (New Haven CT and London, 1994).

Davies, C. S. L., 'Provisions for Armies, 1509–50: A Study in the Effectiveness of Early Tudor Government', *EcHR* n.s. 17 (1964–5), 234–48.

Davies, C. S. L., 'The English People and War in the Early Sixteenth Century', in A. C. Duke and C. A. Tamse (eds), *Britain and the Netherlands, vi* (The Hague, 1977), 1–18.

Davies, C. S. L., 'England and the French War, 1557–1559', in J. Loach and R. Tittler (eds), *The Mid-Tudor Polity c.1540–1560* (London, 1980), 159–85.

Dawson, J. E. A., *The Politics of Religion in the Age of Mary, Queen of Scots: The Earl of Argyll and the Struggle for Britain and Ireland* (Cambridge, 2002).

Decavele, J. and Peteghem, P. Van, 'Ghent "Absolutely" Broken', in J. Decavele (ed.), *Ghent: In Defence of a Rebellious City* (Antwerp, 1989), 107–33.

Delaborde, J., *Gaspard de Coligny, Amiral de France*, 3 vols (Paris, 1879–82).

Desachy-Delclos, S., 'Les élites militaires en Rouergue au XVIe siècle', *Annales du Midi* 108 (1996), 9–27.

Dickin, E. P., 'Embezzled Church Goods of Essex', *Transactions of the Essex Archaeological Society*, n.s. 13 (1913–14), 157–71.

Douglas, A., 'Midsummer in Salisbury: The Tailors' Guild and Confraternity 1444–1642', *Renaissance and Reformation* 25 (1989), 35–51.

Drévillon, H., *L'individu et la guerre. Du Chevalier Bayard au Soldat Inconnu* (Paris, 2013).

Drury, J. L., 'More Stout than Wise: Tenant Right in Weardale in the Tudor Period', in D. Marcombe (ed.), *The Last Principality: Politics, Religion and Society in the Bishopric of Durham 1494–1660* (Nottingham, 1987), 71–100.

Duff, G., 'Some Early Scottish Book-Bindings and Collectors', *Scottish Historical Review* 4 (1907), 430–42.

Duffy, C., *Siege Warfare: The Fortress in the Early Modern World 1494–1660* (London, 1996 edn).

Duffy, E., *The Voices of Morebath: Reformation and Rebellion in an English Village* (New Haven CT and London, 2001).

Dunham, W. H., *Lord Hastings' Indentured Retainers 1461–83*, Transactions of the Connecticut Academy of Arts and Sciences 39 (New Haven CT, 1955).

Dunn, A., 'Inheritance and Lordship in Pre-Reformation England: George Neville, Lord Bergavenny (c.1470–1535)', *Nottingham Medieval Studies* 48 (2004), 116–40.

Dunthorne, H., *Britain and the Dutch Revolt 1560–1700* (Cambridge, 2013).

Dyer, A., 'Appendix: Ranking Lists of English Medieval Towns', in D. M. Palliser (ed.), *The Cambridge Urban History of Britain*, i: *600–1540* (Cambridge, 2000), 747–70.

Dyer, C., *An Age of Transition: Economy and Society in England in the Later Middle Ages* (Oxford, 2005).

Edelmayer, F., *Söldner und Pensionäre: das Netzwerk Phillipps II. im Heiligen Römischen Reich* (Vienna, 2002).

Edwards, D., 'The Escalation of Violence in Sixteenth-Century Ireland', in D. Edwards, P. Lenihan, and C. Tait (eds), *The Age of Atrocity: Violence and Political Conflict in Early Modern Ireland* (Dublin, 2007), 34–78.

Ellis, J., 'Archery and Social Memory in Sixteenth-Century London', *Huntington Library Quarterly* 79 (2016), 21–40.

Ellis, S. G., 'Henry VII and Ireland, 1491–1496', in J. F. Lydon (ed.), *England and Ireland in the Later Middle Ages* (Blackrock, 1981), 237–43.

Ellis, S. G., *Tudor Frontiers and Noble Power: The Making of the British State* (Oxford, 1995).

Ellis, S. G., 'The Tudors and the Origins of the Modern Irish States: A Standing Army', in T. Bartlett and K. Jeffery (eds), *A Military History of Ireland* (Cambridge, 1996), 116–35.

Ellis, S. G., *Ireland in the Age of the Tudors: English Expansion and the End of Gaelic Rule* (London, 1998).

Ellis, S. G., *Defending English Ground: War and Peace in Meath and Northumberland, 1460–1542* (Oxford, 2015).

Eltis, D., 'Towns and Defence in Later Medieval Germany', *Nottingham Medieval Studies* 33 (1989), 91–103.

Eltis, D., *The Military Revolution in Sixteenth-Century Europe* (London, 1995).

Emmison, F. G., *Tudor Secretary: Sir William Petre at Court and Home* (London, 1961).

Falls, C., *Elizabeth's Irish Wars* (London, 1950).

Finch, M. E., *The Wealth of Five Northamptonshire Families 1540–1640*, Northamptonshire RS 19 (Oxford, 1956).

Firth, C. H., 'The Ballad History of the Reigns of Henry VII and Henry VIII', *TRHS* 3rd ser. 2 (1908), 21–50.

Firth, C. H., 'The Ballad History of the Reigns of the Later Tudors', *TRHS* 3rd ser. 3 (1909), 51–124.

Firth, J. F., *Coopers Company, London: Historical Memoranda, Charters, Documents, and Extracts, from the Records of the Corporation and the Books of the Company, 1396–1858* (London, 1848).

Fissel, M. C., *English Warfare, 1511–1642* (London and New York, 2001).

Fowler, K. A., 'News from the Front: Letters and Despatches of the Fourteenth Century', in P. Contamine, C. Giry-Deloison, and M. H. Keen (eds), *Guerre et société en France, en Angleterre et en Bourgogne xive–xve siècle* (Lille, 1991), 63–92.

Fox, A., 'Rumour, News and Popular Political Opinion in Elizabethan and Early Stuart England', *HJ* 40 (1997), 597–620.

Frauenholz, E. von, *Entwicklungsgeschichte des Deutschen Heerwesens*, 2 vols in 3 (Munich, 1935–7).

Frost, R. I., *The Northern Wars: War, State and Society in Northeastern Europe, 1558–1721* (Harlow, 2000).

Fuller, T., *The Church-History of Britain; The History of the University of Cambridge; The History of Waltham-Abby* (London, 1655).

Gairdner, J., 'On a Contemporary Drawing of the Burning of Brighton in the Time of Henry VIII', *TRHS* 3rd ser. 1 (1907), 19–31.

Gardiner, J. and Allen, M. J. (eds), *Before the Mast: Life and Death Aboard the Mary Rose* (Portsmouth, 2005).

Gelabert, J., 'The Fiscal Burden', in R. Bonney (ed.), *Economic Systems and State Finance* (Oxford, 1995), 539–79.

Gillett, E. and MacMahon, K. A., *A History of Hull*, 2nd edn (Hull, 1989).

Girtin, T., *The Golden Ram: A Narrative History of the Clothworkers' Company* (London, 1958).

Glete, J., *Warfare at Sea, 1500–1650: Maritime Conflicts and the Transformation of Europe* (London, 2000).

Glete, J., *War and the State in Early Modern Europe: Spain, the Dutch Republic and Sweden as Fiscal-Military States, 1500–1660* (London, 2002).

Glover, E., *A History of the Ironmongers' Company* (London, 1991).

Glover, E., *Men of Metal: History of the Armourers and Braziers of the City of London* (London, 2008).

González de León, F., '"Doctors of the Military Discipline": Technical Expertise and the Paradigm of the Spanish Soldier in the Early Modern Period', *Sixteenth Century Journal* 27 (1996), 61–85.

Good, J., *The Cult of St George in Medieval England* (Woodbridge, 2009).

Goring, J. J., 'The General Proscription of 1522', *EHR* 86 (1971), 681–705.

Goring, J. J., 'Social Change and Military Decline in Mid-Tudor England', *History* 60 (1975), 185–97.

Goss, C. W. F., 'The Parish and Church of St Martin Outwich, Threadneedle Street', *Transactions of the London and Middlesex Archaeological Society*, n.s. 6 (1932), 1–91.

Gould, J. D., *The Great Debasement: Currency and the Economy in Mid-Tudor England* (Oxford, 1970).

Grant, A., 'Foreign Affairs under Richard III', in J. Gillingham (ed.), *Richard III: A Medieval Kingship* (London, 1993), 113–32.

Grapperhaus, F. H. M., *Alva en de tiende penning*, 2nd edn (Deventer, 1984).

Griffiths, P., *Lost Londons: Change, Crime and Control in the Capital City, 1550–1660* (Cambridge, 2008).

Griffiths, R. A., *Sir Rhys ap Thomas and his Family: A Study in the Wars of the Roses and Early Tudor Politics* (Cardiff, 1993).

Grummitt, D., *The Calais Garrison: War and Military Service in England, 1436–1558* (Woodbridge, 2008).

Gunn, S. J., 'The Regime of Charles, Duke of Suffolk, in North Wales and the Reform of Welsh Government, 1509–25', *Welsh History Review* 12 (1985), 461–94.

Gunn, S. J., 'The Duke of Suffolk's March on Paris in 1523', *EHR* 101 (1986), 596–634.

Gunn, S. J., 'The French Wars of Henry VIII', in J. Black (ed.), *The Origins of War in Early Modern Europe* (Edinburgh, 1987), 28–51.

Gunn, S. J., *Charles Brandon, Duke of Suffolk, c.1484–1545* (Oxford, 1988).

Gunn, S. J., 'The Act of Resumption of 1515', in D. T. Williams (ed.), *Early Tudor England: Proceedings of the Fourth Harlaxton Symposium* (Woodbridge, 1989), 87–106.

Gunn, S. J., 'Chivalry and Politics at the Early Tudor Court', in S. Anglo (ed.), *Chivalry in the Renaissance* (Woodbridge, 1990), 107–28.

Gunn, S. J., 'Wolsey's Foreign Policy and the Domestic Crisis of 1527–8', in S. J. Gunn and P. G. Lindley (eds), *Cardinal Wolsey: Church, State and Art* (Cambridge, 1991), 149–77.

Gunn, S. J., 'War, Dynasty and Public Opinion in Early Tudor England', in G. W. Bernard and S. J. Gunn (eds), *Authority and Consent in Tudor England: Essays presented to C. S. L. Davies* (Aldershot, 2002), 131–49.

Gunn, S. J., 'Archery Practice in Early Tudor England', *PP* 209 (2010), 53–81.

Gunn, S. J., *Henry VII's New Men and the Making of Tudor England* (Oxford, 2016).

Gunn, S. J., Grummitt, D., and Cools, H., *War, State, and Society in England and the Netherlands, 1477–1559* (Oxford, 2007).

Gunn, S. J., Grummitt, D., and Cools, H., 'War and the State in Early Modern Europe: Widening the Debate', *War in History* 15 (2008), 371–88.

Gutierrez, N. and Erler, M., 'Print into Manuscript: A Flodden Field News Pamphlet (British Library Ms Additional 29506)', *Studies in Medieval and Renaissance History* n.s. 8 (1986), 187–230.

Guy, J. A., *The Cardinal's Court: The Impact of Thomas Wolsey in Star Chamber* (Hassocks, 1977).

Haemers, J. and Verbist, B., 'Het Gentse gemeenteleger in het laatste kwart van de vijtiende eeuw: Een politieke, financiele en militaire analyse van de stadsmilitie', *Handelingen der Maatschappij voor Geschiedenis on Oudheidkunde te Gent* 62 (2008), 291–325.

Haigh, C. A., *English Reformations: Religion, Politics, and Society under the Tudors* (Oxford, 1993).

Hale, J. R., 'Sixteenth-Century Explanations of War and Violence', *PP* 51 (1971), 3–26.

Hale, J. R., 'On a Tudor Parade Ground: The Captain's Handbook of Henry Barrett 1562', in his *Renaissance War Studies* (London, 1983), 247–90.

Hale, J. R., *War and Society in Renaissance Europe, 1450–1620* (London, 1985).

Hale, J. R., *Artists and Warfare in the Renaissance* (New Haven CT and London, 1990).

Halstead, R., *Succinct Genealogies of the Noble and Ancient Houses of Alno or de Alneto etc* (London, 1685).

Hammer, P., *Elizabeth's Wars: War, Government and Society in Tudor England, 1544–1604* (Basingstoke, 2003).

Hanlon, G., *The Twilight of a Military Tradition: Italian Aristocrats and European Conflicts, 1560–1800* (London, 1998).

Harari, Y. N., *The Ultimate Experience: Battlefield Revelations and the Making of Modern War Culture, 1450–2000* (Basingstoke, 2008).

Harris, B. J., *Edward Stafford, Third Duke of Buckingham, 1478–1521* (Stanford CA, 1986).

Hasler, P. W., *The House of Commons 1558–1603*, 3 vols (London, 1981).

Hayward, M., *Rich Apparel: Clothing and the Law in Henry VIII's England* (Farnham, 2009).

Heath, B. J., *Some Account of the Worshipful Company of Grocers of the City of London*, 3rd edn (London, 1869).

Helgerson, R., *Forms of Nationhood: The Elizabethan Writing of England* (Chicago IL, 1992).

Henne, A., *Histoire du règne de Charles-Quint en Belgique*, 10 vols (Brussels, 1858–60).

Heuvel, C. van den, *'Papiere Bolwercken': De introductie van de Italiaanse stede-en vesting-bouw in de Nederlanden (1540–1609) en het gebruik van tekeningen* (Alphen aan den Rijn, 1991).

Hewerdine, A., *The Yeomen of the Guard and the Early Tudors: The Formation of a Royal Bodyguard* (London, 2012).

Hicks, M. A., 'The 1468 Statute of Livery', *HR* 64 (1991), 15–28.

Hicks, M. A., 'Lord Hastings' Indentured Retainers?', in his *Richard III and his Rivals: Magnates and their Motives in the Wars of the Roses* (London, 1991), 229–46.

Hildred, A. (ed.), *Weapons of Warre: The Armaments of the Mary Rose*, 2 vols (Portsmouth, 2011).

Hillen, H. J., *History of the Borough of King's Lynn*, 2 vols (Norwich, 1907).

Hindle, S., *The State and Social Change in Early Modern England, 1550–1640* (Basingstoke, 2000).

Hocquet, J.-C., 'Venice', in R. Bonney (ed.), *The Rise of the Fiscal State in Europe c.1200–1815* (Oxford, 1999), 381–415.

Hoop Scheffer, D. de and Klant-Vlielander Hein, A. J., *Vorstenportretten uit de eerste helft vande 16de eeuw: Houtsneden als propaganda* (Amsterdam, 1972).

Hooper, W., 'The Tudor Sumptuary Laws', *EHR* 30 (1915), 433–49.

Hope, W. H. St J., *Cowdray and Easebourne Priory* (London, 1919).

Horowitz, M. R., 'Henry Tudor's Treasure', *HR* 82 (2009), 560–79.

Horrox, R. E., *Richard III: A Study of Service* (Cambridge, 1989).

Hoskins, W. G., *The Age of Plunder: The England of Henry VIII 1500–47* (London, 1976).

Housley, N., *Religious Warfare in Europe 1400–1536* (Oxford, 2002).

Hoyle, R. W., 'Lords, Tenants and Tenant Right in the Sixteenth Century: Four Studies', *Northern History* 20 (1984), 38–63.

Hoyle, R. W., 'Thomas Master's Narrative of the Pilgrimage of Grace', *Northern History* 21 (1985), 53–79.

Hoyle, R. W., 'An Ancient and Laudable Custom: The Definition and Development of Tenant Right in North-Western England in the Sixteenth Century', *PP* 116 (1987), 24–55.

Hoyle, R. W., 'Customary Tenure on the Elizabethan Estates', in R. W. Hoyle (ed.), *The Estates of the English Crown, 1558–1640* (Cambridge, 1992), 191–203.

Hoyle, R. W., '"Shearing the Hog": The Reform of the Estates, c.1598–1640', in R. W. Hoyle (ed.), *The Estates of the English Crown, 1558–1640* (Cambridge, 1992), 204–62.

Hoyle, R. W., 'Resistance and Manipulation in Early Tudor Taxation: Some Evidence from the North', *Archives* 20 (1993), 158–76.

Hoyle, R. W., 'The Origins of the Dissolution of the Monasteries Reconsidered', *HJ* 38 (1995), 275–305.

Hoyle, R. W., 'War and Public Finance', in D. N. J. MacCulloch (ed.), *The Reign of Henry VIII: Politics, Policy and Piety* (Basingstoke, 1995), 75–99.

Hoyle, R. W., 'Taxation and the Mid-Tudor Crisis', *EcHR* n.s. 51 (1998), 649–75.

Hoyle, R. W., *The Pilgrimage of Grace and the Politics of the 1530s* (Oxford, 2001).

Hunter, J., *Hallamshire*, ed. A. Gatty (London, 1869).

Hunter, J., *South Yorkshire*, 2 vols (Wakefield, 1974 edn).

Hurren, E., 'Cultures of the Body, Medical Regimen, and Physic at the Court of Henry VIII', in T. Betteridge and S. Lipscombe (eds), *Henry VIII and the Court: Art, Politics and Performance* (Farnham, 2013), 65–89.

Ives, E. W., 'Patronage at the Court of Henry VIII: The Case of Sir Ralph Egerton of Ridley', *Bulletin of the John Rylands Library* 52 (1970), 346–74.

James, S. E., *Kateryn Parr: The Making of a Queen* (Aldershot, 1999).

Jansen, S. L., *Political Protest and Prophecy under Henry VIII* (Woodbridge, 1991).

Jenkins, R. G., 'On the Gates of Boulogne, at Hardres Court, in the parish of Upper Hardres', *AC* 4 (1861), 43–56.

Johnson, A. H., *The History of the Worshipful Company of the Drapers of London*, 5 vols (Oxford, 1914–22).

Johnson, F. R., 'Notes on English Retail Book-Prices, 1550–1640', *The Library* 5th ser. 5 (1950), 83–112.

Jones, D. W., *War and Economy in the Age of William III and Marlborough* (Oxford, 1988).

Jones, E., 'England's Icelandic Fishery in the Early Modern Period', in D. J. Starkey, C. Reid, and N. Ashcroft (eds), *England's Sea Fisheries: The Commercial Fisheries of England and Wales since 1300* (London, 2000), 105–9.

Jones, J. G., *Beirdd yr Uchelwyr a'r Gymdeithas yng Nghymru c.1536–1640* (Denbigh, 1977).

Jones, J. G., *Concepts of Order and Gentility in Wales, 1540–1640* (Llandysul, 1992).

Jones, M. K. and Underwood, M. G., *The King's Mother: Lady Margaret Beaufort Countess of Richmond and Derby* (Cambridge, 1992).

Jones, P. E., *The Butchers of London: A History of the Worshipful Company of Butchers of the City of London* (London, 1976).

Jurkowski, M., 'Parliamentary and Prerogative Taxation in the Reign of Edward IV', *Parliamentary History* 18 (1999), 271–90.

Kaptein, H., *De Hollandse textielnijverheid 1350–1600: Conjunctuur en continuïteit* (Hilversum, 1998).

Keegan, J., *The Face of Battle: A Study of Agincourt, Waterloo and the Somme* (London, 1991 edn).

Keen, M., *Origins of the English Gentleman: Heraldry, Chivalry and Gentility in Medieval England, c.1300–c.1500* (Stroud, 2002).

Kent, J. R., *The English Village Constable, 1580–1642: A Social and Administrative Study* (Oxford, 1986).

Kerridge, E., *Textile Manufactures in Early Modern England* (Manchester, 1985).

Kerry, C., *A History of the Municipal Church of St Lawrence, Reading* (Reading, 1883).

Kesselring, K. J., *Mercy and Authority in the Tudor State* (Cambridge, 2003).

Kesselring, K. J., *The Northern Rebellion of 1569: Faith, Politics, and Protest in Elizabethan England* (Basingstoke, 2007).

King, A., '"What Werre Amounteth": The Military Experience of Knights of the Shire, 1369–1389', *History* 95 (2010), 418–36.

King, A., 'The Anglo-Scottish Marches and the Perception of "The North" in Fifteenth-Century England', *Northern History* 49 (2012), 37–50.

King, P., 'Eight English Memento Mori Verses from Cadaver Tombs', *Notes and Queries* n.s. 28 (1981), 494–6.

Knecht, R. J., *Renaissance Warrior and Patron: The Reign of Francis I* (Cambridge, 1994).

Knevel, P., *Burgers in het geweer: De schutterijen in Holland, 1550–1700* (Hilversum, 1994).

Knüsel, C., 'Activity-Related Structural Change', in V. Fiorato, A. Boylston, and C. Knüsel (eds), *Blood Red Roses: The Archaeology of a Mass Grave from the Battle of Towton, AD 1461* (Oxford, 2000), 103–18.

Koenigsberger, H. G., *The Government of Sicily under Philip II of Spain: A Study in the Practice of Empire* (London, 1951).

Kowaleski, M., 'Fishing and Fisheries in the Middle Ages: The Western Fisheries', in D. J. Starkey, C. Reid, and N. Ashcroft (eds), *England's Sea Fisheries: The Commercial Fisheries of England and Wales since 1300* (London, 2000), 23–8.

Kowaleski, M., 'Warfare, Shipping and Crown Patronage: The Impact of the Hundred Years War on the Port Towns of Medieval England', in L. Armstrong, M. M. Elbl, I. Elbl, and L. D. Armstrong (eds), *Money, Markets and Trade in Late Medieval Europe: Essays in Honour of John H. A. Munro* (Leiden and Boston MA, 2007), 233–54.

Kümin, B. A., *The Shaping of a Community: The Rise and Reformation of the English Parish c.1400–1650* (Aldershot, 1996).

Kümin, B. A., 'Late Medieval Churchwardens' Accounts and Parish Government: Looking beyond London and Bristol', *EHR* 119 (2004), 87–99.

Kümin, B. A., 'The Secular Legacy of the Late Medieval English Parish', in C. Burgess and E. Duffy (eds), *The Parish in Late Medieval England*, Harlaxton Medieval Studies, 14 (Donington, 2006), 95–111.

Lacey, K. E., 'The Military Organization of the Reign of Henry VII', in M. Strickland (ed.), *Armies, Chivalry and Warfare in Medieval Britain and France: Proceedings of the 1995 Harlaxton Symposium* (Stamford, 1998), 234–55.

Lander, J. R., 'The Hundred Years War and Edward IV's 1475 Campaign in France', in his *Crown and Nobility, 1450–1509* (London, 1976), 220–41.

Latimer, J., *Sixteenth-Century Bristol* (Bristol, 1908).

Lawton, D. A., 'Scottish Field: Alliterative Verse and Stanley Encomium in the Percy Folio', *Leeds Studies in English* n.s. 10 (1978), 42–57.

Le Gall, J.-M., 'Les combattants de Pavie, Octobre 1524–24 février 1525', *Revue historique* 671 (2014), 567–96.

Le Mené, M., 'L'économie angevine sous Louis XI', in B. Chevalier and P. Contamine (eds), *La France de la fin du xve siècle: renouveau et apogée* (Paris, 1985), 51–60.

Lee, F. G., *The History, Description and Antiquities of the Prebendal Church of the Blessed Virgin Mary of Thame* (London, 1883).

Lehmberg, S. E., *The Reformation Parliament, 1529–1636* (Cambridge, 1970).

Lesger, C., *Handel in Amsterdam ten tijde van de Opstand: Kooplieden, commerciële expansie en verandering in de ruimtelijke economie van de Nederlanden ca.1550–ca.1630* (Hilversum, 2001).

Llewellyn, N., 'Claims to Status through Visual Codes: Heraldry on Post-Reformation Funeral Monuments', in S. Anglo (ed.), *Chivalry in the Renaissance* (Woodbridge, 1990), 145–60.

Llewellyn, N., *Funeral Monuments in Post-Reformation England* (Cambridge, 2000).

Lloyd, C. and Thurley, S., *Henry VIII: Images of a Tudor King* (Oxford, 1990).

Loades, D. M., *Mary Tudor: A Life* (Oxford, 1989).

Loades, D. M., *The Reign of Mary Tudor*, 2nd edn (London, 1991).

Loades, D. M., *The Tudor Navy: An Administrative, Political and Military History* (Aldershot, 1992).

Loades, D. M., *Two Tudor Conspiracies*, 2nd edn (Bangor, 1992).

Loades, D. M., *The Life and Career of William Paulet (c.1475–1572), Lord Treasurer and First Marquis of Winchester* (Aldershot, 2008).

Loades, D. M., *The Making of the Elizabethan Navy 1540–1590: From the Solent to the Armada* (Woodbridge, 2009).

Lomas, R., 'The Impact of Border Warfare: The Scots and South Tweedside, c. 1290–c. 1520', *Scottish Historical Review* 75 (1996), 143–67.

Losada, J. C., *San Quintín. El relato vivo y vibrante de las campañas del conde de Egmont en la convulse Europa de Felipe II* (Madrid, 2005).

Lowe, B., *Imagining Peace: A History of Early English Pacifist Ideas, 1340–1560* (University Park PA, 1997).

Lowe, B., 'A War to End All Wars? Protestant Subversions of Henry VII's Final Scottish and French Campaigns (1542–45)', in D. Wolfthal (ed.), *Peace and Negotiation: Strategies for Coexistence in the Middle Ages and the Renaissance* (Turnhout, 2000), 185–94.

Lynn, J. A., *Women, Armies and Warfare in Early Modern Europe* (Cambridge, 2008).

Lysons, D. and Lysons, S., *Magna Brittania, VI, Devonshire* (London, 1822).

MacCaffrey, W. T., 'Parliament and Foreign Policy', in D. M. Dean and N. L. Jones (eds), *The Parliaments of Elizabethan England* (Oxford, 1990), 65–90.

MacCaffrey, W. T., 'The Newhaven Expedition, 1562–63', *HJ* 40 (1997), 1–23.

MacCulloch, D. N. J., *Tudor Church Militant: Edward VI and the Protestant Reformation* (London, 2000).

McDermott, J., *Martin Frobisher: Elizabethan Privateer* (New Haven CT and London, 2001).

McFarlane, K. B., 'War, the Economy and Social Change: England and the Hundred Years' War', *PP* 22 (1962), 3–13.

McGurk, J. J. N., *The Elizabethan Conquest of Ireland* (Manchester, 1997).

McIntosh, M. K., *Controlling Misbehaviour in England, 1370–1600* (Cambridge, 1998).

McIntosh, M. K., *Poor Relief in England 1350–1600* (Cambridge, 2012).

McLaren, M.-R., *The London Chronicles of the Fifteenth Century: A Revolution in English Writing* (Woodbridge, 2002).

MacMahon, L., 'Chivalry, Military Professionalism and the Early Tudor Army in Renaissance Europe: A Reassessment', in D. Trim (ed.), *The Chivalric Ethos and the Development of Military Professionalism* (Leiden, 2003), 183–212.

Maddern, P. C., *Violence and Social Order: East Anglia 1422–1442* (Oxford, 1992).

Mallett, M. E. and Hale, J. R., *The Military Organisation of a Renaissance State: Venice, c.1400 to 1617* (Cambridge, 1984).

Mallett, M. E. and Shaw, C., *The Italian Wars 1494–1559* (Harlow, 2012).

Manning, R. B., *Hunters and Poachers: A Cultural and Social History of Unlawful Hunting in England 1485–1640* (Oxford, 1993).

Manning, R. B., *Swordsmen: The Martial Ethos in the Three Kingdoms* (Oxford, 2003).

March, A. E. W., *A History of the Borough and Town of Calne* (Calne and London, 1903).

Marius, R., *Thomas More* (London, 1993 edn).

Martínez, M., *Front Lines: Soldiers' Writing in the Early Modern Hispanic World* (Philadelphia, 2016).

Maryfield, P., *'Love as Brethren': A Quincentenary History of the Coopers' Company* (London, 2000).

Massarette, J., *La vie martiale et fastueuse de Pierre-Ernest de Mansfeld (1517–1604)*, 2 vols (Paris, 1930).

Mathew, D., 'The Cornish and Welsh Pirates in the Reign of Elizabeth', *EHR* 39 (1924), 337–48.

Mayhew, G., 'Rye and the Defence of the Narrow Seas: A Sixteenth Century Town at War', *Sussex Archaeological Collections* 127 (1984), 107–26.

Meek, E. L., 'The Career of Sir Thomas Everingham, "Knight of the North", in the Service of Maximilian, duke of Austria, 1477–81', *HR* 74 (2001), 238–48.

Megson, B., *Such Goodly Company: A Glimpse of the Life of the Bowyers of London, 1300–1600* (London, 1993).

Merriman, M. H., *The Rough Wooings: Mary Queen of Scots 1542–1551* (East Linton, 2000).

Michon, C. (ed.), *Les conseillers de François Ier* (Rennes, 2011).

Millar, G. J., 'Henry VIII's Colonels', *Journal of the Society for Army Historical Research* 57 (1979), 129–36.

Millar, G. J., *Tudor Mercenaries and Auxiliaries 1485–1547* (Charlottesville VA, 1980).

Miller, D., *The Landsknechts* (London, 1976).

Miller, H., 'Subsidy Assessments of the Peerage in the Sixteenth Century', *Bulletin of the Institute of Historical Research* 28 (1955), 15–34.

Miller, H., *Henry VIII and the English Nobility* (Oxford, 1986).

Moffett, R., 'Military Equipment in the Town of Southampton during the Fourteenth and Fifteenth Centuries', *Journal of Medieval Military History* 9 (2011), 167–99.

Monier-Williams, R. H., *The Tallow Chandlers of London*, 4 vols (London, 1970–7).

Mooney, L. R., 'Lydgate's "Kings of England" and Another Verse Chronicle of the Kings', *Viator* 20 (1989), 255–89.

Moreton, C. E., *The Townshends and their World: Gentry, Law and Land in Norfolk c.1450–1551* (Oxford, 1992).

Moreton, C. E., 'Mid-Tudor Trespass: A Break-in at Norwich, 1549', *EHR* 108 (1993), 387–98.

Morgan, R., *The Welsh and the Shaping of Early Modern Ireland 1558–1641* (Woodbridge, 2014).

Murphey, R., *Ottoman Warfare 1500–1700* (London, 1999).

Murphy, N., 'Henry VIII's First Invasion of France: The Gascon Expedition of 1512', *EHR* 130 (2015), 25–56.

Murphy, N., 'Violence, Colonisation and Henry VIII's Conquest of France, 1544–46', *PP* 233 (2016), 13–51.

Najemy, J. M., *A History of Florence 1200–1575* (Oxford, 2006).

Nall, C., *Reading and War in Fifteenth-Century England from Lydgate to Malory* (Cambridge, 2012).

Nef, J. U., 'War and Economic Progress 1540–1640', *EcHR* 12 (1942), 13–38.

Neuschel, K. B., *Word of Honor: Interpreting Noble Culture in Sixteenth-Century France* (Ithaca NY and London, 1989).

Niccoli, O., *Prophecy and People in Renaissance Italy* (Princeton NJ, 1990).

Nicolle, E. T., 'The Capture of Sark by the French in 1549 and its Re-Capture in 1553, by a Flemish Corsair', *Bulletin annuel de la Société jersiaise* 10 (1923–7), 157–73.

Norris, M. M., 'The 2nd Earl of Rutland's Band of Men-at-Arms, 1551–2', *HR* 68 (1995), 100–16.

North, T., *A Chronicle of the Church of St Martin in Leicester* (London, 1866).

O'Brien, P. K. and Hunt, P. A., 'The Rise of a Fiscal State in England, 1485–1815', *HR* 66 (1993), 129–76.

O'Malley, G., *The Knights Hospitallers of the English Langue 1460–1565* (Oxford, 2005).

Oldland, J., 'Wool and Cloth Production in Late Medieval and Early Tudor England', *EcHR* n.s. 67 (2014), 25–47.

Orme, N., 'Church and Chapel in Medieval England', *TRHS* 6th ser. 6 (1996), 75–102.

Orme, N. and Webster, M., *The English Hospital 1070–1570* (New Haven CT and London, 1995).

Ormrod, W. M., 'The Domestic Response to the Hundred Years War', in A. Curry and M. Hughes (eds), *Arms, Armies and Fortifications in the Hundred Years War* (Woodbridge, 1994), 83–101.

Ormrod, W. M., 'England in the Middle Ages', in R. Bonney (ed.), *The Rise of the Fiscal State in Europe c.1200–1815* (Oxford, 1999), 19–52.

Outhwaite, R. B., 'The Trials of Foreign Borrowing: The English Crown and the Antwerp Money Market in the Mid-Sixteenth Century', *EcHR* n.s. 19 (1966), 289–305.

Owen, H. and Blakeway, J. B., *A History of Shrewsbury*, 2 vols (London, 1825).

Oxford Dictionary of National Biography, ed. H. C. G. Matthew and B. Harrison, 60 vols (Oxford, 2004).

Pablo, J. de, 'Contribution à l'étude de l'histoire des institutions militaires huguenotes, II. L'armée huguenote entre 1562 et 1573', *Archiv für Reformationsgeschichte* 48 (1957), 192–216.

Palliser, D. M., *The Age of Elizabeth: England under the Later Tudors, 1547–1603*, 2nd edn (London, 1992).

Parker, G., *The Army of Flanders and the Spanish Road 1567–1659* (Cambridge, 1972).

Parker, G., *The Military Revolution: Military Innovation and the Rise of the West, 1500–1800* (Cambridge, 1988).

Parker, G., *The Grand Strategy of Philip II* (New Haven CT and London, 1998).

Parrott, D., *The Business of War: Military Enterprise and Military Revolution in Early Modern Europe* (Cambridge, 2012).

Patarino, V. V., 'The Religious Shipboard Culture of Sixteenth and Seventeenth-Century English Sailors', in C. A. Fury (ed.), *The Social History of English Seamen, 1485–1649* (Woodbridge, 2012), 141–92.

Payling, S., 'War and Peace: Military and Administrative Service amongst the English Gentry in the Reign of Henry VI', in P. R. Coss and C. Tyerman (eds), *Soldiers, Nobles and Gentlemen: Essays in Honour of Maurice Keen* (Woodbridge, 2009), 240–58.

Pepper, S., 'Warfare and Operational Art: Communications, Cannon and Small War', in F. Tallett and D. Trim (eds), *European Warfare 1350–1750* (Cambridge, 2010), 181–202.

Pepper, S. and Adams, N., *Firearms and Fortifications: Military Architecture and Siege Warfare in Sixteenth-Century Siena* (Chicago IL, 1986).

Peter, R. and Peter, O. B., *The Histories of Launceston and Dunheved* (Plymouth, 1885).

Pettegree, A., *The Invention of News: How the World Came to Know about Itself* (New Haven CT and London, 2014).

Pevsner, N., Grundy, J., and Linsley, S., *The Buildings of England: Northumberland* (London, 1992).

Phillips, G., *The Anglo-Scots Wars 1513–50* (Woodbridge, 1999).

Phillips, G., 'To Cry "Home! Home!": Mutiny, Morale and Indiscipline in Tudor Armies', *Journal of Military History* 65 (2001), 313–32.

Phythian-Adams, C. V., 'Rituals of Personal Confrontation in Late Medieval England', *Bulletin of the John Rylands Library* 73 (1991), 65–90.

Pognon, E., 'Les plus anciens plans des villes gravés et les événements militaires', *Imago Mundi* 22 (1968), 13–19.

Polwhele, R., *The History of Devonshire*, 3 vols (London, 1793–1806).

Postan, M. M., 'Some Social Consequences of the Hundred Years War', *EcHR* 12 (1942), 1–12.

Postan, M. M., 'The Costs of the Hundred Years' War', *PP* 27 (1964), 34–53.

Potter, D. L., 'The Treaty of Boulogne and European Diplomacy, 1549–50', *HR* 55 (1982), 50–65.

Potter, D. L., *War and Government in the French Provinces: Picardy 1470–1560* (Cambridge, 1993).

Potter, D. L., 'Foreign Policy', in D. N. J. MacCulloch (ed.), *The Reign of Henry VIII: Politics, Policy and Piety* (Basingstoke, 1995), 101–33.

Potter, D. L., *Un homme de guerre au temps de la Renaissance: la vie et les lettres d'Oudart du Biez, maréchal de France, gouverneur de Boulogne et de Picardie (vers 1475–1553)* (Arras, 2001).

Potter, D. L., 'Mid-Tudor Foreign Policy and Diplomacy: 1547–63', in S. Doran and G. Richardson (eds), *Tudor England and its Neighbours* (Basingstoke, 2005), 106–38.

Potter, D. L., *Renaissance France at War: Armies, Culture and Society c.1480–1560* (Woodbridge, 2008).

Potter, D. L., *Henry VIII and Francis I: The Final Conflict, 1540–47* (Leiden and Boston MA, 2011).

Potter, G. R., *Zwingli* (Cambridge, 1976).

Power, G., *A European Frontier Elite: The Nobility of the English Pale in Ireland, 1496–1566* (Hanover, 2012).

Powis, J., 'Guyenne 1548: The Crown, the Province and Social Order', *European Studies Review* 12 (1982), 1–15.

Prestwich, M., *Armies and Warfare in the Middle Ages: The English Experience* (New Haven CT and London, 1996).

Puddu, R., *El soldado gentilhombre* (Barcelona, 1984).

Quatrefages, R., 'A la naissance de l'armée moderne', *Mélanges de la Casa de Velázquez* 13 (1977), 119–59.

Quatrefages, R., 'La Proveeduría des Armadas: de l'expédition de Tunis (1535) à celle d'Alger (1541)', *Mélanges de la Casa de Velázquez* 14 (1978), 215–47.

Quatrefages, R., 'Etat et armée en Espagne au début des temps modernes', *Mélanges de la Casa de Velázquez* 17 (1981), 85–103.

Rachfahl, F., *Wilhelm van Oranien und der niederländische Aufstand*, 3 vols (The Hague, 1906–24).

Ramsay, G., *The City of London in International Trade at the Accession of Elizabeth I* (Manchester, 1975).

Rapple, R., *Martial Power and Elizabethan Political Culture: Military Men in England and Ireland, 1558–1594* (Cambridge, 2009).

Raven, J. J., 'Tholdman', *Proceedings of the Suffolk Institute of Archaeology* 10 (1898–1900), 394–8.

Raymond, J., *Henry VIII's Military Revolution: The Armies of Sixteenth-Century Britain and Europe* (London and New York, 2007).

Redlich, F., *The German Military Enterpriser and his Work Force: A Study in European Economic and Social History*, 2 vols (Wiesbaden, 1964–5).

Reid, R. R., 'The Date and Authorship of Redmayne's "Life of Henry V"', *EHR* 30 (1915), 691–8.

Rentet, T., 'Network Mapping: Ties of Fidelity and Dependency among the Major Domestic Officers of Anne de Montmorency', *French History* 17 (2011), 109–26.

Rice, R. G., 'The Household Goods, etc, of Sir John Gage of West Firle, Co. Sussex, KG, 1556', *Sussex Archaeological Collections* 45 (1892), 114–27.

Rich, E. E., 'The Population of Elizabethan England', *EcHR* n.s. 2 (1950), 247–65.

Richardson, T., 'The Bridport Muster Roll of 1457', *Royal Armouries Yearbook* 2 (1997) 46–52.

Richmond, C., '1485 and All That, or What Was Going On at the Battle of Bosworth', in P. W. Hammond (ed.), *Richard III: Loyalty, Lordship and Law* (London, 1986), 172–209.

Richmond, C., *The Paston Family in the Fifteenth Century: Fastolf's Will* (Cambridge, 1996).

Rimer, G., Richardson, T., and Cooper, J. P. D. (eds), *Henry VIII: Arms and the Man* (Leeds, 2009).

Roberts, M., 'The Military Revolution, 1560–1660', in his *Essays in Swedish History* (London, 1967), 195–225.

Robson, R., *The English Highland Clans: Tudor Responses to a Medieval Problem* (Edinburgh, 1989).

Rodger, N. A. M., *The Safeguard of the Sea: A Naval History of Britain, volume 1, 660–1649* (London, 1997).

Rodger, N. A. M., 'The Law and Language of Private Naval Warfare', *Mariner's Mirror* 100 (2014), 5–16.

Rodríguez-Salgado, M. J. (ed.), *Armada 1588–1988* (London, 1988).

Rodríguez-Salgado, M. J., *The Changing Face of Empire: Charles V, Philip II and Habsburg Authority, 1551–1559* (Cambridge, 1988).

Rogers, C. J. (ed.), *The Military Revolution Debate: Readings on the Military Transformation of Early Modern Europe* (Boulder CO, 1995).

Rogers, N., 'The Cult of Prince Edward at Tewkesbury', *Transactions of the Bristol and Gloucester Archaeological Society* 101 (1983), 187–9.

Rogg, M., '"Zerhauen und zerschnitten, nach adelichen Sitten"? Herkunft, Entwicklung und Funktion soldatischer Tracht des 16. Jahrhunderts im Spiegel zeitgenössischer Kunst', in B. R. Kroener and R. Pröve (eds), *Krieg und Frieden. Militär und Gesellschaft in der Frühen Neuzeit* (Paderborn, 1996), 109–35.

Romer, H., *Herrschaft, Reislauf und Verbotspolitik. Beobachtungen zum rechtlichen Alltag der zürcher Solddienstbekämpfung im 16. Jahrhundert* (Zürich, 1995).

Roosens, B., 'Het arsenaal van Mechelen en de wapenhandel (1551–1567)', *Bijdragen tot de geschiedenis* 60 (1977), 175–247.

Rosenfeld, P., 'The Provincial Governors from the Minority of Charles V to the Revolt', *Anciens Pays et Assemblées d'Etats* 17 (1959), 3–63.

Rospocher, M., 'Songs of War: Historical and Literary Narratives of the "Horrendous Italian Wars" (1494–1559)', in M. Mondini and M. Rospocher (eds), *Narrating War: Early Modern and Contemporary Perspectives* (Bologna, 2013), 79–97.

Ross, J., 'Essex County Society and the French War in the Fifteenth Century', in L. Clark (ed.), *Conflicts, Consequences and the Crown in the Late Middle Ages*, The Fifteenth Century 7 (Woodbridge, 2007), 53–80.

Ross, J., *John de Vere, Thirteenth Earl of Oxford (1442–1513): 'The Foremost Man of the Kingdom'* (Woodbridge, 2011).

Rowlands, E. I., 'Terwyn a Thwrnai', *National Library of Wales Journal* 9 (1955–6), 295–300.

Rowse, A. L., *Tudor Cornwall* (London, 1941).

Rublack, U., *Dressing Up: Cultural Identity in Renaissance Europe* (Oxford, 2010).

Russell, C. S. R., 'Parliament and the King's Finances', in C. S. R. Russell (ed.), *The Origins of the English Civil War* (London, 1973), 91–116.

Russell, C. S. R., *The Causes of the English Civil War* (Oxford, 1990).

Russell, F. H., *The Just War in the Middle Ages* (Cambridge, 1975).

Rye, W., 'An Old Cannon at the Great Hospital, Norwich', *NA* 16 (1905–7), 85–90.

Sablon du Corail, A., 'Les étrangers au service de Marie de Bourgogne: de l'armée de Charles le Téméraire à l'armée de Maximilien (1477–1482)', *Revue du Nord* 84 (2002), 389–412.

Sablon du Corail, A., 'L'État princier à l'épreuve. Financer et conduire la guerre pendant la crise de l'État bourguignon (1477–1493)', *Revue historique* 679 (2016), 549–76.

Sandberg, B., *Warrior Pursuits: Noble Culture and Civil Conflict in Early Modern France* (Baltimore MD, 2010).

Saul, A., 'Great Yarmouth and the Hundred Years War in the Fourteenth Century', *Bulletin of the Institute of Historical Research* 52 (1979), 105–15.

Saul, N., *English Church Monuments in the Middle Ages* (Oxford, 2009).

Saunders, A. D., 'Norham Castle and Early Artillery Defences', *Fort* 25 (1997), 37–61.

Sawyer, A. C., 'The Tyranny of Alva: The Creation and Development of a Dutch Patriotic Image', *De zeventiende eeuw* 19 (2003), 181–210.

Scarisbrick, J. J., *Henry VIII* (Harmondsworth, 1971 edn).

Schanz, G., *Englische Handelspolitik gegen Ende des Mittelalters*, 2 vols (Leipzig, 1881).

Schaufelberger, W., *Der Alte Schweizer und sein Krieg. Studien zur Kriegsführung vornehmlich im 15. Jahrhundert*, 2nd edn (Zürich, 1966).

Schaufelberger, W., *Marignano: Strukturelle Grenzen eidgenössischer Militärmacht zwischen Mittelalter und Neuzeit* (Zürich, 1993).

Schnitter, H., *Volk und Landesdefension. Volksaufgebote, Defensionswerke, Landmilizien in den deutschen Territorien vom 15. bis zum 18. Jahrhundert* (Berlin, 1977).

Schnurmann, C., *Kommerz und Klüngel: der Englandhandel Kölner Kaufleute im 16. Jahrhundert* (Göttingen, 1991).

Schofield, R., 'Taxation and the Political Limits of the Tudor State', in C. Cross et al. (eds), *Law and Government under the Tudors: Essays presented to Sir Geoffrey Elton on his Retirement* (Cambridge, 1988), 227–55.

Schofield, R., *Taxation under the Early Tudors 1485–1547* (Oxford, 2004).

Schröcker, A., *Die deutsche Nation: Beobachtungen zur politischen Propaganda des ausgehenden 15. Jahrhunderts* (Lübeck, 1974).

Scott, D., *The Stricklands of Sizergh Castle* (Kendal, 1908).

Sessions, W. A., *Henry Howard, the Poet Earl of Surrey: A Life* (Oxford, 1999).

Sgroi, R. C. L., 'Piscatorial Politics Revisited: The Language of Economic Debate and the Evolution of Fishing Policy in Elizabethan England', *Albion* 35 (2003), 1–24.

Sharpe, R. R., *London and the Kingdom*, 3 vols (London, 1894–5).

Shaw, W. A., *The Knights of England*, 2 vols (London, 1906).

Shepard, A., *Meanings of Manhood in Early Modern England* (Oxford, 2003).

Sheppard, J. B., 'The Canterbury Marching Watch with its Pageant of St. Thomas', *Archaeologia Cantiana* 12 (1878), 27–46.

Sherer, I., *Warriors for a Living: The Experience of the Spanish Infantry during the Italian Wars* (Leiden, 2017).

Sherlock, P., *Monuments and Memory in Early Modern England* (Aldershot, 2008).

A Short-Title Catalogue of Books printed in England, Scotland, & Ireland and of English Books Printed Abroad, 1475–1640, ed. A. W. Pollard, G. R. Redgrave, W. A. Jackson, F. S. Ferguson, and K. F. Pantzer, 2nd edn, 3 vols (London, 1976–91).

Shrank, C., *Writing the Nation in Reformation England, 1530–1580* (Oxford, 2004).

Sicking, L., *Neptune and the Netherlands: State, Economy, and War at Sea in the Renaissance* (Leiden, 2006).

Sieber-Lehmann, C., *Spätmittelalterlicher Nationalismus: die Burgunderkriege am Oberrhein und in der Eidgenossenschaft* (Göttingen, 1995).

Slack, P. A., *Poverty and Policy in Tudor and Stuart England* (London, 1988).

Smith, A. H., 'Militia Rates and Militia Statutes 1558–1663', in P. Clark, A. G. R. Smith, and N. Tyacke (eds), *The English Commonwealth 1547–1640: Essays in Politics and Society presented to Joel Hurstfield* (Leicester, 1979), 93–110.

Smith, H. P., *The History of the Borough and County of the Town of Poole*, 2 vols (Poole, 1948–51).

Smith, L. B., *Henry VIII: The Mask of Royalty* (London, 1971).

Smith, R. D. and DeVries, K., *The Artillery of the Dukes of Burgundy 1363–1477* (Woodbridge, 2005).

Smuts, M., 'Organized Violence in the Elizabethan Monarchical Republic', *History* 99 (2014), 418–32.

Smyth, A., 'Almanacs and Ideas of Popularity', in A. Kesson, E. Smith, A. Smyth, and J. Daybell, *The Elizabethan Top Ten: Defining Print Popularity in Early Modern England* (Farnham, 2013), 125–33.

Sombart, W., *Krieg und Kapitalismus* (Munich, 1913).

Stabel, P., 'Militaire organisatie, bewapening en wapenbezit in het laatmiddeleeuwse Brugge', *Revue belge de philologie et d'histoire* 89 (2011), 1049–73.

Starkey, D. R., 'Intimacy and Innovation: The Rise of the Privy Chamber, 1485–1547', in D. R. Starkey (ed.), *The English Court from the Wars of the Roses to the Civil War* (London, 1987), 71–118.

Starkey, D. R., *Henry: Virtuous Prince* (London, 2008).

Stayer, J. M., *Anabaptists and the Sword* (Lawrence KS, 1972).

Stephens, W. E., 'Great Yarmouth under Queen Mary', *NA* 29 (1946), 143–54.

Stewart, D., 'Disposal of the Sick and Wounded of the English Army during the Sixteenth Century', *Journal of the Royal Army Medical Corps* 90 (1948), 30–8.

Stewart, D., 'Sickness and Mortality Rates of the English Army in the Sixteenth Century', *Journal of the Royal Army Medical Corps* 91 (1948), 23–35.

Stirland, A. J., *Raising the Dead: The Skeleton Crew of Henry VIII's Great Ship, the Mary Rose* (Chichester, 2000).

Stone, L., *The Crisis of the Aristocracy 1558–1641* (Oxford, 1965).

Stone, L., *The Causes of the English Revolution* (London, 1972).

Stone, L., 'Interpersonal Violence in English Society 1300–1980', *PP* 101 (1983), 22–33.

Stoyle, M., *Circled with Stone: Exeter's City Walls 1485–1660* (Exeter, 2003).

Strickland, M. and Hardy, R., *From Hastings to the Mary Rose: The Great Warbow* (Thrupp, 2005).

Stubbs, S., *A Souvenir Guide: Little Moreton Hall, Cheshire* (Swindon, 2015).

Sutherland, N. M., *The Huguenot Struggle for Recognition* (New Haven CT, 1980).

Sutton, A. F., *The Mercery of London: Trade, Goods and People, 1130–1578* (Aldershot, 2005).

Swanson, H., *Medieval Artisans: An Urban Class in Late Medieval England* (Oxford, 1989).

Tallett, F., *War and Society in Early Modern Europe, 1495–1715* (London, 1992).

Tallett, F. and Trim, D. (eds), *European Warfare, 1350–1750* (Cambridge, 2010).

Taylor, J. G., *Our Lady of Batersey* (Chelsea, 1925).

Tazón, J. E., *The Life and Times of Thomas Stukeley (c.1525–78)* (Aldershot, 2003).

Thiery, D., 'Plowshares and Swords: Clerical Involvement in Acts of Violence and Peacemaking in Late Medieval England, c. 1400–1536', *Albion* 36 (2004), 201–22.

Thirsk, J., *Economic Policy and Projects: The Development of a Consumer Society in Early Modern England* (Oxford, 1978).

Thomas, D., 'Leases of Crown Lands in the Reign of Elizabeth I', in R. W. Hoyle (ed.), *The Estates of the English Crown, 1558–1640* (Cambridge, 1992), 169–90.

Thomas, K. V., *The Ends of Life: Roads to Fulfilment in Early Modern England* (Oxford, 2009).

Thompson, I. A. A., '"Money, Money and Yet More Money!" Finance, the Fiscal-State, and the Military Revolution: Spain 1500–1650', in C. J. Rogers (ed.), *The Military Revolution Debate: Readings on the Military Transformation of Early Modern Europe* (Boulder CO, 1995), 273–98.

Thompson, P., *The History and Antiquities of Boston* (Sleaford, 1997 edn).

Thomson, G. S., *Lords Lieutenants in the Sixteenth Century* (London, 1923).

Thrupp, S., *A Short History of the Worshipful Company of Bakers of London* (London, 1933).

Tielhof, M. van, *De Hollandse graanhandel, 1470–1570: Koren op de Amsterdamse molen* (The Hague, 1995).

Tilly, C., *Coercion, Capital and European States, AD 990–1990* (Oxford, 1990).

Tittler, R., 'The English Fishing Industry in the Sixteenth Century: The Case of Great Yarmouth', *Albion* 9 (1977), 40–60.

Tittler, R., *Architecture and Power: The Town Hall and the English Urban Community c.1500–1640* (Oxford, 1991).

Tittler, R., *The Reformation and the Towns in England: Politics and Political Culture, c.1540–1640* (Oxford, 1998).

Tlusty, B. A., *The Martial Ethic in Early Modern Germany: Civic Duty and the Right of Arms* (Basingstoke, 2011).

Tooley, R. V., 'Maps in Italian Atlases of the Sixteenth Century', *Imago Mundi* 3 (1939), 12–47.

Tracy, J. D., *Emperor Charles V, Impresario of War* (Cambridge, 2002).

Tracy, J. D., *Balkan Wars: Habsburg Croatia, Ottoman Bosnia, and Venetian Dalmatia, 1499–1617* (Lanham MD, 2016).

Trim, D., 'The "Foundation-Stone of the British Army"? The Normandy Campaign of 1562', *Journal of the Society for Army Historical Research* 77 (1999), 71–87.

Trim, D., 'Seeking a Protestant Alliance and Liberty of Conscience on the Continent, 1558–85', in S. Doran and G. Richardson (eds), *Tudor England and its Neighbours* (Basingstoke, 2005), 139–77.

Troeyer, P. B. De, *Lamoraal van Egmont: Een critische studie over zijn rol in de jaren 1559–64 in verband met het schuldvraagstuk*, Verhandelingen van de Koninklijke Academie voor Wetenschappen, Letteren en Schone Kunsten van België, Klasse der Letteren 40 (Brussels, 1961).

Tucker, M. J., *The Life of Thomas Howard, Earl of Surrey and Second Duke of Norfolk, 1443–1524* (London, 1964).

Tudor-Craig, P., 'Henry VIII and King David', in D. Williams (ed.), *Early Tudor England: Proceedings of the 1987 Harlaxton Symposium* (Woodbridge, 1989), 183–205.

Turner, H. L., *Town Defences in England and Wales: An Architectural and Documentary Study, AD 900–1500* (London, 1970).

Vanhemelryck, F., *De criminaliteit in de ammanie van Brussel van de late middeleeuwen tot het einde van het Ancien Régime (1404–1789)*, Verhandelingen van de Koninklijke Academie voor Wetenschappen, Letteren en Schone Kunsten van België, Klasse der Letteren 97 (Brussels, 1981).

Varley, T., *Cambridge County Geographies: Isle of Wight* (Cambridge, 1924).

The Victoria History of Hampshire and the Isle of Wight, ed. H. A. Doubleday and W. Page, 6 vols (London, 1900–14).

The Victoria History of the County of Sussex, ed. W. Page et al., 9 vols in 11 (London, 1905–).

Virgoe, R., 'Sir John Risley (1443–1512), Courtier and Councillor', *NA* 38 (1981–3), 140–8.

Vos, A., 'The Humanism of Toxophilus: A New Source', *English Literary Renaissance* 6 (1976), 187–203.

Wadmore, J. F., *Some Account of the Worshipful Company of Skinners of London, being the Guild or Fraternity of Corpus Christi* (London, 1902).

Wagner, J. V., *Graf Wilhelm von Fürstenberg (1491–1549) und die politisch-geistigen Mächte seiner Zeit* (Stuttgart, 1966).

Wake, J., *The Brudenells of Deene*, 2nd edn (London, 1954).

Walker, S. K., *The Lancastrian Affinity 1361–1399* (Oxford, 1990).

Watts, J., 'Polemic and Politics in the 1450s', in M. L. Kekewich et al. (eds), *The Politics of Fifteenth-Century England: John Vale's Book* (Stroud, 1995), 3–42.

Webb, H. J., *Elizabethan Military Science: The Books and the Practice* (Madison WI, 1965).

Webb, J., *Great Tooley of Ipswich: Portrait of an Early Tudor Merchant* (Ipswich, 1962).

Weever, J., *Ancient funerall monuments within the united monarchie of Great Britaine, Ireland, and the islands adiacent* (London, 1631).

Weikel, A., 'The Rise and Fall of a Marian Privy Councillor: Sir Henry Bedingfield 1509/11–1585', *NA* 40 (1987–9), 73–83.

Welch, C., *History of the Worshipful Company of Pewterers of the City of London, based upon their own Records*, 2 vols (London, 1902).

Welch, C., *History of the Cutlers' Company of London*, 2 vols (London, 1916–23).

Wheeler, J. S., *The Making of a World Power: War and the Military Revolution in Seventeenth-Century England* (Stroud, 1999).

White, D. G., 'Henry VIII's Irish Kerne in France and Scotland', *The Irish Sword* 3 (1958), 213–35.

White, H. T., 'The Beacon System in Kent', *Archaeologia Cantiana* 46 (1934), 77–96.

Whittle, J., 'Lords and Tenants in Kett's Rebellion 1549', *PP* 207 (2010), 3–52.

Willems, B., 'Militaire organisatie en staatsvorming aan de vooravond van de Nieuwe Tijd: Een analyse van het conflict tussen Brabant en Maximiliaan van Oostenrijk (1488–1489)', *Jaarboek voor Middeleeuwse Geschiedenis* 1 (1998), 261–86.

Williams, G., *Renewal and Reformation: Wales, c.1415–1642* (Oxford, 1997).

Williams, N., *The Maritime Trade of the East Anglian Ports 1550–1590* (Oxford, 1988).

Winchester, B., *Tudor Family Portrait* (London, 1955).

Withington, P., 'Introduction—Citizens and Soldiers: The Renaissance Context', *Journal of Early Modern History* 15 (2011), 18–27.

Wood, A., *The 1549 Rebellions and the Making of Early Modern England* (Cambridge, 2007).

Wood, A., *The Memory of the People: Custom and Popular Senses of the Past in Early Modern England* (Cambridge, 2013).

Wood, J. B., *The King's Army: Warfare, Soldiers and Society during the Wars of Religion in France, 1562–1576* (Cambridge, 1996).

Wooding, L., *Henry VIII* (Abingdon, 2009).

Wrigley, E. A. and Schofield, R., *The Population History of England, 1541–1871: A Reconstruction* (London, 1981).

Xenakis, S., *Gewalt und Gemeinschaft: Kriegsknechte um 1500* (Paderborn, 2015).

Youings, J., *The Dissolution of the Monasteries* (London, 1971).

Young, P. and Holmes, R., *The English Civil War: A Military History of the Three Civil Wars 1642–1651* (London, 1974).

Younger, N., *War and Politics in the Elizabethan Counties* (Manchester, 2012).

Youngs, D., *Humphrey Newton (1496–1536), An Early Tudor Gentleman* (Woodbridge, 2008).

UNPUBLISHED THESES

Davies, C. S. L., 'Supply Services of the English Armed Forces, 1509–1550', University of Oxford D.Phil. Thesis (1963).

Ford, L. L., 'Conciliar Politics and Administration in the Reign of Henry VII', University of St Andrews Ph.D. Thesis (2001).

Fox, C. M., 'The Royal Almshouse at Westminster c.1500–c.1600', Royal Holloway University of London Ph.D. Thesis (2013).

Goring, J., 'The Military Obligations of the English People, 1509–1558', University of London Ph.D. Thesis (1955).

Jones, E. T., 'The Bristol Shipping Industry in the Sixteenth Century', University of Edinburgh Ph.D. Thesis (1998).

Trim, D., 'Fighting "Jacob's warres": English and Welsh Mercenaries in the European Wars of Religion: France and the Netherlands, 1562–1610', King's College London Ph.D. Thesis (2003).

INTERNET RESOURCES

Early English Books Online: <http://eebo.chadwyck.com>.

England's Immigrants Project: <http://www.englandsimmigrants.com>.

Hodgkins, A., 'Reconstructing Rebellion: Digital Terrain Analysis of the Battle of Dussindale (1549)', *Internet Archaeology* 38 (2015), <http://dx.doi.org/10.11141/ia.38.3>.

Index

Places in England, Ireland, and Wales are given in their sixteenth-century counties.

Printed and bound by CPI Group (UK) Ltd, Croydon, CR0 4YY